Using C++

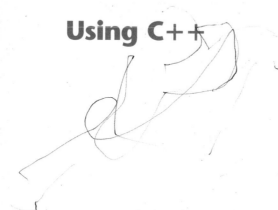

Using C++
An Introduction to Programming

Julien Hennefeld
Brooklyn College of the City University of New York

Charles Burchard
Penn State Erie—The Behrend College

PWS Publishing Company

I(T)P **An International Thomson Publishing Company**

*Boston • Albany • Bonn • Cincinnati • London • Melbourne • Mexico City
New York • Paris • San Francisco • Singapore • Tokyo • Toronto • Washington*

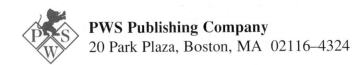

PWS Publishing Company
20 Park Plaza, Boston, MA 02116–4324

I⦗T⦘P ®
International Thomson Publishing
The trademark ITP is used under license.

Printed in the United States of America.
00 01 — 10 9 8 7 6 5 4

*This book is printed on recycled,
acid-free paper.*

Sponsoring Editor: *David Dietz*
Production Editor: *Andrea Goldman*
Manufacturing Coordinator: *Andrew Christensen*
Marketing Manager: *Nathan Wilbur*
Editorial Assistant: *Kathryn Schooling*
Copyeditors: *Andrea Goldman, Lorretta Palagi*
Composition/Art: *The PRD Group*
Cover Design: *Peter Blaiwas*
Interior Design: *Sandra Rigney*
Text Printer and Binder: *R.R. Donnelley & Sons–
    Crawfordsville*
Cover Printer: *Phoenix Color Corp.*

For more information, contact:
PWS Publishing Company
20 Park Plaza
Boston, MA 02116

International Thomson Publishing Europe
Berkshire House
168-173 High Holborn
London WC1V 7AA
England

Thomas Nelson Australia
102 Dodds Street
South Melbourne, 3205
Victoria, Australia

Nelson Canada
1120 Birchmont Road
Scarborough, Ontario
Canada M1K 5G4

International Thomson Editores
Campos Eliseos 385, Piso 7
Col. Polanco
11560 Mexico D.F., Mexico

International Thomson Publishing GmbH
Königswinterer Strasse 418
53227 Bonn, Germany

International Thomson Publishing Asia
221 Henderson Road
#05-10 Henderson Building
Singapore 0315

International Thomson Publishing Japan
Hirakawacho Kyowa Building, 31
2-2-1 Hirakawacho
Chiyoda-ku, Tokyo 102
Japan

Library of Congress Cataloging-in-Publication-Data

Hennefeld, Julien O.
    Using C++: an introduction to programming /
    Julien Hennefeld, Charles Burchard.
        p.   cm.
    Includes index.
    ISBN 0–534–95591–6
    1. C++ (Computer program language)   I.
    Burchard, Charles.   II. Title.
QA76.73.C153H457   1998
005.13'3–dc21   97–31817
                                              CIP

I would like to thank my wife, Marianne, my children, Maggie and Dan, and my canine associate, Zoe, for bearing with me and sustaining me during the difficult stretches of work on the book.

Julien Hennefeld

I would like to thank my wife, Marge, for "running the ship" while I was off on this venture, and my children, Sarah and Emmy, for providing some laughs when I was taking it all too seriously.

Chuck Burchard

Contents

4   Selection Using if and if..else   65

5   Functions and Program Design   95

6   The String Data Type and More Output Formatting   131

Preface

Intended Audience

This book can be used in a number of different types of C++ programming courses. Its clarity, readability, and wealth of illustrative examples make it especially suitable for use in a CS1 course for beginning programmers. Concisely written, the book ultimately is comprehensive and includes more material than can be covered in a single semester by beginners. Thus, it may be used in a single-semester, faster-paced course for computer science majors or students with prior programming experience, or it may be used in a two-semester sequence for beginners and nonmajors. Since it covers almost all of the material recommended for the Advanced Placement A and B exams, it is especially suitable for secondary-level courses. Moreover, it can be used both in courses that limit coverage to procedural C++ and in courses that will eventually cover a significant amount of the object-oriented features of the language.

Content Approach

Basics

At the beginning, we teach C++ as a "better C," because it is an easier and more convenient language in which to write basic programs. We strongly emphasize control structures and writing and designing with functions, and encourage students to build onto a library of useful functions that they can reuse. We discuss problem solving and program design using a four-step method, and make frequent use of pseudocode and top-down development. Because extended, detailed discussions of program development can work well in the classroom but become tedious and visually overwhelming on the printed page, we keep discussions of program development focused and streamlined.

Should Objects Be Taught Early?

Currently, the question of how early to introduce object orientation in the first course is hotly debated. We believe that it is important for students to become proficient in applying and implementing C++ classes by the end of a two-semester sequence, but our experience has been that discussing the syntax for declaring and implementing C++ classes too early confuses students more than it enlightens them. After all, C++ is a hybrid language, and using its complicated object-oriented overlay effectively presupposes quite a bit of mastery of its procedural features. Furthermore, object orientation's extensive overhead is geared toward safely handling the complexity of large programming projects. For many short and medium-size programming problems, object orientation is not appropriate and, when applied to such problems, does not give a convincing introduction to the power and usefulness of object-oriented programming. Further, we are convinced that object-oriented design is a difficult topic that cannot be taught effectively until students have had ample practice in using and implementing objects.

Early Approach to Objects

We do believe, however, that it is possible to give students a *meaningful perspective* on the role and importance of object orientation at the outset. Consequently, in Chapter 1, we present a general discussion of software engineering issues with a comparison of how the procedural and object-oriented paradigms deal with the complexity of large-scale programming projects. In later chapters, we introduce students to objects gradually, by showing them how to use some powerful, predefined classes when the need for these classes arises and is pedagogically appropriate. (These classes are discussed in detail later in this preface.)

Treatment of Class Declaration and Implementation

In regard to teaching about the declaration and implementation of classes, we have taken great care to avoid introducing too many syntactic and conceptual topics at one time. Further, we introduce a given topic, not merely for the sake of coverage but because the particular class under discussion provides real motivation for the topic. Our approach is to split the initial coverage of class declarations and implementations into two closely related chapters. In Chapter 18, we begin exploring important syntactic and conceptual issues in object orientation by showing students how to write client programs based on reading the declaration sections of four different classes. By deferring the details of implementing these classes, we are able to provide more substantive examples of classes and, consequently, more effectively demonstrate the power of object orientation. Then, in Chapter 19, at which time students have had ample practice in using classes and reading their declarations, and have an appreciation for the power they provide, we discuss how to implement and modify the classes of Chapter 18. In Chapter 20, we give an informal discussion of designing with objects by describing actual problems and the kind of analysis and reasoning that an experienced programmer might apply to the problem. There are several classes in Chapter 20 that students will work with in the exercises.

Use of Standard Predefined Classes

The classes that we have targeted for students to use before any treatment of class declaration and implementation are (1) a subset of the ANSI/ISO Draft C++ Standard `String` class, which provides a far superior alternative to `char*`; (2) the built-in `ifstream`, `ofstream`, `istream`, and `ostream` classes required for file handling; (3) a subset of the ANSI/ISO Draft C++ Standard `Vector` class, which provides a safe, more powerful alternative to arrays; and (4) a `Matrix`, or two-dimensional `Vector`, class. Although we decided to use the previously mentioned classes primarily because we believe they make for the clearest and best pedagogy, our approach also strongly reflects recent trends in C++ instructional guidelines and is consistent with an emerging international standard for C++. First, using these classes provides the student with a suitable level of prepackaged programming power. Second, the `String`, `Vector`, and `Matrix` classes are specified by Educational Testing Service's Advanced Placement Computer Science (APCS) Committee for the AP Computer Science exams. (We anticipate that these APCS guidelines will have a major impact on the teaching of C++ in introductory courses at all levels.) Third, the `String` and `Vector` classes are clearly specified as part of the ANSI/ISO Draft C++ Standard and have already been implemented by several commercial C++ vendors.

Vectors Versus Arrays

Although we recommend the use of vectors as a safer, more convenient alternative to arrays, we introduce arrays and discuss their shortcomings before we cover vectors, and we stress that arrays and vectors have far more similarities than differences. Further, we give guidelines for rewriting programs that use vectors as programs that use arrays. Finally, the implementation of the Vector class "over top of" arrays is developed fully later in the book so that students can eventually see the close connection between the two.

Order and Flexibility of Coverage of Topics

To accommodate a variety of different preferences, we have built a reasonable amount of flexibility into the book by including titled paragraphs that point out when it is possible, if so desired, to skip ahead to a related topic in a later chapter. A few examples are listed:

- We did not want to introduce all the selection structures at once in Chapter 4, so the switch statement, which is not a necessity, is not covered until Chapter 12. At the end of section Section 4.4, however, we point out that it is possible to jump ahead to Section 12.1 for an introduction to the switch statement.

- We feel that the single most important programming topic in a first course is functions. In C++, the taxonomy of function types and variations is extensive. We discuss this through several chapters, rather than attempt to cover too many function topics at once. In particular, we have deferred a detailed treatment of reference parameters until Chapter 9, rather than including them in Chapter 5, which covers both void and value-returning functions with value parameters. Section 5.7 briefly introduces reference parameters for use in data input functions, but coverage of this section is optional.

- Recursion is treated separately in Chapter 25 but introduced briefly in Section 10.7, which gives a scenario for early coverage of recursion.

- Sections 22.1 and 23.1–23.7 give a non-object-oriented treatment of pointers and linked lists and can be covered, if desired, any time after Chapter 13.

- Chapter 27 on inheritance can be covered any time after Chapter 19.

Pedagogical Approach

A common problem faced by instructors is finding a textbook that students will actually read and understand so that more class time can be devoted to clarification, elaboration, and integration of material, rather than to "covering" basic material that students should have learned from the book. Consequently, in writing *Using C++*, we have given serious thought to how students actually assimilate technical material. Our goal has been to make this book clear, concise, and focused by stripping down the discussion to what is essential, since too much explanation can be just as bad as too little. Furthermore, we try to foster "active reading," by asking the reader, right in the body of the chapter, not just in the Exercise section, either to determine the output of a sample program fragment or to fill in one or two blank lines in a program whose purpose has been described. This self-testing approach gives readers a basis for determining whether they need to review material before progressing. It also provides confidence-building reinforcement for correct responses. Perhaps most important, it creates a framework that can facilitate the readers' active entry into the material.

Exercises

We believe that rich exercise sets are a vital feature of any introductory programming text. We provide three kinds of exercises in most chapters:

1. Short, objective "self-check" exercises that are designed to give students feedback on key concepts and to demonstrate an important aspect of the material. These exercises give students the kind of written practice that is often tested on exams.

2. Programming assignments whose length and level of difficulty range from short to moderate. More than one of these can be assigned for each chapter.

3. Longer, more difficult programming assignments that could be used for individual or group projects.

Software Provided on the PWS Web Site

1. We provide two short library files, ourtools.h and myfuns.h, that are used throughout the text. These files may be down loaded from the following URL: http://www.pws.com/comsci.html.
   a. ourtools.h provides the following:
      - *Simplified floating point output formatting* To avoid the syntactic baggage and confusing semantics of setiosflags and public data members of ios such as ios::fixed, etc., we provide the functions fixed_out, scientific_out, and default_out, which are first introduced in Chapter 3. The only one that we make extensive use of is the fixed_out function.
      - vprn This is an output stream that is used as a "virtual printer." Its use is first discussed in Section 2.5. In the early chapters preceding files and arrays, students can use this output destination to process input from the

monitor and send output, as a neatly formatted table, to another destination. (The implementation of this stream is trivial and is explained in Chapter 11.)

■ *An Assert function* This function, specified by the APCS Committee, facilitates assertions with meaningful output messages for assertions that fail.

b. myfuns.h contains implementations of a small number of useful functions from early chapters. Students are encouraged to add other useful functions to this library.

2. We provide three library files, bastring.h, bavector.h, and bamatrix.h, which contain, respectively, our implementations of the String, Vector, and Matrix classes discussed earlier. (Complete documentation can be found in bastring.doc, bavector. doc, and bamatrix.doc in Appendix E.)

The five library files mentioned include all implementation code. This avoids the issue of separate compilation and building projects. Although these issues are important for large software projects, we believe that the small size of programs (even the longer projects) in introductory courses does not warrant the added complications of building projects for separate compilation. Instructors who prefer to split interface (.h) and implementation (.cpp) can have students do so as an exercise. Note, however, that the Vector and Matrix classes are templated and, as such, are not separately compilable by most compilers.

Many other Draft Standard compatible String and Vector classes are also available via the Internet, and we will provide relevant information via PWS's Web site (http://www.pws.com/comsci.html). We anticipate that these classes, if not the entire Draft Standard, will already be included in many C++ compliers when the book goes to press.

Acknowledgments

We are very indebted to Eric Bach, Indira Malik, and Ray Morin for suggesting revisions and for their help with proofreading and exercise solutions.

We would also like to express our appreciation to the following reviewers whose comments and criticisms helped shape the book:

■ Don Bailes, *East Tennessee State University*

■ Manuel E. Bermudez, *University of Florida*

■ George Converse, *Southern Oregon State College*

■ Ken Collier, *Northern Arizona University*

- Charles Dierbach, *Towson State University*
- H. E. Dunsmore, *Purdue University*
- Mohamed Y. Eltoweissy, *University of Pittsburgh–Johnstown*
- Susan L. Keenan, *Columbus State University*
- Anil Kini, *Texas A & M University*
- Thomas Kisko, *University of Florida*
- Daniel Ling, *Okanagan University College*
- Bonnie MacKellar, *Western Connecticut State University*
- John S. Mallozzi, *Iona College*
- Jeff McKinstry, *Point Loma Nazarene College*
- John Motil, *California State University–Northridge*
- Jean-Claude Ngatchou, *Jersey City State College*
- Rayno Niemi, *Rochester Institute of Technology*
- Ingrid Russell, *University of Hartford*
- Janet M. Urlaub, *Sinclair Community College*
- David C. Wallace, *Illinois State University*
- Wayne Wallace, *University of Wisconsin–Oshkosh*

In addition, we would like to thank the following people at PWS: Mike Sugarman, Executive Editor, for bringing about our collaboration; David Dietz, our editor, for his superb job in guiding this project; and Andrea Goldman for her excellent work as production editor.

Chuck Burchard
Julien Hennefeld

1

Overview of Computers and Problem Solving

1.1 Computers and Computer Science

Computers   A *computer* is an electronic machine that can perform calculations and process large amounts of data at incredible speeds. Today, the fastest computers can perform more than a billion operations per second, and even moderately priced desktop computers perform several million instructions per second.

The *abacus*, a primitive calculating device dating back to 2000 B.C., represented numbers by a system of rows of beads that were strung along wires attached to a frame. Abacus users performed simple arithmetic calculations by moving beads by hand. By contrast, the modern digital computer uses a large collection of minute electronic switches to represent not only numbers and other kinds of data but also the set of instructions for processing the data.

The modern digital computer is made possible by the use of the *binary number system*,[1] which represents information as sequences of 0s and 1s, and *binary logic* (also called *Boolean logic*), which performs computations and operations on this information. These 0s and 1s, called *binary digits*, or *bits*, can be implemented on a computer by a sequence of electronic switches, where each switch that is OFF corresponds to a 0 and each switch that is ON corresponds to a 1. While some switches are used as *memory* for storing information, others are connected to form *logical circuits* that perform computations. The operations of the

---

[1] Appendix F, "Binary Representation of Integers," contains a brief introduction to binary numbers.

circuits are based on the fact that Boolean logic has two values — TRUE, which can be represented by a switch being ON, and FALSE, which can be represented by a switch being OFF. In short, the incredible speed of a computer results from the fact that the processing is performed as a rapid-fire sequence of electronic pulses.

Data   ***Data*** is information that describes objects and events. This information usually takes the form of words (or text), numbers, graphical images, and even sound. In a computer, data is stored in memory in binary form and is processed by the computer's logical circuitry.

Programming Languages   A list of instructions that causes a computer to perform a particular task is known as a ***computer program***. A computer program must be written in a precise fashion in one of the many computer languages that have been invented since the advent of modern computers.

Low-Level Languages (Machine and Assembly Languages). In a sense, the only language that a computer can "understand directly" is ***machine language***. Instructions in machine language consist of sequences of 0s and 1s that control the operation of the computer's logical circuitry. For example, a typical instruction in a machine language might be

```
0100 1010 0101 0011
```

As you might imagine, writing programs in machine language is extremely tedious. ***Assembly language*** is an easier-to-read-and-write version of machine language that uses English-like commands such as ADD, MOV, and LOAD and decimal numbers in place of sequences of bits. Be aware that the details of machine and assembly language vary for different kinds of computers.

High-Level Languages. High-level languages such as COBOL, BASIC, FORTRAN, Pascal, SmallTalk, C, C++, and Java were invented to make computer programming easier. These languages use instructions that are similar to ordinary English and vary little, if at all, from one type of computer to another. For example, a typical instruction in C++ might be

```
wage = hours * rate;
```

Compilers   All the programs in this book are written in C++. You might wonder how a computer can execute a program written in a high-level language like C++ if it can only understand its own machine language. The answer is that the computer must be supplied with a translating program, called a ***compiler***. The compiler translates a program written in C++ or another high-level language (referred to as source code) into a list of instructions in machine language (referred to as object code). In other words, a compiler converts source code, the language understood by the programmer, into object code, the language directly understood by the computer.

Algorithms and Efficiency Issues An ***algorithm*** for solving a problem is a step-by-step list of instructions that, when carried out, produces a solution to that problem. Some important algorithms are those that solve substantive problems that arise frequently. For example, the problem of sorting, or arranging in order, a list of numbers (from smallest to largest) or a list of names (alphabetically) arises over and over again.

To get a better sense of what algorithms are about, consider how you might solve the following problem.

■ **PROBLEM** Sort a list of 100 social security numbers. Each social security number is on an index card. Write down a description of your method as a list of instructions to be carried out by someone who is not necessarily very creative (or even smart), but who can follow very clear, step-by-step instructions. *Spend at least five minutes trying to write down your algorithm before reading on!*

Solution There are quite a few standard sorting algorithms. A very simple algorithm, known as the ***selection sort***, is similar to what many people might do naturally. Take a look to see if what you wrote down is similar to the selection sort algorithm, a somewhat incomplete description of which follows

- Go through the deck a first time to find the card with the smallest number; then place that card on top of the deck.

- Go through the 99 bottom cards of the deck to find the one with the smallest number; then place it second from the top of the deck.

- Go through the 98 bottom cards of the deck to find the one with the smallest number; then place it third from the top of the deck.

- Continue in this fashion until all the cards have been put in order.

Do you see anything in this description that needs further clarification or detailing? Exercise 1.6 asks you to discuss what instructions need further details and provide them.

It turns out that a computer program that uses the selection sort is fine for sorting a list of 100 social security numbers, because it will take at most a few seconds of computer time. However, when it comes to sorting a list of 10,000 social security numbers, the issue of **algorithm efficiency** comes into play. On a typical PC, a slow algorithm like the version of selection sort just given might require several minutes to do this task, whereas a different sorting algorithm, such as the Quicksort algorithm, might require less than a minute.

Selection sort and some other simple sorting algorithms are covered in detail in Chapter 14, and quicksort is covered in Section 26.4.

What Is Computer Science?   Computer science consists of a number of overlapping areas. Here is a list of some of its main branches.

- **Programming Languages** This broad area consists of the techniques for programming in a particular language, the comparative analysis of different languages, as well as the study of the design and implementation of existing and new programming languages. New languages are needed for specialized kinds of programming tasks. Also, principles for designing and creating programs are continually evolving, and existing languages may not be well suited to applying these new principles.

- **Algorithms and Algorithm Efficiency**   As we have already mentioned, for certain types of problems, some algorithms are much faster than others. On a more theoretical level, there are techniques for evaluating and describing the efficiency, or *complexity*, of an algorithm and even for determining whether a particular algorithm is the "best possible."

    An important practical application of the study of algorithms and their complexity has been the invention of secure methods, called *encryption schemes*, for sending private, sensitive data over a public channel such as a telephone line or the Internet. If unauthorized persons (who do not have the "key" used for decoding) were to intercept a copy of the transmission, they would not be able to decode it because the current algorithms for attempting to decode a message without the key require a prohibitive amount of computer time — perhaps thousands of years.

- **Software Engineering** This applied area of computer science deals primarily with principles that improve and optimize the development, operation, maintenance, and eventual retirement of large-scale programming projects. Large-scale software may contain millions of lines of code and is the product of many software analysts and designers, as well as large numbers of programmers working over long periods of time — possibly years — known as the software's life cycle. Software engineering is discussed in more detail in Section 1.5.

- **Computer Architecture** This area, which is the domain of both computer scientists and electrical engineers, deals with how computer systems are designed and constructed. Of particular concern are the design of and communication among processors, memory, and other hardware. These topics are discussed further in Section 1.3.

- **Operating Systems** This area deals with the interface between the user and the hardware that makes up a computer system. A graphical operating system (e.g., Windows) enables the user to communicate with and manipulate a computer's hardware by pointing and clicking on the computer's screen using a mouse. An operating system is actually a collection of programs that manage the resources of a computer, including the processor, input and output, and memory, and that maintain security and detect equipment failures.

- **Networking** This branch, which overlaps the field of data communications, addresses the problems of linking computers so that users can conveniently and safely share resources. Networks can range in size considerably, from a small number of linked computers in a single office, to a fairly extensive network such as that for a large banking system, to the enormously large network known as the Internet (which perhaps deserves to be considered an area of study in its own right).

- **Artificial Intelligence** Practitioners in this field attempt to program computers to perform tasks that would seem to require human intelligence. It was once a commonly held view that computers, while very fast, could not really think, because they could only follow orders and had to be given totally unambiguous, step-by-step instructions for anything that they did. However, recent accomplishments in artificial intelligence have been quite impressive. These accomplishments have included chess-playing programs that play at or above the level of the best human players in the world and voice-recognition programs that can recognize spoken words and convert them into writing. Other endeavors in this field, such as decoding the actual *meaning* of spoken language and translating from one human language to another, have thus far been rather disappointing. The distinction between human thought and what a computer can achieve continues to be the subject of intense debate.

- **Databases** Computers are used extensively to store, maintain, and provide access to large collections of data, known as *databases*. The study of databases focuses on how to organize and manage data so that it can be efficiently updated and accessed, and how to provide security so that unauthorized persons cannot alter or access the contents of a database.

1.2 A Brief History of Computing Devices

The first general-purpose, purely electronic digital computer, called ENIAC and built in 1946, was an enormous device that contained 18,000 vacuum tubes, occupied an entire 50-ft by 30-ft room, and weighed more than 30 tons. ENIAC was built for the U.S. Army to make calculations for weather predictions and ballistics tables. The first commercial computer, UNIVAC I, was introduced in 1951 and also took up an entire room. Its cost at the time was $500,000. Since those early days, enormous advances have been made in electronics technology. Perhaps the most remarkable breakthrough was the miniaturization of electronic circuits, allowing a circuit containing hundreds of thousands of switches to be etched onto a silicon chip the size of a fingernail. Today a computer that sits on a desktop, known as a microcomputer, can cost under $1,000 and yet have far more computing power than did earlier computers that filled entire rooms and were affordable only by large organizations.

Here is a brief history of computing devices starting from the abacus of 2000 B.C. up to the current PC.

- **Purely Mechanical Devices** (2000 B.C.) The abacus came into use. (1620 A.D.) The first slide rule was developed by Edmund Gunter, based on work done a few years earlier by John Napier. (1642) Blaise Pascal introduced an arithmetic machine that used wheels and gears to add and subtract and, with much more manual labor, could also multiply and divide; unfortunately, it was not very accurate. (1673) Gottfried Leibniz created a much easier-to-use and more accurate arithmetic machine, based on Pascal's ideas. (1805) Joseph Jacquard invented a loom that was controlled by the forerunner of the computer program; this "program," consisting of metal cards with holes punched in them, was attached to a weaving loom, and the type of pattern woven by the loom was specified by where the holes were punched in the cards. (1842) Charles Babbage began but did not complete work on a general-purpose, steam-powered computing machine, which he called the analytical engine. Many of his ideas have been used in the organization of current computers.

- **Transistion from Partly Electric to Purely Electronic Devices** (1890) Herman Hollerith devised a method for recording U.S. census data, which used punched cards to represent data and electric sensors for tabulating the data. (1924) IBM was formed from the company that Hollerith had started. (1939) John Atanasoff built the first truly electronic computer, but it was very specialized, performing only limited kinds of numerical calculations. (1946) ENIAC, the first general-purpose electronic computer, was built.

- **First Generation of Commercial Computers (1951–1958)** These computers used vacuum tubes as the electronic component in computer circuitry. (1951) UNIVAC I, the first commercial computer, was marketed. (1957) FORTRAN, the first high-level programming language, was invented.

- **Second Generation (1958–1964)** These computers used transistors (invented in 1948), which were smaller and more reliable than vacuum tubes, for the computer circuitry. (1958) The IBM 7090 reached the market.

- **Third Generation (1964–1970)** These computers used integrated circuits rather than transistors as the basic electronic component. Integrated circuits package transistors and wiring onto a thin wafer of silicon called a *chip*. This packaging eliminates the need to individually wire components to a circuit board and, thus, reduces manufacturing costs. (1964) IBM introduced its System 360 series of mainframe computers. (1965) Digital Equipment Corporation (DEC) introduced its minicomputers, which were larger than today's PCs but quite a bit smaller and more affordable than mainframes.

- **Fourth Generation (1970–Present)** These computers use large-scale integrated circuits, which place the logic circuitry of an entire computer onto a single silicon chip, called a *microprocessor*. (1971) Intel Corporation released the world's first microprocessor, the Intel 4004, which contained 2300 transistors (compared with several million in recent Intel microprocessors). (1976) DEC introduced its VAX minicomputer, the most successful minicomputer in history, with the possible exception of its immediate ancestor, the PDP-11. (1977) Apple Computer Company was founded. (1981) IBM introduced the personal computer (PC). (1984) Apple introduced the Macintosh, a computer with a graphical user interface (GUI) and a mouse. (1989) Microsoft introduced Windows for IBM PCs and compatible machines.

1.3 Physical Components — Hardware

The basic components of a computer system are shown in the diagram on the next page. The arrows indicate the direction of the flow of data.

CPU and Main Memory The heart of a computer is its central processing unit (CPU) and its main memory, which, as indicated in the following diagram, are usually stored in the same case or cabinet. For data to be processed by the computer, it must first be read into main memory and then processed by the CPU.

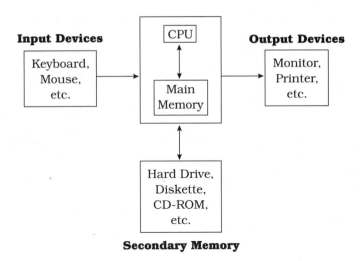

Data can be read or transferred into main memory in two ways. One way is by using an *input device* such as a keyboard or mouse, and the other is by reading data from a *secondary memory* source, such as a diskette, hard drive, or CD-ROM.

Main Memory Versus Secondary Memory   Main memory is ***volatile***, meaning that its contents cease to exist when you switch off the computer's power. Secondary memory, on the other hand, is nonvolatile — its contents remain stored even when computer power is off. Secondary memory devices such as magnetic disks and tapes are often removable and can be used to transfer data and programs from one computer to another.

RAM Versus ROM   In addition to main memory, also known as "random access memory," or RAM, there is ROM, which stands for "read-only memory." ROM is permanent memory and cannot be altered by your programs. The information in ROM, which is set by the computer manufacturer, helps guide the CPU in its internal functioning, including its ability to interpret machine language.

Memory Size (Units of Measurement)   Several terms are commonly used to specify unit amounts of computer memory. The smallest unit of memory is a ***bit*** (or ***binary digit***), which can store a 0 or a 1. A ***byte*** contains eight bits — for example, 01001011 is a typical byte. Because one byte can store only a very limited amount of information (that is, a single letter or a whole number no greater than 255), the storage capacity of a computer is discussed in terms of ***K*** (for ***kilobyte***), ***M*** or ***meg*** (for ***megabyte***), and ***G*** or ***gig*** (for ***gigabyte***). One *K* is approximately 1000 bytes, one *meg* is approximately 1000 K (or one million bytes), and one *gig* is approximately 1000 M (or one billion bytes). Desktop microcomputers purchased today contain at least 32 megs of main memory and several gigabytes of secondary memory.

Input Devices   Computer users usually input information by typing it at the computer keyboard and pointing with a mouse (or possibly a trackball). Information can also be input from the secondary memory devices discussed later in this section. Other input devices include a scanner, for scanning graphical images such as photographs, and a joystick, often used in computer games. Newer technologies also allow users to input information by touching a pressure-sensitive screen or speaking into a microphone. The latter input method is a common component of multimedia computers.

Output Devices   The most commonly used output devices are the video screen of a monitor, a printer, or a secondary memory device. Some computer applications also send output to a plotter for drawing pictures or graphs or to a sound card, a device that provides digital sound reproduction through internal or external speakers.

Secondary Memory   Suppose that you have just typed a program into the computer. This program currently resides in main memory, which will be erased when you turn off the computer. To save your program for future use, you must save it to a secondary storage device. Microcomputers generally use magnetic disks and tapes to store information in magnetic form. Optical disks that store information readable by beams of laser light are also becoming affordable as secondary storage media. The hardware that reads from or writes to a disk (or tape) is known as a **disk** (or **tape**) **drive**. The disk drive functions something like a cassette recorder — programs can be stored and retrieved in much the same way that music can be recorded and played back using a cassette recorder.

Magnetic disks can be removable or fixed and have a wide range of storage capacities. A *floppy disk* is a small (usually 3½ inch in diameter) removable disk, encased in hard plastic, with a typical storage capacity of 1.44 to 2.88 megabytes of memory. A **hard disk** is a rigid metal disk that is usually permanently installed inside the computer or a case attached to the computer. A hard disk's two big advantages over a floppy disk are its greater speed, enabling the computer to access data more quickly, and its much larger memory capacity, which today is typically several gigabytes. The distinction between floppy and hard disks is no longer as clear as it once was — some manufacturers now produce removable high-speed, 3½-inch hard disks with storage capacities of several hundred megabytes.

CD-ROM (Compact Disk-Read Only Memory) drives use the same optical laser technology as the familiar audio CD-ROMs. CD-ROM disks for computers have traditionally been read-only memory (ROM) devices, though writeable CD-ROMs with memory capacities of several gigabytes are becoming affordable.

1.4   Writing Programs: A First View

Computers Programs   Computers can do only what they have been given explicit instructions to do. Thus, when you need to write a program to solve a particular problem, *you*, not the computer, must come up with a step-by-step method for solving it, and then translate your method into a precise list of instructions written in a programming language. The writing of computer programs draws on a programmer's general problem-solving skills and is both an art and a science, requiring discipline, creativity, and practice.

Stages in Problem Solving (as Applied to Writing Programs)

1.   Problem specification   Before attempting to solve a problem, make sure you understand precisely what the solution should accomplish. What sort of input will be used, and what result or output will be produced? (At this stage you need not be concerned about the details of the process of achieving the desired result.) Especially for larger programs, the time spent coming up with a clear specification of the problem will be well rewarded.

2.   Solution design   To figure out a general process that can be used to achieve the desired result, it can be helpful to make up several sets of sample data and then analyze in detail what steps you perform when you solve the problem for those particular sets of data. As described in Section 1.1, the detailed list of steps or instructions for carrying out the general process is known as an algorithm.

An algorithm can be as compact as a single formula — for example, the formula $A = \pi r^2$ for finding the area, A, of a circle given its radius, r. Or, an algorithm may consist of a more extensive list of steps such as that given for the selection sort shown in Section 1.1.

When trying to solve a complicated problem, the programmer might have difficulty finding a correct algorithm right away. It is often a good idea, then, to start the solution process by subdividing the problem into smaller, more manageable subtasks. Such an approach is called *top-down design*.

3. Implementation, coding, and documentation After an algorithm has been developed, it must be translated into a computer program. *Implementation* is the process of translating an algorithm into working commands or instructions — frequently referred to as *code* — in the specific computer language being used. *Documentation* consists of explanatory comments that describe what the program should accomplish and explain how various segments of the code are designed.

4. Testing and debugging Even if a computer program runs and produces a correct result for one set of data, you cannot necessarily conclude that the program is correct. You should test the program for many sets of input that are designed to cover all scenarios. The process of *debugging* a program removes errors, or *bugs*, from the program. (The term "bug" comes from the well-documented case of a technician solving a malfunction in a first-generation computer by actually removing a moth from the machine's electronic circuitry.)

In Chapters 4, 5, and 9, we consider problem solving in relation to writing programs in greater detail.

1.5 Writing Programs: A Broader View

The Early Days of Programming In the 1950s, when computers were first commercially available, and again in the early 1980s, when personal computers were in their infancy, it was not uncommon for a complicated piece of software, created especially for a particular business or company, to be written by a single programmer. Too often, however, that programmer would write poorly documented code that used clever, often obscure, tricks and whose overall structure was difficult to follow. Consequently, if that programmer left the company, for whatever reason, it could be very difficult for a different programmer to take on the job of maintaining and upgrading that particular software.

Software Engineering *Software engineering* is the branch of computer science that deals with designing, documenting, coding, maintaining, and upgrading large programming projects. Large pieces of software can consist of hundreds of thousands, if not millions, of lines of code and are some of the most complex of human creations. Such projects are, of necessity, the work of large teams of programmers working under the direction of several project managers, who, in turn, are responsible to managers at even higher levels of the project. It is vital that code written by one team be readily understandable by other teams and their managers and that the work of all teams can be smoothly integrated by the managers at the higher levels to produce the desired end product.

Some general goals for software design are to ensure that software is

1. Reliable The software should be correct; it should work not just for some cases, but for all intended uses.

2. Easy to write There should be standard methodologies for analyzing a complex problem and designing a solution for it.

3. Easy to understand and use As we have described, portions of code produced by one team will be integrated with work done by other teams and managers. Thus, each portion must be written in ways that specify precisely what it will accomplish and how it can be integrated with other parts of the project.

4. Easy to upgrade Software is constantly being improved, both to fill new needs and to keep up with the competition. For example, the word processing program known as WordPerfect, first released in the early 1980s, has evolved over the years into its eighth major version.

General Techniques for Achieving Software Engineering Goals Although the general principles of software engineering have been developed with an eye toward coordinating the work of teams of programmers, these same principles are helpful to a single programmer working alone to produce even a small (100 or 200 lines) program. After all, this programmer will need to make the problem more manageable by breaking it down into smaller pieces and then joining and coordinating the work done by these different pieces. Four somewhat overlapping techniques that are important in software engineering are

1. Abstraction and top-down design In a complex program, the amount of detail can be intimidating if you try to deal with all of it at once. A better approach is to think in more abstract terms and use top-down design, first describing in a general way a list of subtasks that could be used to solve the problem. Once this outline is in place, you can fill in the details for how to accomplish each of these subtasks. Further, when working on the details of any one subtask, you will not need to think about the details of the other subtasks.

2. Reuse of well-tested code You should not have to repeatedly "reinvent the wheel," especially when new programming problems contain elements that are similar to problems you have already solved. When possible you should try to reuse thoroughly tested pieces of code that were written previously either by others or by you. Similarly, when you write new code, you should structure the new code so that portions of it can be readily extracted for reuse in future programs.

3. Modularity Modularity refers to subdividing a larger object into smaller pieces that are somewhat *self-contained* and *self-standing*. For example, when a TV set is manufactured, the different components of the set are produced and tested separately and then assembled into a whole TV set. Similarly, in programming, modularity means producing (that is, coding) and then testing the different parts of the program separately and then piecing together those different parts. Modularity works well with the top-down approach — the subtasks identified in top-down design will either be implemented as new pieces of code or as modifications to previously written pieces of code.

4. Information hiding The general goal of information hiding is to allow safe use of a device or construct, without requiring that the user understand the inner workings of that device. A good example of this concept is the remote control for a television, which enables the user to turn the set on or off, change channels, change the volume, and so on, merely by pressing the correct button; the user need not have any real knowledge of the inner workings of either the remote control or the television itself.

Information hiding enables a programmer to reuse previously written code without requiring that this programmer understand, let alone slog through the details of, how the code was written. Instead, the focus is on providing the programmer with clear instructions on what the code will accomplish and how to use it. The mechanism for providing the user with instructions for the reuse of code is known as an *interface*.

1.6 Procedural Versus Object-Oriented Programming

Programming Paradigms and C++ A programming *paradigm* is a general framework or model for designing and organizing programs. Two different programming paradigms currently in use are the procedural paradigm and the object-oriented (OO) paradigm. The procedural paradigm, which is the older of the two, has been used successfully to write many large and useful pieces of software. This paradigm, however, has been found inadequate in its handling of very large software projects. In response to these inadequacies, the OO paradigm was developed as a more powerful and reliable way to deal with the enormous complexity of large-scale programming projects.

Earlier languages, such as C, COBOL, FORTRAN, BASIC, and Pascal, were designed for procedural programming. C++, a recent extension of the once dominant C language, not only improves the procedural features of C, but, much more important, also adds powerful OO capabilities. Consequently, C++ has become the language of choice in industry.

More on How Procedural Programming Manages Complexity   In the procedural paradigm, primary emphasis is given to the sequence of actions that will be used to solve the problem. A complex program is first ***modularized*** as a collection of subtasks that manipulate data. In procedural languages like C, each subtask will usually be performed by a *function*, which is a named block of code that performs a specific subtask. Then, the main body of the program can act as an outline, consisting mostly of instructions that call on the functions to perform their designated subtasks. (The actual code for implementing the functions is not given in the main body but elsewhere.)

To appreciate the advantage of procedural programming, imagine a nonmodularized program, without function calls, whose main body consists of several hundred lines of code. Now imagine instead a second, modularized version of this program, with a much shorter main body of perhaps a dozen or so lines of code, that acts as an outline of the overall logical structure of the program. Because of the brevity of the main body, and also by virtue of good documentation, such as function names that reflect what subtasks these functions are performing, this second version of the program will be much easier to understand than its nonmodularized counterpart.

Basic Ideas of Object-Oriented Programming   In object-oriented programming, data plays a more primary role than it does in procedural programming. In object-oriented design, the basic building block is an ***object***. An object binds together data and the various functions (known as member functions) that the object uses to interact with other objects. This binding together of data and functions into an object is known as ***encapsulation***, and the data type for such an object is known as its ***class***. An object-oriented program is one in which various objects interact, in well-specified and safely controlled ways, through their member functions. (These abstract notions will become clearer as you work with classes and functions throughout the book.) As you will see, object-oriented programming is effective in part because program objects can be set up to closely mirror objects from the physical or real world.

More on the Advantages of Object-Oriented Programming   The advantages of the object-oriented paradigm stem in great measure from the following aspects of objects:

1.   Objects mirror the real world.   In object-oriented program analysis and design, a software engineer identifies the objects that are needed to solve the problem and describes how these objects are interconnected and how they interact in the problem solution. The real-world aspect of objects makes this process more natural than the procedural approach of thinking in terms of how functions manipulate data.

2. Objects promote safety. Through encapsulation, objects carefully restrict access to data, and thereby reduce the chances of accidental or incorrect alteration of data. Because data is the central focus of object-oriented programming, this safety feature is a powerful asset in producing reliable software.

3. Objects facilitate code reuse. OO extends the concept of code reuse by setting up large coordinated and integrated blocks of code (procedural programming uses lots of smaller, separate pieces of code). More specifically, OO facilitates the reuse of code that has already been thoroughly tested for reliability. This reuse is accomplished in two main ways:

(a) **Classes** In object-oriented C++, the main organizational construct is the class, which can be thought of as a blueprint for creating a particular type of object. Once designed, implemented, and tested, a given class can be used to create many specific objects of that class.

(b) **Inheritance** Using the object-oriented mechanism of *inheritance*, a programmer can use an existing class (that is, part of the solution of one or more problems) as the base from which to create a new class that is part of the solution of a new problem. This new class "inherits" all the features of the old class, but the programmer can add features to the new class to address the different aspects of the new problem.

4. Objects facilitate testing and program upgrades. The tightly controlled binding of data and functions into an object makes an object relatively independent of the program in which it will be used. Thus, objects can be tested independently and modified and upgraded in ways that have minimal impact on other objects in the program.

Why Learn Procedural Programming at All? If object-oriented programming has all these fantastic advantages over procedural programming, then why should your C++ education deal with procedural programming at all? There are three main reasons:

1. Object-oriented C++ presupposes procedural C++. C++ is a *hybrid* language in that it has both procedural and object-oriented features. Moreover, to write or even modify the code for objects, you will need to become proficient at procedural programming.

2. Object orientation in C++ has a lot of "overhead." Object orientation is intended to handle the complexity of large programs. It approaches a problem by first creating elaborate structures (the classes from which objects are created) that, in C++, require lots of code. For many shorter types of programming problems, this elaborate preparation either doesn't apply or results in a longer and more complicated solution than could be achieved by a procedural program.

3. Object orientation is only one programming paradigm. Object orientation, while considered by many to be a great advance in programming methodology, has not and will not entirely replace procedural programming or other significant programming paradigms that we have not mentioned, such as the functional and logic programming paradigms. A good software engineer should be well versed in multiple paradigms.

■ Exercises

1. Briefly explain how a computer represents information by means of electronic switches.

2. Define or describe the following:

computer	assembly language
computer program	machine language
programming language	source code
compiler	machine code

3. Name at least three high-level programming languages other than C and C++.

4. What is a byte? Approximately how many bytes are in 1 K of memory? In 1 meg of memory? In 1 gig of memory?

5. Define or describe the following:

microprocessor	RAM
silicon chip	ROM
volatile memory	

6. In the description of the selection sort algorithm in Section 1.1, which instructions need additional details?

7. Define or describe the terms *algorithm* and *algorithm complexity*.

8. List the five basic types of hardware and give examples of each.

9. List the four stages in problem solving as applied to writing programs.

10. What are some general goals of software engineering?

11. What is a programming paradigm? What are two currently popular programming paradigms?

12. Give two ways in which the C++ programming language improves on C. Is C++ a pure object-oriented language?

13. Define or describe

modularity	encapsulation
information hiding	inheritance

2

Introduction to C++

A *computer program* consists of a list of instructions written in a *computer language*. All the programs in this book are written in C++. In this chapter, we introduce some of the basics of C++.

2.1 A First Program

■ **EXAMPLE**

```
// height.cpp
// Convert height in feet to inches.
#include <iostream.h>

void main()
{
    int feet, inches;
    feet = 6;
    inches = feet * 12;
    cout << "Height is " << inches << " in.";
}
```

When this program is *run,* the computer screen will display

```
Height is 72 in.
```

Discussion   A line that begins with // is a *comment*. Comments do not affect how the program runs, but instead are used to explain various aspects of the program to a human reader; this type of explanation is known as *documentation*. The comment in the first line gives the name of the file containing the program, and the comment in the second line briefly describes what the program does. The third line of the program

```
#include <iostream.h>
```

is a *compiler directive,* which directs the compiler to include the *library file* iostream.h. This particular library file contains resources needed by any C++ program that receives information from the keyboard or that sends output to the screen. (*Note:* You may also hear library files referred to as *header files* because the compiler directives for including them generally appear at the head, or top, of the program.)

The remainder of the program consists of a *void function* called main, which you can think of as the main control center for program execution. Every program must have a function called main. The *body* of main (or any function) is enclosed in curly braces. The following table summarizes the actions of the first three statements of the program.

Statement	*Memory*		*Action(s)*
int feet, inches;	feet ?	inches ?	Creates two named int memory cells with no specific initial values
feet = 6;	feet 6	inches ?	Assigns the value 6 to the memory cell named feet
inches = feet * 12;	feet 6	inches 72	Retrieves the contents of the memory cell named feet, multiplies it by 12, and stores the result in the memory cell named inches

The final statement produces the output that appears on the computer screen. ▮ ▬

Keywords   Certain words such as int and void have predefined meanings in C++ and are known as *keywords*. They are also called *reserved* words because they are reserved for use by the C++ language itself and may not be used by a programmer for other purposes. A list of C++ reserved words is given in Appendix A.

Variables In processing data, a computer program usually must keep track of the values of certain quantities or **variables** stored in computer memory. We can conveniently refer to these quantities by symbolic **variable names** rather than their actual memory addresses.

Legal Variable Names A variable name must begin with a letter or underbar (_) and may contain only letters, digits, and the underbar. Except in special situations, the use of the underbar to begin a variable name should be avoided. An additional restriction is that the special class of keywords reserved for use by C++ cannot be used as variable names. (Appendix A lists these reserved words.) Variable names may be as long as you like, but only the first 32 characters are significant. The compiler distinguishes between upper- and lowercase letters, so feet, Feet, and FEET are all different variable names. In this book we avoid using uppercase letters in variable names, a practice that is followed by many C++ programmers. Some legal variable names are

    feet   sum   Tax1993   FINAL   average_score

Some illegal names for variables are:

1993Tax	Begins with a digit
valid?	Punctuation not permitted
average.score	Punctuation not permitted
average score	Spaces not permitted

Declaration of Variables Every variable that appears in a C++ program must have its data type declared. To declare the data type of each variable, a program should list each data type used followed by a list of variables of that type. In the previous program the statement

    int feet, inches;

declared the variables feet and inches as variables of type int. Variables of type int can take on only whole number values such as 7, 45, 0, or −36. Moreover, for most compilers, values of type int will be between −32,768 and 32,767, inclusive (or, for some compilers, between −2,147,483,648 and 2,147,483,647). In this chapter we consider only variables of type int. In later chapters, we consider variables of other types.

Assignment Statements An ***assignment statement*** stores a value in the memory location reserved for a variable. For example,

```
feet = 6;
```

is an assignment statement that assigns 6 to the memory location known symbolically as `feet`. The second and third statements in the body of the `height.cpp` program's `main` function are assignment statements.

The general form of an assignment statement is

```
variable = expression;
```

where the expression may be a constant, a variable, or a more complicated arithmetic expression.

When the computer reaches an assignment statement, it evaluates the expression on the right side of the assignment operator (=) and assigns the result to the single variable on the left side of that operator.

In C++ the symbols for addition and subtraction are the usual symbols (+ and −), but the symbol for multiplication is *. C++ also uses two division symbols, / and %, which have different meanings and are discussed in Chapter 3.

Output Statements The last statement of the previous program

```
cout << "Height is " << inches << " in.";
```

produces output that is displayed on the monitor. In a statement beginning with `cout` (pronounced "C out"), each item in double quotes is treated as a message and is output exactly as it is shown; any item not in double quotes must therefore be a variable or an expression, and the value of that variable or expression is output. Note also that each separate item to be output is preceded by the ***output operator*** <<. Any program that produces screen output must include the library file `iostream.h` because `cout` is predefined in that file.

You may use `cout` and the << operator to output a message. To do so, enclose the message in double quotes ("). (Note that a double quote is typed using only a single keystroke.)

```
cout << "Hello";
```

```
Hello.
```

Screen

Or you may use `cout` and << to output the value of a variable or an expression.

```
n = 7;
cout << n << n+9;
```

```
716
```

Screen

You can use cout and << to output messages, variables, and expressions in any order. The output items will be displayed one after another with no space between them, as in the preceding example. If you want a space to appear between a message and the value of a variable or expression, you can include a space as the first or last character of the message.

■ EXAMPLE   Suppose the variable area has the value 20. The statements

```
cout << "area is" << area;
cout << " area is " << area;
```

will produce the output

```
area is20 area is 20
```

Note that spaces outside the double quotes marks (like those in the first line of the example) are ignored.   ■ ▬

■ QUESTION   What will be the output of the following program segment?

```
x = 8; y = 6;
cout << x << y;
cout x << " " << y;
```

Answer

```
868 6
```

■ ▬

*cout **and New Lines***   The preceding example and question illustrate that separate cout statements do not necessarily produce separate lines of output. One way to cause the computer to begin a new line of output is to use the endl *manipulator*. Manipulators are special instructions that we send to cout with << in order to manipulate the way that data is displayed. The endl manipulator causes the printing cursor to move to the beginning of the next line. Some illustrations of `endl` are given in the next two questions.

■ **QUESTION**   What will be output be each of the following program fragments? (These fragments are from the program stored on the PWS Web site as `yd_2_ft.cpp`.)

1.

```
yards = 8;
feet = 3* yards;
cout << yards << " yd. is";
cout << feet << " ft.";
```

2.

```
yards = 8;
feet = 3* yards;
cout << yards << " yd. is";
cout << endl;
cout << feet << " ft.";
```

Answer   **1.**

```
8 yd. is24 ft.
```

2.

```
8 yd. is
24 ft.
```

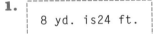

Empty Output Lines   The `endl` manipulator may be placed anywhere in a `cout` statement. If the cursor is already at the beginning of an output line, another `endl` in the statement will cause the cursor to drop to the beginning of the next line, creating a blank output line.

■ **QUESTION**   What will these segments output?

1.

```
cout << "Yes";
cout << endl << "No";
```

2.

```
cout << "Yes" << endl;
cout << endl;
cout << "No";
```

3.

```
cout << "Yes";
cout << "No";
```

Answer   **1.**

```
Yes
No
```

2.

```
Yes

No
```

3.

```
YesNo
```

■ QUESTION What will be output by the following complete program? Give the output with the *exact* messages and spacing.

```cpp
// cents.cpp
// Convert nickels and dimes to cents.
#include <iostream.h>

void main()
{
    int nickels, dimes, cents;
    nickels = 3;
    dimes = 7;
    cents = 5 * nickels + 10 * dimes;
    cout << nickels << " nickels and ";
    cout << dimes << " dimes " << endl;
    cout << "= " << cents << " cents ";
}
```

Answer

```
3 nickels and 7 dimes
= 85 cents
```

2.2 Punctuation and Style

Correct punctuation is essential for a program to run. By contrast, the use of spacing, blank lines, indentation, comments, and meaningful identifiers within a program won't affect whether it runs, though it will affect how easily a person understands the program.

Semicolons In a C++ program, a semicolon is used to end a statement. In the two full programs that you have seen so far, each statement in the body of main ended with a semicolon. For now, the rule for semicolons is to put one after each statement within the body of main.

Paired Symbols You have probably noticed that C++ programs contain items that must be *bracketed* by enclosing them between special symbols. Messages in cout statements, for example, must be enclosed in double quotes. Similarly, the body of main begins with a left *curly brace* ({) and ends with a right curly brace (}). Even the heading of the main function contains a pair of parentheses, although the significance of these parentheses will not be clear until we explore functions in more detail.

Commas The comma is actually an operator in C++. For now we will use it only to separate variables in a type declaration statement.

■ **QUESTION** Put the appropriate punctuation in the following program and then give the output.

```cpp
// yd_2_ft.cpp
   Convert yards to feet.
#include <iostream.h>
void main
{
    int feet yards;
    yards = 8
    feet = 3*yards;
    cout << yards << " yd. = << feet << " ft.";
)
```

Answer The correct code, with highlighted changes, is

```cpp
// yd_2_ft.cpp
// Convert yards to feet.
#include <iostream.h>

void main()
{
    int feet, yards;
    yards = 8;
    feet = 3 * yards;
    cout << yards << " yd. = " << feet << " ft.";
}
```

The output will be | 8 yd. = 24 ft.

Use Meaningful Variable Names and Identifiers Any name that you make up for use in a program is known as an ***identifier***. For example, each variable name is an identifier. In Chapter 3 we will need to create identifiers for other program components, but the same rule that you learned for legal variable names in Section 2.1 applies to any identifier that a programmer creates.

When creating a variable name or some other identifier, you should use a name that is not only legal but also meaningful — the name should remind you of the concept to which it refers. Thus, inches is a better variable name than x to represent the number of inches.

Keywords Versus Standard Identifiers   In Section 2.1 we discussed keywords, identifiers whose use is reserved for the C++ language. You cannot use these words for identifiers that you create. (See Appendix A for a complete list.)

Certain standard identifiers are used quite frequently in C++ programs. Some commonly used standard identifiers are main, cin, and cout. Although it is legal to use a standard identifier for a name that you make up, doing so will interfere with the identifier's predefined meaning within the program. So, avoid using standard identifiers for names that you make up.

Spaces, Blank Lines, and Indentation   Two rules must be followed with regard to spaces.

1. At least one space must separate any two identifiers in the program.

2. No spaces may be placed within an identifier or compound symbol such as <<.

Thus, inch es would not be a legal identifier, and < < would not be recognized as the output operator.

Additional spaces, especially in the form of indentation and blank lines, can and should be used to make the program more readable. These additional spaces, however, are for the human eye only — the computer is guided in determining where one statement ends and the next one begins solely by punctuation, keywords, and standard identifiers. Thus, program yd_2_ft.cpp would run perfectly well even if it were typed as

```
// yd_2_ft.cpp
#include <iostream.h>
void main (){int feet, yards;
yards=8;feet=3*yards;
cout << yards << " yd. = " << feet << " ft.";}
```

Comments   Another important way to make a program easier to understand is to include **comments**. Comments are messages inserted within the program to benefit the reader of the program. Comments may explain the purpose of the program, clarify individual steps, or provide useful information such as the author's name and the identifier of the file containing the program. Comments are ignored completely by the compiler.

There are two ways to place a comment in a program. One is to preface the comment with //. This is illustrated in the first two lines of the correct version of yd_2_ft.cpp in this section. A comment prefaced with // extends only to the end of the line. Multiline comments can be bracketed by /* and */ as in

```
/* yd_2_ft.cpp
   Written by: The Two Authors
   Purpose: Convert yards to feet.
*/
```

NOTE It is good style to include the file identifier, your name, and a brief statement of purpose at the beginning of a program. Your instructor may specify additional information and a particular format for this introductory *documentation*.

Letter Case and Identifiers Because the C++ compiler distinguishes between upper- and lowercase letters in identifiers, Age, age, and AGE are interpreted by the compiler as three different identifiers. Therefore, you must type keywords and standard identifiers exactly as given. (VOID and Cout are not the same as void and cout, respectively.)

When creating our own identifiers, we will follow some basic stylistic guidelines. The first of these applies to making up variable names: We will not use uppercase letters, and we will use the underbar between individual words of multiple word identifiers. Thus, for the variable that records the federal tax paid in 1993, we will use fed_tax_paid_93 rather than other legal possibilities such as FedTaxPaid93 and FED_TAX_PAID_93.

Capitalization and String Literals Sequences of characters enclosed in double quotes (the messages that we displayed via cout, for example) are called *string literals*. These messages are obviously case sensitive — the following cout statements produce different outputs.

```
cout << "who is bjarne stroustrup?";
cout << "Who is Bjarne Stroustrup?";
```

2.3 Memory Cells and More on Assignments

When a program runs, each declared variable is given a memory location (which you can think of as a memory cell). For example, when the program cents.cpp of Section 2.1 is run, three memory cells are created. After the first three assignment statements, memory can be depicted as follows:

nickels   dimes   cents

3	7	85

Changing the Value of a Variable   The memory cell of a variable will hold only the current value of the variable, *not* previous values.

■ **QUESTION**   What will be output by the following program segment?

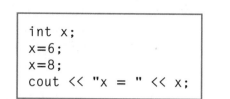

Memory for x

~~6~~
8

Answer

```
x = 8
```

Output

Note that x is first assigned the value 6. The next statement assigns x the new value 8, erasing the previous value of x. The `cout` statement displays only the current contents of the variable x.   ■ ■■

Only Variable on Left Affected   Recall that an assignment statement assigns a value to the variable to the left of the assignment operator (=). Thus, a statement like

```
num1 = num2;
```

replaces any value currently in `num1` by the value currently in `num2`, but it does not affect the value of `num2`.

■ **QUESTION**   What will be output by the following program fragment (from `asnmnt.cpp`)?

```
num1 = 5;
num2 = 14;
num1 = num2;
cout << num1 << endl;
cout << num2 << endl;
```

Answer   In the following line-by-line memory trace, a dash means that the variable has not had its value changed by the current statement.

```
   14
   14

  Output
```

```
num1 = 5;
num2 = 14;
num1 = num2;
cout << num1 << endl;
cout << num2 << endl;
```

```
   5
   -
  14
   -
   -
```

```
   -
  14
   -
   -
   -
```

num1   num2

Same Variable on Both Sides   The variable on the left side of an assignment statement may also appear on the right. In such situations, the current value of that variable is used in the calculation (on the right side of the equal sign) of the new value of that variable.

■ **EXAMPLES**
1. `count = count + 1;`   increases the value of `count` by 1

2. `sum = sum + x;`   increases the value of `sum` by x, but does not change the value of x

3. `num = 3 * num;`   triples the value of `num`

CAUTION   The left side of an assignment statement must consist of a single variable. Thus, the statement `x + 4 = y;` is illegal.   ■ ▬

■ **QUESTION**   What will be output by the following code fragment?

```
hours = 40;
rate = 5;
pay = hours * rate;
cout << hours << " " << rate << " " << pay << endl;
rate = rate + 1;
cout << hours << " " << rate << " " << pay << endl;
pay = hours * rate;
cout << hours << " " << rate << " " << pay << endl;
```

Answer
```
40 5 200
40 6 200
40 6 240
```

Discussion Notice that the original value of pay (200) was output by the second cout statement because at that point pay had not been assigned a new value yet. The statement rate = rate + 1; changes the value of rate. The value of pay is not changed until the second time that the statement pay = hours * rate; is executed.

2.4 Interactive Programs

Obviously, the height.cpp program in Section 2.1 is not very useful. Every time it is run, it will perform the same computation and produce the same output. A more useful program would allow the *user* (the person who runs the program) to enter a value of her own choosing for feet. Such a program is called **interactive**.

Input Statements We would like to allow the user to enter values from the keyboard while the program runs. We can do this by using a statement beginning with cin (pronounced "C in") and the input operator >>. When it executes a cin statement during the run of a program, the computer will pause until the user types in a value (or values) and presses the Enter key.

■ **EXAMPLE**

```
// ft_2_in.cpp
// Convert input number of feet to inches.
#include <iostream.h>

void main()
{
   int feet, inches;
   cout << "Enter number of feet: ";
   cin >> feet;
   inches = 12 * feet;
   cout << "That's " << inches << " inches." << endl;
}
```

When this program is run, the computer will display the following prompt on the output screen

```
Enter number of feet:
```

and will pause with the cursor blinking. The computer is waiting for the user to enter a value for feet. After the user types a value and presses the Enter key, the computer will input that value from `cin`, assign the value to `feet`, and then resume program execution. For example, typing 5 and pressing the Enter key would have the same effect as the assignment statement `feet = 5;`. Two sample runs of the program are

```
Enter number of feet: 5
That's 60 inches.
```

```
Enter number of feet: 24
That's 288 inches.
```

Discussion   Notice that the user inputs, 5 and 24, are underlined in the above program runs. Throughout this text, *all user inputs will be underlined* to distinguish between user inputs and program outputs. When running an interactive program, however, you simply type your inputs when prompted — there is no way for you to underline your inputs as you enter them.

Prompts   When writing an interactive program, you should precede each input statement with an output statement, called a ***prompt***, that will display a message to let the user know what kind of value to enter. That was the purpose of the statement

```
cout << "Enter number of feet: ";
```

in the previous program.

Generally, you should not place an `endl` at the end of a `cout` statement that displays a prompt. If you were to use `endl`, the user input would appear on the screen line following the prompt.

Cascading Input   The last line of the previous program

```
cout << "That's " << inches << " inches." << endl;
```

shows that you can output several items with one `cout` statement. This method is known as ***cascading*** the `<<` operator. Similarly, you can input several values with one `cin` statement by cascading the input operator (`>>`). Thus, it would be possible to use an output/input statement pair like

```
cout << "Enter number of nickels and dimes: ";
cin >> nickels >> dimes;
```

to input values for `nickels` and `dimes` from `cin`. When that input statement is executed, the computer will wait until the user has entered two integer values, separated by at least one space, and then pressed the Enter key.

Input Versus Output Streams There is a good way to remember which operator, << or >>, is the input operator and which is the output operator: The arrows point from the data's source to its destination.

```
cin >> yards
```

The data is flowing from the keyboard *toward* the variable `yards`.

```
cout << feet
```

The data is flowing *from* the variable `feet` to the screen.

`cin` and `cout` are two examples of **streams**, which you can think of as paths for the flow of data. The standard input stream, `cin`, flows from the keyboard to a program. The standard output stream, `cout`, flows from a program to the screen. Both `cin` and `cout` are predefined in `iostream.h`.

QUESTION Suppose we want a program to convert an input number of nickels and dimes into a total number of cents. A sample run of the program would look like

```
Enter number of nickels and dimes: 3 7
3 nickels and 7 dimes = 85 cents
```

Complete the blanks in the following program to produce the output shown.

```cpp
// cents2.cpp
// Convert input number of nickels and dimes
// to cents.
#include <iostream.h>

void main()
{
    int nickels, dimes, cents;
    cout << "Enter number of nickels and dimes: ";
    cin _____;
    cents = 5 * nickels + 10 * dimes;
    cout _____;
}
```

Answer   From the previous discussion, the `cin` statement is

```
cin >> nickels >> dimes;
```

To determine what the second `cout` statement is, let us analyze the second line of output by underlining what is output verbatim and shading what resulted from the output of a variable.

```
3 nickels and 7 dimes = 85 cents
```

Thus, one correct version of the second output statement is

```
cout << nickels << " nickels and "
     << dimes << " dimes = "
     << cents << " cents " << endl;
```

Discussion   The previous statement contains eight output items, making the statement too long to fit nicely on one line. You will frequently encounter this situation. You can spread a single `cout` statement over several lines by breaking it immediately before or after the `<<` operator. Or you can make each line a separate statement as in

```
cout << nickels << " nickels and ";
cout << dimes << " dimes = ";
cout << cents << " cents " << endl;
```

The indentation in the first version helps to indicate that these three lines are all one statement. In the second version, each of the three separate `cout` statements must end with a semicolon.   ▪ ▬

2.5   Using a Virtual Printer

Printing on Paper   You should find out the basic techniques provided by your computer system and C++ implementation for printing on paper both a program's source code and typical runs of that program.

Advantages of a Virtual Printer   In the programs presented so far, user inputs and program outputs have appeared on the monitor. The texts of such program runs can then be printed in their entirety on paper. However, in situations in which the user is repeatedly prompted for input, you may want to print on paper only the processed outputs, omitting the prompts and user inputs. To do this, you can have the program send the processed output to a ***virtual printer,***[1] which is actually a disk file.

---

[1] In some C++ implementations (e.g., Turbo C++ 3.0 for DOS), output can easily be sent directly from a program to an actual printer. However, for Windows implementations, direct printer output from a C++ program requires advanced techniques that are beyond the scope of this text.

Then, after program execution is completed, you can open that file and print its contents on paper.

Using a Virtual Printer The file `ourtools.h`, available from the PWS Web site, provides an easy way to use a virtual printer. Program output that you send to this virtual printer will actually go to the `c:\vprinter.out` file. To use this virtual printer, you need to

1. Place the include directive

    ```
    #include "a:\ourtools.h"
    ```

    with the other include directives at the beginning of your program.

2. Send to `vprn`, rather than to `cout`, any output that you want to go to the virtual printer.

3. After your program has completed execution, open and print the contents of the file `c:\vprinter.out`.

■ **EXAMPLE** The following program sends some of its output to the monitor and some to the virtual printer.

```
// use_vpr1.cpp
// A virtual printer example
#include <iostream.h>
#include "a:\ourtools.h"

void main()
{
    int m, n;
    cout << "Enter a two digit number: ";
    cin >> m;
    cout << "Enter a two digit number: ";
    cin >> n;
    vprn << m << " * " << n << " = " << m*n << endl;
}
```

If the user were to enter 15 and 27, the input and output appearing on the monitor would be:

```
Enter a two digit number: 15
Enter a two digit number: 27
```

and the virtual printer output would be

```
15 * 27 = 405
```

Discussion   Note that in the first #include directive, iostream.h, is enclosed in angular braces, while in the second, a:\ourtools.h is enclosed in double quotes. The difference is that iostream.h is a standard library file in C++, whereas ourtools.h is a programmer-defined library file written by the authors.[2] The compiler needs to know whether included files are standard or programmer defined, and this information can be indicated by using <..> or "..".

The output to the virtual printer does not accumulate over several runs. Each time you run a program that sends output to vprn, the previous contents of the virtual printer will be erased at the beginning of program execution. ■ ▆

Path Information   The include directive for ourtools.h specifies the full path, "a:\ourtools.h", assuming that you have copied this file from the PWS Web site to a disk in the a: drive. You do not need to give the full path if you have provided path information to your operating system. (Instructions for providing path information vary by compiler and operating system.) In the remaining examples in this text, we do not give full path information for programmer-defined include files.

■ Exercises

1. Which of the following identifiers are legal? Which are illegal, and why?
   (a) FinalScore   (b) final score
   (c) final_score   (d) sales_1995
   (e) 1995_sales   (f) total$$

---

[2] The contents of ourtools.h, are short and simple. Creating the virtual printer actually requires *only a single line of code*, which is explained in detail at the end of Section 11.8.

2. Insert the appropriate punctuation and operators in the following program.

```
// exr2.cpp
#include iostream.h

·void main
{
    int feet, inches
    feet = 5
    inches = 12 * feet
    cout inches
```

3. What output will the following code fragment produce?

```
x = 5;
y = 8;
cout << "x equals " << x << endl;
cout << x << y << endl;
cout << y << "equals y" << endl;
```

4. What output will the following code fragments produce?

(a)
```
num = 10;
x = 5;
cout << num;
cout << x;
cout << num << endl;
```

(b)
```
num = 10;
x = 5;
cout << num << ' ';
cout << x << ' ';
cout << endl;
cout << num << endl;
```

(c)
```
x = 4;
y = 6;
y = y + x;
x = x + 1;
cout << "x = " << x
        << endl;
cout << "y = " << y
        << endl;
```

(d)
```
num1 = 2;
num2 = 9;
num1 = num1 + 1;
num2 = num2 + num1;
cout << "num1 = " << num1
        << endl;
cout << "num2 = " << num2
        << endl;
```

5. Complete the following program fragment so that it produces the output given to its right.

```
dimes = 4;
pennies = 6;
tot_cents = _____
_____
_____
```

```
4 dimes and 6 pennies
equals 46 cents.
```

6. What output would the following program produce on the terminal and the virtual printer?

```
#include <iostream.h>
#include "ourtools.h"

void main()
{
  cout << "When this program has finished execution," << endl;
  vprn << "I see that you followed instructions! You" << endl;
  cout << "open the file vprinter.out on drive C." << endl;
  vprn << "know how to get virtual printer output." << endl;
}
```

Programming Problems

7. Write an interactive program that converts yards into inches. Here are two typical runs.

```
Enter number of yards: 4
4 yards = 144 inches
```

```
Enter number of yards: 6
6 yards = 216 inches
```

Run 1   *Run 2*

8. Write an interactive program that asks the user to input a number of dimes and a number of quarters. The program should then calculate and output the total number of cents.

9. Write a program that asks the user to input the length and width of a rectangle. The program should output both the area and the perimeter of the rectangle.

10. Rewrite the program solution to any of the previous three exercises so that your name, the user input(s), and the program-calculated output(s) are displayed, with appropriate messages, on the virtual printer.

3

More on the Elements of C++

So far the only data type we have used is `int`. In this chapter you will learn to use other built-in data types — `long` for large integers, `float` for values with a fractional part, and `char` for single characters. You will also study several arithmetic operators and their rules of precedence. Finally, you will learn to use a simple form of the `for` loop so that your programs can input and process several groups of data in one run.

3.1 A First Look at Syntax Errors

Before a C++ program can be run, the compiler must translate the program into machine language. As part of the compilation process, the compiler checks that the program contains no violations of the C++ syntax (or grammar) rules. Such violations are called ***syntax errors*** or, because they are detected during compilation, ***compile-time errors***. Some common types of syntax errors are misspelled keywords, incorrect or missing punctuation, and undeclared variables.

■ **EXAMPLE**   The following program (shown with line numbers) contains three syntax errors. Type it in, save it, and try to compile it.

```
1   // errors.cpp
2   #include <iostream.h>
3   void main()
```

```
 4  {
 5      int n;
 6      cout << "Hello" << endl;
 7      N = 2;
 8      cout << "n eqalls " << n
 9      cout << "So long << endl;
10  }
```

One compiler, Turbo C++ 4.5 for Windows, produces the following list of line numbers and syntax errors.

```
 7: Undefined symbol 'N' in function main()
 9: Statement missing ; in function main()
 9: Unterminated string or character constant in function main()
10: Compound statement missing } in function main()
```

Discussion   Notice that the compiler had reached line 9 by the time it caught the missing semicolon from line 8 — many compiler error messages are "late" like this one. The final two error messages are due to the missing closing quote on the string "So long". Although only one syntax error occurred on lines 9 and 10, the compiler could not recover from the error on line 9 and began to produce misleading error messages from that point on. The compiler did not detect the misspelling, "eqalls", on line 8 because that word was part of a string literal. ■ ▆

Dealing with Compiler Error Messages   The compiler does a good but not perfect job of diagnosing syntax errors, so you should become familiar with some of its limitations. First, error messages (e.g., "missing semicolon") are frequently late, and one syntax error (e.g., "unterminated string") can cause the compiler to begin producing error messages where no actual error exists. Second, the compiler does not diagnose some errors at all. For example, if you forget to close a comment begun with /*, the compiler will view the remainder of the program as a comment. Third, the compiler often correctly detects a syntax problem, but gives a cryptic error message rather than an easy-to-understand diagnosis. For these errors you will need help from your instructor until you have sufficient experience to catch them yourself.

A good approach to dealing with compiler error messages is to use the compiler's first error message as a guide to repairing the first actual syntax error, then compile again. Continue this repair–compile process until your code is free of syntax errors.

3.2 The long **Integer Data Type**

In Chapter 2 you saw the int data type, which has a range of $-32,768$ (or -2^{15}) to $32,767$ (or $2^{15}-1$) for many versions of C++. The most useful additional integer data type is long, which can store integers between $-2,147,483,648$ (or -2^{31}) and $2,147,483,647$ (or $2^{31}-1$), inclusive. (For some C++ compilers, this is also the range for int.)

■ **EXAMPLE**   The following program produces the correct output when salary and bonus are declared to be of type long, but would produce an incorrect output if salary and bonus were declared to be of type int.

```
// bonus.cpp
#include <iostream.h>

void main()
{
    long salary, bonus;
    salary = 32767;
    bonus = 8000;
    cout << "Salary plus bonus is $";
    cout << salary + bonus << endl;
}
```

```
Salary plus bonus is $40767
```
Output

CAUTION (Wraparound) If both salary and bonus had been of type int, the output would have been

```
Salary plus bonus is $-24769
```

The reason for this incorrect calculation is **wraparound**. int values higher than 32,767 "wrap around", as if arranged around a circle, starting over again at the leftmost end of the negative int values. Thus,

$$32767 + 1 = -32768, \quad 32767 + 2 = -32767, \quad 32767 + 3 = -32766$$

and so on.

You might wonder why we use the int data type at all if long can handle a much larger range of values. The reason is that variables of type long require four bytes of memory (int variables require only two bytes), and operations on longs take more time than operations on ints. Thus, when you are sure type int will suffice, it is better to use int than long.

3.3 The float and double Data Types

The float Data Type   A variable of type float is much more inclusive than one of type int or long. Not only can a float variable be assigned an integer value in the ranges used by int and long, but a float variable can also be assigned fractional values and much larger values. Some float values are:

   4.3   −52.97   2.33333   −123000000000.   0.0000003

In C++, float values can store six digits of precision.

float Values and Exponential (Scientific) Notation   When a float value has a very large (e.g., −123000000000.) or very small (e.g., 0.0000003) absolute value, the float value should be expressed in *exponential* or *scientific notation*. For example,

1. −123000000000 can be expressed as −1.23e11, where the e11 means to multiply 1.23 by 10^{11}; that is, move the decimal point 11 places to the right, appending zeros as needed.

2. 0.0000003 can be expressed as 3e−7, which means to multiply 3 (or 3.0) by 10^{-7}, in effect moving the decimal point seven places to the left.

In C++, the exponent of a float value can be between −38 and +38, inclusive.

CAUTION   When you type a float value as part of program code, you should include a decimal point or use exponential notation. As an example of what can go wrong, the assignment statement x = 1230000000000; does not store 1.23e12 in x. Instead, the compiler assumes that 1230000000000 is a long value, and because this value exceeds LONG_MAX, its value is corrupted as a result of wraparound. For more on this phenomenon, see the program flt_wrp.cpp from the PWS Web site.

Outputting float ***Values: Default Format***   In default output (i.e., in the absence of formatting specifiers) of a float value, the *computer* will examine the value to output in order to determine how many digits to display and whether to use ordinary decimal notation or exponential notation.

■ **EXAMPLE**   The following program fragment (from floatout.cpp) produces the output to its right.

```
cout << 4.5 << endl;
cout << -.375 << endl;
cout << 10.6666666 << endl;
cout << 67800000.0 << endl;
cout << 523000000000 << endl;
cout << 523000000000. << endl;
cout << 0.000098 << endl;
```

Program fragment

```
4.5
-0.375
10.6667
6.78e+07
3308957184
5.23e+11
9.8e-05
```

Output

Discussion   The third line shows that, by default, decimal values are displayed to, at most, six digits of accuracy. In the fourth line of output, 6.78e+07, the e+07 means that 6.78 is to be multiplied by 10^7. Similarly, 0.000098 is displayed as 9.8e-05 which is 9.8×10^{-5}, and indicates that the decimal point should be moved five places to the left. The fifth line of output, 3308957184, emphasizes the point made previously: a value with no decimal point or exponent (523000000000) is assumed to be an integer. Some compilers will give a warning about the fifth cout statement. For example, the Turbo C++ 4.5 compiler gives the warning

```
Constant is long in function main()
```
■ ▄▄

Specifying the Output Format for float ***Values***   Suppose that a float variable x has the value 10.6667 and you want its output given to two decimal places. By default, the statement cout << x; outputs 10.6667. To override the default output format, you have two options:

Method 1: Use C++'s Built-in Formatting Capability.   C++'s built-in methods for outputting numbers to a desired number of decimal places are complicated and difficult to explain.[1]   For example, to ensure that x

---

[1] Appendix G contains information on output formatting functions such as setiosflags and setprecision, which are provided by the library file iomanip.h.

will be output accurately to two decimal placed (10.67) you would need to write:

```
cout << setiosflags (ios::fixed | ios::showpoint)
     << setprecision(2);
cout << x;
```

Method 2 (Simpler): Use `fixed_out` **from** `ourtools.h`.   The `fixed_out` statement from the file `ourtools.h` provides a much simpler way for the programmer to specify the number of decimal places to be used in outputting `float` values. The effect of `fixed_out (cout, n);` is that, until further notice, `float` variables output to the monitor will be in fixed-point, or ordinary, decimal form, with n digits after the decimal place. For example, if x has the value 10.6667, then the statements

```
fixed_out (cout, 2);
cout << x;
```

ensure that the output will be 10.67 rather than (the default output) 10.6667.

Again, *be aware that* `fixed_out` *is not part of standard C++ but, instead, is contained in the file* `ourtools.h` *on the PWS Web site.*[2] Thus, in order to use `fixed_out` in a program, not only must `ourtools.h` be copied to your "work disk" or your hard drive, that program must also contain the include directive #include "ourtools.h".

■ **QUESTION**   Fill in the blank lines in the following program so that each `cout` statement produces the output shown to its right.

```
// fltfrmt.cpp
#include <iostream.h>
#include "ourtools.h"
```

---

[2] `fixed_out` is not difficult to write and is entirely portable from one C++ implementation to another. Its details are given at the end of Section 11.9.

```
void main()
{
    float x, y;
    x = 25.37691;
    y = 44.31;
    ─────────────────
    cout << x << endl;      25.377
    cout << y << endl;      44.310
    ─────────────────
    cout << x << endl;      25.4
    cout << y << endl;      44.3
}
```

Answer   The missing lines are

```
        fixed_out(cout,3);
        fixed_out(cout,1);
```

Using fixed_out *with Other Streams*   The fixed_out statement can be used to format output that is sent to other destinations. The general form is

```
        fixed_out (stream-name, n);
```

Thus, for example, the statements

```
        fixed_out(cout, 3);
        fixed_out(vprn, 4);
```

will specify, respectively, that until further notice, float values output to the monitor will be given to three decimal places, whereas those output to the virtual printer (see Section 2.5) will be given to four decimal places.

The fixed_out formatting statement (and its more complicated equivalent, given in method 1) is said to be *persistent* because it will remain in effect until it is overridden by another formatting statement.

Mixed-Type Expressions   When an arithmetic expression contains computations involving different data types, that expression is called a *mixed-type expression*.

Arithmetic Operations That Mix int **and** float.   If an arithmetic operation mixes an operand of type int and one of type float, the result is of type float. Of course, if both operands are of the same type, the result is also of that type. Thus, if x is of type float and n of type int

```
x + n // is of type float
n * 4 // is of type int
n + 4.0 // is of type float
```

More generally, when it is legal to mix two different types in an operation, the result is of the more inclusive type. Thus, when you add an int value and a long value, the result is of type long.

Assignment Statements That Mix floats **and** ints.   Both of the following are legal:

1. Assigning an integer expression to a variable of type float. This is *perfectly safe.*

2. Assigning a float value to an integer variable. When doing this, be aware that the fractional portion of the float value will not be stored in the integer variable — it will be truncated because an integer variable cannot store a fractional part. For example, if n is of type int, then

    ```
    n = 4.5; // assigns 4 to n
    ```

■ **QUESTION**   What will be the output of the following code fragment from mix_asn.cpp?

```
int m, n;
float x, y;
m = 3.0;
n = 12.7;
x = m;
x = x + .5;
m = x + 1;
y = x + 1;
cout << m << " " << n << endl;
cout << x << " " << y << endl;
```

Answer

```
4 12
3.5 4.5
```

■ **QUESTION**   The following program converts inches to centimeters. What will the run look like if the user inputs 4 for inches?

```
// in_2_cm.cpp
// Convert inches to centimeters.
#include <iostream.h>

void main()
{
    int inches;
    float centimeters;
    cout << "Enter number of inches: ";
    cin >> inches;
    centimeters = 2.54 * inches;
    cout << inches << " in. equals ";
    cout << centimeters << " cm." << endl;
}
```

Answer   The run will be

```
Enter number of inches: 4
4 in. equals 10.16 cm.
```

Note that in the absence of formatting specifiers, the value calculated for centimeters (in this case, 10.16) is output as is.   ■ ▬

Other Floating-Point Types   For calculations requiring more than six digits of precision or a wider range of exponents than −38 to +38, the data types double and long double are available. The following chart shows the storage sizes, exponent ranges, and digits of precision of these types in Turbo C++.

Floating-Point Data Types

Type	Size (bits)	Exponent range	Precision (digits)
Float	32	−38 to 38	6
Double	64	−308 to 308	15
Long double	80	−4932 to 4932	19

3.4   More on Numerical Operators

The Division Operator, /   When the / operator is used to perform division, the data types of the operands can affect the result of the computation. This is detailed in the following two cases.

1. *When both operands are integer types*, the operator / returns the integer quotient, throwing away the remainder. Thus,

$$9/2 \ = \ 4 \quad \text{and} \quad 9/10 \ = \ 0$$

Although there are situations when you need to calculate a quotient without remainder (such as in converting a height given in inches to feet and inches), *this operator is also a common source of programming errors because, in ordinary mathematical notation, 9/2 = 4.5.*

2. *When at least one of the operands is of type* float, the operator / performs ordinary division and the result is of type float. Thus,

$$9.0/2 \ = \ 4.5 \quad \text{and} \quad 9/10.0 \ = \ 0.9$$

The Remainder (or Modulus) Operator %   When using this operator, both operands must be integer types. This operator returns the remainder (or modulus) of the first operand divided by the second. Thus,

$$9\%2 \ = \ 1 \quad \text{and} \quad 9\%10 \ = \ 9$$

■ QUESTION   Evaluate each of the following.

1. 26 / 4   **2.** 26 % 4   **3.** 26 / 4.0

Answer   **1.** 6   **2.** 2   **3.** 6.5   ■ ▬

■ QUESTION   Fill in the blanks so that when the input is 75 the following fragment (from inches.cpp) produces the output shown. The variables inches and feet are both of type int.

```
cin >> inches;
feet = inches _____;
cout << feet << " ft. "
     << inches _____ << " in.";
```

```
6 ft. 3 in.
```

Output

Answer   The completed lines are

```
feet = inches  / 12;
      << inches  % 12 << " in.";
```

Rules of Precedence

QUESTION   Consider 2 + 3 * 4. Is the resulting value equal to 20 because (2 + 3) * 4 = 20? Or is it equal to 14 because 2 + (3 * 4) = 14?

Answer   It is equal to 14 because in C++ (as in algebra) multiplication has higher precedence than addition, so multiplication is performed first.

Precedence Table

Precedence	*Numerical operators*
Higher	*, /, %
Lower	+, −

(Operations with the Same Precedence)   When an expression with no parentheses contains two operators of the same precedence from the preceding table, the computer performs those operations in order from left to right.

(Parentheses Take Precedence)   Operations within parentheses are performed first. Use parentheses when you need to alter the normal precedence order. Thus, if you wanted the computer to multiply $a + b$ by c, you would use (a + b) * c.

QUESTION   Evaluate each of the following.

1. 1 + 2 * 3 + 4   **2.** 6 + 5 / 2 * 3

3. 1 + 2 * (3 + 4)   **4.** (6 + 5) / (2 * 3)

Answer   **1.** 11   * is performed first because it has higher precedence than +.

2. 12   / is performed before * because of the left to right rule. + is performed last because it has lowest precedence.

3. 15   The operations are performed right to left because parentheses take precedence, and * takes precedence over the first +.

4.   1   The parentheses override the usual precedence rules for /, *, and +.

QUESTION   How would you write the formula $q = \dfrac{a+b}{c+d}$ as a C++ assignment statement?

Answer   q = (a + b) / (c + d); [*Note:* q = a + b / c + d; is not correct because the right side would be evaluated as $a + (b/c) + d$.]   ■ ▬

Getting the Decimal Quotient of Two int Variables   You can convert an integer operand to be of type float in a calculation by putting that operand in parentheses and preceding it by the keyword float. Thus, if m and n are of type int, the expression float(m)/n performs ordinary division. If x and y are of type float and m and n are of type int with m=9 and n=2, then the following fragment will produce the output shown.

```
x = float(m) / n;
y = m / n;
cout << "x = " << x << endl;
cout << "y = " << y << endl;
```

```
x = 4.5
y = 4
```
Output

Type Casts   In the first line of the preceding fragment, the value of m is *cast* to type float. That is, putting m in parentheses and preceding it by the keyword float causes m to be treated as a float value. Note, however, that in the next statement m is still of its original type, int.

PROBLEM   **(Integers and Percentages)**   Suppose that in an election for class president, the variable voters, represents the total number of students who voted and that Smith_count represents the number of students who voted for Smith. The following *incorrect* fragment *attempts* to convert the fraction of the votes that Smith got into a percent given to the nearest tenth.

```
Smith_pct = Smith_count / voters * 100;
fixed_out(cout,1);
cout << "Smith got " << Smith_pct <<
     "% of the votes." << endl;
```

QUESTION   1.   What will the output be when voters and Smith_count are both of type int, Smith_count = 10, and voters = 80. Note that 10/80 = 0.125, which we want to output as 12.5%.

2. Correct the first line of this fragment.

Answer   **1.** `Smith got 0.0% of the votes.`

2. The problem occurs because when the computer evaluates the expression `Smith_count / voters * 100`, it first performs the integer division, `Smith_count / voters` (which is $10/80 = 0$), then multiplies that result by 100. Two common correct answers are

```
Smith_pct = 100.0 * Smith_count / voters;
Smith_pct = float(Smith_count) / voters * 100;
```

Note that both answers ensure that the first operand for / is of type `float`.

Some other instructive *incorrect* attempts are

```
Smith_pct = 100 * Smith_count / voters;
Smith_pct = 100 * float(Smith_count / voters);
```

The first statement assigns 12.0 (instead of the desired 12.5) to `Smith_pct`, while the second assigns 0.0.   ▨ ▬

3.5 Arithmetic Assignment Operators as Abbreviations

Each of the numerical operators, =, −, *, /, and %, can be combined with the assignment operator to create an **arithmetic assignment** operator. These operators are +=, −=, *=, /=, and %=. Each consists of two keystrokes and may not contain embedded spaces.

▨ **EXAMPLES**   **1.** `total_tax += state_tax;` is equivalent to, but shorter than, `total_tax = total_tax + state_tax;`

2. `count = count − 1;` can be written as `count −= 1;`

3. `principal = principal * (1.0 + int_rate/12);` can be written as `principal *= (1.0 + int_rate/12);`   ▨ ▬

REMARK Arithmetic assignment operators are not necessary, but they are commonly used to abbreviate assignment statements in which the variable to the left of the assignment operator also appears in the expression on the right.

CAUTION In an arithmetic assignment operator, the arithmetic operator precedes the assignment operator. (This is easy to remember — notice the order of the words in "arithmetic assignment" operator.) Reversing the order of the individual operators may cause either a syntax error or an unexpected result at run-time. For example,

1. `rate =/100.0;` contains a syntax error. The expression `/100.0`, which appears to the right of the assignment operator, is syntactically incorrect because the operator `/` requires an operand on both its left and right. A correct version of the statement is `rate /= 100.0;`.

2. `salary =+ bonus;` does *not* contain a syntax error. However, this statement is equivalent to `salary = +bonus;`, so `bonus` is assigned to `salary` rather than added to it.

■ **QUESTION** Give the output of the following fragment (from `asn_ops.cpp`).

```
int a; float y;
a = 10; y = 3.7;
a += 3;
y *= 4.0;
cout << a << " " << y;
a =- 1;
cout << " " << a;
```

Answer

```
13 14.8 −1
```

      ■ ▬

Precedence of Arithmetic Assignment Operators All assignment operators have lower precedence than the normal arithmetic operators. This ensures that the expression to the right of the assignment operator is evaluated before the assignment or arithmetic assignment is performed.

■ **EXAMPLE** If the `float` variables `balance` and `int_rate` contain 1000.00 and 0.05, respectively, then the statement

```
balance *= 1.0 + int_rate;
```

updates `balance` to 1050.00, because `+` is evaluated before `*=`.

      ■ ▬

3.6 Named Constants

User-Defined Named Constants A *constant* is a value that is fixed, either permanently or for some long term. Examples would be the number of centimeters per inch (permanent) and the maximum number of credits that a student may take per semester (long term). Within a C++ program you declare a **named constant** by using the const keyword as in

```
const float CM_PER_IN = 2.54;
const int MAX_CREDITS = 19;
```

Constants, like variables, are named memory locations. Unlike variables, however, the value of a constant remains fixed throughout the program. Statements within a program must not attempt to alter the value of a constant.

Constants and Style The rules for creating identifiers, given in Section 2.2, also apply to making up names for constants. In this text, we follow the common practice of using uppercase letters in constant identifiers, while continuing the practice of using lowercase letters in variable identifiers. These stylistic conventions make it easy to tell whether an identifier is a constant or a variable.

■ **EXAMPLE** Consider the following program.

```
// yd_2_m.cpp
// Convert input number of yards to meters.
#include <iostream.h>

void main()
{
    const float METERS_PER_YARD = 0.9144;
    float yards, meters;
    cout << "Enter distance in yards: ";
    cin >> yards;
    meters = yards * METERS_PER_YARD;
    cout << "That's " << meters << " meters."
         << endl;
}
```

A typical program run is

```
Enter distance in yards: 100
That's 91.44 meters.
```

When to Use Named Constants   There are three main reasons for using constant identifiers.

1. Referring to a certain fixed value by name can help make a program easier to understand. For example, the descriptive name METERS_PER_YARD would mean more to most readers than the "mystery number" 0.9144.

2. Certain well-known, frequently used constants (such as 3.14159) are easy to mistype, and the compiler does not catch this kind of error. Referring to such constants by name (PI in this case) ensures that within a given program we always use the same value for the constant.

3. A constant is assigned its value only once in a program, but may be referred to many times in the program. Therefore, if, at a later date, the value of a constant (for example, MAX_CREDITS) is changed, the program can be updated easily.

When Not to Use Named Constants   Some constants are easy to recognize and to type, and their values are permanently fixed. An example is 60, the number of seconds in a minute. In this case, it is easier to use the literal constant, 60, than the symbolic name SECONDS_PER_MINUTE.

Some Predefined Constants   C++ contains many **predefined constants**. Because these constants are defined in library files, the user needs some experience to know where to find them. For example, INT_MIN, the lower bound on values of type int, and LONG_MAX, the upper bound on values of type long, are defined in the file limits.h.

```
// consts.cpp
#include <iostream.h>
#include <limits.h>

void main()
{
    cout << INT_MIN << endl;
    cout << LONG_MAX << endl;
}
```

```
-32768
2147483647
```

Output

CAUTION   If limits.h were not included in the preceding program, the compiler would not recognize the constant identifiers referred to in main. The compiler diagnoses an "unknown identifier" when you have misspelled an identifier, forgotten to declare it, or, in the case of predefined identifiers, failed to include the proper header file.

3.7   The `char` Data Type

A variable of type `char` can store any *single* character value. Some familiar examples of a character value are a letter, a digit, or a punctuation mark. Character values in a program are enclosed in *single* quote marks. (In Chapter 2 you saw that messages, also called string literals, are enclosed in *double* quote marks.)

■ EXAMPLE In the following code fragment (from `ltrgrade.cpp`) `grade` is a variable of type `char`.

```
char grade;
cout << "Enter your grade: ";
cin >> grade;
cout << "You received a grade of "
     << grade << endl;
```

Typical program runs would be

```
Enter your grade: C
You received a grade of C
```

```
Enter your grade: A-
You received a grade of A
```

Discussion   The `char` variable `grade` can store only a single character. In the second run, the statement `cin >> grade` extracts and stores in `grade` only the character `'A'`; the `'-'` remains in the stream, `cin`, from which it will be the next character, if any, input.   ■ ▬

Assigning Values to `char` ***Variables***   To assign `grade` a value through an assignment statement, you would need to place single quote marks around the value, as in

```
grade = 'B'; // stores B without quotes
```

Whitespace Characters   Characters that produce empty (white) space when output, such as blanks, newline characters, and horizontal tabs, are known as ***whitespace*** characters. Whitespace characters are used to separate data inputs to a program. When reading a value into a `char` variable, the computer scans over whitespace characters. Thus, if `x`, `y`, and z are of type char, the following program fragment could produce the given run. (The character ' ↵ ' in the typical run indicates that the user pressed the Enter key.)

```
cout << "Enter 3 chars: ";
cin >> x >> y >> z;
cout << x << y << z;
```

Program fragment

```
Enter 3 chars: ____M#  ↵
        ? ↵
M#?
```

Typical run

Internal Representation of Characters Each character is represented by a one-byte (8-bit) code. Personal computers use the American Standard Code for Information Interchange, known commonly as ASCII (pronounced "as-key"). For example, the letter 'A' is represented internally as binary 01000001 which is decimal 65. Similarly, '$' is $00100100_2 = 36_{10}$ and '7' is $00110111_2 = 55_{10}$. Appendix B contains a table of characters and their ASCII codes.

Type Casts with *char* and *int* Type casts can also be used to convert between characters and their ASCII codes. If ch is a char, then int(ch) will be its ASCII code, and if n is an integer from 0 to 255 (the range of ASCII codes), char(n) will be the character having ASCII code n.

■ **EXAMPLE** The following fragment (from char2int.cpp) produces the given output.

```
cout << 'B' << int('B') << endl;
cout << char(63) << 63 << endl;
cout << ('Y'+1) << endl;
cout << char('Y'+1) << endl;
```

Program fragment

```
B66
?63
90
Z
```

Output

Lexicographic Ordering of Characters All ASCII characters are in an *extended alphabetical* or *lexicographic ordering* based on their ASCII codes. Thus, 'x' < 'z' because the ASCII code for 'x' (120) is less than that of 'z' (122). Similarly, when comparing two uppercase letters, the < operator obeys the normal alphabetical order. However, < *should not be used to compare an upper- and a lowercase letter!* Do you see why?

3.8 Escape Sequences

In Section 2.1, you saw that output statements can contain messages, or **string literals**, enclosed between double quote characters. But what if we want to display a string literal such as

```
She replied, "You can quote me."
```

If we were to try

```
cout << "She replied, "You can quote me."";
```

we would get a syntax error message indicating that the compiler expects a semicolon after the second double quote mark. The compiler does not assume that the second double quote is part of the string literal; it assumes that this double quote ends the string literal. We can resolve this misunderstanding by using the backslash character, \, to cause an "escape" from the way the compiler normally interprets characters. In the statement

```
cout << "She replied, \"You can quote me.\"";
```

the **escape sequence**, \", lets the compiler know that the double quote character is part of the string literal.

Because a single backslash character appearing in a string literal is not displayed by a cout statement, special treatment is required to display a message such as

```
Read the file c:\windows\readme.txt.
```

The correct cout statement is

```
cout << "Read the file c:\\windows\\readme.txt.";
```

The first backslash in \\ introduces an escape sequence, and the second indicates that '\' is to be printed.

Control Characters   Other escape sequences cause the compiler to put special characters, called **control characters**, on the output stream. For example, the escape sequence \n causes output to move to the beginning of a new line. In fact, '\n' is called the **newline character**. (It may seem strange at first, but *two* keystrokes produce a *single* character in this case.) The escape sequence \a causes the computer's speaker to beep, though for historical reasons, '\a' is called the **bell character**. Some other useful control characters are given in Appendix C.

■ QUESTION What is the output of the following program fragment?

```
cout << "This code\nuses the\n";
cout << "newline character\n";
cout << "and makes the speaker beep\a.";
```

Answer

```
This code
uses the
newline character
and makes the speaker beep.
```
The speaker beeps as the last line is displayed.

■ ■

Using \n in Place of end1   The end1 manipulator is not necessary when the newline control character, '\n', can be made the last character of a string literal. If, however, the last output on a line is the value of a variable, use the end1 manipulator to begin a new line.

3.9   A First Look at for Loops

A powerful feature of the computer is its ability to execute the same group of statements a number of times. This process is called *looping*, and the group of statements that is executed repeatedly is known as the *loop body*. To present more interesting applications involving looping in Chapters 5 and 6, we now discuss a simple, special case of the for loop, known as a *count-controlled* loop. (See Chapters 7 and 8 for a more detailed discussion of for loops as well as while loops and do..while loops.)

Loop Header   The *header* of a for loop is the line given at the top, beginning with the keyword for. It is used to specify how many times the loop body will be executed.

Form of a Count-Controlled for Loop

```
for (i=1; i<= final_value; i=i+1)
    {
    statements of the loop body
    }
```

Action of a Count-Controlled for Loop   In a for loop with the above kind of header, the loop body will be executed first with i=1, then with i=2, then with i=3, and so on, until finally it is executed with i=final_value. Thus, the loop body will be executed final_value times altogether. The variable used in the header of the above for loop is known as the *loop control variable* or *LCV* for short.

■ **EXAMPLE** In the following program, note that 3 is used as final_value, so the loop will be executed three times. The output of the program is shown to its right.

```
// test.cpp
#include <iostream.h>

void main()
{
    int i;
    for (i=1; i<=3; i=i+1)
        {
        cout << "Testing " << i << endl;
        }
    cout << "So long.\n";
}
```

```
Testing 1
Testing 2
Testing 3
So long.
```

Output

■ **QUESTION** (**Multiplication by 4 Table**) Complete the following fragment (from mult4.cpp) so that it produces the output shown to its right.

```
int i;
cout << "mult. by 4\n";
for (i=1; _____; i=i+1)
    {
    cout << "4 x " << i << " = ";
    cout << _____ << endl;
    }
```

Program fragment

```
mult. by 4
4 x 1 = 4
4 x 2 = 8
4 x 3 = 12
    .
    .
    .
4 x 9 = 36
```

Output

Answer Note that we want the loop body executed nine times — first with i=1, then with i=2, and so on, up to i=9. Thus, the missing piece of the loop header is i<=9. The missing piece of the loop body is the calculation for four times the current value of i, so it should be 4*i.

More Descriptive Names for the LCV   Although the loop control variable often has a single letter name, like i, programmers sometimes use a more descriptive name. For example, in a loop used to process a number of employees, it would make sense to use an LCV such as emp, which is short for employee.

Abbreviated Statement to Update the LCV by 1   In a for loop header, you can abbreviate the update statement i=i+1, as follows:

```
i++ // same effect as i=i+1
```

The typing convenience of this abbreviation is more obvious when an update statement like student=student+1 is abbreviated as student++.

Using a for ***Loop to Process Several Input Data Groups***   A particularly important application of the simple for loop is to enable a single program run to input and process several groups of data. The following program fragment (from pay.cpp) inputs hours and rate and then calculates and outputs pay for each of three employees.

```
int emp; // employee
int hrs;
float rate;

for (emp=1; emp<=3; emp++)
    {
    cout << "Enter hours and rate: ";
    cin >> hrs >> rate;
    cout << "Pay = $" << hrs * rate << endl;
    }
```

■ **EXAMPLE**   **(Letting the User Specify the Number of Iterations)**   The previous for loop was limited to processing a predetermined number of employees (three), where the number 3 was decided on by the programmer. The following program fragment (from pay2.cpp) is more flexible than the preceding fragment because it allows the user to specify the number of data groups to be input. The following program fragment also uses the LCV to display the employee number with the prompt and improves readability by displaying a blank line before each prompt.

```
cout << "How many employees? ";
cin >> num_emps;
for (emp=1; emp<=num_emps; emp++)
   {
   cout << endl;
   cout << "Enter hours and rate for employee "
        << emp << ": ";
   cin >> hrs >> rate;
   cout << "Pay = $" << hrs * rate << endl;
   }
```

A sample run, with the user inputting 2 for the number of employees, is

```
How many employees? 2

Enter hours and rate for employee 1: 12 4.75
Pay = $57

Enter hours and rate for employee 2: 16 9.93
Pay = $158.88
```

A Slightly More General *for* ***Loop*** The following loop header is more general in that it shows that the loop control variable need not start at 1.

```
for (LCV=initial_value; LCV<=final_value; LCV++)
```

For example, the header

```
for (numb=15; numb<=30; numb++)
```

would have the loop body executed first with numb=15, then with numb=16, and so on, up through numb=30.

3.10 Errors

The three general categories of errors are (1) syntax, (2) run-time, and (3) logical. As you will see, logical errors are the most dangerous because the computer does not detect them and thus gives no warning.

Syntax Errors Syntax errors (violations of the C++ grammar rules) were discussed in Section 3.1. These errors are caught by the compiler at compile time. The most common kinds of syntax errors are misspelled keywords and identifiers, incorrect or missing punctuation, and undeclared variables.

Run-Time Errors A *run-time* error (also called an *execution error*) is an error that is not caught during the compilation stage, but instead is caught by the computer during the running of the program. For example, the compiler would not produce a syntax error for the statements

```
c = 0;
y = x / c;
```

When the program is run, however, the computer would terminate execution and display a run-time error message such as

```
Floating point: Divide by zero
```

Logical Errors A *logical error* is an error in the design of the program. Logical errors do not generally produce error messages. A simple example of a logical error is the use of an incorrect formula. For example, to compute the average of *b* and *c*, suppose you used the statement

```
avg = b + c / 2;
```

Using this statement, the program would calculate that the average of 60 and 80 was 100. Although the calculation is incorrect, the statement is syntactically correct and causes no run-time error. The computer will not catch the error — *you* will have to catch it by examining the program run!

More complex kinds of logic errors often occur in situations where the actual logical flow of the program may be quite different from what the programmer intended. We examine such situations in later chapters on selection and looping.

■ Exercises

1. Describe the three types of errors in a program and when they are detected.
2. Write the following numbers in ordinary (fixed-point) decimal notation.
   (a) `1.4372e+03`   (b) `5.46E-01`
   (c) `5.46E-03`   (d) `1.4372e+06`

3. Suppose x is of type `double` and has the value 824.176. Give the output of

```
fixed_out(cout,1);
cout << x << endl;
fixed_out(cout,2);
cout << x << endl;
```

4. Give the value of each of the following.

(a) `13 / 4`   (b) `13 / 4.0`   (c) `13 % 4`

(d) `float(13)/4`   (e) `float(13/4)`   (f) `13.0 % 4.0`

5. Suppose the `int` variables a, b, and c have values a=49, b=5, and c=3. Find

(a) `a % b * c + 1`   (b) `a % (b * c) + 1`

(c) `24 / c*4`   (d) `a / b % 2`

(e) `7 + 2 / c - 1`   (f) `48 / (c * 2) * 4`

6. Suppose m is of type `int` and x is of type `float`. Give the final value of m and x in

(a) `m = 3;`   (b) `x = 9 / 2 + 1.3;`
  `x = 7.9 + m;`   `m = x;`

7. Rewrite the following assignment statements using the appropriate arithmetic assignment operator, or indicate why this cannot be done.

(a) `x = x - 0.01;`

(b) `seconds = 60 * minutes + seconds;`

(c) `wage = hours * rate;`

8. Rewrite each of the following expressions without using the arithmetic assignment operators.

(a) `salary += bonus;`

(b) `seconds -= 1;`

(c) `annual_int_rate /= 100.0;`

(d) `total_cost *= (1.0 + SALES_TAX_RATE);`

9. Write a C++ statement for each of the following algebraic expressions.

(a) $\dfrac{x + y}{2w}$ (b) $\dfrac{1}{2}(5x - 3y)$

10. Fill in the blank in the following program fragment so that the output will be 4 3 6.

```
num = 436;
ones = num % 10;
tens = (num / 10) % 10;
hundreds = _____;
cout << hundreds << ' '
     << tens << ' ' << ones << endl;
```

11. Give the output of the following program fragment.

```
m = 7; p = 13;
m = m + p;
p = m - p;
m = m - p;
cout << m << ' ' << p << endl;
```

12. If bonus and salary are both of type int, what is wrong with the following fragment? (*Hint*: Assume 16-bit integers.)

```
bonus = 4000;
salary = 30000 + bonus;
```

13. Give the output of the following fragment if assets is of type
    (a) float   (b) double

```
assets = 3124567.98;
cout << "You're worth $" << assets << endl;
fixed_out(cout,2);
cout << "You're worth $" << assets << endl;
```

14. Consult the ASCII table in Appendix B to give the output of the following fragment.

```
cout << char(36) << char(57) << endl;
cout << int('P') << ' ' << int('t') << endl;
```

15. Give the output of the following code fragment.

```
int n;
for (n=1; n<=3; n=n+1)
   {
   cout << n << " Hi ";
   cout << "there." << endl;
   }
cout << "Bye now." << endl;
```

16. Write an experimental program to determine the output of the program fragment of the previous exercise when

    (a) a semicolon is placed immediately after the for loop header.

    (b) the matching curly braces are removed.

    Can you explain the resulting output?

17. Give the run of the following fragment if the user inputs are 3, 7, 12, and 5.

```
int n, times, total, curr;
cout << "How many times: ";
cin >> times;
total = 0;
for (n=1; n<=times; n=n+1)
   {
   cout << "Enter an int: ";
   cin >> curr;
   total = total + curr;
   cout << curr << " " << total << endl;
   }
```

Programming Problems

18. Write an interactive program that converts kilograms to pounds (1 kg = 2.2 lb). A sample run would look like

```
Enter number of kilograms: 6
6 kilograms = 13.2 pounds
```

19. Write an interactive program that converts an input number of quarters and dimes into a dollar total. A sample run would look like

```
Enter number of quarters and dimes:  5 2
5 quarters and 2 dimes equals $1.45.
```

20. Write an interactive program that converts ounces into pounds and ounces. For an input of 39 ounces, the output should be

```
39 oz. = 2 lb. 7 oz.
```

21. Write an interactive program that converts seconds to hours, minutes, and seconds. For an input of 7903 seconds, the output should be

```
7903 sec. = 2 hr. 11 min. 43 sec.
```

22. Write an interactive program that determines the fewest coins required to make change using quarters, dimes, nickels, and pennies. For an input of 196 (cents) the output should be

```
7 quarters
2 dimes
0 nickels
1 pennies
```

23. Rewrite the solution to any of the preceding programming problems using the `for` loop technique of Section 3.9 to input and process several data groups. Allow the user to specify the number of data groups.

24. Write a program to print Fahrenheit and Celsius temperature equivalents for Fahrenheit temperatures between 85° and 95°, inclusive. Display the Celsius temperature accurate to the nearest tenth degree. (*Hint:* Use the `fixed_out` function.)

25. Write a program to print Celsius and Fahrenheit temperature equivalents for Celsius temperatures between –10° and 10°, inclusive. Display both Fahrenheit and Celsius temperatures as whole numbers.

4

Selection Using `if` and `if..else`

T he programs discussed up to now have been limited in what they accomplish because they use only a few simple features of C++.

In this chapter we introduce some additional features of C++, the `if` and `if..else` statements and logical expressions and operators. These features give a program the capacity to make decisions — that is, to perform a test and then take the appropriate course of action depending on the outcome of the test. This capacity is known as *selection*.

4.1 One-Way Selection Using `if`

An `if` statement is used when you want the computer to perform some action conditionally — that is, only when a certain condition is true. Here are two examples of `if` statements.

1. `if (age >= 18) cout << "may vote";`

2. `if (month == 4) days_in_month = 30;`

These statements are interpreted as follows:

1. If the value stored in `age` is greater than or equal to 18, then display the message `may vote`. Note that the mathematical symbol $\geq$ is indicated by a two character sequence, `>=`, in C++.

2. If the value stored in the variable `month` is equal to 4, then assign 30 to the variable `days_in_month`. We will have more to say about the difference between comparison for equality (`==`) and assignment (`=`) later in this section.

General Syntax and Action of `if`

```
if (condition) action statement
```
or

```
if (condition)
    action statement
```

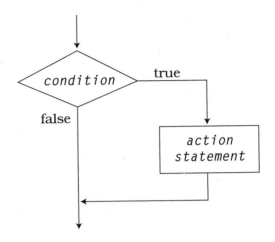

In the preceding general syntax format and flowchart, the condition must be a *logical expression* — an expression that is either true or false. For example, `age >= 18` is true when `age` has the value 20 and is false when `age` has the value 17. The condition must be enclosed in parentheses, and the action statement may appear on either the same line or the following line. The action statement should be indented if it appears on the next line.

If the condition is true, the computer executes the action statement and then proceeds to the next statement in the program. If the condition is false, the computer proceeds directly to the next statement in the program *without* executing the action statement!

Relational Operators   C++ has six *relational operators* for comparing integer, floating-point, and character values. These relational operators have lower precedence than the arithmetic operators +, −, *, /, and % introduced in Section 3.4.

Relational operator*	Meaning
>	Is greater than (comes after)
<	Is less than (comes before)
==	Is equal to
>=	Is greater than or equal to (at least)
<=	Is less than or equal to (no more than)
!=	Is not equal to

*Note that == consists of two keystrokes with no space in between. The same is true of >=, <=, and !=.

■ **QUESTION**   When the following code fragment is executed, what will be printed for each given value of `age`?

```
if (age >= 18) cout << "of age" << endl;
cout << "good luck" << endl;
```

     1.   age = 25   **2.**   age = 14   **3.**   age = 18

Answer   **1.**

```
of age
good luck
```

2.

```
good luck
```

3.

```
of age
good luck
```

■ **QUESTION**   If x = 5, y = 2, and `count` = 31 when the computer reaches the following code fragment, what will be printed?

```
if (x + y > 8) count = count + 1;
cout << count;
```

Answer

```
31
```

Because the action statement is not executed, `count` remains at 31.

4.2   Selecting from Two Alternatives Using `if..else`

In one-way selection, the computer performs a test and then executes either the action statement or no statement at all, depending on the outcome of the test. In two-way selection, the computer performs a test and then executes exactly one of two statements. If the condition is true, the computer executes the statement following the condition; if the condition is false, the computer executes the statement following the keyword `else`. We will refer to these statements, respectively, as the true and false alternatives.

■ **QUESTION**   When the fragment is executed, what will be output for each value of `score`?

```
if (score >= 60)
    cout << "You pass." << endl;
else
    cout << "You fail." << endl;
cout << "Have a nice day!" << endl;
```

1. score = 54   **2.** score = 73

Answer   **1.**

```
You fail.
Have a nice day!
```

2.

```
You pass.
Have a nice day!
```

■ **QUESTION**   Suppose baseballs are priced at 10 dollars each if at least 5 are purchased and 12 dollars each otherwise.

1. Complete the `if..else` statement in the following program fragment from `cost.cpp`.

2. Show what the program run will look like if the user inputs 3 for the number of balls.

3. Show what the program run will look like if the user inputs 20 for the number of balls.

```
void main()
{
    int number, cost;
    cout << "Number purchased: ";
    cin >> number;
    if (number < 5)
        cost = _____;
    else
        cost = _____;
    cout << number << " baseballs cost $" << cost;
}
```

Answer   **1.**
```
if (number < 5)
    cost = 12 * number;
else
    cost = 10 * number;
```

2.

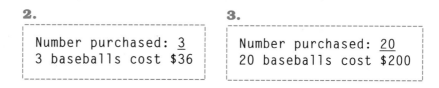

```
Number purchased: 3
3 baseballs cost $36
```

3.

```
Number purchased: 20
20 baseballs cost $200
```

Format for `if..else`   Notice the indentation format in the baseball program fragment. The true and false alternatives are each indented three spaces to display the structure of the two-way selection. Although the C++ compiler does not require any specific amount of indentation, consistent use of indentation makes the program more readable. The general syntax and action are

General Syntax and Action of `if..else`

```
if (condition)
    statement1
else
    statement2
```

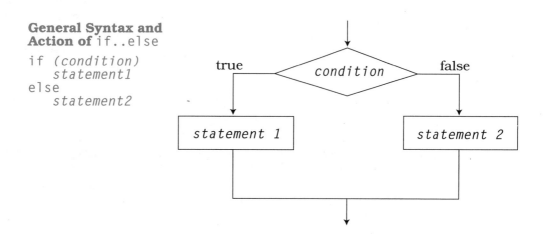

Compound True or False Alternatives   Each alternative of an `if..else` statement contains a single statement. *Whenever the true or false alternative consists of more than one statement, you must place those statements between curly braces, { and }, in order to make those statements into a single* ***compound statement***.

■ **EXAMPLE**   Let us return to the baseball cost program in which a discount is given for purchases of at least five balls. Suppose we wish to output not only the cost but also either the message `Discount` or the message `No discount`. Because the true and the false alternatives will each contain two statements, we need to use curly braces. This is illustrated by the following code fragment from `cost2.cpp`.

```
if (number >= 5)
    {
    cout << "Discount" << endl;
    cost = 10 * number;
    }
else
    {
    cout << "No discount" << endl;
    cost = 12 * number;
    }
```

Discussion   Individual statements such as `cost = 10 * number;` end with a semicolon. Compound statements begin with { and end with }.

If the true alternative consists of multiple statements, failure to place these statements between curly braces will result in a compile-time error. If the false alternative consists of multiple statements, failure to enclose those statements in curly braces will result in a logic error. (See Exercise 4.10.) ■ ▬

Logical Expressions and Logical Values   A *logical expression* is an expression that is either true or false. For example, the condition in an `if` statement is a logical expression.

Until recently, C++ did not have explicit *logical values* named true and false for handling logical expressions. Instead, C++ used, and still does allow the use of, integer values — 1 for true and 0 for false. That is, a logical expression that is true evaluates to 1, and a logical expression that is false evaluates to 0. There is one additional detail that you should be aware of — when the compiler is expecting a logical value, it will interpret any nonzero integer value as true.

The `bool` Data Type   As part of the recent draft standard, a data type named `bool` (after the British logician, George Boole) was added to C++. This data type has only two values, `false` and `true`, which are really just named constants for the integer values 0 and 1. We will use this data type whenever we want to store the result of a logical expression. If your compiler does not yet have a built-in `bool` data type, use the file `bool.h` on the PWS Web site.

PITFALL   (Don't Use = Instead of ==)   When you write an `if` condition that tests for equality, be careful to use the comparison operator, `==`. When you mistakenly use the assignment operator, `=`, to test for equality, the compiler will execute the statement differently than you intended.

(*Note*: Many compilers will give a warning message when an `if` condition contains the assignment rather than the intended equality comparison operator.) For example, in the following code fragment, no matter what value is stored in `month` just before the `if` statement is executed, the output will always be `April`!

```
if (month=4) // SOS! Should be (month==4)
    cout << "April";
else
    cout << "Not April";
```

The output from this program will always be `April` because the assignment operator, `=`, assigns 4 to `month`, so the `if` condition, `month=4`, then has the value 4. Because C++ considers any nonzero value to be true, the true branch is executed.

4.3 The Logical Operators: AND (&&), OR (||), NOT (!)

Logical Operators   The logical operators && (AND), || (OR), and ! (NOT) are used to form compound logical expressions. For example, an `if` statement can have a compound logical expression such as in

```
if ((sex=='f' || age > 25)) && years > 5) . . .
```

&& **(AND)**   An expression of the form p && q has the value `true` only when both p and q are `true`; otherwise, it has the value `false`.

|| **(OR)**   An expression of the form p || q has the value `true` provided that at least one of p and q is `true`; otherwise, it has the value `false`.

! **(NOT)**   An expression of the form !p has the value `true` when p is `false`; otherwise, it has the value `false`.

■ **EXAMPLE**   **(AND)**   The ABC Company gives two tests to each job applicant. An applicant is hired if he scores at least 65 on both tests; otherwise, he is rejected. The following fragment uses the correct compound `if..else` test to determine whether an applicant is hired or rejected.

```
if (score1 >= 65 && score2 >= 65)
    cout << "Hire";
else
    cout << "Reject";
```

NOTE   The operator precedence table provided later in this section shows that the relational operator >= has higher precedence than the logical operator &&. Thus, it is not necessary to parenthesize the individual logical expressions in the compound if..else test.   ■ ▬

■ EXAMPLE   (AND)   In the town of Paduka, a woman is eligible to be a firefighter if her height is between 65 and 75 inches, inclusive. Mathematically, we can write

$$65 \le height \le 75$$

To translate this into a syntactically correct C++ if..else statement, however, we must use the && operator to combine the two conditions on height.

```
if (65 <= height && height <= 75)
    cout << "Eligible";
else
    cout << "Not eligible";
```

We could also write this compound logical condition as

```
if (75 >= height && height <= 65) . . .
```
   ■ ▬

■ EXAMPLE   (OR)   The XYZ Company gives two tests to job applicants. At this company, an applicant is hired if she scores at least 90 on either test; otherwise she is rejected. Here is the statement we could use.

```
if (score1 >= 90 || score2 >= 90)
    cout << "Hire";
else
    cout << "Reject";
```
   ■ ▬

■ QUESTION   (Negating a Compound && **Condition)**   Consider the Paduka Fire Department again, where a woman is eligible to become a firefighter if her height is between 65 and 75 inches, inclusive. In the following if statement, we want the true branch to output "Not eligible" and the else branch to output "Eligible".

```
if (_____)
    cout << "Not eligible";
else
    cout << "Eligible";
```

Complete the condition in the following two ways.

1. Using the NOT operator

2. Using the || operator to express the negation of p && q

Answer   1.   `if (!(65 <= height && height <= 75))`

Notice that two sets of parentheses are necessary. The inner set specifies that the condition to be negated is the complete compound condition that it encloses.

2.   `if (height < 65 || height > 75)`

In general, not (p and q) can be negated as not p or not q.

■ **QUESTION**   For the XYZ Company job application problem (in which a job applicant is hired if he scores at least 90 on either of two exams), write a logical condition that is true when the applicant should be rejected, and false when he should be hired. Do this two different ways:

1. Using the ! and || operators

2. Using the && operator

Answer   1.   `! (score1 >= 90 || score2 >= 90)`

Using !, simply negates the original compound logical expression.

2.   `(score1 < 90 && score2 < 90)`

To be hired, at least one of the two test scores must be at least 90, so the applicant is rejected if both are below 90.

Binary Versus Unary Operators   Notice that the logical operators && and || each requires two operands, but the ! operator takes only one. Operators that require two operands are called **binary**, while those that require only one are called **unary**. The + and − operators have both binary and unary forms.

Operator Precedence Table (Updated)

Operator	Description
! + −	Logical NOT, unary plus, minus
* / %	Multiplication, quotient, remainder
+ −	Addition, subtraction
<< >>	Stream insertion and extraction
< <= > >= == !=	Relational
&&	AND
||	OR
= *= /= %= += −=	Assignment

Note: In the table an operator has higher precedence than those that appear below it. For example, * has higher precedence than >>, which has higher precedence than &&.

Most operators are grouped (associated) left to right. The exceptions in this table are the unary and assignment operators.

Some Comments on the Precedence Table

- All relational operators have higher precedence than && and ||. Therefore, the programmer need not put parentheses around each of the two >= conditions in `if (score1 >= 65 && score2 >= 65)`.

- Additional parentheses can be used to override the rules of precedence or to make clear the intended order of evaluation.

- && has higher precedence than ||. The following Adults Only example illustrates the need for additional parentheses when || is the intended main connective in a compound condition involving both || and &&.

■ **EXAMPLE**   **(Pitfall: Failing to Override Operator Precedence)**   At the Adults Only Corporation a person is hired if he is at least 21 years of age and scores over 85 on either of two tests. Note that

```
if (age >= 21 && score1 > 85 || score2 > 85)
    cout << "Hired";
```

is incorrect because a 15-year-old with a score of 88 on the second test would be hired. The problem stems from the fact that && has higher precedence than ||, so the computer evaluates the expression as if it were typed

```
if ((age >= 21 && score1 > 85) || score2 > 85)
    cout << "Hired";
```

■ **QUESTION** Use extra parentheses to write the correct `if` statement for the previous example.

Answer
```
if (age >= 21 && (score1 > 85 || score2 > 85))
    cout << "Hired";
```

Using `bool` *Variables to Simplify Selection Statements* A complex logical expression can often be simplified and clarified by using one or more `bool` variables to store the values of parts of the expression.

■ **EXAMPLE** Consider again the example of the Adults Only Corporation, where a person is hired if he is at least 21 years of age and scores over 85 on either of two tests. Suppose we need to determine whether an applicant is or is not hired, and if not, give the reason for not hiring. The following sequence of statements accomplishes this.

```
bool tests_ok;
tests_ok = (score1 > 85 || score2 > 85);
if (tests_ok && age>=21)
    cout << "Hired";
if (!tests_ok)
    cout << "Reject - low tests";
if (age<21)
    cout << "Reject - under age";
```

Discussion Storing the value of the compound expression

```
(score1 > 85 || score2 > 85)
```

in the `bool` variable `tests_ok` has two advantages. First, it simplifies the compound statement used to decide whether to hire and avoids the problem of operator precedence that occurred in the previous example. Second, the value of `tests_ok` can be used in the second `if` statement to tell why the applicant was rejected without reevaluating the preceding compound expression.

4.4   Linear Multiway Selection Using a Nested `if` Statement

When either the true or the false branch of an `if` statement is itself an `if` statement, the entire statement is called a ***nested*** `if` statement.

■ QUESTION   In the following nested `if` statement (from `compare.cpp`), what will be output when

1. x = 5, y = 9   2. x = 6, y = 4   3. x = 8, y = 8

```
if (x > y)
    cout << "x is larger";
else // Fact: x <= y
    if (x < y)
        cout << "y is larger";
    else
        cout << "x equals y";
```

Answer
1. Because the condition x > y is false, the computer will execute the matching `else` branch, which is itself an `if..else` statement. Because the test x < y is true, the computer will output `y is larger`.

2. Because the first logical expression x > y is true, the computer will output `x is larger`.

3. Because both x > y and x < y are false, the output will be `x equals y`.

Discussion   Note that in the previous nested `if` statement, the computer will execute the `cout` statement following the first `if` test that evaluates to true. In the event that neither `if` test is true, then the computer will execute the final `else` alternative.   ■ ▬▬

A Better Format for the Previous Fragment   Recall that if we change the indentation by adding extra spaces, computer execution will not be affected. The following equivalent code will better reflect that we are selecting from a list of three alternatives.

```
if (x > y)
    cout << "x is larger";
else if (x < y) // Fact: x <= y
    cout << "y is larger";
else
    cout << "x equals y";
```

We will refer to such a construct as a *linear three-way* selection because the three-way selection statement is aligned to clearly indicate the three alternatives.

Linear Multiway Selection You may use the following construct to select exactly one of a list of several alternatives.

```
if (condition 1)
    statement 1;
else if (condition 2)
    statement 2;
    .
    .
    .
else
    statement n;
```

The computer will check the conditions in sequential order. When it reaches a condition that is true, it executes the statement associated with that condition and then transfers control to the statement immediately following the linear *n*-way selection statement. In the event that none of the conditions is true, the computer will execute the statement associated with the final else.

Note that a statement for any of the alternatives could be a compound statement. Of course, braces would be needed to mark the statements for that alternative.

■ QUESTION The char variable suit contains one of the letters 'C', 'D', 'H', or 'S' to represent the suit (clubs, diamonds, hearts, or spades) of a card. Write a linear five-way selection statement to output one of the five messages: "clubs", "diamonds", "hearts", "spades", or "Invalid suit".

Answer

```
if (suit == 'C')
    cout << "clubs";
else if (suit == 'D')
    cout << "diamonds";
else if (suit == 'H')
    cout << "hearts";
else if (suit == 'S')
    cout << "spades";
else
    cout << "Invalid suit";
```

Code fragment from `suit.cpp`

■ **QUESTION**   The following fragment is intended to assign the `char` variable `grade` the value 'H' if `score` is at least 95, 'P' if `score` is under 95 but at least 60, or 'F' if `score` is under 60.

    1. Explain what is wrong with the fragment.

    2. Rewrite the fragment correctly.

```
if (score >= 60)
    grade = 'P';
else if (score >= 95)
    grade = 'H';
else
    grade = 'F';
```

Answer

    1. The order of the conditions is such that *all* scores of 60 or more are given a grade of 'P'. The second condition is evaluated *only if* `score` is less than 60.

    2. Two possibilities are

```
if (score>=60 && score<95)
    grade = 'P';
else if (score>=95)
    grade = 'H';
else
    grade = 'F';
```

```
if (score>=95)
    grade = 'H';
else if (score>=65)
    grade = 'P';
else
    grade = 'F';
```

Note that the solution on the right is clearer and more compact than the one on the left.

Linear Multiway Selection Using `switch`

C++ provides another, more specialized statement, `switch`, that can sometimes be used for performing linear multiway selection. We have deferred the introduction of this statement until Chapter 12, but, if you want, you can look ahead to Section 12.1 for an introduction to its syntax and application.

4.5 More General Nested Selection

Linear multiway selection is not always the best way to code complex selection problems. For some problems, other more general selection structures may reflect more clearly the algorithmic structure of the solution.

EXAMPLE In a certain state, drivers are assessed points for traffic violations. Teenaged drivers who have six or more points are given a test to determine their eligibility to drive; older drivers who have nine or more points are subject to a review of their eligibility, which may or may not include a test. Give the output of the following nested selection code (from drvtst.cpp) when age and points are, respectively:

1. 21 and 7 **2.** 16 and 7 **3.** 19 and 0 **4.** 48 and 10

```
if (age <= 19)
   if (points < 6)
      cout << "OK\n";
   else
      cout << "Test\n";
else // age > 19
   if (points < 9)
      cout << "OK\n";
   else
      cout << "Review\n";
```

Answer The outputs are:

1. OK **2.** Test **3.** OK **4.** Review

Discussion   The structure of the preceding code reflects a two-way selection, teen-aged or older driver; for each of these two alternatives, an additional two-way selection determines whether a review is necessary.   ▪ ▬▬

One can rightly argue that, because only three outputs for the preceding code fragment are possible, a linear nested three-way selection is a good structure to use. Using a three-way selection, however, involves some trade-offs — although the three-way selection is shorter, it contains compound logical expressions. Exercise 4.20 asks you to write this three-way structure.

Verifying Input   A nested selection statement can be used to trap invalid inputs (with a warning message) so that processing is applied only to valid inputs.

▪ **QUESTION**   Complete the following program segment (from `pass.cpp`) that outputs "out of range" if `score` is less than 0 or greater than 100; "You pass" if `score` is 60 or greater (but at most 100); or "You fail" if `score` is less than 60 (but at least 0).

```
cin >> score;
if (_Score<0 || score>100_____)
    cout << score << " is out of range.";
else // Fact: score is between 0 and 100, incl.
    if (__60<=score<=100____)
        cout << "You pass.";
    else
        cout << "you fail.";
cout << endl;
```

Answer   The two missing logical expressions are

1. `score < 0 || score > 100`

2. `score >= 60`

The second condition could be written as

`score >= 60 && score <= 100`

but the condition `score <= 100` is redundant — the condition of the outer `if` statement would have trapped any scores that are out of range.   ▪ ▬▬

Obviously, the preceding selection statement can be restructured as a linear three-way selection to clearly reflect the three alternatives — invalid, pass, or fail. The following program, however, illustrates the advantage of top-level, two-way selection to distinguish between valid and invalid inputs when the processing of valid inputs is more complex.

■ **QUESTION**   The following program prompts for and inputs hours and rate, then outputs either an error message or the employee's wage.

1. Give the output when the inputs for hours and rate are
   (a) −5 and 8.50   (b) 50 and 10.00   (c) 10 and 3.50

2. Describe in words the way an employee is compensated for overtime.

```
// wages.cpp
#include <iostream.h>
#include "\ourtools.h"

void main()
{
    const float MIN_WAGE = 5.35;
    int hours;
    float rate, wages;

    cout << "Enter hours worked and hourly rate: ";
    cin >> hours >> rate;
    if (hours >= 0 && rate >= MIN_WAGE)
        { // valid inputs for hours and rate
        if (hours <= 40)
            wages = hours * rate;
        else
            wages = 40*rate + (hours-40)*2.0*rate;
        fixed_out (cout, 2);
        cout << "Wages = $" << wages << endl;
        }
    else // hours and/or rate invalid
        cout << "INPUT ERROR(S).\n";
}
```

Answers   **1.** **(a)**

```
Enter hours worked and hourly rate: -5 8.50
INPUT ERROR(S).
```

(b)

```
Enter hours worked and hourly rate: 50 10.00
Wages = $600.00.
```

(c)

```
Enter hours worked and hourly rate: 10 3.50
INPUT ERROR(S).
```

2. An employee receives her hourly rate for each hour up to and including 40 and double her hourly rate for each hour over 40. Note that the calculation for `wages` when `hours` is at least 40 pays double only for those hours that are in excess of 40. A common mistake is to calculate

```
wages = 2 * rate * hours;
```

which pays double for *every* hour worked and would probably put the company out of business if many employees worked overtime!

4.6 Problem Solving Applied to Writing Programs

We now consider the four general problem-solving stages first discussed in Section 1.4 in relation to the task of writing programs.

1. **Problem specification (understanding the problem)** Do you understand what the program is supposed to do? What form should the output take? What information must be read in to produce the output?

2. **Solution design (developing an algorithm)**
    (a) **Consider specific cases.** For many problems, a way to get started is to *work out by hand or with a calculator* the outputs for several different inputs. Can you describe the formula(s) or process that you need to convert input into output?

(b) **Use top-down design.** Try to subdivide the problem into smaller, more manageable subtasks and then figure out how to accomplish each of these subtasks.

(c) **Try imitating.** Can you imitate code that you've already seen, changing only some of the variable names and some of the fixed values? Are there any additional complications? If so, focus on how to handle them.

(d) **Write pseudocode.** *Pseudocode* is a mixture of ordinary English, mathematical formulas, and actual C++ code. Writing a pseudocode draft of your program can help you implement top-down design. It enables you to write code for those details that you have decided on while leaving in somewhat vague form the details that need more work. Sometimes you will find it useful to write additional pseudo-code drafts — known as *refinements* — with more details worked out, for either the entire program or only some of the more difficult subtasks.

3. **Coding the algorithm** You must ultimately translate your solution method into a complete program using the correct C++ syntax.

4. **Testing and debugging** Although your program may run successfully for one set of inputs, the program is not necessarily correct. Your program should be tested (that is, run) for other sets of inputs designed to cover all types of scenarios. A *test oracle* is a set of inputs designed to test all possible execution paths of your program. For example, when using an `if..else` statement with a condition such as `if(age<=18)`, make sure that you test inputs on either side of the boundary value (18 in this case) as well as the boundary value itself.

To illustrate the preceding steps, we discuss them in the context of two different problems.

■ **PROBLEM** Write a program that takes as input an employee's hours worked and regular pay rate and outputs the employee's wages for the week. Calculate an employee's wages as follows: She receives her regular rate for the first 40 hours, 1.5 times her regular rate for each hour between 40 and 50 hours, and double her regular rate for each hour over 50. *For invalid inputs, in addition to outputting the message "INPUT ERROR(S)," further diagnostic messages should appear specifying which input value was out of range or that both were out of range.*

Understanding the problem   This program will be quite similar to the previous program, `wages.cpp`. The input is the same. The output, though, is potentially different because

1. the formula for determining pay is somewhat different, and

2. the diagnostic messages for invalid inputs are more specific.

Developing an algorithm   You can prepare much of the basic framework for this program *by imitating* `wages.cpp`, but perhaps you would gain insight into the problem by beginning with some hand calculations. You should be methodical about such calculations, subdividing them into the cases that will be used for your *test oracle*.

Valid Input Cases

	Case	Hours	Rate	Hand calculations
I	40 hours or less	30	12.00	first 30 hours 30 * $12 = $360
II	Between 40 and 50 hours	45	12.00	first 40 next 5 hours hours 40 * $12 + 5 * $18 = $570
III	Over 50 hours	58	12.00	first 40 next 10 next 8 hours hours hours 40 * $12 + 10 * $18 + 8 * $24 = $852

Let us also consider the different cases that would cover all the possible kinds of diagnostic error messages.

Invalid Input Cases

	Hours	Rate	Diagnostic Messages
IV	10	2.00	`rate = 2.00 is less than minimum wage`
V	−3	12.00	`hours = −3 is invalid`
VI	−3	4.00	`rate = 4.00 is less than minimum wage` `hours = −3 is invalid`

Pseudocode   First, we write pseudocode that provides a top-down outline for the entire program. Note that each of the italicized items describes in English a task that still must be converted into computer code. Then we will write a refinement that provides further details for the three-way selection to find wages subtask.

Pseudocode outline for the entire program

```
Input data
if (hours >= 0 && rate >= MIN_WAGE)
    { // valid input
    Do a 3-way selection to calculate wages
    fixed_out (cout, 2);
    cout << "Wages = $" << wages << endl;
    }
else // hours and/or rate invalid
    {
    cout << "INPUT ERROR(S)" << endl;
    Do tests to give more specific error diagnostics
    }
```

Pseudocode for the three-way selection to calculate wages

```
if (hours <= 40)
    Pay straight rate for each hour
else if (hours <= 50)
    pay 1.5 times rate for hours over 40
else
    pay overtime using two levels
```

Coding the algorithm   Exercise 4.28 asks you to write the wages program based on the given pseudocode. Before doing so, you might find it helpful to write a pseudocode refinement for the subtask "Do tests to give more specific error diagnostics" for invalid input.

Testing and debugging   A test oracle should include input from each of the cases described earlier and also the two boundary cases for valid input when the number of hours is either 40 or 50.   ■ ▰▰

Prototype Solutions   Problems of any size will often involve complex details that can become mental blocks because you find them distracting (e.g., tedious, detailed output formatting) or intimidating (e.g., a complicated mathematical formula). One way that you can surmount such mental blocks is to concentrate on producing a ***prototype solution***. A prototype solution is a correct solution of a simplified version of the original problem. This simplified solution may neglect (temporarily) certain exceptional or particularly problematic details of the original problem. When you are satisfied that the prototype solution is correct, you can then concentrate on improvements that address those problematic details you originally deferred.

■ **PROBLEM**　Input the number of a month; if the input is 2 (February), also input the year. Then, output the number of days in and the name of the month; if the month is February, also output the year.

Understand the problem　Here, it is helpful to consider some sample runs.

```
Enter month (1-12): 13
13 is not a valid month.

Enter month (1-12): 1
There are 31 days in January.

Enter month (1-12): 2
For February, also enter the year: 1998
There are 28 days in February, 1998.

Enter month (1-12): 2
For February, also enter the year: 2000
There are 29 days in February, 2000.

Enter month (1-12): 4
There are 30 days in April.
```

Sample runs

Develop an algorithm　The specific cases for this problem and the core of its solution are contained in the familiar algorithm, "Thirty days hath September, April, June, and November. All the rest have 31, save February, which hath . . . (something about 29 days during a leap year and 28 the rest of the time)." Determining whether February has 28 or 29 (leap years only) days is the only troublesome detail. A possible top-level algorithm in pseudocode is

Pseudocode for the entire program

Prompt for and input the number of the month
`if` (month *is not valid*)
　　Display an error message

```
else
   {
   if (month==2)
      Prompt for and input the year

   Determine the number of days in month
   and assign this value to ndays

   Display ndays
   Display the name of month
   }
```

Let us consider two subtasks that require some thought. For convenience, we begin with the simpler of these two subtasks.

1. **Display the name of a month given its number.** This is a 12-way selection that can be written by imitating the card suit example of Section 4.4.

2. **Determine the number of days in a (valid) month.** This is a three-way selection based on the "Thirty days hath . . ." algorithm. In pseudocode it can be written something like

   Pseudocode for determining the number of days in a month

   ```
   if (month is 9, 4, 6, or 11)
      ndays = 30;
   else if (month is 2)
      {
      Determine whether Feb. has 28 or 29 days.
      }
   else // all other valid months
      ndays = 31;
   ```

Another deeper level of refinement is required for the subtask of determining whether February has 28 or 29 days.

3. **Determine the number of days in February for a given year.**
   (a) **Suppose you don't know the method for doing this.** Then you will not be able to write the complete program. However, you could write a simplified prototype program that takes care of everything else, but postpones this difficulty by

outputting "28 or 29 days" when the month is February. Then, when you find out how to handle February, you can write the complete, correct program.

(b) **Leap year explained.** Leap years are years in which February has 29 days instead of 28. The device of leap year was invented to keep the calendar in sync with the "true time of year" because a year has approximately 365¼ days. If there were no leap years (that is, if February always had 28 days), then every four calendar years, the calendar date would gain approximately one day on the "true time of year." Because a year is not exactly 365¼ days, but actually slightly less, most, but not all, years divisible by 4 have been made leap years. The rule that is used to keep the calendar in sync is

Rule

> y r is a leap year if
> (it is divisible by 4)
> AND
> ((it is NOT a centennial) OR (it is a centennial divisible by 400))

Thus, noncentennial years that are divisible by 4, like 1992 and 1996, are leap years, and centennial years that are divisible by 400 are leap years. So, centennial years like 2100, 2200, and 2300, which are not divisible by 400, are not leap years.

Code the algorithm Exercise 4.29 asks you to write the complete program based on this top-down pseudocode and its refinements for the more difficult subtasks.

Testing and debugging A thorough test oracle for the above prototype will include as input data (1) Each of the months 1, 3, 4, 5, . . . , 12; (2) at least one month less than 1 and one month greater than 12; and (3) for input month 2 (February) (a) a year divisible by 4, but not divisible by 100; (b) a year not divisible by 4; (c) a year divisible by 100, but not 400; and (d) a year divisible by 400.

■ Exercises

1. Fill in the blanks in the following statement so that it outputs whether or not age is under 21.

```
if (_____)
    cout << _____;
else
    cout << age << " is not under 21.";
```

2. The following program fragment is written in poor style. Explain what is wrong with it and rewrite it.

```
if (age >= 65)
    cout << "You may retire.";
if (age < 65) else
    cout << "Keep working.";
```

3. Find the error(s) in the following code fragment.

```
if (age >= 18);
    cout << "You may vote.";
else
    cout << "You may not vote.";
```

4. What will be output by the code fragment on the right when x = 1 and y = 5? when x = 0 and y = 6?

True _false_

```
if (!(x<2 && y<6))
    cout << "true";
else
    cout << "false";
```

5. What will be output by the following code fragments when x=6, y=6 and n=7?

(a)
```
if (x>5 && y>10 || n>10)
    cout << "OK";
else
    cout << "Maybe";
```

(b)
```
if (x>5 || y>10 && n>10)
    cout << "YES";
else
    cout << "NO";
```

6. Give the outputs for parts (a) and (b) of Exercise 4.5 when x=2, y=3, and n=12.

7. Give the output of the following program fragment when `yr` is
   (a) 1995   (b) 1996   (c) 1900   (d) 100

```
if (yr%4==0 && (yr%400==0 || yr%100!=0))
   cout << " leap\n";
else
   cout << " no\n";
```

8. (a) Fill in the blank in the following fragment so that someone who is younger than 16 and over 76 inches tall is advised to "Play basketball!" and all others are told "More information needed".

```
cin >> age >> height;
if (_____)
   cout << "Play basketball!";
else
   cout << "More information needed";
```

   (b) Rewrite the preceding code fragment so that the true branch displays the "More info..." message. (*Hint*: Use the || operator in the condition.)

9. What output does the fragment below produce when `num` is 1? 2? 3? 17? What corrections must you make so that this fragment will not produce extra output when the input is 1 or 2?

```
if (num==1)
   cout << "uno";
if (num==2)
   cout << "dos";
if (num==3)
   cout << "tres";
else
   cout << "Sorry. I'm just"
        << "starting Spanish";
```

10. Only one of the following code segments will compile.
    (a) Identify the segment that will not compile and explain why not.
    (b) Give the output of the code segment that *will* compile for
        (i)   hrs = 30 rate = 10.00
        (ii) hrs = 45 rate = 10.00

```
if (hrs <= 40)                    if (hrs > 40)
   pay = hrs*rate;                   cout << "Bonus - ";
else                                 pay = hrs*rate + 100;
   cout << "Bonus - ";            else
   pay = hrs*rate + 100;             pay = hrs*rate;
cout << "Pay = $" << pay;         cout << "Pay = $" << pay;
```

11. In the following code fragment length, width, and height are integers, weight is a float, and width_ok, too_high, and load_ok are of type bool. Give the code fragment's output for the following values:

	length	width	height	weight
(a)	12	8	7	30
(b)	20	10	10	30
(c)	20	15	12	50
(d)	30	12	16	40

```
width_ok = width < 15;
too_high = height > 13;
load_ok = weight < 45 && weight/(width*length)<0.2;

if (width_ok && !too_high && load_ok)
   cout << "OK to cross bridge\n";
else
   {
   cout << "Do not cross bridge!\n";
   if (!load_ok)
      cout << "Excessive weight or load factor.\n";
   if (!width_ok || too_high)
      cout << "Too wide or too high\n";
   }
```

12. Give the output of the nested selection structure on the right when

   (a) x = 3 and y = -5
   (b) x = 0 and y = 10
   (c) x = -5 and y = -1
   (d) x = -10 and y = 1

```
if (x>=0)
   if (y>=0)
      cout << "Quadrant I";
   else
      cout << "Quadrant IV";
else
   if (y>=0)
      cout << "Quadrant II";
   else
      cout << "Quadrant III";
```

13. Which logical expressions are redundant in the selection statement to the right? (*Hint:* Consider the four quadrants in the *xy*-plane.)

```
if (x>=0 && y>=0)
    cout << "Quadrant I";
else if (x>=0 && y<0)
    cout << "Quadrant IV";
else if (x<0 && y>=0)
    cout << "Quadrant II";
else if (x<0 && y<0)
    cout << "Quadrant III";
```

14. Improve the efficiency and style of the following program fragment.

```
if (age>=18 && sex=='F') cout << "Adult female";
if (age>=18 && sex=='M') cout << "Adult male";
if (age<18 && sex=='F') cout << "Juvenile female";
if (age<18 && sex=='M') cout << "Juvenile male";
```

15. The code fragment on the left reads and processes a Fahrenheit temperature. Complete the code fragment on the right so that, for any input, it produces the same output as that on the left.

```
cin >> F;
if (F<-40 || F>110)
    cout << "No way";
else if (F>32)
    cout << "Melt";
else
    cout << "Freeze";
```

```
cin >> F;
if _____
    cout << "Melt";
else if _____
    cout << "Freeze";
else
    cout << "No way";
```

16. (a) Write a linear nested selection statement to output "Ace", "Jack", "King", "Queen", or "Invalid rank", depending on whether the char variable rank contains 'A', 'J', 'K', 'Q', or none of these.

    (b) Modify the above selection statement to allow the value of rank to be either upper- or lowercase.

Programming Problems

For each of the following problems, use the `for` loop technique presented in Section 3.9 so that a single run of the program processes a user-specified number of input data groups.

17. (a) Write a program in which the user inputs her age and the output states whether or not she is a teenager.

    (b) Write a version of this program that outputs "Invalid age!" if the user enters an age that is negative or over 110.

18. (a) Tee shirts are on sale for $12 each if fewer than three are purchased, $10 each if at least three, but less than ten are purchased, and $7 if at least ten are purchased. Write a program to input the number of shirts and output the total cost of the shirts.

    (b) Write a version of this program that limits customers to purchases of at most two dozen tee shirts (with a warning message for attempts to purchase more) and that prints an error message if the input is negative.

19. Write a program that inputs three exam scores, then outputs both the smallest and the largest of the three scores.

20. Rewrite program drvrtest.cpp (see the beginning of Section 4.5) using a three-way selection statement.

21. The sum of the lengths of any two sides of a triangle is greater than the length of the third side. Write a program to input three lengths; then tell whether or not they could be the lengths of the sides of a triangle.

22. Write a program that inputs the suit ('C', 'D', 'H', or 'S') and rank (1, 2, . . ., 13) of a card and then outputs the rank and suit, in words. For example, the inputs 'D' and '1' would result in the output Ace of Diamonds and the inputs 'H' and 'Q' would result in the output Queen of Hearts.

23. Write a program to input an employee's gross pay, then output the tax to be withheld and the net pay. Tax will be withheld at the rate of 10% on the first $200, 15% on the next $400, and 20% on anything over $600.

Longer Assignments

24. A point (x, y) in the plane can be classified nine ways by its relationship to the x- and y-axes. It may be at the origin, on the positive or negative x- or y-axis, or in quadrants I, II, III, or IV (see Exercise 4.12). Discuss whether this problem is better suited to linear multiway selection or more general nested selection, then write a program to classify points input by the user.

25. Write a program to input a long integer, then print it with commas if it has more than three digits. For example, −2036 and 1234567890 would be printed as −2,036 and 1,234,567,890, respectively.

26. (a) At Enlightened State University (ESU) students pay $250 per credit, with a maximum per-semester tuition fee of $3,350. Additionally, a student must take at least 12 credits to be considered full time, and no student may take more than 20 credits. Write a program that inputs the student's number of credits, then outputs that student's status (part or full time) and tuition. Print appropriate error messages if the input is negative or greater than 20.

    (b) At ESU, nonresident students pay $450 per credit with a maximum per-semester tuition fee of $6,000. Modify the program of part (a) to input both the residency status (N or R) and the number of credits, then output whether the student is part or full time, resident or nonresident, and the student's total tuition.

27. Write a program that inputs the coefficients, A, B, and C, of the quadratic $Ax^2 + Bx + C$ and then outputs whether the quadratic has two distinct real zeros, two equal real zeros, or no real zeros. Indicate also if the inputs are the coefficients of a linear, rather than a quadratic, equation.

28. Code and test the overtime pay algorithm that was developed in Section 4.6.

29. Code and test the days per month algorithm that was developed in Section 4.6.

30. Write a program that allows the user to enter the two-letter abbreviation for one of the states in the U.S. and then output the full name of the state. (*Hint:* Read a single character at a time, and use nested multiway selection statements.)

5

Functions and Program Design

All of our programs thus have been quite simple. To solve a more complicated programming problem, you should start by dividing that problem into smaller subtasks and then writing a separate block of code, in the form of a *function*, for each subtask. This way, you can systematically write the program in smaller, more manageable pieces, instead of trying to deal with the complexity of the entire program all at once.

A *function*, which is a named block of code, is like a small program that performs some well-defined subtask. Like a program, a function is usually given data to process in connection with that subtask and can have its own variables. In this chapter we discuss two broad categories of functions in detail:

1. Functions that calculate a single value based on the data they are given and then return that value. Such functions are called *value-returning functions*.

2. Functions that display information based on the data they are given, but do not return any value. Because these functions do not return any value, they are called *void functions*.

In Section 5.7, we briefly discuss a third category of functions, *data input functions*, whose task is to prompt for and input data. Data-input functions are a type of void function and are discussed in more detail in Chapter 9.

An important part of this chapter's discussion of functions concerns *value parameters*, which are a special kind of variable that a function uses to receive the data that it will process. Although most of the discussion of parameters in this chapter is devoted to value parameters, we introduce a second kind of parameter, **reference parameters**, that will be used by the data input functions of Section 5.7. (If you wish, you can then jump ahead to Chapter 9, where reference parameters are covered in greater detail and used by functions other than data-input functions.)

We begin in Section 5.1 by considering some **predefined functions** that are packaged in the library file math.h as a standard part of C++. Then we discuss the syntax for creating new functions of your own that you can use as building blocks in program design.

Our discussion of program design with functions stresses the following:

- **Reuse of Reliable Code** You need not reinvent the wheel at each turn. If a subtask can be performed by calling a built-in function, using the built-in function is certainly easier and safer than writing the code yourself. (These functions have been written and thoroughly tested by experts.) As you will see in Section 5.8, you can also package functions that *you* have written in your own library files so that you can reuse them.

- **Top-Down Design** In top-down design, program complexity is reduced by subdividing the original problem into smaller, more manageable subtasks. C++, like most programming languages, supports top-down design by allowing a program to be written with its main function's body acting somewhat like a supervisor. That is, main can call other functions that you have written, but the actual code for these functions is given elsewhere in the program. This approach streamlines main by making it like an outline. Further, this approach makes writing, debugging and updating a program easier, because the overall program structure will be more **modular**. That is, the program is built from pieces of code that tend to be more self-contained.

- **Information Hiding** *Information hiding* refers to a phenomenon encountered in everday life as well as in programming — namely, the ability to use a construct without having to think about or even know how it is implemented. One common example is using a telephone without understanding data communications or the physics of analog sound. Another is using a word processor without knowing how text and formatting codes are stored in the computer. Predefined functions also employ information hiding. For example, you can use the predefined function sqrt in a call such as sqrt(2) to find the square root of 2, even though you may not know an algorithm for finding square roots. As you will see, C++ syntax encourages information hiding in functions that you write by allowing you to separate what a function does and how to use it from how to write the code to implement it.

5.1 Some Predefined Functions and the Library File `math.h`

Before we discuss how to write your own functions, we will consider using some predefined mathematical functions from the standard library file, `math.h`. Any program that uses a function from a library file must have an `include` statement specifying that library file. Otherwise, the compiler will be unable to locate the function. A program using any of the basic mathematical functions from the library file `math.h` requires the `include` statement

```
#include <math.h>
```

(Recall that the `include` statement for a nonstandard library file, such as `ourtools.h`, enclosed the file in double quote marks instead of angular brackets.)

Function Call, Arguments, and Return Value A *function call* is a program statement or expression that transfers control to a function so that the function will perform its particular subtask. For example, in the following statement, which uses the `sqrt` function of `math.h` to assign the square root of 49 to `y`,

```
y = sqrt (49); // function call
```

the function call is highlighted. Any value that a function call supplies to the function is known as an ***argument*** of the function call, whereas a result calculated and returned by the function call is known as the ***return value***. Thus, for the previous call, the argument is 49 and the return value is 7.

The general syntax for a function call is the name of the function, followed by a parenthesized list of arguments (if any), in which commas separate multiple arguments.

```
function-name (argument1, argument2, . . . .)
```

■ **QUESTION** The square root of 2 to 15 significant digits is 1.41421356237310. In the following program, the output statements use the default formatting (to, at most, six significant digits). What will the output be?

```
// sqroot.cpp
#include <iostream.h>
#include <math.h>

void main()
{
    int x;
    x = 2;
    cout << sqrt(9) << endl;
    cout << sqrt (10*x + 5) << endl;
    cout << sqrt(x) << endl;
}
```

Answer

```
3
5
1.41421
```

Form of an Argument   The argument supplied to sqrt can be a variable, a constant, or even an expression. Thus, sqrt(x), sqrt(9), and sqrt(10*x + 5) are all valid calls of sqrt.

Mixing Numeric Types with sqrt   The sqrt function expects an argument of type double, but can also accept an int, long, or float argument. In such cases, a copy of the argument will be converted to a double (in a temporary memory location) and then passed to the function. Further, the double result can be assigned to an int, long, or float variable, though precision may be lost.

Some Commonly Used Functions* from *math.h*

Function	Returns	Examples
abs(n)	the absolute value of n (an int)	abs(-12) is 12 abs(3) is 3
atan(x)	the angle (in radians) whose tangent is x (*Note:* 45° is 0.785398 radians.)	atan(0.0) is 0 atan(1.0) is 0.785398
ceil(x)	the smallest integer not less than x	ceil(5.1) is 6.0 ceil(-0.9) is 0.0
exp(x)	*e* to the x power (e^x)	exp(1.0) is 2.71828 exp(2.5) is 12.1825

(continued)

Function	Returns	Examples
cos(x)	the cosine of x (x is radians) (*Note:* 90° is 1.57080 radians.)	cos(0.0) is 1.0 cos(1.5708) is 0.0
fabs(x)	the absolute value of x	fabs(-10.3) is 10.3
floor(x)	the largest integer not greater than x	floor(99.99) is 99.0 floor(-13.0) is −13.0
labs(l)	the absolute value of l (a long)	labs(-40000) is 40000
log(x)	the natural (base *e*) logarithm of x	log(2.71828) is 1.0 log(12.1825) is 2.5
log10(x)	the base 10 logarithm of x	log10(1000.0) is 3.0
pow(x,y)	x to the y power (x^y)	pow(3.0,4.0) is 81.0 pow(81.0,0.25) is 3.0
sin(x)	the sine of x (x in radians)	sin(1.57080) is 1.0
sqrt(x)	the square root of x	sqrt(81.0) is 9.0 sqrt(3.0) is 1.73205
tan(x)	the tangent of x (x in radians)	tan(0.785398) is 1.0

*Except for abs and labs, all arguments and return values are of type double.

QUESTION Give the values returned by floor(x + 0.5) when x has the value

(a) 5.7   (b) 8.1   (c) 4   (d) 2.5

Answer   (a) 6   (b) 8   (c) 4   (d) 3

ceil **and** floor **and Rounding**   The ceil function returns the smallest integer not less than its argument, and the floor function returns the largest integer not greater than its argument. For example, both ceil(5.1) and ceil(6.0) return 6; and floor(5.9) and floor(5.0) return 5. Although C++ has no built-in round function to return the integer nearest to its argument, floor(x+0.5) will always return the integer nearest to x, as illustrated by the preceding question.

The pow **Function**   The pow function has two arguments; the first argument is the base and the second is the power. For example, pow(2,5) returns the value 32 (= 2⁵), and pow(10,-3) returns 0.001 (= 10⁻³).

The Constant Pi   One of the most important constants in mathematics is pi, the ratio of circumference to diameter of any circle. When using pi in a program, you should create a named float constant, PI, with the value 3.141592. (Exercise 5.13 presents a method for creating a more accurate double version of pi.)

QUESTION (**Precalculus**)   How would you complete the following program fragment (from sine.cpp), which will output the sine of an angle when the angle is input in degrees? (Note that `angle` must be converted to radians before it can be passed to the `sin` function.) *Hint:* Because an angle of one degree equals $\pi/180$ radians, an angle of d degrees will equal $d*(\pi/180)$ radians. Assume `PI` has been defined as a named constant.

```
float degs, radians;
cout << "Enter angle (in degrees): ";
cin >> degs;
radians = _____;
cout << "Sine of " << degs << " degrees = "
     << _____ << endl;
```

Answer   The first blank should contain `degs * PI / 180`. The second should contain `sin(radians)` because the `sin` function should be applied to the radian measure of the angle.   ■ ▬

PITFALL: ABSOLUTE VALUE   Three different functions can be used to calculate absolute value — `abs`, `labs`, and `fabs`. These functions take arguments of type `int`, `long`, and `double`, respectively, and return a result of the same type as the argument. The results of calls such as `abs` `(-10000000)` and `labs` `(-6.789)` are essentially meaningless because the arguments are not of the appropriate types.

5.2 Writing Value-Returning Functions

Although built-in libraries provide a number of useful functions, many situations will require you to write your own functions. When writing a function, it is customary to write it in *two separate pieces*: a **declaration** and a **definition**.

■ **EXAMPLE**   The following program defines and uses the function `dollar_value` to convert a specified number of dimes and quarters into a dollar amount. Note the placement of the **declaration** of `dollar_value` (before `main`) and the **definition** (after `main`).

```
// dollars.cpp
// Convert dimes and quarters to dollars.
#include <iostream.h>
#include "ourtools.h"

float dollar_value (int d, int q);      ←——————— function declaration
// return dollar value of d dimes and q quarters

void main()
```

```
{
    int dimes, quarters;
    float dollars;
    fixed_out (cout, 2); // for monetary amounts

    cout << "Enter number of dimes and quarters: ";
    cin >> dimes >> quarters;
    dollars = dollar_value (dimes, quarters);          ←————— function call
    cout << dimes << " dimes and " << quarters
         << " quarters" << " equals $"
         << dollars << endl;
}

float dollar_value (int d, int q)          ←—————— header ⎫ function
{ return 0.10*d + 0.25*q; }                ←——————  body ⎬ definition
```

A typical program run is:

```
Enter number of dimes and quarters: 3 8
3 dimes and 8 quarters equals $2.30
```

Function Declaration A function **declaration** (also called a **function prototype**) is placed in the declaration section, before the main function. With its accompanying comment, the declaration specifies what the function accomplishes and what a programmer needs to know to write a call to that function. The syntax for the function declaration and an example declaration follow.

Syntax:

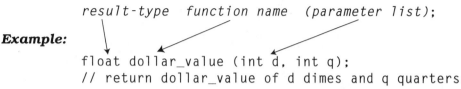

result-type   function name   (parameter list);

Example:

```
float dollar_value (int d, int q);
// return dollar_value of d dimes and q quarters
```

The preceding function declaration specifies that the function result will be of type float, the function name is dollar_value, and the function takes two arguments of type int; the comment explains what the function accomplishes.

Function Definition The function **definition** specifies, in code, the details of how the function performs its subtask.

Header   Customarily the function definition *header* and the function declaration are written exactly the same except that *the declaration is followed by a semicolon.* (Including the semicolon in the definition header will produce a syntax error.)

Body   The *body* contains the actual code that carries out the function's task. The execution of a *return* statement in the function body returns the single value calculated by the function to the point in the program where the function was called.

Parameters Versus Arguments   *Arguments* appear in the function call, whereas *parameters* are variables that belong to the function and appear in the function's declaration (or, equivalently, in the function's definition header). A function's value parameters are used to receive data supplied in the calling statement.

Parameter and Argument Matching   When the computer begins to execute a function call, it creates a memory cell for each value parameter and then copies the value of the matching argument into that cell. Arguments and parameters are matched, in order, from left to right. That is, the first parameter is assigned the value of the first argument, the second parameter is assigned the value of the second argument, and so on. Suppose that during a run of dollars.cpp the user inputs 3 for dimes and 8 for quarters. In the following diagram we use arrows, for assignment, to illustrate the fact that the first parameter (d) gets the value of the first argument (dimes) and that the second parameter (q) gets the value of the second argument (quarters).

Call

```
dollars = dollar_value (dimes, quarters);
                         3         8
```

Execution of Call

```
float dollar_value (int d, int q)
   {                   3      8
      return 0.10*d + 0.25*q;
   }
```

Be aware that when the computer finishes executing a function call, it deletes the memory cells that it created for that function's value parameters.

PITFALL: ARGUMENT ORDER   Recall that parameters and arguments are matched by order. Thus, when you are writing a call to a function you must be careful to give the arguments in the same order as the parameters with which they will be paired with.

■ **QUESTION** Note that in the function declaration

```
double dollar_value (int d, int q);
```

the parameter for the number of dimes is listed first. Suppose that in the program dollars.cpp the last cout statement in the body of main is replaced by

```
cout << dimes << " dimes and " << quarters
     << " quarters" << " equals $"
     << dollar_value (quarters, dimes) << endl;
```

What would the screen display be if the user again entered the values 3 and 8?

Answer

```
Enter dimes and quarters   3 8
3 dimes and 8 quarters equals $1.55
```

Discussion As indicated in the following diagram,

Call
```
dollars = dollar_value (quarters, dimes);
```
8   3

Execution of Call
```
float dollar_value (int d, int q)
{
        return 0.10*d + 0.25*q;
}
```
8 3

the value of quarters will be assigned to the parameter d and the value of dimes will be assigned to the parameter q, resulting in incorrect output.

■ ■

Local Variables Just as it can declare its parameters, a programmer-defined function can declare its own variables and constants in the body of the definition. These variables and constants are said to be *local* because they are accessible only by statements within the function. As with parameters, the memory for a function's local variables is created when the computer begins executing the function call and is deleted upon completion of the call.

■ **EXAMPLE**   Note that in the following program the body of the function declares and uses the local variable larger.

```
// max.cpp
#include <iostream.h

int max (int a, int b);
// Return the larger of a and b.

void main()
{
    int a, b;
    cout << "Enter two integers: ";
    cin >> a >> b;
    cout << "The larger is " << max(a,b) << endl;
}

int max (int a, int b);
{
    int larger;
    if (a > b)
        larger = a;
    else
        larger = b;
    return larger;
}
```

■ **QUESTION**   What would be another version of the body of max that does not need the local variable larger, but instead uses two return statements?

Answer
```
    if (a > b)
        return a;
    else
        return b;
```

■ **PROBLEM**   At Enlightened State University, students receive grades of Honors, Pass, or Fail rather than the usual letter grades. The function grade returns

'H', 'P', or 'F' depending on whether `avg` merits a grade of Honors (at least 92), Pass (at least 65, but less than 92), or Fail (less than 65). Write the definition of the function `grade` whose declaration is:

```
char grade (float avg);
```

Solution Both of the following definitions are possible solutions:

```
char grade (float avg)
{
    char grd;
    if (avg >= 92)
        grd = 'H';
    else if (avg >= 65)
        grd = 'P'
    else
        grd = 'F';
    return grd;
}
```

```
char grade (float avg)
{
    if (avg >= 92)
        return 'H';
    else if (avg >= 65)
        return 'P'
    else
        return 'F';
}
```

Argument and Parameter Names A value parameter's name may be the same as or different from a matched argument variable's name because matching is done by order and not similarity of names. Be aware that even if an argument variable and its matched parameter have the same name, they are two different variables, each with its own memory cell.

There are good reasons *not* to require an argument to have the same name as its parameter. For instance, a programmer who calls a function from a library may not know the names of the function's parameters. This situation results from information hiding rather than the programmer not being sufficiently knowledgeable! As an example, you've been using the `fixed_out` function, but you probably don't know the names of its parameters. As long as you have information about the function's parameter types, result type, and intended action, you can use the function effectively.

What Is Meant by the Scope of a Variable During program execution when a variable or a parameter (which is a kind of variable) is declared, a particular memory cell is associated with it. The ***scope of a variable*** or parameter is the portion of the program in which statements can use that variable to refer to that particular memory cell.

Scope for Various Kinds of Variables

- **Value Parameters and Local Variables** The scope of a function's parameters and local variables is limited to the body of that function.

- **Variable Declared in** main A variable declared at the top of the body of main has its scope limited to the body of main. Be aware that *a variable's scope does not include the bodies of functions that are called by* main.

What If a Variable Is Used Outside Its Scope?   When a programmer writes a statement that uses a variable outside its scope, one of the following two problems will occur:

1. **The compiler will generate an "Unknown Identifier" error message** when there is no declaration of a variable or a parameter by that same name whose scope includes the problematic statement. For example, in program max.cpp, if the variable larger had been declared in main, but not as a local variable of the function max, then the compiler would have produced an error message for each occurrence of larger in the body of max.

2. **An unintended memory cell will be used** if the program contains another declaration of a variable with that *same name* and the problematic statement is within the scope of that other variable.

■ QUESTION

1. Suppose that function main declares a variable named x and that a function, fnc, which has a local variable named x, is called by main. Is this legal? What will happen when the computer executes a statement in the body of fnc that uses x?

2. Suppose that main declares a variable named y and fnc has neither a parameter nor a local variable named y. What will happen if a statement in the body of fnc uses y?

Answer

1. Yes, this is legal. The computer will use the memory cell for the local variable declared in fnc for statements within the body of fnc that refer to x.

2. This scenario will produce an "Unknown Identifier" error message during compilation because the program does not contain a declaration for y with the body of fnc as its scope. ■ ▬

Memory for Value Parameters and Local Variables   When the computer begins to execute a function's calling statement it creates

1. a memory cell for each value parameter, then copies the argument that is matched with the value parameter into this cell, and

2. a memory cell for each local variable.

When a statement in the body of a function is executed, these memory cells are used for any references to value parameters or local variables. Upon completion of the execution of the function's body, the memory cells for all the function's value parameters and local variables are erased.

Security Feature of Value Parameters   When you rent a video, the video is protected so that you cannot erase or record over any portions of the video. Value parameters offer a similar sort of protection. When a function is called, the execution of the call will not alter the value of any argument that is matched with a value parameter. This security feature is a consequence of the value parameter having its own memory cell, which receives a *copy* of the value of the matched argument. Thus, a statement in the function body that changes the value of a value parameter is really changing its *copy* of the matching argument, *not* the argument itself.

Protecting Against Side Effects   A ***side effect*** is said to occur when one portion of a program disrupts what was done by another portion. Some protection against side effects is provided by the security feature of value parameters and the fact that each variable has its own scope. (However, see the Short Stays R Us Hospital example at the PWS Web site for an illustration of an unpleasant side effect.)

5.3   Program Design with Value-Returning Functions

Two related reasons for writing your own functions within a program are

1. to **simplify** the body of `main` so that `main` acts somewhat like a supervisor in that it can call functions to perform some subtasks (whose details are given elsewhere in the program), or it can also carry out some subtasks itself, and

2. to **modularize** the program — pieces of the program corresponding to different subtasks can be handled by separate functions.

This approach makes writing, debugging, and updating programs easier because the overall program structure is clearer when `main` delegates subtasks to functions, and complications or errors in a subtask can be traced to the function that handles that subtask.

Eventually you will learn to write functions that can handle all programming subtasks. For now, however, only subtasks corresponding to the calculation and return of a single value will be delegated to functions.

Keeping Focused   Once you have subdivided a longer problem into subtasks and written a first level of pseudocode, you should begin to make decisions about (1) which subtasks you will write all the code for in the `main` body, (2) which subtasks you will accomplish by a call to a function that you will write later, and (3) which subtasks are complicated enough to warrant further thought.

■ **PROBLEM**   In Professor Maximillian's course, each student takes four exams. A student's letter grade is determined by first calculating her weighted average as follows:

$$\text{wtd\_avg} = \frac{(\text{score1} + \text{score2} + \text{score3} + \text{score4} + \text{max\_score})}{5}$$

(This counts her maximum score twice as much as each of the other scores.) Her letter grade is then an A if `wtd_avg` is at least 90, a B if `wtd_avg` is at least 80 (but under 90), a C if `wtd_avg` is at least 70 (but under 80), a D if `wtd_avg` is at least 60 (but under 70), or an F if `wtd_avg` is under 60.

The following table presents four pseudocode statements with decisions for each statement about how to handle the subtask described.

Pseudocode	*Decisions*
1. Prompt for and input the scores.	Put this code in `main`.
2. Calculate `wtd_avg`.	This subtask requires further thought.
3. Determine the letter grade.	Use a call to the function `grade`, similar to that of Section 5.2.
4. Output `wtd_avg`. and grade.	Put this code in `main`.

Calculating `wtd_avg` ***(subtask 2)***   The only complicated subtask is that of finding `wtd_avg`. For that subtask, we first must find `max_scr`, the maximum of the four scores, and then use the formula for `wtd_avg`. To find `max_scr` we can have a contest among the four scores, similar to the "final four" in a basketball tournament. That is, the larger of `scr1` and `scr2` will face off against the larger of `scr3` and `scr4`. For these three face-offs we will use three calls to the function `max` that was discussed in the previous program.   ■ ■■

■ **QUESTION**   How would you complete the following program fragment (from `weighted.cpp`) to input and calculate the weighted average of four exam scores, then display the average accurate to the nearest tenth?

```
// weighted.cpp
// Find weighted average of and letter
// grade for four exam scores.
#include <iostream.h>
#include <math.h>
#include "ourtools.h"

int max (int a, int b);
// return max of a and b

char grade (float avg);
// return grade for avg:

void main()
{
    int scr1, scr2, scr3, scr4;
    int max_scr, max12, max34;
    float wtd_avg;
    char ltr_grade;

    // Prompt for and input the scores.
    cout << "Enter 4 scores: ";
    cin >> scr1 >> scr2 >> scr3 >> scr4;

    // Calculate wtd_avg.
    _____;
    _____;

    max_scr = max(max12, max34);
    wtd_avg = (scr1+scr2+scr3+scr4+max_scr)/5.0;

    // Determine grade
    _____;

    // Output wtd. avg. and grade
    fixed_out(cout,1);
    cout << "Weighted average: " << wtd_avg;
    cout << "   Grade " << ltr_grade << endl;
}
```

Answer   The missing lines are

```
max12 = max(scr1, scr2);
max34 = max(scr3, scr4);
ltr_grade = grade (wtd_avg);
```

Discussion   Function `max` is called three times, with different arguments each time. This example further illustrates the claim of the previous section that the argument name doesn't have to be the same as the corresponding parameter name — in this case it would be impossible.

The definitions of the functions `max` and `grade` are not shown. Exercise 5.10c asks you to write the function `grade`.   ■ ▬

5.4 Void Functions and Program Design

All the functions discussed thus far have returned a value. To further modularize these programs (so that most or all of the subtasks are done by function calls from `main`), you will need to write functions that perform subtasks other than returning a value. C++ uses *void functions* for such subtasks.

Some Primary Uses of *Void* Functions   Void functions can be used for:

1. Calculating and outputting a result, all from within the body of the function.

2. Outputting final results that were calculated earlier in the program. (The body of such a function usually consists of several `cout` statements.)

3. Displaying useful output other than program calculations. Examples of this are detailed instructions for input; a summary of what the program will accomplish; or warnings or error messages. (Such functions are usually parameterless.)

4. "Pretty printing" — that is, taking extra care to display information (usually program-calculated output) in some standard or especially readable format. Pretty printing is a specialized form of uses 2 and 3.

Void Functions   A *void function* does not return a value; it has `void` as its result type. For example, the next program contains the following declaration of a `void` function:

```
void print_dollar_value(int d, int q); // declaration
```

The call to a void function is a complete statement in itself. By contrast, the call to a value-returning function is part of an expression in an assignment or output statement. Note that the following program contains the stand-alone call

```
print_dollar_value(dimes, quarters); // call
```

■ **EXAMPLE** (Use 1: Calculating and Outputting a Value) The following program converts an input number of dimes and quarters into a dollar amount.

```
// dollars2.cpp
#include <iostream.h>
#include "ourtools.h"

void print_dollar_value (int d, int q);
// print dollar value of
// d dimes and q quarters.

void main()
{
    int dimes, quarters;
    cout << "Enter number of dimes and quarters: ";
    cin >> dimes >> quarters;
    print_dollar_value(dimes, quarters);
}

void print_dollar_value(int d, int q)
{
    float dollars;
    dollars = 0.10*d + 0.25*q;
    cout << d << " dimes and " << q << " quarters = ";
    fixed_out (cout, 2);
    cout << '$' << dollars << endl;
}
```

A typical run of the program is:

```
Enter number of dimes and quarters: 3 8
3 dimes and 8 quarters equals $2.30
```

Value-returning Versus *void* **Functions** The void function print_dollar_value does not return the value of its local variable dollars to the body of main for printing there. Instead, the body of print_dollar_value contains the cout statement to print the value of dollars.

In general, if you need to calculate and print a value, how do you decide whether to write the function as a void function that prints the value itself or as a value-returning function? A good rule of thumb is the following: If the value is also needed in later computations or outputs, write a value-returning function; otherwise, write whichever version you prefer. (Note that in the previous program, either way is okay.)

■ **EXAMPLE**   (Use 2: A void **Function to Display Grade Information**)   Note that the weighted.cpp program of Section 5.3 can be further modularized by replacing the three lines of code to output the weighted average and letter grade with the function call

```
display_results(wtd_avg, ltr_grade);
```

■ **QUESTION**   Give the definition of display_results.

Answer

```
void display_results(float wtd_avg, char ltr_grade)
{
    fixed_out(cout,1);
    cout << "Weighted average: " << wtd_avg;
    cout << " Grade " << ltr_grade << endl;
}
```

Parameterless Functions   The void function print_dollar_value had two parameters. A function may also be *parameterless*, as is the void function do_intro of the next program. Note the empty parentheses in both the declaration and the call.

```
void do_intro(); // declaration
do_intro(); // call
```

■ **EXAMPLE**   (Uses 3 and 1: Fahrenheit–Celsius Conversion)   Here is a typical run of a program that converts from Fahrenheit to Celsius or vice versa:

```
   CELSIUS <———> FAHRENHEIT CONVERTER
THE TWO CONVERSION FORMULAS ARE
    F = 1.8 * C + 32
    C = (5.0/9) * (F — 32)
Is input Celsius or Fahrenheit? (F/C): F
Enter number of degrees: 80
80 F = 27 C
```

This program contains three void functions. The first function, do_intro, is parameterless; it displays, for the user's information, the formulas used in converting between Fahrenheit and Celsius. The other two void functions, change_F2C and change_C2F, have degrees as a parameter; each is responsible for using the correct formula and then printing the final line of output appropriately. Here is the program.

```cpp
// temps.cpp
#include <iostream.h>

void do_intro();
void change_C2F(int C);
void change_F2C(int F);

void main()
{
    char scale; // Cels or Fahr
    int degrees;
    do_intro();
    cout << "Is input Celsius or Fahrenheit? (F/C): ";
    cin >> scale;
    cout << "Enter number of degrees: ";
    cin >> degrees;
    if (scale=='c' || scale=='C')
        change_C2F(degrees);
    else
        change_F2C(degrees);
}

// Function definitions go here . . .
```

Here are the definitions of the functions do_intro *and* change_F2C. Exercise 5.7 asks you to write the definition of change_C2F.

```cpp
void do_intro()
{
    cout << "CELSIUS <——> FAHRENHEIT CONVERTER\n";
    cout << "THE TWO CONVERSION FORMULAS ARE:\n";
    cout << "    F = 1.8 * C + 32" << endl;
    cout << "    C = (5.0/9) * (F - 32)" << endl;
}
```

```
void change_F2C(int F)
{   int C;
    C = (5./9.) * (F-32) + 0.5; // add 0.5 to round
    cout << F << " F = " << C << " C" << endl;
}
```

Different Function Call in Each Branch   In the previous program each branch of the if statement required a different formula and form for the output statement, so each branch consisted of a different void function call to calculate and print the result. The branches of a linear nested if statement commonly contain or consist of function calls. However, do not confuse this kind of if statement in the body of main with the technique of implementing a single function by use of an if statement in the function body as was done, for example, in the grade function of Section 5.2.

■ **PROBLEM**   **(Use 4: Pretty Printing)**   We want to display dates in the standard form mo/day/yr, with a leading zero for the month and day when these numbers are only single digits. Some examples are

Month	Day	Year	Display
5	6	1998	05/06/1998
12	2	2000	12/02/2000
3	9	1995	03/09/1995

■ **QUESTION**   Study the following main function (from date1.cpp) and the preceding display. How would you complete the definition of function format_date?

```
void main()
{
    int month, day, year;
    cout << "Enter month day and year: ";
    cin >> month >> day >> year;
    format_date (month, day, year);
    cout << endl;
}
```

```
void format_date (int mon, int day, int yr)
// Print date in mon/day/yr format, with a
// leading zero for a single digit month or day.
{
    if (mon < 10)
        cout << '0';
    cout << mon << '/';
    if (day < 10)
        _____;
    cout << _____;
}
```

Answer   Note that the body of format_date uses its parameters rather than the matching variables of main. Thus, this function must use yr rather than year. The completed lines are

```
        cout << '0';
    cout << day << '/' << yr;
```

5.5   Functions Calling Other Functions

In C++, the body of a function definition can contain a call to any other function whose declaration has been provided prior to the point of the call. Thus, if you place all the function declarations together before main and all their definitions together after main (as we normally do), then the body of any one of the function definitions can contain calls to any of the other functions. (These functions can also call library functions provided the appropriate libraries have been included at the top of the program.)

■ **EXAMPLE**   In the following program, date2.cpp, the body of the format_date function contains calls to the print_2d function in order to print the month and day in two-digit form (with a leading zero if necessary). Notice how the logic of format_date is much clearer than it was in the version of the previous section.

```
void format_date (int mon, int day, int yr);
// Print date in mon/day/yr format, with a
// leading zero for a single digit month or day.

void print_2d (int n);
// print n as a 2-digit number
```

```
void main()
{
    int month, day, year;
    cout << "Enter month day and year: ";
    cin >> month >> day >> year;
    format_date (month, day, year);
    cout << endl;
}

void print_2d (int n)
{
    if (n < 10)
        cout << '0';
    cout << n;
}

void format_date (int mon, int day, int yr)
{
    print_2d(mon); cout << '/';
    print_2d(day); cout << '/' << yr;
}
```

Order of Definitions and Declarations   You can give the function declarations or their definitions in any order you choose. Thus, for example, you could interchange the order of the declarations of format_date and print_2d, or you could place the definition of print_2d after the definition of format_date. (Of course, if a program contains many user-defined functions, it would be good style to present the declarations and definitions alphabetically by function name.)

5.6 Using Function Stubs in Program Development

Function Stubs   A *function stub* is simply a function definition that returns a "phony" value. This type of function can be useful in programming problems, when you need to compute a value, but there is no built-in function to do the computation, and you don't have immediate access to a formula or algorithm for the computation. Although function stubs return a phony value, they enable you to progress in the development of the program because you can (1) write a program that runs and that can be tested for the overall flow of control, (2) test other portions of a program that depend on the function that is written as a stub, and (3) achieve a good stopping place in writing a program that is still incomplete — you need only to replace each stub with an actual function.

■ **EXAMPLE** **(Monthly Car Loan Payment)** Write a program to determine whether a car loan is approved. The inputs to the program will be the amount of the loan, the annual rate of interest (as a percent), the lifetime of the loan in months, and the applicant's yearly income. The loan is approved if the applicant's monthly income is at least four times the monthly payment. Here are two sample runs. (Note that the monthly payment is given only if the loan is approved.)

```
Amount of loan: $18900
Annual interest rate (%): 9.25
Loan lifetime in months: 60
Annual income: $36300
LOAN APPROVED!
The monthly payment is $394.63
```

```
Amount of loan: $27800
Annual interest rate (%): 10.7
Loan lifetime in months: 36
Annual income: $21000
LOAN DENIED.
Have a nice day.
```

Pseudocode Here is a top-level pseudocode algorithm with some decisions about how to handle the subtasks.

Pseudocode	**Decisions**
1. Prompt for and input all loan information.	Use `cin-cout` statements in `main`.
2. Calculate the monthly payment.	Call a value-returning function. For now, make it a stub.
3. Decide whether to approve or reject the loan and output the decision and loan amount.	Call a `void` function, passing monthly payment and annual income to it.

The Stub for the Payment Calculation Function Don't be alarmed if you don't know the formula for computing the *equal* monthly payments — most people don't. The formula is complicated by the fact that you pay interest *continuously* on the unpaid principal (which does *not stay fixed*).

The function stub should have parameters to receive whatever quantities are needed to do the actual calculation for the monthly payment. Thus, the function stub should have parameters for (1) the amount of the loan, A, (2) the annual rate of interest, r, and (3) the lifetime of the loan in months, m. We will have this function stub return the value 0. Here is the stub.

```
double payment(double A, double r, int m)
{
    return 0;
}
```

Below we give a main function that uses the stub for the payment function.

```
void main()
{
    double amount, rate, annual_income,
            monthly_payment;
    int months;

    // Get inputs from loan applicant
    cout << "Amount of loan: $";
    cin >> amount;
    cout << "Annual interest rate (%): ";
    cin >> rate;
    cout << "Loan lifetime in months: ";
    cin >> months;
    cout << "Annual income: $";
    cin >> annual_income;

    // calculate monthly payment
    monthly_payment = payment(amount, 0.01*rate, months);

    // Approve/deny the loan, then display decision
    decide_loan (monthly_payment, annual_income);
}
```

Exercise 5.12a asks you to write the decide_loan function, change the value returned by the stub for payment, and then test this version of the program. In this way, you will see how to test the rest of the program even though you haven't written a correct version of the payment function. Then Exercise 5.12b asks you to replace the body of the payment function with the correct code for calculating the payment and test the program with several input data groups.

■ **QUESTION**   The formula for monthly payment, *MP*, is

$$MP = \frac{r \times A/12}{1 - (1 + r/12)^{-m}}$$

where A = the loan amount
r = the annual interest rate (as a decimal)
m = the lifetime of the loan in months.

Complete the definition of the `payment` function. (*Hint:* Calculate the numerator and denominator separately and use the `pow` function from `math.h`.)

```
double payment(double A, double r, int m)
{
    double num, den;
    num = r * A/12;
    den = _____;
    _____;
}
```

Answer   The completed lines are

```
den = 1 - pow(1 + r/12, -m);
return num/den;
```

Notice that the body of `payment` contains a call to the library function `pow`. This is another example of a function calling a function.   ■ ■■

5.7   Reference Parameters and Data Input Functions

Thus far in our discussion, a function call statement could not change the value of any variables that were its arguments because the only kind of parameter that we have used is the value parameter. A second kind of parameter, known as a ***reference parameter***, allows a calling statement to change the value of a variable in the calling statement. Perhaps the simplest use of reference parameters is to further streamline the body of a program's `main` function by enabling data to be input using a single function call — the actual `cin` and `cout` statements will appear in the body of the definition of that function.

For example, in the program `temps.cpp`, of Section 5.4, the data is input using four statements in `main` (two `cout`-`cin` statement pairs). A way to further streamline `main` would be to replace those four statements by the following function call:

```
get_temp_data (scale, degrees);
```

and to define the `get_temp_data` function as follows:

```
void get_temp_data (char& scl, int& dgrs)
{
    cout << "Is input Celsius or Fahrenheit? (F/C): ";
    cin >> scl;
    cout << "Enter number of degrees: ";
    cin >> dgrs;
}
```

The ampersand after a parameter's type (highlighted) lets the compiler know that the parameter is a reference parameter. A reference parameter does not receive its own memory cell, but instead shares the memory cell of its matching argument. *Thus, any statement in the body of the function that gives a value to a reference parameter will actually give the value to the matching variable argument of the function call.*

Exercise 5.9 asks you to experiment with the preceding `get_temp_data` function. Later, Exercise 5.12c asks you to write a `get_loan_data` function to input the data in the car loan program of Section 5.6.

More on Reference Parameters   If you would like to study reference parameters in greater detail, you can go to Section 6.1 on string variables and then jump to Chapter 9.

5.8   Saving and Reusing Your Own User-Defined Functions

You have already seen how to use functions from the library file `ourtools.h` at the PWS Web site. For example, we have frequently used `fixed_out` from that file. Whenever you write a new function that you feel will be useful in future programs, you can add its definition to this library. Or you can create your own separate libraries of related functions. Then, you can reuse a function in a program without rewriting either its declaration or its definition — just include `myfuns.h` (or the name of your own library file) so that the program has access to the function.

The Structure of a Library File   The library file `myfuns.h` at the PWS Web site illustrates a common way to structure library files that are not too large.

```
// myfuns.h
#ifndef _MYFUNS_H
#define _MYFUNS_H

#include <math.h>


Definitions of functions provided
 by myfuns.h go here.


#endif
```

Avoiding Duplicate Function Definitions Note the three highlighted compiler directives beginning with the test #ifndef _MYFUNS_H. This test at the top of a library file protects against duplicate definition errors. A duplicate definition error might occur if another library file, othrfuns.h, contained the directive #include "myfuns.h" and if a program contained directives to include both of these library files. In that situation, if myfuns.h did not have the #ifndef test, then the compiler would be asked *twice* to compile the function definitions from myfuns.h, resulting in a duplicate definition error.

Be aware of the following point of syntax: The name chosen for the symbol in the #ifndef directive is arbitrary. However, the name _MYFUNS_H conforms to a fairly standard convention observed by C++ programmers for naming compiler symbols.

Systematic Testing of Functions As a rule, you should never add a function to a library without thoroughly testing it. Because any program can be a consumer of the library's contents, you want to be certain that the library provides only quality products. The for loop introduced in Section 3.9 can be used to input function arguments repeatedly, call the function, and, in the case of a value-returning function, display the result.

■ **EXAMPLE** The following program fragment (from dollars3.cpp) tests the dollar_value function written in Section 5.2. The number of tests and the arguments for each test are input by the user.

```
int i, num_tests;
int dimes, quarters;

cout << "How many function tests? ";
cin >> num_tests;
for (i=1; i<=num_tests; i++)
    {
    cout << "Enter number of dimes and quarters: ";
    cin >> dimes >> quarters;
    fixed _out (cout, 2); // for monetary amounts
    cout << dimes << " dimes and " << quarters
         << " quarters" << " equals $"
         << dollar_value (dimes, quarters) << "\n\n";
    }
```

When applying the preceding technique, keep in mind that the test is only as good as your test oracle. ■ ▬

Using Copy and Paste to Add Functions to a Library   You don't need to retype a function definition to add it to the `myfuns.h` file or another of your personal function library files. Most text editors provide features for copying text from one file and pasting it into another.

5.9 Other Useful Library Functions

C++ contains many standard libraries of functions in addition to `math.h`. In this section we first consider some functions from the library file `ctype.h` for character classification and conversion. We also briefly introduce simulation using functions from the library file `stdlib.h` to generate pseudorandom numbers.

■ **EXAMPLE**   **(Character Classification)** To test whether a character is a letter, you can use the `isalpha` function from `ctype.h` and write

```
if (isalpha(ch)) . . .
```

Note how much clearer and more concise this test is than the equivalent

```
if (('a'<=ch && ch<='z') || ('A'<=ch && ch<='Z')) . . .
```
■ ▬

■ **EXAMPLE**   **(Character Conversion)** When writing a user-friendly program that allows single-letter responses to be entered in either upper- or lowercase, you can simplify the coding by converting these responses to upper case before processing them. The following program fragment (from `temps2.cpp`) achieves both user-friendliness and simplicity by converting the user input to uppercase.

```
cout << "Enter degrees and scale (C or F): ";
cin >> degrees >> scale;
scale = toupper(scale);
if (scale=='C') . . .
```

In the `if` condition, you need not check whether `response` is `'c'`.

Simulation and Pseudorandom Numbers

Computers are often used to simulate random processes, simple examples of which would be flipping a coin or rolling a pair of dice. (A very complex example would be the flight simulators on which pilots and astronauts train.)

Because a computer executes algorithms consisting of well-defined, predictable sequences of steps, the computer cannot behave randomly. However, a computer can execute algorithms to produce long sequences of numbers that *appear* to be random. The numbers in these sequences are called **peudorandom** numbers, and the algorithm that produces them is known as a **pseudorandom number generator**. For simplicity, we will use the term *random* in place of the term *pseudorandom.*

In C++, the library file `stdlib.h` contains a parameterless random number generation function, `rand`. Each time that `rand` is called, it returns a pseudorandom integer in the range 0 through `INT_MAX`.

Seeding the Random Number Generator

The following `main` function (from `rnd.cpp`) outputs ten pseudorandom numbers.

```
void main ()
{
    int i;
    for (i=1; i<=10; i++)
        cout << rand() << ' ';
    cout << endl;
}
```

Each time you run `rnd.cpp`, *it will output the same sequence of numbers,* because the pseudorandom sequence starts with the same number each time. This outcome would certainly be a problem in a program that used the pseudorandom number sequence to simulate a card game — the user would be dealt the same hand every time the program ran!

The solution to this problem is to **seed** the (well-encapsulated) random number generator — that is, we will give the generator an integer "seed" from which to "grow" its sequence of numbers. Seeding can be done by calling the `void srand` function `stdlib.h`, using some seed as the argument.[1] Of course, we want this seed to vary from one run to another so that the sequence of numbers produced by the generator will vary from one run to another. A standard method for doing this is to use the computer's internal clock.

The library file `time.h` contains a function, `time`, that uses the computer's internal clock to return the `unsigned long` (32-bit) integer that is the number of seconds elapsed since 12:00:00AM, GMT, January 1, 1970. For our purposes, it will suffice to provide an argument of 0 to this function and then pass the return value to the `srand` function as follows:

```
srand (time(0)); // seed the R.N.G
```

■ **EXAMPLE**   The following program simulates rolling a pair of fair six-sided dice ten times. The outputs of the program are, for all practical purposes, indistinguishable from several rolls of an actual pair of dice.

```
// roll2.cpp
#include <iostream.h>
#include <stdlib.h>
#include <time.h>

void main()
{
    int i;
    int dots1, dots2;
    srand(time(0)); // seed R.N.G.
    for (i=1; i<=10; i++)
        {
        dots1 = rand()%6 + 1;
        dots2 = rand()%6 + 1;
        cout << "Roll: " << dots1
                << " and " << dots2 << " = "
                << (dots1+dots2) << endl;
        }
}
```

```
Roll: 2 and 1 = 3
Roll: 4 and 5 = 9
Roll: 1 and 3 = 4
Roll: 1 and 5 = 6
Roll: 4 and 1 = 5
Roll: 4 and 3 = 7
Roll: 6 and 5 = 11
Roll: 3 and 2 = 5
Roll: 1 and 1 = 2
Roll: 2 and 5 = 7
```

Sample run

----

[1] Borland and Turbo C++ provide a parameterless seed function, `randomize`, in the `stdlib.h` library, which can be used in place of `srand`.

Discussion   Notice that the value of rand()%6 will be between 0 and 5 inclusive, so adding 1 produces a value between 1 and 6, inclusive. Subsequent runs of the program will produce different results.   ■ ▬▬

PITFALL: srand   The random number generator should be seeded *once and only once* in a program run. Multiple calls to srand can cause the random number generation algorithm to behave in a noticeably nonrandom fashion. Thus, you should not place the call to srand within the body of the for loop of the program roll2.cpp. (Give it a try so that you will recognize the problem if you ever make this mistake.)

■ **Exercises**

1. Give the value of
   (a) abs(-34)   (b) fabs (-5.12)   (c) log10(1000.0)
   (d) pow(2.5,2)   (e) pow(2,6.0)   (f) pow(10.0,4)
   (g) sqrt(2.25)   (h) ceil(sqrt(140.3))   (i) floor(log10(123.7))

2. Give the value of
   (a) 9/4   (b) float(9/4)   (c) 9 / float(4)
   (d) 9 / ceil(4.5)   (e) int(9.5) / 4   (f) 9 / 4.0

3. What is the value of ceil(log10(abs(m))) when m, an int, has the value
   (a) −100   (b) 99   (c) −5   (d) 12345

4. Look up the ctype.h library file in your on-line or printed help files to get information on the isdigit, isalnum, and ispunct functions. Then, give the output of the following program segment when the value of ch is
   (a) '4'   (b) '?'   (c) 'G'

   ```
   if (isdigit(ch))
       cout << "digit" << endl;
   if (isalnum(ch))
       cout << "alnum" << endl;
   if (ispunct(ch))
       cout << "punct" << endl;
   ```

5. Given that m and n are of type char and have the values '7' and 'P', respectively, give the value of the following:
   (a) isupper(n)   (b) islower('n')   (c) isalpha(m)
   (d) isalpha('m')   (e) toupper(m)   (f) tolower(n)
   (g) int(m)   (h) char(60)   (i) char(n - 2)

6. If x and n are of type `double` and `int`, respectively, give the output of the program fragment on the right when x and n have the values

    (a) 1.2536 and 2

    (b) 1.2536 and 3

    (c) 12536.0 and –3

```
pow10 = pow(10,n);
x = x * pow10;
cout << x << ' ';
x = floor(x + 0.5);
cout << x << ' ';
x = x / pow10;
cout << x << endl;
```

7. Write the definition of function `change_C2F` of the program `temps.cpp`.

8. Find all the syntax errors in the following program.

```
#include <iostream.h>

void main()
{
    int num1, num2;
    cout << "Enter two integers: ";
    cin >> num1 >> num2;
    cout << "Max = " << max(num1, num2) << endl;
}

int max (int a, int b);
{
    if (num1 > num2)
        return a;
    else
        return b;
}
```

9. The program `temps2.cpp` at the PWS Web site implements the temperature conversion program of Section 5.4 with the `get_temp_data` function of Section 5.7.

    (a) Run this program for several different temperatures and scales, and record the results.

    (b) Remove the ampersands in the declaration and definition of `get_temp _data`, then run the program with the same data you used in part a. You should get different results. Explain.

Programming Problems

10. Write the definitions of the functions whose declarations and descriptions are given on the next page. Use the technique of Section 5.6 to test your solutions systematically.

(a) `int min (int a, int b);`
   `// Return the minimum of a and b.`

(b) `float pay (int hrs, float rate);`
   `// Return pay, where hours over 40 are`
   `// paid at 1.5 times the regular rate.`

(c) `char grade (float avg);`
   `// Return a grade of 'A', 'B', 'C', 'D', or 'F'`
   `// using 90, 80, 70, and 60 as cutoffs.`

(d) `void personal_info ();`
   `// Display your name, age, and semester`
   `// standing neatly formatted, with labels.`

(e) `void display_pt (float x, float y);`
   `// Display the point with coordinates`
   `// x and y in the form (x, y).`

(f) `bool is_leap (int yr);`
   `// Return true if yr is a leap year, false`
   `// otherwise.` (*Hint*: See Exercise 4.8 of Chapter 4.)

(g) `double round (double x, int n);`
   `// Return x rounded to n decimal places.`
   `// (`*Hint*`: See Exercise 5.6.)`

(h) `int mins_past_midnight (int hour, int minute, char meridian);`
   `// Return number of minutes past midnight for the time`
   `// with the given hour, minute, and meridian`
   `// ('A' or 'P', for AM or PM).`

(i) `double hypotenuse (double leg1, double leg2);`
   `// Return the length of the hypotenuse of a`
   `// right triangle having legs of length leg1`
   `// and leg2.`

(j) `int random_int (int low, int high);`
   `// return a random integer between low and`
   `// high, inclusive.`

11. Add the `is_leap` function of the previous exercise to the `myfuns.h` library. Then write a program that repeatedly inputs a year, calls the `is_leap` function from the library with the input year as the argument, and then outputs whether the year is a leap year.

12. Complete the Car Loan program of Section 5.6 as follows:

   (a) Write the `decide_loan` function assuming that a loan is approved only if the monthly payment is no more than 25% of the applicant's gross monthly income. Change the `payment` function stub to return $350. Try different inputs to test your `decide_loan` function.

   (b) Replace the body of the `payment` function by the code given in the text. Test the program with several well-chosen input data sets.

   (c) The `main` function of the program is cluttered by the `cout` and `cin` statements for the subtask of prompting for and getting the input data. Write a data-input function, `get_loan_data`, to handle this task, and call it from `main`.

13. You do not need to remember 15 digits of accuracy to create a `double` version of the constant pi. Instead, use the formula $\pi = 4 \cdot$ `arctan(1.0)`. Write a program to create this constant and display all 15 digits of it. (You may wish to add this constant to one of your own library files.)

14. Rewrite the program `weighted.cpp` of Section 5.3 using a data input function, `get_scores`, to prompt for and input the four exam scores.

15. Rewrite the program `date2.cpp` of Section 5.5 using a data input function, `get_date`, to prompt for and input the month, day, and year.

16. Write a program that inputs a weight in kilograms, then calls a `void` function, `convert_to_lb_oz`, to output the equivalent weight in pounds and ounces, accurate to the nearest ounce. (One kilogram equals 2.2 pounds.) For example, if the input is 3.0 kg, the output would be 3 kg = 6 lb. 10 oz.

17. Input the radius of a circle (or sphere) and output its area and circumference (or volume and surface area) by calling a `void` function, `display_circle_info` (or `display_sphere_info`).

18. Write a program that inputs a `long` integer, then calls an `int`-valued function, `num_digits`, that returns the number of digits in its `long` parameter. Test this function using inputs having different numbers of digits, as well as zero and negatives. (*Hint*: Consider Exercise 5.3.)

19. When a ball is thrown up at an angle of θ degrees and with initial velocity V_0 the height of the ball after t seconds is

$$h(t) = V_0 t \sin\theta - 16t^2$$

Write a program to input the initial angle and velocity with which a ball is thrown and a time t in seconds, then output the height of the ball t seconds after it was thrown. Use a `float`-valued function, `height`, to calculate the height, and a `void` function, `display_info`, to output the user inputs and the calculated height.

20. Rapid Delivery charges by weight for delivery of packages. The delivery charge for the first pound is \$3.00 and \$0.50 is added onto the charge for each additional four ounces. For example, a package weighing more than 16 but at most 20 ounces costs \$3.50 to deliver; a package weighing more than 20 but at most 24 ounces costs \$4.00 to deliver; etc. Write a program that inputs the weight of a package in ounces, then outputs the charge for delivery. (Use a `float`-valued function, `delivery_charge`, and a `void` function, `display_delivery_charge`.)

21. Given a distance in meters, output the equivalent distance in miles, yards, and inches, accurate to the nearest inch. (There are 1.093613 yards per meter.) For example, if the input is 10,000 meters, the output would be

        10000 m. = 6 mi. 376 yd. 5 in.

You may want to use the functions whose declarations are

```
double meters_to_yards (double meters);
// convert m meters to yards

void display_mi_yd_in (double meters);
// display meters as miles, yards,
// and inches, rounded to nearest inch
```

22. Write a program that uses pseudorandom numbers to "draw" a user-specified number of cards from a standard deck of 52. Output for a given card will look like

    Five of diamonds or Queen of hearts

    (*Hints*: Write parameterless value-returning functions suit and rank, each of which calls rand. You may output the same card more than once.)

23. The area of a triangle can be calculated from the lengths a, b, and c of its sides using **Hero's formula**:

    $$\text{area} = \sqrt{s(s-a)(s-b)(s-c)} \text{ where } s = \frac{(a+b+c)}{2}$$

    (*Note*: If a, b, and c cannot be the lengths of the sides of a triangle, then the quantity $s(s-a)(s-b)(s-c)$ will be negative or zero.)

    Write a program to input the lengths of the sides of a triangle; then output the area of the triangle or a message saying that the lengths cannot be those of the sides of a triangle. (Use a float-valued function called tri_area.)

Longer Assignments

24. For optimal aerobic benefit, a person should maintain a heart rate between 60% and 80% of his or her maximal heart rate — this range is called the aerobic target zone. A person's maximal heart rate (MHR) is calculated as MHR = 220-age and k percent of maximal heart rate is given by the formula

    0.01* k * (MHR — RP) + RP

    where RP is the person's resting pulse rate.

    Write a program to input a person's age and resting pulse rate, then output that person's maximal heart rate and aerobic target zone. The lower and upper pulse rates of the target zone should be accurate to the nearest whole number. (Use an int-valued function to return MHR and a void function to display the lower and upper ends of the aerobic target zone, rounded to the nearest integer.)

25. Write a program to input the coefficients A, B, and C of the quadratic equation $Ax^2 + Bx + C = 0$; then determine whether or not the equation has real zeros. If the equation has real zeros, determine whether they are distinct, then calculate and output the zeros. (*Hint*: Display the output values with default formatting.)

26. Given a metric distance and the time (in minutes and seconds, accurate to the nearest hundredth of a second) that a runner took to cover that distance, output the runner's average pace per mile, accurate to the nearest hundredth of a second. For example, in 1997, Haile Gebresilasie set a world 10,000-m record of 26:31.32. A sample run would look like

```
Enter meters run: 10000
Enter time for the run (mm:ss.hh): 26:31.32
Average pace per mile: 4:16.09
```

27. Input a time specified as the hour (1–12), minute (0–59), and the meridian ('A' or 'P' for A.M. or P.M.); then output that time in the form HH:MM A.M./ P.M. Then enter a nonnegative number of minutes and output the time that is that number of minutes later than the original time. A sample run would look like

```
Enter hours, minutes, and (A)m or (P)m: 10 5 P
The time is 10:05 PM
Enter a number of minutes (>0): 200
After 200 minutes, the time will be 1:25 AM
```

28. Write a program that inputs the maximum monthly loan payment that a customer can afford, the lifetime of the loan in months, and the annual interest rate. Using continuous compounding, determine the maximum amount the customer can borrow. (*Hint:* Use a function stub.)

6

The `String` Data Type and More Output Formatting

In the early days of computing, computers were used almost exclusively for large-scale numerical calculations. Now, however, much of their use involves processing non-numeric data for tasks ranging from making medical diagnoses to maintaining mailing lists.

This chapter introduces the nonnumeric `String` data type that stores sequences of characters. It also discusses techniques for formatting output (especially in table form) and the use of special characters known as *escape sequences*. The chapter ends with a program design problem that uses multiway selection, functions, and strings.

6.1 A First Look at String Variables

Suppose you want a variable, let us call it `last_name`, that can store someone's last name as its value. A name is a sequence, or *string*, of characters. For example, the name "Doright" is a string of seven characters. Unfortunately, C++ does not currently provide a standard string data type — C++ relies on the C library `string.h` for handling character strings. Proper string handling using `string.h`, however, requires knowledge of topics (arrays and pointers) that aren't normally covered until late in an introductory computer science course. Additionally, the way you would use `string.h` to work with strings is inconsistent with the way you use built-in data types like `int`, `float`, and `char`.

Fortunately, the proposed ANSI/ISO[1] draft C++ standard does provide a string data type. (Some compilers already include this type — in

---

[1] American National Standards Organization/International Standards Organization

131

Turbo C++ and Borland C++ for Windows 3.1 or 95/NT, a string data type is provided by the library file `cstring.h`[2].) As an alternative, the PWS Website contains a library file, `baString.h`, that implements a subset of the draft standard string class.

Using `baString.h`, a variable declared to be of type `String` can store *variable-length sequences* of characters. That is, the amount of memory reserved for a `String` variable is automatically increased or decreased as the program runs to fit the particular string of characters currently stored in that variable.

■ **EXAMPLE** The statements

```
String last_name;
last_name = "Jones";
```

declare a `String` variable `last_name` and assign it the value `Jones`.

You can visualize memory for `last_name` as a sequence of consecutive bytes, each holding one character. After the assignment statement is executed this memory will look like

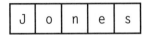

■ **EXAMPLE** (**Using** `cin >>` **to Read a Value into a** `String` **Variable)** Suppose the user entered `N` for `initial` and `Doright` for `last_name` during a run of the following program.

```
// name.cpp
// Prints your last name and initial.
#include <iostream.h>
#include "baString.h"

void main()
```

---

[2] Users of Turbo C++ for Windows or Borland C++ may replace the include statement for `"baString.h"` by `#include <cstring.h>` in order to use the `string` class provided by Borland. However, the library file `baString.h` uses the identifier `String` rather than `string` for the class. Therefore, you must either (1) change all occurrences of `String` to `string` (using your editor's global find and replace capability) or (2) make `String` a synonym for `string` by placing the statement

```
typedef string String;
```

immediately after the include directive for `<cstring.h>`.

Similar modifications will enable you to use any other draft standard compliant `string` class that is available to you.

```
{
    char initial;
    String last_name;
    cout << "Enter first initial: ";
    cin >> initial;
    cout << "Enter your last name: ";
    cin >> last_name;
    cout << last_name << ", " << initial << '.'
        << endl;
}
```

A run of the program would look like

```
Enter first initial: N
Enter your last name: Doright
Doright, N.
```

When Quotes Are Needed Recall that when entering a character value in response to a run-time prompt, you do not enclose the character in single quotes, whereas you must put single quotes around a character value that appears in a source code statement. Similarly, a String value input to a program at run time is not enclosed in double quotes, but String values appearing in program code must be delimited by double quotes, as in

```
    last_name = "Jones"; // double quotes required!
```

If the double quotes were removed in the above statement, the compiler would assume that Jones was a variable name or some other identifier.

How cin >> **Works for** String **Variables** To read a string value from cin and store it in a String variable, the computer (1) skips over leading whitespace, (2) reads non-whitespace characters, one at a time, into the memory allocated for the String variable, and finally (3) stops reading characters upon encountering whitespace (which is not read into the String).

CAUTION You cannot use cin >> to read a string with embedded whitespace, such as the blank in John Doe. The following fragment illustrates this sometimes inconvenient feature of the String data type.

```
cout << "Enter name: ";
cin >> full;
cout << "Name is " << full;
```

```
Enter name: John Doe
Name is John
```
Sample run

The computer read the value "`John`" into the variable `full`, because reading was terminated by the space between `John` and `Doe`. A correct technique for reading a string with embedded whitespace into a single `String` variable will not be covered until Section 6.5. For now we will use separate variables to get around this problem as in the following fragment.

```
String first, last;
cout << "Enter name (First Last): ";
cin >> first >> last;
cout << first <<' ' << last << endl;
```

for which a typical program run is

```
Enter name (First Last): John    Doe
John Doe
```

Notice that the user may type any amount of whitespace between input string values when separate `String` variables are used in a `cin` statement.

The + Operator and String Concatenation   The + operator will *concatenate,* or join, string or character values. The + operator is said to be *overloaded,* because, in addition to its usual use for adding numeric values, it can also be used to concatenate strings.

EXAMPLE   The program

```
// names.cpp
#include <iostream.h>
#include "baString.h"

void main()
```

```
{
    char init; // first initial
    String first, last, // names
           first_and_last, // first last
           last_and_init; // last, init.

    cout << "Your name (First Last): ";
    cin >> init; // get first letter
    cin >> first; // then rest of first name
    first = init + first; // restore first letter
    cin >> last;

    last_and_init = last + ", " + init + '.';
    first_and_last = first + ' ' + last;
    cout << last_and_init << endl;
    cout << first_and_last << endl;
}
```

produces the typical run

```
Your name (First Last): Alphred Omega
Omega, A.
Alphred Omega
```

Strings as Function Parameters and Result A function can have parameters of type String and can return a String as its result.

■ **QUESTION** How would you complete the definition of the function name (from the program name_fn.cpp) so that if first, init, and last had the values "Alf", 'N', and "Omega", respectively, the value returned by the function would be "Alf N. Omega"?

```
String name (String first, char init, String last)
{
    String temp;
    temp = _____;
    _____;
}
```

Answer   The missing lines are

```
temp = first + ' ' + init + ". " + last;
return temp;
```

The `String length` ***Function***   The following program fragment (from `length.cpp`) and its output illustrate how to determine the number of characters stored in a string variable.

```
String greeting;
int len;
greeting = "Madam, I'm Adam.";
len = greeting.length();
cout << greeting << endl;
cout << "Length is " << len << endl;
```

```
Madam, I'm Adam.
Length is 16
```
Output

Note the syntax used in calling the `length` function to find the length of the string value stored by the `String` variable `greeting` and assign it to the `int` variable `len`.

```
len = greeting.length();    // correct call
len = length(greeting);     // illegal syntax
```

In general, if `str` is of type `String`, the expression `str.length()` returns the number of characters in `str`. You will learn more about this syntax for a function call (using dot notation) in Section 10.6.

■ **QUESTION**   How would you complete the following fragment (from `fourltr.cpp`) that will determine whether or not an input word is a four-letter word?

```
String word;
cout << "enter a word: ";
cin >> word;
_____
   cout << "A four letter word" << endl;
else
   cout << "Not a four letter word" << endl;
```

Answer   `if (word.length() == 4)`

6.2 Numeric Output in Table Form

The `setw` manipulator, which is used to control horizontal alignment of output, is found in the library `iomanip.h` (which stands for "input/output manipulators").

Syntax of `setw`   In a statement of the form

```
cout << setw(width) << expr;
```

width should have an integer value and *expr* can be an expression with either a numeric or a string value. Then, the value of *expr* will be output with its rightmost character at the right end of a **zone** of *width* spaces. The output is said to be right-justified. Be aware that `setw` is not **persistent** — that is, it affects only the next value to be output.

■ **EXAMPLE**   Consider the following code fragment and its output.

```
cout << "1234567890" << endl;
cout << setw(7) << 46 << endl;
cout << setw(7) << "Smith" << endl;
cout << "Jones" << endl;
cout << "AB" << setw(7) << "CDEF" << endl;
```

```
1234567890
        46
     Smith
Jones
AB    CDEF
```

Code fragment from `setwdemo.cpp`

Output

Discussion   `setw(7)` causes `46` and `Smith` to be output with their rightmost character in column 7, but because `setw` is not presistent, `Jones` is output flush left. Note that `setw` creates the output zone *starting from the current output position*. Thus, in the last `cout` statement, `AB` uses up two spaces, and then `setw(7)` creates a zone of width 7. Hence the right end for this zone will be column 9 — that is why the `F` of `CDEF` is in column 9.

■ ■

■ **EXAMPLE**   The `setw` manipulator is often used to more effectively align output in column(s). In the following code fragments (from `table.cpp`), `float` variables a, b, and c have values of 14.6, 8.7, and –12.5, respectively.

1.

```
cout << "TABLE\n";
fixed_out (cout,1);
cout << a << endl;
cout << b << endl;
cout << c << endl;
```

2.

```
cout << "TABLE\n";
fixed_out (cout,1);
cout << setw(5) << a << endl;
cout << setw(5) << b << endl;
cout << setw(5) << c << endl;
```

Here are the outputs. Note how much better the output of fragment (2) looks with the decimal points aligned.

1.
```
TABLE
14.6
8.7
−12.5
```

2.
```
TABLE
14.6
8.7
−12.5
```

■ **QUESTION**   **(Two-Column Numeric Output)**   Suppose a= 8, b= 20, and c= −5 in the following fragment from twocol.cpp. In the output,

1. What column will the D of "SQUARED" be in?

2. How many blank spaces will be between the R of "NUMBER" and the S of "SQUARED"?

3. What will the entire output be?

```
cout << "NUMBER" << setw(10) << "SQUARED" << endl;
cout << setw(6) << a << setw(10) << a*a << endl;
cout << setw(6) << b << setw(10) << b*b << endl;
cout << setw(6) << c << setw(10) << c*c << endl;
```

Answer

1. The D of "SQUARED" will be in column 16, because outputting NUMBER uses up six spaces and then setw(10) creates a zone of width 10, with its right end in column 16 (i.e., 16 = 6 + 10).

2. There will be three blank spaces, because "SQUARED" has seven letters and is output right-justified in a zone of width 10.

3. The entire output is

```
NUMBER   SQUARED
     8        64
    20       400
    −5        25
```

■ **QUESTION**   What changes would you make to the previous program fragment if you wanted to have five blank spaces between the headings "NUMBER" and "SQUARED" and again have the units digits of the two columns aligned under the R and D, respectively?

Answer Because the number of letters in "SQUARED" is 7, and 7 + 5 = 12, you would change all the setw(10) format specifications to setw(12).

■ **QUESTION** The following program produces the table of square roots shown to its right. Note that there are two blank spaces between N and the s of sqrt and that each square root has its rightmost digit under the N. How would you fill in the missing lines?

```
// sqrts.cpp
#include <iostream.h>
#include <iomanip.h>
#include <math.h>
#include "ourtools.h"

void main()
{
    int n;
    cout << _____;
    fixed_out (cout, 3);
    four (n=1; n<=10; n++)
        {
        cout << _____ << n;
        cout << _____;
        cout << endl;
        }
}
```

N	sqrt(N)
1	1.000
2	1.414
3	1.732
4	2.000
5	2.236
6	2.449
7	2.646
8	2.828
9	3.000
10	3.162

Answer The completed lines are

```
cout << " N  sqrt(N)" << endl;
    cout << setw(2) << n;
    cout << setw(8) << sqrt(n);
```

6.3 Tables with Strings in the First Column

■ **QUESTION** In the following fragment, name is of type String and age is of type int.

```
cout << "NAME" << setw(12) << "AGE" << endl;
cout << name << setw(16-name.length()) << age << endl;
```

1. In what column will the E of AGE be output?

2. If name = "Doe" and age = 24, what will the output be?

3. If name = "Hillerman" and age = 8, what will the output be?

Answer   1. The E of AGE will be in column 16, because NAME uses up four spaces, and then setw(12) creates a zone of width 12 — the right edge of this zone is in column 16, because 4 + 12 = 16.

2.
```
NAME        AGE
Doe          24
```

3.
```
NAME        AGE
Hillerman     8
```

In (2) Doe uses the first three columns, and because name.length() is 3, the setw format specification is equivalent to setw(16-3) or setw(13). Thus, the right end of the zone created by this setw is column 16, because 3 + 13 = 16. The value of age is output right justified in this zone. Similarly, in (3), Hillerman uses the first nine columns, and then setw creates a zone with its right end in column 16, because 9 + (16-9) = 16.

The next example uses the general technique that

```
cout << name << setw( x - name.length() )
```

creates a zone with its right end in column x whenever the String variable name contains fewer than x characters.

■ **EXAMPLE**   **(Keyboard Input with Virtual Printer Output in Table Form)**   Honors students at ESU may work in the Tutoring Center for $4.55 per hour. The following main function (from pay.cpp) inputs information on student tutors from the keyboard and outputs to the virtual printer a neatly formatted table of information on the student tutors.

```
void main()
{
    const float RATE = 4.55;
    int tutor, num_tutors;
    int hours;
    String name;

    cout << "How many tutors worked this week? ";
    cin >> num_tutors;
```

```
vprn << "NAME" << setw(12) << "HOURS"
    << setw(10) << "PAY" << endl;

for (tutor=1; tutor<=num_tutors; tutor++)
    {
    cout << "Tutor's name and hours worked: ";
    cin >> name >> hours;
    fixed_out (vprn,2);
    vprn << name << setw(16-name.length()) << hours
        << setw(10) << hours*RATE << endl;
    }
}
```

The user screen and virtual printer output for a typical run are

```
How many tutors worked this week? 3
Tutor's name and hours worked: Fritz 7
Tutor's name and hours worked: Eve 24
Tutor's name and hours worked: Isabella 2
```

User screen

```
NAME        HOURS       PAY
Fritz           7     31.85
Eve            24    109.20
Isabella        2      9.10
```

Virtual printer output

6.4   cin **and** cout **Are Streams**

Streams   A **stream** is a sequence of data that comes from a particular *source* and is available and waiting to be moved to a particular *destination.*

The cin **Stream**   The data for the cin stream comes from user keyboard input; this data will wait in cin's "holding area," or **buffer**, until it is read into a program's variables (cin's particular *destination*). Statements of the form

```
cin >> var1 >> var2 >> . . .;
```

are used to move the data from `cin` into one or more program variables. The program examples so far have made simple use of the `cin` stream in that as soon as the user entered data into the `cin` stream, this data was immediately read into program variables. In more complicated examples that we will consider in the next section, data might remain in `cin`'s buffer for a while before being read into program variables.

Depicting the Current State of the `cin` ***Stream***   A diagram to depict the `cin` stream's current state should indicate clearly what is the sequence of data that is still waiting to be read (or moved) into program variables. The diagram should also indicate data items that have recently been moved. Thus, in our diagrams, the sequence of data still waiting to be moved will be unshaded, whereas data items recently moved (and no longer part of the `cin` stream) will be shown to the left in shading.

Depicting the Newline Character ↵   We will use the symbol ↵ to depict the newline character that corresponds to the user pressing the Enter key. Be aware that ↵ is a whitespace character. We will use the ↵ symbol in the succession of snapshots of the current state of `cin` for the program fragment given below.

```
cout << "Enter hours worked: ";
cin >> hrs;
cout << "Enter rate: ";
cin >> rate;
cout << "Pay is $" << hrs*rate;
```

```
Enter hours worked: 30
Enter rate: 8
Pay is $240
```
Sample run

Data that has recently been removed from the `cin` stream is in the left column and shaded. Note that `cin >> . . .` does *not* remove a trailing newline character from the `cin` stream.

cin	When?
30↵	After user enters 30
30↵	After computer executes `cin >> hrs;` (Note that the trailing ↵ is still in `cin`.)
30↵8↵	After user enters 8
30↵8↵	After computer executes `cin >>rate;`

The computer stops after the prompt `Enter rate:` because of the way the statement `cin >> rate;` works — the computer cannot finish executing the statement `cin >> rate;` until the `cin` stream contains some numeric data that the user must enter.

cout **and** *vprn* **Streams** For `cout`, data is moved from the program to the monitor (destination), whereas for `vprn`, data is moved from the program to the file `C:\vprinter.out` (destination). We do not need diagrams for the current state of `cout` and `vprn` because for these streams data does not linger — instead, data items are moved immediately.

6.5 Reading Strings with Embedded Whitespace

As was already mentioned in Section 6.1, we cannot use `cin >>` to read strings like `John Doe` that contain interior, or embedded, whitespace. Instead, we can use the void `getline` function (provided by `baString.h`) described below.

The `getline` **Function** The call `getline(cin, str_var)` reads all characters (including whitespace) from the current character of the input stream `cin` up to, but not including, the next newline character, ↵, stores these characters in `str_var`, then discards ↵ from `cin`.

Thus, the following fragment can be used to read the user's name into the `String` variable `name`. In the run given to the right, `name` would receive the value `Jane Doe`.

```
cout << "Enter your name: ";
getline (cin, name);
```

```
Enter your name: Jane Doe
```

■ **QUESTION** (**Mixing** `cin` **and** `getline` **for** `String` **Input**) Recall that `cin >> str_var;` scans over leading whitespace characters, if any, then reads in only the non-whitespace characters preceding the next occurrence of whitespace in `cin`. Give the output, with exact spacing, for the following program if the user enters HAVE A NICE DAY.

```
// message.cpp
#include <iostream.h>
#include "baString.h"

void main()
```

```
{
    String first, rest;
    cout << "Enter a message: ";
    cin >> first;
    getline (cin, rest);
    cout << first << endl;
    cout << rest << endl;
}
```

Answer

```
Enter a message: HAVE A NICE DAY
HAVE
  A NICE DAY
```

Note that the first character stored in `rest` is a space, because after the computer executes the statement `cin >> first;` the contents of `cin` are

HAVE A NICE DAY↵   ■ ■■

A Special Case of `getline` When the next character in `cin` is the newline character, then the call `getline (cin, str_var)` assigns the null string (that is, no characters) to `str_var`.

Inputting a Number and then a `String` *with Embedded Spaces* The correct way to do this is tricky! Let us first look at an incorrect attempt.

■ **EXAMPLE**   **(An Incorrect Attempt)** In the following program fragment (from `nochars.cpp`), `age` is of type `int` and `name` is of type `String`. The fragment is intended to allow the user to input her age, 46, and her name, Jane Doe. However, as indicated by the sample run, something goes wrong.

```
cout << "Enter your age: ";
cin >> age;
cout << "Name (first last): ";
getline (cin, name);
cout << name << ", you don't look "
     << age << ".\n";
```

```
Enter your age: 46
Name (first last): , you don't look 46.
```

Sample run

Discussion   Notice that the user, Jane Doe, did not get a chance to enter her name. Just before the computer executes `getline(cin, name);` the state of `cin` is 46 ↩. Thus, as mentioned in the special case, `getline` assigns a string with no characters to `name`. ■ ▬

Using `cin.ignore` *to Skip the Rest of an Input Line*   To make the above code work correctly, we need to skip over the end-of-line character so that it won't be read by `getline`. Placing the function call statement

```
cin.ignore (80, '\n');
```

before the call to `getline` will accomplish this, and thus prevent *getline* from reading the null string into `name`. This statement says to ignore, or skip over, the next 80 characters of `cin`, but to *stop immediately* after skipping over `'\n'`, if it is encountered in `cin` before 80 characters have been skipped. (Be aware that values other than 80 and `'\n'` can be passed to `ignore`. However, in the situation at hand, the end-of-line character is the one we want to skip, and it is highly unlikely that the user would have typed many, if any, characters between her age and the carriage return that terminates that input line.)

The following code fragment from `name_age.cpp` illustrates a correct way to allow the user to enter his or her age, then name.

```
cout << "Enter your age: ";
cin >> age;
cout << "Name (first last): ";
cin.ignore (80, '\n');
getline (cin, name);
cout << name << ", you don't look "
     << age << "\n";
```

```
Enter your age: 46
Name (first last): Jane Doe
Jane Doe, you don't look 46.
```

Sample run

The above sample run is correct because after execution of `cin >> age;` the only character remaining in `cin` is ↩, and after execution of `cin. ignore (80, '\n');` there will be no characters in `cin`. Because `cin` is empty, the computer will wait for user input when executing `getline (cin, name)`. After the user enters `JaneDoe`↩ in response to the prompt for first and last name, the characters in `cin` will be Jane Doe←. Thus, the statement `getline (cin, name);` will read Jane Doe into `name` and, as usual, remove the trailing end-of-line character.

Using `getline` ***After*** `cin >>`   Using `getline` to read strings with embedded spaces requires the kind of careful handling that should be done any time the `getline` statement follows an input using `cin >>`. In the previous example, the `cin` statement was used to input an integer, but the same problem would have existed had the `cin` statement been used to input a `float`, a `char`, or even a `String` without embedded spaces.

6.6 A Program Design Involving Strings

▦ **PROBLEM**   Write a program to output the name of any positive one- or two-digit integer (1 through 99) in words.

Understand the problem.   Only 99 valid inputs are possible for this problem. Systematically listing some inputs and the corresponding outputs is a good start toward a solution. Consider the table of input/output pairs given at right.

Input	Output
3	three
11	eleven
17	seventeen
25	twenty-five
50	fifty
76	seventy-six

Develop an algorithm.   A "brute-force" approach to the problem would be a 99-way selection. Keep in mind, however, that a solution that works is not necessarily a good or even an acceptable solution. In designing a solution, you should look for common or redundant subtasks — these subtasks can then be modularized as functions and reused throughout the solution.

The words for the numbers from 1 through 13 contain no redundancy; further, the words for 14 through 19 aren't all simply the words for 4 through 9 with the suffix *teen* appended (e.g., fifteen and eighteen). Thus, a 19-way selection for choosing the word for the numbers 1 through 19 seems acceptable. However, the words for the numbers from 20 through 99 all involve the word for a decade (twenty, thirty, . . . , ninety) followed, except in the case of the decades themselves, by a hyphen and the word for the second, or units, digit of the number. Thus, we might arrive at the following subtasks:

1. Determine the word for 1 to 19:

2. Determine the word for 20 to 99:
　　(a) Determine the word for the decade.
　　(b) Determine the word for the units digit, if it is not 0.

Subtasks (1) and (2b) overlap. For example, the numbers 5 and 35 both require the word *five* to be printed. So it makes sense to split subtask (1) into two separate subtasks:

　　(a) Determine the word for a digit (1 to 9).
　　(b) Determine the word for 10 to 19.

Thus, a pseudocode algorithm to store the word for a two-digit number n in word is

---

```
input n
t = the tens digit of n
u = the units digit of n
if (n <= 9)
   word = the word for the digit u
else if (n <= 19)
   word = the word for 10+u
else
   {
   word = the word for the decade 10*t
   if (u>0)
     word = word + '-' + the word for the digit u
   }
```

The underlined, italicized phrases suggest calls to String-returning functions with the following declarations:

```
String word_for_digit(int d);
// return word for d, d=1,2,...,9

String word_for_10_plus(int u);
// return word for 10+u, u=0,1,...,9

String word_for_decade(int t);
// return word for 10*t, t=1,2,...,9
```

Code, test, and debug the program.   We leave these important phases of the program design to you. Extending the solution to handle three or more digits is discussed in the exercises.   ▪ ▬

▪ Exercises

1. Give the exact output of the following program fragments.

(a)
```
int m, n;
m =  431;
n = -57;
cout << "ABCDEFG" << endl;
cout << setw(6) << m << endl;
cout << setw(6) << n << endl;
cout << setw(4) << m << endl;
cout << setw(2) << n << endl;
```

(b)
```
int k, m, n, p;
k = 675; m = -2; n = 18; p = 5;
cout << "ABCDEFGH" << endl;
cout << setw(4) << k;
cout << setw(4) << m;
cout << endl << setw(4) << n;
cout << setw(4) << p << endl;
```

2. Give the exact output of the following program fragment.

```
float x, y;
x = -3.8412; y = 47.162;
cout << "ABCDEFG" << endl;
fixed_out(cout,1);
cout << setw(6) << x << endl;
cout << setw(6) << y << endl;
fixed_out(cout,3);
cout << setw(6) << x << endl;
fixed_out(cout,2);
cout << setw(3) << y << endl;
```

3. List which `include` files are required by the program fragment of Exercise 6.2 and for what specific features of the code.

4. Give the exact output of the following program fragment.

```
String first, last, full;
first = "Alfredo";
last = "Eyenstine"
full = last + ", " + first;
cout << full << endl;
full = full + " Q."
cout << full << endl;
```

5. Write and test a function, `month_name`, that returns the name of a month given its number.

6. Implement and test the function `LFI_name` whose declaration and description are

```
String LFI_name (String first, char init, String last);
// Return the full name in the form LAST, FIRST INIT.
```

7. Implement and test the function whose declaration and description are

```
int value_in_cents (String cname);
// return value in cents of a coin
// given its name, cname, in lower-case
```

8. Explain what is wrong with the following program fragment and how you would correct it so that it produces runs like the sample.

```
String model;
char ans;
cout << "Do you own a computer? (Y/N): ";
cin >> ans;
if (ans=='Y' || ans=='y')
    {
    cout << "What model? ";
    cin >> model;
    cout << "The " << model << " is a great machine.\n";
    }
```

```
--------------------------------------------------
| Do you own a computer? (Y/N): y                |
| What model? ACME 786DX8 500Mhz                 |
| The ACME 786DX8 500Mhz is a great machine.     |
--------------------------------------------------
```

9. Given that `name` is of type `String` and `balance` is of type `double`, write a statement or statements to print `name` left aligned beginning in column 1 and `balance` right aligned ending in column 28, with two digits to the right of the decimal point. Some sample output would be

```
-------------------------------------
| Wealthy, I. M.      1234567.89    |
| Poor, Pat                 5.98    |
|   ↑                          ↑    |
-------------------------------------
   col 1                      col 28
```

Programming Problems

10. Write a program that asks the user to input the name, age, and sex of each of three employees. The virtual printer output will be a table formatted as follows:

```
-------------------------------------
| Name                 Age  Sex     |
| Doe, Jane             25   F       |
| Smith, Raoul          31   M       |
| Moore, Mary Lou       19   F       |
-------------------------------------
```

11. Extend the solution of the student tutor problem of `pay.cpp` as follows:
    (a) Input the student's first and last names, and output them in the form Last, First.
    (b) Students are paid more for advanced semester standing — they receive an extra $0.25 per hour for each semester beyond three but not beyond eight. Include each student's semester standing as part of the input, and output both the student's semester standing and hourly rate.

12. Complete the coding and testing phases of the problem design of Section 6.6.

13. Using the pseudocode of Section 6.6, write and test a function, `word_for_2digits`, that takes a positive integer less than 100 as its argument and returns the `String` that is the word for that number.

Longer Assignments

14. (a) Write and test a function, `words_for_3digits`, that takes a positive integer less than 1,000 as its argument and returns the `String` that is the word or words for that number.

(b) Write a program that displays, in words, the name of any (long) integer input by the user. (*Hint*: Use the words_for_3digits function of the above exercise.)

15. Write a program that inputs the number of quizzes you have taken this semester, then, for each of the quizzes, input the maximum points possible, your score, and the title of the quiz. The virtual printer output will be a summary consisting of (a) a well-formatted table containing all inputs as well as your percentage (to the nearest tenth) and letter grade for each quiz and (b) your average quiz percentage and letter grade. Typical virtual printer output is

```
QUIZ           TITLE                    YOUR PERFORMANCE
 1    Arithmetic Operators in C++         26/ 30 = 86.7% B
 2    Nested Selection                    35/ 45 = 77.8% C
 3    Inputting String variables          38/ 40 = 95.0% A
Quiz average: 86.5 B
```

Virtual printer output

16. Write a program to produce itemized bills for customers of Computers 'R' Us. The program will input the customer's name, the number of items purchased, and for each item, the item name, the quantity purchased, and the unit price. A typical bill, printed on the virtual printer, will look like

```
********************************************************
                  COMPUTERS 'R' US
Customer: ESU Comp. Sci. Dept.

      ITEM                      UNIT PRICE        COST
- - - - - - - - - - - - - - - - - - - - - - - - - - - -
10    1.2Gb Maxtop hard drive       198.95     1989.50
40    16Mb SIMM                      79.90     3196.00
25    Mantis Spreadsheet Software    99.99     2499.75
 5    CRU Notebook Computer        2370.00    11850.00
- - - - - - - - - - - - - - - - - - - - - - - - - - - -
                                  TOTAL       19535.25
```

7

The Three C++
Looping Constructs

C++ has three looping constructs: `for` loops, `while` loops, and `do..while` loops. In Section 3.9 we considered some examples of count-controlled `for` loops. Next we give a fuller treatment of `for` loops as well as introducing `while` and `do..while` loops. In this chapter we discuss the following types of applications:

Type of application	*Preferred loop*
Have the *loop generate* and *process* a fixed-step list of data values, e.g., 11, 13, 15, 17, 19, which has fixed step 2.	▪ `for` loop
Have the *user input* the data values to be processed.	▪ `for` loop if the number of data groups to be input is known in advance ▪ `while` or `do..while` loop if the *user* must *signal* when to stop entering data

In Chapter 8, we will discuss more general looping tasks, in which the loops are controlled by conditions that test for completion of the looping task.

7.1 Some Preliminaries

Counting and Summing Variables   Loops are frequently used to count and sum. The following questions and examples show how counting and summing variables are implemented. Subsequent examples will illustrate counting and summing with loops.

■ **QUESTION**   What is the output for each of the following fragments?

1.

```
count = 0;
count = count + 1;
count = count + 1;
count += 1;
cout << count;
```

2.

```
sum = 0;
sum = sum + 8;
sum = sum + 3;
sum += 15;
cout << sum;
```

Answer

1.   The value of count is given an initial value of 0; count is then incremented by 1 three times. Thus, the output is 3.

2.   The output is 26 because the values 8, 3, and 15 are added onto the initial value 0. ▨ ▬

Initialization of Variables   The variables count and sum in the preceding code fragments accumulate values by adding onto their current values. This process requires that count and sum have starting, or initial, values. The process of giving a variable an initial value is called ***initialization***.

Fixed-Step List of Values   When each next term in a list is obtained by adding (or subtracting) the same fixed number, we will call it a fixed-step list (also known as an arithmetic sequence). For example, the three lists 12 15 18 21, 30 25 20 15 10, and 1 2 3 4 5 6 are all fixed-step lists. The fixed steps are 3, –5, and 1, respectively.

7.2   while **Loops and Fixed-Step Lists**

Syntax and Action of while

```
while (condition)
    loop body
    statement
```

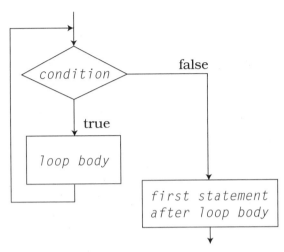

The while loop works as illustrated by the preceding flowchart. The computer starts by testing the condition. If the condition is true, the entire loop body is executed; then control is returned to the top to retest the condition. This process is repeated as long as the condition is true. The first time the computer evaluates the condition as false, control passes to the first statement after the loop body.

■ **EXAMPLE**   **(Generating and Processing the List 1 2 3)**   The following fragment will produce the given output.

```
n = 1;
while (n <= 3)
    {
    cout << "Test " << n
        << endl;
    n = n + 1;
    }
cout << "So long";
```

```
Test 1
Test 2
Test 3
So long
```
Output

Discussion   During the first, second, and third executions of the loop body, n has the values 1, 2, and 3, respectively, which are output. The loop body is not executed a fourth time because the test n <= 3 fails when n is 4. In a fixed-step while loop, the variable that takes on the value in the list is called the ***loop control variable***. Note that in this kind of while loop, the test condition is given in terms of the final value of the control variable.

■ ■

■ **QUESTION** **(Generating and Processing a List with Step = 2)** Complete the program fragment to give the output shown. (The number of iterations is known — in Section 7.3, we will redo this loop as a for loop, the preferred way.)

```
n = ____;
while _____
    {
    cout << n "squared = "
         << n*n << endl;
    n _____;
    }
```

```
11 squared = 121
13 squared = 169
15 squared = 225
17 squared = 289
19 squared = 361
```
Output

Answer Note that this loop can be thought of as generating and processing the fixed-step list 11 13 15 17 19. The line of code before the loop (the initialization of n) should be n = 11. The test condition while(n <= 19) should use the final value in the list. The update should be n=n+2 (or n+=2).

■ ■■

Step-Controlled Loops We will refer to a loop as ***step controlled*** if it has a loop control variable that takes on the values from a fixed-step list, and its exit condition is *solely in terms of the final value of that list*. Of course, a count-controlled loop is a step-controlled loop with step equal to one.

CAUTION: Curly Braces for the Loop Body Be aware that if you do not put curly braces { } around the intended loop body, the compiler will use the single statement following the loop header as the loop body even if indentation seems to indicate that several statements are in the loop body. To program defensively, you should always enclose the loop body in curly braces.

■ **QUESTION** What will be the output of the following syntactically correct program fragments?

1.

```
x = 0;
while (x < 10)
    x = x+1;
    cout << x << endl;
cout << "Done\n";
```

2.

```
x = 0;
while (x < 10)
    cout << x << endl;
    x = x+1;
cout << "Done\n";
```

Answer   **1.**   **2.**

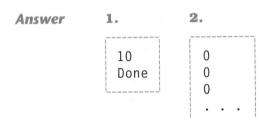

```
10                0
Done              0
                  0
                  . . .
```

Discussion   The indentation indicates that two statements were intended to make
up the loop body in both (1) and (2). However, in each fragment, because
there are no curly braces, the compiler assumes that the loop body is
the single statement immediately following the `while` header.

In (1) the loop body x = x+1; is repeated as long as the test x < 10
is true; then, when x becomes 10, the loop is exited, and control passes
to the statement immediately after the loop body, namely, `cout << x <<
endl;`. In (2) we have an infinite loop. The loop body `cout << x << endl;`
is repeated indefinitely — the loop control variable never changes because the statement x = x+1; is not part of the loop body! (See Section
8.6 for more on infinite loops.)   ■ ▬

Stopping an Infinite Loop   How you stop an infinite loop (and, in fact,
whether you can even do this reliably) depends on your operating system.
Windows 95/NT users can press Ctrl+Alt+Del and then click on End
Task; DOS users can press Ctrl+Break and follow the instructions. Unfortunately, Windows 3.1 users face a more difficult situation and may
have to use Ctrl+Alt+Del to reboot.

Silent Infinite Loop   If you were to run a program containing the infinite
loop of fragment (2), above, it would be obvious from the rapid-fire printing
that there was an infinite loop. A more difficult situation to diagnose is
one in which the computer is trapped in an infinite loop that does not
produce any output. Such an infinite loop is called *silent* (although the
term *invisible* seems more appropriate). The following fragment (from
`silent.cpp`) produces a silent infinite loop.

```
n = 0; sum = 0;
while (n != 15)
    {
    n += 2;
    sum += n;
    }
cout << "sum = " << sum << endl;
```

If the computer is not responding to keyboard entries when you think that a program run is finished, you should suspect a silent infinite loop.

7.3 for **Loops and Fixed-Step Lists of Data Values**

A commonly used form of the for loop, where LCV stands for the loop control variable, is the following:

```
for (initialize LCV; test LCV; update LCV)
    {
    statements of the loop body
    }
```

Advantages of a for ***Loop*** Any step-controlled while loop, can be written more cleanly as a for loop, because all the loop control information (initial value, test condition, and update) can appear in the for loop header instead of being spread out in three different locations as in the while loop. Writing a step-controlled loop as a for loop allows a reader to see at a glance the values of the control variable for which the loop will be executed. Using this method is also safer because the programmer is less likely to accidentally omit the initialization or update statement.

■ **EXAMPLE** The following while and for loops produce the same output.

```
n = 1;
while (n <= 3)
    {
    cout << "Time " << n
         << endl;
    n = n + 1;
    }
```

```
for (n=1; n<=3; n++)
    {
    cout << "Time " << n
            << endl;
    }
```

■ **QUESTION** How would you fill in the blanks so that each of the following loops produces the output at right?

```
11 squared = 121
13 squared = 169
  . . .
21 squared = 441
```

```
for (n=11; n<=21; n+=2)
    {
    cout << n << " squared = "
            << n*n << endl;
    }
```

```
n=11;
while (n<=21)
    {
    cout << n << " squared = "
            << n*n << endl;
    n=n+2;
    }
```

Answers

```
for (n=11;  n<=21;  n=n+2)
```

```
n=11;
while (n<=21)
        n=n+2;
```

■ **QUESTION**   The Shirts-to-Go retail store has just received a new supply of shirts. Preliminary market research indicates that the profit obtainable at a given sales price x can be calculated using the formula *profit* = x(100 – 3x). We want to produce the following tabular output for integer sales prices ranging from $10 to $30.

```
PRICE         PROFIT
  10            700
  11            737
  12            768
   .              .
   .              .
   .              .
  30            300
```

In the program that follows, the control variable price will take on values from the list 10, 11, 12, . . . ,30, and profit will be calculated from the current value of price. Note that the setw manipulator is used for proper alignment of the values in the two columns of output. Fill in the blanks in the following program.

```cpp
// shirts.cpp
// Prints price-profit table for prices from $10 to $30.
#include <iostream.h>
#include <iomanip.h> // for setw

void main()
```

```
{
    int price, profit;

    cout << "PRICE" << setw(10) << "PROFIT" << endl;
    for (price = 10; price <= 30; price += 1)
        {
        profit = Price*(100-3*price);
        cout << setw(5) << price
            << _____
        } // end for
}
```

Answer The missing lines are

```
profit = price * (100 - 3*price);
    << setw(10) << profit << endl;
```

Decrementing the Loop Control Variable The loop control variable may be updated by decrementing. For example, the for statement

```
for (i=10; i>=0; i=i-2)
    cout << i << ' ';
```

would output 10 8 6 4 2 0.

char **Control Variables** A loop control variable may be of type char as well as of any integer type. For example, the following program fragment produces the given output.

```
char ltr;
for (ltr='A'; ltr<='F'; ltr=ltr+1)
    cout << ltr;
cout << endl;
```

```
ABCDEF
```
Output

The loop control update statement ltr = ltr+1 increases the ASCII value of ltr by 1, so that ltr contains the next letter of the alphabet.

The ++ and -- Operators The *increment* (++) and *decrement* (--) operators increase or decrease a variable by one. Because of their convenience, ++ and -- are used extensively by C++ programmers, particularly for updating loop control variables.

■ **EXAMPLE**   The following program fragments produce the outputs below them.

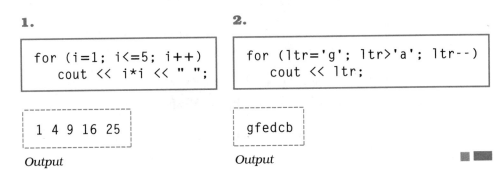

1.

```
for (i=1; i<=5; i++)
    cout << i*i << " ";
```

```
1 4 9 16 25
```
Output

2.

```
for (ltr='g'; ltr>'a'; ltr--)
    cout << ltr;
```

```
gfedcb
```
Output

Prefix and Postfix Forms of ++ and --   The ++ and -- operators each have two forms, called *prefix* and *postfix*. The prefix form is placed before the expression to be incremented or decremented, as in ++i and --ltr, and has a somewhat different meaning than the postfix form. You may see both forms of these operators if you look at C++ code in the literature, but for now, we will use only the postfix form of these operators.

Review of Flow of Control   Before the first execution of the for loop body, the computer checks the test condition using the initial value of the control variable. (If this first test is not satisfied, the loop body will not be executed at all.) Also after each execution of the loop body, the control variable is automatically updated and then the test condition is checked. Thus, for example, if the header of a for loop is

```
for (i=1; i<=9; i++)
```

then the loop control variable i will have the value 10 *after* the loop is exited.

CAUTIONS

1.   An "out of sync" header can result either in the loop being skipped or in an infinite loop. For example, fragment (a) will produce no output because the first test of the condition, using the initial value of the control variable, is false; and (b) will result in an infinite loop, outputting 5 6 7 8 . . . , because the test condition never becomes false.

(a)

```
for(i=1; i>=10; i++)
    { cout << i << " "; }
```

(b)

```
for(i=5; i>0; i++)
    { cout << i << " "; }
```

2. Don't alter the control variable within the loop body when the for loop header updates the control variable.

```
for (i=1; i<=10; i=i+1)
    {
    cout << i << " ";
    i = i + 2;          ←──────────── Don't do this!
    }
```

3. Don't put a semicolon after the for header, because doing so would cause any statements after the semicolon to be outside the loop. Consequently, the loop (with an "empty" body) would be executed, after which the intended loop body would be executed only *once*. (See Exercise 7.1 for an example.) ■ ▬

7.4   for **Loops to Input Groups of Data**

■ **EXAMPLE**   The next program will use the variable sum to compute the sum of four numbers input by the user. For example, if the user were to enter the numbers 17, 13, 20, and 8, the program run could look like

```
Enter number: 17
Enter number: 13
Enter number:   20
Enter number:  8
Average = 14.5
```

Here is the program.

```
// avginpt.cpp
// Find average of 4 input ints.
#include <iostream.h>

void main()
```

```
{
    int i, number, sum;
    sum = 0;  ←─────────────────── initialize
    for (i=1; i<=4; i+=1)
       {
       cout << "Enter number: ";
       cin >> number;  ←────────── get one number
       sum += number;  ←────────── process number
       }
    cout << "Average = "  ←──────┐
       << sum/4.0 << endl;  ←─────┘ } print the final result
}
```

Which Variables to Initialize   A variable that is given a starting value *before* a loop or in the header of a for loop is said to be *initialized*. For example, in the previous program, the statement sum = 0; initialized sum to 0.

In general, a variable should be initialized if its updated value is calculated in terms of its current value. Thus, counting and summing variables must always be initialized. Note that you need not initialize number to 0 because it is assigned a new value that does *not* depend on its current value.

CAUTION   If you did not initialize sum to 0, its starting value would be unpredictable; the value would be whatever value was in the memory allocated for it, which could be a value left over from a previous program run. (See Exercise 7.6.) If you forget the statement sum = 0; some compilers may give a warning such as, Possible use of 'sum' before definition in function main().

General Form   Interactive programs using for loops to process information for a certain number of people, items, or groups of data have the following top down design:

> *Before*   Initialize any variables that count or sum.
>   Output any headings.
> *During*   for (i=1; i<= _____; i=i+1)
>   {
>   cout-cin combination(s) to get the information on
>   one person or item
>   Process the information for that person or item
>   } // end for
> *After*   Output any final tallies or results.

Variable Limits   You can increase the flexibility of a program by using variable(s) for the initial and test values of the loop control variable. A common application allows the user to specify how many groups of data will be entered.

■ **EXAMPLE**   In the following program, the user is asked to input the number of employees (num_emps) to be processed. Note the use of the variable num_emps in the test emp<=num_emps. Using the variable num_emps gives the program flexibility — the user does not have to change any lines in the program to run it for different numbers of employees.

```cpp
// payroll.cpp
// Calculate each employee's wage and
// the total payroll.
#include <iostream.h>
#include "ourtools.h"
#include "baString.h"

void main()
{
    int emp, num_emps, hours;
    float rate, wage, total_wages;
    String name;

    cout << "PAYROLL PROGRAM\n";
    cout << "How many employees? ";
    cin >> num_emps;
    total_wages = 0.0;
    fixed_out(vprn, 2);
    for (emp=1; emp<=num_emps; emp+=1)
        {
        cout << "Employee's last name: ";
        cin >> name;
        cout << "Hours worked and rate: ";
        cin >> hours >> rate;
        wage = hours * rate;

        _____


        } // end for
    vprn << "Total payroll: $" << total_wages
        << endl;
}
```

■ **QUESTION**   How would you fill in the blanks in program `payroll.cpp` so that the virtual printer output will be each employee's name and wage and also the total payroll?

Answer
```
vprn << name << " $" << wage << endl;
total_wages += wage;
```
■ ▬

7.5 More on Designing for Loops

General Advice   Here are some questions to ask yourself when working on a problem that requires a loop.

1. Where are the data values coming from? Are they input by the user or are they generated by a loop control variable? What is the preferred loop?

2. Can you imitate a similar loop or program? If so, what are the additional twists?

3. What variables are needed besides the loop control variable? What quantities must you keep track of?

■ **QUESTION**   How would you write a program to find the sum of the squares of the first 100 integers, that is, the sum of

$$1^2 + 2^2 + 3^2 + \ldots + 100^2$$

A laborious method would be to have the user input each of these integers. A much better method would be to use the current value of the loop control variable to express the current term to be added to the sum. That is, view this problem as processing the list $1, 2, 3, \ldots, 100$, and interpret "processing" as "add the square of the control variable to a sum." Fill in the blank line in the following program.

```
// sumsqrs.cpp  Find sum of first 100 squares.
#include <iostream.h>
void main()
{
    int i;
    long sum;
    sum = 0;
    for (i=1; i<=100; i++)
        { _____ }
    cout << "Sum of first 100 squares is " << sum << endl;
}
```

Answer   Recall that for each execution of the loop body, we want to use the control variable i to express the term to be added to sum. Hence, the loop body should be

```
{ sum = sum + i*i; }
```

Note that if sum were declared to be of type int, its value could overflow.

             ■ ▬

■ **PROBLEM**   Write a program that allows the user to input the name and test score for each of four students. The output to vprn should give

- the name and score for only those students scoring over 90
- the average for only those students scoring over 90
- the average for the entire class.

Format the output so that if the user inputs the following data

```
Enter last name and score: Smythe 92
Enter last name and score: Chang 85
Enter last name and score: Bird 95
Enter last name and score: Johanson 82
```

the output to vprn is

```
STUDENTS SCORING OVER 90
Smythe   92
Bird     95
AVERAGE FOR OVER 90 STUDENTS: 93.5
AVERAGE FOR THE ENTIRE CLASS: 88.5
```

Some new twists in this problem are that

1. two different summing variables are necessary — one for scores over 90 and one for all scores.

2. you must protect against dividing by zero because the number of students scoring over 90 may be 0.

The complete program is

```
// exam.cpp
// Process names and exam scores of 4 students.
#include <iostream.h>
#include "ourtools.h"
#include "baString.h"

void main()
```

```
{
    String name;
    int student, score, ct_over_90;
    double sum, sum_over_90;

    sum = 0;
    ct_over_90 = 0;
    sum_over_90 = 0;
    vprn << "STUDENTS SCORING OVER 90\n";

    for (student=1; student<=4; student+=1)
        {
        cout << "Enter last name and score: ";
        cin >> name >> score;
        sum += score;
        if (score > 90)
            {
            ct_over_90 += 1;
            sum_over_90 += score;
            vprn << name << " " << score << endl;
            }
        } // end for

    if  (ct_over_90 > 0)
        {
        vprn << "AVERAGE FOR OVER 90 STUDENTS: "
             << sum_over_90 / ct_over_90 << endl;
        }
    else
        vprn << "\tNONE\n";
    vprn << "AVERAGE FOR THE ENTIRE CLASS: "
         << sum / 4.0 << endl;
}
```

■ **EXAMPLE**   **(Finding the Largest)**   Suppose we wish to find the largest, or maximum, number from a list of five *positive* integers that are entered by the user. An algorithm can be developed using the following ideas.

Use a variable called max_so_far. Initialize max_so_far with the first number; then give each of the remaining numbers a chance to replace the current value of max_so_far. The final value of max_so_far will be the maximum.

Here is a pseudocode version of this algorithm. (*Note*: It is common practice when writing pseudocode to omit braces and rely on indentation to indicate the extent of a loop body or branch of a selection statement.)

Before	Initialize max_so_far with the first number.
During	for (i=2; i<=5; i+=1)
	Input a number from cin.
	Test whether it is larger than max_so_far, and
	if so, replace max_so_far with this number
After	Output the value of max_so_far.

Here is the actual program.

```cpp
// maxof5.cpp
// Finds maximum of five positive integer inputs.
#include <iostream.h>

void main()
{
    int i, num, max_so_far;
    cout << "Enter number: ";
    cin >> max_so_far;
    for (i=2; i<=5; i+=1)
        {
        cout << "Enter number: ";
        cin >> num;
        if (num > max_so_far)
            max_so_far = num;
        } // end for
    cout << "The maximum is " << max_so_far << endl;
}
```

Discussion   1. A shortcut we could use in the previous program would be to replace the loop header and the cout and cin statements before the loop header with the following two lines:

```cpp
max_so_far = -1; // or max_so_far = INT_MIN;
for (i=1; i<=5; i+=1)
```

In this method, instead of initializing max_so_far with the first input number, we initialize it with an artificially small value that we know will be replaced by the first actual input number. Note that the control variable goes from 1 to 5 rather than from 2 to 5. A *danger* of this type of shortcut is that if the artificial initial value is never replaced, it will be printed as the maximum.

2.   Whichever method is used, max_so_far must be given an initial value because the process of updating max_so_far depends on its current value.   ■ ■■■

■ **PROBLEM**   Suppose a gardener has 100 feet of fencing and wishes to enclose a rectangular garden alongside her house. Drawing a diagram, we find that the area of the garden equals $x(100 - 2x)$.

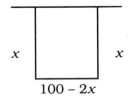

1.   Write a program that will produce the following table of values and the maximum area. (Note that the user will have to scan the table to find the x that gives the maximum area.)

2.   Improve the program so that the computer determines and outputs the value of x that gives the maximum area.

```
Value of x          Area
           10         800
           11         858
            .           .
            .           .
            .           .
           44         528
           45         450
Maximum area is 1250
```

Sample run for (1)

■ **QUESTION**   Which two programs from this chapter will be helpful for writing the program of part 1? What are the added twists? Write the pseudocode.

Answer   The program shirts.cpp generates a table of values from a for loop control variable, and the previous program, maxof5.cpp, determines the maximum of a list of values. The main new twist is that the maximum value that you want to find is from a list whose values are calculated from a loop control variable, *not* from a list of user inputs.

The pseudocode for 1 is

Before	Print the table heading.
	`max_so_far = -1; // initialization`
During	`for (x=10; x<=45; x+=1)`
	Compute the `area` for this value of `x`.
	Print `x` and the associated `area`.
	Update `max_so_far` by testing it against `area`.
After	Print the maximum area.

Exercise 7.14 asks you to write the programs for parts 1 and 2.

7.6   while **Loops Versus** do..while **Loops**

do..while **Syntax**	*while* **Syntax**
`do {`	`while (condition)`
statements of	`{`
loop body	*statements of*
`}`	*loop body*
`while (condition);`	`}`

Note that a do..while *condition terminates with a semicolon, whereas a* while *condition does not.*

Because the condition in a do..while loop is at the bottom of the loop, the condition is tested *after* each execution of the loop body. (do.. while loops are examples of ***post-test*** loops.) Thus, the loop body is always executed a first time. By contrast, the condition in a while loop is tested *before* each execution of the loop body. (while and for loops are examples of ***pre-test*** loops.) The body of a while or for loop will not execute at all if the condition is false when first evaluated.

QUESTION   What would be the output produced by each of the following loops? (*Hint:* It will not be the same for both loops.)

1. ***From*** *post.cpp*

```
x = 99;
do {
   cout << x << endl;
   x = x+1;
   }
while (x < 0);
```

2. ***From*** *pre.cpp*

```
int x;
x = 99;
while (x < 0)
   {
      cout << x << endl;
      x = x+1;
   }
```

Solution   The body of a do..while loop is always executed at least once because it is post-tested. Segment 1 will produce the output 99, whereas segment 2 will produce no output.   ■ ■.

7.7   Sentinel-Controlled Data Input with while **and** do..while **Loops**

The applications we have discussed thus far have not used any of the additional flexibility that while and do..while loops provide. In this section, we use while and do..while loops to write data input loops for which the for loop is not appropriate.

When a for loop is used to process groups of input data, the for loop header normally specifies in advance the number of data groups. By contrast, in a data sentinel-controlled loop, the user can terminate data entry whenever he or she chooses by entering an appropriate signal known as a *sentinel*. In this section we present two different types of sentinel-controlled data input loops, which we call types **A** and **P**.

Type A: Asking Whether the User Wants to Continue   Suppose that on this run the user wishes to find the sum of 15, 47, 43, and 25. In the following program, each time the user has entered a data group and the computer has processed it, the user is asked whether he or she wants to continue.

```cpp
// findsum2.cpp
// Find sum of any number of inputs.
#include <iostream.h>

void main()
{
    int sum, num;
    char ans;
    sum = 0;
    do {
        cout << "Enter number: ";          } prompt for and
        cin >> num;                        } read data group
        sum = sum + num;    ←———————————————— process the data
        cout << "   Continue? (y/n) ";     } find out if the user
        cin >> ans;                        } wants to continue
        }
    while (ans != 'n' && ans != 'N');  ←————— test user response
    cout << "Sum = " << sum << endl;
}
```

Here are two sample runs to calculate the sum of $15 + 47 + 43 + 25$. In run 2, however, the user's carelessness causes the sum to be calculated incorrectly. Do you see the user's mistake?

1.

```
Enter number: 15
    Continue? (y/n) y
Enter number: 47
    Continue? (y/n) Y
Enter number: 43
    Continue? (y/n) t
Enter number: 25
    Continue? (y/n) N
Sum = 130
```

2.

```
Enter number: 15
    Continue? (y/n) y
Enter number: 47
    Continue? (y/n) 43
Enter number:    Continue? (y/n) y
Enter number: 25
    Continue? (y/n) n
Sum = 90
```

Note that the condition `while (ans != 'n' && ans != 'N');` allows the user to type the response in either lowercase or uppercase. Alternatively, you could use the `toupper` function from the library file `ctype.h` in `while (toupper(ans) != 'N');`. Also, the logical expression is written in such a way that data entry continues if the user accidentally types a character other than `y` or `n`. For example, in sample run 1, the user accidentally typed `t` in response to the question about continuing, yet control did not pass out of the loop.

CAUTION Sample run 2 illustrates a drawback of this looping technique. At some point, the user may become hasty, forget to answer the question "`Continue?`", and, instead, input the next data value. In sample 2 this happens when the user enters "43" instead of "y." The first character, 4, of the user input 43, is read into the `char` variable `ans`, the test condition evaluates it as true, and the remaining character, 3, of the input value is read as the value of `num`. Sample run 2 in effect computes $15 + 47 + 3 + 25$, which equals 90.

Type P: *`while` **Loop with Phony Data Sentinel*** In some situations you may be able to eliminate the `y` or `n` question after each data group has been processed. This method eliminates the amount of data input by the user and avoids the problem that arose in sample run 2. In the following program fragment (from `findsum1.cpp`), the user signals the end of data input by typing the "phony value" –1 as a sentinel.

```
sum = 0;
cout << "Enter number (negative to quit): ";
cin >> num;
while (num >= 0)
    {
    sum = sum + num;
    cout << "Enter number (negative to quit): ";
    cin >> num;
    }
cout << "Sum = " << sum << endl;
```

Action of Type P Loops   In the preceding program fragment, note the
cout-cin combination that appears immediately before the while loop.
This method is known as ***priming the loop***, because any variable that
appears in the while condition must already have a value when the loop
condition is first tested. In previous while loop examples, we initialized
the loop control variable by assigning it a value; here we initialize the
loop control variable by reading a user input into it.

Notice that the cout-cin combination occurs twice — once immediately before the loop to prime it and once at the bottom of the loop body.
The cout-cin at the bottom gets the next value of num so that it is ready
to be tested by the while condition. This bottom cout-cin looks ahead
to see if the next input is the sentinel or an actual data value. Additionally,
the while condition prevents processing the sentinel (adding it to
sum) — when the user inputs −1 to quit, the loop body is not executed
for that value of num.

■ **EXAMPLE**   As input for program receipt.cpp, a cashier enters the data for each of
the customer's purchases. Each data group consists of an item name
(possibly more than one word), the price of the item, and the quantity of
that item being purchased. The phony item name xyz is used as a sentinel
value. Here is the screen display for a typical run and the sales receipt
that it produces (on the virtual printer).

```
Enter item name or xyz to stop: rake
    Enter price per item and quantity: 19.50 1
Enter item name or xyz to stop: shovel
    Enter price per item and quantity: 14.50 2
Enter item name or xyz to stop: light bulb
    Enter price per item and quantity: 3.50 6
Enter item name or xyz to stop: xyz
```

User screen display

```
1 rake $19.50
2 shovel $29.00
6 light bulb $21.00
Total bill is $69.50
```

Virtual printer output

■ **QUESTION**   How would you fill in the missing lines in the following program?

```cpp
// receipt.cpp
#include <iostream.h>
#include "ourtools.h"
#include "baString.h"

void main()
{
    String item;
    int quantity;
    float price, cost, sum;

    fixed_out (vprn, 2);
        // for monetary amounts sent to vprn
    sum = 0.00;
    cout << "Enter item name or xyz to stop: ";
    getline(cin, item);
    while (item != "xyz")
        {
        cout << "   Enter price per item and quantity: ";
        cin >> price >> quantity;
        cin.ignore (80, '\n');
        cost = price * quantity;
        sum += cost;
        vprn <<  quantity << " " << item
             << " $" << cost << endl;
        _____

        _____

        }
    vprn << "Total bill is $" << sum << endl;
}
```

Answer   The missing lines are

```
cout << "Enter item name or xyz to stop: ";
getline (cin, item);
```

Discussion   Notice the use of `cin.ignore (80, '\n);` to skip over the rest of the input line consisting of the item price and quantity purchased. This ensures that the next input statement, `getline (cin, item);`, begins reading from a new line of input rather than reading the trailing end-of-line marker from the line of numeric inputs. (See Section 6.5 for a review of this technique.)

General Form for Type P Data Sentinel Loops

---

prompt and input (to get first part of first data group)
`while` (first part != sentinel)
    {
    (prompt and) input rest, if any, of current data group
    process current data group
    prompt and input (to get first part of next data group;
                          may need `cin.ignore` if `getline` is used)

    }

Comparison of Type A and Type P Loops   Type A loops have simpler logic than type P loops, and type A loops provide the user with clearer instructions. Type A loops can also be used in situations where no "phony" data value exists. (For example, suppose a program processes integer inputs *regardless* of their value — what could one possibly use for a sentinel value?) However, type A loops require more data entry than type P loops.

7.8 Debugging Strategies

Suppose that your program either did not run at all, or ran, but gave an output that seemed incorrect. Here are some debugging steps that you could take.

1. Reread the program to find any obvious errors such as incorrect syntax or errors of types that are common to the programming constructs you are using. For example, when using a `for` loop, make sure that all variable initializations are done correctly; if the loop does nothing, check for a semicolon immediately after the loop header.

2. Do some sort of trace to determine the changes in the values of important variables. You could use three kinds of traces; the first two are computer assisted, and the third is done entirely by hand.

   (a) **Inserting Extra** cout **Statements** Place these statements at strategic locations in your program to determine the values of key variables at various times. Then, rerun your program and examine the output. (You may want to print a hard copy.) Once you've corrected your program, you should remove the extra output statements or at least make them into comments.

   (b) **Using the Built-in Debugging Tools** Many modern C++ program development environments provide interactive debugging tools. These tools allow you to step through program execution one statement at a time, examining the effect of each statement on any variables you've chosen to "watch." (The details of using these tools will vary from one system to another.)

   (c) **Hand Tracing** This important technique can be used when you need to study your program without the distraction of sitting at the computer. Furthermore, skill at hand tracing increases your awareness of what pieces of program code will do, so you can improve your ability to write programs that have fewer errors. Hand tracing is also invaluable for studying new algorithms.

■ **EXAMPLE** (Hand Tracing) Suppose that when the following program fragment (from trace1.cpp) is executed, the user inputs the following six numbers: 5, 30, 10, 40, 15, and 29. What will the virtual printer output be?

```
for (i=1; i<=3; i++)
   {
   cout << "Enter a number: ";
   cin >> num1;
   num2 = num1 + 2;
   num1--;
   vprn << num1 << " " << num2 << endl;
   cout << "Enter a number: ";
   cin >> num2;
   } // end for
vprn << num1 << " " << num2 << endl;
```

Suggested Memory Table Method

1. Draw a column for each variable. A variable's current value will be the value *farthest* down in that variable's column.

2. Draw a horizontal line each time you begin a new execution of the loop body, or when you exit from the loop.

During a hand trace, each time you execute a statement that changes the value of a variable, you should update the memory table. Each time you execute an output statement, you should write down the output produced.

Here is what the memory table would look like at the time the first output statement is executed.

i	num1	num2
1	5	7
	4	

The first output statement then prints 4 7 on the virtual printer. By the time you have finished the hand trace, the memory table will be

i	num1	num2
1	5	7
	4	30
2	10	12
	9	40
3	15	17
	14	29

Note that you cannot determine what the output will be just by looking at the final version of the memory table because this table does not indicate where the output statements occurred. The complete virtual printer output will be

```
4  7
9  12
14  17
14  29
```

■ **QUESTION**   How would you produce a hand trace of the following loop (from trace2.cpp), and give its output?

```
n = 1;
sum = 0;
do {
    sum = sum + n*n;
    n = n + 2;
    }
while (n < 8);
cout << "Sum = " << sum
        << endl;
```

Answer   Trace

Loop Iteration	Calculation for *sum*	*sum*	*n*
		0	1
1	$(0 + 1^2)$	1	3
2	$(1 + 3^2)$	10	5
3	$(10 + 5^2)$	35	7
4	$(35 + 7^2)$	84	9

Sum = 84

Output

In summary, this loop found the sum $1^2 + 3^2 + 5^2 + 7^2$.   ■ ■■

■ **Exercises**

1. What will be output by each of the following program fragments?

(a)
```
for (i=1; i<=3; i=i+1)
    cout << "Hi ";
    cout << "there.\n";
cout << "Bye\n";
```

(b)

```
for (j=20; j>=5; j=j-3)
    { cout << j << ' '; }
```

(c)

```
for (j=20; j>=5; j=j+7);
    { cout << j << ' '; }
```

(d)

```
for (j=20; j>=5; j=j+7)
    { cout << "Again\n"; }
```

(e)

```
for (j=20; j<=5; j=j-4)
    { cout << "Again\n"; }
```

2. If i and sum are of type int, and ltr is of type char, what will be the output of

(a)

```
sum = 0;
for (i=1; i<=4; i+=1)
    {
    sum = sum + i*i;
    cout << i << ' ' << sum << endl;
    }
cout << "done\n";
```

(b)

```
sum = 0;
for (i=1; i<=4; i+=1)
    {
    sum = 0;
    sum = sum + i;
    }
cout << sum << endl;
```

(c)

```
for (ltr='Z'; ltr>'P'; ltr=ltr-2)
    { cout << ltr; }
cout << "/\n";
```

3. Complete each program fragment so that it produces the output given to its right.

(a)

```
j=1; k=1;
for (i=1; i<=8; i++)
    {
    _____ = j+k;
    cout << sum << ' ';
    j=k;
    k=_;
    }
```

```
2  3  5  8  13  21  34  55
```

Output

(b)

```
prod = 1;
for (i=1; _____; i++)
    {
    prod = _____;
    cout << "2^" << __ << "="
         << _____ << endl;
    }
```

```
2^1=2
2^2=4
2^3=8
2^4=16
2^5=32
2^6=64
```
Output

(c)

```
prod = __;
for (_____; ____; i++)
    {
    prod = _____;
    cout << i << _____;
    cout << endl;
    }
```

```
2!=2
3!=6
4!=24
5!=120
6!=720
7!=5040
```
Output

4. Use the memory table method of Section 7.8 to determine the output of

   (a)

   (b)

```
p=30;
for (i=5; i>0; i--)
    {
    p = p-2;
    cout << p << ' ';
    if (p%4==0)
        cout << "OK";
    cout << '\n';
    }
```

```
int i, m, p;
m=5;
for (i=1; i<=3; i=i+1)
    {
    p = m - 2;
    m = m + p;
    p += 6;
    if (m>p)
        cout << p;
    else
        cout << m;
    cout << endl;
    }
cout << m << ' ' << p;
```

5. In the hand trace of Section 7.8, what would the virtual printer output be if the fourth statement in the loop body were changed from `num1--;` to `num1 = num2 - 1;`?

6. (a) Write a program that uses the variable sum to find the sum of the first 50 integers. Run the program *twice*. Each run should produce exactly the same output.

(b) Now remove the initialization sum = 0; and then save, compile, and run your program two more times. Explain the results.

7. What will be output by each of the following code fragments?

(a)

```
n=1;
while (n<=9)
    {
    n = n + 5;
    cout << n
        << endl;
    }
```

(b)

```
n=1;
while (n<=9)
    {
    cout << n
        << endl;
    n = n + 5;
    }
```

(c)

```
n=1;
while (n<=9)
    cout << n
        << endl;
    n = n + 5;
```

(d)

```
n=1;
while (n>9)
    {
    n = n + 5;
    cout <<n<< endl;
    }
```

(e)

```
n=1;
do {
    n = n + 5;
    cout << n << endl;
    }
while (n>9);
```

8. If a while loop is reached, is it certain that the loop body will be executed at least once? Answer the question for a do..while loop.

Programming Problems

9. Write a program to output the table at right to the virtual printer. [*Hint*: Celsius = 5/9 × (Fahrenheit – 32).]

Fahrenheit	Celsius
32	0.0
34	1.1
.	.
.	.
100	37.8

10. Write a program to loop through the ASCII codes from 0 to 127, displaying all punctuation characters and their ASCII codes.

11. Write a program that will evaluate the function $y = 4x^2 - 16x + 15$, with x going from 1 to 2 in steps of 0.1. For each x, give the value of y and the message POSITIVE or NOT POSITIVE. Format the output in the form

```
┌─────────────────────────────────────────────┐
│  x value    y value                          │
│     1.0       3.00    POSITIVE               │
│     1.1       2.24    POSITIVE               │
│      .         .         .                   │
│      .         .         .                   │
│     2.0      -1.00    NOT POSITIVE           │
└─────────────────────────────────────────────┘
```

12. Write a program to calculate the sum

$$S(N) = 1 + 1/2 + 1/3 + \ldots + 1/N$$

for each of several positive values input by the user. For accuracy, use the `double` or `long double` data type.

13. When a ball is thrown upward at an angle of θ *degrees* and with initial velocity V_0 the height of the ball after t seconds is

$$h(t) = V_0 t \sin\theta - 16t^2$$

Using an initial velocity of 144 feet per second and $\theta = 60$ degrees, write a program to output a *table* giving the height of the ball for each value of t from 0.5 to 8.0, in increments of 0.5 seconds.

14. Write both versions of the maximum area problem given in Section 7.5.

15. For any of the functions of Exercise 5.10, write a test program that uses a type A input loop to (1) input repeatedly the arguments to be passed to the function, (2) call the function with those arguments, and then (3) output the result of the function call.

16. Write a program that uses a sentinel (type P) loop to input several positive integers. The program will then output the number of inputs, the smallest and largest input, and the sum and mean of the inputs.

17. Write a program to input a positive integer N, then print all of its proper divisors (greater than 1 but less than N), and then print the number of proper divisors of N and their sum.

Longer Assignments

18. Write a program that uses a sentinel (type P) loop to input repeatedly a positive integer and tell whether the input integer is *deficient, perfect,* or *abundant.* For example,

     6 is *perfect* because $1 + 2 + 3 = 6$
     15 is *deficient* because $1 + 3 + 5 < 15$
     24 is *abundant* because $1 + 2 + 3 + 4 + 6 + 8 + 12 > 24$

(*Hint*: Consider the previous exercise.)

19. Write an interactive program to grade a class of students. Use a sentinel-controlled input similar to that of `receipt.cpp` to input and process each student's name and three exam scores. The program will find each student's average and determine whether the student passed (at least 60 percent) or failed. The first part of the virtual printer output will be a table of labeled, properly aligned columns giving each student's name, three grades, average (accurate to the nearest tenth), and a message (`passed` or `failed`). The second part of the output will give the class size, the number of students who passed, and the name and average of the student with the highest average.

20. Write an interactive program for the Sales-R-Us Company to process and print payroll information about its employees. For each employee, the program should read in the employee's name, hours worked, and base pay rate. For example, a typical data group might be

    ```
    Dough, Johan 50 9.00
    ```

    An employee's gross wage is computed at the regular rate for the first 40 hours worked and 1.5 times the regular rate for each hour over 40. An employee's tax is withheld at the rate of 10% on the first $200 and 20% on anything over $200.

    The first part of the (virtual printer) output will be a table giving the relevant information for each employee.

Name	Hours Worked	Base Rate	Gross Wage	Net Tax	Wage
Dough, Johan	50	9.00	495.00	79.00	416.00
. . . etc. . . .					

    The second part of the (virtual printer) output will give (1) the total gross for all employees, (2) the total tax withheld from all employees, (3) the average net pay, and (4) the name and gross pay for the employee with the largest gross. (You may assume only one employee has the largest gross pay; there is not a tie.)

21. Write a program to input a sentence, one word at a time, terminated by `.`, `!`, or `?`. Then, output the number of words in the sentence, the average word length, and the longest word in the sentence. For simplicity, assume that the only punctuation marks within the sentence are `,` and `;`, and separate each punctuation mark from the preceding word by a space. Thus, a sample input sentence would be

    ```
    Alas , there was no more fuel ; we began losing
    altitude rapidly !
    ```

22. Write a program to determine the number of days by which two dates (of the form mm-dd-yy) differ. [*Hints:* Use the functions `days_in_month` and `is_leap_year` (from Problem 2 in Section 4.6) in combination with `for` loops. You may also use the functions `day_of_year` and `days_left_in_year` that,

given a date, return, respectively, the days elapsed and the days left in a given year.]

23. Various algorithms can determine the day of the week on which a given date fell or will fall. One method for determining the day of the week for a particular date is to combine the result of the previous exercise with the fact that January 1, 1900, fell on Monday. Write a program to determine the day of week for a given input date.

8

More on Loops

In this chapter we continue the discussion of loops begun in the previous chapter. We also consider more general looping tasks and applications and several loop-related issues.

8.1 More General Task-Controlled Loops

The loops of the previous chapter terminated upon completion of one of two tasks.

1. A fixed-step loop control variable reached a predetermined value

2. A data input loop encountered a sentinel value.

These two special categories of loops can be applied to many computational tasks. However, loops can carry out tasks that do not fall into either of those two categories. In such situations, it is useful to think of a loop in terms of its task as follows:

while (*task not completed*)   do
    loop body   *loop body*
                      while (*task not completed*);

■ **PROBLEM** The sum of the squares $1^2 + 2^2 + 3^2 + \cdots$ eventually goes over 1000. Write a program to find the integer whose square first puts the sum over 1000. The output should be of the form

```
Sum first goes over 1000 when _____ squared is added.
Sum is _____.
```

Variables and Loop Exit Test We need a variable, n, to go up by steps of 1 in order to generate the squares 1^2, 2^2, 3^2, and so on. We also need a variable, sum, to keep track of the sum of the squares. The loop exit test is obviously

```
while (sum <= 1000)
```

Solution **Pseudocode** Here is pseudocode for the problem solution.

```
initialize n and sum to 0
while (sum <= 1000)
    {
    increase n by 1
    add n² to sum
    }
print the results
```

Code Here is the full program.

```cpp
// over1000.cpp
// Finds first square to put sum over 1000.
#include <iostream.h>

void main()
{
    int n, sum;
    n=0;
    sum=0;
    while (sum <= 1000)
        {
        n++;
        sum = sum + n*n;
        }
    cout << "Sum first goes over 1000 when "
        << n << " squared is added.\n";
    cout << "Sum is " << sum << ".\n";
}
```

Note that this loop is not step controlled because the variable, n, which goes up by fixed steps of 1, is not the variable in the loop exit test. A do..while version of this program would be identical except the loop would be headed by do and the test, while (sum <= 1000), would be at the bottom of the loop.

Guidelines for Constructing a Task-Controlled Loop   Let us apply the problem-solving guidelines of Section 4.6, focusing on issues that are important in loops.

1. **Understand the problem.** What do you want the loop to accomplish? What do you want to be true by the end of the loop? Can you systematically work through particular instances of the problem by hand?

2. **Develop the looping algorithm.**
    (a) **Variables Needed and the Loop Exit Test** Do you need a variable that goes up or down by a fixed step? Do you need other variables? What variable(s) will be needed in the loop condition? What is the loop condition?
    (b) **Before and After** What loop-related tasks are performed *before* the loop (such as initialization or headings) and *after* the loop (such as output of final tallies).
    (c) **Loop Body** Each execution of the loop body should make some progress toward achieving completion of the task, such as processing the next term. For such a loop, how is the next term generated, and how is it processed?
    (d) **Pseudocode** Write a top-down outline or pseudocode, including any needed initializations.

3. **Write the complete code for the loop.** Your pseudocode and the work you do in steps 1 and 2 will lead you to the complete code.

4. **Test the loop.** Design several data sets for which you can predict or hand calculate the output, including some that test special cases. Check that the loop does what it is supposed to. Pay particular attention to the first and last execution of the loop.

■ **EXAMPLE**   (**Compound Interest**)   If $500 is invested at 4.5% compounded annually, after how many years will the balance first exceed $1,000?

1. **Understand the problem.** Doing the calculations for just the first few years, in a systematic fashion, can provide a great deal of insight into the problem. For example:

Year	Balance at the end of year
1	500 + .045 * 500 = 500 + 22.50 = $522.50
2	522.50 + .045 * 522.50 = $522.50 + $23.51 = $546.01

etc.

2. Develop the looping algorithm.

(a) Needed Variables and Loop Exit Test We need a variable `balance` to keep track of the balance, plus interest, at the end of every year. We also need a variable `year` to count the years. The loop condition is obviously

```
while (balance <= 1000)
```

(b) Before and After The variables `year` and `balance` must be initialized *before* the loop. The program contains no loop-related output before the loop. The final values of `year` and `balance` will be printed *after* the loop, in the specified format.

(c) Loop Body Each time through the loop, the value of `balance` must be increased by 4.5% times its current value, and `year` must be increased by 1.

(d) Pseudocode Here is the pseudocode.

```
initialize year to 0 and balance to 500
while (balance <= 1000)
    {
    increase balance by .045 * balance
    add 1 to year
    }
print year and balance
```

3. Write the complete code for the loop.
The following program fragment (from `cmpdint.cpp`) is the code for the `while` version.

```cpp
const float RATE = 0.045; // 4.5%
float balance;
int  year;

balance = 500;
year = 0;
```

```
while (balance <= 1000.00)
   {
   balance = balance + RATE * balance;
   year++;
//   cout << year << '\t' << balance << endl;
   }
cout << "Balance over $1,000 at end of year "
      << year << endl;
fixed_out (cout, 2);
cout << "Balance was " << balance << endl;
```

4. **Test the loop.** The comment within the loop body is an output statement that was used during program debugging and then changed into a comment when the program was judged to be correct. (See Section 7.8, "Debugging Strategies.")

Discussion   In many loops it matters whether a statement to increment a variable (like year++;) appears at the top or the bottom of the loop body. In the previous program, however, note that the two (uncommented) statements in the loop body could have had their order switched because the variable year does not appear in the assignment statement for balance.

The do..while version is identical to the while version except for the placement of the while test and the addition of the keyword do.

Off-by-One Errors   An *off-by-one error* occurs when a counter is off by 1 or when something is done one time too many or one time too few. Here are three examples.

1. If year were initialized to 1 in the previous compound interest program, then the program would output the wrong value for the year in which the balance goes over $1,000 — it would be too large by 1.

2. For the program that finds when the sum of squares first goes over 1000, if the order of the two lines in the loop body were switched, the value output for n would be too large by 1.

3. The following loop prints one more comma than is intended.

```
for (i=1; i<=5; i++)
   { cout << i << ","}
```

    1, 2, 3, 4, 5

Intended Output

Protecting Against Off-by-One Errors Although there is no magic formula for avoiding off-by-one errors, here are some important factors to consider:

- ***Order*** Note where a key variable should be incremented in relation to the other statements in the loop body.

- ***Initialization*** Check whether the initial value of a key variable is correct or should be one greater or less.

- ***Relational Operator*** Pay close attention to the relational operator in the loop exit test. For example, whether you use < or <= can make a difference of one execution of the loop body.

- ***First and Last Execution of Loop Body*** Analyze what will happen during the first and last executions of the loop body. For example,
  - in the incorrect loop, whose intended output was the integers 1 through 5, separated by commas, the final execution of the loop body outputs 5,. The simplest way to produce the intended output is to use a `for` loop to output 1, 2, 3, 4, and then to output 5 separately after that loop.
  - in the incorrect version of the program to find when the sum of squares first goes over 1000, consider the last execution of the loop body — the value of n whose square first puts sum over 1000 is added to sum, and *then* n is *incremented*, making it 1 too large.

■ **EXAMPLE** **(Ulam's Conjecture)** The following statement is known as Ulam's conjecture, named after the mathematician S. Ulam.

CONJECTURE: Regardless of the starting integer, the following process will always eventually produce the integer 1.

- Start with any positive integer greater than 1.
- If the current integer is even, divide it by 2; if it is odd, multiply it by 3 and add 1.
- Obtain successive integers by repeating this process as long as the current integer is not 1.

  1. **Understand the problem.** When 26 is the starting integer, the sequence will be 26 13 40 20 10 5 16 8 4 2 1. You should try some other starting values, like 21 and 96.

  2. **Develop the looping algorithm.**
     (a) ***Variables and Loop Exit Test*** Let us use a single variable n to run through all the values in the Ulam sequence. Thus, n will start at the number whose Ulam sequence we want, and each execution of the loop body should calculate and

print the next number in the Ulam sequence. The exit condition is obviously `while (n != 1)`.

(b) **Before and After** The variable n must be initialized *before*
the loop — we can get it from the user in order to make the
program flexible. We should print a brief message with the
value of n immediately before the loop. There is no loop-
related output after the loop body.

(c) **Loop Body** Each execution of the loop body should calculate and print the next number in the Ulam sequence.

(d) **Pseudocode** Here is the pseudocode using a `do..while`
loop.

```
prompt for and get the starting value for n
output n
do {
    calculate the next number, n, in the Ulam sequence
    output n
    }
while (n != 1);
```

We leave completion of this program as an exercise.

Choosing Between *while* **and** *do..while*

- For many looping tasks, both loops work equally well, and the
  `do..while` version is identical to the `while` version except for the
  location of the loop exit test and the addition of the keyword `do`.

- If there is the possibility of a situation in which you do not want
  the loop body executed even once, then the `while` loop must be used.
  For example, in the loop for Ulam's conjecture, if the user were to
  specify 1 as the starting integer, the `while` version would give the
  correct output, but the `do..while` version would not. (Do you see
  why?)

- As you will see in the next few sections, if a variable in the loop exit
  test receives its first value in a natural way during the first execution
  of the loop body, then the `do..while` loop is usually much better.

- If you are reading code, you can tell at a glance whether a loop with
  the keyword `while` is a `while` or a `do..while` loop, by noting whether
  or not the `while` test is followed by a semicolon — the `while` test in
  a `do..while` loop must be followed by a semicolon.

8.2 Using do..while Loops to Trap Input Errors

A common cause of faulty program output is the entry of incorrect data. ("Garbage in, garbage out" is a familiar programming maxim.) Although the programmer cannot be guaranteed that the user will not make mistakes when entering data, the programmer can use certain techniques to gain some protection against such errors.

One technique is to include clear prompts so that the user knows the precise form for the inputs. A second technique is to include program code to detect and trap mistakes. A program that contains such safeguards is said to be **robust** because it is strong in the sense of being resistant to *some* forms of bad data. The do..while loop is commonly used to force the user to input a data value within some specified range. The loop does so by not letting execution get beyond the loop until the user enters a data value of the required form.

■ **EXAMPLE** Look for a possible weakness in the following program fragment (from letter1.cpp) that is intended to determine whether an input capital letter is in the first half (A–M) or the second half (N–Z) of the alphabet.

```
cout << "Enter capital letter: ";
cin >> ch;
if (ch >= 'A' && ch <= 'M')
    cout << ch << " in first half of alphabet.\n";
else
    cout << ch << " in second half of alphabet.\n";
```

Here is a run of the program in which the user failed to heed the prompt to enter a capital letter.

```
Enter capital letter: d
d in second half of alphabet.
```

In the following robust program fragment (from letter2.cpp), note the use of a do..while loop to force the user to enter a capital letter. Execution does not get beyond the loop until the user enters an uppercase letter.

```
do {
    cout << "Enter capital letter: ";
    cin >> ch;
    }
while (ch<'A' || ch>'Z');
if (ch >= 'A' && ch <= 'M')
    cout << ch << " in first half of alphabet.\n";
else
    cout << ch << " in second half of alphabet.\n";
```

Here is a typical run of the preceding robust code.

```
Enter capital letter: d
Enter capital letter: $
Enter capital letter: D
D in first half of alphabet.
```

Trapping Input Errors — *do..while* **Versus** *while*   Although the previous example could have used a `while` loop, such a code would be somewhat awkward. Because the variable `ch` is used in the test condition, this variable must already have a value before the `while` loop is encountered the first time. Thus, a `while` loop version would need a priming `cout-cin` before the loop as well as `cout-cin` in the loop body. The `do..while` loop version is simpler.

8.3   Multiple Reasons for Loop Exit

When there are two or more possible reasons for exiting a loop, a compound condition is used in the loop exit test. Usually in such situations, the program should include an `if..else` statement after the loop to determine which condition caused the exit.

■ **EXAMPLE**   **(Die Rolling Game)**   Write a program to simulate a game in which you roll a single die until you get a 1 or a 6. If you get a 6 first, you win $1 for each roll; if you get a 1 first, you lose $1 for each roll. Here are two sample runs.

```
2 3 2 4 2 5 4 4 3 2 6
You win $11
```

```
5 2 1
You lose $3
```

The following code fragment, from rolls.cpp, produced these runs:

```
srand(time(0)); // init r.n.g.
rolls = 0;
do {
    dots = rand()%6 + 1;
    rolls++;
    cout << dots << ' ';
    }
while (dots!=1 && dots != 6);
cout << endl;

if (dots == 1)
    cout << "You lose $";
else // dots == 6
    cout << "You win $";
cout << rolls << endl;
```

Note that a do..while loop works better than a while loop because the variable, dots, in the loop exit test receives its first value in the body of the loop. Note also that a for loop would not be appropriate because the number of loop iterations cannot be determined in advance.

■ ▬

Boolean Flag A bool variable that is used to keep track of whether some event has occurred is called a *boolean flag* or simply a *flag*. Boolean flags are often used in loop exit tests. For example, the next program uses the boolean flag guessed_it to keep track of whether the user has supplied the correct answer yet.

■ **EXAMPLE** **(Bounded Number of Tries)** Write a program in which the user is given a maximum of three tries to enter the capital of Alaska. If the user fails to provide the correct answer by the third try, he or she is then told the correct answer. Write the program so that it produces the following two sample runs.

```
Give capital of Alaska: Fairbanks
Give capital of Alaska: Nome
Give capital of Alaska: Frostbite Falls
You did not get it in three tries.
The capital is Juneau
```

```
Give capital of Alaska: Anchorage
Give capital of Alaska: Juneau
Nice work! You got it in 2 tries.
```

Here is the program.

```
// statecap.cpp
#include <iostream.h>
#include "bool.h"
#include "baString.h"

void main()
{
    String state, capital, guess;
    int tries; // number of guesses
    bool guessed_it; // was guess correct?

    state = "Alaska";
    capital = "Juneau";
    tries = 0;
    do {
        tries++;
        cout << "Give capital of " << state << ": ";
        getline (cin, guess);
        guessed_it = (guess == capital);
        }
    while (!guessed_it && tries<3);

    if (guessed_it)
        cout << "Nice work! You got it in "
            << tries << " tries.\n";
    else
        {
        cout << "You did not get it in three tries.\n";
        cout << "The capital is " << capital << endl;
        }
}
```

Discussion   Using `bool` variable `guessed_it` avoids a redundant string comparison. If the last statement of the loop body was eliminated, the loop exit test and the following `if` test would both require comparing `guess` and capital, as in

```
while (guess!=capital && tries<3);
if (guess == capital)
```

The statement getline (cin, guess); is needed instead of cin >> guess;, because the latter would not correctly input city names (like Frostbite Falls) containing embedded spaces. ■ ▬

■ **PROBLEM** Randomly generate an integer with exactly three digits, all of which are distinct.

Various algorithms can be used for solving this problem; two of these algorithms follow. In each, n is the three-digit integer, and hd, td, and ud are, respectively, its hundreds, tens, and units digits.

Algorithm A	*Algorithm B*
| ```
do {
    generate n, 100 <= n <= 999
    extract hd, td, and ud from n.
    }
while (hd, td, ud are not distinct);
``` | ```
generate hd, 1 <= hd <= 9
do
    { generate td, 0 <= td <= 9}
while (hd==td);
do
    { generate ud, 0 <= ud <= 9}
while (ud is the same as hd or td);
``` |

Question Write the compound exit conditions for the final while loop of each algorithm.

Answer Algorithm A   (hd==td || hd==ud || td==ud)
Algorithm B   (ud==hd || ud==td)   ■ ▬

8.4 Mid-Loop Exit Using the break **Statement**

In Section 8.3 we looked at loops with multiple exit conditions. The logic of such loops can be simplified whenever one of the exit conditions is a bound on the number of times the loop body should be executed. In such cases, the loop can be written as a for loop to handle the bound on the number of executions — the other loop exit test(s) can be placed within the body of the loop as the test(s) in an if statement that has a *break statement* as its action. When the computer executes a break statement inside the body of a loop, the loop is exited with control transferred to the first statement beyond the loop. *Be aware that an LCV will retain whatever value it had at the time the break statement was executed.*

■ EXAMPLE   The following fragment, from `capital2.cpp`, redoes the state capital problem using a `for` loop.

```
state = "Alaska";
capital = "Juneau";
for (tries=1; tries<=3; tries++) // with break
    {
    cout << "Give capital of " << state << ": ";
    getline (cin, guess);
    if (guess == capital)
        break;
    }

if (tries <= 3) // early exit
    cout << "Nice work! You got it in "
            << tries << " tries.\n";
else
    {
    cout << "You did not get it in three tries.\n";
    cout << "The capital is " << capital << endl;
    }
```

Discussion   Note how the `if..else` statement determines the cause of the loop exit. If the exit is caused by the user giving the correct answer, the `break` statement leaves `tries` at its current value (which is <=3). However, if the user does not get the correct answer within three tries, the `break` statement is not executed and the `for` loop is exited normally, with `tries` taking on the value 4. (See Section 7.3 for a discussion of the final value of a `for` loop control variable.) In general, the `if` test after the loop can use the same test that is used in the `for` loop test condition, namely,

```
if (LCV <= bound) // early exit
```
■ ■■

Bounded Number of Tries: Advantages of for *with* break   You can use this method to produce code that has clearer logic than a `while` or `do..while` loop with multiple exit conditions. The reasons for these advantages are as follows: (1) All the loop control statements relating to the LCV (initialization, test, and update) are placed in the `for` loop header, instead of spread out over three locations. (2) The boolean flag can be eliminated. (3) You don't have to worry about whether to initialize the LCV at the starting value or at one less. (For example, if the maximum number of tries will be three, `tries` must be initialized to 1 (not 0 as was the case in the `do..while` version).

■ **PROBLEM** **(Testing an Odd Integer for Primality)** A positive integer greater than one is said to be *prime* if it has no divisors other than itself and one. (For example, 17 is prime, but 15, which is divisible by both 3 and 5, is not.) To determine whether an odd integer $n > 1$ is prime, you need only test as divisors all odd integers, beginning with 3, that are less than or equal to the square root of n. For example, to determine whether 71 is prime, first note that $\sqrt{71}$ is between 8 and 9. Thus, you need only test 3, 5, and 7 as divisors. Note that 9 is not on the list of test divisors, because 9 is greater than $\sqrt{71}$.

We want to write code that will determine whether or not an odd input integer greater than 1 is prime. If it is not prime, we want the output to give the smallest proper divisor. Here are two sample runs.

```
Enter odd n > 1: 71
Prime
```

```
Enter odd n > 1: 91
A divisor is 7
```

To write the code, we will use three variables — n for the odd integer being tested for primality; td, which will take on the values of the test divisors; and td_bound, which will be an integer upper bound on the test divisors. Before reading on, try to write the code. (*Hint:* Let td_bound be $\sqrt{n}$, and use the test (n % td) == 0 to determine whether td is a divisor of n.)

The following code fragment is from prime.cpp, a program that solves the problem stated above.

```cpp
td_bound = floor(sqrt(n)); // integer upper bound
for (td = 3; td <= td_bound; td += 2) // with break
   {
   if (n % td == 0) // exact divisor, so
      break; // exit the loop
   }
if (td <= td_bound)
   cout << "A divisor is " << td << endl;
else
   cout << "Prime\n";
```

■ **QUESTION** For the following values of n, give the values that td_bound and td will have at the time of the if test after the loop.

1. 83   **2.** 115

Answer   **1.**   td_bound will be 9, and td will be 11.

2.   td_bound will be 10, and td will be 5.   ■ ▬▬

Style Issues and *break*   Unless there are strong reasons for using break, it is better style to place all the loop exit tests in the loop header (or the while part of a do..while loop) rather than to bury them in the loop body. So, don't overuse break. However, we do recommend the use of break for a loop task involving a bounded number of tries, because using break this way simplifies the loop's logic. *It is important to give the comment in the* for *loop header to make it clear that a break statement is in the loop body.*

8.5 Nested Loops

In Chapter 4 we looked at nested selection, a structure in which an if or if..else statement is completely contained within the true or false branch of another if or if..else statement. Similarly, when one loop structure is completely contained in the body of another, the loops are said to be nested.

■ **EXAMPLE**   Consider the following program fragment (from points.cpp), which will compute separate point totals for males and females. The user repeatedly inputs data groups such as 24 m and 47 f, where the first item of the group is the point total and the second is the sex of the person who achieved it. The sex may be entered as m, M, f, or F.

```
male_sum = 0; fem_sum = 0;
do {
    cout << "Enter number of points: ";
    cin >> points;
    do {
        cout << "Enter sex (m or f): ";
        cin >> sex;
        sex = toupper(sex);
        }
    while (sex!='M' && sex!='F');
    if (sex=='F')
        fem_sum += points;
    else
        male_sum += points;
    cout << "Continue? (y or n): ";
    cin >> ans;
    }
while (toupper(ans) != 'N');
```

Discussion   The inner `do..while` loop does the error trapping and allows the input to be either lowercase or uppercase (though the prompt said "m or f"), and the outer `do..while` loop allows the user to enter multiple data groups. ▪ ▬

Nested *for* **Loops**   In nested `for` loops, the entire outer loop body is executed for each of the values of the outer loop control variable. Thus, for *each* value of the outer loop control variable, the inner `for` loop will run through *all* of its values.

▪ **QUESTION**   What will be printed by the following fragment from `nest1.cpp`?

```
for (n=2; n<=4; n++)
    {
    for (i=6; i<=7; i++)
        cout << n << " " << i << endl;
    cout << "i is now " << i << endl;
    }
cout << "n is now " << n << endl;
```

Answer

```
2 6
2 7          ⎫  printed when n = 2
i is now 8   ⎭
3 6
3 7          ⎫  printed when n = 3
i is now 8   ⎭
4 6
4 7          ⎫  printed when n = 4
i is now 8   ⎭
n is now 5      printed after exit from outer loop
```
▪ ▬

Nested Loops of Different Types   In the previous two program fragments, the outer loop was the same type (`do..while`, then `for`) as the inner loop, but any looping structure can be nested within any other.

Row-by-Row Processing   An important application of nested loops is in using an outer loop to process a number of rows, when the processing for each row itself requires a loop.

■ **EXAMPLE**   Write a program segment to generate a right triangle with `num_rows` rows of asterisks, such that the first row has one asterisk, the second has two, the third has three, and so on, and where the rightmost asterisks from each row are right-aligned. A sample run for a user input of 5 is given at right.

```
How many rows (1-20): 5
    *
   **
  ***
 ****
*****
```

A pseudocode algorithm is

Input a value for `num_rows`
```
for (r=1; r<=num_rows; r++)
    {
    Indent the appropriate number of spaces (loop needed)
    Print r asterisks
    drop cursor to a new line
    }
```

Note that the number of spaces to indent *decreases* by 1 each time `r` *increases* by 1. Thus, with a little inspiration, you might realize that on row number `r`, you must indent `num_rows - r` spaces, which can be done with a `for` loop that prints `num_rows - r` spaces.

Here is the actual code from program `asterisk.cpp`.

```cpp
cin >> num_rows;
for (r=1; r<=num_rows; r++)
    {
    // indent by printing num_rows-r spaces
    for (i=1; i<=num_rows-r; i++)
        cout << ' ';
    // print r asterisks
    for (i=1; i<=r; i++)
        cout << '*';
    // drop cursor to a new line
    cout << endl;
    } // end for
```

Discussion   Some of the pseudocode has been included as comments in the actual code. This practice is useful when the logic of a portion of a program is tricky.   ■ ■■

■ PROBLEM   A triangle is a right triangle if the lengths of its sides obey the Pythagorean theorem, that is, if the sum of the squares of the lengths of its two shorter sides (called the legs) equals the square of the longer side (called the hypotenuse). For example, a triangle with sides of length 5, 12, and 13 is a right triangle because $5^2 + 12^2 = 25 + 144 = 169 = 13^2$. Further, any triple (a, b, c) of integers is called a *Pythagorean triple* if a and b are the lengths of the legs of a right triangle and c is the length of its hypotenuse

Generate and output in the form (a, b, c) all Pythagorean triples for which $a \le b \le 100$, and output the number of such triples.

Understand the problem.   This problem has no input — a loop or loops must be used to generate the possible Pythagorean triples. One approach would be to generate every possible pair (a, b) where $1 \le a \le b \le 100$.

The output consists of ordered triples in the form (a, b, c), and because there may be many of these, it would be wise to print several per line.

As usual, hand calculations will be helpful. The following table gives some values for a and b, the lengths of the legs of a right triangle; the calculations for c, the length of the hypotenuse; and the decision about whether (a, b, c) is a Pythagorean triple. Two of these calculations are left for you to complete.

a	b	Calculation of c	Pythagorean triple?
2	3	$c^2 = 2^2 + 3^2 = 4 + 9 = 13$	No. $c = \sqrt{13}$ is not an integer.
3	4	$c^2 = 3^2 + 4^2 = 9 + 16 = 25$	Yes. $c = \sqrt{25}$ is an integer.
10	20	$c^2 = 10^2 + 20^2 = 100 + 400 = 500$	No. $c = \sqrt{500}$ is not an integer.
7	24	$c^2 = $ _____	Yes. _____
12	12	$c^2 = $ _____	No. _____

Develop an algorithm.   In the preceding table, five pairs of the form (a, b) have been used for illustration purposes. The program, however, must generate all possible pairs. That is, for each value of a from 1 through 100, the program must generate all values of b that are greater than or equal to a, but no larger than 100. This suggests nested loops — the outer loop will generate each value of a, and the inner loop will generate all values of b to be paired with a particular value of a.

Thus, a pseudocode algorithm is

```
num_triples=0;
```

```
for (a=1; a<=100; a++)
   for (b=a; b<=100; b++)
     {
     Calculate c such that a² + b² = c².
     if (c is an integer)
        {
        Output (a, b, c)
        num_triples++;
        }
     }
Output num_triples
```

Code the algorithm. Coding the algorithm is left as Exercise 8.32. For the calculation of c, you can use the `sqrt` function from `math.h`.

Testing and debugging. Because the problem has no user input, no test oracle exists. How can you be confident that the program output is correct? One possible strategy is the following:

> Output *all* values of a, b, and c to the virtual printer. Examine these values of a, b, and c and verify that those and only those for which c has no fractional part are displayed on the monitor as Pythagorean triples.

However, for the given problem, this method will generate far too much virtual printer output. For testing purposes, you might experiment by replacing 1 and 100 with other values. ▪ ▬

Simplifying Nested Loops with a Function Call

Often code containing nested loops can be written more clearly by replacing the inner loop with a function call. For example, consider the problem of outputting all odd primes between 100 and 200. A nested loop version that uses some of the code from Section 8.4 is

```
for (n=101; n<=199; n=n+2)
   {
   td_bound = floor(sqrt(n)); // integer upper bound
   for (td = 3; td <= td_bound; td += 2) // with break
      {
      if (n % td == 0)
         break; // exit the loop
      }
   if (td > td_bound)
      cout << n << ' ';
   }
```

A better method is to write a `bool`-valued function `is_prime`. A call to this function will then replace the body of the outer `for` loop.

```
for (n=101; n<=199; n=n+2)
   {
   if (is_prime(n))
      cout << n << ' ';
   }
```

Writing a program to print all primes between two user inputs is left as Exercise 8.31.

8.6 Fixed-Step Loops with Floating Point Step

Numerical Inaccuracies in Floating-Point Calculations Many fractions or decimals (like 1/3 or 0.1) can cause trouble because they do not have an exact binary representation. For example, the value that the computer calculates for `(1.0/3.0) * 3.0` is not exactly 1! (To check this, use program `unequal.cpp` at the PWS Web site.)

Two dangers in floating point, fixed-step loops are (1) infinite loops and (2) loops that are "off-by-one" in the number of executions of the loop body.

Infinite Loop The following program produces an infinite loop.

```
// trouble1.cpp
#include <iostream.h>

void main()
{
   float x;
   x = 0;
   while (x!=1)
      {
      cout << x << endl;
      x = x + 0.1;
      }
}
```

```
0
0.1
0.2
0.3
0.4
0.5
0.6
0.7
0.8
0.9
1
1.1
1.2
 .
 .
 .
```

Output

The behavior of the preceding program might seem puzzling because the output suggests that x actually took on the value 1 and that the loop should therefore have terminated after 0.9 was output. But recall that for x of type `float`, the statement `cout << x;` outputs x rounded to six significant digits. In the preceding output, the values of x are rounded off to six decimal places. To get a better idea of what is going on internally, let us output x to more decimal places, say, eight. We can do this by including the file `<iomanip.h>` and placing the statement

```
cout << setprecision(8);
```

immediately before the `while` loop, as is done in program `trouble2.cpp`, to produce the following output.

```
0
0.1
0.2
0.30000001
0.40000001
0.5
0.60000002
0.70000005
0.80000007
0.9000001
1.0000001
1.1000001
        .
        .
        .
```

Now it is clear why the loop did not terminate. The actual values used for x in the test `while (x!=1)` were never exactly 1.

Rule

> Never use a loop condition that tests for exact inequality or exact equality of two floating point values.

■ **QUESTION**   We want to modify the program `trouble1.cpp` so that it outputs the values 0 through 0.9.

1. If the condition is changed to while (x <= .9), what will the output be? (*Hint:* Look at the output of trouble2.cpp.)

2. Fix the while condition so the output will be 0 through 0.9.

Answer
1. 0 through 0.8.

2. There are many ways to fix the while condition to achieve the output 0 through 0.9. One way is to use while (x <= .95). More generally, use while (x <= final_value + step/2). ■ ■■

■ **QUESTION** How would you fill in the blanks in the for loop of the program safeloop.cpp that follows so that it protects against an off-by-one error and outputs the table to the right?

```
1.0 squared is 1.00
1.2 squared is 1.44
1.4 squared is 1.96
1.6 squared is 2.56
1.8 squared is 3.24
2.0 squared is 4.00
```

```
// safeloop.cpp
#include <iostream.h>
#include "ourtools.h"

void main()
{
    float x;
    for (x = 1.0; _____; _____)
        {
        fixed_out(cout,1);
        cout << x << " squared is ";
        _____
        cout << x*x << endl;
        }
}
```

Answer The missing lines are

```
for(x = 1.0; x <= 2.1; x = x+0.2)
fixed_out(cout,2);
```

Note that the exit condition x <= 2.1 was obtained by adding the value of step/2 to the final value (x <= 2 + .2/2 produced x <= 2.1). ■ ■■

▦ Exercises

1. Give the output of the following fragment when m = 20 and when m = 50.

```
do {
    cout << m/2 << ' ';
    cout << m%2 << endl;
    m = m/2;
    }
while (m>0);
```

2. Give the output of the following code fragment when m = 4, when m = 7, and when m =10.

```
q = m;
while (q + m <= 24)
    {
    q = q + m;
    cout << q << ' ';
    }
```

3. Give the output of the following code fragment when limit is (a) 40 and (b) 100.

```
int n, sum, limit;
n=0; sum=0;
while (sum <= limit)
    {
    n++;
    sum = sum + n*n;
    }
cout << "sum first exceeds " << limit
        << " when you add " << n << " squared\n";
cout << "Sum is " << sum << endl;
```

4. What would the outputs of the preceding fragment be if it were written incorrectly, with the order of the two statements in the loop body reversed?

5. The following code fragment implements the Euclidean algorithm for calculating the greatest common divisor, or *gcd*, of two non-negative integers, a

and b. Trace its output when **(a)** a = 35, b = 21; **(b)** a = 10, b = 12; **(c)** a = 90, b = 108.

```
while (b>0)
    {
    r = a%b;
    a = b;
    b = r;
    cout << a << ' ' << b << ' ' << r << endl;
    }
cout << "gcd is " << a << endl;
```

6. **(a)** Using the code from `prime.cpp`, write a `bool`-valued function, `is_prime`, and add it to the library `myfuns.h`. (*Note:* Be sure to add code to the function so that it can also handle even integers.)

   (b) Write a program that uses a sentinel-controlled input loop to thoroughly test your `is_prime` function.

7. Write program fragments to output the first n positive integers, with each integer

   (a) preceded by two asterisks. (For example, if $n = 3$, output `**1**2**3`.)

   (b) surrounded by two asterisks. (For example, if $n = 3$, output `**1**2**3**`.)

   (c) separated by two asterisks. (For example, if $n = 3$, output `1**2**3`.)

8. Give the output of the following program fragment when **(a)** k = 2 **(b)** k = 3, and **(c)** k = 5.

```
i=1; m=1;
while (m < 50 && i != 5)
    {
    m = m*k;
    i++;
    cout << m << ' ';
    }
if (m<50)
    cout << "IN\n";
else
    cout << "OUT\n";
```

9. **(a)** Give the output of the following program fragment when (i) m = 35, n = 21; (ii) m = 10, n = 12; (iii) m = 90, n = 108.

```
save_m=m; save_n=n;
do {
    rem = m%n; m = n; n = rem;
    }
while (n>0);
cout << save_m/m*save_n << endl;
```

(b) In general, what is the final value output by the preceding program fragment?

10. Rewrite the following program fragment using a do..while loop with multiple exit conditions and no break statement.

```
for (day=1; day<=7; day++)
    {
    cout << "Noon temp: ";
    cin >> temp;
    if (temp<=32) break;
    }
if (temp <= 32)
    cout << "Freezing on noon of day " << day;
else
    cout << "No freezing noons this week."
```

11. (a) Give the output of the following program fragment when the user inputs are 20, 30, 40, and -1.

```
cout << "Max: "; cin >> max;
sum = 0;
while (max > 0)
    {
    i=1;
    do {
        sum += i; i+=2;
        }
    while (sum < max) ;
    cout << i << ' ' << sum << endl;
    cout << "\nMax: "; cin >> max;
    }
```

(b) If the statement `sum = 0;` were moved to immediately precede the inner `do..while` loop, what would be the output of the program fragment (for the same user inputs)?

12. What will be output by each of the following program fragments?

(a)

```
for (i=0; i<=2; i++)
   {
   cout << i << ' ';
   for (ch='A'; ch<='M'; ch+=3)
      cout << char(ch+i);
   cout << endl;
   }
```

(b)

```
for (r=2; r<=5; r++)
   {
   for (c=2; c<=5; c++)
      cout << setw(3)
           << r*c;
   cout << endl;
   }
```

13. Write program fragments that use nested `for` loops to produce outputs like the following, making sure that the user input is between 3 and 12.

(a)
```
Rows: 5

*
**
***
****
*****
```

(b)
```
Rows: 4

*
***
*****
*******
```

(c)
```
Rows: 4

****
***
**
*
```

Programming Problems

14. Write a program that inputs a single digit and then outputs a message saying whether that digit is even or odd. The fragment should include an error trap that ensures the input character is a digit. Write the fragment so that it contains no redundant character comparisons and so that the computer beeps whenever the user inputs a character other than a digit.

15. Write a program that will repeatedly generate three-digit numbers all of whose digits are unique. (Use algorithm A from the end of Section 8.3, with a `bool`-valued function `all_unique` that tells whether the function's `int` parameter consists of three distinct digits.)

16. Write a program to find the smallest n such that $1^2 + 3^2 + 5^2 + \cdots + n^2$ exceeds 1000. Display both n and the corresponding sum.

17. The program `asterisk.cpp` of Section 8.5 contains nested `for` loops. Simplify the nested loops by replacing the inner `for` loops with calls to a function that handles the task of printing a given character (a space or asterisk) a specified numbers of times.

18. Rewrite the loop of program `prime.cpp` as a `while` or `do..while` loop without using the `break` statement.

19. Write and test a function that uses a loop to count and then return the number of digits in its `long` parameter. Does the function work if it receives a negative argument?

20. For the sum $S(N) = 1 + 1/2 + 1/3 + \cdots + 1/N$, write a program to calculate the smallest integer, N, such that $S(N) > MAX$, where `MAX` is a user input. (For accuracy, use the `double` or `long double` data type.) Does your code work if `MAX` is large, say 10 or 15?

21. Write a program that will print the Ulam sequence for an input integer. Format the output so that it contains no more than ten numbers per line. The output should also give the length of the sequence. A typical run is

```
Enter an integer greater than one: 148
Ulam sequence of 148:
148    74    37    112    56    28    14     7    22    11
 34    17    52     26    13    40    20    10     5    16
  8     4     2      1
Length was 24
```

22. A famous number sequence is the Fibonacci sequence 1, 1, 2, 3, 5, 8, 13, 21, . . . , in which each element (beyond the first and second) is the sum of the previous two elements. Write a program that inputs a positive integer, n, then outputs the smallest Fibonacci number that exceeds n and its position in the Fibonacci sequence. A sample run is

```
Enter n>0: 100
144 is the smallest Fibonacci number greater than 100
It is the 12th Fibonacci number.
```

23. (a) Mexico's population in 1997 was 97.6 million and growing at the rate of 1.84% annually. If Mexico were to retain its 1.84% rate of growth, what is the first year in which its population would be over 120 million?

    (b) The U.S. population in 1997 was 268 million and growing at an annual rate of 0.89%. If Mexico and the United States were to maintain these rates of population growth, what is the first year in which the population of Mexico would exceed half that of the United States? What would the countries' respective populations be in that year?

24. At the beginning of 1998, Joe invested $100,000 at a rate of 5% compounded annually. At the end of each year, just after the interest has been added on, Joe intends to withdraw $12,000. What will be the first year at the end of which his balance will not permit such a withdrawal? What will be the balance then? Print a table that, for each year, gives the year, the balance after interest is added, and the balance after Joe's $12,000 withdrawal.

25. The radioactive substance strontium 90 has a decay rate of 2.4% per year.

    (a) Suppose you start with 50 grams of strontium 90. Write a program to determine the number of grams (to the nearest tenth) that remain after each year over a ten-year period.

    (b) Write a program to determine the half-life of strontium 90, that is, the number of years after which half of the original amount of strontium 90 has decayed. Your output should be of the form

    ```
    Strontium 90 half-life between m and n years
    ```

    where n is the smallest integer number of years after which less than half of the original amount is left.

26. When a ball is thrown upward at an angle of θ degrees and with initial velocity V_0, the height of the ball after t seconds is

    $$h(t) = V_0\, t \sin\theta - 16\, t^2$$

    How long will it take (to the nearest 0.1 second) for a ball thrown upward at an initial velocity of 144 ft. per second and at an angle of 60 degrees to reach its maximum height? What is that maximum height? How long (to the nearest 0.1 second) until the ball hits the ground? Print a table giving the time and the ball's height at 0.1-second intervals.

27. What is the largest factorial you can store in a variable of type long? (*Hint:* If x*y > LONG_MAX, then LONG_MAX/x < y.)

28. Use the gcd function of Exercise 8.6 in a program that repeatedly inputs the numerator and denominator of a fraction then outputs the fraction in reduced form.

29. Produce the bits (in reverse order) of the binary equivalent of a non-negative integer. (*Hints:* See the algorithm for decimal to binary conversion in Appendix F. When choosing between a pre-test or post-test loop, consider that $0_{10} = 0_2$.)

Longer Assignments

30. Write a program to print the prime factorization of a positive 32-bit integer. For example, if the input is 1960, the output will be

```
  1960 = 2^3 * 5 * 7^2
```

where $2\hat{\ }3$ represents 2^3.

31. Write a program to display all primes between two positive integers entered by the user.

32. (a) Code the Pythagorean triple generating algorithm of Section 8.4. Display all triples with legs whose lengths are between a user-specified minimum and maximum length.

    (b) Many of the triples generated by the given algorithm are multiples of another triple. For example, (6, 8, 10) and (9, 12, 15) are multiples of (3, 4, 5). Use a gcd function based on the Euclidean algorithm to determine whether the three integers of a given triple have a common factor and, if so, do not print that triple.

33. Write a program to simulate flipping a coin n times, where n is a user input. Output the longest streak of consecutive heads and the longest streak of consecutive tails. [*Hint*: Test this for small (<= 100) values of n, printing the result of each flip.]

    Can you also output the longest streak in which each flip alternates between heads and tails?

9

Functions with Reference Parameters

In Chapter 5 we began our discussion of functions and their use in program design. Recall that many subtasks were handled by function calls in `main`, with the code to implement these functions given elsewhere, thus keeping the body of `main` streamlined. There were, however, some kinds of subtasks that we were not yet ready to implement as functions, but which we will now discuss.

There are two types of parameters: *value parameters*, which have the safety feature that a function call cannot change the value of an argument matched with a value parameter, and *reference parameters*, which do allow a function call to change the value of a matched argument. In Chapter 5 we fully discussed value parameters and then, in Section 5.7, briefly introduced reference parameters. In this chapter we fully treat reference parameters, starting from the beginning, in case you skipped Section 5.7. As you will see, reference parameters greatly extend our ability to use functions to carry out subtasks. We will be able to further streamline `main` by using a function call (1) to handle the `cout` and `cin` statements for prompting for and reading input and (2) to handle subtasks, which, as part of their processing, increment or, in even more general ways, update variable(s) from the function call.

We also discuss the use of global constants and then present a systematic way to do hand tracing of code involving function calls.

213

9.1 Reference Parameters and Data Input Functions

Data Input Functions   When the code to read in keyboard input requires two or more pairs of `cout`-`cin` statements, you should consider handling this subtask by using a data input function call in `main`. Otherwise, these `cout` and `cin` statements clutter and obscure the `main` function's overall logical structure. As you will see, the variables that appear in the call to a data input function must be matched with reference parameters.

Reference Parameters and the Ampersand (&)   A reference parameter allows a function call to give a value to or update the current value of a variable argument appearing in the call. The ampersand, &, is used to let the compiler know that a parameter is a reference parameter. You must place the ampersand between the parameter's data type and its name in both the function declaration and the corresponding definition header. For example, in the following declaration, note that both the parameters, `f_name` and `party`, are reference parameters:

```
void get_voter_data(String& f_name, String& party);
```

(The parameter type `String&` is read "string reference.")

How a Reference Parameter Works   A reference parameter does not receive its own memory cell. Instead, it shares the memory cell of the matching argument from the calling statement. Further, this matching argument must be a variable rather than a constant or other expression. Within the function body the reference parameter becomes an alias for the matching variable in the calling statement. *Thus, any statement from the body of the function, which gives a value to a reference parameter, will actually give that value to the matching variable of the function call.*

   For example, in the following program, the function calling statement

```
get_voter_data(first_name, party);
```

matches `main`'s variable `first_name` with the parameter `f_name`. Then the statement

```
cin >> f_name;
```

in the body of the function will actually read the input value into `main`'s variable, `first_name`.

■ **EXAMPLE**   **(Campaign Letter)**   Local politician Alex Hundt believes in the personal touch in his campaign literature. Thus, his current campaign letter uses the voter's first name and party affiliation. The program to print this "personalized" campaign letter will use the function `get_voter_data` to input a voter's first name and party affiliation. Here is the definition of `get_voter_data`.

```
void get_voter_data(String& f_name, String& party)
{
    cout << "Enter voter's first name: ";
    cin >> f_name;
    cout << "Enter voter's party affiliation: ";
    cin >> party;
}
```

If Hundt's clerical worker were to enter Janice and Democrats, then the letter to Janice would appear as follows. (A different voter would receive the same letter, except with his or her own name and party.)

Dear Janice:
        If you are familiar with my record, you know
that I am not afraid to make tough decisions.
Rest assured that on the School Bond Issue, I will
work tirelessly to provide the highest quality
education for our youngsters, while keeping
property taxes as low as possible. To be effective
I especially need the support of Democrats like
yourself.

Sincerely,
Alex Hundt

Here is the program (minus function definitions) to generate the campaign letter.

```
// politic.cpp
#include <iostream.h>
#include "baString.h"

void get_voter_data (String& f_name, String& party);
// Get voter's first name and party affiliation

void do_campaign_letter (String f_name, String party);
// Print a "personalized" form letter.

void main()
```

```
{
    String first_name, party;
    get_voter_data(first_name, party);
    do_campaign_letter(first_name, party);
}
```

Discussion   Be aware that in the function `do_campaign_letter`, both parameters are value parameters, because this function does not give values to `first_name` and `party`, but merely uses their existing values.   ■ ▬

Decision: Same Name or Different Name   It does not matter whether a reference parameter and the matching variable in the call have the same name or different names — either way the memory cell of the variable in the call is used. For example, consider the following statements from the body of `get_voter_data`.

Statement	*Action*
`cin >> f_name;`	reads the input value into `main`'s `first_name`
`cin >> party;`	reads the input value into `main`'s `party`

Type Matching for Arguments and Reference Parameters   The following argument-parameter matching rule stems partly from the fact that a reference parameter uses the memory of the matching variable from the function call, whereas a value parameter has more latitude because it gets its own memory cell.

Argument-Parameter Matching Rule

> *Reference Parameters*   An argument matched with a reference parameter must be a variable. Moreover, the reference parameter and its matched argument *usually* must be of *exactly* the same type — the sole exception to exact matching for reference parameters is discussed in Section 11.9.
>
> *Value Parameters*   By contrast, argument and value parameter matching is less strict; the argument need not even be a variable, and its type may be any type that can be assigned to a variable whose type is that of the parameter.

Rewriting Other Data Input Code as Functions   In many of the programs from earlier chapters, `main` could easily have been streamlined more by using a data input function call to handle the `cout-cin` statements needed to obtain the input.

For example, in the car loan program of Section 5.6, the eight lines of code in `main` that prompt for and input data could be written as the single call

```
get_loan_data(amount, rate, months, annual_income);
```

Similarly, in the `payroll.cpp` program of Section 7.4, the four lines of `cout-cin` code can be replaced by the call

```
get_emp_data(name, hrs, rate);
```

Be aware, however, that in data sentinel programs with `while` loops (see Section 7.7), the splitting of `cout-cin` statements for a data group's input slightly complicates using a data input function call. Rather than discuss the technique for handling this complication, we leave this kind of data input code in `main`.

■ **EXAMPLE** (A User-Friendly `get_length` **Function**) Suppose we want to enter a length consisting of a `float` value followed by the scale, either inches or centimeters. For convenience, we will allow the user to input the scale as "in" or "cm" — all we really need is the first letter. We can put the details of this input into a function, `get_length`, whose declaration is

```
void get_length (float& len, char& scale);
// Input a length and scale (cm or in)
// Return scale as 'C' or 'I' and scan
// over any other chars on the input line.
```

and whose implementation is

```
void get_length (float& len, char& scale)
{
    String rest;
    cout << "Enter length and scale (cm. or in.): ";
    cin >> len >> scale;
    scale = toupper(scale);
    getline (cin, rest); // of chars on line
}
```

In response to the input prompt, the user could enter 7.5 inches as any of 7.5in, 7.5 In., 7.5 inches, or just 7.5 I. The input routine is robust enough to handle any of these formats, yet none of the details of the subtask are in main. Further, the function could use the error trapping method of Section 8.2 to ensure that the user entered either inches or centimeters for the scale.   ▪ ▬

Functions That Calculate More than One Value   You can use a void function with reference parameters for subtasks other than data input. For example, in the next problem the void function with reference parameters calculates several values and assigns those values to variables in main.

▪ **QUESTION**   How would you write a definition for a function, do_circle_calcs, with parameters r, A, and C, so that the call

do_circles_calcs (rad, area, circum);

will calculate the area and circumference of a circle of radius rad and assign those values to area and circum, respectively?

Answer   The definition of do_circle_calcs (from circle.cpp, at the PWS Web site) is

```
void do_circle_calcs (float r,
                      float& A, float& C)
{
    const float PI = 3.14159
    A = PI * r * r;
    C = 2 * PI * r;
}
```

Notice that r is a value parameter.   ▪ ▬

9.2   Incrementing a Variable with a Function Call

Another common use of reference parameters is to enable a function to increment one or more of the variable arguments of the function call, especially summing or counting variables.

▪ **EXAMPLE**   Consider the following fragment from the main function of the program payroll.cpp (Section 7.4). We will rewrite main by using two functions. The function get_emp_data will prompt for and input an employee's data, and the function `process_emp` will handle the (highlighted) code to process that employee's data. Note that as part of this processing, `total_wages` must be increased by an amount equal to the current employee's `wage`.

```
total_wages = 0.0;
for (emp=1; emp<=num_emps; emp+=1)
    {
    cout << "Employee's last name: ";
    cin >> name;
    cout << "Hours worked and rate: ";
    cin >> hours >> rate;
    wage = hours * rate;
    vprn << name << " $" << wage << endl;
    total_wages += wage;
    } // end for
vprn << "Total payroll: $" << total_wages
        << endl;
```

The definition of `process_emp` is

```
void process_emp (String name, int hrs, float rate,
                    float& total)
{
    float pay;
    pay = hrs * rate;
    vprn << name << " $" << pay << endl;
    total += pay;
}
```

In the program below, `main` will contain the call

```
process_emp(name, hours, rate, total_wages);
```

Here, because `total` is a reference parameter and is matched with `total_wages`, the effect of the statement

```
total += pay;
```

in the body of `process_emp` will be to add `pay` to `total_wages`.

Here is the `main` function of program `payroll2.cpp`, the rewritten version of `payroll.cpp`. Its `for` loop is much more concise than that of `payroll.cpp`.

```
void main()
{
    int emp, num_emps, hours;
    float rate, total_wages;
    String name;

    cout << "PAYROLL PROGRAM\n";
    cout << "How many employees? ";
    cin >> num_emps;
    fixed_out(vprn, 2);
    total_wages = 0.0;
    for (emp=1; emp<=num_emps; emp+=1)
        {
        get_emp_data (name, hours, rate);
        process_emp (name, hours, rate, total_wages);
        }  // end for
    vprn << "Total payroll: $" << total_wages
         << endl;
}
```

PITFALL: OMITTING & FOR AN INTENDED REFERENCE PARAMETER
When a reference parameter is intended, omitting the & can have significant, undesirable consequences.

■ **QUESTION**   Suppose that & had been omitted when declaring the type of the parameter `total` in the `process_emp` function. How would the output differ?

Answer   The last line of the output would have been

```
Total payroll: $0.00
```

because `main`'s variable, `total_wages`, would have been matched with a value parameter and thus would not have its value changed by any of the calls to `process_emp`. ■ ▬

Using a Function to Change a Variable in the Calling Statement
There are two ways to change a variable in a statement that calls a function. One is to use a reference parameter as discussed in this chapter.
    A second method is to use a value-returning function within an assignment statement as discussed in Chapter 5. For example, if `find_this`

is a value-returning function, and if b and sum are variables from main, then the statements

```
b = find_this(x,y);
sum = sum + find_this(x, y);
```

would change the values of b and sum by assignment.

In some situations, either of these methods is okay. However, you should be aware of the following style rule, which restricts the use of value-returning functions.

Style Rule for Value-Returning Functions

> A value-returning function should be used only when the sole purpose of the function is to *calculate and return a single value.* The body of a value-returning function should not read in or print out any values (except possibly during the debugging stage).

Furthermore, in later chapters we will use reference parameters as an efficient way to pass certain kinds of large data structures to functions. A value-returning function with such a reference parameter should not alter that parameter.

■ **QUESTION** Suppose the program payroll2.cpp were rewritten to use a value-returning function, find_pay, in the call

```
total_wages += find_pay(name, hours ,rate);
```

Here, find_pay calculates the employee's wage, prints the employee's name and pay, and then return's the value of pay to main, where it is added onto total_wages by the above assignment statement. Comment on this design in light of the preceding style rule for value-returning functions.

Answer This design would get the job done, but it is in bad style — the body of a value-returning function should not contain any output statements.

■ ▬

9.3 More General Variable Updating by Using Function Calls

In a sense, all the uses of reference parameters discussed thus far have involved using a function call to update the value of a variable. Even data input functions like get_voter_data from Section 9.1 updated the values of first_name and party, which, prior to the function call, were uninitialized (garbage) values.

Swapping Two *int* Values   Suppose x and y are int variables storing the values 5 and 9, respectively. We want to write code to swap, or interchange, the values stored in x and y. Note that the code

```
x = y; // x is overwritten!
y = x;
```

does not work — the first statement erases the starting value of x, so that both x and y will equal 9 after these two statements have executed.

The correct way to switch the values of x and y is to use another variable, say temp, to *temporarily* store the starting value of x before assigning the value of y to x. The correct code is

```
temp = x;
x = y;
y = temp;
```

A mnemonic device for remembering this code is: Notice that temp appears on the *left* side of the first statement and on the *right* side of the last statement. Also notice that one of the two diagonals has x and the other has y.

In the following diagram, the contents of x, y, and temp are shown before and after each of the preceding three assignment statements.

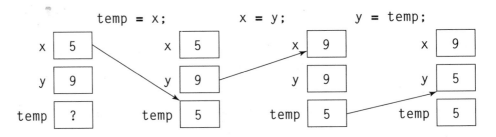

The swap function given in the next program swaps the String values stored in its two *reference* parameters s and t. Thus, a call such as

```
swap (w1, w2);
```

actually swaps the contents of the variables w1 and w2, because s and t are aliases for (use the same memory cells as) w1 and w2, respectively.

■ **PROBLEM**   **(Alphabetizing Words)**   The following program fragment from alpha3.cpp alphabetizes three input words as illustrated in the accompanying sample runs. Notice that the statement

```
if (w1 > w2) swap(w1, w2);
```

will ensure that w1 and w2 are in alphabetical order. Study the sample runs, then complete the missing line from main and write the definition of swap.

```
Enter 3 words: ram ewe lamb
ewe lamb ram

Enter 3 words: screw pulley cog
cog pulley screw
```

Sample runs

```
void swap (String& s, String& t);
// Swap contents of s and t.

void main()
{
    String w1, w2, w3;
    cout << "Enter 3 words: ";
    cin >> w1 >> w2 >> w3;
    if (w1 > w2) swap(w1,w2);
    if (w1 > w3) swap(w1,w3);
    // alphabetically smallest word is now in w1.
    _____;
    cout << w1 << ' ' << w2 << ' ' << w3 << endl;
}
```

Solution The completed statement from main is

```
if (w2 > w3) swap(w2, w3);
```

and the definition of swap is

```
void swap (String& s, String& t)
{
    String temp;
    temp = s;
    s = t;
    t = temp;
}
```

Note that temp must be declared as a local variable.

Templates and the Need for Flexibility   You cannot use the previous swap function to swap the values of two int variables because a reference parameter and its matching argument must be of the same type. You could, however, write a second, structurally similar swap function having two int reference parameters. (In the next chapter, you will see that in C++, under certain circumstances, *several functions can have the same name.* Such functions are said to be ***overloaded***.) Additionally, to swap the values of two float variables, you could write a third swap function having two parameters of type float&.

Certainly, though, it would be better if a single swap function could be defined and then called to swap two String, int, or float values, without your having to write a different version of the function for each data type you might need to swap. In the next chapter, we will discuss how to use ***template functions*** to accomplish this.

Decision: Reference or Value Parameter   If you want a variable argument in a function call to be initialized or updated by the called function, then the matching parameter in the function must be a *reference* parameter.

■ **QUESTION**   Study the following sample runs and code fragment (from fracs.cpp). How would you fill in the blanks in the function declarations?

```
Enter a fraction (num/den): 9/15
9/15 reduces to 3/5

Enter a fraction (num/den): 21 / 7
21/7 reduces to 3

Enter a fraction (num/den): 5/8
5/8 reduces to 5/8
```

Sample runs

Fragment from fracs.cpp

```
void reduce (_____ num, _____ den);
// reduce if necessary

void get_frac (_____ num, _____ den);
// input num and den
```

```
void put_frac (_____ num, _____ den);
// output num/den

void main()
{
   int numerator, denominator;
   cout << "Enter a fraction (num/den): ";
   get_frac (numerator, denominator);
   put_frac (numerator, denominator);
   cout << " reduces to ";
   reduce (numerator, denominator);
   put_frac (numerator, denominator);
   cout << endl;
}
```

Answer   Reference parameters are needed in get_frac (data input functions always use reference parameters for variables receiving input) and in
reduce, where we want potentially new values to be assigned to the arguments, numerator and denominator, of the call. Functions that output
previously calculated results take value parameters. Thus, the completed
lines are

```
void reduce (int& num, int& den);
void get_frac (int& num, int& den);
void put_frac (int num, int den);
```

9.4 Global Constants

In the programs we have presented thus far, all the user-defined constants and variables have been local to functions, including the function
main. Constants, variables, and other identifiers may be declared *globally*
by placing their declarations after the program's include statements and
before the function declarations. The scope of a global constant or variable is the entire program.

WARNING   For now, a good style rule is *not* to declare any global *variables* in your programs because global variables greatly increase the risk
of side effects. For a dramatic example of a side effect caused in part by
global variables and resulting in the death of a patient, see the Short
Stays R Us Hospital example at the PWS Web site in oh_oh.cpp. In that
example, the side effect is caused by a global variable and an intended
local variable (which the programmer forgot to declare), both having the
same name. As a consequence, code in the function body that was in-

tended to give a value to the intended local variable actually changed the value of the global variable.

Global Constants Are Good Style   It is generally a good idea to declare *constants* globally. When a constant is needed locally in several different locations, not only is it more convenient to give its definition just once, but it is also easier to check that the value of the constant is typed correctly because you need only look in one place. *Be aware that no side effects can result from a global constant*, because its value cannot be changed by any program statement.

■ **EXAMPLE**   Consider the following sample runs and program. (Notice that the constant CM_PER_IN is defined globally because it is needed by both the conversion functions.)

```
Enter a length and scale (cm or in): 7.25 in
7.25 in. = 18.415 cm.

Enter a length and scale (cm or in): 42cm.
42 cm. = 16.5354 in.
```

Sample runs

```cpp
// convert.cpp
#include <iostream.h>
#include <ctype.h>
#include "baString.h"

const float CM_PER_IN = 2.54; // global constant

void get_length (float& len,
                 char& scale);
// Input a length and scale (cm or in)
// Return scale as 'C' or 'I' and skip
// over any other chars on line.

void convert_in2cm(float len);
// Convert a length in in. to cm. and display it.
```

```
void convert_cm2in(float len);
// Convert a length in cm. to in. and display it.

void main()
{
    float len;
    char scale;
    get_length (len, scale);
    if (scale=='I')
        convert_in2cm(len);
    else
        convert_cm2in(len);
}

void convert_in2cm(float len)
{
    cout << len << " in. = "
        << len*CM_PER_IN << " cm.\n";
}

void convert_cm2in(float len)
{
    cout << len << " cm. = "
        << len/CM_PER_IN << " in.\n";
}

void get_length (float& len, char& scale)
{
    cout << "Enter length and scale (cm. or in.): ";
    cin >> len >> scale;
    scale = toupper(scale);
    cin.ignore (80, '\n'); // ignore rest of line
}
```

Again, note that CM_PER_IN was declared as a global constant by placing its const declaration after the program's include statements and before the function declarations.

9.5   Hand Tracing

To understand parameter passing, it is helpful to have a systematic method for hand tracing program execution when both value and reference parameters are involved. We present such a method in this and the next section.

■ **QUESTION**   What will be printed by the following program?

```cpp
// trace1.cpp
#include <iostream.h>

void junk (int x, int& y);

void main()
{
    int x, y;
    x = 4; y = 20;
    cout << x << ' ' << y <<" in main\n";
    junk (x, y);
    cout << x << ' ' << y <<" in main\n";
    junk (x, y);
    cout << x << ' ' << y <<" in main\n";
}

void junk (int x, int& y)
{
    x = x + 2;
    y = y + 5;
    cout << x << ' ' << y <<" in junk\n";
}
```

Answer

```
4 20 in main
6 25 in junk
4 25 in main
6 30 in junk
4 30 in main
```

Output

Here is a hand trace for the previous program.

```
Memory of main    │  Memory of junk
 ┌───┬───┐        │
 │ x │ y │        │
 ├───┼───┤ ─ ─ ─ ─│─ ─ ─ ─ ─ ─ ─ ─ ─ ─ ─ ─ ─ ─ ─ ─ ─ ─ ─ ─
 │ 4 │20 │        │
 └ ─ ┴ ─ ┘ ─ ─ ─ ─│─ ─ ─ ─ ─ ─ ─ ─ ─ ─ ─ ─ ─ ─ ─ ─ ─ ─ ─ ─
                  │        junk( x,    y )      1st call
                  │               ↓     ‖
                  │      params  ┌x┐    y
                  │              ├─┤
                  │              │4│
 │  25  │         │              │6│
 ─ ─ ─ ─ ─ ─ ─ ─ ─│─ ─ ─ ─ ─ ─ ─└─┘─ ─ ─ ─ ─ ─ ─
                  │        junk( x,    y )      2nd call
                  │               ↓     ‖
                  │      params  ┌x┐    y
                  │              ├─┤
                  │              │4│
 │  30  │         │              │6│
                  │              └─┘
```

Hand Trace Format Note that we:

1. Used the left side of the page for the memory cells of the function main and the right side for the memory cells of the function junk.

2. Aligned each function parameter directly underneath the corresponding argument of the calling statement. The down arrow (↓) for a value parameter indicates that the value parameter receives the value of its corresponding argument. The vertical equals symbol (‖) for a reference parameter indicates that the reference parameter uses the memory cell of the corresponding argument.

3. Used dashed horizontal lines to separate different function calls.

■ **QUESTION** What will be printed by the following program?

```cpp
// trace2.cpp
#include <iostream.h>

void funk (int& x, int y);

void main()
{
    int a, b, w;
    a = 0; b = 0; w = 0;
```

```
      funk (a, b);
      cout << a << ' ' << b << ' ' << w << '\n';
      a += 20;
      w += 20;
      funk (a, b);
      cout << a << ' ' << b << ' ' << w << '\n';
   }

   void funk (int& x, int y)
   {
      int w;
      w = 5;
      x++;
      y = w + 2;
      cout << x << ' ' << y << ' ' << w
           << " in funk\n'';

   }
```

Answer

```
1 7 5 in funk
1 0 0
22 7 5 in funk
22 0 20
```

Here is the trace.

9.6   Tracing with Order Switched

■ **QUESTION**   What will be printed by the following program?

```
// trace3.cpp
#include <iostream.h>

void jumble (int& x, int& y, int z);

void main()
{
    int a, b, c;
    a = 10; b = 20; c = 30;
    jumble (b, c, a); // note the unnatural order
    cout << a << ' ' << b << ' ' << c << '\n';
    jumble (c, a, b); // another unnatural order
    cout << a << ' ' << b << ' ' << c << '\n';
}

void jumble (int& x, int& y, int z)
{
    x++;      y += 2;      z = z + 3;
    cout << x << ' ' << y << ' ' << z << '\n';
}
```

Answer

```
21 32 13
10 21 32
33 12 24
12 21 33
```

Here is the trace.

Memory of main			Memory of jumble
a	b	c	
10	20	30	
			jumble(b, c, a) 1st call
			$\parallel$ $\parallel$ ↓
			x y z
			10
	21	32	13
			jumble(c, a, b) 2nd call
			$\parallel$ $\parallel$ ↓
			x y z
			21
12		33	24

■ Exercises

1. Give the output of

```
void some_fun (int p, int& q);

void main()
{
    int m=0, n=0;
    some_fun (m, n);
    cout << m << ' ' << n;
}

void some_fun (int p, int& q)
{   p = 5; q = 10; }
```

2. Give the output of

```
void other_fun (int& p, int& q, int& r);

void main()
{
    int m=8, n=13, p=21;
    other_fun (m, n, p);
    cout << m << ' ' << n << ' ' << p << endl;;
}

void other_fun (int& p, int& q, int& r)
{
    int t=p; p=q; q=r; r=t;
}
```

3. Give the output of

```
void str_fun (String& s1, String s2);

void main()
{
    String r="ABRA", s="CAD";
    str_fun (s, r);
    cout << r << ' ' << s << endl;
```

```
        str_fun (r, s);
        str_fun (s, "KAZAMM");
        cout << r << ' ' << s << endl;
    }


    void str_fun (String& s1, String s2)
    {   s1 = s1 + s2;   }
```

4. Give the output of

```
void junk (int& n);

int c = 5; // global

void main()
{
    int a=7;
    junk (a);
    cout << a << ' ' << c << endl;
    junk (a);
    cout << a << ' ' << c << endl;
}

void junk (int& n)
{
    n = n + c;
    c = c + n;
}
```

5. What would be output by the program of the previous exercise if:
   (a) The statement int c = 5; were inserted at the beginning of the function junk?
   (b) The statement int c = 3; were inserted at the beginning of the function main?

6. Write a function to convert kilograms to pounds and ounces, accurate to the nearest ounce. (*Hint*: There are 0.45 kilograms per pound.)

7. Write a function to convert a total number of inches to yards, feet, and inches without altering the total number of inches.

8. Write a function that sorts its three string parameters in alphabetical order. (*Hint*: Use the swap function of Section 9.3.)

Programming Problems

9. Rewrite the Car Loan program of Section 5.6 using the `get_loan_data` function (described in Section 9.1) to prompt for and input the loan amount, annual interest rate, loan lifetime, and annual income.

10. Rewrite the `payroll.cpp` program of Section 7.4 using the `get_emp_data` function described in Section 9.1 to prompt for and input each employee's name, hours, and pay rate.

11. Write a program to prompt for and input the total amount of a customer's purchases and the amount of money tendered by the customer. Then, determine the fewest number of bills (ones, fives, tens, and twenties) and coins (pennies, nickels, dimes, and quarters) to return to the customer in change. (*Hints*: Use a function for determining the number of dollars and the number of cents to return in change. Use one function for determining the number of bills of each denomination to return and another for determining the number of coins of each denomination to return.)

12. Write and test functions to convert rectangular coordinates to polar, and vice versa. To convert polar coordinates (r, θ) to rectangular coordinates (x, y), use the equation:

$$x = r\cos\theta \quad \text{and} \quad y = r\sin\theta$$

13. Write a program that uses the functions `add`, `sub`, `mul`, and `div` to compute the sum, difference, product, and quotient, respectively, of two complex numbers.

14. The Livelong Insurance Company offers insurance policies at low premiums because it insures only applicants who smoke fewer than six cigarettes per day and weigh under 180 pounds. Write a program that will process a list of applicants, where input for each applicant consists of name, number of cigarettes smoked daily, and weight. The virtual printer output should include:

- Each applicant's name, number of cigarettes smoked daily, and weight, along with a message stating whether the applicant has been ACCEPTED or REJECTED. If the applicant has been rejected, the reason(s) should be printed.

- The average number of cigarettes smoked daily and the average weight for those applicants who have been accepted and those who have been rejected.

Longer Assignments

15. Do Exercise 5.27 of Chapter 5 using a function to input the time and a function to update the time by a number of minutes.

16. Do Exercise 6.15 of Chapter 6 using a function to prompt for and input the information for each quiz.

17. Do Exercise 6.16 of Chapter 6 using a function to prompt for and input the name, quantity purchased, and unit price of each item.

18. Do Exercise 7.20 of Chapter 7 using a function to prompt for and input each employee's name, hours worked, and pay rate.

19. Write a program that will generate, but not display, a three-digit "target" number that has three distinct digits. (*Hint*: Use one of the algorithms at the end of Section 8.3.) Then, input a maximum of eight user guesses and, for each guess, output the number of "hits" and "matches" in the guess. Stop when the user guesses the correct number or runs out of guesses.

    For example, if the target number is 427, the guess 207 has one hit (7) and one match (2), the guess 749 has two matches (4 and 7), and the guess 327 has two hits (2 and 7).

10

More on Functions

This chapter contains several function related topics. First, we present a method for documenting function parameters in order to clarify the flow of data into and out of the function. Then, we introduce the use of **structure charts** for designing a program and also for documenting its top-down structure. The remaining sections of the chapter are devoted to special kinds of functions — overloaded functions, functions with default arguments, function templates, member functions, and recursive functions. In later chapters we will use the power and flexibility provided by these special kinds of functions.

10.1 Documenting Parameters — IN, OUT, or IN-OUT

Parameters and Data Flow Data flows into and out of a function by way of the function's parameters. Knowing whether a function has value parameters or reference parameters gives some information about the **data flow**, but it does not tell the whole story. You can document a function's data flow, and thus enhance its clarity and readability, by placing an appropriate comment, //IN, //OUT, or //IN-OUT, after each parameter's declaration.

1. IN **Parameters** A value parameter is always used to pass the argument's value IN to a function. Thus, value parameters are also referred to as *IN parameters*.

2. **OUT Parameters versus IN-OUT parameters** A reference parameter is used to pass a value back *out* of the function to the matched argument. This can occur in two situations:

   (a) OUT When the value passed back to the argument is not based on the previous value of the matched argument. For example, when a "get data" function reads values into a reference parameter, that parameter is an *OUT parameter*.

   (b) IN-OUT When the value passed back is an update of the value of the argument that was passed into the function at the time of the function call. For example, when a function updates a counter that is a reference parameter, that parameter is an *IN-OUT parameter*.

■ **QUESTION** (**Reducing a Fraction**) After looking at the following sample run and the fragment of source code (from `fracs.cpp`), how would you fill in the blanks with int or int&, and indicate which parameters are IN, OUT, and IN-OUT?

```
Enter a fraction (num/den): 9/15
9/15 reduces to 3/5
```

Sample run

Fragment from `fracs.cpp`

```
void get_frac (_____ num,  // _____
               _____ den); // _____
void reduce (_____ num,  // _____
             _____ den); // _____
void output_frac (_____ num,  // _____
                  _____ den); // _____
void main()
{
    int numerator, denominator;
    cout << "Enter a fraction (num/den): ";
    get_frac (numerator, denominator);
    output_frac (numerator, denominator);
    cout << " reduces to ";
    reduce (numerator, denominator);
    output_frac (numerator, denominator);
    cout << endl;
}
```

Answer   The completed lines are

```
void get_frac (int& num,  // out
                   int& den); // out
void reduce (int& num,  // in-out
                int& den); // in-out
void output_frac (int num,  // in
                     int den); // in
```

■ **QUESTION**   **(The** reduce **Function)**   In preparation for the next section (on structure charts), how would you fill in the blanks in the following definition of the reduce function? Note that reduce calls the gcd function (from myfuns.h) in order to find the greatest common divisor of two integers.

```
void reduce (int& num, int& den)
{
    int gc_div;
    gc_div = _____;
    num = num/gc_div;
    _____;
}
```

Answer   The completed lines should be

```
gc_div = gcd(num,den);
den = den/gc_div;
```

■ ▬

10.2 Structure Charts

A *structure chart* is a diagram that depicts the top-down structure of a program and that includes an analysis of data flow between functions. It can be used as a form of documentation as well as a tool in designing the program.

■ **EXAMPLE**   Below is a structure chart for the fracs.cpp program of the previous section. Starting from the box on the left, the function get_frac assigns values to main's variables numerator and denominator. The call to reduce then (potentially) modifies the values of numerator and denominator. Finally, in the rightmost box, the function output_frac displays the reduced fraction.

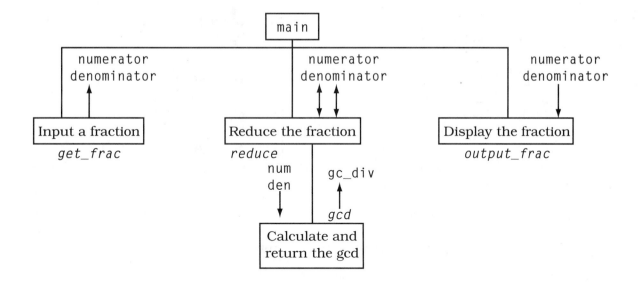

REMARK Notice the difference between the use of an up arrow to indicate OUT parameters from the function get_frac and to indicate a return value from the gcd function. ▪ ▬

Some Structure Chart Conventions Used in This Book

1. **Boxes** Each box contains a description of what that program segment does.

   (a) When the action in a box is carried out by a function, heavy lines will be used for the box border.

   (b) Otherwise, a dashed line will be used for the border.

2. **Function names** The function name will be placed *under* the box if the function is void, but *over* the box if the function returns a value.

3. **Arrows and data flow for a parameter** We will use down arrows (↓) for IN parameters, up arrows (↑) for OUT parameters or the value returned by value-returning functions, and double arrows (↕) for IN-OUT parameters.

■ **PROBLEM** **(Using a Structure Chart in Program Design)** In a certain course that is marked on a pass-fail basis (where pass requires an average score of 60 or better), each student has taken two tests. Write a program that prints each student's name, scores, average, and grade, and then prints how many students passed and the highest score on each test.

Here is a sample run showing the interactive dialog on the monitor and the program's output to the virtual printer.

```
How many students? 3
Last name: Adams
Scores:     60 70
Last name: Bond
Scores:     75 40
Last name: Clark
Scores      70 82
```

Interactive dialog

```
Adams   60 70 65.0   Pass
Bond    75 40 57.5   Fail
Clark   70 82 76.0   Pass
2 students passed.
Highest score on exam 1: 75
Highest score on exam 2: 82
```

Virtual printer output

A pseudocode algorithm for this problem is

Get the number of students, num_students.
initialize pass_count and max1, max2
for (i=1; i<=num_students; i++)
    get_data   Get a student name and two scores.
    find_mark   Find and print a student's average and mark;
                    update pass_count if necessary.
    update_maxes   Update max1 and max2 if necessary.
print_summary   Print final summary (after the loop).

QUESTION Study the preceding pseudocode algorithm for the problem. Then, give a next level of pseudocode by completing the function call statements using the arguments

```
name, score1, score2,
pass_count, max1, max2
```

Put a down, up, or up-down arrow over each argument in a function call to indicate whether that argument corresponds to an IN, OUT, or IN-OUT parameter, respectively.

Answer Here is the next level of pseudocode.

```
cin >> num_students;
pass_count = 0;
max1 = -1; max2 = -1;
for (i=1; i<=num_students; i++)
```

```
    {
              ↑        ↑        ↑
    get_data (name, score1, score2);
              ↓        ↓        ↓       ↕
    find_mark (name, score1, score2, pass_count);
                       ↓        ↓       ↕       ↕
    update_maxes (score1, score2, max1, max2);
    }
              ↓        ↓        ↓
print_summary (pass_count, max1, max2);
```

Here is the structure chart based on the previous pseudocode.

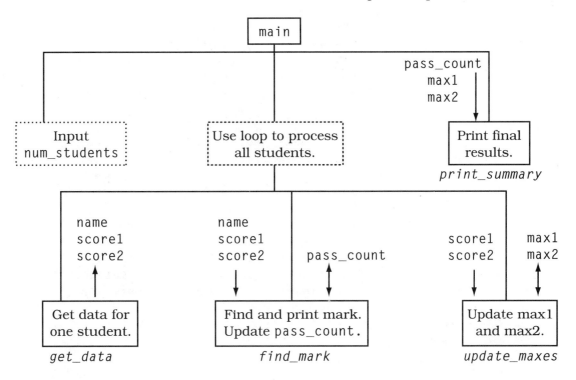

Here are the definitions of all the functions, including main, from the program class.cpp.

Function Declarations from class.cpp

```
void get_data (String& name,         // out
               int& scr1, int&scr2); // out
```

```
void find_mark (String name,           // in
                int scr1, int scr2,    // in
                int& count);           // in-out

void update_maxes (int scr1, int scr2,     // in
                   int &max1, int& max2); // in-out

void print_summary (int pass_count,        // in
                    int max1, int max2);   // in
```

Main Function of *class.cpp*

```
void main()
{
    int num_students;
    String name;
    int score1, score2,
        max1, max2,
        pass_count;

    cout << "How many students? ";
    cin >> num_students;

    pass_count = 0;
    max1 = -1;  max2 = -1;
    for (int i=1; i <= num_students; i++)
        {
        get_data (name, score1, score2);
        find_mark (name, score1, score2, pass_count);
        update_maxes (score1, score2, max1, max2);
        }
    print_summary (pass_count, max1, max2);
}
```

Function Definitions from *class.cpp*

```
void get_data (String& name,        // out
               int& scr1, int&scr2) // out
{
    cout << "Last name: "; cin >> name;
    cout << "Scores:     "; cin >> scr1 >> scr2;
}
```

```
void find_mark (String name,         // in
                int scr1, int scr2, // in
                int& count)          // in-out
{
    float avg;
    avg = (scr1 + scr2) / 2.0;
    fixed_out(vprn,1);
    vprn << name << setw(10-name.length()) << scr1
        << setw(3) << scr2 << setw(5) << avg;
    if (avg >= 60)
        {
        vprn << " Pass\n";
        count++;
        }
    else
        vprn << " Fail\n";
}

void update_maxes (int scr1, int scr2,   // in
                   int &max1, int& max2) // in-out
{
    if (scr1 > max1) max1 = scr1;
    if (scr2 > max2) max2 = scr2;
}

void print_summary (int pass_count,      // in
                    int max1, int max2) // in
{
    vprn << pass_count << " students passed.\n";
    vprn << "Highest score on exam 1: " << max1 << endl;
    vprn << "Highest score on exam 2: " << max2 << endl;
}
```

NOTE In main, we used the shortcut method for initializing max1 and max2. If you wanted to use score1 and score2 to initialize max1 and max2, you would need to process the first student separately before the loop.

10.3 Overloaded Functions

Functions that share the same name are said to be *overloaded*. Function overloading can simplify the job of thinking up names for two or more functions that perform different versions of essentially the same task — such functions can all be given the same name. C++ allows different functions to have the same name (i.e., to be overloaded) as long as their declarations differ with regard to either the *number* of parameters or the *data type* of at least one parameter. Thus, the compiler must be able to use the *function signature* — the number and types of arguments in the function call — to determine which version of the function to call.

■ **EXAMPLE**   **(Overloaded** round **Function)**   The file myfuns.h on the PWS Web site contains two different functions with the name round. Their declarations are

```
double round (double x);
    // round to the nearest integer

double round (double x, int d);
    //round to d decimal places
```

The one-parameter version of round is provided because it nicely complements the ceil and floor functions that are provided in math.h. (See the discussion of ceil, floor, and rounding in Section 5.1.) The two-parameter version is provided as a useful generalization of the one-parameter version. See myfuns.h for the two-parameter version's definition.

In a program that includes the file myfuns.h and in which a, b, and x are of type double, the following statements have the indicated effect.

```
x = 56.3762;
a = round(x);    // a becomes 56 (x unchanged)
b = round(x, 2); // b becomes 56.38 (x unchanged)
```

However, if myfuns.h had contained only the declaration and definition of the two-parameter version of round, then

```
a = round(x);    // would be illegal
a = round(x, 0); // would round to nearest int
```

■ **PROBLEM**   Two different formulas for the area of a triangle are:

1.   Base and height formula:

$$\text{area} = \frac{\text{base} * \text{height}}{2}$$

2.   Three sides (Hero's) formula:

$$\text{area} = \sqrt{(s(s{-}a)(s{-}b)(s{-}c))}$$

where *a*, *b*, and *c* are the three sides and $s = \dfrac{a+b+c}{2}$

Note that for a 3, 4, 5 right triangle the base is 3 and the height is 4, so the area, calculated by the base-height formula, is 6. You should verify that the more complicated Hero's formula also gives area equal to 6.

Write a program that can compute the area of a triangle from its base and height as well as from the lengths of its sides.

■ **QUESTION** Complete the missing lines of main in the following program fragment (from tri_over.cpp). Note that the program declares both a two-parameter and a three-parameter version of the function tri_area.

```
double tri_area (double base, double height);
// Base & Height formula
double tri_area (double a, double b, double c);
// Three Side formula

void main()
{
    float base, height,
          s1, s2, s3,
          area;

    cout << "Enter base and height of a triangle: ";
    cin >> base >> height;
    area = _____;
    cout << "Area = '' << area << endl;
    cout << "Enter lengths of sides of a triangle: ";
    cin >> s1 >> s2 >> s3;
    cout << "Area = " _____;
}
// function definitions
 .  .  .  .  .  .  .  .  .  .  .  .  .
```

Answer The missing lines are

```
        area = tri_area(base,height);
        cout << "Area = " << tri_area(s1, s2, s3) << endl;
```

The program tri_over.cpp at the PWS Web site is nearly complete — the two tri_area functions are coded as stubs. Exercise 10.13 asks you to write the actual definitions of these functions. ■ ▬

Exact Match of Data Types Not Necessary If the data types of the arguments in a function call do not exactly match the data types of the parameters in the declaration, the compiler will look for a "closest fit" among the version(s) of the function. Thus, if only one function has the name max, and this function has the declaration

```
double max (double x, double y);
    // return larger of x and y
```

then max could be called with int arguments. However, if the program had also declared the second version of max

```
int max (int m, int n);
```

then a call of max with int arguments would use this second version because the match would be exact. (The only difference would be minor — the data type of the returned value would be int instead of double.)

By contrast, if a program declared *only* the int version of max, then a call to max with arguments of type double would be the closest fit, but the passing of double arguments to int parameters would, in most cases, result in lost precision.

math.h **Does Not Use Overloading**　After seeing overloaded functions, you might wonder why math.h gives different names (abs, labs, fabs, fabsl) to each of its versions of the absolute value function, instead of overloading the single name abs. The reason is historical — much of the math.h library was created in the days of C, when function overloading was not permitted.

10.4　Functions with Default Arguments

In some situations you can declare and define a single function with *default arguments* instead of giving two or more different function declarations and definitions. A function with default arguments can be called without all of its arguments specified in the call. When arguments are unspecified in a call, the corresponding parameters receive the default values.

■ **EXAMPLE**　(**The** round **Function**)　It is desirable for each of the following calls to be legal:

```
a = round(x);
b = round(x, 2);
```

This can be achieved either by:

  1. Overloading two round functions. Declare and define *two* different round functions as was done in myfuns.h and discussed in the previous section.

2. Writing a single round function with default parameter(s). Declare and define the following version of round, with d as a default parameter having default value d = 0.

```
double round(double x, int d = 0);
```

Thus, the call round(x) would actually be the call round(x,0) because the default value, 0, would be supplied for the second argument.

The *definition* of this round function would be identical to the myfuns.h two-parameter version.

Ambiguity You cannot declare both the default argument version and the overloaded versions of round because doing so would create an ambiguous situation for the compiler — the compiler cannot decide which version to execute for a call such as

```
m = round(x,2); // ambiguous if both default and
                //  overloaded versions declared
```

The `getline` *Function and Default Arguments* We have used the getline function in statements like getline (cin, sentence); to read all characters up to the end of an input line into a String variable. This function has a third parameter whose default value is the newline character, '\n'. We can specify a different value for this third parameter in the call to getline.

■ **EXAMPLE** If sentence is of type String, a typical run of the following code fragment

```
cout << "Enter some text, terminated by #:\n";
getline (cin, sentence, '#');
cout << "You entered:\n";
cout << sentence << endl;
```

(from sentence.cpp) would be:

```
Enter some text, terminated by #:
This sentence is too
long to fit on
one line# so it's on three.
You entered:
This sentence is too
long to fit on
one line
```

Discussion　In the run, `getline` stops reading characters when it encounters its third parameter, `'#'`. The function removes the `'#'` from `cin`, and the remaining characters following `'#'` are still in `cin`.

Rules for Functions with Default Arguments

1. Any parameters for which default arguments are specified must follow those for which no default arguments are specified.

2. Default values are specified in a function's *declaration* but are *not* repeated in its *definition*.

The declaration

```
int sum (int a, int b, int c=0, int d=0);
```

obeys the first of these rules, but the following declarations do not.

```
int sum (int a, int b=0, int c, int d=0);
int sum (int a=0, int b=0, int c, int d);
```

■ QUESTION　The function `sum` whose declaration is `int sum (int a, int b, int c=0, int c = 0);` returns the sum of its parameters. How would you write its definition, then give the output of the fragment?

```
cout << sum (10, 9) << ' ';
cout << sum (3, 4, 5) << ' ';
cout << sum (2,4,6,8) << endl;
```

Answer　The function definition would be

```
int sum (int a, int b, int c, int d)
{ return a+b+c+d; }
```

and the output of the fragment would be 19 12 20.

Note that the default argument values are *not* repeated in the function definition.

■ QUESTION　How would you write the declaration and definition of a single `draw_line` function such that the following code fragment will produce the given output?

Code Fragment (from `lines.cpp`)

```
draw_line (10);
draw_line (8, '#', 2);
draw_line (6, '+', 0);
draw_line (4, '*');
draw_line (8);
```

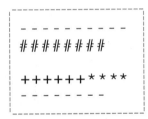

Output

Answer   The declaration and function description could be

```
void draw_line (int len, char ch='-', int nls=1);
// Draw a line consisting of len copies of the
// character ch, followed by nls newline characters.
```

and the corresponding function definition is

```
void draw_line (int len, char ch, int nls)
{
    int i;
    for (i=1; i<=len; i++)
        cout << ch;
    for (i=1; i<=nls; i++)
        cout << '\n';
}
```

Discussion   This single version of the draw_line function can handle calls with one, two, or three arguments. You could write three different versions of draw_line, but doing so requires more coding and more memory for the source and object code.

Notice that the default values of ch and nls are not repeated in the header of the function definition.

Overloaded Functions Versus Default Arguments   When writing a function that has more than one form, you must decide whether to write overloaded versions of it or one version using default arguments. Default arguments are not appropriate when the different versions of the function:

1.   Take different data types. (Recall the max functions of Section 10.3.)

2.   Require different algorithms or formulas. (Recall the tri_area functions of Section 10.3.)

Otherwise, the use of default arguments is an option that saves writing redundant code.

10.5 Function Templates

Recall from Section 10.3 on function overloading that you may write and call, all in the same program, a number of different max functions — one to find the larger of two int values, another for two float values, another for two String values, and so on. Writing the declarations and definitions for each of these individual max functions is not difficult because the statements are so similar. Each definition has the following form:

```
Type max (Type a, Type b)
{
    if (a > b)
        return a;
    return b;
}
```

Thus, to write the definition of a max function for a particular data type, you would replace the word Type with the actual data type. Although writing each individual max function is not difficult, it is tedious and seems needlessly repetitious because all these definitions have a single pattern. In a powerful language like C++, one might expect to find, and indeed does find, a shorter approach — using function templates.

Function Templates   A *function template* is not an actual function, but rather a pattern that the compiler can use to generate actual functions. For example, with a max function template, we can specify the "pattern" or template for a generic max function. Then, the compiler can use this template to generate those actual max functions that are needed by a particular program. Function templates are another example of code reuse, because one template can be used to generate many actual functions.

Function Template Syntax   To tell the compiler that a declaration and its definition will be a function template, the declaration and the definition must both begin with a line like

```
template <class Type>
```

Then the rest of the declaration and definition header would use the word Type in place of an actual data type. (Be aware that the choice of the identifier, Type, in the template is arbitrary. We could just as well have used another identifier. Some other common choices are DataType, CType, EType, or simply T.)

■ **EXAMPLE**   The following program contains the declaration and definition of a max function template.[1] The ways in which this function template differs from an ordinary max function declaration and definition have been highlighted. The sample runs show max functions that have been called and correctly executed for three different data types.

---

[1] Borland and Turbo C++ users must change the function name from max to Max (or something similar), because Borland provides a max template function in the library <stdlib.h>, which is included by baString.h.

```
// max_tpl.cpp
// Illustrate a template function
#include <iostream.h>
#include "baString.h"

template <class Type>
Type max (Type a, Type b);
// Return the larger of a and b.

void main()
{
    float f1=3.14, f2=4.5;
    int i1=99, i2=99;
    String w1="first", w2="SECOND";

    cout << max (f1, f2) << endl;
    cout << max (i1, i2) << endl;
    cout << max (w1, w2) << endl;
}

template <class Type>
Type max (Type a, Type b)
{
    if (a > b)
        return a;
    return b;
}
```

```
4.5
99
first
```

Run

How Actual *max* **Functions Are Created from the Template**   During compilation of the previous program, whenever the compiler detects a call to max, it uses the max function template and the data type of the arguments to generate an actual max function. The compiler substitutes the data type of the arguments for each occurrence of the identifier, Type, which is very much like a parameter.

For the previous program, the compiler generates three actual max functions, one for each of the types — float, int, and String. However, the compiler does not generate an actual max function for other data types such as double or char because the program contains no calls to max having double or char arguments.

Templates Are Used in Sorting   *Sorting*, the topic of Chapter 14, is the process of arranging a list of values in numeric order (for numbers) or alphabetic order (for strings). Because the details of coding a sorting algorithm can be tricky, you should code a sorting algorithm only once, as a template function, and leave to the compiler the task of creating the actual sorting functions needed to sort lists of `int`s, `float`s, `double`s, or `String`s. In programming languages that do not have templates, the programmer must write each of these actual sorting functions.

10.6   Member Versus Free Functions

In Chapter 6 we first encountered two situations that required us to use the somewhat unusual dot notation. In Section 6.1, the statement

```
len = greeting.length();
```

assigned the length of the `String` variable `greeting` to the `int` variable `len`. In Section 6.5, the statement

```
cin.ignore (80, '\n');
```

skipped over all characters up to and including the end-of-line character of the current input line. As you will see in subsequent chapters, dot notation is used frequently in connection with data types that are classes.

A Class's Variables Are Known as Objects   A ***class*** is a powerful kind of data type that binds together both data and the functions for operating on that data. A class's data and functions are known, respectively, as its ***member data*** and its ***member functions***. An ***object*** is any variable whose data type is a class. Thus, for example, because the `String` data type is a class, all `String` variables are objects. As you will learn in the next chapter, `cin` is a predefined (in the library file `iostream.h`) input stream object. Some standard C++ classes that we will consider in the next chapter are `ifstream` and `ofstream` (for input from and output to disk files). In later chapters, you will learn to use author-defined `Vector` and `Matrix` classes.

Member Function Calls   An object of a particular class has access to member functions of that class. The syntax for a member function call is

arguments (if any)
↓

object_name.mem_function (   )

In the following fragment (from `length.cpp`), note the use of dot notation in the two calls to the `String` class member function `length`.

```
String city1, city2;
city1 = "Erie, PA";
city2 = "Brooklyn, NY";
len1 = city1.length();
cout << city1 << ' ' << len1
     << endl;
cout << city2 << ' '
     << city2.length() << endl;
```

```
Erie, PA 8
Brooklyn, NY 12
```

Output

Be aware that the call

```
len1 = length(city1); //syntax error
```

would be incorrect, because the call of a member function must use dot notation. The object, which is an *implicit argument,* should not be within the parentheses, but should appear to the left of the dot. A member function can also have *explicit arguments* that are placed within the parentheses — this was the case with cin's ignore member function.

Rationale for Dot Notation   The following two reasons are behind the somewhat strange syntax used in member function calls.

1. **Active versus passive data**   Member function syntax places the data object (which is an implicit argument) before the function, instead of after it. This notation is in keeping with a central idea of object-oriented programming (OOP), which shifts the roll of data from passive to active. For example, in OOP, you can think of the call

    ```
    len_str = str.length();
    ```

    as sending a message to the object str to execute its length member function. Here, the object str is the active agent because it executes its length member function. By contrast, in the call

    ```
    y = sqrt(x);
    ```

    the variable x is acted on by the free function sqrt — the free function is the active agent.

2. **Resolving ambiguity when different functions have the same name**   It is permissible for member functions that are coded differently and belong to different classes to have the same name. For example, in the next chapter you will see that the classes ifstream and ofstream each have their own somewhat different

open functions. The compiler can resolve any potential ambiguity by using the class of the calling object to determine which open member function to call.

10.7 Recursive Functions

A *recursive* function is a function whose definition contains one or more calls to itself. Recursion tends to be used when a problem can be repeatedly reduced to smaller and smaller versions of itself, until finally a reduced version is reached that is small enough to be solved directly. Although many students find recursion confusing at first, it is an important programming tool that can make many seemingly difficult problems surprisingly easy to solve.

Early Coverage of Recursion   If you wish, you can now jump ahead to Sections 1 and 2 of Chapter 25, which cover recursive functions. Section 25.3 can then be studied in conjunction with, or any time after, the discussion of binary searches in Section 14.2.

▥ Exercises

1. Document each of the parameters of the following functions, from the program payroll2.cpp of Section 9.2, as IN, OUT, or IN-OUT.

```
void get_emp_data (String& name,  // _____
                   int& hrs,      // _____
                   float& rate);  // _____

void process_emp (String name,    // _____
                  int hrs,        // _____
                  float rate,     // _____
                  float& total);  // _____
```

2. Create a structure chart for program politic.cpp of Section 9.2.

3. Create a structure chart for program payroll2.cpp of Section 9.2.

4. Write definitions for the following overloaded rand_int functions.

```
int rand_int (int n);
// return a random int between 0 and n−1, inclusive.
```

```
int rand_int (int a, int b);
// Given a <= b, return a random int
// between a and b, inclusive.
```

5. Write the declaration and definition of a `swap` function template.

6. Could you use a default parameter to write a single version of the `rand_int` functions of Exercise 10.4? If so, discuss which approach is better.

7. What will be output by each of the following program fragments? (See Section 10.4 for the definition of `draw_line`.)

(a)

```
for (row=1; row<=3; row++)
   {
   draw_line (3-row, ' ', 0);
   draw_line (row, '<', 0);
   draw_line (row, '>');
   }
```

(b)

```
for (row=1; row<=4; row++)
   {
   draw_line (row, 'x', 0);
   draw_line (1, ' ', 0);
   draw_line (5-row, 'x');
   }
```

8. Complete the sample run of the following code.

```
String s1, s2, s3, s4;
cout << "Enter some text: ";
cin >> s1;
getline (cin, s2);
getline (cin, s3, 's');
cin >> s4;
cout << s1 << ' ' >> s1.length() << endl;
cout << s2 << ' ' >> s2.length() << endl;
cout << s3 << ' ' >> s3.length() << endl;
cout << s4 << ' ' >> s4.length() << endl;
```

Enter some text:
<u>What should I</u>
<u>enter to stop this?</u>
What

Sample run

Programming Problems

9. Test the functions of Exercise 10.4, and add their definitions to `myfuns.h`.

10. Test the function template of Exercise 10.5, and add its definition to `myfuns.h`.

11. Rewrite the program `weighted.cpp` of Section 5.3 so that (a) the input of scores is handled by the function `get_scores`, (b) the output of the weighted average and letter grade is handled by the function `print_results`, and (c) the calculation of the weighted average is done by the function `weighted_avg`. Draw a structure chart for your program design.

12. (a) Modify the program `payroll2.cpp` of Section 9.3 so that (i) employees are paid time-and-a-half for hours in excess of 40, and (ii) the wage calculation of `process_emp` is handled by a call to a `float`-valued function, `wages`.

   (b) Draw a structure chart for the program of part (a).

13. Complete the program `tri_over.cpp` of Section 10.3.

14. Rewrite the program `tri_over.cpp` so that the user is first asked whether the inputs will be the triangle's base and height or the lengths of its three sides. Then, call the appropriate overloaded `get_inputs` function to prompt for and input these values, and call the appropriate overloaded `tri_area` function to calculate the triangle's area.

15. (a) Write a program that inputs the dimensions, border, and fill characters for a rectangular box, then draws two boxes. The first box will be drawn as specified by the user inputs; the second will be twice as wide, two rows shorter, and use the `draw_box` function's default border and fill characters, '+' and ' ', respectively. A typical run is given at the right.

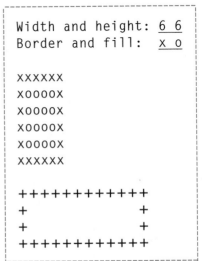

```
Width and height: 6 6
Border and fill:  X O

XXXXXX
XOOOOX
XOOOOX
XOOOOX
XOOOOX
XXXXXX

+++++++++++
+         +
+         +
+++++++++++
```

   Use a `get_box_info` function to prompt for and input the user specifications for the box, and a `draw_box` function to draw a box with given dimensions, border, and fill characters. The `draw_box` function should call the `draw_line` function of Section 10.4.

   (b) Draw a structure chart for the program.

16. Write a program to input some text, then output the number of lines, the total number of characters on all the lines, the average number of characters per line, and the shortest and longest lines. (*Hint:* Use a sentinel-controlled loop and terminate input by the sentinel line "DONE.")

17. Write a program to input some text, then output the number of words, the average number of characters per word, and the longest and shortest words. Include punctuation as part of a word. (Terminate input with the sentinel word "DONE.")

11

Text Files and Streams

In all of the programs we have considered thus far, data has been entered interactively — that is, typed in while the program is running. With this technique, if the same data is needed later for another program, the user has to retype it. Clearly, this technique is undesirable when large amounts of data are needed. For example, a large company would certainly not want to retype all its employee data each time a program needed to process this data.

Files provide an efficient means for storing data so that it can later be used by any number of programs. A file is a collection of related data items that is stored on an external storage device such as a disk or hard drive and given an external file name for reference. In this chapter, we consider *text files,* which consist of sequences of ASCII coded characters.

You have already seen how the built-in streams `cin` and `cout` are used for the flow of data into and out of programs. In this chapter we discuss how to use *file stream variables* to act as a "pipeline" for the flow of data between an external file and a program. When the external file is used to provide input for the program, an *input* file stream variable is needed, whereas when the external file receives output from the program an *output* file stream variable is needed.

11.1 Creating a Text File

You can create text files of data using the same text editor that you use to create C++ programs. The identifier you give the text file is called the file's *external file name.* Suppose you want to create the following file containing payroll information (identifier, hours worked, and hourly rate) for employees Eve, Lou, and Pat, and save it with the file name wages.dat.

You start as if you were going to type in a new program. First you create a new file and give it the file identifier wages.dat. Then instead of typing program code, you type the file data; finally, when you are finished, you save the file.

```
Eve 40 8
Lou 35 9
Pat 38 7
```
wages.dat

Stream Variable Versus External File Name Note that wages.dat is not a legal variable identifier in C++. Thus, when writing a C++ program that uses the data in wages.dat for input, you must make up a name for a *stream variable* that will be used to refer to wages.dat within the program. A good choice for this stream variable is one that indicates the associated file's contents and its use. For example, wages_in is good because it indicates both the file's contents and its use (for input rather than output.)

11.2   Stream Variables Are Objects

Recall from Section 10.6 that an **object** is a powerful kind of variable that binds together both data and the functions for manipulating that data. Note the following facts about file stream variables and objects:

- A file stream variable is an object.
- The data type of an object is known as its **class**. (We say that an object *belongs* to its class.)
- The data type of a stream variable is ifstream if it is used for input from a file and ofstream if it is used for output to a file.

Thus, the declaration for the input file stream variable wages_in would be:

```
ifstream wages_in;
```

■ QUESTION   As just mentioned, a file stream variable is an object. To what class does the object wages_in belong?

Answer   An object's class is the same as its data type. Thus, the answer is ifstream.

Member Functions and Dot Notation   An object of a particular class has available to it various functions known as the member functions of that class. As already discussed in Section 10.6, the syntax for calling a member function is

arguments (if any)

$\downarrow$

object_name.member_function (   )

The class `ifstream` has many member functions. In this chapter we consider four of `ifstream`'s most basic (file handling) member functions — `open`, `close`, `fail`, and `eof`. Here is a typical call to each of these functions when the input file stream variable is `wages_in`.

```
wages_in.open("wages.dat");
wages_in.close();
if (wages_in.fail()) . . .
while (!wages_in.eof()) . . .
```

Note that `open` and `close` are `void` functions (their calls stand alone), whereas `fail` and `eof` return a value (generally used in a test condition). Also note that `open` is the only one of these functions that takes an argument.

11.3 Input from a File Stream: The Header Technique

File with a Header   Recall from Sections 3.9 and 7.4 that a user can enter a number to determine how many data groups a `for` loop will read. Similarly, we can include such a number as the first item in an external file. In an external file, this number is called a **header**. To include a header in an external file, the person who creates the data file must know how many data groups are to be processed.

Because the details of reading from an external file are simpler when the file has a header than when it doesn't, our first program will use `exam.dat`, an external file with a header, to provide the input data. The header (i.e., the first value) of `exam.dat` tells how many scores follow. For example, `exam.dat` could contain

```
6 85 92 100 81 79 95
```

or it could contain

```
8
85 92 100 81
79 95 63 74
```

Opening a File for Input   The library file `fstream.h` contains the data type `ifstream` and its member functions. A program that uses a file as input must (1) include the library file `fstream.h`, (2) declare the input file stream variable, and (3) attach the input file stream variable to an actual external file. Thus, a program that uses the input file stream exams_in with the attached external file exam.dat must include the following lines:

```
#include <fstream.h>
ifstream exams_in; // declares the file stream variable
exams_in.open("exam.dat") // attaches stream variable
                          // to an external file
```

Be aware that after a call to the open function the *file pointer*, which has the job of pointing to the next item to be read from the file, is set to the first item of the file. In Section 11.5 we take a more detailed look at how a file pointer works.

Using >> to Read from a File Stream   Once a file has been opened for input, the extraction operator >> can be used with the attached stream variable in much the same way it is used to read from the standard input stream cin. For example, in the program shown in the following example, the statement

```
exams_in >> num_exams;
```

reads the header (the number of exam scores) from the file stream exams_in attached to the external file exam.dat.

Closing a File Stream   After a program has finished reading from a file, the file stream should be closed by using the close member function. The statement

```
exams_in.close();
```

detaches the stream from the external file exam.dat so that no further data can be read from the file (unless the file is opened again).

■ **EXAMPLE**   Calculate and print the average of the integer exam scores in the file exam.dat, which has a header as illustrated at the beginning of this section. In the following program the code needed to declare the stream variable and open and close the associated file is highlighted, and the statements using the extraction operator >> are italicized.

```
// average.cpp
// Read and average exams from data file with header.
#include <iostream.h>
#include <fstream.h> // for ifstream data type

void main()
```

```
{
    int score, sum;
    float avg;
    int ct; // count for loop control
    int num_exams; // data file header
    ifstream exams_in;

    exams_in.open("exam.dat");
    exams_in >> num_exams; // read the header
    sum = 0;
    for (ct = 1; ct <= num_exams; ct++)
    {
        exams_in >> score;
        sum += score;
    }

    avg = float(sum) / num_exams;
    cout << "There were " << num_exams << " exams.\n";
    cout << "Average score = " << avg << endl;
    exams_in.close();
}
```

The program produces the following output for the given data file.

```
6
85 92 100 81 79 95
```

exam.dat

```
There were 6 exams.
Average score = 88.6667
```

Program output

Discussion   To change the preceding program so that it reads input from a different external file, say, exam3.dat, we need only change the argument passed to the open member function. For example,

```
    exams_in.open("exam3.dat");
```

If the data file is not in the current directory, this information must be passed to the open member function. For example, if exam.dat were in the cmpsc101 directory of the a: drive, the call to open would be

```
    exams_in.open("a:\\cmpsc101\\exam.dat");
```

The double backslashes in the string argument passed to open are necessary! Remember that the backslash indicates an escape sequence, and to make a backslash character part of a string, it must itself be given in an escape sequence.

PITFALL (Typing `cin >>` **When Reading from a File Stream)**   In the program `average.cpp`, suppose the first statement to read input from the file is typed as

```
cin >> num_exams; //intended: exams_in >> num_exams;
```

In this case, you would see no activity on the user screen at run-time. While you wait for the computer to process the data file, the computer is actually waiting for you to enter a value from the keyboard for `num_exams`. Like infinite loops, this is a mistake that all programmers, novices and experts alike, make from time to time.

PITFALL (Nonexistent File)   Another common source of trouble is an `open` statement that refers to an external file that does not exist (or cannot be found in the current drive/directory). Unfortunately, unless you include some error-checking code, the program will give you no warning that something is wrong. Instead of terminating program execution with an error message, the program will execute in an unpredictable way, almost certainly producing a result different than what you intended. Variables that were supposed to receive input from the file will receive "garbage" values. At times, a nonexistent file can even cause an infinite loop!

Protecting Against a Nonexistent External File   Fortunately, C++ does provide various ways for you to ensure that a program which attempts to open a nonexistent file will terminate with an error message, thus avoiding a run that produces unreliable results without any warning. We use the `ifstream`'s member function, `fail`, which returns 1 if the `open` member function failed and 0 if it succeeded. Both of the following two methods place an error-checking test immediately after an `open` operation in order to protect against a nonexistent file.

One Method (Using `cerr` **and** `abort`**)**   If `exam.dat` does not exist (or cannot be found in the current drive/directory) the program will display the message `Unable to open file.` on the user screen along with a message that the program is being aborted.[1]

---

[1] In some versions of C++, if the file specified in the `open` function call does not exist, an empty file of the specified name will be created at run-time, and the `fail()` function will then return "false." If this is the case with your version of C++, always include a second argument, `ios::nocreate`, in the call to `open`, as in

```
exams_in.open("exam.dat", ios::nocreate);
```

This will ensure that a nonexistent file is not created "on the fly" and that `fail()` returns "true" as desired.

```
exams_in.open("exam.dat");
if (exams_in.fail())
    {
    cerr << "Unable to open file.\n";
    abort();
    }
```

Note that `cerr` is a predefined (in `iostream.h`) output stream that flows to the monitor. The error message could have been sent to the monitor via `cout`, but it is common practice among C++ programmers to send critical error messages by way of `cerr`. The predefined (in `stdlib.h`) `void` function `abort` is called to terminate a program.

A Shorter Method (Using an `Assert` Function) A compact and more general-purpose method for protecting against this and many other errors is to use an `assert` function, which allows you to specify an error message to be displayed if a stated assertion is false. We have provided such a function, `Assert`, as part of the `ourtools.h` library. (Be aware that the predefined library, `assert.h`, also contains an `assert` function, with a lowercase *a*. This function, however, is not as useful as our `Assert` function because it does not allow you to specify an error message as a parameter. When you use `assert`, the resulting error message can be somewhat cryptic, particularly to the user of your program.)

Here is the protection code, using our `Assert` function.

```
exams_in.open("exams.dat");
Assert(!exams_in.fail(),"Unable to open file.");
```

This method also outputs the message "Unable to open file." in the event that the `open` statement attempts to open a nonexistent file.

Our `Assert` Function Explained The `Assert` function takes two arguments: (1) a logical expression that we assert is true and (2) a string literal that is displayed as an error message if the assertion fails. When an `Assert` statement executes, if the logical expression is false, the error message is displayed and program execution is aborted; if it is true, program execution continues normally. It is important to note that the logical expression passed to `Assert` uses the `!` operator to assert that the `open` operation did *not* fail.

11.4 Input from a File: The End-of-File Technique

It is not always convenient to provide a header at the beginning of a file. If the file contains a large number of data groups, it would be easy to miscount them and thus give an incorrect header. Also, the addition or deletion of data groups requires the header to be changed accordingly. As an alternative to the header method, a sentinel value can be placed at the end of the data file. When reading from files, however, an even more flexible technique uses neither header nor sentinel — instead, the program detects when an attempt to read past the end of the file has occurred.

The `eof` Member Function The `int`-valued `eof` (end-of-file) member function tests whether the end of an input file stream has been passed. The value returned by `eof` is 1 when, and only when, an input operation has attempted to read past the end of the file; it is 0 otherwise.

The `ws` Manipulator The whitespace manipulator, `ws`, is provided in the `iostream.h` library file. The purpose of this manipulator is to scan over whitespace characters, stopping when a non-whitespace character has been encountered. The following example shows that you can use the `ws` manipulator to ensure that a `while` loop that tests for end-of-file will not execute one time too many.

■ **EXAMPLE** In the following program, assume that the external file `wages.dat` (as given in Section 11.1) has been saved in the current directory.

```cpp
// wages.cpp
#include <iostream.h>
#include <fstream.h> // for ifstream class
#include "ourtools.h" // for Assert
#include "baString.h"

void main()
{
    String name;
    int hours, rate, pay;
    ifstream wage_in;
    wage_in.open("wages.dat");
    Assert(!wage_in.fail(), "Unable to open file.\n");

    while (!wage_in.eof())
```

```
    {
        wage_in >> name >> hours >> rate;
        pay = hours * rate;
        cout << name << " $" << pay << endl;
        wage_in >> ws;
    }

    wage_in.close();
}
```

The program `wages.cpp` will produce the following user screen output:

```
Eve $320
Lou $315
Pat $266
```

Discussion   The last statement of the loop body

```
    wage_in >> ws;
```

scans over any whitespace from the current position in `wage_in`. This statement may seem redundant because whitespace is automatically skipped when reading the next data value from an input stream with the `>>` operator. This statement does, however, perform a crucial task the third (and last) time it is executed. Before its execution, all the data in the file has been read, but no attempt has been made to read past the end of the file, which means that `eof` will return 0. However, executing the statement `wage_in >> ws` after all data has been read *causes an attempt to read past the end of the file*. Thus, in the subsequent loop exit test, `eof` returns 1, and the loop terminates.

In the absence of the statement `wage_in >> ws` the `while` loop will *execute an extra time*. Because there is no more data to read, the values of `name`, `hours`, and `rate` during this fourth iteration will be unpredictable. This issue is illustrated in detail in Section 11.5.   ■ ■

A Standard Format for the End-of-File Technique Loop Header   In the previous programming example, the critical statement `wage_in >> ws` appears at the *bottom* of the `while` loop body, and is thus executed immediately before the `while` loop test `!wage_in.eof()` at the *top* of the loop. As standard practice, we will combine these two statements in the loop header to clearly indicate that they are executed consecutively.

```
while (wage_in >> ws && !wage_in.eof())
{
    wage_in >> name >> hours >> rate;
    pay = hours * rate;
    cout << name << " $" << pay << endl;
}
```

The preceding `while` loop header says, in effect, "As long as it is possible to (1) skip over whitespace and (2) not move past the end of the file, execute the loop body again."

■ **QUESTION**   The following program reads students' names and test scores from the external file `scores.dat`. Each data group consists of a student's name (last name, first name) followed by two scores on the next line. The program prints each student's name and whether she or he passed or failed (passing requires an average of at least 60). The program also counts the number of students who passed and who failed. Fill in the blanks.

```
// scores.cpp
#include <iostream.h>
#include <fstream.h> // for ifstream class
#include "ourtools.h" // for Assert
#include "baString.h"

void main()
{
    ifstream scores_in;
    String name;
    int score1, score2;
    int passcount, failcount;

    scores_in._____; // open file
    Assert(_____,"Unable to open file.");

    passcount = failcount = 0;
    while (_____)
    {
        getline (_____, name);
        scores_in >> _____>>_____;
        scores_in._____; // skip rest of line
```

```
            if ((score1+score2)/2 >= 60)
               {
               cout << name << " passed\n";
               passcount++;
               }
            else
               {
               cout << name << " failed\n";
               failcount++;
               }
            }

         scores_in.close();
         cout << passcount << " students passed.\n";
         cout << failcount << " students failed.\n";
      }
```

Answer   The completed lines are:

```
         scores_in.open("scores.dat"); // open file
         Assert(!scores_in.fail(),"Unable to open file.");
         while(scores_in >> ws && !scores_in.eof())
            getline (scores_in, name);
            scores_in >> score1 >> score2;
            scores_in.ignore(80,'\n'); // skip rest of line
```

Discussion   **1.** Notice the use of the standard format for the end-of-file loop header.

2. Because each name contains embedded whitespace, it must be read with the getline function rather than the extraction operator >>.

3. The statement scores_in.ignore(80,'\n'); ensures that the getline function begins reading from a new line of the stream scores_in rather than from the end of the current input line (see Section 6.5).

11.5   How a Text File Is Stored

A text file is stored as a sequence of ASCII characters, including control characters (newline, tab, etc.). For example, cpp source code files are text files.

Newline Characters and End of File   When you create a file with a text editor, each time you press the ENTER key (↵) a newline character is placed into the file. As we have done previously, we denote this newline character pictorially by using ↵. To indicate the end of a file, we will use ||.

File Pointer   When a program executes the open member function for an input file stream variable, a ***file pointer*** (which we denote by a vertical arrow, ↑) is positioned on the first character of the file attached to the stream. Thus, if program wages.cpp of Section 11.4 uses the wages.dat file of Section 11.1, after the statement wage_in.open("wages.dat") is executed, the file and file pointer will be

E	v	e		4	0		8	←	L	o	u		3	5		9	←	P	a	t		3	8		7	←	

↑
pointer

■ **QUESTION**   In the program wages.cpp, give the location of the file pointer after the first execution of

    1. wage_in >> name >> hours >> rate;

    2. wage_in >> ws;

Answer   After statement 1, the file pointer will be on the first newline character. After statement 2, it will be on the L at the beginning of the second line of the stream.

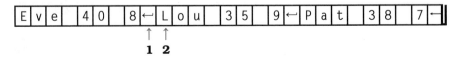

       ↑ ↑
      1 2

The eof ***Member Function***   The eof member function returns 1 when, and only when, an input statement has attempted to read past the end of file; before that it will return 0. Thus, when the loop condition

    while (!wages_in.eof())

is tested, the loop body will be executed again if and only if no attempt has been made to read past the end of the file.

■ **QUESTION**   In the program wages.cpp (p. 264), give the position of the file pointer and the value of wage_in.eof() immediately after the third execution of

1. `wage_in >> name >> hours >> rate;`

2. `wage_in >> ws;`

Answer   After 1, the file pointer is positioned on the last newline character, and the value of `wage_in.eof()` is 0. After 2, the position of the file pointer is meaningless (because of the attempt to read past the end of the file), but it helps to depict it as being positioned just past the end of the file. At this point, the value of `wage_in.eof()` is 1.

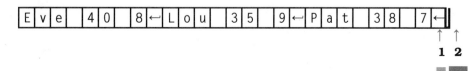

■ **EXAMPLE**   Suppose the `ifstream` variable `ints_in` is

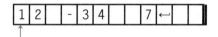

and the following program fragment (from `extra_in.cpp`) is executed:

```
cout << "Contents of ints.dat:\n";
while (!ints_in.eof())
    {
    ints_in >> n;
    cout << n << ' ';
    }
```

The output will be

```
Contents of ints.dat:
12 -34 7 7
```

After three executions of the loop body, the file pointer is positioned on the newline character (↵), so the loop exit test `!ints_in.eof()` evaluates to 1 (!0), and the loop body is executed a fourth time. The fourth execution of the statement `ints_in >> n` scans whitespace, thus running past the end of the file, and fails to read a new value for `n`. The output statement displays the current value of `n` (still 7), and the loop exit test evaluates to 0 (!1).

Discussion　　As in `ints.dat`, sometimes multiple whitespace characters follow the last piece of data in the file. The person who created the file would not see these characters precisely because they *are* whitespace.　■　■■

Seeking the End of a File

Seeking the End of a File　　The previous example illustrates that before checking the value of `eof()`, it is necessary to actively **seek** the end of a file, as discussed in the previous section. The statement to accomplish this task, `ints_in >> ws`, can be placed at the end of the loop body, or it can be placed in the *standard end-of-file loop header* discussed in the previous section.

The program `ints_in.cpp` is the same as `extra_in.cpp` except that it contains the loop header

```
while (ints_in >> ws && !ints_in.eof())
```

When `ints_in.cpp` is run using the file `ints.dat` as input, it produces the correct output:

```
Contents of ints.dat:
12 -34 7
```

11.6 Entering the External File Identifier Interactively

A user might want to run the same program a number of times for different data files without having to edit the program for each run by changing the file name in the call to the `open` member function. The next program fragment, from `input_id.cpp`, shows how a `String` variable can be used to store the external file name and pass this information to the `open` member function.

```
String file_id;
ifstream wage_in;

cout << "Please enter file ID: ";
cin >> file_id;
wage_in.open (file_id.c_str());
Assert(!wage_in.fail(), "Can't open that file.");

. . .   etc.  . . .
```

If the user typed `wagesjan.dat` in response to the prompt, the call

```
wage_in.open (file_id.c_str());
```

would have the same effect as

```
wage_in.open("wagesjan.dat");
```

The `c_str( )` ***Member Function***   The argument passed to `open` is `file_id.c_str()` rather than simply `file_id`. This argument is used because `open` requires an argument whose type is an "old style" C string, not a C++ `String` variable (of the `String` data type proposed by the Draft C++ standard). Anticipating this problem, the Draft standard `String` data type provides a member function, `c_str()`, to return, in the old style C format, the character sequence stored in a `String` variable.

11.7   Protecting Against Bad Data

The data file `scores.dat` consists of each student's last name and test score (with 100 being the highest possible score). Suppose this file contains some bad data. For example, it might contain the data group

```
Smith
542
```

Obviously, Smith's score of 542 is incorrect. When data is being read from an external file, we cannot use the `do..while` looping technique of Section 8.3 to force the input of an appropriate value. We can, however, use an `if..else` test to filter data so that good data is processed and certain bad data is rejected with a warning message. For example, we might use an `if..else` statement as follows:

```
while (scores_in >> ws && !scores_in.eof())
    {
        scores_in >> name >> score;
        if (0<= score && score <= 100)
            {
            . . . process data group . . .
            }
        else
            cout << "BAD DATA " << name << ' '
                 << score << endl;
    }
```

REMARK   Note that this attempt to protect against bad data is limited in its effectiveness. For example, suppose that the person creating the file typed 48 when Smith's score was actually 84. The if test would not detect this mistake. This simple form of error trapping will detect only values that are out of range.

11.8   Sending Output to a File

So far we have directed program output to the user screen or the printer, both of which are physical devices, or to a virtual printer, which is a fixed file on the hard drive and whose previous contents get overwritten each time it is used. There is another possibility: We can direct the output to an arbitrary, named file on disk. In this way, program output can be stored for future printing or for use as input to another program.

Creating an Output File Stream   An output stream whose destination is a disk file is called an ***output file stream***.

Declaration   An output file stream is a variable of the data type ofstream that is predefined in the fstream.h library file.

The open **Member Function**   An ofstream variable is attached to a specific external file by passing the external file name to the ofstream variable through its open member function. If this external file does not exist, open creates it and positions the output stream pointer at the beginning of the file. If this external file *does* exist, there are two possibilities:

1.   If the file is not a *write-protected* or *read-only* file, open erases its current contents, then positions the file pointer at the beginning of the file. (A file could be write protected because it is on a floppy disk whose write-protect notch is locked, or it has been marked read only via a DOS command or a Window's utility.)

2.   If the file is write protected or read only, the open operation fails.

The fail **Member Function**   The fail member function returns 1 if the open operation failed, and returns 0 if it succeeded.

The close **Member Function**   The close member function of an ofstream variable performs these operations:

1.   Sends any data currently in the stream to the external file.

2.   Saves the external file.

3.   Detaches the external file from the ofstream variable so that no further data can be written to the file.

■ QUESTION   The program `sqrt_tbl.cpp` produces the given user screen output and the disk file `a:\sqrts.tbl` of integers and their square roots (to three decimal places).

```
Opening output file . . .
Writing to output file . . .
Output file closed.
```

User screen output

```
 2 1.414
 3 1.732
 4 2.000
 .
 . etc.
 .
20 4.472
```

`a:\sqrts.tbl`

Complete the missing lines in the main function of `sqrt_tbl.cpp`.

```
void main()
{
    _____; // declare sqrt_out
    int n;
    cout << "Opening output file . . .\n";
    sqrt_out.open(_____);
    Assert(_____,
           "Unable to open output file.");

    fixed_out(_____, 3);
    cout << "Writing to output file . . .\n";
    for (n=2; n<=20; n++)
        _____ << n << ' ' << _____ << endl;
    sqrt_out.close();
    _____<< "Output file closed.\n";
}
```

Answer   The missing lines are:

```
ofstream sqrt_out; // declare sqrt_out
sqrt_out.open("a:\\sqrts.tbl");
Assert(!sqrt_out.fail(),
       "Unable to open output file.");
fixed_out(sqrt_out, 3);
   sqrt_out << n << ' ' << sqrt(n) << endl;
cout << "Output file closed.\n";
```

Discussion

1. The three lines of user screen output are not necessary, but they prevent the program from running "silently." These lines are particularly useful during program testing and debugging, and the statements that produce them can be commented out later.

2. Notice that the `fixed_out` function can be used to format floating point numbers sent to an output file stream.

3. Suppose that, after running this program, you made `a:\sqrts.tbl` a read-only file, then changed the loop exit test to `n<=99`. When you ran this updated program, the screen output would be

```
Opening output file . . .
Unable to open file for output.
```

and the file `a:\sqrts.tbl` would be unchanged.   ■ ▬

Updating a File   Suppose that the file `wage1.dat` contains employee names and weekly salaries, as shown to the right. We want to add a $25 bonus to each employee's salary and save the new salaries on disk. With text files, we cannot read from and write to the same file. (An `ifstream` can only be read from; an `ofstream` can only be written to.) Thus, we must store the new salaries in a second file. We will read from the

Thorne, Hank
400
Dark, Joan
503
. . . etc. . .

original salary file one data group at a time, update the salary, and then write the updated data group to the second file. The following program fragment (from `update.cpp`) accomplishes this task:

```cpp
String name;
int wage;
ifstream old_wages;
ofstream new_wages;

old_wages.open("wage1.dat");
Assert(!old_wages.fail(),"Cannot open wage1.dat.");
new_wages.open("wage2.dat");
Assert(!new_wages.fail(),"Cannot open wage2.dat.");

while (old_wages >> ws && !old_wages.eof())
```

```
{
   getline (old_wages, name);
   old_wages >> wage;
   old_wages.ignore (80, '\n'); // skip rest of line
   wage = wage + 25;;
   new_wages << name << endl
              << wage << endl;
}

old_wages.close();
new_wages.close();
```

Exercise 11.9 asks you to modify `update.cpp` so that the original external file contains the updated information by the end of the run.

The Virtual Printer The virtual printer output stream, `vprn`, introduced in Section 2.5, is actually just the disk file `c:\vprinter.out`. This stream is declared and opened for output by the single statement (from `ourtools.h`):

```
ofstream vprn ("c:\\vprinter.out");
```

which is a shorter way of writing

```
ofstream vprn;
vprn.open ("c:\\vprinter.out");
```

11.9   Streams as Parameters (With a Brief Introduction to Inheritance)

We begin this section by discussing how to pass a file stream as an argument in a function call. Then, to explain a rule for writing functions with some flexibility in the type of argument they can take, we briefly introduce the concept of inheritance.

Syntax Restriction: File Streams Must Be Reference Parameters
When a file stream is an argument in a function call, its matching parameter must be a reference parameter for two reasons:

1.   After a function call with a file stream as argument, we normally want the stream in its altered state. For example, if a call reads one data group from a stream, we want the argument's file pointer to have been advanced.

2.   A file stream is potentially too large to be copied in memory as is done with value parameters.

■ PROBLEM In the program `update.cpp` of the previous section, all file input and output is handled directly in the function `main`. Although the details of this I/O are relatively simple, it would be better to modularize the program by writing functions to handle the subtasks of reading from `wage1.dat` and writing to `wage2.dat`. The `main` function of the improved program, `update2.cpp`, would then look like the following. (User-defined functions that have file streams as parameters are highlighted.)

```cpp
void main()
{
    String name; int wage;
    ifstream old_wages;
    ofstream new_wages;

    old_wages.open("wage1.dat");
    Assert(!old_wages.fail(),"Cannot open wage1.dat.");
    new_wages.open("wage2.dat");
    Assert(!new_wages.fail(),"Cannot open wage2.dat.");

    while (!old_wages.eof())
        {
        get_emp_info (old_wages, name, wage);
        put_emp_info (new_wages, name, wage+25);
        }
    old_wages.close();
    new_wages.close();
}
```

Of course, `main` must be preceded by the declarations of these highlighted user-defined functions and followed by their definitions. In the following declarations for the `get_emp_info` and `put_emp_info` functions, notice that both `ins` and `outs` are reference parameters.

```cpp
void get_emp_info (ifstream& ins, // in-out
                   String& name,  // out
                   int& wage);    // out
// Input name and wage from stream ins.

void put_emp_info (ofstream& outs, // in-out
                   String name,    // in
                   int wage);      // in
// Output name and wage to stream outs.
```

■ **QUESTION**   Study the input statements of `update.cpp` (Section 11.8) and the declaration of the function `get_emp_info`, above. Then write the body of `get_emp_info` as it would appear in the definition of the function.

Answer   Note that the code in the body of `get_emp_info` is the same as that of the `main` function of `update.cpp`, except that the input stream is the parameter `ins` rather than the variable `wages_in`. The body of `get_emp_info` is thus:

```
{
    getline (ins, name);
    ins >> wage;
    ins.ignore (80, '\n');
}
```

Making `get_emp_info` **More Flexible**   Suppose you want to use the function `get_emp_info` to get data from the keyboard. Of course, you would need to prompt the user and could do so in this manner:

```
cout << "Enter employee's name on one line,\n"
     << "then his/her wage on the next: ";
get_emp_info (cin, name, wage);
```

Unfortunately, if this is the only change you make, you will get an error message when you attempt to compile this code. The cause of this error is that the argument, `cin`, is of type `istream_withassign`, which does not match `ifstream`, the type of the first parameter of `get_emp_info`. (This is our first mention of `cin`'s data type. Because `cin` is predefined in `iostream.h`, we haven't had any reason to declare its type.)

Fortunately, this problem has a solution — you should also change `ifstream` to `istream` in the declaration of `get_emp_info`. Then, the revised function will be flexible enough so that either of the following calls can be made:

```
get_emp_info (old_wages, name, wage);
get_emp_info (cin, name, wage);
```

The rule that allows this flexibility in the previous function calls can be stated as follows:

Rule for Flexibility of File Stream Arguments

> For a function to be flexible enough to take either `cin` or an input file stream as an argument, the type of the matching stream parameter must be `istream`. (Similarly, for a function to take either `cout` or an output file stream as an argument, the matching stream parameter must be of type `ostream`.)

Inheritance and Stream Parameters   Inheritance is a complex subject, but a brief discussion of it will help explain why the input (output) stream parameter in the previous rule must be of type `istream` (`ostream`).

A main goal of inheritance is the creation of new, more specialized classes from a **base class** by the addition of extra features such as additional data members and member functions. A new class that is created from a base class is called a **descendant class**. A descendant class inherits the features of its base class and may contain additional, more specialized features.

Some Examples of Base and Descendant Classes   The base class for all input streams is `istream`. One descendant of `istream` is `ifstream`, the class for more specialized input streams — namely, those that are *input file* streams. Be aware that the `ifstream` class extends the functionality of the `istream` class. For example, the `open` function is a member of the `ifstream` class but not the `istream` class. Another descendant of `istream` is `istream_withassign`, the data type of `cin`.

Similarly, `ostream` is a base class for all output streams, and has as descendant classes `ofstream`, for *output file* streams, and `ostream_withassign`, the data type of `cout`.

General Flexibility Rule for Reference Parameters   In a function call, an argument that is matched with a reference parameter must be either the same type as, or a descendant type of, that reference parameter. (Of course, in the body of the function definition, only the features of the reference parameter's class may be used.)

The rationale for this rule is that the reference parameter, when considered as a stand-in for its matching argument, may use only those features that it shares with its argument. (You have already seen in Chapter 9 that a reference parameter uses the argument's memory cell.) Thus, the parameter must not be more specialized (i.e., have more features) than its argument.

The `fixed_out` **Function**   The definition of the `fixed_out` function, from `ourtools.h` is

```
void fixed_out (ostream& out, int d)
{
    if (d<0) d=0;
    out << setiosflags (ios::fixed | ios::showpoint)
        << setprecision(d);
}
```

Notice that its parameter is of type ostream&, so that either a file stream or the standard output stream cout can be the first argument in a call to fixed_out.

11.10 More Member Functions for Stream Input/Output

Input and output streams have many member functions. Many of these control the way output is displayed and are quite tedious to use. The authors have provided fixed_out and related functions in ourtools.h to enable you to control the output of floating point numbers without learning the tedious (and, at this point, unnecessary) details of these member function calls. (If you are curious about these details, look at the code in ourtools.h.)

However, some easy-to-use stream member functions are available (in iostream.h) that facilitate solutions to some tricky input and output problems. The following table summarizes those we will need in later chapters. In the given typical calls, outs represents an output stream, and ins an input stream.

Function	*Action*	*Typical Call*
fill	Specify the character for filling any unused columns of an output zone.	outs.fill('.');
get	Read the next character from an input stream, *whitespace included.*	ins.get(ch);
putback	Put a character back at the front of an input stream, making it the next character to be read from the stream.	ins.putback(ch);

■ **PROBLEM** Military time is given as a four-digit number. For example, 0530 ("oh five thirty hours") represents 5:30 A.M., whereas 1730 ("seventeen thirty hours") represents 5:30 P.M. The following code fragment (from `octerror.cpp`) attempts to read and display military times.

Program fragment

```
int m_time:
cout << "Military time: ";
cin >> m_time;
cout << "You entered: ";
cout << m_time << endl;
```

```
Military time: 0000
You entered: 0
Military time: 1730
You entered: 1730
Military time: 0530
You entered: 344
```

Sample runs

The sample runs clearly indicate problems with both input and output. First, 0000 is read correctly, but is not displayed as a four-digit number. Second, the third input, 0530, is apparently not even read correctly. We will tackle these problems separately, beginning with the first one, which is the easier of the two.

■ **EXAMPLE**   The following code fragment uses `cout`'s `fill` member function to display a military time stored in an integer variable, `m_time`, as a four-digit number, padded on the left with zeros.

```
cout.fill('0'); // use 0 for fill char
cout << setw(4) << m_time << endl;
cout.fill(' '); // reset fill char
```

■ ▬

Inputting Integers with Leading Zeros   In C++ an integer read from a stream with the extraction operator is *not* read as a decimal integer *if it begins with a leading zero*. This is the source of the error in reading the military time 0530 — the leading zero indicates that 530 is a base 8 (octal) number. Thus, the decimal value of the input is $5 \times 8^2 + 3 \times 8^1 + 0 \times 8^0 = 5 \times 64 + 24 = 344$. To input four-digit military times, we need more control of the input process than the extraction operator alone provides. An algorithm is

Algorithm for reading a
four-digit military time

```
do at most 3 times
   cin >> ch;
   if (ch is not '0')
      put ch back into cin;
      break out of the loop
cin >> m_time;
```

By the time execution reaches the statement cin >> m_time; the next character to be read is either not a zero, or it is the fourth zero of the input 0000.

■ **QUESTION** Complete the following function (from militime.cpp) to input a four-digit military time.

```
void get_militime (istream& ins, // in-out
                   int& mt)       // out
{
    int i;  char ch;
    // scan up to 3 leading zeros
    for (_____)
       {
       ins >> ch; // read non-whitespace character
       if (ch != '0')
          { // ch is not a leading '0', so
          _____; // put it back
          _____; // exit the loop
          }
       }
    // read the time
    ins >> mt;
}
```

Answer The missing lines are

```
        for (i=1; i<=3; i++)
            ins.putback(ch); // put it back
            break;           // exit the loop
```

■ **PROBLEM** Write a program to read a line of input and count the spaces in it. A typical run of the program is

```
Enter a line of text:
Here it is — the line of text.
There were 7 spaces.
```

We want to count spaces, which are whitespace characters, so using the extraction operator (which skips whitespace when reading from a stream) will not solve the problem. Furthermore, we need to know when we have reached the end of the input line, but the newline character \n is also whitespace.

■ QUESTION Fill in the blanks in the following program fragment (from `spaces.cpp`) to read an input line one character at a time and count the number of spaces in the line.

```
cout << "Enter a line of text:\n";
spaces = 0;
cin._____;
while (_____) // while not end-of-line
    {
    if (ch == ' ')
        spaces++;
    _____;
    }
cout << "There were " << spaces << " spaces.\n";
```

Answer The missing lines are

```
cin.get(ch);
while (ch != '\n') // while not end-of-line
    cin.get(ch);
```

■ Exercises

1. Suppose the `ifstream` variable `emps_in` is

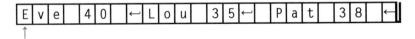

where ↑ indicates the file pointer. If `name` and `age` are of type `String` and `int`, respectively, give the output of the following program fragment, and indicate the position of the file pointer after each execution of statements a and b.

```
while (!emps_in.eof())
    {
    emps_in >> name >> age; // statement a
    emps_in >> ws;          // statement b
    cout << name << ' ' << age << endl;
    }
```

2. In the following code fragment, `line` is of type `String`. What is its output if `emps_in` is the `ifstream` variable of the previous exercise?

```
while (!emps_in.eof())
    {
    emps_in >> line;
    cout << line << ' ' << line.length() << endl;
    }
```

3. (a) What problem occurs when the following fragment is executed for the ifstream variable emps_in of the previous two exercises?

```
while (!emps_in.eof())
    {
    getline (emps_in, line);
    cout << line << ' ' << line.length() << endl;
    }
```

   (b) What change(s) in the while condition will eliminate this problem, and what will be the resulting output?

4. Write a free function, file_size, to return the number of characters in the text file whose external name is the parameter of the function. For example, if the disk file nameage.dat contains

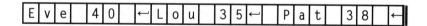

   then the value return by file_size(nameage.dat) will be 24.

5. Write a complete program to copy the file old.dat to new.dat one character at a time. Print an error message and terminate program execution if there is a problem with opening either file.

6. Redo the previous exercise, with the following modifications:
   (a) Enter the external names of the source and destination files interactively.
   (b) Copy one complete line at a time.

Programming Problems

7. Write a program that will read integers from a file whose name you enter interactively. The program will then output to the monitor (a) the number of integers read, (b) the smallest and largest of the integers, and (c) the sum and average (to the nearest 0.1) of the integers.

8. Rewrite the program class.cpp of Section 10.2 so that input is read from the file student.dat and output is displayed on the monitor.

9. Rewrite the program `update.cpp` of Section 11.8 so that at the end of the program run, the original input file contains the updated wage information. (*Hint:* Write a function, `copy_file`, that copies its `ifstream` parameter, `src_in`, to its `ofstream` parameter, `dest_out`.)

10. Write a program that inputs a positive integer N, then writes to the disk file `primes.dat` all odd primes less than or equal to N. The primes should be arranged 10 per line, right justified in six columns. Use a `bool` function `is_prime` that determines whether its single `int` parameter is or is not prime. (*Hint:* Use the primality testing algorithm of Section 8.6.)

    Test your program by running it for small values of N (100, 300) before running it for large values of N.

11. Write a program that reads names in the form `FIRST MI. LAST` from the file `fmlnames.dat`, puts the names in the form `LAST, FIRST MI.`, then writes them to the file `lfmnames.dat`. Use the following code fragment and function calls as part of your main function.

```
get_name (names_in, first, mi, last);
while (!names_in.eof())
    {
    rebuild (first, mi, last, full_name);
    put_name(names_out, full_name);
    get_name (names_in, first, mi, last);
    }
```

12. Write the definitions of the following overloaded `prepare_file` functions as described in comments. Test the functions, then add them to `myfuns.h`.

```
void prepare_file (ifstream& ins, String file_id);
// Open the ifstream object ins as the disk file whose
// identifier is file_id. If open fails, print a message
// that the file cannot be opened for input, then exit.

void prepare_file (ofstream& outs, String file_id);
// Open the ofstream object outs as the disk file whose
// identifier is file_id. If open fails, print a message
// that the file cannot be opened for output, then exit.
```

13. Modify the program `update.cpp` of Section 11.9 to use the `prepare_file` functions of the previous exercise.

14. Write a program that allows the user to input the quantity and type (P, N, D, Q, H, $) of each of several coins on one line. The output will be the quantity and type of each coin, followed by the total value of all the coins. A sample run

```
Enter coins: 30N 25d   10Q   2$
30 N
25 d
10 Q
2 $
Total value is $8.50
```

is shown to the right. (*Hint*: Use the istream get and putback member functions.)

15. Rent-A-Wreck, Inc., keeps information on each of its rental cars in the file cars.dat. Each line of the file consists of the three-symbol serial number for a car and the number of miles that car has been driven to date. Write a program to read information from cars.dat and produce two output files, under50.dat and 50plus.dat. These files should contain, respectively, the serial numbers of cars that have been driven under 50,000 miles and cars that have been driven at least 50,000 miles. Sample files are shown.

A10	51029
A20	14293
A30	4123
B10	61770
B30	82001
C05	9182
C20	90910
C30	100301

cars.dat

A20
A30
C05

under50.dat

A10
B10
B30
C20
C30

50plus.dat

12

The switch **and** enum **Statements**

In certain situations, the switch statement provides a cleaner way to do multiway selection than the more general nested if. After discussing some basics of the switch statement, we show its use in menu-driven programs. We also demonstrate its use in a major application, a program that acts like a pocket calculator.

We also briefly discuss the use of the enum statement to create enumerated data types, which are the only data types, besides char and integer types, that can be used as cases in switch statements. Enumerated types can sometimes improve the readability of code, but they are often not convenient to use, because their values cannot be input or output unless the programmer writes explicit translation code.

12.1 switch **Statement Syntax**

Basic Format and Action   The basic format for the switch statement is

```
switch (selector-expression)
    {
    case case-value-1: statement(s)-1
                    break;
    case case-value-2: statement(s)-2
                    break;

    .

    .
    case case-value-n: statement(s)-n
                    break;
    default: default-statement(s)
    } // end switch
```

The break statement transfers control to the end of the switch statement.

where the *selector-expression* and the distinct, constant values, *case-value-1, case-value-2, . . . , case-value-n* are all of the same **ordinal type** — that is, a type whose values can be listed in order. In C++ the ordinal types are all the integer types, char, and the programmer-defined enumerated types (to be introduced in Section 12.3). The floating-point types and String data type are not ordinal types.

The action of this statement can be described as follows: If the value of the *selector-expression* equals the *case-value* given for one of the *n* cases, then the statement(s) for that case are executed, and control passes to the first statement after the switch statement; otherwise, the *default-statement(s)* are executed before control passes to the first statement after the switch.

■ **EXAMPLE** The following main function, from trnslat2.cpp, gives the Spanish word for a positive integer entered by the user. (As you can see, its knowledge of Spanish is very limited.)

```
void main ()
{
    int num;
    cout << "Enter a positive integer: ";
    cin >> num;

    cout << "The Spanish word is ";
    switch(num)
        {
        case 1: cout << "uno";
                break;
        case 2: cout << "dos";
                break;
        case 3: cout << "tres";
                break;
        default:
            cout << "???\n"
        } // end switch
    cout    << '.' << endl;
}
```

```
Enter a positive integer: 2
The Spanish word is dos.

Enter a positive integer: 5
The Spanish word is ???.
```

Sample runs

Using the `default` ***Option with*** `switch`   If none of the case values in a `switch` statement match the value of a selector expression, the statement(s) specified after the keyword `default` are executed. This is illustrated by the second of the preceding sample runs.

If the default option was omitted, as in the following code fragment, from `trnslat1.cpp`,

```cpp
cout << "The Spanish word is ";
switch(num)
    {
    case 1: cout << "uno";
            break;
    case 2: cout << "dos";
            break;
    case 3: cout << "tres";
    } // end switch
cout << '.' << endl;
```

then the output for any input integer other than 1, 2, and 3, would be

```
The Spanish word is .
```

PITFALL   (Omitting Needed `break` **Statements)**   If a case that is executed does not end with a `break` (or `return`) statement, then the computer will execute the code for the next case as well, continuing until it comes to a `break` (or `return`) statement or the end of the `switch`. For example, when `num` has the value 1, the `switch` statement in the following fragment (from `nobreak.cpp`) produces the inappropriate output.

```
The Spanish word for 1 is unodostres???.
```

```
cout << "The Spanish word for " << num << " is ";
switch(num)
    {
    case 1: cout << "uno";
    case 2: cout << "dos";
    case 3: cout << "tres";
    default: cout << "???";
    } // end switch
cout << '.' << endl;
```

Listing Cases with the Same Action Together If several different cases of a switch statement are to execute the same statements, you can list them together. For example, the following `switch` statement (from `daysmon0.cpp`) outputs a message about the number of days in `month`.

```
switch (month)
    {
    case 4: case 6: case 9: case 11:
        cout << "30 days";
        break;
    case 3: case 5: case 7:
    case 8: case 10: case 12:
        cout << "31 days";
        break;
    case 2:
        cout << "28 or 29 days";
        break;
    default: // invalid months
        cout << "Invalid value for month.";
    } // end switch
```

Exercise 12.7 asks you to rewrite the previous fragment using a nested `if` instead of the `switch` statement. You should be impressed by how much clearer and easier to read the `switch` version is.

*switch **More Limited Than Nested*** `if` Although the `switch` statement can lead to clearer code than a nested `if` statement, there are many situations in which the `switch` statement is not applicable and nested `if` must be used instead. The `switch` statement's limited applicability is a result of two restrictions. First, the selector must be an ordinal type, meaning that it cannot be of types float or String, among others. Second, the selection test is always for equality and, thus, it cannot test whether the selector has a value less than some case value. An example of a nested if statement that is not suited for coding as a switch statement is

```
if (n < 0)
    cout << "Negative";
else if (n > 0)
    cout << "Positive";
```

■ EXAMPLE   **(Translating Characters to Strings)**   When a switch statement is used in the body of a function to return a value, the break statements can be eliminated because the return statement exits not only the switch statement, but also the function itself. For example,

```
String word_for_suit(char ch)
{
    switch(ch)
        {
        case 'c': case 'C':
            return "CLUBS";
        case 'd': case 'D':
            return "DIAMONDS";
        case 'h': case 'H':
            return "HEARTS";
        case 's': case 'S':
            return "SPADES";
        default:
            return "UNKNOWN SUIT";
        }
}
```

Using a Computation to Set Up a switch *Statement*   Some situations may, at first glance, appear to require a nested if. However, you might be able to use a computation to transform the problem into a form suitable for the use of switch.

Suppose, for example, a student has taken two tests, and his letter grade (A, B, C, D, or F) is assigned using the usual cutoffs, 90, 80, 70, and 60. Note that avg = (scr1 + scr2)/2 gives avg an int value from the list 0, 1, 2, . . . , 99, 100. Here, the large number of cases makes a switch statement impractical. However, if we use an int variable, avg_div10, and assign it a value as follows

```
avg = (scr1 + scr2)/2;
avg_div10 = avg/10;
```

then, avg_div10 will take on a value from the list 0, 1, 2, . . . , 9, 10. Exercise 12.12 asks you to write a char-valued function, grade, that takes two parameters, scr1 and scr2, and uses a switch statement to return the appropriate letter grade.

12.2 switch **and Menu-Driven Programs**

A *menu* is a list of possible options from which the user can choose. In a *menu-driven program*, a loop allows the user to enter menu choices repeatedly until she chooses to quit. The switch statement is commonly used to select the block of code that performs the tasks corresponding to the user's menu choice.

■ **EXAMPLE**   **(An Information Menu for Today)**   Here is a sample run of a program, infomenu.cpp, that allows the user to view information from whichever of the categories she selects.

```
Today's Menu:
Type A for Advice of the Day.
Type W for Today's Weather.
Type S for Sports Scores.
Type Q to quit.

Your choice: W
50% chance of rain.
Your choice: A
Buy low, sell high.
Your choice: Q
You have chosen to exit.
```

The main and process_choice functions are given next. The display_menu function is trivial and can be found at the PWS Web site.

```
void main()
{
   char choice;
   display_menu();
   do {
      cout << "Your choice: ";
      cin >> choice;
      process_choice (choice);
      }
   while (choice != 'Q');
}
```

```
void process_choice (char choice)
{
   choice = toupper(choice);
   switch(choice)
      {
      case 'A': cout << "Buy low, sell high.\n";
                break;
      case 'W': cout << "50% chance of rain.\n";
                break;
      case 'S': cout << "Celtics 104, Bulls 80\n";
                break;
      case 'Q': cout << "You have chosen to exit.\n";
                break;
      default:  cout << "Invalid choice - try again.\n";
                break;
      } // end switch
}
```

■ **PROBLEM**   **(Pocket Calculator Program)**   Write a program to implement a calculator with the following functions: +, *, ^ (for exponentiation), I (to invert
the current value), S (to set the current value), M (to display a menu of
calculator functions), and Q (to quit). A sample session of calculations
will look like the following.

Explanation	*Sample Session*

```
Calculator functions:
  + (add), * (mult), ^ (expo),
  (I)nvert,    (S)et, (Q)uit,
  show this    (M)enu again.
```

Set the current value to 2.5.	<u>S 2.5</u>
	2.5
Cube the current value.	<u>^ 3</u>
	15.625
Invert the current value.	<u>I</u>
	0.064
Multiply the current value by 100	<u>* 100</u>
	6.4
Quit.	<u>q</u>

The following main function, from calcltr.cpp, implements the top level of the solution.

```cpp
void main()
{
    char choice; // menu choice
    double curr_val; // current value of calculator

    display_menu();
    cout << setprecision(15); // see iomanip.h
    curr_val = 0;
    do {
        cin >> choice;
        choice = toupper (choice);
        process_choice (choice, curr_val);
    }
    while (choice != 'Q');
}
```

The current value of the calculator is stored in the double variable, curr_val, and the setprecision manipulator from iomanip.h is used to ensure that up to all 15 digits of precision of curr_val are displayed after each calculation. The display_menu function displays and briefly explains the menu of choices, and the process_choice function executes each valid menu choice.

Here is the beginning of process_choice.

```
void process_choice (char choice,        // IN
                     double& curr_val) // IN-OUT
{
   double num;
   switch (choice)
      {
      case '+': cin >> num;
                curr_val += num;
                break;
      case '*': cin >> num;
                curr_val *= num;
                break;

      . . .
        etc.
```

You are asked to write and test the full calculator program in Exercise 12.17. In Exercises 12.18 and 12.19, you are asked to add further functionality to the calculator.

12.3 **The** enum **Statement**

The char and integer data types of C++ are built-in ordinal data types. Using the enum statement, a programmer can define other ordinal types, known as ***enumerated types***. Although not necessary, enumerated types permit self-documenting code that enhances the readability of a program. Suppose, for example, that the price of theater tickets depends on the day of the week. The statement

```
switch (day)
   {
   case 2: case 3: case 5: case 6:
      price = 6.00; break;
   case 1: case 4: case 7:
      price = 8.00;
   }
```

is difficult to interpret because it is not obvious how much a ticket for a performance on, say, Wednesday costs. It would be easier to understand if we were permitted to write the $8.00 alternative list as

```
case "Sun": case "Wed": case "Sat": // illegal
   price = 8.00;
```

but, unfortunately, it is illegal to use a string value for a case in a switch statement. Fortunately, as you will soon see, the enum statement provides an attractive solution to this problem.

Basic *enum* ***Statement Syntax*** An enumerated type is declared by listing, or enumerating, its values within curly braces. These values *should not be enclosed in double quotes because they are not string values.* Some examples are

```
enum day_type {SUN, MON, TUE, WED, THU, FRI, SAT};

enum suit_type {CLUBS, DIAMONDS, HEARTS, SPADES};

enum batting_result_type
     {OUT, WALK, SNGL, DBL, TRPL, HOMER};
```

Enumerated Values Are Symbolic Constants In effect, the values of an enumerated type are programmer-chosen constant names for the integers, 0, 1, . . . , etc. Thus, SUN, MON, . . . , SAT are symbolic names for the integers 0, 1, . . . , 6, respectively. As with constants defined in a const statement, enumerated values cannot be changed by assignment or input statements. Thus,

```
SUN = 5; // illegal
```

is diagnosed as a syntax error by the compiler.

As a general rule of style, the names of enumerated values are all uppercase because they are symbolic constants.

■ **QUESTION** Given that day is of type day_type, just defined, complete the following switch statement to determine the price of a theater ticket. (Tickets are $8.00 on weekends and Wednesdays and $6.00 all other days.)

```
switch (day)
   {
   case MON: case TUE: case THU: case FRI:
      price = 6.00; break;
   case SUN: case WED: case SAT:
      price = 8.00;
   }
```

Answer   The completed line is

```
case MON: case TUE: case THU: case FRI:
```

Starting with Values Other Than Zero   By default, the values specified in an `enum` are numbered starting at zero. However, it is sometimes desirable to specify a different starting value. For example, in a program to play a card game, the ranks, or values, of face cards can be represented as 2 through 10, then 11 (jack), 12 (queen), 13 (king) , and 14 (ace) . The `enum` statement

```
enum rank_type {JACK=11, QUEEN, KING, ACE};
```

allows a programmer to refer to the rank of a face card by its name rather than its internal integer representation.

Using *enum* ***to Create Symbolic Names for Integers***   Many C++ programmers use the `enum` statement *without a type name* to give symbolic constant names to integer values. For example, the statements

```
enum {CLUBS, DIAMONDS, HEARTS, SPADES};
enum {JACK=11, QUEEN, KING, ACE};
```

give the integers 0, 1, 2, and 3 the symbolic names `CLUBS`, `DIAMONDS`, `HEARTS`, and `SPADES`, respectively, and give the integers 11, 12, 13, and 14 the symbolic names `JACK`, `QUEEN`, `KING`, and `ACE`, respectively.

■ **EXAMPLE**   **(Displaying a Deck of Cards)**   The following fragment, from the file `carddeck.cpp`, displays a card deck in order by suit and rank. Note that `rank` and `suit` are of type `int`, but make use of the symbolic names provided by the `enum` statements given earlier.

```
int rank, suit;
for (suit=CLUBS; suit<=SPADES; suit++)
    {
    for (rank=2; rank<=ACE; rank++)
        {
        display_card (rank, suit);
        cout << ' ';
        }
    cout << endl;
    }
```

Its output is

```
2c  3c  4c  5c  6c  7c  8c  9c  10c  Jc  Qc  Kc  Ac
2d  3d  4d  5d  6d  7d  8d  9d  10d  Jd  Qd  Kd  Ad
2h  3h  4h  5h  6h  7h  8h  9h  10h  Jh  Qh  Kh  Ah
2s  3s  4s  5s  6s  7s  8s  9s  10s  Js  Qs  Ks  As
```

Drawback of Enumerated Types   The values of an enumerated type variable can only be input and output as the integers that they represent. Thus, the statements

```
day_type day;
day = WED;
cout << day;
```

produce the output 3, not WED, and, in response to the statements

```
cout << "Enter the day: ";
cin >> day;
```

the user must type an integer from 0 through 6, inclusive, *not* one of the symbolic names, SUN, MON, etc.

Because of these limitations, enumerated types are most useful as internal documentation and are used sparingly by most programmers. If you must output the symbolic name of an enumerated type value, you must translate the value into a string. A String-valued function such as the following is most useful for this purpose.

```
String day_to_str(day_type day)
{
    switch (day)
        {
        case MON: return "Monday";
        case TUE: return "Tuesday";
        case WED: return "Wednesday";
        case THU: return "Thursday";
        case FRI: return "Friday";
        case SAT: return "Saturday";
        case SUN: return "Sunday";
        }
}
```

Now, the fragment

```
day_type day;
day = WED;
cout << day_to_str(day);
```

would produce the output Wednesday.

■ Exercises

1. Given that word is of type String, what is wrong with the following statement?

```
switch (word)
    {
    case "one":  cout << 'I'; break;
    case "five": cout << 'V'; break;
    case "ten":  cout << 'X';
    }
```

2. Give the output of the following statement if the value of numeral is

   (a) 'I'   **(b)** 'X'   **(c)** 'C'

```
switch (numeral)
    {
    case 'I': cout << 1;
    case 'V': cout << 5;
    case 'X': cout << 10;
    default:  cout << '?';
    }
```

3. Write an enum statement that defines an enumerated type, prism_color, whose values are RED, ORANGE, YELLOW, GREEN, BLUE, INDIGO, and VIOLET.

4. Write a function, as_string, so that the for loop

```
for (prism_color col = RED; col <= VIOLET; col++)
    cout << as_string(col) << endl;
```

will display the colors RED, ORANGE, . . . , VIOLET, one per line.

5. Write a String-valued function, month_abbrev, that uses a switch statement to return the three-letter abbreviation of the month corresponding to its int parameter, month_num. How should the function handle invalid month numbers?

6. Give the output of the following switch statement (from letters.cpp) if the value of ch is

   (a) 'X'   (b) 'R'   (c) '3'

```
switch (ch)
    {
    case 'C': case 'O': case 'Q':
    case 'S': case 'U':
        cout << "All curves\n";
        break;
    case 'B': case 'D': case 'G':
    case 'J': case 'P': case 'R':
        cout << "Curves and straight lines\n";
        break;
    default:  // other uppercase letters
        cout << "All straight lines\n";
    } // end switch
```

7. Rewrite the switch statement from program daysmon0.cpp (see Section 12.1) as a nested if statement.

Programming Problems

8. Write and test a bool-valued function, is_vowel, that returns true or false depending on whether its char parameter is a vowel.

9. Write a program that tells whether an input character is a vowel (a, e, i, o, or u), sometimes a vowel (y), or not a vowel.

10. Write a program that inputs the number of sides of a regular two-dimensional figure, then outputs its name. If the number of sides is less than three, indicate that there is no such two-dimensional figure; if the number of sides is greater than ten, display a message indicating that the name is not known.

11. Write a program to print each uppercase letter of the alphabet along with a message indicating whether the letter is composed of all curves, all straight lines, or curves and straight lines.

12. Write and test a char-valued function, grade, that takes two float parameters, scr1 and scr2. The function will average the two scores, then use a switch statement to return the appropriate letter grade on the 90, 80, 70, 60, scale.

13. At ESU a student's semester standing is based on the number of credits that student has earned, as shown in the table at right. Write and test an int-valued function, semester, that uses a switch statement to return the semester standing that corresponds to its int parameter, credits.

Credits earned	Semester
0 - 14	1
15 - 29	2
30 - 44	3
. . .	. .
105 - 119	8
120 or more	9

14. Write and test an int-valued function, days_in_month, that uses a switch statement to return the number of days in its int parameter, month.

15. Using the following enumerated type and functions

```
enum coin_type {PENNY, NICKEL, DIME, QUARTER, HALF};

String coin_string (coin_type coin);
// Return the string that is the name for coin

int value_in_cents (coin_type coin);
// Return the value, in cents, of coin.
```

write a program to input the quantity of coins of each denomination and output the dollar total of all the coins. A sample run of your program will look like this.

```
Enter the quantity of each type of coin:
penny: . . . 3
nickel: . . 2
dime: . . . 7
quarter: . . 4
half dollar: 1
Total value is $2.33
```

16. Using the following enumerated type and functions

```
enum day_type {SUN, MON, TUE, WED, THU, FRI, SAT};

String day_to_str(day_type day);
// Return the three letter string corresponding to day.
```

```
day_type str_to_day (String dstr);
// Return the day_type value corresponding to the
// three letter string dstr.

day_type day_before(day_type day);
// Return the day before day

day_type day_after(day_type day);
// Return the day after day
```

write a program that repeatedly inputs the three-letter abbreviation of a day, tells whether the day falls during the week or on the weekend, and outputs the abbreviation of the day immediately before and the day immediately after the input day.

Longer Assignments

17. Write and test the calculator program of Section 12.2.

18. Extend the calculator program of Exercise 12.17 by adding menu options C, F, and R. C and F require the program to take the ceiling and floor, respectively, of the current calculator display value, whereas R, followed by an integer value, requires the program to round to a specified number of decimal places.

19. Add division operators, / and %, to the calculator of Exercise 12.17. (*Note*: The % operator in C++ supports only integer division. However, modular division of floating-point numbers is supported by the fmod function from the math.h library.)

20. Write a menu-driven automatic teller program in which the user's bank balance is initialized to $200. The user will then be allowed to make as many transactions as desired from the menu:

```
(B)alance (D)eposit (W)ithdraw e(X)it:
```

Do not allow the user to overdraw. On exiting, print a courteous message and the user's current balance.

21. In the two-person game of Rock-Scissors-Paper, each player selects either 'R', 'S', or 'P'. The winner is determined as follows: Rock breaks Scissors, Scissors cuts Paper, Paper covers Rock. The game is a tie if both players make the same choice. Write a program that randomly generates and processes 10 games. The first part of the output should give the result of each game. A typical result might be

```
S R Rock breaks Scissors. Player 2 wins.
```

The second part of the output should tell how many games were won by each player.

22. Redo Exercise 6.14 using switch rather than extended if statements wherever possible.

23. Write a program that allows the user to enter the two-letter abbreviation for one of the 50 U.S. states, and then outputs the full name of the state. (*Hint*: Read a single character at a time, and use nested switch statements.)

24. Write a program that allows the user to enter the one- or two-letter symbol for a chemical element, then outputs the full name of the element

13

Arrays and the Vector Class

C ++ has always provided the built-in *array* data type as the primary structure for storing a list of items of the same type. However, in light of some major shortcomings of arrays, the very similar, but safer and more powerful, *vector class* is being used increasingly in place of arrays.[1]

In this chapter we consider two common types of situations in which arrays or vectors are useful: (1) When a list of data must be processed *more than once* and (2) when a large number of related counting or summing variables are required.

We begin with some programs that illustrate the basic use of arrays. Then, after pointing out some deficiencies of arrays, we introduce vectors, explaining why they are both safer and more convenient than arrays. We also discuss the modifications that are needed to convert a program using vectors into one using arrays (or vice versa). Finally, for the longer applications, we switch over entirely to vectors as the preferred structure.

13.1 Arrays

An *array* is a *structured data type* consisting of a collection of memory cells for storing a list of values that are *all of the same type* — a list of int numbers, a list of float numbers, or a list of String items. (A String is also a structured data type, and consists of a collection of char memory

---

[1] The C++ version of the Advanced Placement Exams for Computer Science now covers vectors instead of arrays.

cells.) The entire list of data items comprising an array is given a single name.

Suppose `scores` is an array variable that stores four integer values, 79, 86, 72, and 93, as depicted.

scores

scores[0]	79
scores[1]	86
scores[2]	72
scores[3]	93

The memory cells that make up an array are called its **elements** or **components**, or simply **cells**. Each cell has a **subscript**, or **index**, which is used to access the value in that cell. *Be aware that the memory cells of an array are always numbered beginning with zero!*

To specify an individual element of an array, you must give both the name of the array and the subscript. For example, the notation `scores[2]`, read "scores sub 2," refers to memory cell number 2 of the array `scores`. Thus, if `scores` is as depicted, the following statements preform the actions described in comments.

```
scores[2] = scores[2] + 5; // changes scores[2] to 77
cout << scores[3]; // outputs the contents (93) of
                   // scores[3].
```

Declaring an Array   A statement of the form

```
element-type array-name [size];
```

creates an array, *array-name*, of `size` contiguous memory cells of type *element-type*, with subscripts 0, 1, . . . , `size`−1. Thus, the following declarations have the effect indicated in comments.

```
float x[10]; // declare floats x[0]..x[9]
String names[8]; // declare Strings names[0]..names[7]
```

▓ QUESTION   What output will the following program produce?

```
// arydemo.cpp
// Demonstrate array declaration and subscripting.
#include <isostream.h>

void main()
```

```
{
    int x[4]; // Declare array with 4 int cells
             // x[0], x[1], x[2], and x[3]

    // Assign values to these components
    x[0] = 83;
    x[1] = 29;
    x[2] = 70;
    x[3] = x[1] + x[2];

    // Some output:
    cout << x[2]   << ' '
         << x[2+1] << ' '
         << x[2]+1 << endl;
}
```

Answer The program output will be 70 99 71.

After the four assignment statements have been executed, the contents of array x can be depicted as

x[0]	x[1]	x[2]	x[3]
83	29	70	99

An array can be depicted vertically or horizontally. Here we depict it horizontally.

Note that X[2+1] refers to the contents of cell 3, whereas x[2]+1 is the sum of 1 and the contents of cell 2. ▪ ▬

■ **QUESTION** (1) Give a declaration for an array named hourly_rates, which can hold ten float values; (2) then write statements that will assign 7.50 to the first and last cells of that array.

Answer (1) float hourly_rate[10];
         (2) hourly_rates[0] = 7.50;
              hourly_rates[9] = 7.50;

Note that the declaration uses the number of memory cells, 10, but the subscript for the last memory cell is 9, one less. ▪ ▬

Using a *for* ***Loop to Fill an Array*** A for loop, whose control variable is the array subscript, can be used to fill an array interactively. For example, the following code, from io_loops.cpp, stores four input integers in x[0], . . . , x[3].

```
cout << "Enter 4 values: ";
for (i=0; i<4; i++)
    cin >> x[i];
```

■ QUESTION **(Outputting an Array's Contents)**　Assuming that the user enters the values 14, 70, 14, and 68 when the preceding loop executes, fill in the blanks in the following loop so that its output is that shown at right.

```
for (i=0; i<4; i++)
   cout << "x[" << _____ << "] is "
        << _____ << endl;
```

```
x[0] is 14
x[1] is 70
x[2] is 14
x[3] is 68
```

Answer　The completed lines are

```
cout << "x[" << i << "] is "
     << x[i] << endl;
```

■ ▬

■ QUESTION　**(Reversing the Original Order of an Input List)**　In the following `main` function, from `rev_ary1.cpp`, a list of integers is processed twice. The first time, the list of input numbers is read into an array. The second time, it is printed in reverse order by going through the array backwards. After looking at the sample run of the program, fill in the header of the loop, which outputs the array cells in reverse order.

```
Enter number of inputs (up to 25): 6
Enter 6 integers: 18 23 9 77 20 10
Reverse of original order: 10 20 77 9 23 18
```

Sample run

```
void main()
{
   int i, size;
   int numbs[25];

   cout << "Enter number of inputs (up to 25): ";
   cin >> size;
   cout << "Enter " << size << " integers: ";
   for (i=0; i<size; i++)
      cin >> numbs[i];

   cout << "Reverse of original order: ";
   // Second time through array
   for (_____; _____; i--)
      cout << numbs[i] << ' ';
   cout << endl;
}
```

Answer The completed line is

```
for (i=size-1; i>=0; i--)
```

(*Note*: In the sample run, the value of size was 6, which is less than the *declared size*, 25, of numbs.) ■ ▬

Array Parameter Declarations When declaring an array parameter, the array parameter's name must always be followed by the empty square brackets, [ ]. Also be aware of these two facts.

1. **Arrays are automatically passed by reference.** Thus, you do not use & when declaring an array reference parameter. In fact, including & will result in a syntax error.

2. **Arrays cannot be passed by value.** However, beginning an array parameter declaration with the keyword const prevents the function from changing the values of the matching array argument in the function call.

For example, in the next program note the array parameters in the two function declarations:

```
void get_data (int numbs[], int& size);
    // numbs is a reference parameter
void print_reverse (const int numbs[], int size);
    // numbs is protected like a value parameter
```

Efficiency Benefits of Not Using Value Parameters An array can be a large structure, and passing an array parameter by value, if possible, would require the computer to make a duplicate copy of the array's contents. Because array parameters are always passed by reference (or constant reference, when protection is needed), the cost in time and memory of making the copy is eliminated.

■ **EXAMPLE** Program rev_ary2.cpp is a revision of rev_ary1.cpp that uses the functions get_data and print_reverse to read the input into an array and then print it in reverse order. Here is the main function and the definition of the get_data function:

```
void main()
{
    int size;
    int numbs[25];

    get_data (numbs, size);
    cout << "Reverse of original order: ";
    print_reverse (numbs, size);
}
```

```
void get_data (int numbs[], int& size)
{
    int i;
    cout << "Enter number of inputs (up to 25): ";
    cin >> size;
    cout << "Enter " << size << " integers: ";
    for (i=0; i<size; i++)
        cin >> numbs[i];
}
```

13.2   Shortcomings of Arrays

Before introducing the Vector class in the next section, we will point out some problems with arrays that the Vector class has been designed to remedy.

1. Lack of Index Range Checking Suppose that the array numbs has four memory cells allocated by the declaration int numbs[4]. The following code to enter four values and store them in numbs might create a serious problem:

```
cout << "Enter 4 integers: ";
for (i=1; i<=4; i++)
    cin >> numbs[i];
```

The mistake is that no memory cell has been declared for numbs[4]. However, when i=4, instead of stopping execution with an error message, the computer will attempt to put the fourth input value in the memory cell immediately after numbs[3]. Thus, if the user entered the values 11, 3, 19, and 96, memory would look like:

	[0]	[1]	[2]	[3]	. . . . .
numbs	?	11	3	19	96

The danger is that the shaded memory cell that was filled with 96 might (1) belong to another variable, whose value is now corrupted, making the program unreliable, or (2) might belong to some other currently running application program. In the most extreme case, this could necessitate rebooting the computer, and any unsaved work in progress would be lost.

2. **Lack of a Simple Way to Dynamically Resize an Array** During execution of a program, we may want to increase the size of an array in order to accommodate more data. However, resizing an array requires advanced techniques involving pointer variables and dynamic memory allocation and deallocation. These topics are introduced in Chapter 22.

3. **Inconsistent Syntax and Problems Arising with** typedef C++ improved on C by providing the reference parameter. This notation, however, cannot be used consistently, because arrays are automatically passed by reference. Note that the following declaration specifies that both numbs and size are passed by reference.

```
void get_data (int numbs[], int& size);
```

This problem is compounded when a programmer uses a typedef statement such as

```
typedef int Int_array[20]; // Int_array can now be
                           // used as a data type
```

so that the above function declaration can be written as

```
void get_data (Int_array numbs, int& size);
```

Now, neither & nor [] is present to indicate that numbs is passed by reference — the reader can only trust that Int_array really represents an array type.

The *Vector* **Class Solution** As you will see in the remaining sections of this chapter, the Vector class remedies all of the problems of arrays. Before looking at vectors, however, we discuss how to protect against out-of-bounds array subscripts.

Using *Assert* **as a Precaution** One way to protect against the danger of an out-of-bounds array subscript is to precede each statement that alters the value of an array cell by a call to Assert (from ourtools.h). For example, if x is an array of ten floats, then:

```
Assert (0<=i && i<10, "Subscript error");
cin >> x[i];

Assert (0<=i-1 && i<10, "Subscript error");
x[i-1] = x[i];
```

are safe ways to read into x[i] and to assign to x[i-1], respectively.
You might also want to protect against outputting an out-of-bounds

array cell, although *using* an out-of-bounds array cell will not cause the kind of run-time problems that altering such a cell causes.

13.3 Vectors

Obtaining a* Vector *Class Implementation   Be aware that a ***vector class*** is part of the proposed ANSI-ISO draft C++ standard, and is now built into many compilers. However, if your C++ compiler does not contain a vector class, you can use the Vector class implementation contained in the file baVector.h, available at the PWS Web site. (Complete documentation is given in Appendix G and in the file bavector.doc.) This author-defined Vector class is a subset of the one proposed in the draft standard. Another option is to download an implementation from an Internet site.

Version-Dependent Issues

1. Vector **Versus** vector The ANSI-ISO draft standard uses the name vector for the vector class, while the implementation at the Web site uses Vector. (Other implementations may use other names — the Advanced Placement Exams use the name apvector.) If your implementation of the vector class uses a different spelling, you can either (a) use the "global replace" feature provided by most text editors to change the spelling, or (b) use a typedef statement like

    typedef vector Vector;

to make Vector a synonym for vector.

2. Appropriate #include **Statement** Any program using vectors must have an appropriate #include statement for the file containing the implementation of the Vector class. For example, if you use the PWS Web site's implementation of the Vector class your program needs

    #include "baVector.h"

If you use some other implementation, fill in the blank with the appropriate #include directive: _____.

Declaring a Vector Variable   A statement of the form

    Vector<element-type> vector_name(size);

creates a vector variable, *vector_name*, of size size, where *element-type* is the type of element that is to be stored in the vector.

Let us contrast the declaration of numbs as a vector of size 10 with that of numbs as an array of size 10:

```
Vector<int> numbs(10); // declaration as a vector
int numbs[10]; // declaration as an array
```

■ **QUESTION**   Declare a vector of 10 float values called hourly_rates, and assign 7.50 to the first and last components of the vector.

Answer   The declaration would be

```
Vector<float> hourly_rates(10);
```

and the assignment statements would be

```
hourly_rates[0] = 7.50;
hourly_rates[9] = 7.50;
```

■ **EXAMPLE**   The following program uses a vector, rather than an array, to input integers from the keyboard, and display them in reverse order. The changes that have been made to convert from arrays to vectors are shaded.

```
// rev_vct1.cpp
#include <iostream.h>
#include "baVector.h"

void main()
{
    int i, size;
    Vector<int> numbs(25);

    cout << "Enter number of inputs (up to 25): ";
    cin >> size;
    cout << "Enter " << size << " integers: ";
    for (i=0; i<size; i++)
        cin >> numbs[i];

    cout << "Reverse of original order: ";
    // Second time through vector
    for (i=size-1; i>=0; i--)
        cout << numbs[i] << ' ';
    cout << endl;
}
```

Automatic Subscript Range Checking   It is a common error to forget that a vector's (like an array's) subscript range runs from zero to *one less than* the declared size of the vector. For the numbs vector of the previous example, a common mistake would be to write a statement such as

```
cout << numbs[25];
```

Fortunately, vectors have a built-in safety feature called ***subscript range checking*** — at run-time, whenever a statement involving a vector element is executed, the element's subscript is checked to make sure it is within the allowable range for that vector. In the case of the preceding cout statement, the error message

```
***ERROR: Subscript [25] out of range (0..24)
```

would be displayed and program execution would terminate.

Vector Parameter Declarations   A vector parameter declaration generally takes one of the two forms:

1.   Vector<*elt-type*>& *vector-name*

2.   const Vector<*elt-type*>& *vector-name*

As discussed in Section 13.1, for efficiency reasons, pass by reference is preferable to pass by value for large data structures. Note that the const modifier is included when protection is desired.

For example, to rewrite rev_vct1.cpp so that data input and output are done by calls to functions, the declarations for the two functions would be:

```
void get_data (Vector<int>& numbs,
               int& size);
void print_reverse (const Vector<int>&numbs,
                    int size);
```

The complete code for this program is at the PWS Web site in rev_vct2.cpp.

Overview: Vectors Versus Arrays

1.   The syntax for accessing individual memory cells is identical for arrays and vectors — both put the subscript in square brackets. Thus, *vector and array programs to solve the same problem will look very similar.*

2.   To convert an elementary vector program to an equivalent array program you would:

(a) change any declarations of vector variables or parameters to their array equivalents,

(b) remove the #include "baVector.h" directive, and

(c) insert Assert function calls, as discussed in Section 13.2, to provide subscript range checking.

3. Dynamic resizing — that is, changing the size of an array or vector while a program is running — is easier for vectors than for arrays. You can use techniques from Section 22.4 to provide dynamic resizing for arrays.

Reading Data from a File Without a Header When a data file does not have a header, the technique for reading data from the file into a vector differs from the count-controlled input loop of rev_vct1.cpp in two ways:

1. A while loop is used for input.

2. A variable with a meaningful name, say, size, is used to keep track of the number of values read into the vector. size will be initialized to 0 and incremented each time a value has been read and stored in the vector. By the time all the data has been read into the vector, the value of size will be the working size of the array. (For example, see the function get_data of the next program.)

Also, note that once the data has been read into the vector, futher processing of the vector elements can be done using a for loop with size as an upper limit on the control variable.

■ **PROBLEM** The file grade.dat contains the exam scores for each of the students in a class of at most 40 students. We want to write a program that first finds and prints the class average, and then prints each of the scores that is greater than the class average. For example, if the file grade.dat contained the scores 70, 80, 71, 58, 79, and 92, the output would be

```
6 scores read.
Class average = 75.0
Scores above average: 80 79 92
```

A vector is needed because the data must be processed twice — first to find the average, and then to determine which scores are above the average. Let us call this vector scores.

Here is a first draft in pseudocode.

Read the data from the file into the vector scores.
Calculate the class average using a function.
Print the number of scores and the class average.
Process scores *a second time to identify and print*
  those scores that are above the class average.

Here is a refinement.

```
get_data (      );  file will also be opened and closed here
avg = mean (     );
cout << num_scores << " scores read.\n";
fixed_out(cout,1);
cout << "Class average = " << avg << endl;
print_above (      );
```

Before reading on, fill in the arguments in the function calls, and identify each as IN, OUT, or IN-OUT.

The following code is from the program aboveavg.cpp.

```
const int MAX_SCORES = 40; // Global const

void get_data (Vector<int>& scr, // out
               int& size);       // out
// read data from grades.dat into
// scr[0]..scr[size-1]

float mean(const Vector<int>& scr, // in
           int size);              // in
// return mean of scr[0]..scr[size-1]

void print_above(const Vector<int>& scr, // in
                 int size,  // in
                 float x);  // in
// print values in scr[0]..scr[size-1] greater than x

void main()
```

```
{
    Vector<int> scores (MAX_SCORES);
    int num_scores;
    float avg;

    get_data (scores, num_scores);
    avg = mean (scores, num_scores);
    cout << num_scores << " scores read.\n";
    fixed_out(cout,1);
    cout << "Class average = " << avg << endl;
    print_above (scores, num_scores, avg);
}
```

Let us consider the function implementations. While doing so, note that the parameter size is used as a vector subscript only in the get_data function — in the other functions, size is the upper limit of a for loop.

```
void get_data (Vector<int>& scr, // out
               int & size)       // out
{
    ifstream ins;
    ins.open ("grade.dat");
    Assert (!ins.fail(),
            "Can't open grade.dat");

    size = 0;
    while (ins>>ws && !ins.eof())
        {
        ins >> scr[size];
        size++; // another score
        }
    ins.close();
}
```

Note that a single function, get_data, reads the entire contents of the external data file into the vector. In such situations, it is customary to put all file handling statements in that function. Thus, get_data declares the ifstream ins locally, opens the file grade.dat, and, finally, closes the file.

■ **QUESTION**   Fill in the missing portions of the functions `mean` and `print_above`.

```
float mean(const Vector<int>& scr, // in
           int size)               // in
// return mean of scr[1]..scr[size]
{
    int i;
    float sum;

    if (size==0) return 0;
    sum = 0;
    for (i=0; i<size; i++)
        _____;
    _____;
}
```

```
void print_above(const Vector<int>& scr, // in
                 int size,   // in
                 float x)    // in
{
    int i;
    cout << "Scores above average: ";
    _____
        if (scr[i]>x)
    _____;
    cout << endl;
}
```

Answer   The completed lines of `mean` are

```
    sum += scr[i];
return sum/size;
```

and the completed lines of `print_above` are

```
for (i=0; i<size; i++)
    cout << scr[i] << ' ';
```

13.4 Vectors of Counting Variables

Vectors are particularly useful when you are tallying a number of related quantities. By using the vector index, you can directly increment the appropriate counter instead of performing a tedious multiway selection to choose the appropriate counter.

■ **PROBLEM** **(Vote Counting)**   Suppose that in a recently held election, the names of the four candidates, Grey, Mastrekova, Quirot, and Rodal, are stored, one per line, in the file candnams.dat. Suppose further that votes.dat is a file containing the votes cast in that election, in which a 1, 2, 3, or 4 represents a vote for, respectively, Grey, Mastrekova, Quirot, or Rodal. That is, votes.dat consists of a list like:

    1 4 3 2 1 2 4 12 2 . . . etc.

We wish to write a program to process the file votes.dat. The printout should be as follows. (Notice that invalid votes are reported.)

```
Invalid vote: 12
Invalid vote: 5
Invalid vote: 24

CANDIDATE       VOTES
Grey             17
Mastrekova       38
Quirot           24
Rodal            32
```

We will use a vector of Strings, cand_names, to record the candidates' names, and a vector of integers, vote_counts, to count the votes for each candidate. Because the votes are stored as integers 1 through 4, we will use cells 1 through 4 of each vector, and ignore cell 0.

	cand_names		vote_counts
[0]	???	[0]	??
[1]	Grey	[1]	17
[2]	Mastrekova	[2]	38
[3]	Quirot	[3]	24
[4]	Rodal	[4]	32

At the start of the program, the candidate names must be read into cand_names from the candnams.dat file, and cells 1 through 4 of vote_counts must be initialized to 0.

Here is the pseudocode.

Read cand_names *from file* candnams.dat.
Initialize vote_counts *to all zeros.*
tally (vote_counts);
>   This function will use a while loop to read and tally each of the votes; for
>   example, a vote of 3 will increase vote_counts[3] by 1.
print_summary (cand_names, vote_counts)
>   This function will use a for loop to print the contents of the vectors of
>   names and vote counts in table form.

■ **QUESTION**   What kind of parameter (IN, OUT, IN_OUT) should vote_counts be in the
function tally? in the function print_summary? For both functions, give
the technique (value, reference, constant reference) that should be used
to pass vote_counts to the function.

Answer   Because we want tally to change the values of vote_counts from all
zeros to the final totals for each candidate, vote_counts will be an
IN-OUT parameter passed by reference to tally. Because print_summary
does not change vote_counts, it will be an IN parameter of that function.
Because vote_counts is a vector, it should be passed to print_summary
by constant reference rather than by value.   ■ ■■

Here is the program without function implementations.

```
// election.cpp
#include <iostream.h>
#include <fstream.h>
#include <iomanip.h>
#include "baString.h"
#include "baVector.h"
#include "ourtools.h" // for Assert

void get_names (Vector<String>& name); // out
// Read candidate names from file into
// name[1]..name[4]

void initialize(Vector<int>& count); // out
// Initialize count[1]..count[4] to zeros

void tally(Vector<int>& count); // in-out
// Read votes from votes.dat and tally
// using vector of counts, count.
```

```
void print_summary(const Vector<String>& name, // in
                   const Vector<int>& count);  // in
// Output names and vote counts for each candidate

void main()
{
    Vector<String> cand_names (5);
    // names of cand_names 1..4
    Vector<int> vote_counts(5);
    // tally vote_counts for cand_names 1..4

    get_names (cand_names);
    initialize(vote_counts);
    tally(vote_counts);
    print_summary(cand_names, vote_counts);
}
```

Processing a Single Vote We now concentrate on a very important detail of the function `tally` — how to process a vote that has just been input. The statements

```
vot_in >> cand;
if (1<=cand && cand<=4)
    Count 1 more vote for candidate # cand;
else
    count << "Invalid vote: " << cand << endl;
```

first read a number representing a vote for a particular candidate, then either count 1 more for that candidate or display a message that the number read is not valid. (The stream `vot_in` is associated with the file `votes.dat`.) The important detail here is how to write the highlighted pseudocode in C++. An *inefficient* way is to use a four-way selection statement such as

```
switch (cand)
{
    case 1: count[1]++; break;
    case 2: count[2]++; break;
    case 3: count[3]++; break;
    case 4: count[4]++; break;
} // end switch
```

However, this entire `switch` statement can be replaced by the following, much simpler statement:

```
count[cand]++;
```

Here, the value of `cand` (1, 2, 3, or 4) gives the subscript of the element of `count` that is to be incremented.

Here are all of the function implementations.

```
void get_names (Vector<String>& name) // out
{
   int cand;
   ifstream names_in;
   names_in.open ("candnams.dat");
   Assert (!names_in.fail(),
           "Can't open candnams.dat for input");
   for (cand=1; cand<=4; cand++)
      names_in >> name[cand];
   names_in.close();
}

void initialize(Vector<int>& count)    // out
{
   int cand;
   for (cand=1; cand<=4; cand++)
      count[cand]=0;
}

void tally(Vector<int>& count) // in-out
{
   int cand;
   ifstream vot_in;
   vot_in.open ("votes.dat");
   Assert (!vot_in.fail(),
           "Can't open votes.dat for input");

   while (vot_in>>ws && !vot_in.eof())
      {
      vot_in >> cand;
      if (1<=cand && cand<=4)
         count[cand]++;
      else
         cout << "Invalid vote: " << cand
              << endl;
```

```
          } // end while
      vot_in.close();
  }

void print_summary(const Vector<String>& name, // in
                   const Vector<int>& count)    // in
  {
      int cand;
      cout << "\nCANDIDATE    VOTES\n";
      for (cand=1; cand<=4; cand++)
         cout << name[cand] << setw(15-name[cand].length())
              << count[cand] << endl;
  }
```

Subscript Translation   To store annual sales totals for the 11 years from 1990 through 2000, consider the following two possible vector declarations:

```
Vector<float> sales(2001);
   // allocates sales[0]..sales[2000] — wasteful
Vector<float> sales(11);
   // allocates sales[0]..sales[10] — just enough
```

Using the more economical declaration of just 11 memory cells, here is a for loop, with meaningful prompts, that reads each year's sales total into sales. Note how the year is translated into a valid subscript from 0 to 10 by subtracting 1990.

```
for (year=1990; year<=2000; year++)
   {
   cout << "Enter sales total for " << year << ": ";
   cin >> sales[year - 1990];
   }
```

13.5   Parallel Vectors

In the program election.cpp of the previous section, we used two vectors, both with the subscript range 0..4, to keep track of two closely related lists of data — the candidates' names and the number of votes cast for each candidate. Such vectors are called **parallel vectors** because of the relationship between same-subscripted components of the two vectors.

■ PROBLEM   Suppose the file `scores.dat` contains the last name, semester standing, and exam score of each student in Professor Maximillian's class. We want to write a program to find the highest exam score achieved, and then print the name and semester standing of everyone who earned that score. For the given data file, the printout would be as shown below.

`scores.dat`

Smith	2	70
Johnson	7	92
Young	8	75
Cohen	4	92
Bird	5	83
. .	.	.

```
High score 92
Achieved by:
     Johnson (sem. 7)
     Cohen (sem. 4)
```
Program output

The Need for Parallel Vectors We need to store the data in parallel vectors because there can be more than one student earning the highest score. A *first pass* through the vector of scores determines the highest score, and a *second pass* locates each score equal to the highest and prints the name and semester standing of the student who earned it.

For the data file `scores.dat`, the parallel vectors would look like

	names		semesters		scores
[0]	Smith	[0]	2	[0]	70
[1]	Johnson	[1]	7	[1]	92
[2]	Young	[2]	8	[2]	75
[3]	Cohen	[3]	4	[3]	92
[4]	Bird	[4]	5	[4]	83
. .	. . . .	. .	. .	. .	. . .

The following `Vector`, constant, and function declarations and the `main` function are from `highest.cpp`.

```cpp
const int MAX_STDNTS = 30;  // Global const

void get_data (
        Vector<String>& name,  // out -- names
        Vector <int>& sem,     // out -- semesters
        Vector<int>& scr,      // out -- scores
        int& size);    // out
```

```
// read data from scores.dat into cells 0..size-1
// of parallel vectors name, sem, and scr.

int max_score (const Vector<int>& scr, // in
               int N);   // in
// return maximum score in scr[0]..scr[N-1]

void print_achievers (
      const Vector<String>& name, // in -- names
      const Vector<int>& sem,     // in -- semesters
      const Vector<int>& scr,     // in -- scores
      int size,        // in -- size of vectors
      int hi_scr);     // in
// output name and semester of each student
// who earned a score equal to hi_scr.

void main()
{
   Vector<String> names(MAX_STDNTS);
   Vector<int> semesters(MAX_STDNTS);
   Vector<int> scores(MAX_STDNTS);
   int num_stdnts;
   int highest;

   get_data (names, semesters, scores, num_stdnts);
   highest = max_score(scores, num_stdnts);
   cout << "High score " << highest << endl;
   cout << "Achieved by:\n";
   print_achievers(names, semesters, scores,
                   num_stdnts, highest);
}
```

■ **QUESTION**   Complete the missing lines in the implementations of the following functions from the preceding program fragment.

```
void get_data (
      Vector<String>& name, // out -- names
      Vector<int>& sem,     // out -- semesters
      Vector<int>& scr,     // out -- scores
      int& size)   // out
```

```
{
    ifstream ins;
    ins.open ("scores.dat");
    Assert (!ins.fail(), "Can't open scores.dat.");

    size = 0;
    while (ins>>ws && !ins.eof())
        {
        ins >> _____;
        _____;
        }
}
```

```
void print_achievers (
        const Vector<String>& name, // in -- names
        const Vector<int>& sem,      // in -- semesters
        const Vector<int>& scr,      // in -- scores
        int size,      // in -- size of vectors
        int hi_scr)     // in
{
    int i;
    for (i=0; i<size; i++)
        if (_____)
            cout << "    " <<  _____
                  << " (sem. " << _____ << ")\n";
}
```

Answer   The incomplete lines of get_data are

```
ins >> name[size] >> sem[size] >> scr[size];
size++;
```

and the incomplete lines of print_achievers are

```
if (scr[i] == hi_scr)
    cout << "    " << name[i]
          << " (sem. " << sem[i] << ")\n";
```

13.6 Hand Tracing with Vectors

You can improve your understanding of vectors and your ability to debug programs that use vectors if you learn to systematically hand trace code involving vectors.

■ **QUESTION** Suppose vct is a vector of six int components. What will be the contents of vct after execution of the following loop?

```
for (n=0; n<6; n++)
    vct[n] = 5*n + 2;
```

Answer vct [0] [1] [2] [3] [4] [5]
{ 2, 7, 12, 17, 22, 27}

This trace is quite easy because just one vector component is involved in each iteration of the loop body. ■ ▬

■ **QUESTION** (More Difficult) The main difficulty in the next trace is that the action during each iteration of the loop body involves not one, but three vector components. Suppose vct is a vector of six int memory cells whose contents are 35, 18, 10, 24, 47, and 55. What will be the contents of vct after execution of the following loop?

```
for (n=0; n<4; n++)
    if (vct[n] > vct[n+1])
        vct[n+2] = vct[n] + 1;
    else
        vct[n+2] = n;
```

Answer Here is a trace table that does detailed "bookkeeping," which provides a reliable trace. The four columns of the trace table keep track of

1. the current value of the loop control variable, n,

2. the vector components reference in the if test,

3. the assignment statement that is executed, and the vector components that are involved in that assignment, and

4. the current and updated contents of the vector vct.

To aid readability, dashed lines are placed between successive loop iterations.

n	if test vct[n]>vct[n+1]	action statement	vct [0]	[1]	[2]	[3]	[4]	[5]
0	vct[0]>vct[1] 35 > 18	vct[n+2]=vct[n]+1 vct[2] = 35 + 1	35	18	~~10~~ 36	24	47	55
1	vct[1]>vct[2] 18 > 36	vct[n+2]=n vct[3] = 1	35	18	36	~~24~~ 1	47	55

n	if test vct[n]>vct[n+1]	action statement	vct [0]	[1]	[2]	[3]	[4]	[5]
2	vct[2]>vct[3] 36 > 1	vct[n+2]=vct[n]+1 vct[4] = 36 + 1	35	18	36	1	~~47~~ 37	55
3	vct[3]>vct[4] 1 > 37	vct[n+2]=n vct[5] = 3	35	18	36	1	37	~~55~~ 3

The final contents of vct is 35, 18, 36, 1, 37, and 3.   ■ ■■

13.7 Comparing Adjacent Cells (Useful Applications)

Some vector manipulations can be handled by using a for loop to compare each of the pairs of adjacent cells — *one* execution of the loop body will compare the contents of *one* pair of adjacent cells, and then take any necessary action.

Suppose that x is a vector of integers, size contains the number of vector components that are filled, and the integers that x contains are in *increasing* order. For example,

x[0] x[1] x[2] . . . . x[size-1]

| 14 | 14 | 22 | 25 | 25 | 25 | 25 | 38 | 38 | 40 | . . |

■ **PROBLEM** Print each distinct value contained in the ordered vector exactly once. For example, for vector x the output would be 14 22 25 38 40.

Solution Here is the code to solve the first problem.

```
cout << x[0]; // process first cell
for (i=1; i<size; i++)
    if (x[i] != x[i-1])
        cout << setw(3) << x[i];
```

   ■ ■■

First and Last Cells Are Special Frequently, the first cell, last cell, or both the first and last cells of a vector require special consideration. (The middle cells can be handled entirely by the body of the for loop.) The first cell might require extra code *before* the loop as a kind of initialization, whereas the last cell might require extra code *after* the loop.

■ PROBLEM For an ordered vector, print each distinct value and the number of times it occurs. For the previous vector x, the output would be

```
14   2 occurrence(s)
22   1 occurrence(s)
25   4 occurrence(s)
38   2 occurrence(s)
40   1 occurrence(s)
```

Solution This is more difficult than the first problem because each time we encounter a value that is different from the previous value (like the first 22), we don't yet know how many times this new value will occur.

The pseudocode to handle the middle boxes would be

```
if (x[i]==x[i−1])
    increment the count for the length of the current streak
else
    print the contents of x[i−1] and its streak count
    reset streak count to 1
```

This pseudocode is essentially the body of the for loop. Before you read on, see if you can write the entire solution to the second problem — not simply the for loop, but also any statements needed before or after the loop to handle the first and last cells. Note that the last cell requires some attention after the loop.

Here is the code for the second problem.

```
count = 1; // for x[0]
for (i=1; i<size; i++)
   if (x[i] == x[i−1])
      count++;
   else
      {
      cout << x[i−1] << " " << count
           << " occurrence(s)\n";
      count = 1;
      }
cout << x[size−1] << " " << count
     << " occurrence(s)\n";
```

In Exercise 13.6, you are asked to perform a trace of the preceding code using a table like that given in Section 13.6.

13.8   Resizing Vectors

In Section 13.2, you saw what happens if a vector does not have a sufficient number of cells to hold all the data in an external file.

One method for handling this problem is to declare the vector to have a sufficient number of cells to accommodate *any* data file that might conceivably be used as input. This method, however, may waste a great deal of memory if most of the cells are unused except in the case of a few possible input files.

In this section, we explore a superior method, that of resizing the vector *as the program runs*. With this method, whenever all cells of `numbs` are full, we expand it so it can hold more data. How you use this method depends on whether or not the input data file has a header.

Resizing When Using a Header   The following program fragment, from `resize1.cpp`, reads integers from a file with a header into a vector, `numbs`, then outputs them. Program output is given for the file `num2.dat`.

```
void get_data (Vector<int>& numbs); // out
// Resize numbs according to the header in
// num2.dat, then read the data into numbs.

void put_data (const Vector<int>& numbs); // in
// Output elements of numbs.

void main()
{
    Vector<int> numbs; // initially, length is 0

    get_data (numbs);
    cout << "There are " << numbs.length()
        << " elements in numbs. They are:\n";
    put_data (numbs);
}
```

`num2.dat`

```
6
41  68  32
74  55  27
```

```
There are 6 elements in numbs. They are:
41 68 32 74 55 27
```
Output

Notice first that the declaration

```
Vector<int> numbs; // initially, length is 0
```

specifies no size for numbs. In this case, numbs will have an initial length, or capacity, of 0. The get_data function has to change the size of numbs before any data can be read into it.

Second, notice that the vector numbs is the only argument in the calls to get_data and put_data. (This is unlike the get_data and print_reverse functions of program rev_vct2.cpp; in addition to a vector argument, these functions both required an int argument specifying how many vector cells were actually being used.) The Vector class member function length() returns the number of cells in a vector, and because get_data resizes numbs to fit the data exactly, we don't need to pass another argument telling how many cells are filled.

The implementation of the get_data function is

```
void get_data (Vector<int>& numbs) // out
{
    int i, header;
    ifstream nums_in;
    nums_in.open ("num2.dat");
    Assert (!nums_in.fail(),
            "Can't open num2.dat");

    // read header and resize numbs to fit exactly
    nums_in >> header;
    numbs.resize(header);

    // read data into numbs
    for (i=0; i<header; i++)
        nums_in >> numbs[i];
}
```

Here, the statement

```
    numbs.resize(header);
```

calls the Vector class member function resize to change the size of numbs to the size just read into header.

Resizing When Using the Sentinel or End-of-File Techniques

The main function of program resize1.cpp does not need to know whether the get_size function uses a header value or some other information to resize numbs — it merely needs to know that all cells of the vector are filled. The following version of get_data, from resize2.cpp, uses the end-of-file technique to read data from num3.dat, a file with no header.

```
void get_data (Vector<int>& numbs) // out
// Use eof technique to read the data from num3.dat
// into numbs, resizing as needed. When all data has
// been read, resize numbs to fit the data exactly.
{
    int size;
    ifstream nums_in;
    nums_in.open ("num3.dat");
    Assert (!nums_in.fail(),
            "Can't open num3.dat");

    numbs.resize(8); // assume small file to start
    /* trace */ cout << "\nLength=" << numbs.length();

    size=0;
    while (nums_in>>ws && !nums_in.eof())
        {
        if (size >= numbs.length())
            {
            // double vector's capacity
            numbs.resize (2*numbs.length());
            /* trace */ cout << "\nLength=" << numbs.length();
            }
        nums_in >> numbs[size];
        size++;
        }
    // Resize to fit data exactly
        numbs.resize(size);
    /* trace */ cout << "\nLength=" << numbs.length();
    /* trace */ cout << endl;
}
```

A run of `resize2.cpp` for a file `num3.dat` consisting of 18 integers is

```
Length=8                    Tracing output
Length=16                       .
Length=32                       .
Length=18                       .

There are 18 elements in numbs. They are:
 41 68 32 74 55 27 98 64 87 13 19 20 77 99 80 87 82 80
```

Notice that there are three different calls (all highlighted) to `resize` in the body of `get_data`. The first call, `numbs.resize(8);`, creates enough cells to hold at most eight data items. The second call, `numbs.resize (2*numbs.length());`, doubles the size of `numbs` whenever more cells are needed to store data. The third and final call, `numbs.resize(size);`, re-sizes `numbs` so that any unused cells are removed from the vector, thus fitting `numbs` exactly to the amount of data in the input file.

Tracing output has been included in `get_size` for illustration/testing purposes — you can see when and to what size the vector is resized.

Caution with Resize You might wonder why the size of `numbs` is doubled, rather than increased by one, each time more cells are required. The reason for this is that `resize` is a somewhat time- and memory-intensive operation. Each call to `resize` requires that the current vector contents be copied to a new memory location. Resizing in increments of one element would require excessive amounts of copying, although it would never make excessive demands on memory. On the other hand, resizing in increments of, say, 1000, would require less frequent copying, but could make excessive demands on memory. Resizing by doubling maintains a reasonable balance between the amount of copying and the demands on memory.

■ Exercises

1. What will be the contents of v (declared as `Vector <int> v(5);`) after each of the `for` loops in the following code fragment?

```
for (int j=0; j<5; j++)
    v[j] = 2*j + 1;
for (j=3; j>=0; j--)
    v[j] = v[j+1] + j;
```

2. What kinds of errors do the following programs contain?

(a)
```
#include "baVector.h"
void main()
{
    Vector<int> nums;
    for (int i=0; i<3; i++)
        nums[i] = 10 * i;
}
```

(b)
```
#include "baVector.h"
void main()
{
    Vector nums[3];
    for (int i=0; i<3; i++)
        nums(i) = 10 * i;
}
```

3. Give the output of the following program fragments assuming that chs is declared as Vector<char> chs(5);.

(a)
```
for (i=0; i<5; i++)
    chs[i] = 'A' + i;
for (i=0; i<5; i++)
    cout << chs[i];
```

(b)
```
chs[0] = 'Z';
for (i=1; i<5; i++)
    chs[i] = chs[i-1] - 1;
for (i=0; i<5; i++)
    cout << chs[i];
```

4. Given that v[0] through v[5] are 5, 12, 8, 4, 23, and 19, show the contents of v[0]..v[5] after execution of each of the following code fragments.

(a)
```
tmp = v[0];
for (i=0, i<5; i++)
    v[i] = v[i+1];
v[5] = tmp;
```

(b)
```
for (i=0, i<3; i++)
{
    tmp = v[i];
    v[i] = v[5-i];
    v[5-i] = tmp;
}
```

5. Give the output of the following main function.

```
void main()
{
    int len = 4;
    Vector<int> x(len);
    for (int i=0; i<x.length(); i++)
        x[i] = 2*i;
    for (int i=0; i<x.length(); i++)
        cout << x[i] << ' ';
    x.resize(2*len);
    for (int i=len; i<x.length(); i++)
        x[i] = x[i-len] * len;
    for (int i=0; i<x.length(); i++)
        cout << x[i] << ' ';
}
```

6. Set up a trace table similar to that at the end of Section 13.6, then trace through the code fragment at the end of Section 13.7 using the vector x of that section as data.

7. Suppose the parallel vectors names, IQs, and genders ('m' or 'f') contain information on a class of size students. Write a program fragment that will print the names of all female students with IQs over 120.

8. Write the function concat so that it returns a vector that consists of the elements of v1 followed by the elements of v2.

```
Vector<int> concat (const Vector<int>& v1,
                    const Vector<int>& v2);
```

9. (a) Assuming that v1 and v2 have the same length, write the function intertwine so that it returns a vector in which the elements of v1 and v2 are intertwined (the first element of v1 followed by the first element of v2, the second element of v1 followed by the second element of v2, and so on).

```
Vector<int> intertwine (const Vector<int>& v1,
                        const Vector<int>& v2);
```

   (b) Rewrite intertwine so that if v1 and v2 have different lengths, the extra elements of the longer vector are appended to the end of the vector to return.

10. Assuming that v1 and v2 are sorted in increasing order, write the function merge so that it returns a vector that contains all elements of v1 and v2 sorted in increasing order.

```
Vector<int> merge (const Vector<int>& v1,
                   const Vector<int>& v2);
```

Programming Problems

11. The ACME Specialty Store sells five items, with ID numbers 101, 102, . . . , 105. A text file contains several data pairs, one per line, consisting of an item's ID number and the number of units of that item sold. For example, the pair 102 9 means that 9 units of item 102 were sold.

    Write a program that will print a table giving the ID numbers 101 through 105 and the number of units of each that were sold.

12. A consumer research organization has a data file containing the names of stores and the price that each charges for a particular computer monitor. Write a program to determine the lowest price charged for that monitor, and then print two lists.

    ■ **List 1.** The names of all stores charging the lowest price.

    ■ **List 2.** The names and prices for all stores whose price does not exceed the lowest price by more than 10%.

13. A file contains each student's name and raw test score (0–100) for a class of up to 30 students. The teacher has an unusual method of curving the scores. If there are fewer than five scores of 90 or above, up to eight points are added to each raw score; otherwise, up to four points are added to each raw score; but no student may receive a curved score over 100.

Write a program that will first print a list with each student's name and raw score, then print a list with each student's name and curved score. Test your program using a file with at least five scores of 90 or above, and one with fewer than five scores of 90 or above.

14. The first ten Fibonacci numbers are 1, 1, 2, 3, 5, 8, 13, 21, 34, and 55. (Each Fibonacci number greater than one is the sum of the previous two.) Write a program to store at least the first 25 Fibonacci numbers in a vector. Then print a table consisting of each Fibonacci number greater than one, and the ratio of each Fibonacci number to its predecessor.

15. Write a program that will simulate rolling a pair of dice 1000 times, then print a list giving the frequency of each outcome. Format the output as shown at right.

```
Roll   Frequency
 2       - - -
 3       - - -
 .
 .
 .
12       - - -
```

16. Write a program to simulate a lottery drawing in which six different numbers from 1 through 54 are selected at random. A typical output might be:

```
The six numbers are: 3 10 18 24 47 51
```

[*Hint*: Use a vector, drawn, declared as Vector<> drawn(55). Initialize cells 0 through 54 to false, and use true to indicate that a given number has been drawn.]

17. (a) Write a program to output the binary representation of a 32-bit integer input. (*Hint*: Use the "repeated division by two" algorithm of Appendix F to produce and store the bits in a vector, then print the contents of the vector in reverse.)

(b) Modify the program of part (a) to allow the user to specify the base, b, of the output, where $2 \le b \le 8$, then output the base b representation of the input integer.

Longer Assignments

18. A file contains each student's name and raw score. Write a program that will read this information into two parallel arrays and then resize the vectors to fit the data. First compute the class mean, μ, then compute the standard deviation, σ, from the class mean.

The method for computing the standard deviation is as follows: For each student, compute the difference between the student's raw score and the class mean. Then, the standard deviation is

$$\sqrt{(\text{sum of squares of these differences})/(\text{class size})}$$

For example, if the grades were 70, 74, 80, 82, 68, and 76, the mean would be 75.0, and the standard deviation would be

$$\sqrt{\frac{(70{-}75)^2 + (74{-}75)^2 + \ldots + (76{-}75)^2}{6}}$$

Once the mean, μ, and standard deviation, σ, have been computed, assign letter grades as follows:

A $\qquad \mu + \sigma \quad \le$ score
B $\qquad \mu + \sigma/3 \le$ score $< \mu + \sigma$
C $\qquad \mu - \sigma/3 \le$ score $< \mu + \sigma/3$
D $\qquad \mu - \sigma \quad \le$ score $< \mu - \sigma/3$
F $\qquad\qquad\qquad$ score $< \mu - \sigma$

The output should contain (1) a list with each student's name, numerical score, and letter grade; (2) the class average and standard deviation; and (3) a table telling how many students received each letter grade.

19. An external file contains names of customers and amounts of purchases. Some customers may have several entries, but they are grouped together, alphabetically by name, as shown at right.

```
Adams  12
Adams  10
Bond   25
..etc. ..
```

   Write a program that will read in all the data, print each customer's name and purchase total, then output the name of the customer with the largest purchase total.

20. (a) In C++, the largest 32-bit integer is 2,147,483,647. Using vectors to store digits, write a program that can enter, add, and display integers having up to 20 digits. (*Caution*: You must pad input integers having less than 20 digits with leading zeros.) Don't forget to provide for carries when adding.

   A sample run would be

```
Enter a 20 digit integer: 00000098765432101234
Enter a 20 digit integer: 00000000007895678901

00000098765432101234 + 00000000007895678901
= 00000098773327780135
```

   (b) Modify your display function so that leading zeros are not displayed.

   (c) Modify your enter function so that it is not necessary to type leading zeros.

21. Write a program that uses the functions of the previous problem to determine the largest 20-digit Fibonacci number.

14

Searching and Sorting

A rranging a list of values in order is known as *sorting*. For example, we might sort a list of numerical values in increasing order or a list of names in alphabetical order. Locating a particular item in a list is known as *searching*. Searching a sorted list is generally much faster than searching an unsorted list. For example, consider looking up someone's telephone number in an alphabetical directory versus a nonalphabetical one. This is not to imply that you should always sort a list before searching it, because sorting can be quite time consuming. The decision regarding whether to sort a list before searching it depends to some degree on the length of the list and the number of times the list will be searched.

In this chapter we discuss two searching algorithms: (1) the *linear search*, which can be used on any list, and (2) the more efficient *binary search*, which can only be used on *sorted* lists.

We also discuss three elementary sorting algorithms: (1) the *selection sort*, (2) the *bubble sort*, and (3) the *insertion sort*. For a small vector of 100 or fewer items, each of these sorts is quite satisfactory because the sorting time will be only a fraction of a second on today's personal computers. However, the time required to sort a really large vector becomes an important consideration, and it makes sense to use an advanced sorting technique such as *quicksort*, which is discussed in Chapter 26.

Finally, we discuss how to use template functions, first introduced in Chapter 10, to write a sorting or searching function that can be used on vectors of various kinds of items.

14.1 Linear Search

In a linear search (also called a sequential search) of a vector, we start with the first cell of the vector and examine the contents of one cell after another until we either find the desired item or have examined all cells without finding it. The following linear_search function returns either the location (subscript) of the desired item or, if the item is not in the vector, the value −1.

Linear Search Using a Bounded Number of Tries The following version of linear search employs the "bounded number of tries" method introduced in Section 8.3.

```
int linear_search (const Vector<String>& V,
                   String to_find,
                   int size)
// Search V[0]..V[size-1] for to_find.
// Return index where found, or -1 if not found.
{
    int index=0;
    bool found=false;
    while (!found && index<size)
        if (V[index] == to_find)
            found = true;
        else
            index++;

    if (found)
        return index;
    else
        return -1;
}
```

Notice the use of the variables found and index to control the search loop. Initially, found is false, and index is 0, the subscript of the first vector cell. It is helpful to translate the search loop condition, !found && index<size, from C++ into everyday English.

C++	while	(	!found	&&	index<size	)
English	as long as		the desired item has not been found	and	there are more cells to examine	

■ QUESTION   Suppose that `names` and `salaries` are parallel vectors containing `String` and `double` components, respectively. Fill in the blank in the following code fragment that outputs the salary of the employee whose name is input by the user.

```
cout << "Enter name of employee: ":
cin >> name_to_find;

where = linear_search
              (names, name_to_find, num_emps);

cout << name_to_find;
if (where < 0)
    cout << " is not on the payroll.\n";
else
    {
    fixed_out(cout, 2);
    cout << " has salary $" << _____
        << endl;
    }
```

Answer   Because the `names` and `salaries` vectors are parallel, the desired subscript is `where`. Thus, the blank should be filled with `salaries[where]`.

                                                                    ■ ▬▬

Linear Search Using a Mid-Loop Exit   To simplify the logic of (and shorten the code for) the linear search, we use the mid-loop exit technique introduced in Section 8.4. The body of the linear search can then be coded *much more simply* as

```
int index;
for (index=0; index<size; index++)
    if (V[index] == to_find)
        return index;
return -1;
```

14.2 Binary Search (of a Sorted Vector)

A linear sort works well enough for a short list but would be much too time consuming for a long list. If, for example, you want to look up the telephone number for William Phillipson in the Manhattan phone directory, it would be foolish to start with the very first name and continue searching, sequentially, one name at a time. A more efficient method would be to take advantage of the alphabetical ordering of the names to jump to a place in the second half of the phone book.

The binary search is akin to the method you would automatically use to look up a phone number by name. In the binary search, you keep narrowing the search by eliminating half of the remaining list. Of course, you must have a sorted list in order to use binary search.

■ **EXAMPLE**   Suppose we want to search for the name Gil in the following (sorted) vector, V.

Start of vector					Middle						End of vector
V[0]	V[1]	V[2]	V[3]	V[4]	V[5]	V[6]	V[7]	V[8]	V[9]	V[10]	V[11]
Ben	Eva	Fay	Gil	Ida	Jan	Lee	Opy	Pat	Ray	Tim	Una

First, we compare the desired name, Gil, to the contents of the middle cell, V[5]. (*Note:* When there are an even number of cells, we take the middle cell to be that cell just to the left of the midline.) Because Gil is alphabetically less than Jan, we can conclude that if Gil is in the array at all, it must be in the left half — that is, among cells V[0] through V[4].

		Middle		
V[0]	V[1]	V[2]	V[3]	V[4]
Ben	Eva	Fay	Gil	Ida

Segment of V still under consideration

Next, we compare Gil to the contents of the current middle cell, V[2]. Because Gil is greater than Fay, we can narrow the search to the right half of the segment of V still under consideration — that is, cells V[3] and V[4].

Middle	
V[3]	V[4]
Gil	Ida

Segment of V still under consideration

This time, the name we are searching for, "Gil," is equal to the contents of the middle box. Thus, the search finds Gil in V[3].

Binary Search Function   We want the binary_search function to return either the subscript of the cell containing the desired item or −1 if the item is not in the vector. The variables first, last, and mid will keep track of the subscripts of the first, last, and middle cells, respectively, of the segment of the vector still under consideration.

The key test, one that occurs repeatedly in a binary search, compares the item to find with the contents of the middle cell. If the items are equal, the desired item has been found; if the item to find is less than the contents of the middle cell, then the search should be narrowed to the half-segment to the left of the middle cell, shaded in gray.

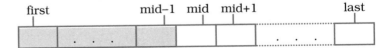

Note that the segment still under consideration can be changed to the left half-segment by assigning `last` a new value, namely, `last = mid − 1`.

■ QUESTION   In the following `binary_search` function, fill in the blank that adjusts the segment still under consideration when `to_find` is *larger* than the contents of `V[mid]`.

```
int binary_search (const Vector<String>& V,
                   String to_find,
                   int size)
{
   int first, mid, last;

   first = 0;  last = size-1;
   while (first<=last)
      {
      mid = (first + last) / 2;
      if (to_find == V[mid])
         return mid;
      if (to_find < V[mid])
         last = mid-1;
      else // to_find > V[mid]
         _____;

      }

   return -1;
}
```

Answer   When `to_find > V[mid]`, we want to narrow the search to the right half-segment. Thus, the completed line is

```
first = mid+1;
```

Hand Traces of Binary Search We did one trace of the binary search before giving the code. Let us do two more traces using a slightly larger vector containing int components. We organize this trace in table form.

V	[0]	[1]	[2]	[3]	[4]	[5]	[6]	[7]	[8]	[9]	[10]	[11]	[12]
	23	35	40	48	57	62	64	75	78	84	87	92	95

Trace When to_find= **48** Each row of the following trace table displays

1. the number of the next execution of the loop body,
2. the values of first and last at the beginning of that execution,
3. the new value calculated for mid,
4. the order relation between to_find and V[mid], and
5. the statement that narrows the search or returns the result of a successful search.

Loop body execution	Vector segment under consideration	mid	Compare to_find and V[mid]	Narrow search or return
1	V[0]..V[12]	6	48 < 64	last=mid−1
2	V[0]..V[5]	2	48 > 40	first=mid+1
3	V[3]..V[5]	4	48 < 57	last=mid−1
4	V[3]..V[3]	3	48 == 48	return 3

Trace When to_find= **82 (Not in the Vector)**

Loop body execution	Vector segment under consideration	mid	Compare to_find and V[mid]	Narrow search or return
1	V[0]..V[12]	6	82 > 64	first=mid+1
2	V[7]..V[12]	9	82 < 84	last=mid−1
3	V[7]..V[8]	7	82 > 75	first=mid+1
4	V[8]..V[8]	8	82 > 78	first=mid+1
first=9 > last=8, causing loop exit				

14.3   Selection Sort

We begin our discussion of sorting with the *selection sort*, which is the easiest sort to understand. The selection sort is similar to the process the average person would go through if asked to sort a list of 40 numbers (or alphabetize a list of 40 names). The basic idea is to first find the smallest number and swap it with the number in position 0. (Remember — vector cells are numbered starting with 0!) Then, restricting our attention to the remaining numbers, we find the next smallest number and swap it with the number in position 1. Continuing in this fashion, once the smallest 39 numbers have been correctly placed in positions 0 through 38, the remaining number must be the largest and belongs at the end of the list (in position 39); thus, the list is sorted.

Let us illustrate the selection sort for the following vector, V.

[0]	[1]	[2]	[3]	[4]	[5]	[6]
53	44	39	12	56	30	48

We use the subscript of the cell that we want to fill correctly to keep track of the sort's progress. To fill each cell, we make a *pass* through the vector (or a remaining portion of it) to find the correct number to put in the cell to be filled.

To correctly fill cell 0, we make a pass through the entire vector to locate the smallest number, V[3], or 12, which is then swapped with the number in cell 0. Then we have

[0]	[1]	[2]	[3]	[4]	[5]	[6]
12	44	39	53	56	30	48

To fill cell 1 correctly, we make a pass through the subvector V[1]..V[6] to locate the next smallest number, V[5], or 30, which is then swapped with the number in cell 1.

[0]	[1]	[2]	[3]	[4]	[5]	[6]
12	30	39	53	56	44	48

To fill cell 2 correctly, we make a pass through the subvector V[2]..V[6] to locate the next smallest number, V[2], or 39, which is then swapped with the number in cell 2. (In an actual run of the sort, this swap is made even though the cell to fill and the cell containing the smallest number are the same!) After cells 3, 4, and 5 have been correctly filled, this vector will be sorted, because the remaining number, the largest, will be in V[6].

Now, let us consider a vector with N numbers and describe what happens during the pass that fills cell ctf ("cell to fill"), with an eye to writing the C++ code for the sort.

v[0] v[ctf–1] v[ctf] v[N–1]

At the start of the pass that will correctly fill cell ctf, the shaded cells from V[0] through V[ctf-1] are already correctly filled with the final sorted values. Thus, we can restrict our attention to V[ctf]..V[N-1]. We need to make a pass through the subvector V[ctf]..V[N-1] to determine the index (call it index_min) of the smallest element of that subvector. Then, we swap the contents of V[ctf] and V[index_min].

In the pseudocode, note that we need only fill cells 0 through N-2. For example, if the vector had seven elements, after cells 0 through 5 (=7−2) are correctly filled, the largest element cannot be anywhere but in the remaining cell, V[6].

Here is the pseudocode.

```
for (ctf=0; ctf<N-1; ctf++)
    {
    Use an inner for loop to find index_min, the index
        of the smallest element in V[ctf]..V[N-1].
    Swap V[ctf] and V[index_min].
    }
```

Here is the actual code.

```
void select_sort (Vector<CType>& V, int N)
// Sort V[0]..V[N-1] in increasing order
{
    int ctf, // cell to fill
        index_min; // index of minimum component
                   // in cells ctf .. N-1

    for (ctf=0; ctf < N-1; ctf++)
        {
        // At start of pass: V[0]..V[ctf-1]
        // contain final sorted values.
```

```
    // Make a pass to find index_min
    index_min=ctf;
    for (int i=ctf+1; i < N; i++)
       if (V[i] < V[index_min])
           index_min=i;

    // Swap contents of cells ctf and index_min
    swap (V[ctf], V[index_min]);

    // At end of pass: V[0]..V[ctf] contain
    // final sorted values.
    }
}
```

Note that for iteration number ctf of the outer loop, the loop body makes a pass through subvector V[ctf]..V[N-1] to find its smallest element, then correctly places it. The inner for loop starts at ctf+1 because index_min was initialized with ctf itself.

■ QUESTION   If you number the passes so that the starting pass is pass number 0, the next pass is pass number 1, and so on, then the pass number will be the same as that of the cell to fill. That is, pass 0 correctly fills cell 0; pass 1 fills cell 1, and so on. Hence, the code for select_sort can be written using a loop control variable named pass. What changes would you need to make in the select_sort function so that it uses a variable named pass instead of the variable ctf?

Answer   Just replace every occurrence of ctf with pass.   ■ ■■

A Complete Program Calling select_sort   The program select1.cpp at the PWS Web site is a complete program that calls select_sort. The program, minus function definitions, is

```
// select1.cpp -- Selection sort
#include <iostream.h>
#include "baVector.h"
// #include "baString.h"

typedef int CType; // vector component type

void get_vector (Vector<CType>& V, int& N);
// Get vector components V[0]..V[N-1] from keyboard
```

```
void put_vector (const Vector<CType>& V, int N);
// Display V[0]..V[N-1]

void swap (CType& a, CType& b);
// interchange a and b

void select_sort (Vector<CType>& V, int N);
// Sort V[0]..V[N-1] in increasing order

void main()
{
    Vector<CType> Vect_to_sort;
    int size;

    get_vector (Vect_to_sort, size);
    cout << "\nBefore sort:\t";
    put_vector (Vect_to_sort, size);
    cout << endl;
    select_sort(Vect_to_sort, size);
    cout << "After sort:\t";
    put_vector (Vect_to_sort, size);
    cout << endl;
}
```

Modifications Required for Sorting Other Data Types Essentially, this same program can be used to enter, sort, and output vectors of Strings, floats, etc. The only modification needed is to change the data type specified in the highlighted typedef statement. In the final section of this chapter, we discuss how to use template functions (first introduced in Section 10.5) to eliminate the need for even this small modification.

14.4 Bubble Sort

Each pass of **bubble sort** consists of a trip through a remaining, potentially out-of-order subvector. During each pass, the contents of successive pairs of adjacent memory cells are compared and, if out of order, switched.

Recall that the selection sort correctly fills cells, starting on the *left* end with cell 0. By contrast, the bubble sort will correctly fill cells, starting at the *right* end with the *last cell*. (Also for the bubble sort there is no advantage to starting the pass numbering with 0, so we will start it with 1.)

Pass 1 of Bubble Sort   Suppose that four numbers, 34, 28, 43, and 15, are stored in cells 0 through 3 of a vector V. We wish to sort those numbers in increasing order. The first pass of bubble sort performs the three comparisons and makes the two switches as indicated in the following table. (When there are four cells, V[0]..V[3], there are only three *adjacent pairs* of cells.)

Comparison	Result	Action		V	[0]	[1]	[2]	[3]
V[0] > V[1]	true	switch			34	28	43	15
V[1] > V[2]	false	none			28	34	43	15
V[2] > V[3]	true	switch			28	34	43	15
					28	34	15	43

At the end of this pass, the highest numbered cell, V[3], must be correctly filled.

Pass 2 of Bubble Sort   Because the largest number is necessarily in V[3], pass 2 is performed on the subvector V[0]..V[2].

Comparison	Result	Action		V	[0]	[1]	[2]	[3]
V[0] > V[1]	false	none			28	34	15	43
V[1] > V[2]	true	switch			28	34	15	43
					28	15	34	43

Pass 3 of Bubble Sort   Because the two largest numbers are now in the correctly filled cells, V[2] and V[3], pass 3 is performed on the subvector V[0], V[1].

Comparison	Result	Action		V	[0]	[1]	[2]	[3]
V[0] > V[1]	true	switch			28	15	34	43
					15	28	34	43

The vector is now sorted. Note that for a vector, V[0]..V[size-1], of size elements, the bubble sort uses size-1 passes to sort the vector. The first pass correctly fills V[size-1], the second correctly fills V[size-2], and so on, until the final pass correctly fills V[1]. This leaves V[0] containing the smallest number. Note that a given pass correctly fills V[size-pass].

■ **QUESTION** The following vector of six components will be in sorted order after fewer than five (size-1) passes. Show the contents of the vector after pass 1, after pass 2, and after pass 3.

36	25	49	21	52	38

Answer
After pass 1:   25 36 21 49 38 **52**
After pass 2:   25 21 36 38 **49 52**
After pass 3:   21 25 36 **38 49 52**

That portion of the vector that the bubble sort guarantees to be correctly filled after each pass is shaded. However, after only three passes, the entire vector is actually sorted.

Discussion The bubble sort is so named because, viewing the vector vertically (with cell 0 at the top), the smaller numbers slowly "bubble" to the top, while larger ones "sink" into place, one by one, at the bottom. Each pass is guaranteed to fill correctly *at least one* more cell. In the previous example, the first pass filled cell 5 with the largest number, 52. The second pass, however, filled cells 2, 3, and 4, with 36, 38, and 49, respectively.

■ ▬

Two Versions of Bubble Sort Next, we present two versions of the bubble sort. The files bubble1.cpp and bubble2.cpp contain complete programs to demonstrate these two versions of the bubble sort.

In version 1, the computer makes size-1 passes to fill correctly cells size-1, then size-2, on down to cell 1, *even if the vector is actually sorted after fewer passes.*

Pseudocode for version 1 of the bubble sort

```
for (pass = 1; pass < size; pass++)
   {
   cell_to_fill = size - pass;
   for (i = 0; i < cell_to_fill; i++)
      if (V[i] > V[i+1])
          switch the contents of V[i] and V[i+1]
   }
```

Let us check the correctness of the upper limit in the inner loop,

```
for (i = 0; i < cell_to_fill; i++)
```

that handles the comparisons and switches during each pass.

When `pass = 1`, `cell_to_fill` is `size -1`. The inner loop compares cells 0 and 1, 1 and 2, and so forth, up to and including cells `cell_to_fill-1` and `cell_to_fill`. Thus, this pass makes `size -1` comparisons and correctly fills `v[cell_to_fill]`.

For each succeeding pass, the upper limit of the inner loop decreases by 1 because `pass` increases by 1.

Version 2 of Bubble Sort (Improved)   Version 1 of the bubble sort can be improved in two ways.

First, note that in the body of the outer `for` loop, `pass` is used only to determine the next value of `ctf` (short for `cell_to_fill`). Because `ctf` goes from `size-1` down to 0 as `pass` goes from 1 to `size`, `ctf` can be used as the control variable for the outer loop. That is,

```
for (ctf=size-1; ctf>0; ctf--)
```

Second, and more important, if a vector can be sorted in fewer than `size-1` iterations of this outer loop, we save time by having the computer make an early exit from the sort. How will the computer know when the vector is already sorted? If the computer makes a pass in which no swaps are needed, then the vector is already sorted.

Pseudocode for version 2 of the bubble sort

```
for (ctf = size-1; ctf > 0; ctf--)
    {
    swaps = 0; // "clear slate" for new pass
    for (i = 0; i < ctf; i++)
        if (V[i] > V[i+1])
            {
            switch the contents of V[i] and V[i+1]
            count one more swap
            }
    exit the outer loop if no swaps were made
    }
```

Here is a complete `bubble_sort` function that implements the algorithm of version 2. The tracing code shown in the box illustrates the action of the sort.

```
void bubble_sort (Vector<CType>& V, int size)
// Sort V[0]..V[size-1] in increasing order
{
    int swaps; // count swaps made on a given ctf
    for (int ctf=size-1; ctf>0; ctf--)
        {
        // At start of pass: V[ctf+1]..V[size-1]
        // contain final sorted values.

        swaps = 0;
        for (int i=0; i<ctf; i++)
            if (V[i] > V[i+1])
                {
                swap (V[i], V[i+1]);
                swaps++;
                }

        // At end of pass: V[ctf]..V[size-1]
        // contain final sorted values.

            cout << "ctf = " << ctf
                << " swaps = " << swaps <<'\t';
            put_vector (V,size); cout << endl;

        if (swaps==0) return;
        }
}
```

Two sample runs for `ints` are

```
/* Sample runs:
Enter data (Ctrl+Z to quit):
70 20 80 30 55 66
Before sort:    70 20 80 30 55 66
ctf = 5 swaps = 4        20 70 30 55 66 80
ctf = 4 swaps = 3        20 30 55 66 70 80
ctf = 3 swaps = 0        20 30 55 66 70 80
After sort:    20 30 55 66 70 80
```

```
Enter data (Ctrl+Z to quit):
10 20 30 90 40 50 60 70 80
Before sort:    10 20 30 90 40 50 60 70 80
ctf = 8  swaps = 5        10 20 30 40 50 60 70 80 90
ctf = 7  swaps = 0        10 20 30 40 50 60 70 80 90
After sort:     10 20 30 40 50 60 70 80 90
```

A sample run for Strings is

```
Enter data (Ctrl+Z to quit):
fox cat bear horse cow elk
Before sort:    fox cat bear horse cow elk
ctf = 5 swaps = 4        cat bear fox cow elk horse
ctf = 4 swaps = 3        bear cat cow elk fox horse
ctf = 3 swaps = 0        bear cat cow elk fox horse
After sort:     bear cat cow elk fox horse
```

14.5 Inserting into a Sorted Vector

Suppose one new entry is to be added to an already sorted vector, V, so that the enlarged vector will also be sorted. An inefficient method would be to place the new entry at the end of the vector and then use the bubble sort on this enlarged vector. A more efficient method takes advantage of the fact that the starting vector is already sorted.

QUESTION Suppose that the vector V is as shown and that size is 8.

V[0]   V[7]

25	31	52	59	72	75	81	83	. . .

If the following loop is executed,

```
for (int i=size-1; i>=0; i--)
    {
    if (V[i] < entry)
        break;
    }
```

what will be the value of i after the loop if entry is

(a) 55   **(b)** 80   **(c)** 94   **(d)** 12

Answer The loop starts at the right end of the vector, V, and is exited either by way of the break statement (the first time V[i] is less than entry) or, if the break statement is never executed, when i becomes −1. Thus, the value of i after control passes out of the for loop will be the index of the cell immediately to the left of the cell into which we would want to insert entry. The answers are

    (a) 2   **(b)** 5   **(c)** 7   **(d)** −1.   ■ ■■

The *insert* Function The insert function inserts one new entry into a sorted vector so that the enlarged vector is also sorted. The heart of the insert function is a for loop that accomplishes the following two things:

1. After the loop, the value of i will be the index of the cell immediately to the left of the cell into which the new entry is to be inserted.

2. The loop shifts some elements to the right to make room for the new entry. For example, if V is the vector of the previous question and entry is 55, here is what V will look like before and after execution of the insert function's for loop. (The shaded cell is where the new entry will be inserted and the final value of i is shown.)

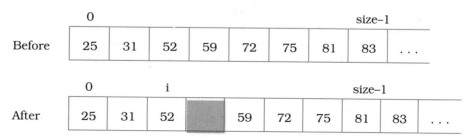

Here is the insert function. Note that after the for loop (highlighted), the new entry must still be inserted and size must be updated.

```
void insert (CType entry, Vector<CType>& V, int& size)
{    // On entry to insert:
    // V[0]..V[size-1] is in sorted order.

    // resize V if necessary
    if (size==V.length())
        V.resize (V.length() + 8);
```

```
      // make room for entry and locate
      // the cell to left of the insertion spot
      for (int i=size-1; i>=0; i--)
         {
         if (V[i] < entry)
            break;
         V[i+1] = V[i];
         }

      V[i+1] = entry; // insert entry
      size++; // update size to account for entry

      // On exit: size has been incremented,
      //          V[0]..V[size-1] is sorted,
      //          and V contains the new entry
   }
```

Insertion Sort   *Insertion sort* sorts a list by making repeated calls to the `insert` function. (Exercise 14.20 asks you to write and test an `insert_sort` function template.) In the following example, the `sort_from_file` function reads and alphabetizes a list of names from a file. It starts by reading the first name from the file into `name_list[0]`; it then reads the second name and inserts it so that the vector `name_list[0]..name_list[1]` is sorted; it then reads and inserts the next name so that the vector `name_list[0]..name_list[2]` is sorted; and so on.

■ **EXAMPLE**   The program `insert.cpp` first uses the function `sort_from_file` to read and alphabetize a list of names from an external file, `fullname.dat`. The program then allows the user to add names to the list, one at a time, alphabetizing as each new name is added. Note that the `insert` function is used both in `sort_from_file` and in the loop that allows the user to add new names interactively.

The main function of the program `insert.cpp` is

```
void main()
{
   Vector<String> name_list;
   String name;
   int size;
```

```
      sort_from_file ("fullname.dat", name_list, size);
      cout << "The names are:\n";
      put_vector (name_list, size);
      cout << endl;

      cout << "\nEnter name (XXX to quit): ";
      getline(cin, name);
      while (name != "XXX")
         {
         insert (name, name_list, size);
         cout << "Enter name (XXX to quit): ";
         getline(cin, name);
         }

      cout << "\nAfter insertions, the names are:\n";
      put_vector (name_list, size);
      cout << endl;
   }
```

For the initial data file, `fullname.dat`, given
to the right, a sample run of `insert.cpp` is

```
Stroustrup, Bjarne
Pascal, Blaise
Hollerith, Hermann
Lovelace, Ada
```

```
The names are:
        Hollerith, Hermann
        Lovelace, Ada
        Pascal, Blaise
        Stroustrup, Bjarne

Enter name (XXX to quit): Wirth, Nicklaus
Enter name (XXX to quit): Babbage, Charles
Enter name (XXX to quit): Newton, Isaac
Enter name (XXX to quit): Pascal, Blaise
Enter name (XXX to quit): XXX

After insertions, the names are:
        Babbage, Charles
        Hollerith, Herman
        Lovelace, Ada
        Newton, Isaac
```

```
Pascal, Blaise
Pascal, Blaise
Stroustrup, Bjarne
Wirth, Nicklaus
```

Notice that the loop to read and insert names does not determine whether a name is already on the list—duplicate names may be added to the list. Exercise 14.22(a), asks you to modify function insert so that it does not add duplicates to the list. Exercise 14.22(b) asks you to use a binary search in function insert in order to determine the value of spot.

14.6   Template Functions for Sorting and Searching

Recall from Section 10.5 that function templates facilitate code reuse by allowing a programmer to write the template for a function once and leave to the compiler the task of producing an actual version of the function for each data type for which the function will be called.

In the C++ code for all of our sorting algorithms, we have used the typedef statement to attach a generic alias, CType, to the actual type of the data to be sorted. Using CType gives us some flexibility when specifying the type of data to sort — we need only change the actual data type specified in the typedef statement when we want to sort a different type of data. However, this approach is limited in the following respect: A given program run cannot use the same sorting function to sort more than one type of data, because the typedef statement binds CType to the specified data type for the entire program. However, the use of CType as a stand-in for the actual data type enables us, with minimal effort, to convert each actual sorting function that we have written into a function template. We need only remove the typedef statement that specifies Ctype, then preface each sorting function declaration and definition with the line

```
template <class CType>
```

Thus, the declarations of the function templates for swap and select_ sort are

```
template <class CType>
void swap (CType& a, CType& b);
// interchange a and b

template <class CType>
void select_sort (Vector<CType>& V, int N);
// Sort V[1]..V[N] in increasing order
```

The definitions of these functions are the same as those given in Section 14.3 *except that* each function definition is immediately preceded by the line

```
template <class Ctype>
```

which tells the compiler that a function declaration or definition is a function template.

Testing the *select_sort* **Template Functions** The program select2.cpp (see the PWS Web site) contains a complete program that tests template versions of the select_sort and swap functions, as well template versions of the get_vector and put_vector functions for interactive vector input and output.

A typical run of the program, showing that the compiler correctly generates both int and String versions of each of the four functions just mentioned is

```
Enter 8 integers, separated by whitespace:
29 59 3 99 20 59 60 12
Before sort:    29 59 3 99 20 59 60 12
After sort:      3 12 20 29 59 59 60 99

Enter 6 strings, separated by whitespace:
dog cat horse rat vole bat
Before sort:    dog cat horse rat vole bat
After sort:     bat cat dog horse rat vole
```

The declarations of the function template and the main function of select2.cpp follow.

```
template <class CType>
void get_vector (Vector<CType>& V, int N);
// get user data for vector V

template <class CType>
void put_vector (const Vector<CType>& V, int N);
// Output V[0]..V[N-1]

template <class CType>
void swap (CType& a, CType& b);
// interchange a and b
```

```
template <class CType>
void select_sort (Vector<CType>& V, int N);
// Sort V[0]..V[N-1] in increasing order

void main()
{
    Vector<int> N(8);
    cout << "Enter 8 integers, separated by whitespace:\n";
    get_vector (N, 8);
    cout << "Before sort:\t"; put_vector (N, 8); cout << endl;
    select_sort(N, 8);
    cout << "After sort:\t"; put_vector (N, 8); cout << endl;

    Vector<String> S(6);
    cout << "\nEnter 6 strings, separated by whitespace:\n";
    get_vector (S, 6);
    cout << "Before sort:\t"; put_vector (S, 6); cout << endl;
    select_sort(S, 6);
    cout << "After sort:\t"; put_vector (S, 6); cout << endl;
}
```

■ Exercises

1. For the vector V whose elements are [40, 20, 30, 20, 35], give the value of
   (a) linear_search (V, 30, 5)
   (b) linear_search (V, 20, 5)
   (c) linear_search (V, 35, 4)

2. For the vector V given at the beginning of Section 14.2, create trace tables similar to those at the end of the section to illustrate the action of the following calls.
   (a) int n = binary_search (V, "Pat", 12);
   (b) int n = binary_search (V, "Una", 12);
   (c) int n = binary_search (V, "Gil", 9);
   (d) int n = binary_search (V, "Hal", 10);

3. For the vector V whose elements are [44, 55, 20, 12, 60, 32], trace the action of the select_sort function of Section 14.3 by giving the values of ctf, index_min, and V[0]..V[5] after each iteration of the outer for loop.

4. For the vector V whose elements are [55, 20, 12, 32, 60, 44], trace the action of the improved bubble_sort function of Section 14.4 by giving the values of ctf, swaps, and V[0]..V[5] after each iteration of the outer for loop.

5. Give a vector of six integers in which only two elements are out of their final sorted positions, but for which the improved bubble_sort function must make the maximum of five passes.

6. Suppose the tracing statement

```
cout << i << ' ';
```

is placed at the beginning of the body of the for loop of the insert function of Section 14.5. What will be the output of the following main function?

```
void main()
{   Vector<String> critters;
    int size = 0;

    insert ("gnu", critters, size); cout << size << endl;
    insert ("boa", critters, size); cout << size << endl;
    insert ("emu", critters, size); cout << size << endl;
    insert ("awk", critters, size); cout << size << endl;
    insert ("yak", critters, size); cout << size << endl;
    insert ("emu", critters, size); cout << size << endl;
    put_vector (critters, size); cout << endl;
}
```

7. Write a function, is_sorted, that determines whether its vector parameter is sorted.

8. Does it make sense to write a general search function that first calls the is_sorted function of the previous exercise in order to decide whether to use a linear or binary search to do the actual searching? Discuss your answer.

Programming Problems

9. Rewrite the linear_search function so that when the parameter to_find occurs more than once in V, the function returns the index of the highest numbered cell that contains to_find.

10. Rewrite the select_sort function so that after k passes, V[N-k]..V[N-1] contain the k largest elements of the vector, in sorted order. (For readability, change some comments and variable names.)

11. The *median* of a sorted vector of numbers can be defined as follows: *For an odd number of numbers, the median is the middle number; for an even number of numbers, it is the average of the two middle numbers.* Write a function that returns the median of the first *N* numbers of a sorted vector.

12. The *mode* of a list of numbers is the number that occurs most frequently in the list. Write a function that returns the mode of a sorted vector of integers.

13. Write the `void` function, `print_all`, whose declaration and description are

```
void print_all (const Vector<String>& last,
                const Vector<String>& first,
                int size,
                String wanted_last);
// Print the last, then first, names of each person
// having wanted_last as last name; if there are no
// such people, print NONE.
```

Write a program to test the `print_all` function by reading an unsorted list of names from a file into parallel vectors, `first` and `last`, then interactively entering several last names to be passed to the `print_all` function.

14. Modify the test program and function of the previous exercise as follows:
   (a) After reading the first and last names into parallel vectors, sort them alphabetically by last name.
   (b) Call `binary_search` from within `print_all` to locate an occurrence of `wanted_last` (if it exists).
   (c) Print the last, then first, names of *all* people having `wanted_last` as their last name.

15. A file contains the name (`Last`, `First`) and age of each student in a class. The names are not in alphabetical order. Write a program to print the names and ages as read from the file, and then print the names and ages in alphabetical order by name. Finally, print the names and ages in decreasing order of age. Be sure that each name is printed with the correct age.

16. Implement and test the following overloaded `binary_search` function template:

```
template <class CType>
void binary_search
    (const Vector<CType>& V,
     Ctype to_find, // item to find
     int size,      // size of V
     int& loc,      // where to_find is or should be placed
     bool& found);  // whether to_find was found
// Search sorted subvector V[0]..V[size-1] for to_find.
// If found is returned true, then to_find is in cell loc;
// If found is returned false, then to_find should be
// placed in cell loc to maintain sorted order.
```

Longer Assignments

17. Redo Exercise 13.18 so that the output consists of (1) the list of names, numerical scores, and letter grades, alphabetized by name; (2) the list of names, numerical scores, and letter grades, in decreasing numerical order by score; (3) the class mean, standard deviation, median, and mode; and (4) a table telling how many students received each grade.

18. Write a telephone directory program that reads names (Last, First) and phone numbers into two parallel vectors, then sorts the vectors alphabetically by name. When the user enters a name in response to a prompt, the program should use a binary search to find the name. If the name is in the directory, it will print the person's phone number; otherwise, it will prompt the user to enter the phone number, then use a modification of the insert function to add the name and number to the vectors. Terminate the program execution when the user enters the name STOP.

19. **(Shaker Sort)** The shaker sort is a somewhat more efficient version of the improved bubble sort. Instead of traversing the vector from top (low index) to bottom (high index) on each pass, the shaker sort alternates — every other pass traverses the vector from bottom to top. Thus, the first pass moves the largest element to the bottom of the vector, the second moves the smallest to the top, the third moves the second largest element into position, etc. Write and test a shaker_sort function.

20. **(Insertion Sort)** The code for using the insert function of Section 14.5 to sort a vector of size components of type CType is

```
int ssv_sz=1; // sorted subvector size
while (ssv_sz < size)
    {
    // V[0]..V[ssv_sz-1] is a sorted subvector.

    CType item_to_insert = V[ssv_sz];
    insert(item_to_insert, V, ssv_sz);

    // (1) ssv_sz has been incremented, and
    // (2) V[0]..V[ssv_sz-1] is a sorted subvector.
    }
```

Using the techniques of Section 14.6, write and test an insert_sort function template.

21. Write a menu-driven program for updating an alphabetized list of names (Last, First) read from a disk file. The menu options are

```
A (followed by a name) — Add name to the list.
D (followed by a name) — Delete name from the list.
P — Print the current list of names.
S (followed by external file name) — Save current list to disk.
Q — Quit.
```

When the user chooses to quit, if the list has been updated since the last save operation, prompt the user about saving. If the file is to be saved, prompt the user for an external file name.

22. (a) Revise the program insert.cpp of Section 14.5 so that if an input name is already on the list (as determined by a call to the binary_search function of Section 14.2), it will not be added to the list.

(b) Repeat part (a), but have the insert function call the overloaded binary_search function of Exercise 14.16 to find the insertion spot for the new entry.

23. A file contains state abbreviations, names, capitals, largest cities, and populations (accurate to the nearest tenth of a million) in alphabetical order by two-letter state abbreviations. Write a program that reads this information into five parallel vectors. Then, write a menu-driven program that allows the user to:

(a) Get all information on a state by entering its two-letter abbreviation.

(b) Get a list of all states
   (i)   whose population is within a specified range.
   (ii) whose capital city begins with a specified letter.
   (iii) whose largest city begins with a specified letter.

24. The file planets.dat contains the name, diameter (mi.), mean distance from the sun (10^6 mi.), number of (earth) days to orbit the sun, and number of (earth) days to rotate on its axis. Read this data into four parallel vectors, then produce four tables of output, the first in alphabetical order by planet name, the second in increasing order of distance from the sun, the third in decreasing order of days to orbit the sun, and the fourth in decreasing order of days for the planet to rotate on its axis.

15

Matrices

S o far all the vectors we have considered have been one dimensional; thus, only one subscript has been needed to specify the desired element. When information fits naturally into a rectangular table, however, we may find it advantageous to store the information in a *two-dimensional vector*, also called a *matrix*. Two subscripts are necessary to specify an element in a matrix — a row subscript and a column subscript. We begin this chapter by considering basic matrix syntax and the use of nested loops for processing matrices.

C++ has no built-in matrix data type, nor is one proposed as part of the ANSI/ISO C++ standard. Instead, a two-dimensional vector can be declared as a vector of vectors. However, we will work with a Matrix[1] class (provided in the file baMatrix.h at the PWS Web site), because it is a good example of how a user-defined class can extend the C++ language and simplify the programmer's work. (Complete documentation is given in Appendix E and at the PWS Web site in the file bamatrix.doc.)

15.1 Matrix Syntax and Nested for Loops

Declaring a Matrix To declare a matrix, the keyword Matrix is followed in angular brackets by the type of values it is to hold, and then by the name of the matrix; optionally, the dimensions of the matrix can also be

---

[1] This class is based very closely on the apmatrix class recommended by the Advanced Placement Computer Science Committee for use in CS1 and CS2.

specified at this time by including them in parentheses, with the number of rows appearing first. For example,

```
Matrix<int> M(3,5);
```

declares a matrix, M, that can store three rows and five columns of int values. Be aware that the top row of M is row 0, and the leftmost column is column 0.

To specify a particular cell of a matrix, the name of the matrix is followed by the desired row and column, each in its own set of square brackets.

■ **QUESTION** The following program fills the matrix M with values that are input by the user.

```cpp
// matdemo.cpp
#include <isostream.h>
#include <iomanip.h>
#include "baMatrix.h"

void main()
{
    Matrix<int> M(3,5);
    int row, col;

    // fill M row by row
    cout << "Type 15 integers, then press ENTER:\n";
    for (row=0; row<3; row++)
        for (col=0; col<5; col++)
            cin >> M[row][col];

    // some output for you to determine
    cout << "M[1][2] = " << M[1][2] << endl;
    cout << "M[2][1] = " << M[2][1] << endl;
    for (col=0; col<5; col++)
        cout << setw(4) << M[1][col];
    cout << endl;
}
```

Suppose the user responds to the prompt for input with the values:

10 20 30 40 50   2 4 6 8 10   13 15 17 19 21

1. Draw a table that depicts M after the code to fill M has been executed.

2. What output will the program produce?

Answer Note that the for loop at the bottom of main outputs row 1, the *second* row of the matrix.

M

	0	1	2	3	4
0	10	20	30	40	50
1	2	4	6	8	10
2	13	15	17	19	21

```
M[1][2] = 6
M[2][1] = 15
    2   4   6   8   10
```
Output

A Function to Find Each Row's Sum We want to modify the previous program so that if a function sum_rows is declared and defined, and if the call sum_rows(M) is inserted as the last line of main, then a run of the modified program will produce the following additional output.

```
Row 0: sum = 150
Row 1: sum = 30
Row 2: sum = 85
```

Pseudocode for sum_rows

```
for (row=0; row < 3; row++)
    {
    find the current row's sum (using a loop)
    output that sum
    }
```

QUESTION Fill in the blanks in the definition of sum_rows.

```
void sum_rows (const Matrix<int>& M)
{
    int row, col, sum;
    for (row=0; row<3; row++)
        {

        _____;
        for (_____)
            sum += _____;
        cout << "_____" << row
                << ": sum = " << _____ << endl;
        }
}
```

Answer　The sum across row number `row` is found by initializing `sum` to 0 and then using an inner `for` loop in which `col` takes on the values 0, 1, . . . , 4, so that `M[row][col]` will take on the five values of that row. Thus, the completed lines are

```
sum = 0;
for (col=0; col<5; col++)
    sum += M[row][col];
cout << "Row " << row
        << ": sum = " << sum << endl;
```

Reading in the Dimensions of a Matrix

In the first program of this chapter, we declared the dimensions of matrix `M` at the outset by

```
Matrix<int> M(3,5);
```

We can also declare a matrix without specifying its dimensions. This allows a program to read the values for the matrix's dimensions and then call the `resize` member function to complete the dimensioning of the matrix. Once the dimensions of a matrix have been specified, either in the initial declaration or in a call of the `resize` function, the member functions, `numrows` and `numcols`, can be called to return the dimensions of the matrix.

■ **EXAMPLE**　The following code, from `matdemo3.cpp`, inputs the number of rows and columns of a matrix, then prompts for and inputs enough data to fill all the rows and columns. Finally, it displays the matrix, one row at a time.

```
void fill (Matrix<int>& M);
void display (const Matrix<int>& M);

void main()
{
    Matrix<int> M; // no rows or cols, yet
    int n_rows, n_cols;

    cout << "How many rows and cols: ";
    cin >> n_rows >> n_cols;
    M.resize(n_rows, n_cols);

    fill (M);
    display (M);
}
```

The definition of the fill function is:

```
void fill (Matrix<int>& M)
{
   int row, col;
   cout << "Enter " << M.numrows() * M.numcols()
        << " values:\n";
   for (row=0; row < M.numrows(); row++)
      for (col=0; col < M.numcols(); col++)
         cin >> M[row][col];
}
```

Thus, if the user enters 2 and 4 for the number of rows and columns, then the fill function will prompt the user to enter eight values.

■ **QUESTION** Fill in the blanks in the function display so that it outputs M in matrix form — that is, with each row displayed on its own line. Note that this function makes use of the member functions numrows and numcols.

```
void display (const Matrix<int>& M)
{
   int row, col;
   cout << "\nMatrix contents:\n";
   for (row=__; row < _____; row++)
      {
      for (col=__; col < _____; col++)
         cout << setw(5) << _____;
      cout << endl;
      }
}
```

Answer The completed lines are

```
   for (row=0; row < M.numrows(); row++)
      for (col=0; col < M.numcols(); col++)
         cout << setw(5) << M[row][col];
```

Row-by-Row Processing When writing code to do row-by-row processing of an entire matrix, you normally use nested loops with an outer loop whose header is of the form for(row = . . .; row++). This keeps the value of row fixed while an inner for loop ranges over each of the columns across that row. Some examples of row-by-row processing are

(1) reading values into a matrix row by row, (2) finding each of the row sums for a matrix, and (3) displaying a matrix. Exercises 15.7 and 15.8 asks you to do some column-by-column processing.

■ **EXAMPLE**   **(Reading from a File with the Number of Rows in a Header)**   In a common type of application, in which a matrix's values are read from a file, the programmer will know the number of columns for the matrix but not the number of rows; the number of rows will be given in the file header. For example, suppose the file sales.dat gives the five-day sales figure for each of its salespersons. We need to create code that opens the file sales.dat for input; reads the header value that gives the number of salespersons; resizes the sales matrix, which had been declared without dimensions; and then reads the rest of the file into the sales matrix as depicted here.

sales.dat

```
18
25 13 29 40 30
  .  .  .
30 30 32 34 28
```

sales

	0	1	2	3	4
0	25	13	29	40	30
1	41	39	38	42	33
.	.	.	.	.	.
.	.	.	.	.	.
17	30	30	32	34	28

■ **QUESTION**   Fill in the blanks in the following code (from sale.cpp) so that it correctly fills the sales matrix with the data from sales.dat.

```cpp
Matrix<int> sales;
int staff_size;
int person, day; // loop control variables
ifstream sales_in;

// Open input file
sales_in.open ("sales.dat");
Assert (!sales_in.fail(),
        "Unable to open sales.dat");

// Read the header value
sales_in >> staff_size;

// Resize sales matrix and read data into it
sales.resize (_____);
for (person=0; person<_____; person++)
   for (day=0; day<5; day++)
      sales_in >> sales[person][day];
```

Answer The completed lines are:

```
sales.resize(staff_size, 5);
for (person=0; person<staff_size; person++)
```

NOTE We have used the descriptive variables `person` and `day` instead of `row` and `col`, respectively. ■ ■

15.2 Program Design with a Matrix and Parallel Vectors

■ **PROBLEM** **(Dropping the Lowest Score)** Professor Fairchild gives four exams and then determines each student's letter grade by averaging the student's three best scores. An A is at least 90, a B is at least 80 but under 90, a C is at least 70 but under 80, a D is at least 60 but under 70, and an F is under 60.

`class.dat` is a file that contains a header value giving the number of students, then, for each student, that student's name on one line, followed by his or her four exam scores on the next line. We want to write a program that outputs all names and scores, then outputs the names, weighted averages, and letter grades. Output to the monitor and the virtual printer will look like this.

```
class.dat

8
Smith, Stew
90 82 75 78
Jones, Jan
85 90 92 98
 . . .
 . . .
Stone, Ed
80 72 74 60
```

```
EXAM PROCESSING STARTED . . .
ALL EXAMS PROCESSED -- Output on virtual printer.
```

Monitor output

```
Smith, Stew      90  82  75  78
Jones, Jan       85  90  92  98
  .   .   .       .   .   .   .
Stone, Ed        80  72  74  60

Grades:
Name          Avg. best 3  Grade
Smith, Stew       83.3       B
Jones, Jan        93.3       A
  .   .   .        .  .       .
Stone, Ed         75.3       C
```

Virtual printer output

In preparation for dropping each student's lowest score, we find each student's lowest score and store it in a vector called lows. For each student, the average of the three top scores can be computed as

((sum of all four scores) — lowest score)/3.0

Data Structures In this program, we use the following parallel data structures.

	names	scores				lows	best 3_avgs
		0	1	2	3		
0	Smith, Stew	90	82	75	78	75	83.3
1	Jones, Jan	85	90	92	98	85	93.3
	. . .	..	..	..	..	..	...
class_size -1	Stone, Ed	80	72	74	60	60	75.3

Here is the pseudocode:

---

get_data: *Read all the data from the external file into* names *and* scores, *and, at the same time, write this information to the virtual printer.*
find_lows: *Find each student's low score and store it in* lows.
average_best3: *Find the average of each student's three best scores.*
print_summary: *Send each student's name, average, and letter grade to the virtual printer.*

Here is the main function from the program class.cpp.

```
void main()
{
    Vector<String> names;
    Matrix<int> scores;
    Vector<int> lows;
    Vector<float> best3_avgs;
    int class_size;

    cout << "EXAM PROCESSING STARTED ...\n";
    get_data (names, scores);

    class_size = names.length();
    lows.resize(class_size);
    find_lows (scores, lows);
```

```
        best3_avgs.resize(class_size);
        average_best3 (scores, lows, best3_avgs);

        print_summary (names, best3_avgs);
        cout << "ALL EXAMS PROCESSED --"
             << "Output on virtual printer.\n";
}
```

Now we consider the functions. The get_data function is given first.

```
void get_data (Vector<String>& names, // out
               Matrix<int>& scores)    // out
{
    ifstream class_in;
    int class_size; //in the data file
    int stud, exam; // loop control variables
    String name;

    class_in.open("class.dat");
    Assert (!class_in.fail(),
            "Unable to open class.dat for input.");

    // Use header value to resize the matrix and vector
    class_in >> class_size;
    names.resize(class_size);
    scores.resize(class_size, 4);

    // read data, store, and print it
    for (stud=0; stud<class_size; stud++)
        {
        class_in >> ws;
        getline (class_in, name);
        names[stud] = name;
        vprn << name << setw(16 - name.length()) << " ";
        for (exam=0; exam<4; exam++)
            {
            class_in >> scores [stud][exam];
            vprn << setw(4) << scores[stud][exam];
            }
        vprn << endl;
        }
}
```

■ **QUESTION** Complete the blanks in function find_lows.

```cpp
void find_lows (const Matrix<int>& scores, // in
                Vector<int>& lows)          // out
{
   int stud, exam; // LCVs
   int curr_low; // low for current student

   for (stud=0; stud < scores.numrows(); stud++)
      {
      curr_low = scores[stud][1];
      for (exam=1; exam<4; exam++)
         if (scores[stud][exam]  < _____)
            curr_low = _____;
      lows[stud] = curr_low;
      }
}
```

Answer The completed lines are

```cpp
if (scores[stud][exam] < curr_low)
   curr_low = scores[stud][exam];
```

■ ▬

■ **QUESTION** The function average_best3 drops the lowest score. Fill in the blanks.

```cpp
void average_best3 (const Matrix<int>& scores,   // in
                    const Vector<int>& lows,      // in
                    Vector<float>& best3_avgs)    // out
{
   int stud, exam; // LCVs
   float curr_tot; // total exam scores for current student

   for (stud=__; stud _____; stud++)
      {
      // total exam scores for this student
      curr_tot = 0.0;
      for (exam=0; exam<4; exam++)
         curr_tot += scores[stud][exam];
      curr_tot -= lows[stud]; // throw out the lowest
      _____ = curr_tot / 3.0; // store avg
      }
}
```

Answer   The completed lines are

```
for (stud=0; stud < scores.numrows(); stud++)
    best3_avgs[stud] = curr_tot / 3.0; // store avg
```

Here is the function `print_summary`. Notice that, for each student, the computer passes the corresponding cell of `best3_avgs` to the function grade.

```
void print_summary (const Vector<String>& names,      // in
                    const Vector<float>& best3_avgs) // in
{
   int stud;
   fixed_out (vprn, 1);

   vprn << "\nGrades:\n";
   vprn << "Name" << setw(20) << "Avg. best 3"
      << "  Grade" << endl;
   for (stud=0; stud<names.length(); stud++)
      {
      vprn << names[stud] << setw(22 - names[stud].length())
         << best3_avgs[stud] << setw(6)
         << grade(best3_avgs[stud]) << endl;
      }
}
```

The highlighted portions of this code contain two different `length` functions calls. First, because `names` is a vector, the size of the vector, `names.length()`, is used by the `for` loop in order to loop through all names, weighted averages, and letter grades. Second, for each value of the loop control variable, `stud`, the contents of the cell `names[stud]` is of type `String`. Thus, `names[stud].length()` gives the number of characters in the name stored in `names[stud]`.

15.3   Mathematical Operations on Matrices (For Students Familiar with Matrix Algebra)

In mathematics, a matrix with m rows and n columns is known as an $m \times n$ *matrix*.

Matrix Addition   If A and B are both $m \times n$ matrices, then the sum A + B is defined by adding corresponding elements. For example,

$$\begin{bmatrix} 3 & 1 \\ 5 & 7 \end{bmatrix} + \begin{bmatrix} 6 & 0 \\ -2 & 1 \end{bmatrix} = \begin{bmatrix} 9 & 1 \\ 3 & 8 \end{bmatrix}$$

Here is a program fragment to find the matrix sum C = A + B, where A and B are both $m \times n$ matrices.

```
for(int row = 0; row < m; row++)
    for(int col = 0; col < n; col++)
        C[row][col] = A[row][col] + B[row][col];
```

Matrix Multiplication   The definition of matrix multiplication is considerably more complicated than that of addition. Be aware that the product of two matrices is defined only when the number of columns of the matrix on the left equals the number of rows of the matrix on the right.

If A is $m \times n$ and B is $n \times p$, then the product matrix, C = A * B is an $m \times p$ matrix, where $C[i,j] = \sum_{k=0}^{n-1} A[i,k] * B[k,j]$. Thus, the i,jth element of C is calculated by taking the dot product of the ith row of A with the jth column of B. For example,

$$\begin{bmatrix} 2 & 3 \\ 5 & 1 \\ 6 & -1 \end{bmatrix} \begin{bmatrix} -1 & 5 & 2 & 1 \\ 3 & 1 & 0 & 1 \end{bmatrix} = \begin{bmatrix} 7 & 13 & 4 & 5 \\ -2 & 26 & 10 & 6 \\ -9 & 29 & 12 & 5 \end{bmatrix}$$

Note that $C[0,1] = 13$ because $2 * 5 + 3 * 1 = 13$.

■ **QUESTION**   Assuming the main function of a program contains the declaration

```
Matrix<int> A, B, Prod;
```

fill in the blanks in the function mult so that the matrix Prod contains the product of the matrices A and B.

```
void mult (const Matrix<int>& A,    // in
           const Matrix<int>& B,    // in
           Matrix<int>& Prod)       // out
{
    if (A. _____ != B. _____)
        { // can't compute A × B
        Prod.resize(0,0);
        return;
        }
```

```
    Prod.resize (A.numrows(), B.numcols());
    for (int row=0; row<Prod.numrows(); row++)
        for (int col=0; col<Prod.numcols(); col++)
            {
            int sum = 0;
            for (int k=0; k<A.numcols(); k++)
                sum += _____
                _____ = sum;
            }
    }
```

Answer   The completed lines are

```
    if (A.numcols() != B.numrows())
    sum += A[row][k] * B[k][col];
    Prod[row][col] = sum;
```

Exercises

1. If M is declared by the statement

   ```
   Matrix<int> M;
   ```

   draw M after execution of each of the following code fragments.

   (a)
   ```
   M.resize(3,4);
   N = 0;
   for (r=0; r<M.numrows(); r++)
       for (c=0; c<M.numcols();  c++)
           { N++; M[r][c] = N; }
   ```

   (b)
   ```
   M.resize(4,3);
   N = 0;
   for (c=M.numcols()-1; c>=0; c--)
       for (r=0; r<M.numrows(); r++)
           { N++; M[r][c] = N;  }
   ```

2. Write code fragments to
   (a) create a 4 × 6 matrix of characters and fill each cell with '?'.
   (b) create a 10 × 2 matrix of strings and fill each cell with "EMPTY."

3. Write the definition of the function whose declaration is

```
void fill (Matrix<int>& M, int fill_val);
// Fill every cell of M with fill_val
```

4. Write the definition of the function whose declaration is

```
void display (const Matrix<int>& M);
// Display M one row per line, with each
// item right-justified in four columns
```

5. Using the functions of the previous two exercises, give the output of the code fragment at right.

```
M.resize(4,4);
fill(M, 0);
for (r=0; r<M.numrows(); r++)
    for (c=0; c<=r; c++)
        M[r][c] = 4*r + c;
display(M); cout << endl;
for (r=0; r<M.numrows(); r++)
    for (c=r+1; c<M.numcols(); c++)
        M[r][c] = M[c][r];
display(M); cout << endl;
```

6. (a) Rewrite the `fill` function of Exercise 15.3 as a function template with `int` replaced by `EType`.

   (b) Redo Exercise 15.2 using the function template of part (a) of this exercise.

7. Write the definition of the function with the following declaration.

```
double col_sum (const Matrix <double> & X, int c);
// If c is a valid column in the matrix X, return the
// sum of the entries in column c; else, return 0.
```

Programming Problems

8. A basketball team with six players has played four games. A file contains the raw data with a typical data group like

```
Smith
12 14 7 10
```

giving a player's name and points scored in each of the four games. Write a program that prints the data in a nicely formatted table, then prints each player's scoring average (accurate to the nearest tenth). Finally, the program prints the number of points scored by the team in each of the four games.

9. Write a program for the previous exercise so that all output is displayed in a single table. Game totals should appear below columns of scores, and individual averages should appear to the right of rows of scores.

10. Suppose a 3 × 3 matrix representing a game of tic-tac-toe contains Xs, Os, and possible blanks. Write a function that determines and prints the outcome of the game. For example, for the game at right, the output should be `Player X won`.

0	0	X
	X	X
X		0

11. You have on file the closing prices of several stocks for each weekday of last week. Write a program that reads the names and prices into a vector and a matrix, respectively. For each stock, the program should print the maximum and minimum price and the day each was achieved. (Make a neat table under suitable headings.) Finally, the program should print the minimum and maximum prices for the entire portfolio.

12. A *magic square* is an n × n matrix such that the sum of every row, column, and diagonal is the same. Write a program that reads in the values for a 3 × 3 matrix and calls a `bool`-valued function, `is_magic`, to test whether the matrix is a magic square.

Longer Assignments

13. Write a program that allows a teacher to use a computer to grade her students' responses to a multiple-choice exam consisting of ten questions numbered 1 through 10, each having an answer from `'A'` through `'E'`.

    The data file should contain two lines for each student — the first has the student's name, and the second the student's answers to the ten questions. A sample line is:

    ```
    John Dough
    A E C A B A D E C B
    ```

    The first line of the data file should be the answer key for the exam, and the second line should be a count of the number of pairs of lines (one pair per student) that follow.

    The output of your program should consist of

    (a) the name and score for each student,

    (b) a summary of the number of correct responses to each question, along with the number of the question, and

    (c) the average score for the class.

14. **(Pascal's Triangle)** The first 5 rows of Pascal's triangle are given on the following page, and a method for storing the values in a matrix is shown to the right of the triangle.

Pascal's Triangle

```
            1
         1     1
       1    2    1
     1   3     3   1
   1    4    6    4    1
```

Matrix Storage

	0	1	2	3	4
0	1				
1	1	1			
2	1	2	1		
3	1	3	3	1	
4	1	4	6	4	1

Notice that row r of the triangle has $r+1$ entries, the first and last of which are 1s, and any other entry in the row is the sum of the two entries in row $r-1$ to its left and right.

Write a program to store the first 12 rows of Pascal's triangle in a matrix and then print the rows one at a time.

15. **(Following a Path Through a Maze)** An example maze data file is given at right. The first two entries of the file are the number of rows and columns in the maze, and each subsequent line contains a single row of the maze. The border of the maze and obstacles within the maze are represented by plus signs. Spaces represent open areas within the maze. A path through the

```
6 12
+++++F++++++
+++++o++  +++
+++   oooo+++
+ + + ++ooo+
+++   ++    oS
++++++++++++
```

maze, from the start, S, to the finish, F, is represented by lowercase ohs. Write a program to read a maze from a file into a matrix. Find and print the coordinates of the start and finish, then follow the path (indicated by ohs) through the maze, printing the coordinates of each location on the path.

16. Using the format of the previous exercise, create a maze, but do not indicate a path through the maze. Then write a program to find a path through the maze from the start to the finish. (*Hint:* Use a vector to keep track of the coordinates of each location on the current path. When your path hits a dead end, use the vector to backtrack, and mark "dead-end" locations with a D.)

17. In a diving competition, each competitor makes ten dives, each of which has a degree of difficulty between 1.8 and 3.6. Each of eight judges awards a score from 0.0 to 10.0 for each dive. The score for a dive is determined by throwing out the low and high scores, then multiplying the sum of the remaining six scores by the degree of difficulty of the dive.

Write a program to read the degree of difficulty and eight scores for each of ten dives from a file. Then output, in table form, the degree of difficulty, individual scores, and final score for each dive. Finally, output the total score for the diver.

18. In Olympic diving, each judge is from a different country. Modify the program of Exercise 15.17 to also input the country of each judge and print this as part of the table. As part of the final statistics, print the country and number of the judge who gave the lowest average scores and of the judge who gave the highest average scores.

19. Write an interactive program that allows two people to play tic-tac-toe on the computer. Store the current state of the board in a 3 × 3 matrix, where each entry is an X, O, or space. Include functions to

    (a) Display the board.

    (b) Request the next move from the appropriate player, and check that it is a legal move. You may assume that X always goes first.

    (c) Determine whether the game is over and why.

20. Write the matrix multiplication program of Section 15.3.

16

String Processing

S ince Chapter 6, we have been using the subset of the ANSI/ISO draft C++ standard string class that is provided in the library file bastring.h.[1] (Complete documentation is given in Appendix E and is available from the PWS Web site in the file bastring.doc.) Until now, we have dealt with string values as a whole. In this chapter, we look at String class functions that enable us to examine and manipulate parts of a string, either one character at a time, or in larger chunks. We also show how to apply these functions to some string processing problems.

In the last section of the chapter, we look briefly at how C++ programmers use the built-in language features, not the String class, for string handling.

---

[1] Users of Turbo C++ for Windows or Borland C++ may replace the include statement for "baString.h" by #include <cstring.h> in order to use the string class provided by Borland. However, the PWS Web site uses the identifier String rather than string for the class. Therefore, it is necessary either (a) to change all occurrences of "String" to "string" (using your editor's global search-and-replace capability) or (2) to make "String" a synonym for "string" by placing the statement

    typedef string String;

immediately after the include directive for <cstring.h>.

Similar modifications will enable you to use any other draft standard-compliant string class that is available to you.

16.1 Accessing Individual Characters

A string variable resembles a vector in that the components are indexed starting at 0 and in that individual characters can be accessed using the subscript operator, [ ].

■ **EXAMPLE** Suppose `name` has been declared to be of type `String`. Then, the following fragment will output the letter h.

```
name = "John";
cout << name[2]; // outputs the letter h
```

After the assignment statement, the contents of `name` would be as shown here.

	[0]	[1]	[2]	[3]	[4]	. . .
name	'J'	'o'	'h'	'n'	?	. . .

■ **EXAMPLE** The following `main` function (from the program `count_e.cpp`) examines a string character by character to count how many e's it contains.

```
void main()
{
    String word;
    int e_count;

    cout << "Enter a word: ";
    cin >> word;

    e_count = 0;
    for (int i=0; i<word.length(); i++)
        if (word[i]=='E' || word[i]=='e')
            e_count++;

    cout << "Number of e's in " << word
         << " is: " << e_count << endl;
}
```

A typical program run is

```
Enter a word: Extraterrestrial
Number of e's in Extraterrestrial is: 3
```

Changing a Single Character   You may change any character in a string simply by assigning a new character to that component of the string. Thus, when the statements at right are executed, the resulting output is wood.

```
String str;
str = "word";
str[2] = 'o';
cout << str;
```

Range Errors with String Subscripts
Be careful not to assign values to individual elements that are beyond the length of the current value of the string variable. For example, the code at right, when executed, produces an error message similar to

```
String str = "hand";
str[4] = 'y';
cout << str;
```

```
String subscript [4] is out of range 0..3
```

■ QUESTION   The following function (from makupper.cpp) replaces all lowercase letters in the string s with their uppercase equivalents. Complete the code by filling in the blanks.

```
void make_upper (String& s) // IN_OUT
{
    for (int i=0; i < _____; i++)
        if (islower(s[i]))
            _____ = _____;
}
```

Answer   The completed lines are

```
for (int i=0; i < s.length(); i++)
    s[i] = toupper(s[i]);
```

Compatibility of String and *char*   As with integer and floating point numbers, we have another instance of one-way compatibility. (Recall that when you assign an int variable a float value, the fractional part of the float value is lost.) You may assign a character to a string variable but not a string (even of length 1) to a character variable. The following statements illustrate various legal and illegal operations.

```
String st, name="Who?";
char ch='x';
. . .
st = "a";    // ok
ch = "a";    // ILLEGAL - a string is not a character.
st = ch;     // ok
ch = st;     // ILLEGAL
ch = name[2]; // ok
ch = '';     // ILLEGAL a char literal can't be empty
st = "";     // ok - null string is valid string value.
```

16.2 Some Applications

Substitution Encoding   In substitution encoding, each letter of the original message is replaced by the letter appearing beneath it in the following key.

```
A B C D E F G H I J K L M N O P Q R S T U V W X Y Z
H M D P W B L Q T Z K C F J S V Y U O G A X R E N I
```

Thus, the message

    JOHN, MEET ME AT THE ZOO.

will be encoded as

    ZSQJ, FWWG FW HG GQW ISS.

The following code, from program `sub_code.cpp`, asks the user to input a message and then outputs the coded message.

```
void encode (const String& msg,
             String& coded_msg);
// Encode msg by substitution.

void main()
```

```
{
    String msg; // the message to encode
    String coded_msg; // the encoded message

    cout << "Enter a message to encode (end with #):\n";
    getline (cin, msg, '#');
    encode (msg, coded_msg);
    cout << "Encoded message is:\n";
    cout << coded_msg << endl;
}
```

■ **QUESTION**   Complete the definition of the function encode by filling in the blanks. (Note that if ch is an uppercase letter, then ch-'A' gives the position of ch in the alphabet, with 'A' at position 0, 'B' at position 1, and so on.)

```
void encode (const String& msg, String& coded_msg)
{
    const String code = "HMDPWBLQTZKCFJSVYUOGAXRENI";
    char ch; // a single char of the msg
    int alpha_pos; // position of char in the alphabet

    coded_msg = msg;
    for (int i=0; i < msg.length(); i++)
        {
        ch = _____; // get ith char
        if (isalpha(ch))
            {
            alpha_pos = toupper(ch) - 'A';
            coded_msg[i] = _____
            }
        }
}
```

Answer   The completed lines are

```
ch = coded_msg[i]; // get ith char
    coded_msg[i] = code[alpha_pos];
```

Playing Fortune Hangman The program `hangman.cpp` allows a user to play Hangman against the computer. Portions of a typical session of Hangman are shown to the right.

The computer selects a word at random from an external file containing 25 words. Then, for each turn, the computer simulates a spin of the wheel of fortune, returning a random multiple of $100 (up to $500). The user then guesses a letter. If the guess is correct, the human's potential earnings are increased by the random dollar amount times the number of occurrences of the letter in the mystery word. If the guess is incorrect, the total earnings are not changed; the incorrect letter is added to the string of incorrect guesses. The user wins if he or she guesses the word with no more than eight incorrect guesses.

```
Word so far: ----------
   Incorrect guesses:
This guess is worth $300
Pick a letter: e

Word so far: -e---e-----
   Incorrect guesses:
This guess is worth $300
Pick a letter: a

Word so far: -e-a-e---a-
   Incorrect guesses:
This guess is worth $400
Pick a letter: s

Word so far: -e-a-e---a-
   Incorrect guesses: s
 .
 .
 .

Word so far: he-adecimal
   Incorrect guesses: stro
This guess is worth $400
Pick a letter: x

Congratulations!
You won $4000
```

The variable `word_so_far` keeps track of the portion of the word that the user has been able to fill in so far. If the word has a length of 9, `word_so_far` starts as `---------`. Further along in the game `word_so_far` might be `-ara-e-e-`.

Here is the pseudocode for the Hangman program's `main` function.

Select a word at random.
Initialize `word_so_far`, `wrong_chars`, *and* `earnings`.
`do {`
　　1. *Display correct and incorrect guesses the user has made so far.*
　　2. *Spin the wheel to determine the value of the next guess, and*
　　　display the value.
　　3. *Process the next guess, updating* `word_so_far`,
　　　`wrong_chars`, *and* `earnings`.

　　`}`
`while` (*less than eight wrong guesses OR* `word_so_far != word`);
Display the final results.

Here is the `main` function:

```
void main()
{
    String word, word_so_far, wrong_chars;
    int spin_amt, earnings;

    select_word (word);
    initialize (word, word_so_far, wrong_chars, earnings);

    print_heading();
    do {
        display_guesses (word_so_far, wrong_chars);
        spin_wheel (spin_amt);
        process_guess (word, word_so_far, wrong_chars,
                        spin_amt, earnings);
        }
    while (wrong_chars.length() < 8 && word != word_so_far;
    display_results (word, word_so_far, earnings);
}
```

The functions for `hangman.cpp` follow.

```
void select_word (String& word)
{
    ifstream words_in;
    words_in.open ("words.dat");
    Assert (!words_in.fail(),
            "Can't open the file of words.");
```

```
    int num_words, // in file
        index; // of the word to choose
    words_in >> num_words;
    srand(time(0));
    index = rand() % num_words;
    for (int i=0; i<=index; i++)
        words_in >> word;
    words_in.close();
}
```

REMARK Alternatively, we could have read all 25 words into a string vector and then selected a vector subscript at random. This approach would be preferable to the preceding function if the program allowed the user to play many games on a single run.

```
void initialize (const String& word,
                 String& word_so_far,
                 String& wrong_chars,
                 int& earnings)
{
    word_so_far = "";
    for (int i = 0; i < word.length(); i++)
        word_so_far = word_so_far + '-';
    wrong_chars = "";
    earnings = 0;
}
```

```
void display_guesses (const String& word_so_far,
                      const String& wrong_chars)
{
    cout << endl;
    cout << "Word so far: " << word_so_far << endl;
    cout << "   Incorrect guesses: " << wrong_chars
         << endl;
}
```

```
void spin_wheel (int& spin_amt)
{
    cout << "This guess is worth $";
```

```
    spin_amt = 100 * (1 + rand()%5);
    cout << spin_amt << endl;
}
```

```
void process_guess (const String& word,
                    String& word_so_far,
                    String& wrong_chars,
                    int spin_amt,
                    int& earnings)
{
    char guess;
    int count;

    cout << "Pick a letter: ";
    cin >> guess;
    count = 0;
    for (int i=0; i<word.length(); i++)
        if (word[i] == guess)
            {
            word_so_far[i] = guess;
            count++;
            }
    if (count>0)
        earnings += (count * spin_amt);
    else
        wrong_chars += guess;
}
```

```
void display_results (const String& word,
                      const String& word_so_far,
                      int earnings)
{
    cout << endl;
    if (word == word_so_far)
        cout << "Congratulations!\nYou won$" << earnings;
    else
        cout << "Sorry, you lost.\nThe word was " << word;
    cout << endl;
}
```

16.3　Automatic Resizing and Concatenation

One way in which the String class differs from the Vector class is in terms of memory allocation. Recall that we had to specify an initial maximum size for a vector variable before any data could be stored in it. Then, we could make the vector larger or smaller, as needed, by calling the Vector class's resize function. Also, we could check on the current maximum size for the vector by calling the class's length function.

Strings Are Resized Automatically　　The situation for strings is different. First, we never have to specify a maximum size for a string variable — the amount of memory available for storing characters in the string grows and shrinks automatically (by fixed amounts, such as 16, 32, or 64, that depend on the particular string class implementation). Second, the String class's length function returns the length, in characters, of the value currently stored in a string variable, *not* the amount of memory currently allocated for that variable. Thus, if the String variable str contains the value short, the value of str.length() is 5; more than 5 bytes of memory may currently be allocated for str, but we need not concern ourselves with the actual amount — this is handled efficiently by the String class.

String Concatenation Using +=　　String concatenation, which you first saw in Section 6.1, provides an example of a string variable growing indefinitely large, without the programmer having to manage the amount of memory allocated for the string. Using the overloaded += operator, we can "grow" a string by repeatedly concatenating other strings or single characters onto it.

▪ QUESTION　A sample run of the program squeeze.cpp follows.

```
Enter a sentence:
A man,    plan, a canal     - Panama!
AmanplanacanalPanama
```

How would you complete the following code fragment from squeeze.cpp so that it grows a string, sqz_sent, that contains all the letters of the input string, sentence.

```
cout << "Enter a sentence:\n";
getline(cin, sentence);
```

```
// Concatenate each letter of the original
// input sentence onto the end of sqz_sent
sqz_sent = "";
for (int i=0; _____; i++)
    if (isalpha(sentence[i]))
        _____;

// Output "squeezed" version of input sentence.
cout << sqz_sent << endl;
```

Answer   The completed lines are

```
for (int i=0; i<sentence.length(); i++)
        sqz_sent += sentence[i];
```

Memory Exhaustion   The limit to how long a string can become is determined by the amount of memory available for a program's data. The program exhaust.cpp at the PWS Web site exhausts all memory available for strings by repeatedly concatenating a string to itself, thus doubling the string's length each time. This program will eventually cause a run-time error, but it will not crash your system.

16.4   String Searching

Using *find* to Search for Substrings   The find function can be used to determine if a substring appears within another string. If the desired substring is found, it returns the starting point of that substring within the target string. If the substring is not found within the string, the find function will return the value NPOS, a named constant defined in the String class. (*Note*: NPOS is defined to be the largest value of type unsigned int, which, for 16-bit integers, is 65535.) The find function takes a second default argument, with default value 0, which tells the function at what position to start the search.

■ **EXAMPLE**   The following fragment, from find.cpp illustrates the use of the find function. Its output is also given.

```
String s ("A rose is a rose is a rose.");
String w ("is");
int pos1, pos2;
pos1 = s.find (w);
pos2 = s.find (w, pos1 + 1);
cout << pos1 << ' ' << pos2 << endl;
```

```
7 17
2 12 65535
-1
```

Output

```
cout << s.find("rose") << ' ';
cout << s.find("rose", 10) << ' ';
cout << s.find("rose", 30) << endl;
pos1 = s.find("thorn");
cout << pos1 << endl;
```

Discussion Notice that the last two calls to the functions find, s.find("rose", 30) and s.find ("thorn") are unsuccessful and, thus, return NPOS. However, the last output value is −1, not 65535. This is because the statement

```
pos1 = s.find("thorn");
```

stored NPOS, an unsigned int, in pos1, a signed int. ■ ▬

■ **EXAMPLE** **(Counting Occurrences of a String)** The following code, from str_ct.cpp, asks the user to input some text, then repeatedly inputs a string to search for in the text, and outputs the number of occurrences of that string.

```
void main()
{
    String text, word;
    int pos; int count;

    cout << "Enter some lines of text (# at end):\n";
    getline (cin, text, '#');

    cout << "\nString to count (XXX to stop): ";
    cin >> word;
    while (word != "XXX")
        {
        pos = 0; count = 0;
        do {
            pos = text.find(word, pos);
            if (pos >= 0)
                {
                count++;
                pos += word.length();
                }
            }
        while (pos >= 0);
        cout << word << " " << count << endl;
```

```
            cout << "String to count (XXX to stop): ";
            cin >> word;
         } // end while
}
```

A sample run of this code is

```
Enter some lines of text (# at end):
A rose is a rose is a rose.
What does this sentence mean?#

String to count (XXX to stop): rose
rose 3
String to count (XXX to stop): is
is 3
String to count (XXX to stop): thorn
thorn 0
String to count (XXX to stop): a
a 4
String to count (XXX to stop): XXX
```

Discussion   Notice that `str_ct.cpp` counts *any* occurrence of the string to count, not just whole words. Thus, the "a" in the word "mean" is counted. Also, the counting is case sensitive — all lowercase a's are counted, but not the first word, "A".

Exercise 16.11 asks you to modify this program so that the user can specify (1) whether to count whole words only and (2) whether to match the case of the string to count. This is more in the spirit of the search feature of text editors and word processors. ■ ▬

16.5 **Manipulating Substrings**

In most of our applications so far, we have manipulated a string one character at a time. To facilitate manipulation of larger portions of a string, the `String` class provides the member functions `insert`, `remove`, and `substr`.

Using the *insert* ***Function***   The `insert` function inserts a string into a host string at a specified position. The call

```
    host_str.insert (pos, str_to_insert);
```

will cause `str_to_insert` to be inserted into `host_str` at position `pos`.

■ **EXAMPLE** The following fragment, from `insert.cpp`, illustrates calls to `insert`.

```
String s, ins;
s = "I like C";
ins = "really ";
s.insert(2,ins);
cout << s << endl;
s.insert(s.length(), "++ better!");
cout << s << endl;
s.insert (0, "As predicted, ");
cout << s << endl;
```

The output of the preceding fragment is

```
I really like C
I really like C++ better!
As predicted, I really like C++ better!
```

The second call shows that a string can be inserted immediately after the last character of the host string, and the last call shows that a substring can be inserted immediately before the first character of the host string.   ■ ■■

Using the *remove* **Function**   The `remove` function removes a portion of a host string. The call

```
host_str.remove (start, len);
```

removes up to `len` characters from `host_str`, beginning with the character in position `start`. It is not an error if `len` exceeds the number of characters from position `start` to the end of `host_str`. In fact, `len` has a default value of `NPOS` (`UINT_MAX`), so the call

```
host_str.remove (start);
```

removes *all* characters of `host_str` from position `start` to the end of the string.

■ **EXAMPLE** The following fragment, from `remove.cpp`, illustrates calls to `remove`.

```
s = "But, that's not all there is to it.";
s.remove (0,5);
cout << s << endl;
```

```
s.remove(14);
cout << s << endl;
s.remove(6,4);
cout << s << endl;
```

The output of the fragment is

```
that's not all there is to it.
that's not all
that's all
```

Using the `substr` **Function**   The form of a call to the `substr` function is the same as that of a call to the `remove` function. However, rather than removing a specified portion of the host string, `substr` returns a copy of that portion of the host string.

■ EXAMPLE   The following code fragment, from `substr.cpp`, produces the given output.

```
s = "A single step begins the journey.";
cout << s.substr (2,11) << endl;
cout << s.substr(21) << endl;
```

```
single step
the journey.
```
Output

16.6   Defining Your Own String Functions

In addition to using the `String` class member functions that we have discussed, you may need to define some of your own string handling functions. Until you have studied the material on classes in Chapters 18 through 20, it is best to write these functions as free functions, rather than as member functions, because writing member functions requires you to alter the `String` class itself.

■ EXAMPLE   **(Trimming Leading and Trailing Spaces)**   Recall that `getline` reads a string with leading, embedded, and trailing spaces. However, if `name1` contains `"Smith, Al"`, and `name2` contains `"  Smith, Al   "`, then the logical expression `name1 == name2` is false. Accordingly, we find it useful to have the functions `Ltrim` and `Rtrim` to "trim" all spaces from the left and right ends, respectively, of a string.

The definition of Rtrim, from trim_fun.cpp, is

```cpp
void Rtrim (String& str) // IN-OUT
{
    int len = str.length();
    if (len == 0) // nothing to do
        return;
    // Find rightmost non-whitespace character
    for (int i=len-1; i>=0; i--)
        if (!isspace(str[i]))
            break;
    // Remove whitespace, if any
    if (i < len-1)
        str.remove(i+1);
}
```

Discussion   The function determines the position, i, of the rightmost non-whitespace character, then removes all characters to its right using a single call to remove. This approach is somewhat tricky — note the screened code, which handles the special cases in which the string is empty, or is not empty, but has no trailing whitespace.

An easier approach, illustrated in the following code fragment, is to repeatedly remove just the rightmost character if it is whitespace.

```cpp
len = str.length();
while (len>0 && isspace(str[len-1])
    {
    str.remove(len-1);
    len--;
    }
```

This second approach, however, while simpler than the first, may not be as efficient. Depending on the implementation of remove, a single call to remove is probably faster than several calls.   ▪ ▬

String Replacement   The String class given in baString.h (see the PWS Web site) does not provide a function to replace one string with another. However, such functions are useful — all word processors and text editors provide flexible "search-and-replace" features.

■ QUESTION   Suppose the String variable message contains a personalized message to "Mr. Smith" in which the name "Mr. Smith" occurs several times. To send the same message to "Mrs. Peterson" would require substituting every occurrence of "Mr. Smith" with "Mrs. Peterson." Does the following code fragment accomplish this task?

```
pos = str.find("Mr. Smith");
if (pos != NPOS)
    {
    str.remove(pos, 9);
    str.insert(pos, "Mrs. Peterson");
    }
```

Answer   No. It would change only the first occurrence of "Mr. Smith" to "Mrs. Peterson." To change all occurrences would require a loop.   ■ ▬

■ QUESTION   How would you complete the following function to replace all occurrences of find_str with rep_str?

```
void replace_all (String& str, // IN-OUT
                  const String& find_str, // IN
                  const String& rep_str)  // IN
{
    int pos;
    pos = str.find(find_str);
    while (pos != NPOS)
        {
        str.remove(pos, _____);
        str.insert(pos, rep_str);
        _____;
        }
}
```

Answer   The completed lines are

```
str.remove(pos, find_str.length());
pos = str.find(find_str);
```
   ■ ▬

Exercise 16.12 asks you to correct a potential problem in the preceding solution. Other exercises ask you to use the String class member functions to write other "free" String handling functions.

16.7 Using char Arrays (Optional)

Without a String class to use, a C++ program can store sequences of characters in an array. C++ has little built-in language support for manipulating char arrays, but the standard library string.h contains many functions for manipulating char arrays.

In this section, we discuss some of the issues involved in using char arrays. We show equivalent statements, using both a String class and char arrays, to declare and manipulate character strings.

Declaration and Storage A char array is declared like any other array type. (See Sections 13.1 and 13.2 for an introduction to arrays.) Some examples are

String **class**	**Array of** *char*
String word; String line; String sntnc, parag;	char word[12]; char line[81]; char sntnc[101], parag[501];

A maximum length must be specified for the char array and, as with other types of arrays, there is no automatic checking for out-of-range subscripts.

Assignment We stated at the beginning of this section that C++ provides little language support for char arrays. This means that many operations that can be performed on the built-in types int, float, char, etc., are not directly supported for char arrays. For example, assignment of one char array to another must be performed using the string copy function, strcpy, from string.h, *not* the assignment operator!

Some examples are

String **class**	**Array of** *char*
word = "Hello" parag = line;	strcpy(word, "Hello"); strcpy(parag, line);

char **Versus** *char* **Array** The String class provides automatic type conversion from char to String. However, a single char is not compatible with a char array. Thus, for example, the call strcpy(word, 'I') will not compile. Use the call strcpy(word, "I") to assign "I" to word.

Internal Representation and the Null Terminator The number of characters stored in a char array will usually be less than the declared size of the array. A special ***null terminator*** character, '\0' (ASCII 0), marks the end of the actual characters of the string. Thus, after execution of the statement

```
strcpy(word, "Hello");
```

the storage for word looks like

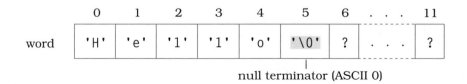

null terminator (ASCII 0)

The screened null terminator character is placed after the last letter, 'o', by the strcpy function, not by the programmer.

Calculating Length   The string length function, strlen, from string.h is used to determine the number of characters in a char array, up to, but not including, the null terminator. For the char array word, above, the value returned by strlen(word) would be 5.

Some comparative examples are

String **class**	**Array of** *char*
len = line.length(); len = String("syzygy").length();	len = strlen(line); len = strlen("syzygy");

Input and Output   The stream I/O operators, >> and <<, function the same for char arrays as for objects of type String. However, because char arrays are not dynamically resized as are Strings, it is critical that the number of characters input not exceed the number of memory cells declared for the destination char array. One way to ensure this is to use the setw manipulator for input, as illustrated in the following comparative examples.

String **class**	**Array of** *char*
cin >> word;	cin >> word; or, a safer method is: cin >> setw(11) >> word;
cout << word << '\n' << sntnc << endl;	cout << word << '\n' << sntnc << endl;

To read a sequence of characters containing leading, embedded, or trailing blanks into a char array, use the istream class's getline member function.

String *class*	Array of *char*
getline(cin, line);	cin.getline(line,80);
getline(cin,parag,'#');	cin.getline(parag,500,'#';

Comparison Rather than the relational operators (<, ==, etc.), the string comparison function, strcmp, from string.h must be used to compare char arrays. strcmp returns a negative, zero, or a positive value, depending on whether its first parameter is less than, equal to, or greater than its second parameter.

Some comparative examples are

String *class*	Array of *char*
if (word > "apple")..	if(strcmp(word,"apple")>0)..
if (line == sntnc)..	if(strcmp(line,sntnc)==0)..
if ("" < line)..	if(strcmp("",line) < 0)..

Concatenation The string concatenation function, strcat, from string.h is used to concatenate one char array onto another. Its function is similar to that of the String operator +=. Some comparative examples are

String *class*	Array of *char*
word = word + ", ";	strcat(word, ", ");
line += word;	strcat(line, word);
line += (word + " ");	strcat(line, strcat(word, " "));

Parameter Passing and Function Return Values A char array is passed as a parameter much like any other type of array, with one significant exception — there is no need to pass a second parameter indicating the number of characters actually stored in the array, because this is indicated in the char array itself by the presence of the null terminator, and can be accessed by calling the strlen function.

Because all arrays are passed by reference, you may want to use the const modifier to ensure that the called function does not alter a char array parameter.

Finally, it is somewhat tricky to write a function whose return type is a char array. To do so, you must carefully apply the pointer variables and dynamic memory allocation techniques that are introduced in Chapter 22.

Some comparative examples are

String **class**	**Array of** *char*
`void encode(String& line);`	`void encode (char line[]);`
`int num_spaces` `   (const String& line);`	`int num_spaces` `   (const char line[]);`
`String upper_case` `   (const String& line);`	(Requires dynamic memory allocation techniques.)

char* **Notation**   The notation char* (read "char pointer") is commonly used for passing char arrays as parameters. For example, the function declaration

        void encode (char line[]);

can be written as

        void encode (char* line);

The meanings of char line[] and char* line are nearly, but not exactly equivalent, and a complete understanding of their meanings requires some knowledge of pointers and dynamic memory allocation, both of which are discussed in Chapter 22.

Function Declarations in *string.h*   If you browse through the on-line help files for the string.h library, you will see the char* notation used extensively. A typical example is its use in the strcpy function, whose declaration is:

        char* strcpy(char* dest, const char* src);

The strcpy function copies the char array src to the char array dest, stopping after the terminating null character has been copied, and then returns the updated value of dest.

Other *string.h* **Functions**   string.h has many more functions that we have not discussed. For example, the strstr function provides some, but not all, of the power of the String class member function find. However, no functions are provided for char arrays that would be similar to the String class member functions insert, remove, and substr. To write your own char array equivalents of these functions, you must understand pointer variables and dynamic memory allocation (see Chapter 22).

Web Site Examples The directory \ch16\charray at the PWS Web site provides some complete program examples that use char arrays to process strings of characters.

■ Exercises

1. Give the output of the following code fragments.

(a)   (b)

```
String s, t1, t2;
s = "ABCDEFGHIJKL";
t1 = s.substr (5,3);
t2 = s.substr(7);
cout << t1 << ' ' << t2;
```

```
String s ("ABRACADABRA");
String w = "AB";
cout << s.find (w) << ' ';
cout << s.find (w, 5) << ' ';
cout << s.find (w, 10) << endl;
cout << s.find("CAD") << ' ';
cout << s.find("cad") << endl;
```

2. Assume that s is of type String. What will be printed by the following code fragment?

```
s = "To every thing there is a season.";
s.remove (9,5);    s.remove(21);
cout << s << endl;
s.insert(9, "purpose"); s += "reason.";
cout << s << endl;
```

3. Assume that s and adj are of type String. What will be printed by the following code fragment?

```
s = "The fox jumped.";
adj = "quick, brown ";
s.insert(4,adj);
s[s.length()-1] = ' ';
cout << s << endl;
s.insert(s.length(), "over the lazy dog.");
cout << s << endl;
```

4. Write a `bool`-valued function, `is_integer`, that tells whether its `String` parameter represents an integer, possibly with a leading plus or minus sign. For example, the values of `is_integer ("123")` and `is_integer ("-1000")` would be true, but the values of `is_integer ("12#")` and `is_integer ("-10.0")` would be false.

5. Write an `int`-valued function, `num_vowels`, that counts the number of vowels in its `String` parameter.

6. Write a free `Ltrim` function to remove all spaces from the beginning of its `String` parameter. For efficiency, make only one call to the `String` class's `remove` function.

7. Write and test a `String`-valued function, `no_punct`, whose return value is its parameter with all punctuation removed.

Programming Problems

8. Write and test the following functions.
   (a) `long to_integer (String s);`
       `// Return the long value that is represented`
       `// by the string s.`
   (b) `String to_string (long n);`
       `// Return the string representation of the`
       `// long value, n.`

9. A palindrome is a string that reads the same forward and backward. Here are two examples of palindromes.

   `Madam, I'm Adam.`
   `Able was I ere I saw Elba.`

   Write a program that will determine whether an input string is a palindrome. (You should consider uppercase and lowercase versions of the same letter to be equivalent, and ignore non-alphabet characters.)

10. Write and test a function, `squeeze_spaces`, that replaces any multiple embedded spaces in its `String` parameter with singles spaces. That is, `squeeze-spaces` would replace the string

    `"Here    are   a lot    of    spaces."`

    with the string

    `"Here are a lot of spaces."`

11. Modify the program `str_ct.cpp` of Section 16.4 so that:
    (a) It counts only whole words.
    (b) It is not case sensitive; that is, it ignores case when counting substrings that match the string to count.

12. In the function `replace_all` of Section 16.6 an infinite loop occurs if the parameter `rep_str` contains a copy of the parameter `find_str`. Modify the function to correct this problem.

13. A file contains a list of words and their opposites, one pair of words per line. Write a program that will output a list giving each word, its opposite, and the letters that those words have in common. If a letter appears more than once in a word and its opposite, it should be listed just once. At the end of this list, output the pair with the most letters in common. (You may disregard the possibility of a tie.) Format the output as follows.

```
Word            Opposite   Common
interesting     boring     inrg
fat             skinny     -
happy           sad        a
tallest         shortest   tes

  . . .           . . .       . .

Pair with most letters in common: _____ , _____
```

14. Redo the program for Exercise 16.13 so that if a letter appears more than once in both words, it is listed the number of times it occurs in both words. For example, "tallest" and "shortest" would have "test" in common.

Longer Assignments

15. Consult a periodic table of the elements to produce a data file of all chemical elements, their symbols, and atomic numbers. Then write a program that inputs a sequence of letters and then prints out all information on the elements (if any) that begin with that sequence of letters. For example, if the input is te, the output will be all information on technetium, tellurium, and terbium.

16. A *Caesar cipher* encodes a message by replacing each letter of the message with the letter that is n positions further along in the alphabet. Letters at the end of the alphabet wrap around to the beginning. Write a Caesar_cipher function that takes a message (consisting of uppercase letters) to encode and an integer n as its parameters, and encodes the message using the n-shift.

17. Modify the Caesar_cipher function of Exercise 16.16 so that it handles digits, lowercase letters, and common punctuation in addition to uppercase letters. (*Hint:* Store all characters to be shifted in a vector, then replace each character of the message by the one that is n positions further along in the vector.)

18. Modify the function of Exercise 16.17 so that the shift amount changes with each character. That is, the first character is replaced by its 1–shift replacement, the second by its 2–shift replacement, and so on.

19. Morse code is a coding scheme that replaces a character by a sequence of dots (·) and dashes (–) as indicated in the table on the next page.

A ·–	G ––·	M ––	S ···	Y –·––	5 ·····
B –···	H ····	N –·	T –	Z ––··	6 –····
C –·–·	I ··	O –––	U ··–	1 ·––––	7 ––···
D –··	J ·–––	P ·––·	V ···–	2 ··–––	8 –––··
E ·	K –·–	Q ––·–	W ·––	3 ···––	9 ––––·
F ··–·	L ·–··	R ·–·	X –··–	4 ····–	0 –––––

(a) Write a program that inputs messages from the keyboard, translates them into Morse code, and stores them in a file. (Ignore characters that are not letters or digits.)

(b) Write a program that reads messages in Morse code from a file and displays the translated messages on the monitor.

20. Write a program that converts Roman numerals into their Arabic equivalents. Assume a maximum of ten Roman numeral digits chosen from

$$M — 1000 \quad D — 500 \quad C — 100 \quad L — 50$$
$$X — 10 \quad V — 5 \quad I — 1$$

21. Write a program to read a file of text and count the occurrences of each word in the file. In counting words, ignore case and all punctuation other than embedded hyphens. Store the words alphabetically in a vector and maintain a parallel vector of counters. Keep the vector of words alphabetized, and use a binary search to find words or to locate where new words should be placed.

22. An unformatted file of text is stored on disk with very basic formatting codes. The formatting codes are <P> to start a new paragraph, <S> to skip a line, <M *n*> to move the left margin to column *n*, and <L *n*> to indicate that subsequent lines are to be at most *n* characters in length.

Write a program that reads the text and formatting codes, then produces the formatted text so that it contains no multiple embedded blanks and paragraphs are indented five spaces.

23. Modify the program of Exercise 16.22 so that lines are fully justified. That is, each line that is not the last line of a paragraph will be filled with just enough spaces so that its rightmost character is on the right margin.

17

Structs

A lthough C++ has relatively few built-in data types, it does allow the programmer to define new data types. One broad category of programmer-defined data types is the **struct**. The struct facilitates **data abstraction**, a powerful mechanism whereby a set of related values, possibly of different data types, can be considered to be a single entity. For example, a "time" consists of an hour, a minute, a number of seconds, and a meridian (A.M. or P.M.). Using a struct, a programmer can define a struct data type, let us call it time_str, so that a *single* variable of type time_str can hold the *four* related data values that make up a time. As another example, in a payroll processing program, an "employee" is an abstraction for the many items of data that must be stored and manipulated in order to produce a complete pay stub for each employee. A struct can be used to bind all these data items together into a single variable.

Although structs are useful in their own right, part of our purpose in presenting them here is to pave the way for an in-depth exploration, beginning in the next chapter, of the more important and also more complicated category of data type, the **class**. Because structs and classes have many similarities, it is helpful to learn about some of their features first in the simpler setting of structs.

17.1 The Basics of Structs

Defining a Struct Data Type Let us begin with a simplified version of data abstraction for "employee". We want to define a struct data type, employee_str, so that a variable, emp, of that type can contain these three data values.

	name	soc_sec	pay_rate
emp	"Hall, Ed"	"140–43–5991"	7.50

The definition of the struct data type, employee_str, is:

```
struct employee_str
    {
    String name;
    String soc_sec;
    float pay_rate;
    };
```

The definition of a struct data type begins with the keyword struct, followed by the name you choose for the data type. (As you can see, we usually end the name of a struct data type with _str.) Then, one or more **data members** are declared within curly braces. Finally, a semicolon terminates the struct definition.

Struct definitions are usually made global by placing them before any function declarations and definitions. In that way, the struct data type will be available to all of the functions, including main, in the file in which it is defined.

Structs Versus Vectors   All data values of a particular vector variable must be of the same type. A struct variable, by contrast, can — and usually does — hold data values of different types. For vectors, subscript notation, [ ], is used to access individual values. For struct variables, a different type of notation, **dot notation**, is used to access the contents of individual data members.

Using Dot Notation to Access Data Members   To access a particular data member of a struct variable, you specify the name of the struct variable, followed by a dot, followed by the name of the desired data member. For example, if emp has been declared to be a variable of type employee_str and contains the data values depicted above, then the following three statements have the effects described by the comments.

```
cout << emp.soc_sec; // outputs 140-43-5991
emp.pay_rate = 9.25; // changes pay rate to 9.25
```

```
employee_str.pay_rate = 4.00; // illegal
                              // employee_str is not a variable
```

■ **EXAMPLE** The following program reads an employee's data into a struct variable, then raises that employee's pay rate by $1, and finally outputs the updated data. Note the calls to two functions that have a struct variable as an argument.

```
// emp.cpp
#include <iostream.h>
#include "baString.h"

struct employee_str
   {
   String name;
   String soc_sec;
   float pay_rate;
   };

void get_data (employee_str& emp);
// Prompt for and read data into emp

void display (employee_str emp);
// Display data in emp

void main()
{
   employee_str emp;
   get_data(emp);
   emp.pay_rate += 1;
   cout << endl;
   cout << "Updated employee data:\n";
   display(emp);
}
```

```
Enter name: Hall, Ed
Enter ID#: 140-43-5991
Enter pay rate $9.57

Updated employee data:
Name: Hall, Ed
ID#: 140-43-5991
Pay rate: $10.57
```

Typical run

The definition of the get_data function is

```
void get_data (employee_str& emp)
{
   cout << "Enter name: ";
   getline(cin, emp.name);
```

```
    cout << "Enter ID#: ";
    cin >> emp.soc_sec;
    cout << "Enter pay rate $";
    cin >> emp.pay_rate;
}
```

Writing the display function is left as Exercise 17.6. ■ ■■

■ **QUESTION** (**A** date_str **Data Type**) How could you create a struct data type, date_str, and a function, display, that will output its date_str type parameter, d, in the form mm/dd/year. That is, if current_date is of type date_str and its contents are

	month	day	year
current_date	5	9	1999

then the call display (current_date); will output 05/09/1999.

Answer The struct data type and the function should be

```
struct date_str
    {
    int month;
    int day;
    int year;
    };
```

```
void display (date_str d)
{
    if (d.month<10) cout << '0';
    cout << d.month << '/';
    if (d.day<10) cout << '0';
    cout << d.day << '/';
    cout << d.year;
}
```

■ ■■

17.2 Vectors of Structs

In this section we again take up a problem from Section 13.5 — that of storing and processing the names, semester standings, and exam scores for a class of several students. In Section 13.5 we used three parallel vectors, name, semester, and score to store three related lists of data. Now, we reduce the data complexity of the problem by creating a single vector, students, each component of which is a struct consisting of a single student's name, semester, and score.

Suppose we define the struct data type student_str as

```
struct student_str {
    String name;
    int semester;
    int score;
    };
```

and the vector students as

Vector<student_str> students(MAX_STDNTS);

where MAX_STDNTS is a global constant. Then, for the data file scores.dat on the left, the contents of students can be as depicted as:

scores.dat

```
Smith       2    70
Johnson     7    92
Young       8    75
Cohen       4    92
Bird        5    83
. .         .    . .
```

	name	semester	score
students [0]	Smith	2	70
students [1]	Johnson	7	92
students [2]	Young	8	75
students [3]	Cohen	4	92
students [4]	Bird	5	83
. . .	. . .	. .	. .

QUESTION Notice that each component of the vector students is a struct. How would you write statements to

1.   Print the semester standing of students[1]?

2.   Assign "Oldman" as the name of students[2]?

3.   Add 5 to the score of students[4]?

Answer Because each vector component is a struct, it is necessary to use dot notation to access the data members of each vector component. The answers are, therefore,

1.   cout << students[1].semester;

2.   students[2].name = "Oldman";

3.   students[4].score += 5;

Discussion   The individual components of students are highlighted to help illustrate that a vector component must be selected by subscripting *before* a data member of that component can be selected using dot notation. The following "solution"

```
cout << students.semester[1];
```

to part 1 is incorrect because dot notation is used on the vector before selecting a component by subscripting.   ■ ▬

■ **QUESTION**   How should you write statements to interchange the contents of students[2] and students[4]? (*Hint:* You can consider a struct variable as a single entity when doing an assignment.)

Answer   We can save several steps by assigning structs as a whole rather than one data member at a time. The necessary statements are

```
student_str temp;
temp = students[2];
students[2] = students[4];
students[4] = temp;
```

■ ▬

The following struct, constant definition, function declarations, and main function are from highest.cpp.

```
struct student_str {
    String name;
    int semester;
    int score;
    };

const int MAX_STDNTS = 30; // Global const

void get_data
        (Vector<student_str>& std, // out
         int& size);     // out
// read data from text file into vector
// of student info, std[0]..std[size-1]

int max_score
        (const Vector<student_str>& std, // in
         int N);    // in
// return max_score in std[0]..std[N-1]
```

```
void print_achievers
        (const Vector<student_str>& std, // in
         int N,           // in
         int hi_scr); // in
// output name and semester of each student in
//   std[0]..std[N-1] earning hi_scr.

void main()
{
    Vector<student_str> students(MAX_STDNTS);
    int num_stdnts;
    int highest;

    get_data (students, num_stdnts);
    highest = max_score(students, num_stdnts);
    cout << "High score " << highest << endl;
    cout << "Achieved by:\n";
    print_achievers(students, num_stdnts, highest);
}
```

■ **QUESTION** How should you complete the missing lines in the following function implementations.

```
void get_data
        (Vector<student_str>& std, // out
         int& size)     // out
{
    ifstream ins;
    ins.open ("scores.dat");
    Assert (!ins.fail(), "Can't open scores.dat.");

    size = 0;
    while (ins>>ws && !ins.eof())
        {
        ins >> _____ >> _____
            >> _____;
        size++;
        }
}
```

```
void print_achievers
        (const Vector<student_str>& std, // in
         int N,         // in
         int hi_scr) // in
{
    int i;
    for (i=0; i<N; i++)
        if (_____)
            cout << "   " << _____ << " (sem. "
                 << _____ << ")\n";
}
```

Answer   The incomplete lines of get_data should be

```
ins >> std[size].name >> std[size].semester
    >> std[size].score;
```

and the incomplete lines of print_achievers should be

```
if (std[i].score==hi_scr)
        cout << "      " << std[i].name << " (sem. "
             << std[i].semester << ")\n";
```

17.3 Nested Structs

Data abstraction takes place on many levels. For example, "student" is an abstraction for a large collection of personal attributes, one of which is the student's birth date. A birth date, in turn, is composed of a month, a day, and a year. In C++, we can model different levels of data abstraction by defining structs whose data members are themselves structs. For example, for the struct type student_str, its data member birth_date is itself a struct.

```
struct date_str
    {
    int month;
    int day;
    int year;
    };
```

```
struct student_str
    {
    String name;
    String IDnum;
    date_str birth_date;
    };
```

Double Dot Notation Suppose that student is a variable of type student_str and contains these values.

	name	ID_num	birth_date		
student	Bond, Earl	130–34–5989	5	22	1968

Then, ***double dot notation*** is needed to give the complete path when accessing data members that are structs within structs. The statements

```
cout << student.name;
cout << " was born in ";
cout << student.birth_date.year;
```

would produce the output Bond, Earl was born in 1968.

Of course, it would be possible to create a struct data type, say, name_str, to store a name as its individual components, first name, last name, and middle initial. Doing this for the preceding example is left up to you as Exercise 17.4.

17.4 Danger of Liberal Access to a Struct's Data

Frequently, a struct type has data members whose values are interrelated. When working with such struct types, the programmer must maintain the relationships among such members.

■ **EXAMPLE** Consider the following code from danger.cpp.

```
struct Time_piece_str
    {
    int hr, min;
    char merid;
    };
```

```
void display(Time_piece_str T);

void main()
{
    Time_piece_str watch;
    watch.hr = 11;
    watch.min = 45;
    watch.merid = 'A';
    cout << "The time is now:   ";
    display(watch); cout << endl;
    watch.min += 40; //danger!
    cout << "40 minutes later: ";
    display(watch); cout << endl;
}
```

Because the programmer neglected to maintain the relationships among the Time_piece_str variable's data members, the program's second line of output is nonsensical.

```
The time is now:   11:45 AM
40 minutes later: 11:85 AM
```

In Exercise 17.7, you are asked to write the display function.

Data Member Access and the Class   Of course, you could write an update function to handle the task of updating a Time_piece_str variable by a certain number of hours and minutes. (In fact, this is Exercise 17.13.) But the liberal access allowed to the data members of a struct still permits the kind of inappropriate modification of data members that we have seen. In the next chapter, you will see how a ***class*** data type can be defined to handle the update automatically and, at the same time, prevent the user of the class from making the type of error just discussed. The user of the class is relieved from having to deal with this task and is prevented from making the kinds of mistakes that go with the task.

17.5   Overloading the +, >>, and << Operators for Fractions

A fraction, which consists of both a numerator and a denominator, can be stored as a single variable using the struct type fraction, whose declaration is

```
struct fraction
{ int num, den };
```

Naturally, we want to write code to input, output, and add `fraction` objects by using the same operators, >>, <<, and +, that we use to input, output, and add variables whose types are built-in numeric types. For example, we want the following code fragment from `fracs3.cpp` (at the PWS Web site) to produce the kind of sample run to its right.

```
cout << "Enter fraction: ";
cin >> g;
cout << "Enter fraction: ";
cin >> h;
f = g + h;
cout << "Their sum is ";
cout << f;
```

```
Enter fraction: 1/4
Enter fraction: 3/8
Their sum is 20/32
```

Typical run

However, for `fracs3.cpp` to produce this run, we must overload the <<, >>, and + operators for the struct data type, `fraction`. If we do not overload these operators, the compiler will produce the error message, "Illegal structure operation" for each of the highlighted lines of the previous code fragment.

Fraction Operations Without Overloading In this next program, which produces the same sort of sample runs as the previous fragment, we have not yet attempted operator overloading. Taking a more elementary approach instead, we define the functions `get_frac`, `sum`, and `put_frac`, and use them in place of the highlighted statements of the previous fragment.

```
// fracs1.cpp
// Input, add, and output fractions
#include <iostream.h>

struct fraction
    { int num, den; };

void get_frac (fraction& f); // out
fraction sum (fraction f1, fraction f2);
void put_frac (fraction f);
```

```
void main()
{
    fraction f, g, h;
    cout << "Enter a fraction: ";
    get_frac(g);
    cout << "Enter a fraction: ";
    get_frac(h);
    f = sum(g, h);
    cout << "Their sum is ";
    put_frac(f);
    cout << endl;
}
```

The definition of get_frac is

```
void get_frac (fraction& f) // out
{
    char slash;
    cin >> f.num >> slash >> f.den;
}
```

and the definition of put_frac is left to you as Exercise 17.8.

QUESTION How should you complete the definition of the sum function? For the sum, use the "quick and dirty" formula a/b + c/d = (ad + bc) / bd, without reducing.

```
fraction sum (fraction f1, // in
              fraction f2) // in
{
    fraction the_sum;
    the_sum.den = _____;
    the_sum.num = _____;
    return the_sum;
}
```

Answer The completed lines of sum should be

```
the_sum.den = f1.den*f2.den;
the_sum.num = f1.num*f2.den + f1.den*f2.num;
```

Overloading the + Operator for `fraction` ***Addition*** In the expression g + h, the sum g + h has two operands, g and h. To make the + operator legal for fractions, we define a function named `operator+`, which has two `fraction` parameters and returns their sum. The declaration of `operator+` is:

```
fraction operator+(fraction f1, fraction f2);
```

Note that `operator+` has two `fraction` parameters and returns a `fraction` result.

Defining `operator+` has the following effect: Whenever the compiler encounters the + operator with operands of type `fraction`, the compiler interprets this as a call to `operator+`. For example, when g and h are fractions, the expression g + h is interpreted as the member function call `operator+(g, h)`.

Here are the function declarations and the body of `main` from program `fracs2.cpp`, which uses an overloaded + operator to add two fractions:

```
void get_frac (fraction& f); // out
void put_frac (fraction f); // in
fraction operator+ (fraction f1, fraction f2);

void main()
{
    fraction f, g, h;
    cout << "Enter a fraction: ";
    get_frac(g);
    cout << "Enter a fraction: ";
    get_frac(h);
    f = g + h; // really a call to operator+
    cout << "Their sum is ";
    put_frac(f);
    cout << endl;
}
```

The definition of `operator+` has exactly the same body as the definition of the `sum` function from the previous program.

■ **QUESTION** The statement f = g + h; is really a call to the function `operator+`. How should you rewrite that statement using explicit function notation to call the function `operator+`?

Answer   f = operator+(g, h);

Although this function notation is closer to how the compiler really handles + for fractions, the + notation is far more preferable. In fact, the whole point of defining `operator+` was to make it legal to use the ordinary + notation when adding fractions. ■ ▬

Overloading *<<* ***and*** *>>* ***for Input and Output of Fractions*** In `fracs3.cpp`, we overload the `>>` and `<<` operators so that a client program can be written as indicated at the beginning of this section; that is, so that client program statements such as `cin >> g` and `cout << f` will be legal.

Definition of `operator>>`   Here is how to overload `operator>>` for the `fraction` data type.

```
istream& operator>> (istream& ins, fraction& f)
{
    char slash;
    ins >> f.num >> slash >> f.den;
    return ins;
}
```

Notice that this definition contains two parameters so that a call can specify (1) which stream the input will be read from (it might be from a file instead of `cin`) and (2) which object the input will be read into. This definition of `operator>>` makes the following code legal.

```
cin >> g; // same call as: operator>>(cin, g);
```

The definition of `operator<<` is similar. The program `fracs3.cpp` contains the full program with +, >>, and << overloaded.

Why the Return Type of `operator>>` ***is*** `istream&`   You may have wondered why the return type of `operator>>` is not `void`, but is instead `istream&`. The short explanation is that this way of defining `operator>>` enables cascading, as in

```
cin >> g >> h;  // legal
```

Written in function notation, the preceding statement is really the nesting of two function calls.

```
operator>>( operator>>(cin, g), h);
```

The value returned by the screened first (or inner) call becomes the first argument for the second (or outer) call of `operator>>`, and this argument must be of type `istream&`. If it were of type `void`, a syntax error would occur.

CAUTION When overloading operators, be sure to make their new meanings consistent with their existing meanings. Thus, using + for addition of fractions or for concatenation of strings makes good sense. On the other hand, using << for multiplication of fractions, while legal, would be pointless and confusing.

■ Exercises

1. (a) Write the definition of a data type name_str, that can store a person's first name, last name, and middle initial.

   (b) Write statements to define a name_str struct variable, user_name, then prompt for and input the data members of this struct, one item at a time.

   (c) Write statements to output the contents of user_name in the form FIRST M. LAST and in the form LAST, FIRST M.

2. Information for all the employees of the ACME company is stored in a variable, company, that is a vector of structs. For example, company might contain

	name	gender	payrate
company[1]	Bond, Al	m	9.50
company[2]	Brock, Ann	f	10.25
company[3]	Doyle, Don	m	8.90
	.	.	.
	.	.	.
	.	.	.

Write a definition for an employee struct and a declaration for the vector company that can store information on 100 employees.

3. Here are the definitions and declarations for creating a variable called employees, which will hold a vector of structs.

```
struct emp_strct {
    String name;
    int     age;
    float   salary;
    }; // end emp_strct

Vector<emp_strct> employees;
```

Suppose that data has been read into the vector, and it has been resized to exactly fit the data. Write program fragments to

(a) print the name and age of the fourth employee in the vector.

(b) print the names of all employees earning over $35,000.

(c) change the salary of the third employee to $40,000.

4. (a) Redefine the `student_str` data type from the end of Section 17.3 so that a student's name is stored in a data member of type `name_str` (of Exercise 17.1).

(b) Write statements that will display the contents of a variable of this `student_str` type in the format:

```
Name:       Good, Johnnie B.
ID number:  149-00-9812
Birth date: 12/7/76
```

5. Write a function, `get_date`, to enter a `date_str` (Section 17.3) in the form `MM/DD/YYYY`. (You may assume that months and days have no leading zeros.)

6. Implement a `display` function to output the contents of its `employee_str` parameter. (See the program `emp.cpp` of Section 17.1.) Use the typical run as a guide for how output should appear.

7. Implement a `display` function to output the contents of its `Time_piece_str` parameter in the format of the program `danger.cpp` of Section 17.4.

8. Implement the `put_frac` function of the program `fracs1.cpp`, Section 17.5. In case the fraction's denominator is 1, do not print the slash or the denominator.

9. Write the definitions for the nested struct data type represented by the following diagram:

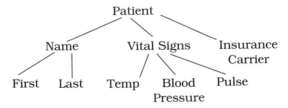

Programming Problems

10. A text file contains bank depositor information. For each depositor, the file contains the depositor's name, account number, type of account (checking or savings), and current balance. Write a program that will print two tables, with the first sorted by name and the second by account number. Each table should contain all the data for each customer.

11. An unsorted text file contains the name, age, and credits earned for each student in a class. Write a program that will print three tables of student

names, ages, and credits earned. The first table should be alphabetical by name; the second should be in order by age, with the youngest listed first; the third should be in order by credits earned with the highest number of credits listed first.

12. A text file contains the name, age, and credits earned for each student in a class and is sorted alphabetically by name. Write a menu-driven program that allows the user to repeatedly choose from the following menu options.

    A <*age*>   List all students of the given age.
    C <*crds*>   List all students having earned at least *crds* credits.
    N <*ltr*>   List all students whose last name begins with the letter *ltr*.
    Q   Quit.

13. Write and test a function that updates its `Time_piece_str` reference parameter by a specified number of hours and minutes passed as value parameters.

Longer Assignments

14. Redo Exercise 14.17 using a vector of structs to store the names, scores, and "curved" letter grades for the students.

15. Redo Exercise 14.18 using a vector of structs to store the names and phone numbers for the students.

16. A text file contains the pre-weekend win–loss records for each of the teams in a Little League. Write a program that will first read the data (team names, wins, and losses) into a vector of structs and print a table giving the team names, wins, losses, and winning percentages. Then, the program should allow the user to update the standings by prompting for and entering the winner and loser of each of the games played during the weekend. After the updating is done, the program should display a new table of standings, in decreasing order by winning percentage.

17. There are seven candidates in a mayoral election in which voters can vote for their top three choices in order of preference. A first-place vote is worth 5 points, a second-place vote is worth 3 points, and a third-place vote is worth 1 point. One text file, `cands.dat`, contains the names of the seven candidates; a second text file, `ballots.dat`, contains one voter's worth of choices per line. Sample files are

    ```
    cands.dat        ballots.dat

    Cane             Hund Spaniel Chien
    Hund             Perro Spaniel Wolff
    Wolff            .
    Chien            .
    Fideau           .
    Perro
    Spaniel
    ```

For example, the first ballot would give 5 points to Hund, 3 to Spaniel, and 1 to Chien.

Write a program that will process all the ballots and then print a table, ordered by decreasing point total, that gives each candidate's name, the number of first-, second-, and third-place votes he or she received, and the candidate's point total.

18. Do Exercise 14.23 using a vector of structs.

19. Do Exercise 14.24 using a vector of structs.

18

Using an Existing Class Given Its Interface

A class is a constructed data type that is either predefined (with its defining code contained in an existing library file) or programmer defined. A program that uses a particular class is called a *client program* of that class, and a variable of a class is known as an *object*. Some of the main features of classes are as follows.

- **Classes can prepackage lots of programming power.** A class binds together not just "related data," as was the case for the structs of the previous chapter, but also its own member functions for manipulating an object's data. This binding of related data and code is known as *encapsulation*.

- **Classes promote safety through a public interface.** A class makes effective use of information hiding (a concept discussed in Section 18.1) by subdividing access into a *public interface* and a *private section*. Client programs access and manipulate an object's data only through calls to member functions that are part of the public interface; client programs are denied direct access to anything in the private section. This arrangement prevents the client programmer from making certain kinds of careless mistakes, especially in situations where a change in one data member necessitates changes to other related data members.

- **Classes can be readily extended.** Classes can be improved, both by adding new public member functions and also by increasing the efficiency of the implementation of its existing features. Further, such improvements can be made in ways that ensure that existing client programs, written for the original version of the class, will run correctly with the new version of the class.

In earlier chapters, when we introduced some predefined classes (String, istream, ifstream, ostream, ofstream, Vector, and Matrix), we made things easier by explaining some of their most useful public member functions *without having you look at the library files of those classes*. In this chapter, however, the focus is on figuring out how to use a class based on a reading of the interface section of a class's library file. To that end, we use the Time_piece, Int_list, and Fraction classes written by the authors and provided at the PWS Web site.

Ultimately, nothing is free. So what is the price to be paid for all of these powerful features of classes? Fortunately, for the client programmer, which is what you will be in this chapter, the main burden is shouldered by the class implementor, who writes the actual implementation code for all the member functions. The task of implementing a class is complicated by some new syntax and by the extra care that must be taken to maintain the distinction between public and private sections.

In the next chapter, you will switch hats and learn some of the new syntax and techniques that are part of the class implementor's trade. This will enable you to modify an existing class and start you on your way to writing the full definition of a class from scratch.

18.1   Information Hiding, Public Interfaces, and Electronic Devices

In a general sense, *information hiding* means that the details of the "inner workings" of a mechanism (say, an electronic device) are concealed and encapsulated in order to provide a simpler and safer way to use the mechanism. The use of public interfaces in classes (to achieve the benefits of information hiding) is similar in spirit to their use in familiar electronic devices. Some common advantages of using public interfaces in both electronic devices and classes are

1. Simplicity The user is not overloaded with details that he does not need to understand or even know about in order to use the mechanism. For example, you have undoubtedly used a compact disc player, but probably do not know how a particular CD player uses laser technology to read the digital coding on a CD and convert it into sound. All of these details are coordinated and executed for you when you press the correct sequence of buttons on the CD player's control panel, which acts as your interface to the inner workings.

Similarly, a client programmer may use calls to public member functions without understanding or even knowing their defining code. Of course, you have already seen this aspect of information hiding in connection with libraries of functions.

2. Safety The user is protected against making certain kinds of errors (some of which may be very dangerous) because she can access the inner workings of the mechanism only in restricted, well-designed ways.

Suppose you open the door of a microwave oven that is running, then insert your hand. You are protected against burning your hand because opening the door will immediately cause the oven to stop emitting microwaves. This coordination of activities (if door opens, then turn off the microwave emitter) is encapsulated in the oven's inner workings. Furthermore, you do not have the kind of unrestricted access to the oven's inner workings that would allow you to keep the microwave emitter on while you open the door. The microwave control panel provides you with the features you need, while restricting access in order to provide some degree of safety.

A class affords similar protection by providing the client with a limited public interface consisting of just those member functions that the client will need, while denying access to functions that are for internal use only — this can protect the client against some kinds of improper manipulations of the inner workings of the class.

3. Extensibility and easy use of improved version The technology used in the internal workings of CD players and microwave ovens improves over time, and their public interfaces (control panels) also evolve. Still, the basic control panel features retain a familiar enough form that someone who knew how to use a previous model can quickly begin using the new and improved model.

With classes, a well-defined public interface makes it easy to ensure that client programs that work with an existing version of a class will still work correctly with a new and improved version of the class.

18.2 Using a Time_piece Class

In this section we demonstrate the use of the Time_piece class contained in the PWS Web site file time_pc1.h. It is illuminating to contrast this class with the struct, Time_piece_str, that was discussed in Section 17.4.

Danger of a Struct's Liberal Access to Data In the program danger.cpp from Section 17.4, an initial time of 11:45 A.M. was updated by adding 40 minutes to it and then the new time was displayed. The statements used to update the watch's time and then display the updated time were

```
watch.min += 40;
cout << "Current time: " << endl;
display(watch);
```

These statements produced the invalid time display:

```
Current time: 11:85 AM
```

In the first program that we will present in this chapter, the Time_piece class will enable a client program to handle such an update safely and simply and *will not allow the preceding type of error to be made.*

Member Data and the State of an Object   Recall that a variable whose type is a class is known as an object. An object's data (just like a struct variable's data) is stored in its data member variables. The Time_piece class that we will declare shortly has the same three data members, hr, min, and merid, that the struct type Time_piece_str had. The **state** of an object, which is the current values of its data members, is depicted in the same way that a struct variable's contents were depicted. Thus, when the clock object stores the data representing the time 11:45 A.M., its state can be pictured as follows.

clock	.hr	.min	.merid
	11	45	'A'

Public Versus Private   A class's interface contains a public section and a private section. The public section lists (that is, gives declarations for) all the member functions that are available to client programs. The first part of the private section gives all the data member declarations; the private section may also contain additional member functions that are for internal use (in the implementation code) only and are *not* available to client programs. (Data members can be made public, but you will rarely have a reason to do so. We follow the standard convention of making all class data members private.)

Access to an Object's Data   Because a class's data members are declared in the private section, an object's data *cannot* be directly accessed by a client program in the same way that a struct variable's data was accessed. Thus, if watch is a struct variable of type Time_piece_str, and clock is a Time_piece object, then we have the following situation.

```
watch.min += 40; // OK. watch is a struct variable
clock.min += 40; // illegal. clock is an object
                 // and its data is private
```

As you will see in Section 18.3, the proper way to gain access to an object's data members is through the use of special functions that are known as *accessor* functions and that must be provided by the class designer in the public section.

Interface of the Time_piece ***Class*** Here is the interface of the Time_piece class as given in the file time_pc1.h.

```
class Time_piece
{
public: // accessible by client programs
    void set(int h, int m, char mrd);
    void update(int h, int m);
    void display();

private: // for internal use only
    int hr, min; // the hour and minute
    char merid;  // meridian: a(m) or p(m)
    void validate();
};
```

Understanding a Class from Its Interface In general, when reading a class's interface, with an eye to writing client programs, you will want to know the following.

1. ***How is the data set up?*** Look for the data members at the top of the private section.

2. ***What public member functions are available?*** Always look carefully at the entire public section.

You will not make any use of member functions that are given in the private section.

Note that the Time_piece class contains

1. three private data members, hr, min, and merid;

2. three public member functions, set, update, and display; and

3. one private member function, validate.

Further Documentation of Public Member Functions To use a class, we often need some form of additional documentation that describes each public member function and provides sample calls and their actions. This documentation might be given as comments in the interface of the class or, more likely, in a printed manual. In the case of standard or predefined C++ classes, additional documentation is usually given in on-line help files accessible from within your particular program development environment.

Further Documentation of Time_Piece Public Member Functions

```
void set(int h, int m, char mrd);
// Set calling object's time,
// where 1 <= h <= 12, 0 <= m <= 59,
// and mrd is 'a', 'A', 'p', or 'P'.
// Example: The call clock.set(2,30,'A');
// sets clock to 2:30 AM.

void update(int h, int m);
// Change calling object's time by h hr and m min.
// Example:  If clock's time is 2:30 AM, the call
// clock.update(4,16) will change it to 6:46 AM.

void display();
// Display calling object's time on the monitor
// Example:  clock.display() will display the time
// stored in clock.
```

■ **EXAMPLE**   (A First Program that Uses the Time_piece Class)   The following program correctly adds an elapsed number of minutes (input by the user) to a starting time and then displays the updated time. Notice that in the highlighted statements dot notation is used for member function calls.

```
// t_pc_ex1.cpp
#include <iostream.h>
#include "time_pc1.h"
   // for Time_piece class

void main()
{
    Time_piece clock;
    int mins_elapsed;
    clock.set(11,45,'A');
    clock.display();
    cout << endl;
    cout << "Minutes elapsed: ";
    cin >> mins_elapsed;
```

```
11:45 AM
Minutes elapsed: 40
New time: 12:25 PM
```

Sample run

```
clock.update(0,mins_elapsed);
cout << "New time: ";
clock.display();
cout << endl;
}
```

Discussion   The update of the clock's time by adding 40 minutes was done by a call to the member function `update`, which automatically handles any changes necessitated by the number of minutes exceeding 59.

Maintaining Data Integrity   A well-designed class protects an object's data members from being invalid or internally inconsistent. This is accomplished in the following three general ways:

1. **Denying direct access to data**   Because data is private, a statement such as

    ```
    clock.min = 68;
    ```

    is illegal.

2. **Encapsulating bookkeeping**   A class should relieve the client programmer of many tedious "bookkeeping" details that, if handled carelessly, could result in mistakes. For example, in the `Time_piece` class of the previous program, a time update is handled by a call to the public member function `update`, which automatically takes care of the interrelatedness of the data members.

3. **Automatic error checking in functions that set values**   The implementation code for any public member function that specifies values to store in an object should check that these values are valid. The `Time_piece` class, for example, automatically terminates the program with an error message if a client program contains a call such as

    ```
    clock.set(5,78,'P');
    ```

When we discuss implementation in the next chapter, you will see that the implementation code for `set` makes a call to the private member function `validate` in order to check that the values it receives as parameters are valid.

■ **QUESTION**   How would you add code to the body of the previous client program so that the output will also state whether the new time is on the hour — that is, the `min` data member is 0.

Answer   You could not do this — it would be impossible! The data members are private, and this particular class has no accessor functions. ▪ ▬

▪ **QUESTION**   How would you complete the following program so that it produces the output shown? (Use a `for` loop to update `watch` in 1-hour and 15-minute increments, from a starting time of 9:00 A.M. to a final time of 2:00 P.M.)

```
// t_pc_ex2.cpp
#include <iostream.h>
#include "time_pc1.h"

void main()
{
    _____ watch;
    int k;
    watch.set(9,0,'A');
    watch._____; cout << endl;
    for (k=1; k<=4; k++)
       {
       watch._____;
       watch._____; cout << endl;
       }
}
```

```
9:00 AM
10:15 AM
11:30 AM
12:45 PM
2:00 PM
```

Output

Answer   The missing lines are

```
Time_piece watch;
watch.display(); cout << endl;
   watch.update(1,15);
   watch.display(); cout << endl;
```

▪ ▬

18.3 An Improved `Time_piece` Class with Accessor Functions

Accessor Functions   In the previous section we discussed the problems that can arise if data members are made public. Still, a client program may need to use the values of a private data member. An *accessor function* allows a client program "read-only" access to a private data member — its value can be retrieved but there is no possibility of changing it. (By contrast, a member function that can alter member data is called a *modifier* function.)

Accessor Function Declarations and the `const` ***Modifier*** Before looking at the improved `Time_piece` class of this section, let us first examine one particular accessor function, `get_hour`, of that class. Its declaration and description are

```
int get_hour() const;
// Return data member hour.
```

Notice the highlighted keyword, `const`, that follows the function's parameter list. This new syntax serves two purposes. First it ensures that the implementation code for the function cannot alter the state of the object. Second, it serves as a form of documentation, clearly informing the reader of the class about whether a member function accesses or alters member data.

In fact, the `const` modifier should be used with any member function that does not alter member data. Such functions are referred to as ***const member functions***. The `display` function is not, strictly speaking, an accessor function, because it does not return member data to a client program. Still, it does not alter member data, so it, too, should have the `const` modifier at the end of its declaration.

An Improved `Time_piece` ***Class*** Recall that the earlier version of `Time_piece` had no accessor functions, and thus, a client program could not even determine whether the current state of an object was exactly on the hour. The file `time_pc2.h` contains an improved `Time_piece` class. Here is the interface for the improved version, with changes highlighted.

```
class Time_piece
{
public:
    // modifier functions
    void set(int h, int m, char mrd);
    void update(int h, int m=0);

    // accessor functions
    int get_hour() const;
    int get_minute() const;
    char get_meridian() const;
    int get_mins_past() const;

    // IO functions
    void display (ostream& outs = cout) const;
    void enter();
```

```
private:
    int hr, min;  // the hour and minute
    int mins_past; // mins past midnite
    char merid; // meridian: a(m) or p(m),

    void validate() const;
    void normalize();
    void set_mins_past();
};
```

Improvements in the New Version of the *Time_piece* Class

1. **Increased public functionality** To its public section we have added:

    - Four accessor functions that permit a client program to access each of the data members. (Note also the additional data member, mins_past.)

    - An enter function that allows a starting time to be entered interactively.

    - The option (via default parameters) to have display output to a disk file or the virtual printer by using a call like clock.display(vprn).

2. **Use of the** const **modifier** The const modifier has been placed at the end of the declaration of every function, public or private, that can access but not alter member data. As discussed earlier, this serves both as a security measure and as documentation.

3. **More efficient implementation** Although this improvement will be largely invisible to the user, you will see in Chapter 19 that the internal implementation of update has been made more modular and more efficient. This has been achieved by adding private member functions normalize and set_mins_past and the private data member mins_past.

4. **Internal documentation** The categorization of public member functions as accessors, modifiers, and I/O functions improves the readability of the class interface.

Be aware that a client program of the original version of the Time_piece class will *still* run as a client of this improved version. To run it, you need only change the #include statement so that it specifies the file that contains the improved class.

■ **QUESTION**   **(Using Accessor Functions)**   The following program asks the user to input the time. It then updates the time by 30 minutes, outputs the new time, and states whether or not the new time is on the hour. If it is on the hour, the new time is printed without minutes. After studying the typical runs, how would you fill in the blanks?

```cpp
// t_pc_ex3.cpp
#include <iostream.h>
#include "time_pc2.h"

void main()
{
    Time_piece clock;
    cout << "Enter a time: ";
    _____;
    cout << "In half an hour it will be: ";
    clock.update(0,30);
    clock.display(); cout << endl;

    cout << "The new time is ";
    if (clock._____ != 0)
        cout << "not on the hour.\n";
    else
        {
        cout << "on the hour.\n";
        cout << "It is " << clock. _____
            << clock._____ << "M\n";
        }
}
```

```
Enter a time: 11:30am
In half an hour it will be: 12:00 PM
The new time is on the hour.
It is 12PM

Enter a time: 2:45 PM
In half an hour it will be: 3:15 PM
The new time is not on the hour.
```

Typical runs

Answer   The completed lines are

```
clock.enter();
if (clock.get_minute() != 0)
   cout << "It is " << clock.get_hour()
        << clock.get_meridian() << "M\n";
```

■ **PROBLEM**   **(Two** `Time_piece` **Objects)**   Write a client program that will input the user's logon and logoff times for an Internet session, then output the length in minutes of the session. Typical runs of the program will look like those given at right.

A top-level algorithm for this problem is

```
Logged on at: 10:50 am
Logged off at: 1:20 pm
Time on net: 150 min.


Logged on at: 9:45PM
Logged off at: 2:00AM
Time on net: 255 min.
```

1. Enter the `logon_time`.

2. Enter the `logoff_time`.

3. Calculate `mins_on_net` (the length of the session).

4. Output `mins_on_net`.

■ **QUESTION**   How would you complete the following code (from `logtime.cpp`), which implements the preceding algorithm? (*Hints*: You will need to access the private data member `mins_past` in order to calculate the length of the Internet session. You may assume that an Internet session lasts less than 24 hours.)

```
Time_piece _____, _____;
int mins_on_net;

cout << "Logged on at: ";
logon_time. _____;
cout << "Logged off at: ";
_____;
mins_on_net = logoff_time._____
              - logon_time._____;
if (mins_on_net < 0) // session went past midnight
   mins_on_net += 24*60;
cout << "Time on net: " << mins_on_net
     << " min.\n";
```

Answer The completed lines are

```
Time_piece logon_time, logoff_time;
logon_time.enter();
logoff_time.enter();
mins_on_net = logoff_time.get_mins_past()
                    - logon_time.get_mins_past();
```

Discussion Access to the private data member `mins_past` of either of the `Time_piece` objects is possible only via the accessor function `get_mins_past`. The statement

```
mins_on_net = logoff_time.mins_past
                    - logon_time.mins_past;
```

will not compile.

18.4   Using an `Int_list` **Class and a Constructor**

The `Int_list` class, contained in the file `int_lst.h`, can be used to store and manipulate lists of integers. Look at the following `Int_list` class interface to determine what its data members are and what public functions are available. Note that its first public function has the same name as the class. Such a function is called a *constructor function*, or simply a *constructor*. We explain shortly the role of constructors.

```
class Int_list {
public:
   // constructor
   Int_list(); // construct a list of length 0

   // accessors
   int length () const;
      // return length of list
   int retrieve (int i) const;
      // retrieve ith list element
      // (first element is in position 1)
   bool contains (int elt) const;
      // return true if list contains elt; else false.

   // modifiers
   void add (int elt);
      // add elt to end of list
   void sort ();
      // sort list in increasing order
```

```
      // output
      void display (ostream& os=cout) const;
         // display list on ostream os

   private:
      int len;     // length of the list
      Vector<int> Elts; // elements of the list
      bool sorted; // true if list is sorted; else false
   };   // end Int_list class interface
```

■ **QUESTION** What are the data members and accessor functions of the `Int_list` class?

Answer   `Int_list` has data members `len`, `Elts`, and `sorted`, and accessor functions `length`, `retrieve`, and `contains`. Some points to note:

1. Data members are never functions.

2. Each call to `retrieve` returns one element of the vector.

3. There is no accessor function for `sorted`.   ■ ▬▬

Constructor Functions and Initialization   Constructor functions are easy to recognize because (1) they are always public functions with the same name as their class and (2) they have no return type. As a matter of style, constructor function declarations are normally positioned at the top of the public section.

An important role of a constructor is to enable a client program's declaration of an object to *also* initialize some of that object's data members. For example, as indicated by the documentation in the public section of `Int_list`, a client program declaration such as

```
      Int_list L;
```

not only reserves memory for the object L, but also assigns the value 0 to its data member `len`. (Although it is not publicly documented, the constructor also initializes the data member `sorted` to true because an initially empty list is sorted.) By contrast, when an object of a class without constructor functions is declared, all of its data members start with uninitialized, garbage values, as was the case whenever a client program declared an object of type `Time_piece`.

Constructor Syntax Peculiarities   The syntax for constructor functions is unlike that of any functions we have encountered thus far. First, the declaration of a constructor function *never has a return type*. Second, even though a constructor is a class member function, *dot notation is never used* in calling the constructor.

■ **EXAMPLE** The following program produces the given output.

```
// tst_lst0.cpp
#include <iostream.h>
#include "int_lst.h"

void main()
{
    Int_list L;
    cout << "L= ";
    L.display(); cout << endl;
    cout << L.length() << endl;
    L.add(30);
    L.add(25);
    L.add(30);
    L.add(99);
    cout << "L= ";
    L.display(); cout << endl;
    cout << L.length() << endl;
}
```

```
L=
0
L= 30 25 30 99
4
```
Output

Discussion The preceeding program and its output illustrate that

1. The Int_list object L is initially empty, with len initialized to 0, because the declaration of L invokes the Int_list class's constructor.

2. add appends its parameter to the end of the list.

3. display outputs list elements separated by spaces, with no trailing line feed. ■ ■■■

■ **PROBLEM** Write a program to input a list of exam scores, terminated by a negative sentinel, then output (1) the number of scores, (2) the scores in the order entered, and (3) the scores in increasing sorted order. A typical program run is:

```
Enter scores (−1 to quit) : 78   85   92
83   90   67   −1
There are 6 scores.
They are: 78 85 92 83 90 67
In order: 67 78 83 85 90 92
```

■ **QUESTION** How should you complete the following program fragment (from tst_lst1.cpp), which uses an Int_list object, scores, to solve the preceeding problem?

```
Int_list scores;
int score;
cout << "Enter scores (-1 to quit) : ";
cin >> score;
while (score >= 0)
    {
    scores._____;
    cin >> score;
    }
cout << "There are " << _____
    << " scores.\n";
cout << "They are: ";
scores.display(); cout << endl;
scores._____;
cout << "In order: ";
_____
```

Answer The completed lines should be

```
        scores.add(score);
    cout << "There are " << scores.length()
    scores.sort();
    scores.display(); cout << endl;
```

Destructors A *destructor function* is the opposite of a constructor function. For the classes that we will be working with in this and the next three chapters, we do not need to write destructor functions. Therefore, we defer a detailed explanation of the destructor to Section 22.6, where writing the destructor for a class is necessary.

18.5 Using a Fraction **Class — More on Constructors**

The interface of the Fraction class given in the file frac_cl1.h is

```
class Fraction  // interface
{
```

```
public:
    // constructors
    Fraction(); // "do nothing" constructor
    Fraction (long n, long d=1);
        // construct Fraction with value n/d

    // accessors
    long get_num() const; // return num
    long get_den() const; // return den

    // modifiers
    void set (long n, long d=1);
        // set calling object to n/d
    void normalize(); // make den positive
    void reduce(); // reduce calling object
    Fraction operator+ (Fraction f2) const;
        // return calling object + f2

    // IO functions
    void enter(istream& ins=cin);
        // input value of calling object from ins
    void display(ostream& outs=cout) const;
        // display calling object on outs

private:
    long num, den; // numerator, denominator
    void validate() const; // that den is not 0
};
```

■ **QUESTION**   The program frac_ex1.cpp enters a fraction, reduces it, then outputs
the reduced fraction and its floating point equivalent. After studying the
typical run of the program, how would you fill in the blanks in the program. (Note that there is a member function that reduces a fraction, but
there is none that returns the floating point equivalent of a fraction.)

```
Enter a fraction (num/den) : 22/16
22/16 reduced = 11/8
and as a decimal = 1.375
```

Typical run

```
// frac_ex1.cpp
#include <iostream.h>
#include "frac_cl1.h"

void main()
{
   Fraction f;
   cout << "Enter a fraction (num/den): ";
   f.enter();
   f.display(); cout << " reduced = ";
   _____;
   f. display(); cout << endl;
   cout << "and as a decimal = ";
   cout << double (_____) / _____
        << endl;
}
```

Answer   To give the decimal equivalent of a fraction, you should use the accessor functions for num and den. The completed lines are

```
f.reduce();
cout << double (f.get_num()) / f.get_den()
```

Overloading the + Operator   The Fraction class has an overloaded + operator, which enables statements like f = g + h. We postpone discussion of both its declaration and definition to Section 19.6.

■ **QUESTION**   **(Adding 5/8 to an Input Fraction)**   After studying the typical run given, how would you fill in the blanks in the following program fragment?

Main Function of frac_ex2.cpp

```
void main()
{
   Fraction f, g, h;
   cout << "Enter a fraction: ";
   g.enter();
   cout << "We'll add 5/8 to that . . \n";
   h._____;
   f = g + h;
   f.reduce();
   g.display();  cout << " + "; h.display();
   cout << " = " ;_____; cout << endl;
}
```

```
Enter a fraction: 1/6
We'll add 5/8 to that . .
1/6 + 5/8 = 19/24
```

Typical run

Answer   The completed lines should be

```
h.set(5,8);
cout << " = " ; f.display(); cout << endl;
```

More on Constructors   A parameterless constructor function that does no explicit initializing, but instead allows garbage initial values for all data members is known as a *do-nothing constructor*. A class that contains no explicit constructor declarations actually has a parameterless, do-nothing constructor that is generated "for free" by the compiler. (Similarly, a class that has no explicitly declared destructor gets one for free, and these free destructors suffice for all the classes we study until Chapter 22.) The Time_piece class has such a default constructor.

On the other hand, a class that explicitly provides at least one constructor does not get any parameterless constructor "for free." Thus, the Fraction class has two constructors with these declarations.

```
Fraction (); // "do nothing" constructor
Fraction (long n, long d=1);
// construct Fraction with value n/d
```

The first is an explicit do-nothing constructor for declaring uninitialized Fraction objects, and the second is an explicit constructor for declaring initialized Fraction objects.

Note that if the Fraction class contained no explicit declaration of a parameterless constructor, then the following declaration in a client program would be illegal.

```
Fraction g; // illegal if at least one constructor
            // but no parameterless constructor
```

Like any function, a constructor may have parameters and even default parameters. (See Section 10.4 for a review of default parameters.) For example, the second Fraction constructor has two parameters so that a Fraction object declaration can specify the initial values for num and den. A default value of 1 is assigned to den if no second argument is given in the declaration.

■ EXAMPLE   For the Fraction class, each of the following declarations is legal in a client program.

```
Fraction f; // creates f with garbage values for
            // f.num and f.den
Fraction h(2,3); // creates h with h.num=2 and h.den=3
Fraction k(7);   // creates k with k.num=7 and k.den=1
```

■ QUESTION What will be the output of the following code fragment?

```
Fraction f(3), g(4,7), h;
f.display(); cout << " and ";
g.display(); cout << endl;
h.display(); cout << endl;
```

Answer   The first line of output will be 3 and 4/7. The second line is unpredictable because the no-argument constructor assigns no values to the member data of h.

Constructors Make It Easier to Add Literals Like 5/8   Be aware that if f and g are of type Fraction, then the statement

```
f = g + 5/8; //illegal
```

does not add the fraction 5/8 onto g! The compiler interprets 5/8 not as a fraction literal, but as the int expression 5/8, which evaluates to 0.

Two methods can be used to add the fraction 5/8 to g:

1. **Declaring a named object, h, to store 5/8** This is what was done in the program fragment from frac_ex2.cpp. Recall that in addition to declaring h, we also needed the following two statements.

   ```
   h.set(5,8);
   f = g + h;
   ```

2. **Constructing a temporary, nameless object** You can add 5/8 to g more simply, in a single statement, as follows.

   ```
   f = g + Fraction(5,8);
   ```

   In this statement, the constructor call Fraction(5,8) constructed a nameless, temporary Fraction object with the value 5/8.

18.6   A New Class: Big_Ulam

Ulam's conjecture, first introduced in Section 8.1, was used to illustrate looping techniques and was the subject of various exercises in that and subsequent chapters. It is an interesting problem to experiment with, because mathematicians have not yet determined whether the sequence terminates for every starting value. However, for the experiments that you perform, you are currently limited to sequences whose values do not "wander" outside the bounds of 32-bit integers, which have at most ten decimal digits.

The file bigulam.h (at the PWS Web site) contains a class, Big_Ulam, that enables client programmers to experiment with Ulam sequences whose values have up to 64 decimal digits! Its interface is

```
class Big_Ulam
{
public:
   Big_Ulam(); // constructor

   // accessors
   int num_digits() const;
       // return number of dec. digits
   bool is_1() const;
       // Return true if object is 1; else false

   // modifiers
   void set(unsigned long n);
       // set object to n
   void update();
       // if object is even, divide it by 2;
       // otherwise, mult by 3 and add 1

   // IO functions
   void enter(istream& ins=cin);
       // enter value of object from keyboard
   void display(ostream& outs=cout) const;
       // display object on monitor

private:
   // vector of decimal digits of object
   // least sig. dig. in cell 1
   // most sig. dig. in cell num_digs
   Vector<int> dgs;

   const int MAX_DIGS; // maximum digits in an object
   int num_digs; // num of digs in object
   void div_2();
   void mul_3();
   void add_1();
};
```

A client program, ulam_tst.cpp, with a small portion of a very long sample run is

```cpp
// ulam_tst.cpp
#include <iostream.h>
#include <iomanip.h>
#include "bigulam.h"

void main()
{
    Big_Ulam U;
    int len=0;
    cout << "Initial Ulam int: ";
    U.enter();
    do {
        U.update();
        U.display(); cout << endl;
        len++;
        }
    while (!U.is_1());
    cout << "\nLength = " << len << endl;
}
```

```
Initial Ulam int: 7777777777777777777777777777777
2333333333333333333333333333332
1166666666666666666666666666666
583333333333333333333333333333
175000000000000000000000000000
87500000000000000000000000000
43750000000000000000000000000
.
.
.
5
16
8
4
2
1

Length = 707
```

Sample run

The exercises provide other experiments that you can try using this class.

■ Exercises

1. Identify and explain the four errors in the following program.

```
#include <iostream.h>
#include "time_pc2.h"

void main()
{
    Time_piece clock;
    clock.set (10, 45, 'a');
    clock.validate();
    cout << "Time: " << clock << endl;
    cout << "Hr: " << clock.hr << endl;
    update (clock, 3, 30);
    clock.display();
}
```

2. Write a code fragment to set a `Time_piece` object, `watch`, to 11:57 P.M., then, six times, update `watch` by 1 minute and display the result. Show what an actual run of your code would look like.

3. Suppose you wanted to update a time (input by the user) in 1-hour increments until the time has passed midnight. Does the `Time_piece` class provide adequate functionality for this task? If so, write the code fragment; if not, tell what member functions you would need.

4. Write a code fragment to display the elements of a sorted `Int_list`, `L`, in reverse order, one element per line.

5. Suppose `L` and `M` are of type `Int_list`. Write a function that will tell whether every element of `L` is also an element of `M`.

6. Given a fraction `f`, write a statement or statements to
   (a) display its reciprocal, or a message that it has none.
   (b) construct and display its reciprocal, `r`, and the product of `f` and `r`.
   (c) store the reduced equivalent of `f` in `f_red`, and tell whether `f` is reduced.
   (d) store the normalized equivalent of `f` in `f_nrm`, and tell whether `f` is normalized.

7. Assume that `fracs_in` (type `ifstream`) and `fracs_out` (type `ofstream`) are open streams associated with the files `fracs.dat` and `nrfracs.dat`, respectively, and that `fracs.dat` contains fractions separated by whitespace. Write a code fragment to read each fraction from `fracs.dat`, print it and its normalized, reduced equivalent on the monitor, and store its normalized, reduced equivalent in `nrfracs.dat`.

Programming Problems

Use the `Time_piece` class of `time_pc2.h` for the following exercises.

8. Replace the include file `time_pc1.h` with `time_pc2.h` in program `t_pc_ex2.cpp`. Run the program and verify that it produces the same output as the original version.

9. Write a program that does the following to test the `Time_piece` class of `time_pc2.h`.
   (a) Enter a starting time, then display it.
   (b) Randomly generate, then display, a time interval, in minutes, between ±2000.
   (c) Six times, update the time by the time interval and display it.
   (d) Six times, update the time by the negative of the time interval and display it.

   Verify that the final value produced by this process is the original starting time.

10. Prompt the user to enter a time followed by the time zone (EST, CST, MST, or PST). Then print a table with the equivalent times in all four time zones.

Use the `Int_list` class for Exercises 18.11 through 18.15.

11. Input a line (or sentence or paragraph) of text, then display alphabetically
    (a) the letters that appear in the text.
    (b) the letters that do not appear in the text.

12. Enter two lines of text, then display in ASCII order
    (a) the characters that appear in *both* lines.
    (b) the digits that appear in *either* line.
    (b) the letters that appear in *neither* line.

13. Write a program to simulate a lottery drawing. Six *different* numbers from 1 to 54 should be selected at random. Typical output might be

   ```
   The numbers are: 47 3 18 24 10 51
   ```

14. Extend the program of Exercise 18.13 so that the user can enter the six numbers he or she played in the lottery, and the program will determine how many of the played numbers are winning numbers.

15. Write and test a function `common_elements` that returns an `Int_list` containing the elements that are common to both of its `Int_list` parameters. The returned list should not contain duplicate elements. The function declaration will be

   ```
   Int_list common_elements (const& Int_list A,
                             const& Int_list B);
   ```

Use the `Fraction` class for Exercises 18.16 through 18.18.

16. Write a program that enters a fraction from the keyboard, then displays it in reduced, normalized form and also as a mixed number. A typical run could be

```
Enter a fraction: 39/-15
Reduced and normalized: -13/5
As a mixed number: -2_3/5
```

17. Write a program that inputs `p`, an integer greater than 1, then displays the reduced equivalent and decimal equivalent of each of the fractions `1/p`, `2/p`, . . ., `p/p`. A sample run could be

```
Enter p>1: 4
1/4 = 0.25
1/2 = 0.5
3/4 = 0.75
1 = 1
```

18. Let `f(n) = 1 + 1/2 + 1/3 + .. + 1/n`. Write a program to display `n` and the reduced fractional representation of `f(n)` for `n = 1, 2, . . . , 10`. For example, when `n` is 4, `f(n)` will be `25/12` (=1+1/2+1/3 +1/4).

Use the `Big_Ulam` class (in the file `bigulam.h`) for Exercises 18.19 through 18.23.

19. The following trace table shows the state of the `Big_Ulam` object `M` after several member function calls. Show the state after each of two more calls to `update`.

Call	State of M		num_digs
	dgs		
	0 1 2 3 4 5 6 7 8 9 . .		
`Big_Ulam M;`	(?, ?, ?, ?, ?, ?, ?, ?, , ,)		?
`M.set(832100002);`	(?, 2, 0, 0, 0, 0, 1, 2, 3, 8, . .)		9
`M.update();`	(?, 1, 0, 0, 0, 5, 0, 6, 1, 4, . .)		9
`M.update();`	(?, 4, 0, 0, 0, 5, 1, 8, 4, 2, 1, . .)		10

20. Change the value of `max_digs` from 64 to 9 in the file `bigulam.h`. Then, run the program of Exercise 18.20 for an input of 800,000,003. Compare the result with that produced for the same input by a program that uses the type `long`. (Recall that `long_max` is less than 2.2 billion.) What feature of data encapsulation does this exercise demonstrate? (**CAUTION:** Restore the value of `max_digs` when you are done with this exercise!)

21. To reduce the number of lines of output, display several terms of an Ulam sequence on the same line, separated by two spaces. Do not split a number across lines. (*Hint*: Use the `num_digits` member function to determine whether to print the next term of the sequence on the same or a new line.)

22. When displaying an Ulam sequence you can reduce the amount of output by displaying only the beginning, end, and length of the sequence. Write a program to display the first ten terms of the sequence, a blank line, then those terms that have fewer than three digits (the end of the sequence), and, finally, the total length of the sequence.

23. For a given user input, display the length of its Ulam sequence and the number of digits of the longest term of the sequence.

Longer Assignments

24. Write a program that displays several important international cities' names on the monitor. The program will then repeatedly allow the user to enter the time in any one of the cities and output the equivalent time in any of the other cities. A typical sample run (without the list of cities) would be

```
Enter time and city: 12:30pm   New York
City (XXX to quit):  Paris
It is 6:30 PM in Paris.
City (XXX to quit): Los Angeles
It is 9:30 AM in Los Angeles.
City (XXX to quit): Tokyo
It is 2:30 AM of the next day in Tokyo.
City (XXX to quit): XXX
```

(*Hint*: Store on disk a list of cities and their time differences from EST, then read them into two parallel arrays or into an array of structs.)

25. Write a fraction addition tutorial. Read pairs of fractions from a file, display them as addition problems, and input the user's answer for the sum. Diagnose the user's answer as correct, incorrect, or not reduced. For each problem the user answers incorrectly, show the individual steps involved in arriving at the correct answer. If the answer is correct other than for reducing, give the user a chance to provide the reduced answer. Keep statistics on the user's work for a given session, and display them at the end of the session.

26. For an Ulam sequence, use a vector to keep track of the number of terms having one digit, two digits, etc. Then print a histogram consisting of the counts for each number of digits.

19

Implementing and Modifying a Class

In the previous chapter we discussed how to use a predefined class based on a reading of its interface. In this chapter you begin to learn how to write or modify class implementations by examining, in detail, the actual implementations for the Time_piece, Int_list, and Fraction classes of the previous chapter.

We also discuss the overloading of operators such as +, <, ==, <<, and >>. Operator overloading enables programmer-defined data types to have the same functionality as built-in data types.

19.1 Packaging a Class in a Header File

One way to package a class is to place both its interface and the member function definitions in a single header file. (For large software projects, the preferred method has the class interface in a header file and implementation details in a separate .cpp file.) To avoid potential duplicate declaration errors, you should use compiler directives, first discussed in Section 5.8 and highlighted in the following framework, for packaging the Time_piece class.

```
// time_pc1.h
#ifndef _TIME_PC_H
#define _TIME_PC_H
#include <iostream.h>
#include <ctype.h>
#include <stdlib.h>
#include "bool.h"
```

```
class Time_piece
{
    public:
        void set(int h, int m, char mrd);
        void update(int h, int m);
        void display();

    private:
        int hr, min;  // the hour and minute
        char merid; // meridian: a(m) or p(m),
        void validate();
};
```

> member function definitions
> go here (in any order)

```
#endif
```

19.2   Defining Member Functions of the First Time_piece **Class**

In this section, you begin to learn how to define member functions by studying the definitions of the Time_piece class's member functions.

Definition of set()   The definition of the Time_piece class's set function is

```
void Time_piece::set(int h, int m, char mrd)
{
    hr=h; min=m; merid=toupper(mrd);
    validate();
}
```

Explanation of a Member Function's Definition

Definition Header   The *definition header* is the same as the function's declaration (in the public section) except that the header must also contain the name of the class followed by the *scope resolution operator*, ::, and it has no terminating semicolon. For example, for the set function of the Time_piece class

```
        void set(int h; int m; char mrd);      ← declaration
        void Time_piece::set(int h; int m; char mrd)      ← header
```

The class name and scope resolution operator, ::, are *not* included in the declarations for individual member functions because all of these declarations are contained within the class interface — that is, the member function declarations are within the scope of their class. By contrast, a member function definition is given outside the class interface, so we need to inform the compiler about which class's function is being defined. Be aware that several classes can be defined in the same file and different classes can have a member function with the same name. (For example, many classes have a set function.)

Definition Body   Recall that each object has its own data members with their own memory cells. *Note that dot notation is not used within the definition body to refer to a calling object's data members.* For example, the three statements in the set function's defining body,

```
hr=h;  min= m;  merid=toupper(m);
```

do not use dot notation. The compiler automatically knows that inside the defining body, any data members with no dot notation are data members of the calling object. The syntax is this way because a member function has no name, such as a parameter, by which to refer to the calling object within the definition body. (In Section 22.3, however, you will see that a member function does have a way to refer indirectly to the calling object.)

Each Object Has Its Own Data Members   Recall from Chapter 18 that each object has its own data members. For example, suppose that clock and watch are both objects of type Time_piece. Then, after the following two statements in a client program:

```
clock.set(9, 30, 'A');
watch.set(11, 5, 'P');
```

clock's and watch's data members will have the following values:

	hr	min	merid			hr	min	merid
clock	9	30	'A'		watch	11	5	'P'

Objects Share Member Functions   Although each object has its own member data variables, all objects of a given class share the same member functions. This results in a significant saving in the amount of machine code generated for a client program that declares several objects of a given class.

Access to Private Member Functions   Client programs can call the public but not the private member functions of a class. By contrast, the body of a member function definition can contain calls to any other member function, public or private, of its class. For example, the last statement in the body of Time_piece::set

```
validate();
```

calls the private Time_piece member function validate to check the validity of each of the data members (hr, min, and merid) of the object that called set.

PITFALL (Neglecting to Resolve Scope) If the highlighted code Time_piece:: were omitted from the preceding definition of set, several compiler errors would result. The compiler would diagnose the identifiers hr, min, and merid, as well as the function validate, as undeclared because no information indicates that these are to be considered members of the Time_piece class. The compiler is unable to resolve the scope, or membership, of these identifiers.

■ **QUESTION** **(The Definition of display)** The public member function display will output the calling object's member data in the proper format. How should you fill in the blanks from its defintion?

```
void _____ ()
{
    cout << ____ << ':';
    if (_____) cout << '0';
    cout << min;
    cout << ' ' << ____ << 'M';
}
```

Answer The header is void Time_piece::display() and the other three blanks should contain hr, min < 10, and merid, respectively. ■ ■

The Definition of validate The private member function validate checks that the data members of the calling object are valid. If they are not valid, it displays the (invalid) time with an error message, then terminates program execution. Its definition is

```
void Time_piece::validate()
{
    bool hr_OK = (1<=hr && hr<=12);
    bool min_OK =(0<=min && min<60);
    bool mrd_OK = (merid=='A' || merid=='P');
    if (!(hr_OK && min_OK && mrd_OK))
```

```
        {
        cout << "Time_piece error: ";
        display(); cout << endl;
        exit(1);
        }
    }
```

Notice that validate has its own local variables, hr_OK, min_OK, and mrd_OK, in addition to having access to the data members hr, min, and merid of the calling object. Further, it will call the public member function display in the event that the calling object's private data is not valid.

The Definition of update   The update function contains no new syntax or ideas, but its implementation is somewhat tedious. update uses a local variable, mins_past, to update the calling object's data members, hr, min, and merid, by the number of hours (h) and minutes (m) passed as arguments in the call. A pseudocode algorithm is

---

1. *Convert* hr, min, *and* merid *to* mins_past *(midnight).*
2. *Add* 60*h+m *to* mins_past.
3. *Adjust* mins_past *so that* 0 <= mins_past < 24*60.
4. *Convert* mins_past *back to* hr, min, *and* merid.

The complete code for update is

```
void Time_piece::update(int h, int m)
{
    int mins_past; // midnight

    // convert to minutes past midnight
    if (hr==12)
      mins_past = min;
    else
      mins_past = 60*hr + min;
    if (merid=='P')
      mins_past += 12*60;

    // add (60*h + m) to mins_past and
    mins_past += 60*h + m;
    // adjust so 0 <= mins_past < 24*60
    mins_past %= (24*60);
```

```
    if(mins_past<0)
       mins_past+=(24*60);

    // convert mins_past to hr, min, merid
    hr = mins_past/60;
    min = mins_past%60;
    if (mins_past < 12*60)
       merid = 'A'; // am
    else
       merid = 'P'; // pm
    if (hr==0) hr = 12;
    if (hr>12) hr -= 12;
}
```

Exercises 19.2 and 19.3 ask you to trace `update` for various values of its parameters and its calling object's member data.

19.3   Defining Accessor Functions and Improving the `Time_piece` **Class**

We begin with the most visible improvement to the `Time_piece` class — the addition of accessor functions. Then we discuss the more subtle improvements, involving an additional private data member, `mins_past`, and two additional private member functions, that make the class's implementation more modular and more efficient.

The interface of the improved `Time_piece` class, with changes from the basic version highlighted, is

Improved `Time_Piece` ***Class from*** `time_pc2.cpp`

```
class Time_piece
{
public:
    // modifier functions
    void set(int h, int m, char mrd);
    void update(int h, int m=0);

    // accessor functions
    int get_hour() const;
    int get_minute() const;
    char get_meridian() const;
    int get_mins_past() const;
```

```
      // IO functions
      void display(ostream& outs = cout) const;
      void enter();

   private:
      int hr, min;  // the hour and minute
      int mins_past; // mins past midnite
      char merid; // meridian; a(m) or p(m);

      void validate() const;
      void normalize();
      void set_mins_past();
};
```

Defining Accessor Functions   The body of an accessor function consists of a single return statement specifying the data member to be returned. For example, the definition of `get_hr` is

```
int Time_piece::get_hr() const
{ return hr; }
```

The definitions of the other three member functions are similar.

Adding a Default Parameter to `display(..)`   Note that `display`'s definition header contains the parameter `outs`, but its default value of `cout` is assigned in the declaration of `display` (in the public section).

```
void Time_piece::display(ostream& outs) const
{
   outs << hr << ':';
   if (min<10) outs << '0';
   outs << min;
   outs << ' ' << merid << 'M';
}
```

Exercise 19.12(a) asks you to modify the `Time_piece` class's `enter` member function so that times can be entered from a file or, by default, from the keyboard.

mins_past **as a Data Member** Notice that mins_past, which was a local variable in the body of update in the first Time_piece class, is now a data member. Each call to enter, set, or update will assign the proper value to mins_past. For example, note the effect of the following two consecutive calls on the state of clock:

Call	hr	min	merid	mins_past
clock.set(5,30,'A')	5	30	'A'	330
clock.update(10,30)	4	0	'P'	960

■ **QUESTION** What will be the new state of clock after execution of the further call clock.update(12)? (*Hint*: clock will go past midnight.)

Answer hr=4 min=0 merid='A' mins_past=240 ■ ▬

Increased Modularity: Two New Private Functions Notice that two private member functions, normalize and set_mins_past, have also been added. These functions can be used by public member functions to avoid duplication of tasks and to achieve a more modular design. set_mins_past converts data members hr, min, and merid to mins_past, a total number of minutes past midnight, whereas normalize converts mins_past to an equivalent hr, min, and merid. Notice that set_mins_past and normalize correspond to steps 1 and 4, respectively, of the pseudocode algorithm for update given in the previous section. The definitions of set_mins_past and normalize are

```
void Time_piece::
            set_mins_past()
{
    if (hr==12)
        mins_past = min;
    else
        mins_past = 60*hr+min;
    if (merid=='P')
        mins_past += 12*60;
}
```

```
void Time_piece::normalize()
{
    hr = mins_past/60;
    if (hr==0) hr = 12;
    if (hr>12) hr -= 12;
    min = mins_past%60;
    if (mins_past < 12*60)
        merid = 'A'; // am
    else
        merid = 'P'; // pm
}
```

■ **QUESTION** What are the missing lines needed to complete the definition of the improved version of Time_piece::set?

```
void Time_piece::set(int h, int m, char mrd)
{
    hr=h; min=m; merid=toupper(mrd);
    _____;
    _____;
}
```

Answer   The missing lines are

```
validate();
set_mins_past();
```

QUESTION   The improved version of Time_piece::update needs to perform only steps 2 through 4 of the pseudocode algorithm given in Section 19.2. What are the missing lines needed to complete its definition?

```
void Time_piece::update(int h, int m)
{
    mins_past += _____;
    _____ %= (24*60);
    if (mins_past<0)
        mins_past+=(24*60);
    _____;
}
```

Answer   The missing lines are

```
mins_past += 60*h + m;
mins_past %= (24*60);
normalize();
```

Discussion   update does not need to convert the data members hr, min, and merid to mins_past — this will have been done by either set or enter, the only public member functions that allow new values to be specified for these data members.

The Public Function *enter( )*   The enter function is quite robust in the latitude it allows the user. Its rules for entering a time from the keyboard are (1) the hour and minute are integers, possibly with a leading zero; (2) a semicolon separates the hour and minute; (3) the meridian will be AM or PM, in either uppercase or lowercase; and (4) zero or more spaces may be placed before the hour, on either side of the semicolon, and between the minute and the meridian.

Thus, 3:15AM could be entered in various forms, such as 3:15am, 03:15 am or 3 : 15 AM.

The actual definition of enter is given in time_pc2.cpp (see the PWS Web site). Although it does not contain any new ideas that relate to defining a member function, it does use some tricky stream processing.

19.4 Implementing the Int_List Class

An Int_list object has three private data members, len, Elts, and sorted. The following trace table shows the state of L, an Int_list object, after each of several member function calls.

State of L after each call:

Calls	len	Elts [0]	[1]	[2]	[3]	[4]	[5]	.	.	sorted
Int_list L;	0	{ }								true
L.add(25);	1	{ ?,	25,	?,	?,	?,	?,	.	. }	true
L.add(30);	2	{ ?,	25,	30,	?,	?,	?,	.	. }	true
L.add(7);	3	{ ?,	25,	30,	7,	?,	?,	.	. }	false
L.sort();	3	{ ?,	7,	25,	30,	?,	?,	.	. }	true
L.add(14);	4	{ ?,	7,	25,	30,	14,	?,	.	. }	false

Notice that the vector Elts, which stores individual list elements, is initially empty, so adding the first element requires that Elts be resized by some fixed amount. Also, cell 0 of Elts is *not* used in this implementation of the class.

The Definition of display()   The display function outputs the elements of the calling object, separated by single spaces, to its ostream& parameter. Its definition is

```
void Int_list::display (ostream& os) const
{
    if (length()==0) return;
    os << Elts[1];
    for (int i=2; i<=length(); i++)
        os << ' ' << Elts[i];
}
```

You may find it unusual that the first element is output before the loop that outputs the remaining elements. This approach ensures that a space is placed only *between* list elements, *not after* each one. Further, when written this way, this code is easily modified so that list elements are separated by a comma and a space, and the whole list is enclosed in parentheses. Thus, an empty list would be displayed as () and the list constructed in the previous trace table would be displayed as (7, 25, 30, 14). Exercise 19.8 asks you to make this modification.

Accessor Function Call or Direct Access to Member Data?   The defining body of a member function can call other member functions (both public and private), and it can also directly access data members. For example, the first statement in the body of `display` could have been written as

```
if (len == 0) return 0;
```

and the `for` loop header could also have used `len` in place of `length()`. Using accessor functions in member function definitions can provide some protection against changes that the class designer may decide to make later. (For example, the length of the list could be stored in the unused cell 0 of the `Elts` vector, eliminating the need for the data member `len`.) On the other hand, depending on your compiler, use of the accessor function might be less efficient than accessing the private data member directly. Don't worry about this point — just be aware that both methods are commonly practiced.

The `Int_list()` ***Constructor***   The declaration

```
Int_list L;
```

not only declares the object L to be of type `Int_list`, it makes L initially empty. There are two ways to define this constructor. One way is

```
Int_list::Int_list()
{ len=0; sorted=true; }
```

In executing this constructor, the computer first allocates memory for the private data members `len`, `sorted`, and `Elts` (which is of type `Vector<int>`), then sets `len` to 0 and `sorted` to true. Because the constructor must *set* rather than *access* the data member `len`, the `length` accessor function cannot be used here.

Constructors and the Initializer List   An important task of a constructor function is to initialize some, if not all, of its data members. A special syntax for doing these initializations is provided by the ***initializer list***.

A second way to define the `Int_List` constructor uses an initializer list.

```
Int_list::Int_list()
    : len(0), sorted(true)          ← initializer list
    {  }
```

An *initializer* gives an initial value to a data member and is of the form

> *data_member (init_val)*

An initializer list consists of one or more initializers, separated by commas, and is always placed between the constructor function header and body. A colon separates the constructor function header from the first initializer.

For constructor function definitions, the use of initializers is preferred over assignment statements because, in certain situations, an initializer is more efficient than an assignment statement. When giving constructor definitions, we will always use initializer lists.

The Definition of `add(..)`   The trace table at the beginning of this section illustrates that `add` must increment `len` and assign the `int` argument passed to it to the next available cell of `Elts`. A few issues, however, require careful handling. The vector `Elts` may need to be resized (see Section 13.8) before the new element can be added, and adding the new element may alter the value of `sorted`.

■ QUESTION   How would you fill in the missing lines to complete the definition of `add`? Assume that `Elts` is resized in increments of 8, as necessary.

```
void Int_list::add(int elt)
{
    len++;
    if (len >= _____)
        Elts._____(Elts.length() + __);
        _____ = elt;
    sorted = sorted &&
                (len==1 || elt >= Elts[____]);
}
```

Answer   The missing lines are

```
    if (len >= Elts.length())
        Elts.resize(Elts.length() + 8) ;
    Elts[len] = elt;
            (len==1 || elt >= Elts[len-1]);
```

Discussion   The last statement of add updates sorted. If sorted is currently false, then adding a new element cannot change this. However, if sorted is currently true, then it remains true if, and only if, the new value of len is 1, or the new element is at least as large as the one in the previous cell, Elts[len-1].   ■ ▬

The retrieve(..) **Function**   The retrieve function returns the ith element of an Int_list object, provided that i is between 1 and len, inclusive. Its definition, which makes use of the Assert function from ourtools.h, is

```cpp
int Int_list::retrieve(int i) const
{
    Assert (1 <= i && i <= len,
            "List subscript out of range.");
    return Elts[i];
}
```

The Definition of sort()   The sort member function obviously sorts the integers in cells 1 through len of the array Elts. The version given in int_list.h uses a version of insertion sort (Section 14.5), though any sorting algorithm will do. The highlighted statements in the following definition show how sort uses and updates the sorted data member.

```cpp
void Int_list::sort()
{
    if (sorted) return;
    int ins_elt; // element to insert
    int ssv_sz; // sorted subvector size
    for (ssv_sz = 2; ssv_sz<=length(); ssv_sz++)
        {
        ins_elt = Elts[ssv_sz];
        for (int i = ssv_sz-1; i>0; i--)
            {
            if (ins_elt >= Elts[i])
                break;
            Elts[i+1] = Elts[i];
            }
        Elts[i+1] = ins_elt;
        }
    sorted = true;
}
```

The Definition of `contains(..)` The `contains` function uses a linear search (see Section 14.1) to determine whether an `Int_list` object contains a particular element. However, `contains` does not return the target element's index, if found.

■ **QUESTION** How should you complete the loop header to complete the definition of `contains`? Keep in mind that cell 0 of the `Elts` vector is not used in this `Int_List` implementation.

```
bool Int_list::contains(int elt) const
{
    for (int i=__; i <= _____; i++)
        if (Elts[i] == elt)
            return true;
    return false;
}
```

Answer The completed loop header is

```
for (int i=1; i <= length(); i++)
```

■ ■■

19.5 Implementing the `Fraction` Class

Here again is the interface for the `Fraction` class of `frac_cl1.h`.

```
class Fraction // interface
{
public:
    // constructors
    Fraction(); // "do-nothing" constructor
    Fraction (long n, long d=1);
        // construct fraction with value n/d

    // accessors
    long get_num() const; // return num
    long get_den() const; // return den

    // modifiers
    void set(long n, long d=1);
        // set calling object to n/d
    void normalize(); // make den positive
```

```
    void reduce(); // reduce calling object
    // Functions that return a new Fraction object
    Fraction operator+ (Fraction f2) const;
        // return calling object + f2

    // IO functions
    void enter(istream& ins=cin);
        // input value of calling object from ins
    void display(ostream& outs=cout) const;
        // display calling object on outs

private:
    long num, den; // numerator, denominator
    void validate() const; // that den is not 0
}; // end Fraction class interface
```

The `set(..)` **Function**   The following definition is for the set function. Notice that it uses the private `Fraction::validate` function in the same way that `Time_piece::set()` uses `Time_piece::validate`.

```
void Fraction::set(long n, long d)
{ num=n; den=d; validate(); }
```

Accessor Functions `get_num()` **and** `get_den()`   These definitions have single statement bodies, { `return num;` } and { `return den;` }, respectively.

■ **QUESTION**   (**The** `display()` **Function**)   How should you fill in the blank in the following definition? Note that, for example, the fractions 3/5 and 4/1 should be displayed as 3/5 and 4, respectively.

```
void Fraction::display(ostream& outs) const
{
    outs << num;
    if (_____)
        outs << '/' << den;
}
```

Answer   The completed blank is `den != 1`.   ■ ■■

■ **QUESTION**   **(The Two-Argument Fraction Constructor)**   Using an initializer list, how should you complete the following definition of the two-argument constructor?

```
Fraction::Fraction (long n, long d)
  : _____ // initializer list
{ validate(); }
```

Answer   The completed initializer list is

```
: num(n), den(d) // initializer list
```
■ ▬

The definitions of `normalize`, `reduce`, and `enter` require no new techniques, and can be found at the PWS Web site. The next section covers overloading operators for the `Fraction` class.

19.6   Overloading Operators for a Class

In Section 17.5 you saw how to overload some operators for struct types as free functions. The situation is somewhat more complicated for classes, because classes, unlike structs, have private data members.

Only Existing Operators Can Be Overloaded   In C++ you cannot create new operators by overloading, but you can overload all the existing C++ operators with the exception of the member access, or dot, operator (.), the scope resolution operator (::), and the comma (,) operator.

Overloading + for the `Fraction` ***Class***   The purpose of overloading the + operator is to make the following type of statement legal for `Fraction` objects `f`, `g`, and `h`:

```
f = g + h;
```

Because the `Fraction` class's data members are private, it is easier to overload `operator+` as a member function of the `Fraction` class than as a "free" function, as we did for the `fraction` struct. Because a member function can be called only by an object of its class, the addition `g + h` is really the call `g.operator+(h)`, in which `g` is the calling object. Thus, the `Fraction` class member function, `operator+`, will have only *one* parameter rather than two, as was the case for the "free" `operator+` function of the `fraction` struct. Accordingly, the declaration of `operator+` for the

Fraction class is

```
Fraction operator+ (Fraction f2) const;
// Return the sum of the calling  Fraction object
// and f2, leaving the calling object unchanged.
```

■ **QUESTION** **(Definition of** operator+**)** The "quick and dirty" calculations for the numerator and denominator of the sum a/b + c/d are

```
numerator = ad + bc
denominator = bd
```

How should you fill in the blanks in the following definition of operator+? (*Hint*: Note that three different fractions appear in the body of the definition, namely, the calling object, the parameter, f2, and the local object, sum, which is used to hold the fraction that will be returned.)

```
Fraction Fraction::operator+(Fraction f2) const
{
    Fraction sum;
    sum.num = _____ + _____;
    sum.den = _____;
    return sum;
}
```

Answer Dot notation is not used for the calling object's data members. By contrast, to access the data members of the parameter f2, we could use either dot notation or the accessor functions for these data members. However, because the data members of the local variable sum are being assigned values, as opposed to merely being accessed, dot notation must be used. Thus, the completed lines are

```
sum.num = den * f2.num + num * f2.den;
sum.den = den * f2.den;
```

Overloading operator< We often want a client program to be able to compare two objects of a class, call them obj1 and obj2, in a statement such as

```
· if (obj1 < obj2) ..
```

To make this use of < legal, we need to overload that class's operator< member function.

■ **QUESTION** Suppose that Student is a class with a name data member and various other data members and member functions. Suppose further that stud1 and stud2 are of type Student and that a client program statement such as

```
if (stud1 < stud2) ..
```

is intended to determine whether the name data member of stud1 is alphabetically prior to the name data member of stud2. How should you complete the following operator< member function definition for the Student class?

```
bool Student::operator< (const Student& rhs) const
{ return _____; }
```

Hints

1. The comparison stud1 < stud2 is equivalent to the call stud1. operator<(stud2), where stud1 is the calling object, and stud2 (the object on the right hand side) is passed to the parameter rhs.

2. Use the name data member to make the comparison.

Answer The completed line is

```
{ return name < rhs.name; }
```

■ ▬

Overloading >> for the Fraction Class The purpose of overloading operator>> is to make the following statement legal for a Fraction, g.

```
cin >> g;
```

We might consider overloading operator>> as a member of the Fraction class, but there is a major flaw with this idea. The left operand of this input statement is an istream object, not a Fraction object, so the calling object is not even of the Fraction class. Further, the istream class is predefined, so we will not tamper with its source code by trying to add a new meaning to its operator>> member function. (It is unlikely that you even have this source code — it is normally distributed only in machine code form.)

The solution is to write operator>> as a free function for the Fraction class. Recall that for the fraction struct, operator>> was a free function and had direct access to a fraction struct's data members. For the Fraction class, however, a free function is *outside* the class's scope, and therefore does not have *direct access* to a Fraction object's data members. In the case of operator>>, this potential difficulty is handled by calling the member function enter, which *does* have access to a Fraction's data members.

■ **QUESTION** **(Definition of** operator>>**)** How should you complete the definition of the free function operator>> for Fraction objects.

```
istream& operator>> (istream& ins, Fraction& f)
{
    f._____;
    return _____;
}
```

Answer The completed lines are

```
f.enter(ins);
return ins;
```

The definition of operator<< is similar for the Fraction class. The declarations (or definitions) of operator<< and operator>> should be placed immediately after the Fraction class interface, so that it is obvious, from a reading of the class interface, that these operators are overloaded for the class.

Overloading >> and << for Other Classes   The technique that we used for overloading << and >> for the Fraction class is applicable to other classes as well. This technique requires that the classes in question have enter and display member functions with parameters of type istream& and ostream&, respectively.

Friend Functions   A *friend* function is a free function whose declaration is given in the public section of a class, preceded by the reserved word friend. *Making a free function a friend of a class gives that function direct access to private members of the class.* Making the free function operator>> a friend of the Fraction class is another way around the problem of direct access to the class's data members num and den.

Friend functions are considered controversial because allowing non-member functions to access private data directly violates the idea of encapsulation. We do not explore friend functions further in this text.

Summary on Overloading Binary Operators

1.   When both operands are objects of the same class, the binary expression is implemented as a member of the class, with the left operand as the calling object and the right operand as a parameter. See, for example, the discussion of overloading + for the Fraction class or overloading < for the Student class.

2. When overloading the stream operators << and >> for I/O of objects of a new class, the operator cannot be a member of the stream class or the new class. Therefore, you must overload << and >> as free functions.

3. The assignment operator, =, is a case unto itself. Each class that you define is automatically provided with a default overloaded assignment operator, which, for many classes, is adequate. For example, we have been using assignment with Fraction objects, even though there is no explicit mention of this operator in the Fraction class. In Chapter 22, you will see why the default assignment operator is not always adequate, and learn how to implement a correct overloaded assignment operator in such situations.

19.7   Defining Member Functions Within the Class Interface

Consider the following Fraction class interface from the file frac_cl2.h. You are already familiar with this class's public member functions — with the exception of the overloaded operator== function, they are precisely those of the Fraction class of frac_cl1.h, first introduced in Section 18.5. (The overloaded free functions, operator>> and operator<<, are also given here — though they are not member functions, they are very important free functions for this class.)

```
class Fraction // interface
{
public:
    // constructors
    Fraction() { };
    Fraction (long n, long d=1)
        : num(n), den(d) // initializer list
    { validate(); }

    // accessors
    long get_num() const { return num; }
    long get_den() const { return den; }

    // functions that alter the calling object
    void set(long n, long d=1)
        { num=n; den=d; validate(); }
    void normalize(); // make den positive
```

```
    void reduce();
    // Functions that return a new Fraction object
    Fraction operator+ (Fraction f2) const;

    // relational  operator(s)
  bool operator== (Fraction f) const
      { return double(num)/den == double(f.num)/f.den;}

    // IO
    void enter(istream& ins=cin);
    void display(ostream& outs=cout) const;
private:
    long num, den; // numerator, denominator
    void validate() const;
}; // end Fraction class interface

// overloaded free functions for stream << and >>
istream& operator>> (istream& ins, Fraction& f)
{ f.enter(ins); return ins; }

ostream& operator<< (ostream& outs, Fraction f)
{ f.display(outs); return outs; }
```

Not only are these the same member functions as provided by frac_cl1.h, but the internal implementations are the same. The difference with this version is that several of the member functions are *defined within the class interface*, rather than outside of it (as was the case in the frac_cl1.h version). Each of the highlighted portions of code is the body of a member function definition. Defining member functions within a class interface has a disadvantage that is offset by several advantages, and there are restrictions on when this can be done.

Disadvantage Placing function bodies within a class interface clutters the interface with information that is not necessary to the user of the class and, in the case of large, complex classes, may be confusing to all but the most seasoned C++ programmers. If a class interface is to include function bodies, it is very important that the client programmer be provided with separate written documentation like that given for the basic Time_piece class in Section 18.2.

Advantages You do not need to use the scope resolution operator when defining a class within its interface. The compiler automatically knows the scope of a function defined within a class interface (and of any member data that the function references).

Of more significance is the way that the compiler generates code for a function defined in its class interface. The compiler *may* generate special *inline* code for the function. Inline code is more compact and executes faster than the code that is normally generated for a function. The compiler decides whether to generate inline code for a particular function; this decision varies from one version of C++ to another.

Restrictions Some compilers generate syntax errors when a function defined within a class interface contains a loop. Further, a function defined within a class interface should consist of at most a few statements and should not contain calls to functions that are not themselves defined inline — the compiler may or may not generate warnings for such a function, but will probably not generate inline code for the function.

■ **QUESTION** Examine the definitions in `frac_cl2.h` of the `Fraction` class member functions that were *not* defined within the class interface. Which of these could have been defined in the class interface rather than outside of it?

Answer None of these functions contains a loop, so the answer depends on the length and content of the function bodies. Because `display` and `normalize` are short and contain no calls to other user-defined functions, they could be defined in the class interface. On the other hand, `enter`, `reduce`, `operator+`, and `validate` all contain calls to user-defined functions, and `enter` consists of several statements.   ■ ■

■ Exercises

1. Suppose that `T` is an object of the improved `Time_piece` class of Section 19.3. Give the value stored in `T`'s `mins_past` private data member after each of the following calls to the `set` member function.

   (a) `T.set(12, 0, 'P');`   (b) `T.set(12, 30, 'a');`

   (c) `T.set(3, 10, 'A');`   (d) `T.set(10, 15, 'p');`

2. For the `Time_piece` object `clock`, give all values that the `mins_past` data member is assigned during execution of the code fragment at right, and determine which private member function does each assignment. Then, give the final value of data members `hr`, `min`, and `merid`.

   ```
   clock.set(3, 0, 'P');
   clock.update(17, 15);
   ```

3. Repeat Exercise 19.2 using the code fragment at right.

   ```
   clock.set(2, 0, 'a');
   clock.update(-30);
   ```

4. Write the definitions of the following Time_piece class member functions:

(a) `void display_short() const;`
```
// Display times in "short" form. That is, display
// times that are "on the hour" without minutes,
// (e. g., display 7:00 PM as 7 PM) and display
// 12:00 AM and 12:00 PM as MIDNIGHT and NOON, resp.
```

(b) `void turn_ahead();`
```
// Turn the calling object one hour ahead.
```

5. Continue the trace table given at the beginning of Section 19.4 by showing the state of the Int_list object L after each of the following calls.

```
L.add(20);  L.sort();  L.add(40);  L.add(5);
```

6. Is the Elts data member of L resized at any time during the above sequence of calls? If so, when? If not, how many more calls to add will cause a resize operation?

7. Write definitions for the following Int_list class member functions.

(a) `bool is_empty() const;`
```
// Return true if the calling Int_list object is
// empty; return false otherwise.
```

(b) `int max_elt() const;`
```
// Return the maximum element of the calling Int_list
// object, or return INT_MIN if the list is empty.
```

8. Modify the Int_list class's display function so that list items are separated by a comma and a space, and the entire list is contained in a single set of parentheses.

9. Give the value of f's private data members, num and den, after each statement of the following code fragment.

```
Fraction f(15, -10);
f.normalize();
f.reduce();
f.set(f.get_den(), f.get_num());
```

10. Write definitions for the following Fraction class member functions.

(a) `void invert();`
```
// Invert the calling Fraction object, or exit with
// an error message if it cannot be inverted.
```

(b) `double as_double() const;`
```
// Return the double equivalent of the
// calling Fraction object.
```

11. Consider the inline definition given in Section 19.7 for the overloaded Fraction class operator, ==. Discuss the pros and cons of the following alternative inline definition.

```
bool operator== (Fraction f) const
{ return num * f.den == den * f.num; }
```

[*Hint*: What happens during the evaluation of (f ==g) when f and g have the values 90,001/100,000 and 180,002/200,000, respectively?]

Programming Problems

12. Copy time_pc2.h to time_pc3.h, then make the indicated modifications to the Time_piece class. Write a program or programs to test the modifications.

    (a) Change the declaration and definition of the enter function so that times can be entered from either a file or the keyboard, with the keyboard being the default input source.

    (b) Overload the stream extraction and insertions operators for I/O of Time_piece objects.

    (c) Overload the relational operators == and != as class member functions.

13. (a) Add the remove function declared here to the Int_list class. Write a test program for it.

```
bool remove (int val);
// If val is in the calling Int_list object, remove
// it and return true; otherwise return false.
```

14. (a) Copy frac_cl2.h to frac_cl3.h, then add member functions to overload operators -, *, /, and != to the Fraction class. You may use the "quick and dirty" calculations:

$$a/b - c/d = (ad - bc)/(bd)$$
$$a/b * c/d = (ac)/(bd)$$
$$(a/b)/(c/d) = (ad)/(bc)$$

    (b) Write a client program to test all of the overloaded arithmetic and stream I/O operators of this modified Fraction class.

15. (a) Copy frac_cl2.h to frac_cl4.h, then overload all the relational operators.

    (b) Modify the selection sort program, select1.cpp, of Section 14.3 to sort a vector of fractions input from the keyboard.

16. (a) Save bigulam.h of Chapter 18 as bigulam2.h.

    (b) Overload operators >> and << for I/O of Big_Ulam objects.

(c) Modify the `BigUlam` constructor to take a single parameter, with default value 64, specifying the maximum number of digits that a `BigUlam` object may have.

(d) Write a version of program `ulam_tst.cpp` (of Chapter 18) that tests the preceding modifications.

(e) Why does it not make sense to overload arithmetic and relational operators for the `Big_Ulam` class?

Longer Assignments

17. Copy `int_lst.h` to `int_lst2.h` and change the implementation of the `Int_list` class as follows. Eliminate the `len` data member, and use the 0 component of the `Elts` vector to store the length of the list. Test this new implementation by using it in the `tst_lst0.cpp` and `tst_lst1.cpp` programs of Chapter 18.

18. Copy `int_lst.h` to `int_lst3.h` and change the implementation of the `Int_list` class as follows.

(a) Replace every direct access to `len` by a call to the accessor function `length`.

(b) Add a private member function, `inc_length`, that adds one to the `len` data member, and replace every direct increment of `len` by a call to `inc_length`.

(c) Test this new implementation of `Int_list` by using it in the `tst_lst0.cpp` and `tst_lst1.cpp` programs of Chapter 18.

(d) Explain how the work of Exercise 19.17 would be made easier if you started with `int_lst3.h` rather than `int_lst.h`. What software engineering principle is illustrated here?

19. Copy `int_lst.h` to `ordinlst.h` and change the `Int_list` class to an ordered integer list class, `Ord_Int_list`, that maintains its elements in increasing order at all times. Test this new class by using it in the `tst_lst0.cpp` and `tst_lst1.cpp` programs of Chapter 18. (*Hint*: Do not sort the `Elts` vector each time an element is added to the list! Instead, use a private `insert` function based on the ideas of Section 14.5.)

20. The "quick and dirty" algorithm used in `frac_cl2.h` for addition of fractions sometimes produce incorrect results for very simple additions. For example, it will not produce 3/200,000 as the sum of 1/100,000 and 1/200,000. Why?

Redo Exercise 19.14 using the `gcd` and `lcm` functions from `myfuns.h` to implement more sophisticated algorithms for fraction computations, and test them using your test program from the same exercise.

21. (a) Why can't a client program use the `setw` manipulator to correctly right-align fractions?

(b) Write a `Fraction` class member function, `length`, that returns the exact number of columns needed to display the calling `Fraction` object. Use this function to redo Exercise 18.17 so that, for any input value, the list of fractions that is output is always right-aligned. (*Hint*: Add to `myfuns.h` a `num_digits` function that returns the number of digits in its `long` parameter.)

20

More Classes for Practice and Application

Thus far we have presented all classes in fairly final form, without discussing the decisions that went into their design. In this chapter we present some new classes for you to add to the "repertoire" of classes that you have available to use in later chapters. The focus in this chapter, however, is to give you some insights into the process that goes into the analysis and design of classes.

We introduce each of these new classes by giving an informal, but detailed, description of objects of the class. Then we show how to use this description of objects of the class to determine what the class's data members and member functions will be. We keep the discussion of the analysis and design of each class informal, because a comprehensive, formal treatment of *object-oriented analysis and design* is beyond the scope of an introductory book.

For each class introduced in this chapter, the PWS Web site contains (1) a complete C++ interface, (2) extensive documentation of the type that would be provided to a client programmer, (3) one or more client programs with sample runs, and (4) implementations of some, but not all, member functions of the class — the remaining implementations are left as exercises.[1]

---

[1] *To the instructor:* Complete implementations of all classes are on the instructor's disk so that, in subsequent chapters, students can use any of these classes, even though they may not have completed the implementation as part of their assigned work.

20.1 A Phone Entry Class

In this section we create a class whose objects are the entries in a computerized phone directory. Consider the following description of a phone entry with respect to the computerized directory of which it is a component.

Description of a Phone Entry A **phone entry** consists of a name, an address, and a phone number, and is a component of a phone directory. A computerized phone directory is stored in a computer and will be modified over time. Keeping phone entries sorted alphabetically by name permits efficient lookups if you need to add or delete an entry or retrieve or change an address or phone number.

For simplicity, we narrow our focus to phone entries from an "internal" directory for a small- to moderate-sized campus or business, so that phone numbers are just four-digit extensions. Further, we do not include the address as part of the entry, though you may want to include it as part of your work on this class.

Design Decisions One approach to designing a class is to identify the significant nouns and verbs in the description of objects of the class. The nouns help identify the data members of the class, and the verbs give some guidance in deciding on the member functions of the class. In general, identifying the member functions of a class is more difficult than identifying its member data.

Member Data In the preceding description of a phone entry, the nouns "name," "address" (which we will ignore), and "phone number" (actually, a four-digit extension) are the attributes that will correspond to data members of the class. Thus, Phone_entry objects will contain only a String, name, in LAST, FIRST form, and a four-digit int extension, extension.

Member Functions The verbs "store," "sort," "search," "retrieve," and "change" in the description of a phone entry give many clues about the member functions that a Phone_entry class must provide. To enable storing, sorting, and searching it must be possible to (1) *read* a phone entry from a file, (2) *write* a phone entry to a file, and (3) *compare* phone entries by name, using relational operators. If a human is to interact with the phone directory from a computer terminal, whether to do lookups or to add and delete entries, it must be possible to (4) *prompt for and input* an entry from the keyboard and (5) *display* an entry on the monitor. Finally, it must be possible to (6) *change* the extension of a given entry.

In the preceding list, it is important to note that there is a different function for *reading* a phone entry from a file (item 1) than for *entering* a phone entry interactively (item 4). This is because interactive input requires prompts that are not needed if you are merely reading from a file.

The *Phone_entry* *Class Interface*   The Phone_entry class interface, from phnentry.h, is

```
class Phone_entry {
public:
   // accessors
   String get_name()   const   { return name; }
   int get_extension() const { return extension; }

   // modifiers
   void set(const String& nm, int xt)
      // set the members of a phone_entry object
      { name=nm; extension=xt; }
   void change_extension (int xt)
      // change the extension of a phone_entry object
      { extension=xt; }

   // IO functions
   void display(ostream& outs=cout) const;
      // write to either the monitor or a file
   void read_from_file(istream& ins);
      // for reading from a file
   void read_from_kbd();
      // for interactive entry, with prompts

   // overload relational operators for sorting
   // and searching phone entries by name
   bool operator == (const Phone_entry& Rhs) const
      { return name == Rhs.name; }
   bool operator != (const Phone_entry& Rhs) const
      { return name != Rhs.name; }
   bool operator < (const Phone_entry& Rhs) const
      { return name < Rhs.name; }
   bool operator <= (const Phone_entry& Rhs) const
      { return name <= Rhs.name; }
   bool operator > (const Phone_entry& Rhs) const
      { return name > Rhs.name; }
   bool operator >= (const Phone_entry& Rhs) const
      { return name >= Rhs.name; }

private:
   String name;
   int extension; // 4 digit extension
}; // end Phone_entry class interface
```

Sample Client Code   The following code, from `phn_tst1.cpp`, illustrates some of the functionality of the `Phone_entry` class.

```
Phone_entry pe1;
pe1.set("Doe, Jean", 2942);
pe1.display();
pe1.change_extension(1400);
cout << "After changes: ";
cout << pe1.get_name() << "  xt-"
     << pe1.get_extension() << endl;

Phone_entry pe2;
cout << "Please input a phone entry:\n";
pe2.read_from_kbd();
cout << pe2 << endl;

if (pe1 < pe2)
   cout << "in order\n";
else
   cout << "out of order\n";
```

A sample run is

```
Doe, Jean            2942
After changes: Doe, Jean xt-1400
Please input a phone entry:
Name (last, first): Darque, John
Extension: 9876
Darque, John         9876
out of order
```

Notice that `Phone_entry` objects can be compared using relational operators. In Chapter 21, we will exploit this capability by creating lists of phone entries that are in alphabetical order by name.

Documentation   The classes of Chapters 18 and 19 were presented without formal documentation, because the use of each class was explained thoroughly in the narratives of those chapters. In this chapter, however, much less information is given about the details of calling member functions of the classes under discussion. Therefore, we should provide some formal documentation for each class. In the interest of saving space in this text, documentation for the classes of this chapter are in text files that are available from the PWS Web site.

Each member function is documented by presenting (1) its declaration, (2) a brief description of the function, (3) any conditions that must be observed by the client of the function, (4) sample calls to the function, with explanations, and (5) notes of special interest or importance. It is important to note that a client programmer can use the class by studying this documentation, without needing to look at the implementation or even the class interface!

■ **EXAMPLE**   For the `Phone_entry` class of this section, extensive documentation is given in the text file `phnentry.doc`. (This documentation is in the form of comments, so it could be appended to the `phnentry.h` file if desired.) As an example, the documentation for the `read_from_file` member function is

```
// void read_from_file(istream& ins);
// Description: Read values from file into calling object.
// Condition(s):
//      The data must be stored in the form:
//                 Last, First dddd
//      where dddd represents the 4 digit extension, and
//      any amount of whitespace may separate the 3 items.
// Sample call: pe1.read_from_file(phon_in);
//      Read values for pe1 from ifstream phon_in
```

Using the `Phone_entry` **Class**   Exercises 20.1 and 20.6 ask you to write client programs that use the `Phone_entry` class. This class will also be used in several examples and exercises in Chapters 21 and 24.

20.2   A Playing Card Class

In this section we create a `Card` class, whose instances are computer models of standard playing cards. The following description of a playing card takes into account that it is a computer model.

Description of a Playing Card   A **playing card** has a suit (clubs, diamonds, hearts, or spades) and a rank (2, 3, . . . , 10, jack, queen, king, or ace). It must be possible to access a card's suit and rank and display a card on the monitor. Because cards are often grouped by suit and ordered by rank, it must be possible to compare two cards, using the suit as the first key (clubs < diamonds < hearts < spades) and the rank as the second. For example, 8 of clubs < 5 of hearts < 8 of hearts. In addition, it must be possible to set the value of an uninitialized card, and it may be useful to be able to generate cards randomly.

The *Card* **Class Interface**   Before discussing some of the design decisions, we present the Card class interface, from card.h, and some client code.

```
// define enumerated constants for ranks and suits
enum { JACK=11, QUEEN, KING, ACE }; // 11, 12, 13, 14
enum { CLUBS, DIAMONDS, HEARTS, SPADES }; // 0, 1, 2, 3

class Card
{
public:
    // accessors
    int get_rank() const { return rank; }
        // return numeric value (2-14) of rank
    int get_suit() const { return suit; }
        // return numeric value (0-3) of suit

    // modifiers
    void set (int r, int s);
        // set card using
        // numbers 2-14 (or enumerated equivalents) as rank
        // numbers 0-3 (or enumerated equivalents) as suit

    void gen_random();
        // randomly generate one of 52 possible cards

    // output
    void display(ostream& outs=cout) const;

    // comparison operators
    bool operator== (Card c) const;
    bool operator!= (Card c) const;
    bool operator< (Card c) const;
    bool operator<= (Card c) const;
    bool operator> (Card c) const;
    bool operator>= (Card c) const;
```

```
private:
   int suit; //    0,     1,     2,     3
            // club, diamond, heart, spade
   int rank; // 2-10, 11,   12,     13,    14
            //            jack, queen, king, ace

   void validate();
      // check that rank and suit are valid, and,
      // if not, print error message and exit
}; // end Card class interface

ostream& operator<< (ostream& outs, Card c)
   { c.display(outs); return outs; }
```

Sample Client Code   The following code fragment, from displ_52.cpp, displays the 52 standard playing cards in standard, or canonical, order.

```
int suit, rank;
Card C;
for (suit=CLUBS; suit<=SPADES; suit++)
   {
   for (rank=2; rank<=ACE; rank++)
      {
      C.set(rank, suit);
      C.display(); cout << ' ';
      }
   cout << endl;
   }
```

Its output is

```
2c 3c 4c 5c 6c 7c 8c 9c 10c Jc Qc Kc Ac
2d 3d 4d 5d 6d 7d 8d 9d 10d Jd Qd Kd Ad
2h 3h 4h 5h 6h 7h 8h 9h 10h Jh Qh Kh Ah
2s 3s 4s 5s 6s 7s 8s 9s 10s Js Qs Ks As
```

Some Design Decisions   This apparently simple class actually presents some rather difficult design decisions. For example, how shall a client programmer specify a card such as, say, the queen of clubs? We could give just the numbers for the rank (12) and suit (0), but this forces the programmer to remember tedious internal details of the class. Using the enum statement to rename integer values provides an excellent solution that still allows the ranks 2, 3, . . . , 10 to be specified directly. (Another alternative would be to specify suits and face cards by their first letter — 'Q' and 'C' for the queen of clubs. Note, however, that this is not satisfactory, because a loop could not run through the suits, and using characters to specify face card ranks is not consistent with using integers for ranks 2 through 10.)

Because a client program will probably not store cards in a file, no file I/O functions have been provided, though you can easily add them if desired. Also, no function is given for reading a card from the keyboard. Exercise 20.4 asks you to implement this function, which can then be used in the program of Exercise 20.7.

There are no explicitly provided constructors, because the compiler-generated no-argument constructor is adequate. A two-argument constructor for constructing cards with initial values would be of limited value. However, a set function for initializing cards *is* necessary. The declaration

```
Vector<Card> deck(52);
```

constructs, via the no-argument constructor, 52 Card objects, deck[0], .., deck[51], that must have a way — the set function — to get initial values.

Practice with the Card **Class** The documentation for the Card class is in the text file card.doc. Exercise 20.2 asks you to complete and test the implementation of the Card class. Exercises 20.4 and 20.7 ask you to write some client programs that use this class. Finally, Exercises 20.13 and 20.14 ask you to complete, test, and use a Card_pile class (see Section 20.4), whose elements, naturally, are Card objects. Exercises in Chapter 21 also make use of the Card class.

20.3   A Checking Account Class

In this section, we design a simple checking account class. A detailed description of a checking account follows:

Description of a Checking Account A **checking account** has (1) an owner; (2) a unique, four-digit personal identification number, or *PIN*, that is known only to the account's owner; and (3) a current *balance*, which (for simplicity) will never be negative.

The *behavior of a checking account* is described below in terms of how the account acts and is acted on.

1. A person *opens* an account by giving his/her name, a unique PIN of their choosing, and an initial positive balance.

2. If an account is open, the account owner
   (a) can *deposit* money into the account,
   (b) can *withdraw* money from and *write checks* against the account, provided that the amount of the withdrawal or check does not exceed the current balance,
   (c) can *close* the account, and receive a check in the amount of the current balance,
   (d) can *inquire* about the current balance of the account, and
   (e) cannot *open* an account having the same PIN.

3. If an account is not open, an error message will be displayed whenever there is an attempt to *deposit* into, *withdraw* from, *write checks* against, *inquire* about, or *close* the account.

The `Check_acct` **Class Interface**   The following `Check_acct` interface is from the file `chk_act.h`. Notice how closely the data members correspond to the nouns and the member functions correspond to verbs in the detailed description of a checking account just given.

```
class Check_acct
{
public:
    // constructors
    Check_acct() : opened(false) { }
    Check_acct (const String& nm, int pin, float bal)
        : owner(nm), PIN(pin), balance(bal), opened(true)
        { }

    // accessors
    String get_owner()    const;
    int    get_PIN()      const;
    double get_balance()  const;
    void   inquire()      const;
    bool   is_open()      const { return opened; }

    // modifiers
    void open (String name, int pin, double amt);
    void cash_check (double amt);
```

```
    void deposit (double amt);
    void withdraw (double amt);
    void close();

 private:
    String owner;    // owner's name
    int PIN;         // personal ID number
    double balance;  // balance
    bool opened; // has account been opened?
 }; // end Check_acct class interface
```

Design Decisions and Sample Code Although the data members and member functions in the Check_acct class interface correspond very closely to the detailed checking account description, the particular details of individual member functions are still not concrete.

Sometimes a good way to pin down such detailed design decisions is to consider the kinds of run-time activity you would want a sample client program (or a portion of it) to generate. The following code fragment illustrates how we might like some of the member functions of the Check_acct class to carry out their subtasks. Keep in mind that this sample code and desired sample run can be written *before* any member functions are actually implemented — it represents the *desired performance* of the class's member functions, not necessarily an actual run!

```
Check_acct acct1;
fixed_out (cout, 2);
acct1.open("Rich, Richy," 4726, 300.00);
acct1.deposit(150.00);
acct1.cash_check(128.50);
acct1.cash_check(400.00);
acct1.inquire();
acct1.withdraw(100.00);
acct1.withdraw(400.00);
cout << "\tAccount owner is: "
     << acct1.get_owner() << endl;
cout << "\tAccount PIN is: "
     << acct1.get_PIN() << endl;
cout << "\tCurrent balance: $"
     << acct1.get_balance() << endl;
acct1.open("Rich, Richy", 4726, 300.00);
acct1.close();
```

```
// Show what happens when account is not open
cout << endl;
acct1.cash_check (50.00);
acct1.deposit(100.00);
acct1.withdraw(100);
cout << "\tAccount owner is: "
     << acct1.get_owner() << endl;
cout << "\tAccount PIN is: "
     << acct1.get_PIN() << endl;
cout << "\tCurrent balance: $"
     << acct1.get_balance() << endl;
acct1.close();
```

The *desired output* of the above code might be

```
OPEN ACCOUNT for Rich, Richy PIN: 4726 Balance $300.00
DEPOSIT $150.00.
CASH CHECK for $128.50
CHECK ERROR: $400.00 exceeds balance: $321.50
BALANCE INQUIRY: $321.50
WITHDRAW: $100.00
WITHDRAW ERROR: $400.00 exceeds balance: $221.50
Account owner is: Rich, Richy
Account PIN is: 4726
Current balance: $221.50
OPEN ERROR: Account already open.
CLOSE ACCOUNT: Check for $221.50 issued to Rich, Richy
CHECK ERROR: Account not open.
DEPOSIT ERROR: Account not open.
WITHDRAW ERROR: Account not open.
Account owner is: NO OWNER
Account PIN is: 0
Current balance: $0.00
CLOSE ERROR: Account not open.
```

Implementing and Using the Check_acct ***Class*** The documentation for this class is in the text file chk_act.doc. Most of the implementation of this class is left to you as Exercise 20.5, which also gives directions for testing your implementation. Exercise 20.8 asks you to write a menu-driven program for managing a checking account, and Exercise 20.9 asks you to extend this program to handle several accounts.

20.4 Descriptions of Additional Classes (for Exercises)

We now describe some of the additional classes for which you will be asked, in the exercises, to complete parts of or all of the design, documentation, and/or implementation and testing.

A *Card_pile* Class A *card pile* consists of 0 to 52 cards. A player can (1) start with an empty pile or a full deck of 52 cards ordered by suit and rank, (2) shuffle the pile, (3) place the pile in standard order, (4) show the top card of the pile, (5) deal the top card from the pile, (6) add a card either to the top or the bottom of the pile, and (7) add another pile either on top of or on the bottom of the pile.

This class will obviously make use of the Card class of Section 20.2. The interface, portions of the implementation, documentation, and test programs are available at the PWS Web site. Exercises 20.13 through 20.15 ask you to complete, test, and apply this class.

A *Student_info* Class This class models a portion of the information that a college or university's information systems department would maintain for each of its students.

Student information consists of (1) a name, (2) a unique ID number (4 digits, for simplicity), (3) a number of credits completed, (4) a number of grade points (4, 3, 2, 1, or 0, respectively, per credit, for an A, B, C, D, or F) earned, (5) a semester standing, which is a function of the number of credits completed, and (6) a grade point average, or GPA, which is a function of the number of credits completed and the number of grade points earned.

For a client program *to manipulate student information* stored in a computer, it must be possible to

1. *initialize* a student's information by providing a name and ID number, or by providing a name, ID number, credits completed, and grade points earned;

2. *access* a student's name, credits taken, grade points earned, GPA, and semester standing;

3. *update* the number of credits and grade points a student has earned, which may result in a change in the corresponding GPA and semester standing;

4. *display* a student's information on the monitor, or write it to a file;

5. *prompt for and input* a student's information from the keyboard;

6. *read* a student's information from a file; and

7. *identify or compare* student information objects by their unique ID numbers

The documentation, implementation, and testing of this class are left to you as Exercises 20.11 and 20.12.

A Basic Date Class, Date   This class is similar in many ways to the Time_piece classes, but it is more complicated. The class interface and documentation and some of the implementation are available at the PWS Web site. Exercise 20.10 asks you to complete the implementation using test programs that are also available at the PWS Web site.

▧ Exercises

Programming Problems

1. (Phone_entry **Class**)   Write a program that reads phone entries from a file into a vector; prints the entries, one per line; sorts the entries alphabetically by name; and then prints them again, one per line.

2. (Card **Class**)   Complete the implementation of the Card class. For testing purposes, use the client programs displ_52.cpp, cardtst1.cpp, and cardtst2.cpp. Sample runs are included with each of these programs.

3. (Card **Class**)   Write a program that determines by simulation how many cards, on average, must be randomly generated to produce $n \leq 52$ distinct cards, where n is a user input.

4. (Card **Class**)
   (a) Add an enter function to the Card class so that a card can be input from a file or, by default, from the keyboard. (*Note*: Allow cards to be entered only in the same format in which they are displayed in the output of program displ_52.cpp.)
   (b) Write a client program to test your enter function.
   (c) Use the enter function to overload the stream extraction operator, >>, and test this operator.

5. (Check_acct **Class**)   Implement and test the Check_acct class of Section 20.3. Study the sample code and output given in that section and the source code and output of accttst1.cpp to do this.

Longer Assignments

6. (Phone_entry **Class**)   Write a menu-driven program that allows the user to manipulate a directory of phone entries read from a file into a sorted vector, using the insert function of Section 14.5 to insert entries as they are read from the file. The user should have options to *add* a new entry by

inputting the name and extension for the entry; *delete* an entry by inputting the name for the entry; *change the extension* by inputting the name and new extension for the entry; or *display* the current list of entries, one per line. When the user chooses to exit, save the updated directory to the original disk file.

7. **(Card Class)** Write a program to generate a hand of 13 unique cards, maintained in sorted order. Then, repeatedly enter a card from the keyboard and determine whether it is in the hand.

8. **(Check_acct Class)** After you have implemented the Check_acct class, write a menu-driven program to manage a checking account. A typical sample run of your code should look like the following.

```
Account in name of: Big Spender
Four-digit PIN:      9120
Open account with    $200
    OPEN ACCOUNT for Big Spender PIN: 9120 Balance $200.00
[C]heck [D]eposit c[L]ose [W]ithdraw: C 29.95
    CASH CHECK for $29.95
    Balance: $170.05
[C]heck [D]eposit c[L]ose [W]ithdraw: w 100.00
    WITHDRAW: $100.00
    Balance: $70.05
[C]heck [D]eposit c[L]ose [W]ithdraw: c 88.13
    CHECK ERROR: $88.13 exceeds balance: $70.05
    Balance: $70.05
[C]heck [D]eposit c[L]ose [W]ithdraw: d 20.00
    DEPOSIT $20.00.
    Balance: $90.05
[C]heck [D]eposit c[L]ose [W]ithdraw: W 100.00
    WITHDRAW ERROR: $100.00 exceeds balance: $90.05
    Balance: $90.05
[C]heck [D]eposit c[L]ose [W]ithdraw: L
    CLOSE ACCOUNT: Check for $90.05 issued to Big Spender
```

9. **(Check_acct Class)** Extend the program of Exercise 20.8 to manage several checking accounts. Of course, each transaction must begin with entry of a PIN. (*Hints*: Store the Check_acct objects in a vector. You may wish to add relational operators to the Check_acct class so that the vector can be kept in order by PIN.)

10. **(Date Class)** The file badate.h contains a basic Date class interface and portions of its implementation. Study the documentation in badate.doc then use the programs datetst1.cpp and datetst2.cpp to complete the implemen-

tation of the class. (*Note*: All files referenced in this exercise are available at the PWS Web site.)

11. (Student_info **Class**)   The file student.h contains the Student_info class interface of Section 20.

    (a) Study the description of a student information object given in Section 20.4, then use the programs studtst1.cpp and studtst2.cpp and their sample runs to complete and test the implementation of the class.

    (b) Write documentation for the Student class similar to that given for the Phone_entry and Date classes.

12. (Student_info **Class**)   Write a program to update student information at the end of a semester. You will need two data files — one containing current information for several students, and another containing update information for those students for the semester. The update information will contain one line per student, consisting of three values — the student's ID, the credits earned, and the grade points earned by that student for the semester. Have the program print all student information before and after the updates, and save the updated student information to a new file.

13. (Card_pile **Class**)   The file cardpile.h contains the interface and partially completed implementation of the Card_pile class, and cardpile.doc contains the documentation for the class. The programs in the files piletst1.cpp, piletst2.cpp, and piletst3.cpp are client programs of the Card_pile class. Study the class documentation, partially completed implementation, and client programs and their output, then complete and test the implementation of the class.

14. (Card_pile **Class**)   Write a program to deal four different five-card poker hands from a shuffled deck of 52 cards, then display each hand. Use a vector, hands, declared as

    ```
    Vector<Card_pile> hands[4];
    ```

    to store the four hands.

15. (Card_pile **Class**)   The card game known as War (in which each player draws a card and the highest card wins) provides opponents no opportunity to apply strategy and skill, and it is rather tedious to play, with a single game sometimes lasting for hours. Such games are better left for a computer to simulate. Write a program to simulate playing this game, and determine, on average, how many cards are played in a typical game. (*Hint*: For testing purposes, just deal each player five cards from the deck, and display tracing output.)

21

Class Templates

Recall that in Chapter 10 we showed how to template a function by using a generic data type, `EltType`, as the data type of one or more of the parameters in the function definition. This templating made the function *more general* by allowing different calls of that function to make different choices for the actual data type of the argument(s) matched with the `EltType` parameter(s).

Similarly, it is possible to template a class by using a generic data type, such as `EltType`, for one of its data members. This makes the class more general by allowing the declaration of an object to specify the actual data type to be used in place of `EltType`.

We begin this chapter by discussing the syntax and techniques for writing a class template. Then we consider three kinds of applications of class templates. First, we redo the `Int_list` class of Chapter 18 as a class template, which we rename `List`, because it can be used to create lists of data types other than just integers. Second, we make this `List` class template even more useful by adding some new member functions to it. Third, we use this improved `List` class and the `Phone_entry` class of the previous chapter to create a complex application that performs phone extension lookups.

21.1 Templating a Class

To focus on the essential details of creating a class template, we begin with a very simple `Float_cell` class. We then show how this `Float_cell` class can be transformed into a generic `Mem_cell` *class template*.

The *Float_cell* **Class**   The Float_cell class models a memory cell for
storage and retrieval of a single float value. It has only one data member
and two member functions. The interface and implementation follow for
the Float_cell class, which is from flt_cell.cpp.

```
class Float_cell   // interface
{
public:
    float retrieve () const;
     void assign (float val);
private:
    float value;
};

// member function implementations
float Float_cell::retrieve () const
{ return value; }

void Float_cell::assign (float val)
{ value = val; }
```

Using the *Float_cell* **Class**   The following main function, also from
flt_cell.cpp, creates and manipulates Float_cell objects x and y.

```
void main()
{
    Float_cell x, y;
    x.assign (2.75);
    cout << x.retrieve() << endl;
    y.assign(−0.003);
    cout << y.retrieve() << endl;
}
```

```
 2.75
−0.003
```

Output

A *Mem_cell* **Class Template**   We now create a Mem_cell class template
that specifies the pattern for creating a class that models the storage
and retrieval of a generic class, or data type, EltType. The interface for
the Mem_cell class template, from mem_cell.cpp, is given here.

```
template <class EltType>
class Mem_cell
{
public:
    EltType retrieve () const;
    void assign (EltType val);
private:
    EltType value;
};
```

The differences between this `Mem_cell` and the `Float_cell` class interfaces are highlighted. In addition to the class name change, the changes include:

1. The placement of the line

   ```
   template <class EltType>
   ```

   before the class interface in order to tell the compiler that this is a class template rather than an actual class.

2. The replacement of each instance of the specific data type, `float`, with the generic data type, `EltType`.

Member Function Implementations   The complete definitions of member functions `retrieve` and `assign` are

```
template <class EltType>
EltType Mem_cell<EltType>::retrieve () const
{ return value; }

template <class EltType>
void Mem_cell<EltType>::assign (EltType val)
{ value = val; }
```

Notice that:

1. The line

   ```
   template <class EltType>
   ```

   must precede each of the class template's member function implementations. (Recall, from Section 10.5, that this is also the case for a "free" function template.)

2. When doing scope resolution, the generic element type must be given with the class template name, `Mem_cell`, as in `Mem_cell <EltType>::`.

__Using   the__ `Mem_cell` *__Class   Template__*   The `main` function from `mem_cell.cpp` illustrates the versatility of a class template. It is given next, along with its output.

```
void main()
{
    Mem_cell<char> c;
    Mem_cell<float> x;
    Mem_cell<String> s;
    c.assign('A');
    x.assign(2.75);
    s.assign("The end.");
    cout << c.retrieve() << endl;
    cout << x.retrieve() << endl;
    cout << s.retrieve() << endl;
}
```

```
A
2.75
The end.
```

Output

The `main` function uses the `Mem_cell` class template to create memory cell objects c, x, and s, which can store and retrieve values of type `char`, `float`, and `String`, respectively.

__Template Classes__   A *__template class__* is a type-specific version of a class that is created by the compiler from a class template. In compiling the three highlighted statements of the previous fragment, the compiler creates three different template classes, one for each of the types `char`, `float`, and `String`.

21.2   List: **A Templated** Int_list **Class**

Using the ideas of the previous section, we can create a `List` class template from the `Int_list` class of Chapters 18 and 19. The `List` class template interface (from `list0.h`) is given here.

```
template <class EltType>
class List {
public:
    // constructor
    List(); // construct a list of length 0
```

```
    // accessors
    int length() const;
        // return the length of the list
    EltType retrieve(int i) const;
        // retrieve ith list element
        // (first element is in position 1)
    bool contains(EltType elt) const;
        // return true if list contains elt, else false

    // modifiers
    void add(EltType elt);
        // add elt to end of list
    void sort();
      // sort list in increasing order

    // output
    void display (ostream& os=cout) const;
        // display list elements on ostream os,

private:
    int len; // size of the list
    Vector<EltType> Elts; // vector of elements
    bool sorted; // true if list is sorted, else false
}; // end List class interface
```

Notice that the name of the class has been changed to List, and that each occurrence of the specific list element type, int, has been replaced by the (highlighted) generic list element type, EltType. (Be aware that not every occurrence of int in the Int_list class represents the type of a list element. The return type of the length function, for example, is not a list element type.)

Using the List ***Class Template*** The syntax for declaring a list of elements of a particular type is like that used for declaring a vector whose elements are of a particular type. The statement

```
    List<float> flt_lst;
```

creates an empty list, flt_lst, of float elements.

■ **EXAMPLE** The following program displays, in ASCII order, the unique characters that appear in a line of text entered by the user.

```
// char_lst.cpp
// Determine the unique characters in a line of text.
#include <iostream.h>
#include "list0.h"

void main()
{
    List<char> ch_lst;
    char ch;
    cout << "Enter a line of text: \n-> ";
    cin.get(ch);
    while (ch != '\n')
        {
        if (!ch_lst.contains(ch))
            ch_lst.add(ch);
        cin.get(ch);
        }
    cout << "That line contains " << ch_lst.length()
        << " different characters.\n";
    ch_lst.sort();
    cout << "They are: ";
    ch_lst.display();
    cout << endl;
}
```

A sample run is

```
Enter a line of text:
-> When in doubt, parenthesize (or punt).
That line contains 20 different characters.
They are: ( ) , . W a b d e h i n o p r s t u z
```

Some List ***Class Member Function Implementations***   Given the implementations of the Int_list class member functions, we can easily create the implementations of the member function templates of the List class template.

■ **QUESTION**   Given the following no-argument Int_list class constructor

```
Int_list::Int_list()
    : len(0), sorted(true) // initializer list
    {  }
```

what are the missing lines of the no-argument constructor of the List class template?

```
_____
_____::List()
    : len(0), sorted(true) // initializer list
    {  }
```

Answer   The completed lines are

```
template <class EltType>
List<EltType>::List()
```

21.3   Improving List by Adding New Member Functions

The existing List class has no member function for removing or replacing an item, and, although the contains member function indicates whether a given item is in the list, it does not return the item's location. To improve the List class template, we add the accessor function, position, whose declaration is

```
int position (EltType elt) const;
    // return position of elt in list,
    // or 0 if not in list
```

and the modifier functions, remove and replace, whose declarations are

```
void remove(int i);
    // remove the ith element from the list

void replace(int i, EltType elt);
    // replace the ith element by elt
```

(*Note*: Recall that list positions start at 1, not 0!)

Finding an Element   Like the contains function, position does a linear search for elt in Elts[1]. . .Elts[len], returning the index of the first cell containing elt, or 0 if no cell contains elt.

■ QUESTION   How should you complete the definition of `position`?

```
_____
int _____::position (EltType elt) const
{
    for (int i=1; i<= length(); i++)
        if (Elts[i]==elt)
            return i;
    return 0;
}
```

Answer   The completed lines are

```
template <class EltType>
int List<EltType>::position (EltType elt) const      ■ ■■
```

Removing an Element   Unlike the `add` member function, which takes
as a parameter the element to be added to (the end of) the list, `remove`
takes as a parameter the index of the element to remove. This provides
a client program with the flexibility either to use `position` to get the index
of an element to be removed, then pass this index to `remove`, or simply
to remove the element at a given list position, without regard for the
element's value.

■ QUESTION   How should you complete the `for` loop that removes the `i`th list element
by left shifting all list elements to the right of the `i`th element?

```
template <class EltType>
void List<EltType>::remove(int i)
{
    Assert (1 <= i && i <= len,
            "List subscript out of range.");
    for (int j__; j_____; j++)
        Elts[j] = Elts[j+1];
    len--;
}
```

Answer   The completed line is

```
for (int j=i; j<len; j++)
```

Discussion   Recall that `add` sometimes must resize data member `Elts` to make room
for the element to be added. When removing an element, if the actual

list size is significantly smaller than the number of cells allocated for Elts, a good memory management practice would be to resize Elts in order to free up this excess memory. We leave this as Exercise 21.10.

Replacing an Element   Replacing the ith list element is a tricky operation, because the replacement may disrupt the order of a sorted list, causing the sorted data member to become false. If the length of the list is only one, replacement cannot alter sorted, and if the list was not sorted before replacement, it is probably not worth the effort to check whether replacement restored the list to order. (This last point is discussed further in Exercise 21.11.) However, careful checking is required if the list length is more than one and the list was sorted *before* replacement. In this case, one of two things could go wrong with the order when elt is placed in Elts[i] — either there is a list element, Elts[i-1], immediately to the left of elt, and elt < Elts[i-1], or there is a list element, Elts[i+1], immediately to the right of elt, and elt > Elts[i-1]. Thus, you need to be sure that there is indeed an element to the left (or right) of elt before checking the inequality; otherwise, a "List subscript out of range" error will occur.

The complete definition of replace, with the code for checking on the status of sorted highlighted, is

```cpp
template <class EltType>
void List<EltType>::replace(int i, EltType elt)
{
    Assert (1 <= i && i <= len,
            "List subscript out of range.");
    Elts[i] = elt;
    if (sorted && len>1) // check new status
        {
        if (i>1 && elt < Elts[i-1]) sorted = false;
        if (i<len && elt > Elts[i+1]) sorted = false;
        }
}
```

The File list.h   The file list.h contains the improved List class template. We apply this List class in the following code.

■ QUESTION   Study the following main function from name_1st.cpp. How would you complete the missing portions of the program run?

Main Function from *name_lst.cpp*

```
void main()
{
    List<String> nm_lst; // list of names
    nm_lst.add("Adam");
    nm_lst.add("Eve");
    nm_lst.add("Ivan");
    nm_lst.add("Maya");
    nm_lst.add("Rhett");
    nm_lst.display(); cout << endl;

    cout << nm_lst.position("Ivan") << endl;
    cout << nm_lst.position("Josh") << endl;
    nm_lst.replace(2, "Erin");
    nm_lst.remove(4);
    nm_lst.display(); cout << endl;
}
```

```
Adam Eve Ivan Maya Rhett
__

0
```

Answer   The completed lines are

```
3
Adam Erin Ivan Rhett
```

21.4 A Phone_entry **List**

Thus far, we have used the List class template to create List template classes only for the char and String data types. In this section we create a list of student phone entries using the Phone_entry class developed in Chapter 20.

Overloaded Comparison Operators   Notice in the definition of the List class member function contains that the relational operator, ==, is used to compare the EltType parameter, elt, to the ith list element. Further, the add and sort member functions use the < and >= relational operators. To make a declaration of the form:

```
List<data-type> L;
```

the type or class represented by *data-type* must have overloaded relational operators ==, <, and >=. In the absence of these operators, the compiler issues an "illegal structure" error message wherever any of these operators is used in the List class implementation.

Recall that all the relational operators are overloaded for the Phone_entry class, so we are ready to proceed.

■ **QUESTION**   The program chng_ext.cpp reads student phone entries from the file stuphon.dat into the list phone_list. It then sorts the entries alphabetically, by name, and displays the entries. Finally, it changes all the phone extensions, then displays the updated phone entries. A sample run is

```
Phone extensions, in order by name:
  Carl, Lewis          2000
  Doe, Jane            1090
  Hillerman, Tonio     3822
  Jagger, Mike         4321
  Ricardo, Lucia       8700

Time to update all phone extensions!
  Carl, Lewis          1010
  Doe, Jane            1020
  Hillerman, Tonio     1030
  Jagger, Mike         1040
  Ricardo, Lucia       1050
```

Study the sample run and the following main function of chng_ext.cpp. How would you complete the missing portions of the main function?

```cpp
void main()
{
    List<Phone_entry> phone_list;
    Phone_entry entry;
    ifstream phones_in;

    phones_in.open("stuphon.dat");
    Assert (!phones_in.fail(),
            "Unable to open stuphon.dat");
    while (phones_in >> ws && !phones_in.eof())
        {
        // read a Phone_entry object from the file
        entry.read_from_file(phones_in);
        // add it to the phone list
        phone_list.add (entry);
        }
```

```
        phone_list.sort();
        cout << "Phone extensions, in order by name:\n ";
        phone_list.display(); cout << endl;

        cout << "Time to update all phone extensions!\n ";
        for (int i=1; i<=phone_list.length(); i++)
            {
            entry = phone_list._____;
            entry.set_extension(1000 + 10*i);
            phone_list._____;
            }
        phone_list.display(); cout << endl;
}
```

Answer   The completed lines are

```
        entry = phone_list.retrieve(i);
        phone_list.replace(i, entry);
```

21.5 Application: Looking Up Phone Extensions

In this section, we apply the `List` class to the problem of processing requests for student phone extensions. The program `get_ext.cpp` repeatedly inputs a student's name (Last, First), then either (1) gives that student's phone extension or (2) displays a message that no listing is available. A portion of a sample run follows.

```
Name (Last, First): Doe, Jane
        The extension is 1090

Another lookup? (Y/N) y
Name (Last, First): Ricardo, Richy
        No listing available.

Another lookup? (Y/N) y
Name (Last, First): Jagger, Mike
        The extension is 4321

    . .  etc.  . .
```

The Main Function   The `main` function of `get_ext.cpp`,

```
void main()
{
    List<Phone_entry> phone_dir;

    load_from_file (phone_dir);
    cout << "Lookup ESU student phone extensions.\n\n";
    process_lookups(phone_dir);
}
```

is very short because the real work is done by the `load_from_file` and `process_lookups` functions, whose declarations and descriptions are

```
void load_from_file
    (List<Phone_entry>& phone_dir);
// Load phone entries from file stuphon.dat
// into the list phone_dir, and put in alpha
// order by name.

void process_lookups
    (const List<Phone_entry>& phone_dir);
// Repeatedly input student names and
// output their phone extensions.
```

We do not present the definition of `load_from_file` — its details are essentially the same as those of the first part of the `main` function of `chng_ext.cpp` that was presented in the previous section.

The process_lookups Function   The pseudocode for `process_lookups` is

```
do {
    Input a name.
    Find the position in phone_dir of the entry for name.
    if (search successful)
        {
        Retrieve the entry for name.
        Output the extension for name.
        }
```

```
        else
            Output message "No listing available."
            See if there is another lookup request.
        }
while (there is another lookup requested)
```

To find the entry for name, we use the List class's position member function. We have only a student's name to use in the lookup, but the position member function takes an argument of type EltType, which, for this problem, is Phone_entry. Recall that the relational operators are overloaded for the Phone_entry class in such a way that Phone_entry comparisons are done *by name only*. That is, any two Phone_entry objects having the same value in their respective name data members will be equal, regardless of the values in their extension data members! Thus, if entry is of type Phone_entry, then the following two statements determine the position of the entry for name in phone_dir.

```
        entry.set(name, 0); // lookup is by name only
        int pos = phone_dir.position(entry);
```

The complete implementation of process_lookups is

```
void process_lookups
    (const List<Phone_entry>& phone_dir)
{
    Phone_entry entry;
    String name;        // to look up
    char ans;           // another lookup?

    do {  // repeatedly process lookups
        // get the name
        cout << "Name (Last, First): ";
        getline(cin, name);

        // look it up
        entry.set(name, 0); // lookup is by name only
        int pos = phone_dir.position(entry);

        // Give extension or message that person is unlisted
        if (pos > 0) // successful search
            {
            entry = phone_dir.retrieve(pos);
```

```
                    cout << "\tThe extension is "
                         << entry.get_extension() << endl;
                }
            else
                cout << "\tNo listing available.\n";

            cout << "\nAnother lookup? (Y/N) ";
            cin >> ans; cin.ignore (80, '\n');
            }
        while (ans != 'n' && ans != 'N');
    }
```

Exercises

Use the following Int_pair class interface, from the file int_pair.cpp, for Exercises 21.1 through 21.8.

```cpp
class Int_pair // interface
{
public:
    // constructors
    Int_pair() { }
    Int_pair (long v1, long v2)
        : val1 (v1), val2 (v2) { }

    // accessors
    long get1 () const { return val1; }
    long get2 () const { return val2; }

    // modifiers
    void set (long v1, long v2);

    // output
    void display (ostream& outs=cout);

private:
    long val1, val2;
};

ostream& operator<< (ostream& outs, Int_pair p)
{  p.display (outs); return outs; }
```

```
void Int_pair::set (long v1, long v2)
{  val1 = v1; val2 = v2; }

void Int_pair::display (ostream& outs)
{  outs << '(' << val1 << ", " << val2 << ')'; }
```

1. Give the output of the following client code fragment.

```
Int_pair p1(5,12), p2;
p2.set (p1.get2(), p1.get1());
p1.display(); cout << endl;
p2.display(); cout << endl;
```

2. Describe the changes that must be made to the Int_pair class interface to make it into a Pair class template for the generic type EType.

3. Write the complete definition of the Pair class template's two-argument constructor. *Hint*: The Int_pair class's two-argument constructor is:

```
Int_pair::Int_pair (long v1, long v2)
    : val1(v1), val2(v2) { }
```

4. Write the complete definition of the Pair class template's display function.

5. What is the difference between a class template and a template class?

6. In order for the compiler to produce a Pair template class for a given class (or data type), what operator must be overloaded for that class (or data type)?

7. Show how to overload the stream insertion operator, <<, for the Pair class template.

8. Recall the Card class of Chapter 20. Assuming that the interface and implementation of the Pair class template are correctly completed, what output will the following code fragment produce?

```
Card c1, c2;
c1.set(2,HEARTS); c2.set(ACE,CLUBS);
Pair<Card> cp (c1, c2);
cp.display();
```

9. Consider the List class template function add whose declaration is

```
void add(EltType elt);
```

(a) What parameter passing method is used?

(b) What are the consequences of this parameter passing method if EltType is a large class such as the Student_info class of Chapter 20?

(c) What would be a better parameter passing technique to use in this situation?

(d) For which other List class member functions would you change the parameter passing technique?

10. Modify the List class's remove function so that excessive unused memory is freed. One way to do this is to resize the Elts vector to half its current length whenever the number of list elements is at most one-third the current length of Elts. However, do not let the length of Elts go under a predetermined minimum of, say, 8.

11. The discussion in Section 21.3 of the List class replace function points out that it is probably not worth the effort to check whether a replacement restores an unsorted list to order.

(a) What is the rationale for this claim?

(b) What other List class member function calls might restore an unsorted list to order?

(c) Write a private member function, check_order, that replace and the functions of part (b) can call to test whether a previously unsorted list has been restored to order, updating sorted accordingly.

Programming Problems

12. Code the interface and implementation of the Pair class template, then test it by creating and manipulating pairs of integers, floats, strings, cards, and fractions.

13. Do Exercise 20.3 using a list rather than a vector of cards.

14. Write a program to read Student_info objects into a list, display the list, sort it by ID number, then display the sorted list.

15. Extend the List class template to a List2 class template by adding the following functions.

```
void add_front (EltType elt);
   // add elt to the front of the list
void add_rear (EltType elt);
   // add elt to the rear of the list
void remove_front();
   // remove the item at the front of the list
void remove_rear();
   // remove the item at the rear of the list
```

16. Exercise 19.19 describes an ordered integer list class, Ord_Int_list. Add the position and remove functions of Section 21.3 to this class, then create an Ordered_list class template.

17. (a) Test the Ordered_list class template of Exercise 21.16 by reading single word strings from the keyboard, storing them in an ordered list, then displaying the list.
    (b) Repeat part (a), but use fractions or dates rather than strings.

Longer Assignments

18. Do Exercise 20.9 using a list or ordered list rather than using a vector of Check_acct objects.

19. Do Exercise 20.12 using a list or ordered list rather than a vector of Student_info objects.

20. (**A** Set **Class**) · Modify and extend the Ordered_list class template of Exercise 21.16 to create a Set class template. A no-argument constructor will create an empty set; add and remove member functions will add and remove individual set elements; a make_empty function will remove all elements; a contains member function will test set membership; and a length function will return the size of the set. You will need to overload operators +, *, and − for set union, intersection, and difference; operator << so that a set is output in curly braces, with members of the set separated by commas; and operators ==, !=, <, <=, >, and >= to take the place of the usual set comparison operators =, ≠, ⊂, ⊆, ⊃, and ⊇.

22

Pointers, Dynamic Memory, and the Vector Class Revealed

In this chapter we introduce the pointer data type, whose variables, as the name indicates, point either to a single memory cell or to a block of cells. Pointer variables allow memory cells to be allocated (created) and deallocated (freed) *dynamically* — that is, while the program is running.

The topics discussed include (1) the `this` pointer and its use in overloading the assignment operator of a class; (2) some connections between pointers and arrays, which explain how arrays are automatically passed by reference and why array indexing starts at zero; (3) how pointers are used to create dynamic arrays, which are arrays whose size can be changed while a program is running; and (4) the implementation of the `Vector` class (used in Chapter 13), which is created from the built-in array data type, but is more convenient to use than arrays.

22.1 Pointer Variables

Two variables are involved in pointing — the variable *that does the pointing* and the variable *that is pointed to*. A *pointer variable* does the pointing by storing the address of the variable that it points to.

Declaring Pointers To declare a pointer variable, place an asterisk between the data type of the variable pointed to and the name of the pointer variable. For example, the statements

```
int* p; // int pointer, p
float *q; // float pointer, q
String * s; // String pointer, s
```

declare pointer variables p, q, and s, which point to memory cells that store, respectively, an int, a float, and a String.

The exact position of the asterisk between the data type and the pointer variable name is not important, but the asterisk must precede each pointer variable in a declaration. Thus, the statement

```
int * p1, *p2, p3;
```

declares p1 and p2 to be of type int pointer, whereas p3 is of type int, *not* int pointer.

Creating a Memory Cell Using the new Operator   Merely declaring a pointer variable, say, ptr, does not create a memory cell for it to point to. The new operator is used to create the memory cell that is pointed to. Thus, if ptr is declared to be of type String*, then the effect of

```
ptr = new String;
```

is (1) to create a String memory cell to which ptr points and (2) to store the address of this memory cell in ptr. You can envision ptr and the memory cell it points to as follows, where the content of the memory cell that ptr points to is an uninitialized, or garbage, value.

Dynamic Memory and the Heap   Memory that is created with the new operator during program execution is referred to as **dynamic memory**. To say that this memory is "created" is somewhat misleading — it is actually allocated, or borrowed, from a reserve of random access memory called the **heap**. As you will see, it is important for dynamic memory that has been previously allocated, but is no longer needed, to be deallocated or freed — that is, returned to the heap.

Accessing a Memory Cell via a Pointer   The memory cell that a pointer variable points to, or **references**, can be accessed by placing an asterisk immediately before the name of the pointer variable. This operation is known as **dereferencing** the pointer variable.

For example, the statement

```
*ptr = "Smith";
```

accesses the memory cell pointed to by ptr, then assigns the value Smith to that cell. After this assignment, memory can be depicted as follows.

Internal Implementation Internally, pointers are implemented by having the memory cell of the pointer variable contain the address of the memory cell that is pointed to. Suppose, for example, that the address of ptr is 1015 and that the memory cell created by the operation new String has address 1242. Then, the effect of

```
ptr = new String;
*ptr = "Smith";
```

can be depicted at the memory address level as shown on the left, or with the simpler diagram shown on the right.

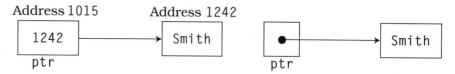

Henceforth, we use the simpler kind of diagram given above because knowing the actual addresses involved is rarely necessary.

Declaring Versus Dereferencing Pointers Note that the asterisk is placed to the left of the pointer variable both when *declaring* the variable and also when *dereferencing* the variable.

■ **QUESTION** What will be printed by the following code from intptrs.cpp?

```
int *p, *q; // pointers to ints
int  x,  y; //

p = new int;
*p = 5;
x = *p + 1;
y = *p;
q = new int;
*q = y + 3;
cout << x << ' ' << y << ' ' << *p
     << ' ' << *q << endl;
```

Answer The output will be

```
6 5 5 8
```

Here is what memory will look like just after execution of this fragment.

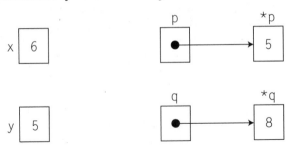

Assigning One Pointer to Another   Suppose pointer variables p1 and p2 both point to memory cells of the same type. The effect of

    p1 = p2;

will be to redirect p1 so that it points to the memory cell pointed to by p2. After execution of the preceding assignment statement, both pointers will point to the same memory cell because they contain the same memory address.

■ **QUESTION**   Suppose p1 and p2 are both of type int*. What will memory look like after the assignment p1 = p2? What will be printed by the following fragment?

```
p1 = new int;
p2 = new int;
*p1 = 86;
*p2 = 45;
p1 = p2;
cout << *p1 << ' ' << *p2 << endl;
```

Answer   Here is a picture of memory after the shaded assignment statement has been executed along with the output of the fragment.

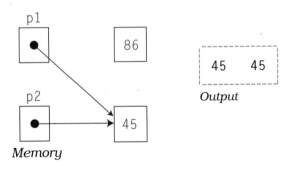

Memory

Discussion Observe that the memory cell originally pointed to by p1 can no longer be accessed because the original value of p1 has been altered. A memory cell to which the pointer has been lost is known as *garbage*. ■ ■

CAUTION If p and q are pointers to the same data type, beware of the big difference between the assignment q = p, which causes q to point to the same cell as p, and the assignment *q = *p, which assigns the value from the cell pointed to by p to the cell pointed to by q.

■ **QUESTION** Suppose the assignment p1 = p2 was replaced by the assignment *p1 = *p2 in the code fragment of the previous question. What output would the fragment produce, and what would memory look like after execution?

Answer The output would be the same, but memory would look like the following.

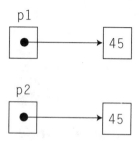

Dynamic Nature of Pointers The memory cells that are pointed to are *not* declared. Only the variables that do the pointing are declared. As you will see, a statement like ptr = new String; can be executed many times within a single program. Each time it is executed, a new memory cell is created. Consequently, there is no fixed number of memory cells that a program can dynamically allocate by using pointer variables.

■ **QUESTION** 1. What will be printed by the following program fragment from strptrs.cpp? Note the memory snapshots at various stages of execution.

2. Can you fill in the blank line with a statement that accesses and prints the contents of the first memory cell created?

```
p = new String;
*p = "Abe";

p = new String;
*p = "Bob";

cout << *p << endl;
_____;
```

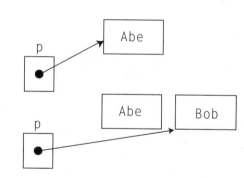

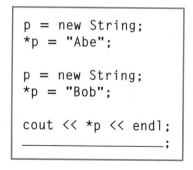

Answer **1.** The output will be Bob

2. No. There is no way to access the contents of the memory cell containing "Abe". When the computer executes p = new String; the second time, it allocates a new memory cell whose address is stored in p. The address of the memory cell containing "Abe" is erased from p.   ■ ▬

In the next chapter, you will learn how to use linked lists to retain access to all the memory cells that have been allocated.

Deallocating a Memory Cell Using delete   When we no longer need a memory cell that is being pointed to, we use the delete operator to *deallocate* the memory cell — that is, return it to the heap. For example, the statement

```
delete p;
```

returns to the heap the memory cell to which p is pointing, making it available for later allocation. (Note how much more descriptive it would be if the delete operator were called recycle!)

Neglecting to Deallocate Dynamic Memory   Proper dynamic memory management is important. Neglecting to deallocate memory that is no longer needed wastes heap memory, thus risking (especially when large blocks of memory are being allocated) the exhaustion of heap memory, which would result in a run-time error.

Be aware, however, that the effects of neglecting to deallocate dynamic memory are not permanent. Each program starts with a fresh store of heap memory, rather than a diminished supply left over by previously run programs.

PITFALL   (Dangling References and delete**)**   Consider the following code fragment (from dangref1.cpp) and its output.

```
int *p;
p = new int;
*p = 1234;
cout << *p << endl;
delete p;
cout << *p << endl;
```

```
1234
1234
```

Output

Notice that even after p has been deleted, p still points to the memory cell that has been deallocated and that is therefore supposed to be available for other uses. A pointer such as this is known as a *dangling reference*, and can be the cause of troublesome program bugs.

The NULL **Pointer** C++ Provides a built-in pointer constant, NULL, that does not point to any memory location. The assignment statement

```
p = NULL; // p points nowhere
```

will set p equal to the NULL pointer.

Using the NULL **Pointer Defensively** After deleting a pointer variable, you should assign the NULL pointer to that variable. For example,

```
delete p;
p = NULL; // defensive programming
```

Because *it is illegal to dereference the* NULL *pointer*, if there is a subsequent attempt to dereference p (such as cout << *p;), the program will stop and a run-time error message will be displayed. When testing and debugging code involving pointers, it is preferable to stop a program with an error message rather than allow a subtle bug involving pointers to go undetected.

Another Source of Dangling References When using delete, care must also be taken that no other pointer is also pointing at the memory cell to be deallocated. For example, if p and q are of type int*, then the output produced by the following statements, from dangref2.cpp, shows that q *still* points to the just deallocated memory cell that was originally pointed to by p.

```
p = new int;
*p = 1234;
q = p;
delete p;
p = NULL;
cout << *q << endl;
```

```
1234
```
Output

22.2 The & Operator

Using & to Obtain the Address of a Memory Cell The *address of* operator, &, returns the address of its (single) operand. Addresses, when stored in pointer variables, are output, by default, in hexadecimal, or base 16.

■ **Example**   The following main function shows how to obtain the address of an integer variable, how to display it in both hexadecimal and in decimal form, and how to assign this address to an integer pointer variable.

Main **Function from** addr_op.cpp

```
void main()
{
    int* p;
    int q = 7;

    // output address of q
    cout << "Address of q (in hex): " << &q << endl;
    cout << "Address of q (in dec): "
        << (unsigned long)&q << endl;

    // make p point to q's memory cell
    p = &q;
    // and display the cell's contents
    cout << "*p = " << *p << endl;
}
```

```
Address of q (in hex): 0x1097241a    ← 32-bit hexadecimal
Address of q (in dec): 278340634     ← 32-bit unsigned decimal
*p = 7
```

Sample run

Discussion   The leading 0x on the address 0x1097241a indicates that the address is in hexadecimal, which, for reasons we do not discuss, is the preferred form when working with actual memory addresses. To output the address in base 10 notation, you must recast the address to unsigned long as was done in the shaded code. (*Note*: When you run this program on your computer, it is unlikely that the address will be the same as that shown here, because a different memory address will probably be used in your run.)   ■ ▬

PITFALL   (Problem That Can Occur When Using & and delete**)**   Inserting the statement

```
delete p; // Danger!
```

as the last statement of the previous program would be a logic error because p points to a memory cell that was allocated ***statically*** at compile-time, not *dynamically* at run-time. (Depending on your compiler, this statement may produce a run-time error.) Statically allocated memory is not allocated from the heap and, thus, cannot be returned to the heap.

22.3 The this **Pointer and the Assignment Operator**

The this ***Pointer*** Every class has as an implicit, private data member, a pointer named this. The address of an object of a class is automatically stored in its this pointer when the object is created. We are going to use the following two aspects of the this pointer.

1. this — gives the address of the object.

2. *this — is the object itself.

The Default Assignment Operator If a class does not explicitly declare an assignment operator, operator=, then the compiler will provide a default version for free. For the classes that we have written so far, the default operator= has been sufficient for successfully carrying out assignment statements in client programs and within member function definitions. However, as you will see in Section 22.5, *the assignment operator must be explicitly declared and defined for any class that has pointer variables as data members* because the default operator= is inadequate for such classes. The general form of the default assignment operator is

```
class_type& operator= (const class_type& Rhs);
```

Note that the client program assignment statement

```
f = g;
```

is really the same as the statement

```
f.operator=(g);
```

Here, the argument g in the call to operator= is the object on the R̲ight-h̲and s̲ide of the assignment, and is passed by constant reference to the parameter Rhs.

In general, the body of the definition of the default operator= function (1) does a member-by-member assignment of each data member from the right-hand side, Rhs, to the calling object and (2) then returns the just assigned calling object. (The return type of operator= is class_type&

rather than void so that assignment can be **cascaded**[1] with other operators.)

An Explicit Version of operator= *for the* Fraction *Class*   We now give, for the Fraction class, an explicit definition of operator= that is equivalent to the compiler-provided default. Note that this definition achieves the member-by-member assignment and the return mentioned earlier.

```
Fraction& Fraction::operator= (const Fraction& Rhs)
{  // do member by member assignment
   num = Rhs.num;
   den = Rhs.den;
   return *this; // return calling object
}
```

Dangers of Self-Assignment   When the default operator= is called by a client program statement such as

```
   x = x;
```

it reassigns to x its current value by reassigning each of its data members, a process known as **self-assignment**. You might assume that this type of statement never happens, but it does, usually in disguised form, in programs that do lots of pointer operations (see Exercise 22.7). Self-assignment accomplishes nothing, and it can be quite time consuming when x is a large data structure.

Although self-assignment would not be costly for objects of the Fraction class, it is instructive to see how to define a Fraction class assignment operator in a way that avoids self-assignment — that is, so that the client program statement

```
   f = f;
```

does not result in an attempt to assign the data members of f to themselves. A similar definition will be used in other classes for which self-assignment must be avoided.

---

[1] If s is a string, the statement

```
   (s = "Shells").insert(3, " se") += " sea shells.";
```

cascades operator=, insert, and operator+=, and results in s containing the string "She sells sea shells." Cascading, although permitted for many data types and operations, can produce cryptic code.

See the programs cascade1.cpp and cascade2.cpp at the PWS Web site for examples of cascading with strings and integers.

■ QUESTION **(Avoiding Self-Assignment in the Definition of** operator=) The following definition of operator= for the Fraction class avoids self-assignment. How should you fill in the blanks?

```
Fraction& Fraction::operator= (const Fraction& Rhs)
{
    if (this != _____) // don't assign to self
    {
    num = Rhs.num;
    den = _____;
    }
    return _____; // return calling object
}
```

Answer To test that the calling object and the object on the right side are different, we can merely test that they have different addresses. Thus, the first blank should contain &Rhs, the address of the parameter. The other two blanks should contain, respectively, Rhs.den and *this.   ■ ▓▓

22.4 Arrays and Pointers

Arrays and pointers are very closely related. In this section, we explore this relationship in order to prepare for our discussion of the implementation of the Vector class in Sections 22.5 and 22.6.

An Array Name Is a Pointer An array is a contiguous block of memory cells, and the array's name is actually the name of a pointer that stores the address of the first of these cells. Thus, the declaration

```
    float x[3];
```

statically allocates three contiguous float memory cells, and x is a pointer containing the address of x[0]. (Be aware that the memory pointed to by x is *not* heap memory.) This is depicted in the following diagram.

For this array x, both x[0] and *x have the same value. To understand why, note that because x points to x[0], the value of the cell pointed to by x is x[0]. Thus the following fragment produces the indicated output.

```
float x[3];
x[0] = 7.24;
cout << x[0] << ' ' << *x;
```

```
7.24  7.24
```
Output

Pointer Arithmetic   In both C and C++, an array variable, x, is really a pointer containing the address of x[0]. This address is known as the array's *base address*. *Pointer arithmetic* allows other array elements to be accessed from the pointer x by adding *integer offsets* to x. That is, x+1, x+2, and so on, are pointers, where the value of x+1 is the address of x[1], the value of x+2 is the address of x[2], and, in general, the value of x+n is the address of x[n], and is said to be the nth offset of x. For example,

```
cout << *(x+i); // same effect as cout << x[i];
```

Thus, array indexing in C and C++ starts at 0, *not* 1, in order to maintain this relationship between the array index and the offset from the base address of the array.

How Arrays Are Automatically Passed as If by Reference   Because an array variable is really a pointer, when an array x is an argument of a function, the function is not passed a duplicate copy of the memory cells of the array, but merely a copy of the address of x[0]. Passing this base address to the function, however, gives *direct access* to all the memory cells of the array. Thus, an array is passed to a function as if by reference.

Creating an Array Dynamically   Arrays can be allocated and deallocated dynamically by using pointer variables. The syntax is only slightly different than that for dynamically allocating and deallocating integers and strings, as illustrated in Section 22.1.

■ **EXAMPLE**   The following code, from dynarray.cpp, dynamically allocates, then fills, displays, and, finally, deallocates an array pointed to by the int pointer a.

```
void main()
{
    int num_cells = 4; // number of array cells
    int* a; // will point to cell 0 of the array
```

```
    // dynamically allocate the array
    a = new int[num_cells];

    // fill it and display its contents
    for (int i=0; i<num_cells; i++)
        a[i] = 10*i + 1;
    for (i=0; i<num_cells; i++)
        cout << a[i] << ' ';
    cout << endl;

    delete [] a;  // deallocate the array
    a = NULL;     // defensive programming
}
```

Discussion Notice that in addition to a data type, the new operator takes an integer, in square brackets, that indicates how many array cells to allocate. The new operator uses the data type and the number of cells to determine exactly how many contiguous bytes of memory to allocate for the array. The square brackets between the delete operator and the address, a, indicate that delete is to return *multiple* memory cells, beginning at address a, to the heap. It might seem logical to supply delete with the number of array cells to be deleted, as in

```
    delete [num_cells] a;
```

However, this is not necessary, and at least one compiler, Turbo C++ 4.5 for Windows, produced the warning "Array size for delete ignored." ▪ ▬

Resizing an Array An advantage of creating an array dynamically rather than statically is that the array can be resized during program execution.

■ **QUESTION** How would you complete the following code (from dblarray.cpp) to double the size of a dynamically allocated array of num_cells integers, whose base pointer is a.

```
// 1) allocate 2*num_cells new cells
int *b;
b = _____;

// 2) copy all elements from a to b
for (i=0; i<num_cells; i++)
    b[i] = a[i];
```

```
// 3) replace a by the new array
_____; // deallocate original array
num_cells = num_cells * 2;
a = b; b = NULL;
```

Answer   The completed lines are

```
b = new int [2*num_cells];
delete [] a;  // deallocate original array
```

22.5   A Simple Vector Class

Our goal in this and the next section is to explain the details of declaring and implementing the templated `Vector` class (of file `bavector.h`) that you began using in Chapter 13. To restrict our focus to the necessary details, we will proceed in stages. In this section, we declare and implement a simplified, nontemplated vector class, `Simple_vector`, that is missing two critical member functions, which are then developed in the next section.

The `Simple_vector` ***Class Interface***   The interface of the `Simple_vector` class, from `smpvct1.h`, is shown here. Notice that a `typedef` statement defines `EltType` and avoids (for now) the syntactical baggage required for templating. As public member functions, the class provides two constructors, an explicitly defined assignment operator, `length` and `resize` functions, and two versions of the overloaded subscript operator, `[]`. There are only two data members — `Elts`, the pointer to a dynamically allocated array of `size` components of type `EltType`, and `size`, the number of array components currently allocated.

```
typedef int EltType; // use typedef rather than templates

class Simple_vector  // class interface
{
public:
    // constructors
    Simple_vector();  // construct vector of length 0
    Simple_vector(int sz); // construct vector of length sz

    // Assignment
    Simple_vector& operator= (const Simple_vector& v);
```

```
    // Accessors
    int length() const;
    // return size of vector

    const EltType& operator[] (int index) const;
    // return non-modifiable subscripted vector elt

    // Modifiers
    EltType& operator[] (int index);
    // return modifiable subscripted vector elt

    void resize (int newsz);
    // change size to newsz
private:
    EltType* Elts; // point to cell 0 of array of elts
    int size;       // size of vector

    void check_range (int index) const;
    // check if index is in valid range
};  // end Simple_vector class interface
```

Implementing the Constructors The zero-argument constructor creates an empty vector, whose array pointer, Elts, is NULL. The one-argument constructor creates a vector of sz elements by dynamically allocating an array of size sz. Notice in the following implementations that all the work is done in initializer lists.

```
Simple_vector::Simple_vector()
    : size(0), Elts(NULL)
    { }

Simple_vector::Simple_vector(int sz)
    : size(sz), Elts (new EltType[sz])
    { }
```

■ **QUESTION** **(Implementing the Assignment Operator)** Recall from the previous section the syntax and action of the assignment operator. How would you complete the following implementation of the assignment operator, keeping in mind that all dynamic memory should be recycled?

```
Simple_vector&
Simple_vector::operator= (const Simple_vector& v)
{
    if ( _____ ) // avoid self-assignment
        {
        delete [] Elts; // get rid of old storage
        size = v.size;   // assign new size
        Elts = _____; // allocate new storage
        // assign new elements, one at a time
        for(int i=0; i<size; i++)
            Elts[i] = v.Elts[i];
        }
    return *this;
}
```

Answer   The completed lines are

```
if (this != &v) // avoid self-assignment
Elts = new EltType [size]; // allocate new storage
```

Inadequacy of the Default Assignment Operator   The following code fragment, from tstassgn.cpp, produces the output shown in 1 when the explicit operator= function, written earlier, is used. However, when the declaration and definition of the explicit assignment operator are commented out of the file (smpvct1.h) containing the Simple_vector class, this code produces the output shown in 2.

```
Simple_vector v1(5), v2;
for (int i=0; i<v1.length(); i++)
    v1[i] = i;

v2 = v1; // Test assignment
cout << "v2 = "; display(v2);

v2[0] = -99;
cout << "v1 = "; display(v1);
```

```
v2 = 0 1 2 3 4
v1 = 0 1 2 3 4
```

1. Explicit operator=

```
v2 = 0 1 2 3 4
v1 = -99 1 2 3 4
```

2. Default operator=

Notice in output 2 that a change to v2 produces a change to v1! When the default operator= function is used, the highlighted assignment statement performs a ***shallow copy***, copying *just the pointer to the array* data member, resulting in v1 and v2 sharing the same array of elements! On the other hand, the operator= function that we wrote earlier in this section performs a ***deep copy***, copying the elements of the array data member so that v1 and v2 have separate copies of the array data member.

■ **QUESTION** **(Implementing** resize**)** Using techniques similar to that for doubling the size of an array (see Section 22.4), how should you complete the missing lines of resize?

```
void Simple_vector::resize (int newsz)
{
    EltType* new_items = new EltType[newsz];
    for (int i=0; i<length() && i<newsz; i++)
        _____ ;

    delete [] Elts;

    _____ ;

    size = newsz;
}
```

Answer The completed lines are

```
    new_items[i] = Elts[i];
  Elts = new_items;
```

■ ■■

Function Notation for Calling operator[] Until now, we have not had occasion to overload the subscript operator, []. Understanding the declaration of an overloaded operator is made easier by translating a "call" to that operator from operator notation into function notation.

■ **QUESTION** Given that v is of type Simple_vector, how would you rewrite the expression v[i] using operator notation?

Answer v[i] is equivalent to v.operator[](i).

■ ■■

Implementing the Subscript Operators The vector component v[index] is stored in cell index of the array data member Elts provided that index is a valid subscript. Thus, the operator[] function has only to check that index is in range and then, accordingly, display either a "subscript out of bounds" error message or return Elts[index]. Because the range checking is handled by the private member function, check _range, the complete implementation is simply

```
EltType& Simple_vector::operator [] (int index)
{
    check_range(index);
    return Elts[index];
}
```

■ QUESTION   What is the missing condition of the private member function, check
_range?

```
void Simple_vector::check_range (int index) const
{
    if (_____)
        {
        cerr << "\n***ERROR: Subscript [" << index
                << "] out of range (" << 0 << ".."
                << (size-1) << ")\n";
        exit(1);
        }
}
```

Answer   The missing condition is index < 0 || index >= size   ■ ■

The const **Versions of** operator[]   Notice that the Simple_vector
class interface also provides a const version of operator[]. It may seem
redundant to provide this second version, because the non-const version
permits a client program either to modify or simply to access a vector
element. However, providing both versions of operator[] is a standard
practice, that is intended to strictly enforce the distinction between accessor and modifier member functions.

Consider the following "free" function, display, from tst_vct1.cpp.

```
void display (const Simple_vector& v)
{
    for (int i=0; i<v.length(); i++)
        cout << v[i] << ' ';
    cout << endl;
}
```

If no const version of operator[] is provided, the highlighted subscripting
operation, v[i], produces the compiler warning "Non-const function
Simple_vector::operator[](int) called for const object." The const
object in question is the parameter v that has been passed by const
reference.

22.6   The Copy Constructor and the Destructor

You have seen that every class has an assignment operator that, if not
explicitly provided by the class implementor, will be generated automati-

cally by the compiler. There are two more such member functions, the *copy constructor* and the *destructor.* The reason why we must provide our own version of these functions for the `Simple_vector` class is that the compiler-provided defaults are inadequate for any class that has dynamically allocated data members.

The Role of the Copy Constructor The copy constructor comes into play in these situations:

1. An argument is passed to a function by value, or a function returns a result by value. In both cases, the copy constructor handles the task of creating the copy.

2. An object declaration specifies an initial value, as in the two equivalent statements:

   ```
   Fraction f(g); // f is initialized to g's value
   Fraction f=g; // alternate syntax
   ```

   (*Note:* Be aware that the second statement is *not* an assignment statement — it is an alternate syntax for constructing f by copy from g.)

3. An initializer list is used in the definition of a constructor. For example, in the `Simple_vector` class's no-argument constructor definition,

   ```
   Simple_vector::Simple_vector()
      : size(0), Elts(NULL)
      { }
   ```

   the highlighted initializers are actually copy constructor calls. The first initializes `size` to 0, and the second initializes `Elts` to `NULL`.

Syntax and Action of the Default Copy Constructor For a class, `class_type`, the general form for the default copy constructor declaration is

   ```
   class_type (const class_type& P);
   ```

and the action is to construct each data member from the corresponding data member of the parameter P.

   Thus, for the `Simple_vector` class, we can achieve the same effect as the compiler-provided default copy constructor by placing the following code in the `Simple_vector` class interface.

```
Simple_vector (const Simple_vector& v)
    : size(v.size), Elts(v.Elts)
    { }
```

This is inadequate because the construction, `Elts(v.Elts)`, merely copies the *pointer* to v's dynamically allocated array of elements — it does not allocate memory for and copy the elements themselves. Thus, the intended "copy" is in reality just another name, or alias, for the argument passed to the constructor.

Implementing the `Simple_vector` **Class Copy Constructor**   A correct implementation of the `Simple_vector` class's copy constructor, from `smp_vct2.h`, is

```
Simple_vector::Simple_vector(const Simple_vector& v)
    : size(v.size), Elts (new EltType[v.size])
{
    for(int i = 0; i < size; i++)
        Elts[i] = v.Elts[i];
}
```

Because the body of this constructor contains a `for` loop for element-by-element copying, the implementation should be given outside the class interface, necessitating the scope resolution in the function header.

The Role of the Destructor   When a variable or object goes out of scope, a *de*structor undoes the work that went into *con*structing the variable or object. (Recall that local variables of a function "cease to exist" when the function call terminates.) *A C++ programmer cannot write an explicit call to a destructor.* Instead, the compiler automatically generates a destructor call each time a local variable or object will cease to exist.

Syntax and Action of the Default Destructor   For a class, `class_type`, the general form for the default destructor declaration is

>   `~class_type ( );`

and the action is to execute the destructor for each data member of the class.

Because destructors cannot be called explicitly, but instead are called implicitly, we can achieve the effect of the compiler-provided default destructor for the `Simple_vector` class by placing the code

```
~Simple_vector ( )
{
    // destructors for size and Elts execute
}
```

in the public section of the `Simple_vector` class interface. (The comment is intended to convey the fact that the constructors for `size` and `Elts` are executed at the end of the body of the destructor, though we see no explicit call.)

Implementing a Correct `Simple_vector` ***Class Destructor*** Because `Elts` is a pointer to a dynamically allocated array, which should eventually be deallocated, a correct destructor will delete this array before the destructor for the variable `Elts` executes. Thus, a correct implementation, if given outside the class interface, would be

`Simple_vector` **Destructor, from** *`smp_vct2.h`*

```
Simple_vector::~Simple_vector()
{
    delete [] Elts;
    // destructors for size and Elts execute
}
```

The `Vector` ***Class Template*** You have now seen the complete details of implementing the `Simple_vector` class. The code for the `Vector` class given in the file `bavector.h` at the PWS Web site is exactly the same except for the extra syntax require for templating.

■ Exercises

1. Draw memory just before execution of each of the output statements in the following code fragment, then give the output of the fragment.

```
char *r, *s, *t;
r = new char; *r = 'R';
s = new char; *s = 'S';
cout << *r << ' ' << *s << endl;
t = r; r = s; s = t;
cout << *r << ' ' << *s << endl;
```

2. Draw memory just before execution of the `delete` statement in the code fragment at right. Explain what happens when the `delete` statement executes.

```
float* fp;
float x = 9.9;
fp = &x;
cout << *fp << endl;
delete fp;
```

3. Draw memory after execution of each of the highlighted assignment statements in the code fragment at right, and give the output produced by the fragment. What pointer variable problem is created by the next-to-last assignment statement?

```
String *p, *q;
p = new String;
q = new String;
*p = "Smith";
*q = *p;
cout << *p << " " << *q << endl;
*p = "Jones";
cout << *p << " " << *q << endl;
p = q;
*q = "Adams";
cout << *p << " " << *q << endl;
```

4. Give the output, if any, of the following code fragments and explain what problem associated with pointer variables is illustrated by the fragments.

(a)
```
int *p;
p = new int;
delete p;
*p = 77;
cout << *p;
```

(b)
```
int *p, *q;
q = new int;
p = q;
delete p;
*q = 0;
cout << *p << ' ' << *q;
```

5. Explain what a dangling pointer reference is and why it can cause problems.

6. What is wrong with the code fragment at right? What error messages does your compiler produce for it? What small change will make the code compile correctly?

```
int* r, s;
r = NULL;
s = new int;
*s = 0;
```

7. What is happening in disguised form in the highlighted statement in the code fragment at right?

```
Fraction f(2,5), *p;
p = &f;
// .. several statements
f = *p;
```

8. For the improved `Time_piece` class presented in Sections 18.3 and 19.3, write explicit versions of (a) the no-argument and copy constructors, (b) the destructor, and (c) the assignment operator. Your versions of these functions should be equivalent to the compiler-provided defaults that were used in those sections.

9. Given that the base address of array `x` is 285156832 (decimal), give the output of the following code fragment.

```
double x[4];
for (int i=0; i<4; i++)
    cout << (unsigned long)(x+i) << endl;
```

10. Without using the subscript operator `[]`, write a `for` loop to assign values entered from the keyboard to `x[0]`, `x[1]`, `x[2]`, and `x[3]`, then write a second `for` loop to display the contents of these cells, one value per line.

11. **(Cascading)**   Determine the output of the following code fragment, then rewrite it without using cascading.

```
String s, t("A string");;
(s = t).insert(2, "short ");
cout << s << endl;
s.remove(8, 7))+=("example.");
cout << s << endl;
```

Programming Problems

12. Write a program that uses a dynamically allocated array, whose size is specified by the user at run-time, to store strings entered by the user, then output them one per line in sorted order.

13. Write a program that uses a dynamically allocated array to store an arbitrary number of integers entered from the keyboard, then display them, 10 per line, each right aligned in a column of width seven. Begin with an array of size 8 and increase the size of the array in increments of 8 whenever more space is required for storage.

Longer Assignments

14. Do Exercise 14.21 using a dynamically allocated array rather than a vector.

15. Redo the `List` class template of Chapter 21 using an array rather than a vector for the `Elts` data member. You will need to write explicit versions of the copy constructor, the destructor, and the assignment operator. Also,

overload the subscript operator [] so that the following pairs of statements are equivalent.

Statement	**Equivalent**
`item = L.retrieve (pos);` `L.replace (pos, elt);`	`item = L[pos];` `L[pos] = elt;`

Write short client programs to test all the member functions.

16. Implement the `Set` class template described in Exercise 21.20 using a dynamically allocated array rather than a vector. Because dynamic memory is involved, you will need to write the copy constructor, the destructor, and the assignment operator.

23

Linked Lists

In this chapter we apply pointer variables and dynamic memory allocation to the task of constructing and manipulating linked lists. For most of the chapter, we focus on the syntax and algorithms for handling linked lists, and we write the code in the form of free functions. In the final section, we combine most of the material that we have developed to create an ordered linked list class template.

23.1 Introduction to Linked Lists

Dynamic Data Structures and Pointers Data structures whose size can change at run-time are said to be ***dynamic***. In Chapters 13 and 15, you saw how to make a Vector or Matrix object grow or shrink by calling the Vector or Matrix class's resize member function. We have also discussed the fact that a String object automatically grows or shrinks to accommodate the characters of the string, with no special work required by the programmer. An Int_List object (see Chapters 18 and 19) also resizes itself automatically as elements are inserted into or removed from the list.

Pointer variables and the new and delete operators are the C++ features that permit the creation of dynamic data structures. One such structure is the linked list. A ***linked list*** consists of ***nodes***. Each node, in turn, consists of data and a pointer that, in most cases, links the node to another node. The following figure gives a depiction of a linked list, with pointers shown as arrows.

Linked Lists Versus Vectors   Although linked lists, like vectors, can grow or shrink to accommodate the data they store, the linked list has one particular advantage over the vector. Suppose we have a vector, names, of 100 last names, sorted alphabetically, and we wish to insert the name "Beck", in order, into names. The following diagram illustrates that before this new entry can be inserted, the contents of cells 2 through 99 will all have to be shifted to the right.

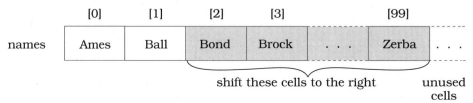

By contrast, if the original 100 names had been stored in an alphabetically ordered linked list, then "Beck" could be inserted much more efficiently by carrying out the following three steps.

1. Create a new node and assign "Beck" to it.

2. Make the arrow from the node containing "Beck" point to the node containing "Bond".

3. Redirect the arrow from the node containing "Ball" so that it points to the node containing "Beck" rather than the node containing "Bond".

The following diagram illustrates the linked list after these three steps have been performed.

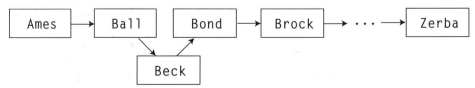

23.2 Pointers to Structs and Classes

A pointer may point to a struct or a class variable. For example, suppose the struct type student_str is declared as follows.

```
struct student_str
    {
    String name;
    int IQ;
    };
```

Then, the following two statements will cause memory to appear as shown.

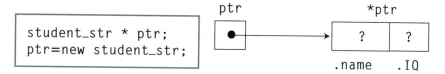

```
student_str * ptr;
ptr=new student_str;
```

The following statements will then assign values to the student_str memory cell, *ptr, as indicated.

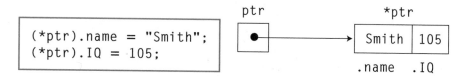

```
(*ptr).name = "Smith";
(*ptr).IQ = 105;
```

CAUTION The parentheses in (*ptr).name are necessary because the dot operator has higher precedence than the dereferencing operator, *.

The -> Operator C++ provides a convenient form of the dereferencing operator, ->, sometimes called the **arrow operator**, that both dereferences a pointer to a struct and accesses a data member of the struct. Using this operator, the preceding two statements can be rewritten as

```
ptr->name = "Smith";
ptr->IQ = 105;
```

■ **QUESTION** Using the -> operator, how should you write a statement to output the name and IQ data members, separated by a space, of the struct pointed to by ptr?

Answer cout << ptr->name << ' ' << ptr->IQ;

Pointers to String Objects The following code fragment and its output show how the -> operator can be used with a String object to call String class member functions.

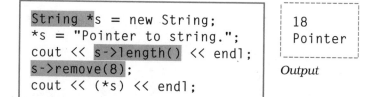

```
String *s = new String;
*s = "Pointer to string.";
cout << s->length() << endl;
s->remove(8);
cout << (*s) << endl;
```

18
Pointer

Output

23.3 Creating a Linked List

For simplicity, let us begin by creating a linked list containing three names. Each name will be contained in a *node*, as shown below.

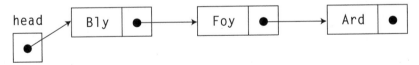

Notice that the last node in the list does not point to any other node. Instead, it contains the NULL pointer, which we depict simply as ●. The NULL pointer is used here as an end-of-list sentinel, which will permit us to use a loop to process an existing linked list.

Defining a Node Type A node that contains a String data member and a pointer to another node is defined as follows.

```
struct NodeType
    {
    String name;
    NodeType *next;
    };
```

Note that in defining NodeType, it is necessary to refer to the type, NodeType, in the declaration of the pointer data member, next! This seemingly circuitous definition is perfectly legal.

■ **EXAMPLE**   We want to write a program to create the linked list shown at the beginning of this section. We use two additional pointer variables:

1. head will point to the first node in the list.

2. last will be repeatedly updated to point to the current last node of the list.

Execution of the following three statements will produce the memory configuration shown at right. (The ? in the node containing Bly indicates that the pointer data member of that node is an uninitialized (garbage) value.)

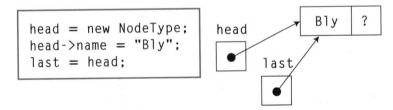

Here is the full program.

```cpp
// create.cpp
#include <iostream.h>
#include "baString.h"

struct NodeType
    {
    String name;
    NodeType *next;
    };

void main()
{
    NodeType *head, *last, *tmp;

    head = new NodeType;      // create first node
    head->name = "Bly";       // fill it
    last = head;              // update last

    tmp = new NodeType;       // create new node
    tmp->name = "Foy";        // fill it
    last->next = tmp;         // link previous node to it
    last = tmp;               // update last

    tmp = new NodeType;       // same as previous 4 lines
    tmp->name = "Ard";        // but with Ard
    last->next = tmp;
    last = tmp;

    last->next = NULL;        // sentinel

    Processing of this linked list would go here.

}
```

■ **QUESTION** Here is a snapshot of memory after the first five assignment statements of the main function of create.cpp have executed.

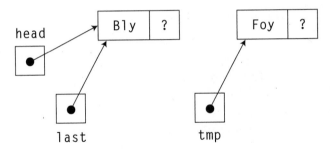

How would you draw a snapshot of memory after execution of

   1.   the sixth statement, `last->next = tmp;`, and

   2.   the seventh statement, `last = tmp;`?

Answer   **1.**   The statement `last->next = tmp;` links the node pointed to by tmp to the list.

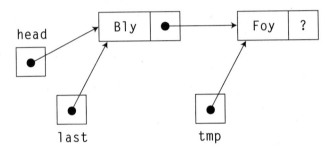

   2.   The statement `last = tmp;` redirects `last` so that it points to the current last node of the list.

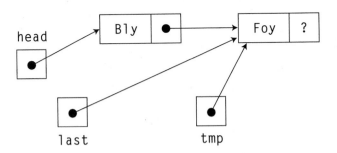

■ **QUESTION**   **1.**   How would you draw a snapshot of memory after execution of the next three statements?

   2.   What effect will the final two statements have?

Answer **1.**

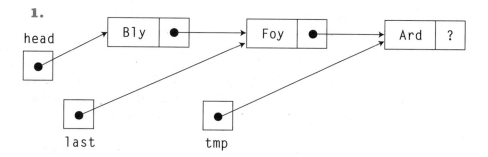

2. The next to last statement will redirect `last` so that it points to the node containing "Ard", and the final statement will set the pointer in the node containing "Ard" to NULL. ■ ■■

■ **QUESTION** What would be output if `ptr` were declared to be of type `NodeType*` and the following two lines were added at the bottom of program `create.cpp`?

```
ptr = head->next;
cout << ptr->name;
```

Answer This would output `Foy` because the assignment statement would cause `ptr` to point to the second node. ■ ■■

23.4 Traversing a Linked List

Traversing a linked list means accessing each of the nodes in the list. In the function `display`, we traverse a linked list of names, printing out each name in the list.

Note that the function must receive the pointer variable that holds the address of the first node of the list. (`NodeType` is as defined earlier.)

```
void display (NodeType *head)
{
    NodeType *ptr = head;
    while (ptr!=NULL)
        {
        cout << ptr->name << endl;
        ptr=ptr->next;
        }
}
```

Let us trace the values of ptr through this loop. Initially ptr is assigned the value of head so that it points to the first node of the list. Each time through the loop, the last statement of the loop body, ptr = ptr->next;, makes ptr point to the next node of the list. This is similar to incrementing a control variable using the statement i=i+1; or i++;. Finally, the loop is exited when ptr takes on the value NULL, which is stored in the pointer data member of the last node of the list.

List Traversal Using a *for* **Loop** The following for loop achieves the initialization, test, and increment just discussed and can be used to implement the body of the display function.

```
NodeType *ptr;
for (ptr=head; ptr!=NULL; ptr=ptr->next)
    cout << ptr->name << endl;
```

23.5   Creating a List Using a Loop

Suppose the file names.dat contains several last names, one per line, as depicted at right.

```
Day
West
Ax
Chen
```

■ **PROBLEM** Fill in the missing blanks in program create2.cpp to create the following linked list.

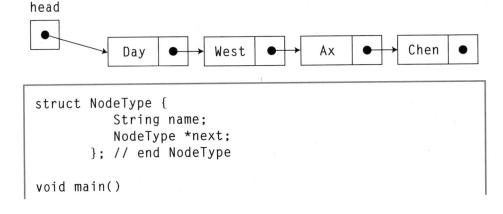

head

```
struct NodeType {
        String name;
        NodeType *next;
    }; // end NodeType

void main()
```

```
{
    NodeType *head, *last, *temp;
    ifstream names_in;
    names_in.open("names.dat");
    assert (!names_in.fail());

    head = NULL;
    while (names_in>>ws && !names_in.eof())
        if (head==NULL) // create and fill first node
            {
            head = new NodeType;      // create first node
            names_in >> head->name;   // fill it
            last = head;              // update last
            }
        else // create, fill, and link a new node
            {
            temp = new NodeType;      // create new node
            names_in >> temp->name;   // fill it
            _____; // link previous node to it
            _____;       // update last
            }

    if (head!=NULL)
        _____;        // sentinel

    names_in.close();

    // Traverse the list
    for (temp=head; temp!=NULL; temp=temp->next)
        cout << temp->name << endl;
}
```

Solution   The completed lines are

```
        last->next = temp; // link previous node to it
        last = temp;    // update last
  last->next = NULL;      // sentinel
```

Discussion

1. Note that if the file names.dat were empty, then the list head created by the statement head = NULL; is called the NULL list, and can be depicted as shown at right.

2. In Exercise 23.10, you are asked to write an interactive program that uses a loop to create a linked list.

23.6   More Linked List Operations

In this section, we write functions to destroy a linked list, compare two linked lists for equality, and copy one linked list to another. For the destroy and copy functions, we need to pass pointer variables as reference parameters, which brings up some initially strange-looking syntax.

Pointers as Reference Parameters   Recall that the display function of Section 23.4 had a parameter, head, of type NodeType*. The argument in the call to display must also be of type NodeType*, and the value of this argument, (the address of a node) is copied into the parameter head — that is, it is passed by value. To indicate that a pointer is to be passed by reference, the & operator is placed after the data type, NodeType*. Thus, the declaration

```
void destroy (NodeType*& head);
```

specifies that head is a reference parameter of type NodeType*. (This is read "NodeType pointer reference.")

Destroy   To destroy a linked list, we will repeatedly remove the first node of the list and delete it, making it available for subsequent allocation.

```
void destroy (NodeType*& head) // in-out
{
    NodeType* temp;
    while (head!=NULL)
        {
        temp = head;
        head = head->next;
        delete temp;
        }
}
```

Comparing for Equality   If two linked lists are equal, then, as we traverse them one node at a time, we should see that the contents of the current nodes of each list are equal, and we must reach the ends of the two lists simultaneously.

```
bool are_equal (NodeType* head1, NodeType* head2)
{
    NodeType *p1 = head1, *p2 = head2;;
    while (p1 != NULL && p2 != NULL)
```

```
        {
        if (p1->name != p2->NAME)
            return false;
        p1 = p1->next;
        p2 = p2->next;
        }
    return (p1==NULL && p2==NULL);
}
```

Copy Copying a source list, pointed to by `head_src`, to a destination list, pointed to by `head_dst`, requires that we traverse the source list, appending a copy of each node of the source list to the end of the destination list. We keep pointers `last_dst` and `next_src` pointing to the last node of the destination list and to the next node of the source list, respectively. We treat as special cases an empty and a one-node source list.

```cpp
void copy (NodeType*& head_dst, NodeType* head_src)
{
    if (head_dst == head_src) // don't copy to self!
        return;

    destroy(head_dst);  // recycle nodes of dest list
    if (head_src == NULL) // nothing to copy
        return;

    // copy first node
    head_dst = new NodeType;
    head_dst->next = NULL;
    head_dst->name = head_src->name;

    // copy rest of nodes
    NodeType* last_dst = head_dst;
        // points to last node of dest list
    NodeType* next_src = head_src->next;
        // points to next node of src list
    while (next_src != NULL)
        {
        // append to the dst list a new node containing
        // the name in the next node of the src list
        NodeType* p = new NodeType;
        p->next = NULL;
        p->name = next_src->name;
        last_dst->next = p;
```

```
                // update pointers to end of dst list
                // and next node of src list
                last_dst = p;
                next_src = next_src->next;
                }
        }
```

23.7   Ordered Linked List Operations

In this section, we assume that we have an alphabetically ordered linked list of names. We give functions for inserting a name in the list and for removing a name from the list.

Inserting Between Two Linked Nodes   Suppose we want to insert a node between two nodes of a linked list. For example, suppose prev and curr (for previous and current) point to two linked nodes, and betw points to an unattached node as shown.

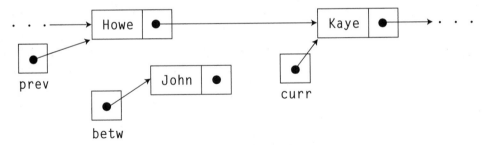

We want to attach the node that betw points to so that it is between the nodes that prev and curr point to.

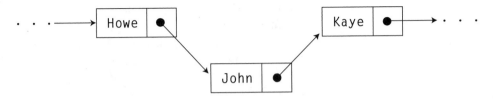

■ **QUESTION**   How should you fill in the blank in the second statement so that the following statements attach the node that betw points to, as depicted?

```
        betw->next = curr; // attaches betw on its right
        prev_____ = ____; // attaches betw on its left
```

Answer   prev->next = betw; // attaches betw on its left   ■ ■

Locating Where the New Node Goes In searching a linked list to insert a new name, we use the pointers prev and curr again. We start prev and curr at the beginning of the list. By the end of the search, prev and curr will point to the two nodes between which the new name is to be inserted.

An important step in searching the list is shifting both the prev and curr pointers one node to the right.

■ **QUESTION** Suppose prev and curr are as depicted here. Which of the following pairs of statements will shift both prev and curr one node to the right, so that prev will point to the node containing "Kaye", and curr will point to the node containing "Most"?

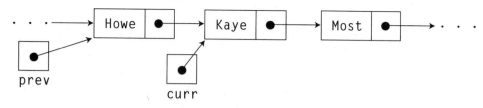

1. prev = curr;
   curr = curr->next;

2. curr = curr->next;
   prev = curr;

Answer Only statements 1 will work. Statements 2 would cause both prev and curr to point to the node containing "Most". ■ ▬

■ **QUESTION** **(Special Case: Searching when** key_name **is known** *not* **to be on the list)**

1. How should you fill in the blank so that prev and curr point to the two nodes between which the node containing key_name should be inserted?

2. If key_name goes at the beginning of the list, where will curr and prev point by the end of the code fragment given next in part 3?

3. If key_name goes at the end of the list, where will curr and prev point by the end of the following code fragment?

```
prev = NULL;
curr = head;
while (curr != NULL)
    {
    if (key_name _____)
        break; // out of loop
```

```
        prev = curr; // shift
        curr = curr->next; // shift
        }
```

Answer

1. `if (key_name <= curr->name)`

2. `curr` will point to the same node as `head`, and `prev` will be `NULL`.

3. `curr` will have the value `NULL`, and `prev` will point to the last node of the list (if there is one). ■ ▬▬

General Case In the general case, `key_name` might be new or it might already be on the list. The general `search` function should have three reference parameters, `prev`, `curr`, and `on_list`; it will return true for `on_list` if `key_name` is on the list, and false if it is not.

```
void search (NodeType* head,   // in
             String key_name,  // in
             NodeType*& prev,  // out
             NodeType*& curr,  // out
             bool& on_list)    // out
{
   prev = NULL;
   curr = head;
   while (curr != NULL)
      {
      if (key_name <= curr->name)
         break; // out of loop
      prev = curr; // shift
      curr = curr->next; // shift
      }
   on_list = (curr != NULL) &&
             (curr->name == key_name);
}
```

■ **QUESTION**

1. If `key_name` is on the list, which of the pointers, `curr` or `prev`, will point to the node containing `key_name` when the `search` function completes execution?

2. If `key_name` is the first name on the list, what values will `curr` and `prev` have when the `search` function completes execution?

Answer
1. curr will point to the node containing key_name.

2. prev will be NULL, and curr will point to the same node as head.

REMARK An exact match of two names requires that neither have any trailing spaces. The Rtrim function, discussed in Section 16.6, can be used to remove any trailing spaces before searching.

The *insert* Function The insert function takes the head pointer and the alleged new name as parameters. The first step of insert is to call search. If search determines that new_name is already on the list, a message will be printed; otherwise, a new node is created for it, and this node, pointed to by betw, is attached. Note that the code for attaching the node that betw points to depends on whether or not this node is to be inserted at the beginning of the list.

```
void insert (NodeType*& head, // in-out
             String new_name) // in
{
   NodeType *prev, *curr, *betw;
   bool on_list;

   search (head, new_name, prev, curr, on_list);
   if (on_list)
      {
      cout << "\t" << new_name
           << " is already on the list.\n";
      return;
      }
   betw = new NodeType;
   betw->name = new_name;
   if (curr ==head) // insert at head of list
      {
      betw->next = head;
      head = betw;
      }
   else                    // insert in middle or at end
      {
      betw->next = curr;
      prev->next = betw;
      }
}
```

■ **QUESTION**　Why is head a reference parameter?

Answer　Because new_name might be inserted at the beginning of the list. In this and only this case would insert change the value of head.　■ ■■

■ **QUESTION**　Why can the same code handle insertions on the middle of and at the end of the list, yet different code is required for an insertion at the beginning of the list?

Answer　When new_name goes at the beginning of the list, the insertion cannot be handled in terms of prev and curr, because prev would have the value NULL and prev->next would not exist. When new_name goes in the middle of or at the end of the list, prev would not be NULL, so prev->next would exist.　■ ■■

The remove **Function**　To remove a node, we begin by calling the search function. If key_name is on the list, search will make curr point to the node that contains key_name — that is, the node to be removed. Before deleting that node, the node before it must be linked to the node after it. Two cases are possible for the position of the node to be removed: (1) It is at the head of the list or (2) it is somewhere in the middle or at the end of the list.

　　Let us consider an example of case (2). Suppose the node containing "Fish" is to be removed. Then, after a call to search, memory would contain

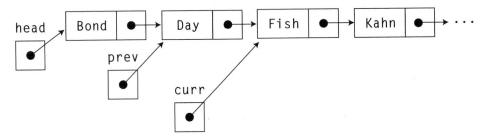

■ **QUESTION**　How should you fill in the blanks to complete function remove?

```
void remove (NodeType*& head, // in-out
             String key_name) // in
{
    NodeType *prev, *curr;
    bool on_list;
```

```
      search (head, key_name, prev, curr, on_list);
      if (!on_list)
         {
         cout << "\t" << key_name
              << " is not on the list.\n";
         return;
         }
      if (curr==head)
         _____;
      else
         _____;
      delete curr;
   }
```

Answer   The complete lines are

```
      head = curr->next;
      prev->next = curr->next;
```

23.8   An Ordered Linked List Class Template

In previous sections of this chapter our presentation of linked list operations has been in the form of pseudocode and free functions. In this section, we incorporate many of these algorithms into an ordered linked list class template. As you will see, the algorithms remain the same, but careful thought must be given to the design of the class, particularly what to make public and what to make private.

Ord_link_list **Class Public Member Functions**   The public section of the Ord_link_list class template's interface is

```
template <class EType>
class Ord_link_list
{
public:
   // constructors and destructor
   Ord_link_list(); // create an empty list
   Ord_link_list (const Ord_link_list& L); // copy constr.
   ~Ord_link_list();
```

```
// assignment
Ord_link_list& operator= (const Ord_link_list& Rhs);

// accessors
bool contains (const EType& elt) const;
    // return true if elt is on list; else false
EType get_data (int i) const;
    // return a copy of the data portion of the ith node
int position (const EType& elt) const;
    // determine the list position of the first
    // node containing elt
bool is_empty() const {return len==0; }
int length() const { return len; }

// modifiers
void destroy ();
    // Deallocate all nodes of the linked
    // list starting at head.
void insert (const EType& elt);
    // If elt is not in the linked list, insert it.
void remove (const EType& elt);
    // If elt is in the linked list, remove it.

// output
void display (ostream& outs=cout) const;
    // Traverse the linked list.

// == and !=
bool operator== (const Ord_link_list& Rhs) const;
bool operator!= (const Ord_link_list& Rhs) const;
```

Because dynamic memory is used for the linked list, the usual copy constructor, destructor, and assignment operator must be provided in place of the compiler-provided defaults. The member functions destroy, insert, remove, display, and operator== are nearly identical to their free function counterparts destroy, insert, remove, traverse, and are_equal, respectively. Notice, however, that each member function has one less parameter than its free counterpart, because the pointer to the head of the list will become a private member of the class, and is always passed implicitly rather than explicitly. Also, the String parameter of several free functions has been replaced by a generic Etype parameter that is passed by constant reference for efficiency.

Ord_link_list **Class Private Members**   The private section of the Ord_link_list class template's interface is

```
private:
   struct NodeType {
            EType    data;
            NodeType* next;
         }; // end NodeType

   NodeType* head; // ptr to first node of list
   int len;        // length of list

   void copy (const Ord_link_list& Rhs);
   // copy Rhs list to calling list

   void search (const EType& elt,
               NodeType*& prev,
               NodeType*& curr,
               bool& on_list) const;
}; // end Ord_link_list class interface
```

Design Decisions   Notice that the NodeType struct that was defined globally in previous sections of this chapter is now encapsulated in the class.
We do this because a client program will not directly manipulate pointers
or nodes. As promised, head, the pointer to the head of the list, is now a
private data member that a client program cannot directly alter. Making
the list length a data member, len, saves the expense of traversing the
list to count nodes whenever a client calls the length accessor function.

The copy and search functions are nearly identical to the free functions of the same names, discussed in detail earlier. The copy constructor
and assignment operator both call copy and, because a client program
can copy a list by using assignment, there is no need to make copy public.
Making it public would not violate encapsulation, but it would clutter
the public interface by adding a redundant function. The search function,
which is called by public functions insert, remove, and contains, has
been made private for purposes of encapsulation. Making search public
would require NodeType to be public (because of the NodeType* reference
parameters), opening the door for client programs to manipulate links
directly. Exercise 23.6 asks you to explain what kinds of problems this
direct manipulation might produce.

Making search private does introduce another design problem, however. A client program will need to locate nodes in order to retrieve the
data in the node. If the location is not given by a pointer, it must be given
by a list position. Thus, accessor functions position and retrieve are
provided for locating the position of a node containing specific data, and
for retrieving a copy of the complete data element. Exercises 23.7 and 23.8

ask you to discuss the advantages and disadvantages of this approach to retrieving and updating the data in a node.

Implementation Details The complete `Ord_link_list` class interface and implementation is available at the PWS Web site in the file `olnklst.h`. We do not discuss the details of the member functions here because most of the code is similar to that of the free functions presented earlier in the chapter. The exercises ask you to consider how you would implement a few of the member functions given the free functions and other information about the private members.

■ Exercises

1. Given that `head` points to a linked list of nodes of type `NodeType` (as defined in Section 23.3), write code fragments to perform these tasks.
   - (a) Count the number of items in the list.
   - (b) Make `last` point to the last node of the list, or `NULL` if the list is empty.
   - (c) Remove the first node from the list.
   - (d) Add a new node containing `"Vark"` to the front of the list.

2. Write declarations for functions that perform the tasks of the previous exercise.

3. Write a code fragment that creates the following linked list:

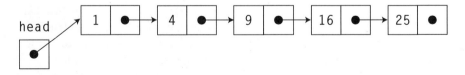

by using a `for` loop with header:
   - (a) `for (int i=5; i>0; i--)`
   - (b) `for (int i=1; i<=5; i++)`

4. Write a function, `prev_ptr`, that returns a pointer to the node immediately before the node pointed to by its parameter.

5. Suppose `p` and `q` are of type `Time_piece*`. (See the Time _piece class interface in Section 18.2.) Give the output of the code fragment at right.

```
p = new Time_piece;
q = new Time_piece;
q->set(3,30,'A');
*p = *q;
q->update(5,30);
p->display(); cout << endl;
(*q).display(); cout << endl;
```

6. Describe two problems that could occur if the private `search` function of the `Ord_link_list` class were made public.

7. How does the efficiency of the `List` class's `retrieve` function compare with that of the `Ord_link_list` class's `retrieve` function?

8. In the following fragment from program `chng_ext.cpp` of Section 21.4, `entry` is of type `Phone_entry` and `phone_list` is of type `List<Phone_entry>`.

```
cout << "Time to update all phone extensions!\n ";
for (int i=1; i<=phone_list.length(); i++)
   {
   entry = phone_list.retrieve(i);
   entry.change_extension(1000 + 10*i);
   phone_list.replace(i, entry);
   }
```

(a) If `phone_list` were of type `Ord_link_list<Phone_entry>`, how would you rewrite the fragment using the `Ord_link_list` class's `retrieve`, `remove`, and `insert` functions?

(b) Compare the efficiency of the two list classes in terms of updating the data in a node.

(c) Discuss the advantages and disadvantages of adding a `replace` member function to the `Ord_link_list` class? Why is this function less problematic for the `List` class?

9. Write the implementations of the following `Ord_link_list` class member functions.

    (a) `operator=`   *Note*: The class's private `copy` function guards against self-assignment.

    (b) `operator==`   *Hint*: Consider the free `are_equal` function of Section 23.6.

    (c) `destroy`   *Hint*: Consider the free `destroy` function of Section 23.6.

    (d) `position`   Why is the `search` function not useful here?

Programming Problems

10. Modify program `create2.cpp` from Section 23.5 so that it creates a linked list of names entered interactively.

11. Use a linked list to display the binary equivalent of a decimal number.

12. Write a function to reverse a linked list "in place." That is, you will create no new nodes — just rearrange the pointers to existing nodes.

13. Suppose the data in each node of a linked list is a struct containing a person's name and age.

(a) Write a function that will make two traversals of the list to delete the node for the first person with the minimum age.

(b) Write a function that will make two traversals of the list to delete the nodes for all people with the minimum age.

14. Write the functions described in the previous exercise, but make only one traversal of the list in each function.

15. Modify the "early exit" version of the bubble sort (from Section 14.4) to sort a linked list.

16. Rewrite program `frac_ex2.cpp` of Section 18.5 with variables f, g, and h declared to be of type `Fraction*`.

Longer Assignments

17. (a) Rewrite program `get_ext.cpp` of Section 21.5 by making `phone_list` an ordered linked list object.

(b) Write a third part of the program to allow the user to update the list by inserting several more phone entries.

18. Do Exercise 20.12 using the `Ord_link_list` class of the chapter.

19. (a) Implement the `Card_pile` class of Section 20.4 using a linked list rather than a vector.

(b) Test your `Card_pile` class by using it to do either of Exercises 20.14 or 20.15.

(c) What advantages does the linked list-based implementation have over the vector-based implementation? Are there disadvantages?

20. Implement the `Set` class template described in Exercise 21.20 using an ordered linked list rather than a vector.

24

Stacks and Queues

S tacks and queues are abstract data types that are of fundamental importance in computer science, not only for their application to a variety of external problems, but also for implementing internal computer operations. For example, compiler implementations use stacks for evaluating expressions and for managing the details of function calls and returns. Queues are used to manage requests for computer resources (processors, printers, etc.) in multiprocessing systems and for other kinds of resources such as airline reservations. The very complex algorithms for routing information through large computer networks and the conglomeration of networks known as the Internet involve many data structures including stacks and queues.

In this chapter we discuss (1) the use of a stack class, including its application to the evaluation of expressions written in *postfix notation*; (2) the use of a queue class and its application to simulation problems; (3) the implementations, using linked lists, of the stack and queue classes; and (4) the use of vectors rather than linked lists for implementing the stack and queue classes.

24.1 Behavior of Stacks and Queues

Both stacks and queues obey strict rules, or disciplines, for insertion, removal, and access of elements. Informally, a stack is like a pile of plates — individual plates are placed on or taken off of the top of the pile only. A queue is like a waiting line — people enter only at the back of the line and leave from the front. (We assume no line jumping or premature exits!)

Stack Behavior A *stack* is a data structure that obeys a ***last-in, first-out (LIFO)*** discipline — the *last* item put *in* the stack will be the *first* taken *out*. That is, items can only be *inserted* at and *removed* from one end of the stack, called the *top*. It is possible to "view," or *access*, the item at the *top* of the stack without removing it. Additionally, it is possible to determine whether the stack is *empty*, to determine its *length* (or size), and to *make* the stack *empty*.

Initially empty stack after inserting `'R'`, *then* `'A'`, *then* `'M'`.

`'M'`	← top
`'A'`
`'R'`

Above stack after removing one item, then inserting `'T'`, *then* `'S'`.

`'S'`	← top
`'T'`
`'A'`
`'R'`

Four consecutive remove operations will then remove, in order, `'S'`, `'T'`, `'A'`, and then `'R'`, leaving the stack empty.

Queue Behavior A *queue* is a data structure that obeys a ***first-in, first-out (FIFO)*** discipline — the *first* item put *in* the stack will be the *first* taken *out*. That is, items can only be *inserted* at one end, called the *rear* or *tail*, of the queue, and *removed* from the other end, called the *front*, of the queue. It is possible to "view," or *access*, the item at the *front* of the queue without removing it. Additionally, it is possible to determine whether the queue is *empty*, to determine its *length*, and to *make* the queue *empty*.

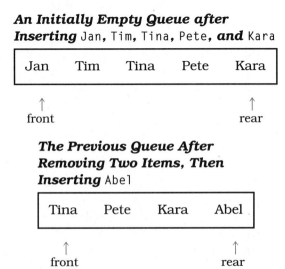

An Initially Empty Queue after Inserting Jan, Tim, Tina, Pete, ***and*** Kara

Jan	Tim	Tina	Pete	Kara

↑ front   ↑ rear

The Previous Queue After Removing Two Items, Then Inserting Abel

Tina	Pete	Kara	Abel

↑ front   ↑ rear

Four consecutive remove operations will then remove, in order, "Tina", "Pete", "Kara", and, finally, "Abel", leaving the queue empty.

Special Terminology for Insertion and Deletion The insert and delete operations on a stack are called ***push*** and ***pop***. (Think of a spring-loaded stack of plates in a cafeteria.) For a queue, the insert and re-move operations are called ***enqueue*** (pronounced "*N-Q*") and ***dequeue*** (pronounced "*D-Q*"), respectively.

24.2 Using a Stack Class

Because our stack and queue classes are implemented as linked lists using dynamic memory, we need to write explicit versions of the construc-tors, destructor, and assignment operators. A complete `Stack` class tem-plate interface (from `stackt.h`) follows that provides the member func-tions discussed in the previous section.

```
template <class EltType>
class Stack
{
public:
    // constructors and destructor
    Stack();                     // construct empty stack
    Stack(const Stack & S );  // copy constructor
    ~Stack(); // destructor

    // assignment
    const Stack & operator = ( const Stack & Rhs );

    // accessors
    const EltType& get_top() const;
        // return top element (NO pop)
    bool is_empty() const { return (top==NULL); }
    int  length()   const { return size; }

    // modifiers
    void push( const EltType & item );
        // push item onto top of stack
    void pop();
      // remove top element
    void make_empty();
        // make stack empty (no elements)
```

```
private:
   struct NodeType {
      EltType data;
      NodeType* next;
      };
   typedef NodeType* NodePtr;

   NodePtr top; // pointer to top element
   int size;    // of stack
};
```

Because the emphasis in this section is on *using* the class, you can ignore for now the information in the private section.

■ **EXAMPLE**   The following main function from usestack.cpp illustrates how the various Stack class member functions are called.

```
void main()
{
   Stack<char> char_stk;
   char ch;

   cout << "Enter characters (# to quit): ";
   cin >> ch;
   while (ch != '#')
      {
      char_stk.push (ch);
      cin >> ch;
      }
   cout << "You entered " << char_stk.length()
        << " characters.\n";

   // Display chars in reverse order of input
   cout << "In reverse order, they are: ";
   while (!char_stk.is_empty())
      {
      cout << char_stk.get_top(); // display top char
      char_stk.pop(); // then remove it from the stack
      }
}
```

A sample run of the program is

```
Enter characters (# to quit): QWERTY#
You entered 6 characters.
In reverse order, they are: YTREWQ
```

■ QUESTION **(Converting Decimal to Binary)** The algorithm for converting a decimal integer to binary by repeated division by two is discussed in Appendix F. The following diagram illustrates the process.

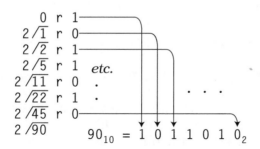

Notice that the remainders, produced from bottom left to top left, are, in effect, stacked up, with the first remainder produced being the last displayed, and the last remainder produced being the first displayed.

The following portion of the main function of dec2bin.cpp implements the algorithm just illustrated. How would you complete the Stack member function calls?

```
unsigned long N; // integer to convert
Stack<int> bits; // declare stack of int bits

cout << "Enter N>=0: "; cin >> N;
```

```
// Push bits, least significant first
do {
   bits._____; // push the remainder
   N = N/2;   // replace N by quotient
   }
while (N>0);

// Display and pop bits, most significant first
while (!_____) // there are more bits
   {
   cout << _____; // display top bit,
   _____; // then remove it from the stack
   }
cout << endl;
```

Answer   The completed calls are

```
        bits.push(N%2); // push the remainder
while (!bits.is_empty()) // there are  more bits
   cout << bits.get_top(); // display top bit,
   bits.pop(); // then remove it from the stack   ▪ ▬
```

24.3   Stacks and Postfix Expressions

You are accustomed to writing mathematical expressions in *infix* form — that is, with the operator between the operands, as in 2 + 5. However, other ways of writing this simple expression are possible. *Prefix*, or *Polish notation* (named after the Polish mathematician Lukasiewsz), places the operator before the operands, as in + 2 5, and *postfix*, or *reverse Polish notation (RPN)*, places the operator after the operands, as in 2 5 +.

Importance of Postfix Notation   Postfix notation is important in computer science for two reasons. First, unlike infix notation, postfix notation requires no parentheses for overriding the default operator precedence rules. Second, postfix expressions are easily evaluated using a stack. In fact, many handheld calculators, particularly earlier versions, use postfix notation precisely because a very simple stack-based architecture can evaluate postfix expressions easily. Further, compilers convert infix expression to postfix for efficient evaluation.

Evaluating Postfix Expressions by Hand   The following table illustrates the steps involved in evaluating an integer postfix expression by hand. On each line, the next expression to evaluate is highlighted.

Expression	Evaluate	Result
30 5 7 + 2 4 * − /	5 7 +	12
30 12 2 4 * − /	2 4 *	8
30 12 8 − /	12 8 −	4
30 4 /	30 4 /	7
7		

Notice that the preceding postfix expression is equivalent to the infix expression

    30 / ((5 + 7) - 2 * 4)

However, for postfix expressions, operator precedence rules are not relevant and, thus, parentheses are not necessary.

The preceding process for evaluating a postfix expression by hand is summarized in the following algorithm.

Algorithm for evaluating a postfix expression by hand

while (*the expression contains operators*)
    1. Scan the expression from left to right until an operator is found.
    2. Evaluate the postfix expression consisting of this operator and the two operands immediately to its left.
    3. Replace the two operands and the operator by this value.

Using a Stack to Evaluate Postfix Expressions The algorithm just given can easily be transformed into an algorithm for evaluating postfix expressions input from the keyboard. The algorithm uses a stack to store operands and the results of intermediate calculations. We refer to a string of contiguous non-whitespace characters as a *token*. A token will be either an operator, an operand, or the termination symbol, '#'.

Algorithm for using a stack to evaluate a postfix expression

Input a token.
while(*the token is not* '#')
    if(*the token is an operand*)
        Push the token onto the operand stack.
    else // *operand is an operator*
        Get the top two operands from the stack.

> *Apply the operator to the operands.*
> *Push the result onto the operand stack.*
> *Input the next token.*
> *Get the final value of the postfix expression from*
> *the top of the operand stack.*

The following table traces the evaluation of the postfix expression 2 5 9 + 11 - * , which is the infix equivalent of 2*((5+9)-11).

Token	Action(s)	Operand stack (bottom → top)
"2"	push (2)	2
"5"	push (5)	2 5
"9"	push (9)	2 5 9
"+"	get top(9), then pop()	2 5
	get_top(5), then pop()	2
	push (5 + 9)	2 14
"11"	push (11)	2 14 11
"-"	get_top(11), then pop()	2 14
	get_top(14), then pop()	2
	push (14 - 11)	2 3
"*"	get_top(3), then pop()	2
	get_top(2), then pop()	
	push (2 * 3)	6
"#"	get_top(6)	6

■ **EXAMPLE**   **(A Postfix Evaluation Program)**   Converting the postfix evaluation algorithm to code requires some auxiliary string handling functions. For example, a function is required to decide whether the token string is an operand, and another is required to "apply" an operator (actually a one-character string) to two integers. Also, before a token can be pushed onto the operand stack, it must be converted from string to integer form.

The following function declarations and `main` function body are from the program `rpn.cpp` (see the PWS Web site).

```
void display_value (Stack<int>& operands);
   // display final value of the expression, or
   // a message that it is not properly formed.

bool is_operator (String s);
// Return true if token is an operator; else false.

int to_int (String s);
// convert the string s to its integer equivalent.

void apply_operator (char op, Stack<int>& operands);
// Apply the operator, op, to the top two
// operands of the stack

void main()
{
    String token;
    Stack<int> operands;

    do_intro();
    cout << "RPN expression: ";

    cin >> token;
    while (token != "#")
        {
        if (is_operator(token))
            apply_operator (token[0], operands);
        else
            operands.push(to_int(token));
        cin >> token;
        }
    display_value (operands);
}
```

The implementations of the auxiliary functions are available at the PWS Web site. ■ ▮▮

■ **QUESTION** **(Equivalent Infix and Postfix Expressions)** The following table presents pairs of equivalent infix and postfix expressions. Study the pairs that are given. How would you complete the table by providing the missing expressions? (*Note*: Write the missing expressions so that the operands appear in the same order as in the equivalent expressions.)

Infix expression	Postfix expression
A + B - C * D	A B C D * - +
	A B + C - D + E -
A * (B + C / (D % E)))	A B C D E % / + *
(A * B + C / D) % E	

Answer   The missing expressions are

$$A + B - C + D - E \quad \text{and} \quad A B * C D / + E \%$$ ■ ▬

24.4 Using a Queue Class

In addition to the necessary constructors, destructor, and assignment operator, the Queue class template of `queuet.h` provides the following member functions, which correspond to those discussed in Section 24.1.

```
// accessors
EltType& get_front() const;
   // return the front item of the queue
bool is_empty() const { return front == NULL; }
int length() const    { return len; }

// modifiers
void enqueue (const EltType& elt);
   // add elt to the end of the queue
void dequeue ();
   // remove the item at the front of the queue
void make_empty();
   // make the queue empty
```

A Simulation Using a Queue   Familiar childhood games such as Tag and Hide and Go Seek involve determining the player who is to be "It." One method has the players stand in a circle while one of the players recites some rhyme to count off players, eliminating every *n*th player, where *n* depends on the number of syllables of the counting rhyme. This process stops when only one player, the one to be "It," remains. This process can be simulated with a queue, even though we usually envision a queue as a line rather than a circle of items. (It is typical of simulations to produce a realistic effect without mirroring the exact details of the actual process.)

Suppose there are seven players, and the counting rhyme has three syllables (e.g., "You are out."). The following diagram depicts the elimination process as simulated by a queue.

Action	*Players remaining*	*Who goes out?*
Count off Bob and Ruth.	Bob Ruth Ned Sam Ari Barb Lucy	
Eliminate Ned.	Ned Sam Ari Barb Lucy Bob Ruth	Ned
Count off Sam and Ari.	Sam Ari Barb Lucy Bob Ruth	
Eliminate Barb.	Barb Lucy Bob Ruth Sam Ari	Barb
Count off Lucy and Bob.	Lucy Bob Ruth Sam Ari	
Eliminate Ruth.	Ruth Sam Ari Lucy Bob	Ruth
etc.	*etc.*	

The function declarations and main function body from whoisit.cpp are

```
void get_players (Queue<String>& players);
// prompt for, input, and store the players'
// names in a queue.

void display_players (Queue<String>& players);
// Display the names of the players.

void determine_who_is_it (Queue<String>& players, int n);
// Eliminate every nth player until only one remains.

void main()
{
    Queue<String> players;
    String name;

    get_players (players);
    display_players (players);
    determine_who_is_it (players, 3);
}
```

■ EXAMPLE   **(The** display_players **Function)**   The Queue class provides no display member function. Instead, the display_players function, declared in the preceding program fragment, removes each name from its Queue parameter, players, displays that name, and then replaces it at the end of the queue. In this way, each name in the queue is displayed, and the queue is restored to its original state on completion of the function. The implementation of the display_players function is

```
void display_players (Queue<String>& players)
{
    String name;

    cout << "\nThe players are:\n";
    for (int i=1; i<=players.length(); i++)
        {
        name = players.get_front();
        cout << name << ' ';
        players.dequeue();
        players.enqueue(name);
        }
    cout << endl;
}
```

■ QUESTION   How would you fill in the blanks to complete the definition of determine_who_is_it?

```
void determine_who_is_it (Queue<String>& players, int n)
{
    String name;
    while (_____)
        {                      // more than one player left
        // count off n-1 players
        for (int i=1; i<n; i++)
            {
            name = players.get_front();
            players.dequeue();
            players.enqueue(name);
            }
```

```
                // eliminate the nth player
                cout << players.get_front() << " goes out.\n";
                _____;
            }
        // tell who is "it"
        cout << _____ << " is it!\n";
    }
```

Answer The completed lines are

```
            while (players.length() > 1)
                players.dequeue();
            cout << players.get_front() << " is it!\n";
```

The implementation of the get_players function can be found at the PWS Web site.

24.5 A Larger Queue Application Involving Simulation

In this section we present a queue application that solves the following simulation problem.

■ PROBLEM A part-time ESU student affairs worker has been given the job of interviewing all students by phone. On a given day, this student works from 1:00 P.M. to 3:00 P.M. using a given list of student phone entries. When the interviewer makes a call, she logs the student's name, phone extension, and the time. If the student is available when the call is made, the interviewer will conduct the interview and record that the student was interviewed; otherwise, she will record that the student was unavailable, move that student's phone entry to the end of the list, and go on to the next call. She stops making calls when either all students on the day's list have been interviewed or it is 3:00 P.M. The list of students that have not been reached when the worker stops making calls will be logged for the next session.

Assume (1) that a call is successful 50% of the time, (2) that the work for a successful call (involving an interview) takes 10 minutes on average, and (3) that an unsuccessful call takes 3 minutes on average. Write a program to simulate this scenario.

Objects to use The solution of this problem calls for objects of three of the classes that we have developed thus far. First, a Queue is the appropriate structure for storing the calls to be made. Second, the entries in the queue will be of type `Phone_entry`, a class developed in Chapter 20. Third, a `Time_piece` object will maintain the current time. In addition, an `istream` object will be used to read the phone entries from the file `esuphons.dat`.

Simulation issues   A simulation clock of type `Time_piece` will maintain the current time. The function `make_call` will simulate making the call by generating a successful call with 50% probability and updating the current time by either 10 (success) or 3 (failure) minutes. Making entries in the log will be simulated by writing the information to the monitor.

Pseudocode   A pseudocode algorithm for our problem is given here. The underlined phrases correspond to free function calls, and the phrases in bold print correspond to operations on the queue of phone calls to be made.

<u>Get the calls to make</u> from `esuphons.dat` and **enqueue them.**
Set the simulation clock to 1 P.M.
`while` (**there are calls to make**, and it is not yet 3 P.M.)
  {
  get the next call to make
  enter the student's name and extension and the time in the log
  <u>make the call</u>, updating the simulation clock appropriately
  `if` (call was successful)
    enter "interviewed" in the log
  `else`
    {
    enter "unavailable" in the log
    add the phone entry to the end of the queue of calls to make
    }
  }
`if` (**not all students interviewed**)
  enter in the log the phone entries for uninterviewed students

---

The `main` Function and Other Function Declarations   The following function declarations and `main` function body are from the program `queueapp.cpp`. All queue object declarations, queue class member function calls, and free functions that pass a queue as a parameter are highlighted.

```
void get_calls_to_make (Queue<Phone_entry>& calls);

void make_call (bool& success, Time_piece& curr_time);
```

```cpp
void log_uninterviewed (Queue<Phone_entry>& uninterviewed);

void main()
{
    Queue<Phone_entry> calls_to_make;
    Phone_entry next_call; // next call to make
    Time_piece curr_time;  // current time
    bool success; // (interviewed or uninterviewed)

    srand(time(0)); // for simulating success/failure of call

    // Read the calls from disk and enqueue them
    get_calls_to_make (calls_to_make);
    cout << "There are " << calls_to_make.length()
        << " calls to be made.\n";

    // begin making calls at 1 PM
    curr_time.set(1,0,'P');

    while (!calls_to_make.is_empty() && curr_time.get_hour()<3)
        {
        // get the next call
        next_call = calls_to_make.get_front();
        calls_to_make.dequeue();

        // log it
        cout << next_call.get_name() << "  X"
            << next_call.get_extension() << " at ";
        curr_time.display();

        // make the call and handle result
        make_call (success, curr_time);
        if (success)
           cout << " interviewed\n";
        else
           {
           cout << " unavailable\n";
           calls_to_make.enqueue(next_call); // try again later
           }
        } // end while

    // log calls that haven't been completed
    if (!calls_to_make.is_empty())
       log_uninterviewed (calls_to_make);
}
```

Definitions of free functions   The definitions of the free functions,
`get_calls_to_make`, `make_call`, and `log_uninterviewed` are

```
void get_calls_to_make (Queue<Phone_entry>& calls)
{
    Phone_entry entry;
    ifstream phones_in;

    phones_in.open("esuphons.dat");
    Assert (!phones_in.fail(),
            "Unable to open esuphons.dat");
    while (phones_in >> ws && !phones_in.eof())
        {
        // read a Phone_entry object from the file
        entry.read_from_file(phones_in);
        // add it to the queue of calls to make
        calls.enqueue(entry);
        }
}


void make_call (bool& success, Time_piece& curr_time)
{
    success = rand()%100 < 50;
    if (success)
        curr_time.update(0,10);
    else
        curr_time.update(0,3);
}


void log_uninterviewed (Queue<Phone_entry>& uninterviewed)
{
    Phone_entry entry;
    cout << "\n\nStudents not yet interviewed:\n";
    while (!uninterviewed.is_empty())
        {
        entry = uninterviewed.get_front();
        uninterviewed.dequeue();
        cout << entry.get_name() << "  X"
             << entry.get_extension() << endl;
        }
}
```

Sample run A typical run of the preceding program, using the file esuphons.dat is

```
There are 13 calls to be made.
Abel, Cane X8947 at 1:00 PM interviewed
Carl, Lewis X2000 at 1:10 PM interviewed
Doe, Jane  X1090 at 1:20 PM unavailable
Hillerman, Tonio X3822 at 1:23 PM interviewed
Igor, Daphne X1050 at 1:33 PM interviewed
Jagger, Mike X4321 at 1:43 PM unavailable
Lewis, Carver X2001 at 1:46 PM interviewed
Knute, Donna X9011 at 1:56 PM unavailable
Ricardo, Lucia X8700 at 1:59 PM unavailable
Snead, Sammy X5178 at 2:02 PM unavailable
Torville, Deanna X5959 at 2:05 PM interviewed
Wynalda, Erica X3901 at 2:15 PM interviewed
Zilcheski, Zack X1091 at 2:25 PM interviewed
Doe, Jane X1090 at 2:35 PM unavailable
Jagger, Mike X4321 at 2:38 PM unavailable
Knute, Donna X9011 at 2:41 PM interviewed
Ricardo, Lucia X8700 at 2:51 PM unavailable
Snead, Sammy X5178 at 2:54 PM unavailable
Doe, Jane X1090 at 2:57 PM unavailable

Students not yet interviewed:
Jagger, Mike  X4321
Ricardo, Lucia  X8700
Snead, Sammy  X5178
Doe, Jane  X1090
```

Exercise 24.13 suggests modifications to make to this program.

24.6   Implementing Stacks and Queues as Linked Lists

In this section we discuss the implementations, using linked lists, of Stack and Queue class templates. These two implementations are similar in many respects, but because the implementation of the Queue class is somewhat more involved than that of the Stack class, we focus on the Queue class implementation.

Queue Class Template Interface   The following `Queue` class template interface is from the file `queuet.h` (see the PWS Web site).

```
template <class EltType>
class Queue {
public:
    // constructor
    Queue()
      : front(NULL), rear(NULL), len(0)
      { }

    // copy constructor
    Queue (const Queue& Q);

    // destructor
    ~Queue();

    // assignment operator
    Queue& operator= (const Queue& Rhs);

    // accessors
    bool is_empty() const { return front == NULL; }
    EltType& get_front() const;
    int length() const { return len; }

    // modifiers
    void enqueue (const EltType& elt);
    void dequeue ();
    void make_empty();

private:
    struct NodeType {
        EltType data;
        NodeType* next;
        };
    typedef NodeType* NodePtr;

    NodePtr front, rear;
    int len;
}; // end Queue interface
```

Private Data Types and Members   The structure of a node, which the client doesn't need to know about, is hidden by defining it in the private section. A `NodePtr` type, which only the implementation uses, is also defined there. Private data members `front` and `rear` point to the front and rear nodes, respectively, of the linked list used to implement the queue, and the private data member `len` records the number of items in the queue. The queue object whose members are, from front to rear, `"Jan"`, `"Tim"`, `"Tina"`, `"Pete"`, and `"Kara"` can be depicted as

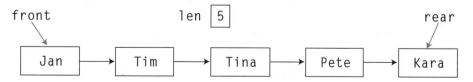

The Constructors, Destructor, and Assignment Operator   Because the queue class is implemented as a linked list, the compiler-provided default constructors, destructor, and assignment operator will be inadequate. We must write explicit versions of these.

The No-Argument Constructor   This constructor must initialize the pointer data members, `front` and `rear`, to `NULL`, and the `len` data member to zero. These initializations are done in an initializer list. The complete implementation of the no-argument constructor is given within the class interface earlier in this section.

The Copy Constructor and Assignment Operator   These must perform a deep copy (see Sections 22.3 and 22.6) of individual nodes from one list, the source, to another, the destination. The details of copying a source list to a destination list are given by the `copy` function of Section 23.6. A simpler method takes advantage of the `Queue` class's `enqueue` member function to attach new nodes to the end of the destination list.

■ **QUESTION**   **(Copy Constructor)**   How should you complete the following copy constructor implementation that uses the pointer, `curr`, to traverse the source queue, `Q`, and the `enqueue` member function to attach nodes to the destination, the calling queue object?

```
template <class EltType>
Queue<EltType>::Queue(const Queue& Q)
    : rear(NULL), front(NULL), len(0)
{
    NodePtr curr; // point to current node of Q
    curr = _____;
    while (curr != NULL)
        {
        // insert data from current node of Q
```

```
                    // at end of queue under construction
                    enqueue (_____);
                    // move to next node of Q
                    curr = curr->next;
                    }
            }
```

Answer   The complete lines are

```
        curr = Q.front;
            enqueue (curr->data);
```

The details of the assignment operator are the same except that it is also necessary to check for self-assignment and return the assigned Queue object.

The Destructor   The destructor must traverse the list, removing each node and using the delete operator to return it to the heap. However, this is precisely what the make_empty member function does. Thus, the destructor can be implemented simply as

```
template <class EltType>
Queue<EltType>::~Queue()
{ make_empty(); }
```

■ **QUESTION**   (make_empty)   The implementation of make_empty can employ the technique given in the linked list destroy function of Section 23.6. Alternatively, it can simply make repeated calls to the Queue class's dequeue function, until the calling Queue object is empty. How should you complete the following implementation, which uses this second technique?

```
template <class EltType>
void Queue<EltType>::make_empty()
{
    while ( _____ )
        _____ ;
    front = NULL;
    rear = NULL; // Optional. Why?
}
```

Answer The completed lines are

```
while (!is_empty())
    dequeue();
```

The `is_empty` **and** `get_front` **Functions** In the implementation of `make_empty`, from the previous problem, the assignment of NULL to `rear` is optional, as indicated in the comment accompanying the program fragment. This is because the `is_empty` function (whose implementation is given in the `Queue` class interface at the beginning of this section) checks only the value of `front` to determine whether the calling `Queue` object is empty.

■ **Question** (`get_front`) How should you complete the implementation of `get_front`.

```
template <class EltType>
EltType& Queue<EltType>:: get_front() const
{
    Assert( _____ ,
        "\"Queue empty\" error in get_front.");
    return front->data;
}
```

Answer If the calling `Queue` object is empty, the `return` statement will produce a (possibly cryptic) run-time error because of the attempt to dereference a NULL pointer. The `Assert` function is used to terminate program execution gracefully in this event. Thus, the completed line is

```
Assert(!is_empty(),
```

Discussion An alternative condition for the first argument to `Assert` is `front!=NULL`, but the `is_empty` function provides a safer solution by hiding the details of whether `front` or `rear` is used to check whether the `Queue` object is empty.

■ **QUESTION** (`enqueue`) The five steps to `enqueue` a new element are (1) allocate a new node, (2) set the data members of the new node, (3) append the new node to the end of the list of nodes, (4) make the `rear` data member point to the new node, and (5) increment the length of the list. How should you complete the code that implements these steps.

Steps

```
template <class EltType>
void Queue<EltType>::enqueue (const EltType& elt)
{
1     NodePtr p = new NodeType;
2     p->data = elt; p->_____;
3     if (is_empty())
          _____ = p;
      else
          _____ = p;
4     rear = p;
5     len++;
}
```

Answer   The completed lines are

```
p->data = elt; p->next = NULL;
    front = p;
    rear->next = p;
```

The *dequeue* **Function**   Like the get_front function, the dequeue function must first determine that the calling Queue object is not empty. Then, the four steps to *dequeue* the front item are (1) use a temporary pointer to "remember" the address of the front node, (2) remove the front node, (3) return the front node to the heap, and (4) decrement the length of the list. The code, with steps numbered, is

```
template <class EltType>
void Queue<EltType>::dequeue()
{
      Assert(!is_empty(),
            "\"Queue empty\" error in dequeue.");
1     NodePtr tmp = front;
2     front = front->next;
3     delete tmp;
      if (is_empty()) rear = NULL; // Optional.
4     len--;
}
```

Steps

Stack **Class Member Function Implementations**   The implementation of the Stack class template as a linked list is similar to that for the Queue class, but somewhat simpler, because all operations take place at the same end of the list, corresponding to the top of the stack. We present here only the constructors, one of which is harder than its Queue class counterpart, and the push member function. Implementations of the other member functions are given in the file stackt.h, which is available at the PWS Web site.

The No-Argument Constructor The no-argument constructor initializes the private data member size to zero, and the linked list pointer, top, to NULL.

```
template <class EltType>
Stack<EltType>::Stack()
    : top(NULL), size(0)
    { }
```

QUESTION How should you complete the implementation of the push member function so that item is inserted at the "top" (front) of the linked list?

```
template <class EltType>
void Stack<EltType>::push(const EltType & item)
{
    NodePtr new_top = new NodeType;
    new_top->data = item;
    new_top->next = _____;
    _____;
    size++;
}
```

Answer The completed lines are

```
new_top->next = top;
top = new_top;
```

The Copy Constructor Recall that the Queue class's copy constructor made repeated calls to the enqueue member function to build up the object under construction. An analogous technique will not work for the Stack class's copy constructor, because repeated calls to the push member function would result in a backwards copy. As a result, we must instead use the linked list copy algorithm of Section 23.6 in the body of the constructor. The complete definition is

```
template <class EltType>
Stack<EltType>::Stack(const Stack<EltType> & S)
    : top (NULL), size(S.size)
{
    if (S.top==NULL) return;

    // S is not empty, so
    // 1) copy top node
    top = new NodeType;
    top->data = S.top->data;
    top->next = NULL;

    // 2) copy remaining nodes
    NodePtr curr = top;
    NodePtr S_curr = S.top;
    while (S_curr->next != NULL)
        {
        S_curr = S_curr->next;
        curr->next = new NodeType;
        curr = curr->next;
        curr->data = S_curr->data;
        }
    curr->next = NULL;
}
```

The implementation of the Stack class's assignment operator requires similar list copying code.

24.7 Implementing Stacks and Queues with Vectors

In this section we consider how to implement a queue using a vector rather than a linked list for storage of the individual elements. Because the implementation of a stack as a vector is similar, but somewhat easier, it is left as Exercise 24.12.

Public Member Functions   The file vqueuet.h contains the interface and implementation of a vector-based Queue class template that provides exactly the same member functions as its linked list-based counterpart.

Private Member Data and Functions The private data members and functions of the vector-based implementation are

```
private:
    int len;       // current length of queue
    int front;     // index of front element
    int rear;      // index of rear element
    Vector<EltType> Elts; // storage for queue elements

    // private helper functions
    void resize_queue(int new_size);
        // resize storage for Elts
    void add_one(int & val) const;
        // add one with wraparound
```

The `len` data member will be used just as it was in the linked list implementation, but the `front` and `rear` data members are now vector indexes rather than node pointers. The use of the private helper functions `resize_queue` and `add_one` are illustrated later in this section.

The No-Argument Constructor The no-argument constructor, whose implementation is given here, simply invokes the constructors for each of the data members, using a named constant, `QDEFAULT_LEN`, to specify the initial amount of vector storage for queue elements.

```
template <class EltType>
Queue<EltType>::Queue()
  : len(0), front(0), rear( -1 ),
    Elts(QDEFAULT_LEN)
  { }
```

Thus, if `QDEFAULT_LEN` is 8, the internal representation of Q after

   Queue<char> Q;

is depicted next. (*Note:* □ represents an uninitialized `char` memory cell.)

len=0		front=0			rear=−1		

Elts

□	□	□	□	□	□	□	□
0	1	2	3	4	5	6	7

The enqueue *and* dequeue **Functions**   Before giving the implementations of the enqueue and dequeue functions, let us look at some diagrams that depict the data members of Q after various enqueue and dequeue operations.

Some Initial Calls to enqueue   After the following six calls to enqueue

```
for (char ch='A'; ch<='F'; ch++)
    Q.enqueue(ch);
```

the internal memory for Q will look like:

len=6   front=0   rear=5

Elts	A	B	C	D	E	F	□	□
	0	1	2	3	4	5	6	7

For each call, the enqueue function has incremented len and rear, and placed the char to be enqueued in Elts[rear].

A Call to dequeue   Now, after execution of Q.dequeue(); the internal memory for Q will look like

len=5   front=1   rear=5

Elts	A	B	C	D	E	F	□	□
	0	1	2	3	4	5	6	7

As one might expect, dequeue has decremented len. However, rather than shifting the remaining elements of the queue (B, C, D, E, and F) one to the left so that the front element is always in Elts[0], dequeue has simply incremented front. Moving the front index is a more efficient algorithm for dequeue than shifting vector elements.

■ QUESTION   Continuing from the above state of Q, how should you show the memory representation of Q after execution of these statements?

```
Q.enqueue('G'); Q.dequeue();
Q.enqueue('H'); Q.dequeue();
```

Answer The internal memory for Q will look like

	len=5			front=3			rear=7	
Elts	A	B	C	D	E	F	G	H
	0	1	2	3	4	5	6	7

"Wraparound" and the add_one **Function** We have now reached a critical issue in the implementation of enqueue. The next enqueue operation cannot increment rear to 8 (an invalid index), but instead must make the value of rear "wrap around" to 0, the index of the next available vector cell. This is precisely where the add_one private member function comes into play. Its definition follows.

```
template <class EltType>
void Queue<EltType>::add_one(int& val) const
{
    val++;
    if (val >= Elts.length())
        val = 0;
}
```

Thus, after execution of

```
for (ch='I'; ch<='K'; ch++)
    Q.enqueue(ch);
```

the internal memory state of Q will be

	len=8			front=3			rear=2	
Elts	I	J	K	D	E	F	G	H
	0	1	2	3	4	5	6	7

Enqueueing When Elts **is Full** The Elts vector is now full, so another call to enqueue will require that it be resized (either by doubling or by adding some fixed number of cells). This task is handled by the resize_queue private member function, which, in the process of resizing, will also copy the current queue elements so that the front element is in Elts[0].

Thus, after executing the statement `Q.enqueue('L');` the internal state of Q will be

len=9			front=0				rear=8					

Elts

D	E	F	G	H	I	J	K	L	□	□	...	□
0	1	2	3	4	5	6	7	8	9	10	...	15

The Implementations of `enqueue` **and** `resize_queue` The implementations of the enqueue and resize_queue functions are

```
template <class EltType>
void Queue<EltType>::enqueue(const EltType & item)
{
    // grow vector if necessary
    if (len >= Elts.length())
        resize_queue(2*Elts.length());

    add_one(rear);     // new rear element
    Elts[rear] = item;
    len++;
}
```

```
template <class EltType>
void
Queue<EltType>::resize_queue(int new_size)
{
    Vector<EltType> temp(new_size); // new storage
    // copy current elements to 0..size-1 of temp
    int j,k=front;
    for(j=0; j < len; j++)
        {
        temp[j] = Elts[k];
        add_one(k);
        }
    Elts = temp; // Update all private data members.
    front = 0;
    rear = len-1;
}
```

Dequeueing When Elts **Is Too Large**   Let us return to our Queue object, Q, and consider its state after four calls to dequeue.

```
    len=5              front=4                rear=8
Elts  ┌─────┬─────┬─────┬─────┬─────┬─────┬─────┬─────┬─────┬─────┬─────┐     ┌─────┐
      │  D  │  E  │  F  │  G  │  H  │  I  │  J  │  K  │  L  │  □  │  □  │ ... │  □  │
      └─────┴─────┴─────┴─────┴─────┴─────┴─────┴─────┴─────┴─────┴─────┘     └─────┘
         0     1     2     3     4     5     6     7     8     9    10   ...    15
```

At this point, only 5 of the 16 memory cells of Elts are in use. A good memory conservation policy would be to halve the memory allocated for Elts whenever the ratio of len to Elts.length() is low enough, say, one-fourth. Thus, one more call to dequeue would reduce this ration to $4/16 = 1/4$, so the internal state of Q would become

```
         len=4            front=0          rear=3
Elts   ┌─────┬─────┬─────┬─────┬─────┬─────┬─────┬─────┐
       │  I  │  J  │  K  │  L  │  □  │  □  │  □  │  □  │
       └─────┴─────┴─────┴─────┴─────┴─────┴─────┴─────┘
          0     1     2     3     4     5     6     7
```

The Implementation of dequeue   The dequeue function's implementation is

```cpp
template <class EltType>
void Queue<EltType>::dequeue()
{
    Assert (!is_empty(),
            "Error: dequeuing an empty queue\n");
    len--;
    add_one(front);
    if (len < Elts.length()/4)
        {
        int new_len = Elts.length()/2;
        if (new_len >= QDEFAULT_LEN)
            resize_queue(Elts.length()/2);
        }
}
```

The remaining member function implementations for the vector-based Queue class template contain no new ideas. You can find them in the file vqueuet.h.

■ Exercises

1. Suppose that a stack S and a queue Q of characters are initially empty. Show S and Q after each iteration of the second `for` loop of the code fragment shown at right.

```
for (char ch='A'; ch<='H'; ch++)
    S.push(ch);

for (int i=1; i<=4; i++)
    {
    S.pop();
    Q.enqueue(s.get_top());
    S.pop();
    Q.enqueue(S.get_top());
    S.push(Q.get_front());
    Q.dequeue();
    }
```

2. Evaluate the following postfix expressions, and show the contents of the operand stack immediately before each of the highlighted operands is input.

   (a) 2 5 9 * 11 `-` +   (b) 2 5 * 9 11 `-` +

   (c) 30 7 % 8 + 2 `/`   (d) 30 7 8 2 % `+` /

3. For each of the following infix expressions, write the equivalent postfix expression. The operands should appear in the same order in both expressions.

   (a) A - B + C / D   (b) (A - (B + C)) / D

   (c) A - (B + C) / D - E   (d) A - B + C / (D - E)

4. For each of the postfix expressions of Exercise 24.2, write an equivalent infix expression. The operands should appear in the same order in both expressions.

5. Write a free function template, `display`, to display the contents of a stack passed by constant reference. Display the elements from left to right, separated by spaces, beginning with the bottom element of the stack.

6. For the linked list-based `Stack` class, write an overloaded version of the `pop` function that will return the popped item as a reference parameter. Do this two ways: (a) by calling other `Stack` class member functions and (b) by directly altering the class's data members.

7. For the linked list-based `Queue` class, write an overloaded version of the `dequeue` function that will return the item removed from the queue as a reference parameter. Do this two ways: (a) by calling other `Queue` class member functions and (b) by directly altering the class's data members.

8. If queue Q is implemented as a vector as in Section 24.7, show the private data members of Q after execution of each of the four `for` loops of the code fragment at right.

```
for (ch='A'; ch<='E'; ch++)
    Q.enqueue(ch);
for (i=1; i<=4; i++)
    Q.dequeue();
for (ch='F'; ch<='K'; ch++)
    Q.enqueue(ch);
for (ch='X'; ch<='Z'; ch++)
    Q.enqueue(ch);
```

Programming Problems

9. Write a program that uses a stack to simulate the use of the backspace key to correct typing mistakes. Each backspace erases the previous character, and consecutive backspaces can be applied in sequence to erase several characters. For example, for the input

> Ms←art←←ny t7←YPO←←←ypos

the corrected input will be

> Many typos

(*Note*: Because ← is not a printing character, use @ for the simulation.)

10. Write a program that uses a stack and a queue of characters to determine whether an input sequence of characters is a palindrome. (Obviously, it is necessary to ignore spaces, punctuation, and letter case.)

11. Use a stack to check for properly balanced grouping symbols (), [], {}. If the symbols are not balanced, explain why not. For example

Input	Analysis
(){}[{()}]	Correct.
({}]()	Mismatched symbols: (and]
{[()]	Unmatched left symbol: {
[()]{})	Unmatched right symbol:)

Longer Assignments

12. Implement the vector-based version of the Stack class template whose interface is given in the file `vstackt.h`. Test your implementation using the menu-driven test program contained in the file `stkt_tst.cpp`.

13. Make the following modifications to the phone interview simulation of Section 24.5.

    (a) Change the interviewer's work hours to 1 P.M. to 5 P.M.

    (b) Place students who are unavailable when called into a separate queue, `call_back`. In a parallel queue, `called_at`, store the time of the unsuccessful call.

    (c) Classes at ESU are 50 minutes long. So, whenever at least 1 hour has passed since the student at the front of the `call_back` queue was called, try that student again before making calls from the `calls_to_make` queue.

14. Use a stack to find a path through a maze. (See Exercises 15.15 and 15.16.)

15. Write a fraction addition tutor. It should prompt the user for the number of problems to be presented, randomly generate them, and provide feedback on each user response. Problems answered incorrectly by the user should be presented again after all problems have been presented once. Also, a final message should tell how many problems were eventually answered correctly. A sample run might look like this.

```
How many problems? 5
4/15 + 9/10 = 37/30
    No!  We'll try that one again later.
1/5 + 1/2 = 7/10
    That's correct.
7/5 + 1/10 = 15/10
    OK, but you forgot to reduce.
2/15 + 2/15 = 4/15
    That's correct.
2/5 + 1/2 = 7/10
    No! We'll try that one again later.

One more try on the ones you missed . . .
4/15 + 9/10 = 35/30
    OK, but you forgot to reduce.
    The correct answer is 7/6.
1/2 + 2/5 = 9/10
    That's correct.

OK. You got 4 out of 5.
```

16. The linked list-based `Queue` class of this chapter has two pointers, `front` and `rear`. However, if the last node of the list contains a pointer to the first node, making the list circular, then only the `rear` pointer is needed, since the front of the list is only one link away. Thus, the private data members of a queue

object whose items are, from front to rear, "Jan", "Tim", "Tina", "Pete", and "Kara" can be depicted as

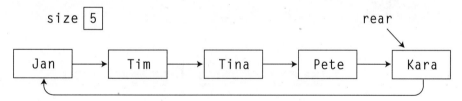

Implement a queue as a circular linked list with a single pointer, last, to the last node of the list of nodes. Test your implementation using the menu-driven test program contained in the file qt_tst.cpp.

25

Recursive Functions

A ***recursive*** function is a function whose definition contains one or more calls to itself. Recursion is applicable when a problem can be reduced repeatedly to smaller and smaller versions of itself, until finally a reduced version is reached that is small enough to be solved directly. By contrast, code that performs repetition without recursion, but instead by means of looping, is known as ***iterative*** code.

A potential drawback of recursion is that some recursive functions are very inefficient in terms of the amount of processing time and internal memory that they require. (For example, see the recursive Fibonacci function in Section 25.5.) Nevertheless, recursive functions can be very useful because *some problems are much easier to solve recursively than iteratively*. For such problems, there are two possible strategies for using recursion:

1. If the recursive solution is fine in terms of efficiency, use that solution.

2. If the recursive solution is too inefficient, then use it as a guide for finding an iterative solution. A recursive solution can always be translated into iterative code. (Well-defined techniques have been created to do this translation, but they are beyond the scope of this book.)

25.1 Writing and Tracing a Recursive Function

Terminal Case In recursion, a problem is reduced repeatedly to simpler and simpler versions of itself, until a reduced version is finally reached that is simple enough to be solved directly — such a final reduced version is known as a *terminal case*. After a terminal case is solved, a solution to the original problem is pieced together by working backwards.

For example, let us consider a recursive solution to the problem of finding 4!. The repeated recursive reductions stem from the recursive equation

$$n! = n*(n-1)!$$

Thus, the problem of finding 4! can first be reduced to that of finding 3!, because 4! = 4*3!. Then, in turn, the problem of finding 3! can be reduced to finding 2!, because 3! = 3*2!. Then, finding 2! can be reduced to finding 1!, because 2! = 2*1!, and we have reached a terminal case, using the fact that 1! is equal to 1. Once this terminal case has been reached, we can work backwards to piece together a solution to the original problem of finding 4!. We discuss how this "piecing together" works in greater detail when we look at the trace of a recursive factorial functional.

Writing a Recursive Function As in looping (where the loop body is coded just once, not repeatedly), the body of a recursive function codes the *recursive reduction step(s) just once*. The terminal case(s) for a recursive function is (are) analogous to loop exit condition(s).

A common form for the body of a recursive function is:

---

if   (*a terminal case*)
    Give a direct solution for this case.
else
    Give a solution to the original problem by using a call (or calls) to the recursive function to solve a "smaller" problem (or problems).

■ **EXAMPLE**   **(Recursive Factorial Function)**   The equation

$$n! = n*(n-1)!$$

can be used as the basis for coding the recursive step, because it gives a solution to the original problem in terms of a smaller version of the problem. Note that the body of the recursive `fact` function (highlighted in the following code fragment) uses the common format just described.

```
// factor1.cpp
#include<iostream.h>

long fact(long n);

void main()
```

```
{
    long n;
    cout << "Enter n>0: ";
    cin >> n;
    cout << n << "! = "
         << fact(n) << endl;
}

long fact(long n)
{
    if(n==1) // terminal case
        return 1;
    else // solve a "smaller" case
        return n * fact(n-1);
}
```

Here is a run to compute 4!.

```
Enter n>0: 4
4! = 24
```

Tracing   As you will soon see, the trace of a recursive function call can be quite complicated. You should keep two important points in mind when tracing a recursive function call. First, none of the recursive calls can be completed until a recursive call for a terminal case has been reached. Second, once a terminal case call has been reached, then earlier recursive calls are completed in the *reverse order* in which they were called because control always returns to the point from which a (now-completed) call was made. The phrase *winding back up* describes this reversal of order for the completion of calls.

Trace of the Call of `fact(4)`   When the program is run to compute 4!, four calls are made to the recursive function `fact`. The first call is to `fact(4)` from `main`. This call cannot be completed immediately because `fact(4)` calls `fact(3)`, which calls `fact(2)`, which calls `fact(1)`. The call to `fact(1)` is the first call that can be completed. Then the computer winds back up and returns the value 1 to the place where `fact(1)` was called. Then the call of `fact(2)` is completed and the value 2 is sent to the place where `fact(2)` was called. Then the call of `fact(3)` is completed, and the value 6 is sent to the place where `fact(3)` was called. Finally, the original call of `fact(4)` is completed.

In the following diagram for fact(4), the recursive calls are indicated by arrows labeled *a, b, c,* and *d,* and the winding back up is indicated by arrows labeled *D, C, B,* and *A.* The value returned by each call is given in bold type within an oval.

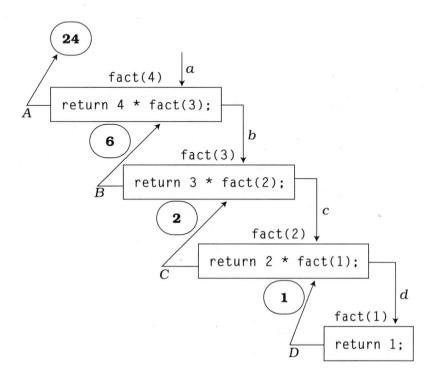

■ **EXAMPLE** **(A Void Recursive Function)** The following code (from the program windup.cpp) is used to take a further look at "winding back up" to complete unfinished calls.

```
void rec_task(int n);

void main()
{
    rec_task(4);
}

void rec_task(int n)
```

```
{
    if(n==1) // terminal case
        cout << n << " GO BACK" << endl;
    else
        {
        cout << n << " hi\n";
        rec_task(n-1);
        cout << n << " bye\n";
        }
}
```

First, the call `rec_task(4)` is started. The computer outputs 4 hi, and then `rec_task(3)` is called. [Note that `rec_task(4)` still has not completed execution.] In starting `rec_task(3)`, the computer outputs 3 hi and then calls `rec_task(2)`, in which it first outputs 2 hi and then calls `rec_task(1)`. `rec_task(1)` is a terminal case because its execution does not produce further calls to `rec_task` — it outputs 1 GO BACK.

The computer must still wind back up and finish all the unfinished calls whose execution has been suspended. It returns to the point in `rec_task(2)` where `rec_task(1)` was called and outputs 2 bye. Then it finishes `rec_task(3)`, by outputting 3 bye, and `rec_task(4)`, outputting 4 bye.

The entire output will be

```
4 hi
3 hi
2 hi
1 GO BACK
2 bye
3 bye
4 bye
```

Diagram for the Trace of `rec_task(4)` In the following diagram, each call gets its own box. The arrows labeled *a, b, c,* and *d* indicate calls; the arrows labeled *D, C, B,* and *A* indicate function returns (during the winding back up process) and point precisely to where control is returned. Be aware that in winding back up, the computer attends to completing each call's unfinished business (shaded in the diagram.) For example, when call `rec_task(1)` is completed, control is passed to the unfinished business of the prior call, `rec_task(2)`. Then, when `rec_task(2)` is completed, control is passed to the unfinished business of `rec_task(3)`, and so on.

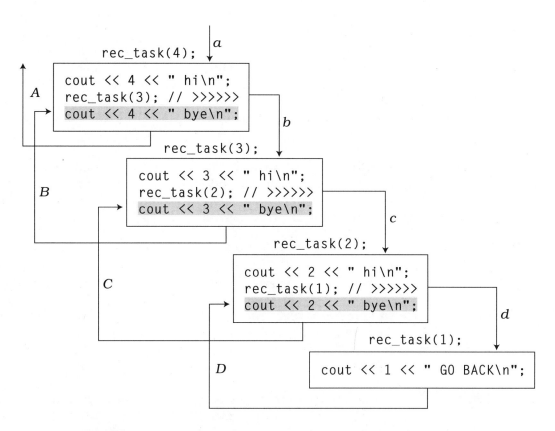

CAUTION Be aware of the possibility of infinite recursion in recursive functions! Even if you include a terminal case, the possibility exists that it will never be reached. (See Exercise 25.5.)

Is Tracing Necessary? It is usually not necessary to do traces of recursive functions that you have written because a properly written recursive function automatically does what needs to be done. Still you should understand how to do a trace. This understanding can help you avoid certain kinds of common errors and also see more quickly when recursive code is likely to be too inefficient.

25.2 Guidelines for Writing Recursive Functions

In this section we present some guidelines for writing recursive functions and illustrate the application of these guidelines to particular problems.

Identify the Reductive Step(s) Solving a problem with recursion involves subdividing it into subtasks such that *at least one of the subtasks is a "smaller" or easier version of the original problem.* You will use a recursive call for the smaller version(s) of the original problem, but you must write the actual code needed for other subtasks.

One common way of reducing a problem to a smaller problem is to get rid of one occurrence of a main difficulty or complication of the problem; this reduces the "size" of the problem by one. Another common strategy is to break the problem into two halves, each of which is easier to solve than the original.

Identify the Terminal Case(s)   The successive reductions must eventually lead to a terminal case and work properly each step of the way. Terminal cases usually correspond to versions of the problem that are so small that they are very easy, if not trivial, to solve.

Two possible pitfalls here are (1) never reaching a terminal case, which is known as ***infinite recursion***, and (2) a reductive step that does not work properly for all input, usually for values that are close to a terminal value. (See Exercise 25.5 for an example of this second pitfall.)

Use Sample Input and Pseudocode   You may find it helpful to consider a specific input and use pseudocode to devise the reductive step for that input. Then translate what you did for that specific input into actual code. Be sure to code the subtasks in the correct order.

■ **QUESTION**   What output will the following loop produce when n has the value 3895? (This question helps lay the groundwork for the recursive function problem that follows it.)

```
while n > 0
    {
    cout << n% 10 << " ";
    n = n/10;
    }
```

Answer   The output, which consists of the digits of n in *reverse* order, separated by spaces, will be 5 9 8 3. (Note that n%10 gives the units digit of an integer, and n/10 removes the units digit. Thus, the first time the loop body is executed, the digit 5 will be output with a blank space after it, and n will then get the new value 389.)   ■ ■■

■ **PROBLEM**   (**Outputting Spaces Between the Digits of an Integer**)   Suppose we want to write a function, print_spaced, that outputs the digits of an integer *in order*, with spaces between digits (e.g., 3895 would be output as 3 8 9 5). Note that the easiest digit to extract, the units digit, is the *last* digit that will be printed. The fact that the order of extraction of digits is the reverse of the desired order of output suggests that a recursive solution might be simpler than an iterative one. (Exercise 25.18 asks you to write an iterative function to solve this problem.)

Sample Input: 3895 The original problem can be subdivided into two subtasks:

1. Print 3 8 9

2. Print a space, then 5

General Coding (Use n instead of 3895.) Subtask 1 will be handled by a call to print_spaced. Note that this recursive call is for a version of the problem that is smaller by one digit. To determine the argument, you must express, in terms of n, how to get 389 from 3895. For subtask 2, you must give the code that prints a space and then extracts and prints the units digit of n.

Terminal Case Single-digit integers are trivial to print with spaces between digits.

■ **QUESTION** Using the preceding analysis, how should you fill in the blanks of the recursive function print_spaced?

```
void print_spaced (long n)
{
    if (n < 10)  // terminal case
        cout << n;
    else // n > 9 -- recursive step
        {
            _____ ;
            _____ ;
        }
}
```

Answer The completed lines are

```
print_spaced(n/10);
cout << " " << n%10;
```

■ **PROBLEM** (**Printing Commas in Numbers**) Write a recursive function to print an integer of type long with commas. For example, the integer 35076802 will be output in the easier to read form, 35,076,802.

■ **QUESTION** For the sample input of 35076802, subdivide the original problem into two subtasks so that one of the subtasks reduces the size of the original problem by one. (*Hint:* Try to get rid of one occurrence of the main complication, which for this problem is the printing of the commas.)

Answer   The subtasks are

1.   Print 35,076

2.   Then print ,802

Writing the complete `print_commas` function is left to Exercise 25.13. In solving this problem

1.   You still must decide on the terminal case. Make sure that you can solve the terminal case directly and that the reductive step works for values close to the terminal case.

2.   You must ensure that necessary leading zeros are not dropped. It might make sense to write a first draft of `print_commas` so that it can handle any integer with no zeros in it, and then modify it slightly to handle numbers like 35076802.   ▨ ▩

■ **QUESTION**   **(Recursive ULAM)**   Recall from Section 8.1 that the Ulam sequence for $n=13$ is 13 40 20 10 5 16 8 4 2 1.

When $n=13$, a way to subdivide the original problem into subtasks is (1) to print 13 and then (2) to print the full Ulam sequence for 40, which is a smaller (*in terms of length*) version of the original problem.

Fill in the blanks in the following recursive Ulam function, which outputs the Ulam sequence for a positive integer n. Note that this function differs from the previous examples in that the recursive step has two options for the recursive call, depending on whether n is odd or even.

```
void Ulam(unsigned long n)
{
   if(n==1) // terminal case
      cout << 1 << endl;
   else
      {
      cout << n << " ";
      if(n%2==0)
         _____; // recursive call
      else
         _____; // recursive call
      }
}
```

Answer   The completed lines are

```
Ulam(n/2); // recursive call
Ulam(n*3+1); // recursive call
```

25.3   Recursion and Vectors

■ **EXAMPLE**   **(Minimum Element of a Vector)**   Suppose that V is a vector of integers and we want vect_min to return the vector's minimum element. Thus, for V = (64, 29, 44, 81, 37, 58, 16, 55), the call

```
cout << vect_min (V, 0, 7);
```

should display 16. Note that the original problem is solved by subdividing the original problem into two subproblems of half the size, one for the left half of the vector, and one for the right half.

```
int vect_min (const Vector<int>& V, int first, int last)
{
   if (first==last) // terminal case
      return V[first];
   // recursive calls
   int min_left = vect_min (V, first, (first+last)/2);
   int min_right = vect_min (V, (first+last)/2 + 1, last);

   // Use results of recursive calls
   // to solve original problem
   if (min_left < min_right)
      return min_left;
   else
      return min_right;
}
```

■ **EXAMPLE**   **(Recursive Binary Search)**   The algorithm for the recursive version of the binary search is essentially the same as that for the iterative version. Note, however, the following differences.

1.   The recursive version requires that first and last be parameters because each recursive call to bin_search must know the first and last indexes of the half of the vector to which the search is restricted.

2.   The loop exit conditions in the iterative version (either in the loop header or in a return statement condition) become the terminal

cases in the recursive version. (Either you have found what you are looking for or the value of `first` exceeds the value of `last`.)

■ **QUESTION** How should you fill in the blanks?

```
int bin_search(const Vector<String>& V,
               String want, int first, int last)
{
    int min;
    mid=(first+last)/2;
    if(first>last)
        return -1; // not found
    if(want == V[mid])
        return mid;
    if(want < V[mid])
        return bin_search(V, want, first, mid-1);
    // want > V[mid]
    return _____ ;
}
```

Answer   The completed line is

```
return bin_search(V, want, mid+1, last);
```

25.4 Recursion and Stacks

As discussed in Chapter 24, a **stack** is a data structure in which new entries are added to the *top*, and entries are deleted from the *top* as well. It is useful to envision a stack as a pile of dishes — when you add a dish to the pile you put it on top, and when you remove a dish from the pile you remove it from the top.

As you will see, the computer uses an internal stack that is part of the processor hardware to implement recursion. For each recursive call, the computer stores information about that call in a **stack frame** that is placed on top of the internal stack. The contents of a stack frame are (1) the return address (r.a.), which is the point in the program where execution resumes when the function has completed, (2) information about the function's parameters, (3) local variables of the function, and (4) in the case of value returning functions, the value returned by the function.

In the following code from `reverse.cpp`, a stack frame is created for each new call to the recursive function `rec_task`. Thus, each time the statement

```
cin >> ch;
```

is executed, the character previously read in is not erased — it is still stored on the stack so that it can be accessed when the computer is winding back up.

■ **QUESTION** What will be the output of the following code (from `reverse.cpp`) if n initially equals 4, and the user successively inputs A, B, C, and D? (*Note*: The Greek letters α and β, with arrows, are used later in this section to indicate return addresses.)

```
void reverse(int n);

void main()
{
    int n = 4;
    reverse(n);
α → cout << endl;
}

void reverse(int n)
{
    char ch;
    cout << "Type a letter: ";
    cin >> ch;
    if (n==1) // terminal case
        cout << ch;
    else
        {
        reverse(n-1);
β → cout << ch;
        }
}
```

Answer The input and output will be

```
Type a letter: A
Type a letter: B
Type a letter: C
Type a letter: D
DCBA
```

Stack Frames for `reverse.cpp` The stack frames stored on the internal stack are shown in the following diagram for each of the four calls to the `reverse` function of the previous question. The return addresses are indicated symbolically by α and β.

This diagram shows the internal stack of information stored for each of the calls to the recursive `reverse` function up to the call that executes the terminal case.

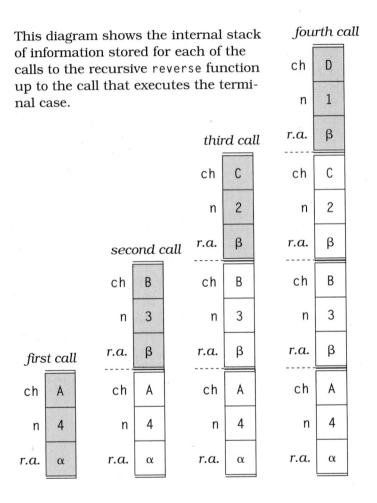

In "winding back up" to the first call (for $n = 4$), the computer keeps completing unfinished calls. In completing the fourth call, the top value for `ch`, `'D'`, is printed, and then the stack frame for that call is destroyed. In completing the third call, the top value for `ch`, `'C'`, is printed, and then the stack frame for that call is destroyed. In completing the second call, the top value for `ch`, `'B'`, is printed, and then the stack frame for that call is destroyed. Finally, the initial call is completed by printing the top value for `ch`, `'A'`, and then destroying the stack frame for that call.

25.5 A Very Inefficient Recursive Function

When the body of a recursive function contains multiple calls to itself, the danger exists that the very same calls will be made not just once, but repeatedly, causing monumental inefficiency. The recursive Fibonacci function, fib, which is discussed next, illustrates how this can happen.

Fibonacci Numbers The Fibonacci numbers are a famous sequence of numbers. The first and second positive Fibonacci numbers are both 1. Thereafter, each Fibonacci number is the sum of the previous two Fibonacci numbers. Here are the first 12 Fibonacci numbers.

1 1 2 3 5 8 13 21 34 55 89 144

If fib_n is used to denote the nth Fibonacci number, the Fibonacci sequence is determined by the following three equations:

$$fib_1 = 1$$
$$fib_2 = 1$$
$$fib_n = fib_{n-1} + fib_{n-2}$$

■ **EXAMPLE** **(Fibonacci Recursively)** Note how naturally the determining equations just given fit the scheme for recursion. The terminal case is (n==1) or (n==2), and finding fib(n) can be reduced to the simpler task of finding the value of fib(n-1) + fib(n-2).

Here is the recursive fib function from rec_fib.cpp.

```
unsigned long fib (int n)
// recursive version
{
    if (n==1 || n==2) // terminal cases
        return 1;
    return fib(n-1) + fib(n-2);
}
```

NOTE The unsigned long data type has been used so that large Fibonacci numbers can be calculated correctly.

Tracing the Call *fib(5)* This trace is somewhat complicated. The call to fib(5) leads to eight additional calls in the following order:

fib(4), fib(3), fib(2), fib(1), fib(2), fib(3), fib(2), fib(1)

as indicated by the following diagram.

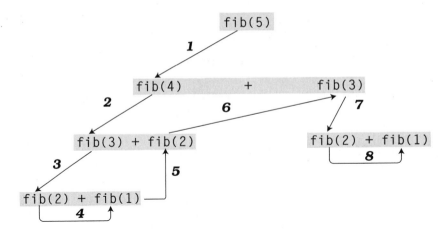

REMARK   Note the inefficiency of this recursive execution. For example, each time fib(3) is executed (twice), the computer evaulates it from scratch. A call to fib(6) would involve three calls to fib(3) and two calls to fib(4), each evaluated from scratch. [Exercise 25.6, part (b), asks you to determine the total number of calls needed to recursively evaluate fib(n).] By contrast, an iterative function could store previously calculated Fibonacci values in a vector [see Exercise 25.6, part (c)].

25.6   A Problem That Is Very Difficult to Solve Iteratively

Finally, we present a famous problem, the ***Towers of Hanoi***, that is easy to solve recursively, but very challenging to solve iteratively.

You have three pegs, A, B, and C, and *n* rings, all of different sizes. Initially, peg A contains all the rings in order of size (with the smallest on top). The object is to move the rings one at a time so that eventually all the rings are on peg C in order of size. All moves must obey the following two rules.

1.   Only the top ring from a peg can be moved.

2.   A larger ring must never be put on top of a smaller ring.

Towers of Hanoi when *n*=3

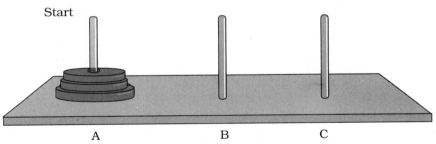

Hand Solution to Towers of Hanoi when *n*=3   The shortest solution requires seven moves. Here are the first four moves of that solution. (1) Move the top ring from A to C. (2) Move ring from A to B. (3) Move ring from C to B. (4) Move ring from A to C. At this point we have

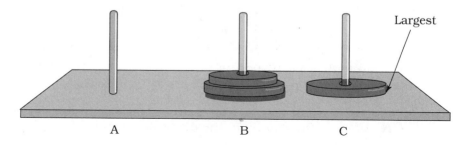

Make sure that you can determine the final three moves.

■ **PROBLEM**   Write a recursive function, move_pile, that will output the moves when peg A has *n* rings that are to be moved to peg C.

Reductive Step   The obvious candidate for a smaller version that reduces the original problem by 1 would be a pile of *n*−1 rings. Again, to figure out the general code let us consider a specific value of *n*, say, *n*=5, and note that the following picture shows how to solve the original problem in terms of a call to move_pile that will move a pile of four rings.

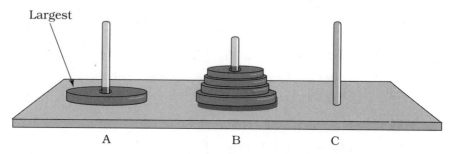

Here is pseudocode for the general reductive step when there are *n* rings, instead of five.

```
else (pseudocode)
    move_pile — to move n − 1 rings from peg A to peg B
    Move the largest ring from A to C
    move_pile — to move n − 1 rings from peg B to peg C
```

Parameters for move_pile   Recursive functions tend not to have many local variables, because the values of a local variable of one call are not accessible in subsequent calls. Furthermore, in the body of move_pile all three pegs figure into the recursive calls. Thus, move_pile should have four parameters — one for the number of rings, *n*, and one for each of the three pegs.

```
void move_pile(int n, char src, char dest, char aux);
// move n rings from the source peg, src, to the
// destination peg, dest, using the auxiliary peg, aux,
// for temporary storage.
```

Note that a call such as move_pile(5, 'A', 'C', 'B') will move the five rings from peg A to peg C.

■ **QUESTION** How should you fill in the blank line in the following function?

```
void move_pile(int n, char src, char dest, char aux)
{
   if(n==1) // terminal case
      cout << "Move " << src << " to " << dest << endl;
   else
      {
      move_pile(n-1, src, aux, dest);
      cout << "Move " << src << " to " << dest << endl;
      move_pile (_____);
      }
}
```

Answer   The completed line is

```
move_pile(n-1, aux, dest, src);
```

25.7 Recursion and Linked Lists

We want to write a function, reverse, that will take a pointer to the head of a linked list and reverse the linked list. If this list is

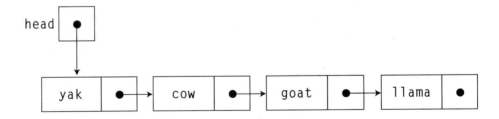

then the call revlist(head); will produce

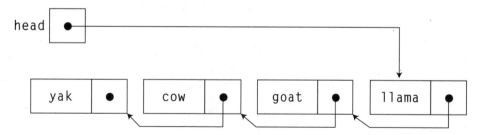

A smaller version of this problem is to reverse the "tail" of the given list — that is, the list consisting of all nodes beyond the first. Thus, for the original list, the result of the statements

```
NodePtr tail = head->next;
reverse(tail);
```

will be

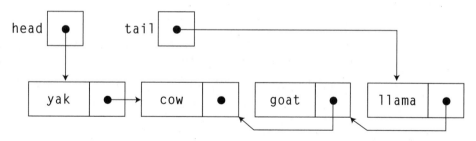

Now, the statements

```
head->next->next = head;
head->next = NULL;
```

will append the original first node, still pointed to by head, to the now-reversed tail, producing

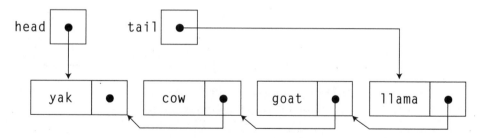

■ **QUESTION**   How should you complete the blank in function `reverse` (from `revlist.cpp`)? (*Hint*: What lists are easy to reverse?)

```
void reverse (NodePtr& head)
{
    if (_____)
        return; // terminal cases

    // reverse the "tail" of the list
    NodePtr tail = head->next;
    reverse(tail);

    // Attach original first node to end of reversed tail
    head->next->next = head;
    head->next = NULL;

    // point head to first node of reversed tail
    head = tail;
}
```

Answer   Because an empty list or a list consisting of a single node is its own reverse, the condition for the terminal cases is

if (head == NULL || head->next == NULL)   ■ ■■

■ Exercises

1. For the recursive function given at right, give the output produced by the following calls.

   (a) `rec_fn(5);`

   (b) `rec_fn(13);`

   (c) `rec_fn(21);`

```
void rec_fn (int n)
{
    if (n<1)
        cout << "Done ";
    else
        {
        rec_fn(n/2);
        cout << n << ' ';
        }
}
```

2. For the call `rec_fn(13)` of Exercise 25.1, draw a trace like that given for the function `rec_task` in Section 25.1.

3. For the following recursive function g, give the value of

    (a) g(3,7)   (b) g(4,-5)   (c) g(-5,7)

```
long g (int n, int m)
{
    long rv; // return value
    if (n<0)
        rv = - (g(-n, m));
    else if (n == 0)
        rv = 0;
    else
        rv = m + g (n-1, m);
    return rv;
}
```

4. For the call g(3,7) of Exercise 25.3, draw a trace like that given for the function fact in Section 25.1.

5. (a) What does the function at right do when n is a positive even integer?

   (b) What does it do when n is a positive odd integer?

   (c) How can you rewrite the terminal case to return the correct sum when n is odd?

```
long sum (int n)
{
    if (n==0)
        return 0;
    else
        return n + sum(n-2);
}
```

6. (a) Draw a trace of the recursive calls in the evaluation of fib(6).

   (b) In general, how many recursive calls are needed to evaluate fib(n). Give your answer as a formula in terms of fib(n).

   (c) Write an iterative program using a vector to find the nth Fibonacci number, where n is an input integer from 1 to 30.

7. Suppose the vector, v, of strings is

v[0]	v[1]	v[2]	v[3]	v[4]	v[5]	v[6]	v[7]	v[8]	v[9]	v[10]	v[11]
Ben	Eva	Fay	Gil	Ida	Jan	Lee	Opy	Pat	Ray	Tim	Una

Give the recursive calls that are made by the binary search function of Section 25.3 to find

    (a) "Pat"   (b) "Ida"   (c) "Tab"

8. Trace the following calls to the `move_pile` function of Section 25.6.

   (a) `move_pile (1, 'A', 'C', 'B');`

   (b) `move_pile (2, 'A', 'C', 'B');`

   (c) `move_pile (3, 'A', 'C', 'B');`

   (d) `move_pile (4, 'A', 'C', 'B');`

   In general, how many steps are required to move *n* disks from a source peg to a destination peg?

9. Write a recursive version of the `linear_search` function of Section 14.1. Will you need three or four parameters? Discuss.

10. Give all output, including tracing output, produced by the following code fragment

```
String str = "Goodbye";
change (str);
cout << str << endl;
```

where the overloaded function, `change`, has the following definitions.

```
void change (String &s)
{
    cout << "One parameter change fn\n";
    change (s, 0, s.length()-1);
}

void change (String &s, int lo, int hi)
{
    cout << "lo = " << lo << " hi = " << hi << endl;
    if (lo < hi)
        {
        char tmp = s[lo];
        s[lo] = s[hi];
        s[hi] = tmp;
        change (s, lo+1, hi-1);
        }
}
```

Programming Problems

11. Add tracing code to function g of Exercise 25.3 so that (a) it displays the values of its parameters, with labels, when the function is entered and (b) it displays its return values just before the function is exited. For example, the statement int n = g(-3,5); should produce the tracing output given at right.

```
m = -3 n = 5
m = 3 n = 5
m = 2 n = 5
m = 1 n = 5
m = 0 n = 5
returning 0
returning 5
returning 10
returnung 15
returning -15
```

12. Use the following definition, in which x is a floating-point number and n is an integer, to write and test a recursive exponentiation function, rec_pow.

$$x^n = \begin{cases} 1/x^n & \text{if } n < 0 \\ 1 & \text{if } n = 0 \\ x \cdot x^{n-1} & \text{if } n > 0 \end{cases}$$

13. Write and test the print_commas function of Section 25.2.

14. Let the greatest common divisor of two non-negative integers, x and y, be denoted by gcd(x, y). Use the following facts from number theory to write a recursive gcd function.

$$\gcd(x, y) = \begin{cases} x & \text{if } y = 0 \\ \gcd(y, x \% y) & \text{if } y > 0 \end{cases}$$

15. Write a recursive function that will return the number of digits in its long parameter. Your function should work for arguments that are negative or zero as well as positive.

16. The following diagram shows how repeated division by two produces, as remainders, the binary digits of a number. However, the digits are produced in reverse order of the desired output order.

$$11_{10} = 10110_2$$

```
      0   r   1
    2/1   r   0
    2/2   r   1
    2/5   r   1
   2/11   r   0
```

(a) Write a print_bin function that will output the bits of its positive long parameter in order.

    (b) Can you modify your function to handle the case where the parameter is zero?

17. **(a)** Using the idea of Exercise 25.16, write a function, `num_bits`, that determines the number of bits in its non-negative `long` parameter.

    (b) Can you come up with a formula in $n > 0$ that gives the number of bits in n?

Longer Assignments

18. Write and test an iterative version of the `print_spaced` function of Section 25.2.

19. Write and test an iterative version of the `print_commas` function of Section 25.2.

20. Write and test a recursive version of the selection sort function template of Section 14.3.

21. Write a recursive function, `rec_display`, to display the items in a stack on a single output line, with the bottom element printed first, and the top element printed last. For efficiency, pass the stack by reference, but make sure the stack has been restored to its original state when the function terminates.

22. Write and test recursive versions of the following linked list functions.

    (a) `build_list`   Build a linked list of strings entered by the user (where the end of input is signaled by the sentinel string `"DONE"`). Each new string should be appended to the end of the list.

    (b) `display`   See Section 23.4.

    (c) `destroy`   See Section 23.6.

    (d) `are_equal`   See Section 23.6.

23. Do the maze traversal program of Exercise 15.16, using a recursive function to find the path through the maze.

26

Advanced Sorting and Efficiency of Algorithms

For a small array or vector (say, 100 elements or less), it doesn't matter which type of sort you use because any sorting algorithm can perform the sort in a very short time. In contrast, for a very large unsorted vector, one of the advanced sorts should be used because they are much quicker than any of the elementary sorts.

We begin this chapter by discussing a standard method for obtaining a "rough measure," known as the *order of magnitude,* of the efficiency of an algorithm. For a particular algorithm, the order of magnitude can be applied to measure both the algorithm's *average case* and its *worst case* efficiency. Then we do order of magnitude calculations for the efficiency of selection sort, the two versions of bubble sort, and the linear and binary searches. Finally we present an advanced sort, known as quicksort, and explain wherein its greater efficiency lies. In a rough sense, quicksort resembles a binary search in that it repeatedly partitions the vector to be sorted into two smaller pieces.

26.1 Efficiency of a Sorting Algorithm

Big-O The term *Big-O* refers to the order of magnitude measure of how quickly an expression in n grows large as n gets large. Big-O provides this measure by focusing on the expression's dominant term and ignoring constant factors.

Expression	Order of magnitude
(a) $n^3 + n^2 - 3$	$O(n^3)$
(b) $4n^2 + 7n + 2$	$O(n^2)$
(c) $8n \cdot \log_2 n + 14n$	$O(n \cdot \log_2 n)$
(d) $2n + 10^7$	$O(n)$
(e) $3 \cdot \log_2 n + 1$	$O(\log_2 n)$

Be aware that n^3 gets larger at a much faster rate than n^2, which, in turn, gets larger at a faster rate than $n \cdot \log_2 n$ does. For example, when $n = 1000$, $n^3 = 1,000,000,000$, whereas $n^2 = 1,000,000$ and $n \cdot \log_2 n$ is approximately 10,000. Thus, when $n = 1000$, expression (a) is significantly larger than (b), even though (b) has larger coefficients; similarly, expression (b) is larger than (c) although (c) has larger coefficients. In turn, the growth rate of (d) is slower than that of (c), and (e) has the slowest growth rate of all of the given expressions.

Order of Magnitude of the Efficiency of a Sort   Computer time during a sort is consumed by the large number of repetitions of certain basic operations, which are closely tied to the number of comparisons of vector elements that the sort must make. Thus:

> The order of magnitude of the efficiency of a sort is Big-*O* of the number of comparisons that the sort makes in sorting a vector of size n. This number of comparisons can be taken as either the *maximum* for all vectors of size n, which describes ***worst case*** efficiency, or the average number for all vectors of size n, which describes ***average case*** efficiency.

As you will see, each of the elementary sorts from Chapter 14 has efficiency of order n^2, both on average and in the worst case, whereas quicksort, covered in this chapter, has average case efficiency of order $n \cdot \log_2 n$. Thus, to sort a very large randomly ordered vector, there is no question that you should use an advanced sort such as quicksort.

Selection Sort Has Order n^2 Efficiency   The code, without comments, for the selection sort algorithm of Section 14.3 is

```
void select_sort (Vector<CType>& V, int N)
{
    int ctf, index_min;
    for (ctf=0; ctf< N-1; ctf++)
```

```
        {
        index_min=ctf;
        for (int i=ctf+1; i<N; i++)
            if (V[i] < V[index_min])
                index_min=i;
        swap (V[ctf], V[index_min]);
        }
    }
```

Let us calculate the number of times the highlighted comparison is performed by selection sort in sorting a vector of size n.

■ During pass 1, when `ctf=0`, it will make $n - 1$ comparisons.

■ During pass 2, when `ctf=1`, it will make $n - 2$ comparisons.

And so on down to the last pass, when it makes one comparison. Thus, the total number of comparisons is

$$n - 1 + n - 2 + \ldots + 3 + 2 + 1$$

The sum of these numbers is the number of terms $(n - 1)$ times the average term $(1 + n - 1)/2$. This product equals $(n - 1)(n)/2$, which equals $(n^2/2) - (n/2)$. Thus, selection sort is of order n^2.

Bubble Sort Has Order n^2 Efficiency Version 1 of bubble sort, from Section 14.4, is given without comments.

```
void bubble_sort (Vector<CType>& V, int n)
{
    int pass, cell_to_fill;
    for (pass = 1; pass < n; pass++)
        {
        cell_to_fill = n - pass;
        for (int i = 0; i < cell_to_fill; i++)
            if (V[i] > V[i+1])
                swap (V[i], V[i+1]);
        }
}
```

The sort will make $n - 1$ passes. The total number of executions of the highlighted comparison will be

$$n - 1 + n - 2 + \ldots + 3 + 2 + 1$$

which is equal to the same sum as in the selection sort and thus also of order n^2.

Average Versus Worst Case   For selection sort and the first version of bubble sort, the number of comparisons depends only on the size of n and not at all on how out of order the original vector is. (Do you see why?)

However, for the improved version of bubble sort, the number of comparisons depends not only on n, but also on the order of the original vector. The *worst case* — that is, the case in which the most comparisons will occur — is any vector for which the smallest value is in the last cell. (Do you see why?)

The *average case* efficiency of a sort or search is a measure of its efficiency as an average over all possible vectors of size n. One way to get at the average case is to determine, mathematically, the average number of comparisons over all possible orderings of a vector of n values. This mathematical analysis can be extremely difficult, even for some fairly simple algorithms, so a more practical, experimental method is often used in estimating the average case order of magnitude. This approach, illustrated in detail in Section 26.3, randomly generates several vectors of size n, counts all comparisons (or some other critical steps) performed by the sort or search, and then calculates the average number of comparisons.

Using mathematical techniques, it can be shown that the average case order of magnitude for the *improved* bubble sort is still n^2, the same as we determined for the worst case. This can be seen intuitively by considering that, for a randomly generated vector, it is quite likely that some of the smaller elements will be far enough to the right that the number of passes required will be close to n, meaning that the "early" exit actually occurs quite late in the sort.

26.2   Efficiency of a Searching Algorithm

Linear Search — Worst and Average Cases Are Both O(n)   The worst case for a linear search of a vector of size n occurs when either the item to find is at the end of the vector or is not in the vector at all. In this case, linear search will make n comparisons. The average case will require $n/2$ comparisons because, on average, the position of the item to find will be in the middle of the vector. Thus, both the worst and the average case efficiency of linear search are of the same order of magnitude, namely, $O(n)$.

Binary Search — Worst and Average Cases are Both O(log n)   Here, the worst case is much easier to analyze than the average case. The worst case happens when the item to find is either not in the vector or is in the last vector cell to be examined. Recall from Section 14.2 that each iteration of the loop of the binary search cuts the segment still under consideration in *half*. Thus, the number of executions of the loop body in the worst case will be *floor* ($\log_2 n$) + 1. To see this more concretely, consider that in a vector of 32 (where 32 = 2^5 or, equivalently, $\log_2 32$ = 5) elements, it will take five halvings of 32 — 16, 8, 4, 2, and 1 — to narrow the segment still under consideration down to a single element, and then one more execution to determine if that element is the item to find. (See Exercise 26.6 for further examination of this log result.) Thus, the binary search is $O(\log n)$ because each execution of the loop body involves at most three comparisons. (It is customary to ignore the base of the log in order of magnitude measurements.)

Although we do not present the argument, the average case behavior of binary search is also $O(\log n)$. Exercises 26.14 and 26.15 ask you to do some experiments with the binary search function and to compare the number of steps performed by both successful and unsuccessful searches.

26.3 A Step-Counting Experiment

In this section, we present a program that determines, by experiment, the average number of comparisons performed by the early exit version of bubble sort in sorting vectors of various sizes. We then relate the results produced by this experiment to the theoretical order n^2 result arrived at in the previous section.

Experimental Design   The central idea of the experiment is to randomly generate a vector of a user-specified size, then increment a counter each time the comparison statement is executed while sorting the vector. We need to consider two issues when deciding how to get a truly representative count from this "generate and sort" process.

First, incrementing a counter for a given step of the sort will require that we modify the sorting function. We use a global counter, comp_ct, so that both the main function and the bubble_sort function have access to the counter. This eliminates the need to pass the counter as a parameter and thus minimizes the amount of modification that must be made to the sorting function itself. Second, to achieve truly random results, we should count the total number of comparisons performed during several iterations of the "generate and sort" process, then take an average over the number of iterations. We make this number of iterations a user input.

The Coding Details   The global variable definition and the main function from bubl_ct.cpp are given here, along with a few sample runs of the program.

```
long comp_ct = 0; // global counter

void main()
{
    int size; // of vector
    int iters; // iterations of sort
    srand(time(0)); // randomize

    cout << "Vector size: "; cin >> size;
    cout << "Iterations:  "; cin >> iters;

    Vector<int> V(size); // vector to sort
    for (int i=1; i<=iters; i++)
        {
        gen_random(V,size);
        bubble_sort(V,size);
        }

    cout << "Avg. comps.: " << comp_ct/float(iters)
        << endl;
}
```

```
Vector size: 40
Iterations: 10
Avg. comparisons: 760.4
```

```
Vector size: 1600
Iterations: 3
Avg. comps.: 1.27547e+06
```

Sample runs

The slightly modified bubble_sort function is:

```
void bubble_sort (Vector<CType>& V, int size)
{
    int swaps; // count swaps made on a given ctf
    for (int ctf=size-1; ctf>0; ctf--)
        {
        swaps = 0;
        for (int i=0; i<ctf; i++)
            if (++comp_ct && V[i] > V[i+1])
```

```
            {
            swap (V[i], V[i+1]); swap_ct++;
            swaps++;
            }
        if (swaps==0) return;
        }
    }
```

Notice that the only modification to the bubble sort code is the highighted statement to increment comp_ct immediately before each execution of the comparison V[i] > V[i+1]. You must use the prefix rather than the postfix version of the increment operator here. Do you see why?

Interpreting the Experimental Results   The following table, which gives the average number of comparisons performed by version 2 of bubble sort for vectors of various sizes, was compiled from several runs of the program. If you were to repeat these experiments, you would get similar but not identical results.

Vector size (n)	Iterations	Average comparisons per sort
10	10	42.45
20	10	180.29
40	10	760.4
80	10	3094.4
160	10	12590.8
320	10	50899.1
800	5	318344
1600	3	1.27547e+06
3200	3	5.11039e+06

We determined in the previous section that both versions of bubble sort were order n^2. The experimental data agrees with this theoretical result. For example, when the vector size is increased from 40 to 160, a factor of 4, the number of swaps increases from 760 to 12,591, a factor of 16.6, or approximately 4^2. Similarly, when the vector size is increased from 80 to 800, a factor of 10, the number of comparisons increases from 3094 to 318,344, a factor of 102.9, slightly more than 10^2. In both cases, *the factor by which the number of comparisons increases is approximately the square of the factor by which the vector size increases,* which is the kind of behavior that $O(n^2)$ algorithms exhibit. Notice that the increase in comparisons is *approximate* rather than exact, because the $O(n^2)$ measure represents any equation of the form $an^2 + bn + c$. The lower-order terms, bn and c, have an effect on the actual increase, although this effect is less noticeable for large n than for small n.

■ **QUESTION** Bubble sort is of order n^2 and makes 318,344 comparisons, on average, to sort a random vector of 800 items. Approximately how many comparisons will it make to sort a random vector of 8000 items?

Answer The number of comparisons should increase by a factor of approximately $(8000/800)^2 = 10^2 = 100$. Thus, we can expect approximately $318,344 \times 100$, or nearly 32 million, comparisons. ■ ■■

In the exercises you are asked to perform step-counting experiments for other algorithms.

26.4 Quicksort

The `quicksort` function presented here is a recursive function. Its body contains calls both to itself and to the function `partition`. You should note that `partition` does most of the work and so, not surprisingly, the difficult coding is contained in `partition`. (Also, be aware that `partition` is not recursive.)

In this section, we describe briefly what a call to `partition` accomplishes, give the body of `quicksort`, and then present all of the details of `partition`. We conclude our discussion of `quicksort` by explaining why it is of order $n \cdot \log_2 n$.

What the `partition` ***Function Accomplishes*** When `partition` is applied to a vector, it rearranges the vector by focusing on the vector's first element, which we will call the ***pivot***. For example, for the vector

42	20	55	59	70	81	32	62	28

the pivot value is 42.

A call to `partition` accomplishes the following:

1. It ultimately puts the pivot in its correct position.

2. It moves the elements in the vector so that by the end of the call

(a) all elements smaller than or equal to the pivot are to the left of the pivot, and

(b) all elements larger than the pivot are to the right of the pivot.

After a call to partition, the preceding vector will look as follows, with the pivot in the fourth cell of the vector.

Vector after call to partition

32	20	28	42	70	81	59	62	55

■ **QUESTION** Suppose partition is applied to the vector

58	73	65	24	32	90	86	17	20	88	30

1. In which cell will 58 end up?

2. Will 65 end up to the left or right of 58?

3. In exactly which cell will 65 end up?

Answer

1. 58 will end up in its correct cell — the sixth from the left.

2. 65 will end up somewhere to the right of 58.

3. You cannot answer this question until you have more details on how partition works. ■ ▬

The Declaration of partition partition has four parameters — the vector to be sorted, the vector's first and last indexes, and the index of the cell in which the pivot will end up. Two of these are reference parameters — the vector itself (because partition will do some rearranging) and part_index (the index of the cell in which the pivot will end up). Here is the declaration for partition.

```
void partition (Vector<EType>& V,
                int first, int last,
                int& part_index);
```

The quicksort Function After partition has been applied a first time to the original vector, the pivot will be in its correct place.

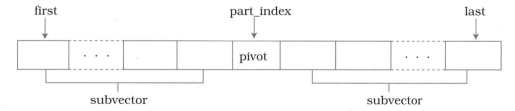

Thus, `partition` reduces the original problem to that of sorting two shorter subvectors. This sorting can be done through two separate recursive calls to `quicksort`.

■ **QUESTION**   How should you fill in the blank in the body of `quicksort`? Note that `quicksort` has three parameters — the name of the vector to be sorted and its first and last indexes.

```
void quicksort (Vector<EType>& V,
                int first, int last)
{
   if (first >= last) // terminal case
      return;

   int part_index;
   partition (V, first, last, part_index);
   quicksort (V, first, part_index-1);
   quicksort (_____);
}
```

Answer   The second call to `quicksort` sorts the subvector to the right of the pivot. The first index for this subvector is `part_index + 1`; the last index remains unchanged. Thus, the missing line should read

```
quicksort (V, part_index+1, last);
```

Details of `partition`   You might imagine that `partition` would first determine the correct position for the pivot and then do all its switching, but it works the other way around. By the time the correct position for the pivot is determined, most of the switching has already been done.

Recall that values larger than the pivot must end up to its right, and values smaller than or equal to the pivot must end up to its left. In `partition`, each value from the left side of the vector that is larger than the pivot is switched with a value from the right side that is smaller than or equal to the pivot.

The `partition` **Algorithm**   `partition` uses a left marker and a right marker. At the start, the left marker is at the left end, and the right marker is at the right end. (The vector shown here is the same one used earlier in our discussion of `partition`.)

At the start

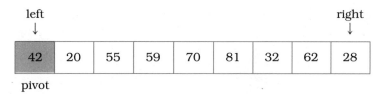

Move the left marker to the right until you find the first element that is larger than the pivot. Move the right marker to the left until you find the first element that is less than or equal to the pivot.

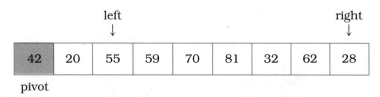

Then switch these two values (in this case, 55 and 28).

After the first switch

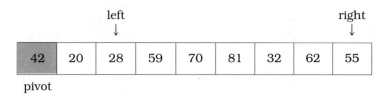

Next, move the left marker farther to the right until you find the next element that is larger than the pivot. Move the right marker farther to the left until you find the next element that is less than or equal to the pivot. Then switch these two values (in this case, 59 and 32).

After the second switch

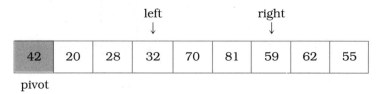

Next, move the left marker to the right until you find the next element that is greater than the pivot. Move the right marker to the left until you find the next element that is less than or equal to the pivot. This time, however, you do not switch these values, because the right marker has crossed over the left marker

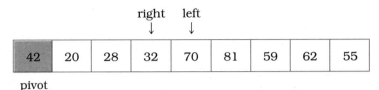

pivot

The final step is to switch the pivot with the value in the cell marked by the right marker.

At the conclusion of `partition`

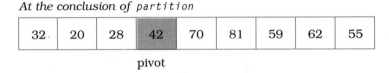

pivot

The `partition` **Function**   We use a do..while loop to keep switching larger values from the left side with smaller or equal values from the right side. The condition while (left < right) will determine whether the markers have met or crossed over.

Note that the final switch is done after the do..while loop. After the final switch, part_index is assigned the subscript for the correct position of pivot. Thus, part_index is a reference parameter of the function so that this subscript value is communicated back to quicksort.

```
void partition (Vector<EType>& V,
                int first, int last, int& part_index)
{
    EType pivot = V[first];
    int left = first;
    int right = last;

    do {
        while (V[left] <= pivot && left<last) left++;
        while (V[right] > pivot) right--;
        if (left < right)
            swap (V[left], V[right]);
        }
    while (left < right);

    swap (V[first], V[right]);
    part_index = right;
}
```

Why the Average Case for `quicksort` ***is O(n • log₂ n)*** It is useful to analyze `quicksort` in terms of levels in the following way:

- **Level 1** The first call to `partition` on the full vector of size n. Essentially n comparisons of vector elements will occur because each of the other vector elements will be involved in a comparison to the pivot. (See the `while` condition.)

- **Level 2** The two calls to `partition` — one for each of the subvectors created by level 1. Again, because every element of the original vector of size n (except the pivot elements of each of the subvectors) is involved in one comparison with a pivot element, essentially n comparisons will occur at this level.

- **Level 3** The four calls to partition — one for each of the four subvectors created by the end of level 2. Again, essentially n comparisons will occur.

And so on for each of the levels.

The total number of comparisons for the full sort is essentially the product of the number of comparisons at each level times the number of levels. Statistically, for a random vector of size n, most of the time the splitting into two pieces by `partition` will be "roughly" in half. Therefore, the total number of levels will be of order $\log_2 n$, similar to the binary search. Thus, the total number of comparisons will be of order $n \times \log_2 n$

The Worst Case for `quicksort` ***is O(n²)*** Ironically, `quicksort` is least efficient when sorting a vector that is already sorted. This is because the splitting at each call of `partition` is not into two roughly equal subvectors. For example, the first call of `partition` splits the original vector into one subvector of size 1 and a second of size $n - 1$. This same kind of thing happens for each call. Thus, the number of levels will be n, with n comparisons in each level, giving a total of n^2 comparisons for the full sort.

Quicksort is the first sort or search we have presented for which the worst case and average case efficiencies have different orders of magnitude.

Going Deeper As mentioned previously, order of magnitude is a *rough measure*. If two algorithms for the same problem have *different* orders of magnitude for the average case, then the algorithm with the smaller order of magnitude will tend to be more efficient for a large instance of the problem. However, when two algorithms for the same problem have the *same* order of magnitude for the average case, it is sometimes the case that one algorithm is nevertheless significantly better on average then the other. For example, there is a sort known as **heap sort** that is $O(n \cdot \log n)$ in both the average and the worst case. Thus, it might seem that heap sort is definitely preferable to quicksort, whose worst case is $O(n^2)$. However, *more careful analysis and step-counting experiments show that, on average, quicksort requires about half as many steps as heap sort.*

Avoiding the Worst Case for `quicksort`   There are several modified versions of quicksort whose worst case is $O(n \cdot \log n)$. One version avoids the worst case by having the `partition` function randomly choose a pivot value from the subvector to be partitioned, then swap it into the first cell of this subvector before carrying out the partition. However, this version is not quite as efficient on average as the original quicksort because of the overhead required for the random number generation, which is significantly more time consuming than a comparison or swap.

■ EXERCISES

1. How many swaps does selection sort make in sorting a vector of *n* items?

2. How many comparisons will the first version of bubble sort make in sorting a random vector of 20 items? in sorting a vector of 20 items that are in increasing order?

3. Answer Exercise 26.2 for the second (early exit) version of bubble sort.

4. Compare the number of comparisons made on average by the two versions of bubble sort in sorting random vectors of size 10, 40, and 800.

5. Why is it crucial that the *prefix* rather than the *postfix* version of the increment operator be used to increment `comp_ct` in the `bubble_sort` function of the program `bubl_ct.cpp` in Section 26.3?

6. For the program fragment at right, determine the final value of `ct` for several values of *n*. How does the value of `ct` compare to *floor*$(\log_2 n) + 1$?

```
ct = 0;
while (n>0)
    { n /= 2; ct++; }
```

7. Show what each of the following vectors will look like after one call to `partition`, and give the value returned in the reference parameter, `part_index`.

	0	1	2	3	4	5	6	7	8
V	55	40	58	32	20	12	29	80	70

	0	1	2	3	4	5	6	7	8
W	40	40	58	32	40	12	40	80	40

8. Trace the effect of `quicksort` on the following vectors.

(a)

42	20	55	59	70	81	32	62	28

(b)

1	2	3	4	5	6	7

(c)

5	6	4	7	3	1	9	2	8

Programming Problems

9. Write a program to (a) read words (at least 25) from a file into a vector; (b) print the vector; (c) use quicksort to sort the vector; and (d) print the vector in alphabetical order.

10. Write a program to (a) read phone entries (see Section 20.1) from a file into a vector; (b) print the vector, one component per line; (c) use quicksort to sort the vector; and (d) print the vector in alphabetical order, one component per line.

Longer Assignments

11. (a) Modify the program `bubl_ct.cpp` so that it also determines the average number of swaps made in sorting a random vector of a given size.

    (b) Create a table like that given in Section 26.3 to display the data of part (a).

    (c) Use the table of part (b) to determine whether the number of swaps required by bubble sort to sort a random vector is $O(n^2)$.

    (d) Use the table of part (b) to estimate the number of swaps bubble sort will make in sorting a random vector of size 10,000.

12. Write a program to determine the average number of comparisons and swaps made by quicksort in sorting a random vector of size n. Let the user input the vector size and the number of iterations of the "generate and sort" process. Create a table like that given in Section 26.3 to display the data. At what point does the performance of quicksort break even with that of bubble sort?

13. (a) Modify the program of Exercise 26.12 to determine the number of comparisons and swaps required by quicksort to sort a vector that is already sorted. Compile a table of data like that of the previous two exercises.

    (b) Modify the program of part (a) to determine the number of comparisons and swaps required by quicksort to sort a vector that is in reverse sorted order. Compile a table of data like that of the previous two exercises.

    (c) Use the tables of data that you compiled in parts (a) and (b) to show that quicksort is $O(n^2)$ in these cases.

14. **(a)** Write a program that determines the average number of comparisons that binary search makes during an unsuccessful search of a vector of n items. (*Hints*: For each i from 0 to $n - 1$, fill cell i of the vector with the value $2*i$. Then, determine the total number of comparisons made by the binary search in searching for each of $-1, 1, 3, 5, \ldots, 2n - 1$.)

    (b) Modify the program of part (a) to determine the average number of comparisons made by a binary search during a successful search of a vector of n items.

15. Use the program of Exercise 26.14 to answer the following questions.

    (a) How does the number of comparisons for a successful binary search compare to that for an unsuccessful binary search?

    (b) What happens to the number of comparisons when the vector size is doubled? When it is squared? How do you explain these results?

27

Inheritance

In this chapter, we discuss some of the ways in which inheritance, a central technique of object-oriented design and programming, is used to create new classes from existing ones. You will see how to use inheritance to create a new class from an existing class by (1) adding new member functions, (2) adding new data members, and (3) overriding or even hiding some member functions of the existing class. A further issue that arises with inheritance is whether to make data members of a class private or to relax this access restriction somewhat. Although the full power of inheritance requires techniques that go beyond the scope of this book, the examples presented will give you some sense of the power of inheritance.

27.1 Introduction to Inheritance

Using the object-oriented mechanism of *inheritance*, a programmer can reuse an existing class (that is part of the solution of one or more problems) as the *base class* from which to create a new, *derived class* (that is part of the solution of another, similar problem). The derived class, also known as the *child class*, inherits all the features of its base class, also called the *parent class*, but can have its own "customized" variations on and extensions of the base class. Notice that the parent–child relationship for classes is somewhat analogous to the parent–child relationship for people — a child inherits the physical and behavioral features of a parent, but always with variations.

The Is-A Relationship   The derived class ***is a*** version of the base class. For example, a square *is a* (special type of) rectangle, and an undergraduate student (likewise, a graduate student) *is a* student. These relationships can be illustrated by diagrams as follows:

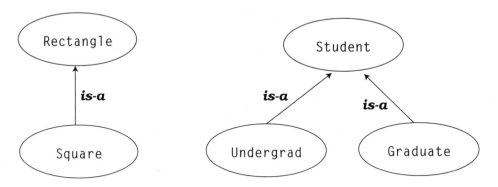

In these diagrams, the "is-a" relationship can be replaced by "derived-from." Note that the arrow points from the derived class to the base class.

Abstract Classes   Both `Rectangle` and `Square` are concrete classes, where an object of type `Square` is a special `Rectangle` whose length and width are equal. On the other hand, the `Undergrad` and `Graduate` classes are two different versions of the somewhat abstract notion of "student." In fact, the class `Student` is too abstract to deal with concretely — it is only feasible to create objects from its more concrete derived classes.

Advantages of Inheritance   Inheritance supports good software engineering practice in three main ways.

1. **Reusing code**   A given problem solution may require a class that is very similar to an existing class. Using inheritance to create this new problem-specific derived class from the existing base class is a way of reusing the code of the base class. If the code for the base class is extensive and complex, a great deal of time is saved through reuse.

2. **Reliability**   Creating a new class via inheritance from a well-tested base class is more reliable than writing a new class from the ground up. Only the new features of the derived class, not its inherited features, must be thoroughly tested.

3. **Information hiding**   Software engineers can write well-documented classes with the intention that these classes be used not only as components of a particular problem solution, but that

they be used as base classes by other programmers. In this way, the demands on the designer of the derived class(es) to understand the details of the base class's code can be minimized. In fact, as you will soon see, the programmer may not even have access to the base class's source code!

Class Hierarchies Just as objects model the real world, a hierarchy, or "family tree," of classes models the classification of closely related objects. As an example, an employee is an abstraction for various specific classes of employees. There are salaried employees and employees who are paid by the hour. Commissioned employees receive a base salary plus a commission that is calculated from their sales, and are thus a special type of salaried employee. Further, employees who are paid by the hour can be further categorized as full time or part time.

27.2 A Better Time_piece **Class by Inheritance**

■ **PROBLEM** Write a tutorial program that will do each of the following, three times: (1) display a time in 24-hour format (hh:mm, where $0 \leq$ hh ≤ 23); (2) ask the user to input the equivalent time in the 12-hour, A.M./P.M. format; (3) tell the user whether the input is correct, and, if not, display the correct answer. A sample run might look like this.

```
Convert 17:30 into AM/PM format: 7:30 pm
Wrong. The answer is 5:30 PM
Convert 1:15 into AM/PM format: 1:15AM
Correct.
Convert 9:00 into AM/PM format: 9:00 am
Correct.
```

A Better Time_piece ***Class*** The solution of the problem just stated requires time piece objects whose values can be compared for equality (using the == operator) and whose values can be output in 24-hour format (e.g., 17:30 rather than 5:30 P.M.). Rather than start from scratch, we can reuse the Time_piece class (of Chapters 18 and 19) to create, via inheritance, a Btr_Time_piece class that provides this additional functionality.

The following client code fragment, from tutor.cpp, uses this Btr_Time_piece class and produces the kind of sample run given earlier.

```
Btr_Time_piece clock, time;

clock.set(5, 30, 'P');
for (int i=1; i<=3; i++)
    {
    cout << "Convert ";
    clock.display_24hr();
    cout << " into AM/PM format: ";
    time.enter();
    if (time==clock)
        cout << "Correct.\n";
    else
        {
        cout << "Wrong. The answer is ";
        clock.display(); cout << endl;
        }
    clock.update (7, 45);
    }
```

The new constructor call and member function calls are highlighted. Notice the calls to the base class's set, enter, display, and update functions — these are members of the Btr_Time_piece class by inheritance.

The Btr_Time_piece **Class Interface**   The following class interface is also from tutor.cpp. The highlighted code indicates that the Btr_Time_piece class is derived from the Time_piece class by public inheritance. (A derived class can also be created through protected or private inheritance, but that is a more advanced issue that we do not tackle.)

```
class Btr_Time_piece : public Time_piece
{
public:
    void display_24hr();
        // display time in 24 hour format
    bool operator== (Btr_Time_piece T);
        // return true if times are equal; else false
};
```

Although you don't see the member functions of the base class, Time_piece, in the above interface, a Btr_Time_piece object still has access to these inherited member functions.

Implementing the display_24hr ***Member Function*** The Btr_Time_piece class does *not* have access to the private data members of the Time_piece class. However, it does inherit the Time_piece class's get_mins_past function, which can be used, as illustrated here, to display a time in 24-hour format.

```
void Btr_Time_piece::display_24hr()
{
    int mins = get_mins_past();
    cout << (mins/60) << ':';
    mins = mins%60;
    if (mins<10) cout << '0';
    cout << mins;
}
```

Implementing operator== Two times are equal if they have the same hour, minute, and meridian. These data members can be accessed via the corresponding accessor functions.

```
bool Btr_Time_piece::operator== (Btr_Time_piece T)
{
    return ( get_hour() == T.get_hour() &&
             get_minute()  == T.get_minute() &&
             get_meridian() == T.get_meridian() );
}
```

The Protected Access Specification

The preceding function body would be simpler — and perhaps more efficient — if the accessor function calls could be replaced by direct access to the private data members hr, min, and merid of the base class. The base class can grant this direct access to any of its descendants by specifying that its data members are **protected** rather than private. It is important to note that a client program cannot directly access members of a class that are either private or protected.

The file time_pc3.h (available at the PWS Web site) makes the formerly private members of the Time_piece class protected.

```
class Time_piece
{
public:

    // modifier functions
    void set(int h, int m, char mrd);

            etc.
  protected:
    int hr, min;  // the hour and minute
    int mins_past; // mins past midnite
    char merid; // meridian: a(m) or p(m),

            etc.
};
```

■ **QUESTION**   How could you rewrite the `operator==` function if `private` were changed to `protected` in the `Time_piece` class?

Answer   The return statement in the body could be coded as

```
return (hr==T.hr && min==T.min && merid==T.merid);
```

Dangers of Providing Protected Access   The preceding version of the `Btr_Time_piece operator==` function uses details that are specific to the implementation of the `Time_piece` class. If the names of any of the data members of the `Time_piece` class were changed, the preceding version of `operator==` would no longer work. However, the first version of `operator==` would still work, because it relies only on the public interface to the `Time_piece` class, and the public interface should never change in ways that break client code or descendant classes.

27.3   Another Descendant of the `Time_piece` **Class**

In this section, we create a descendant of the `Time_piece` class (of `time_pc2.h`) that has an additional data member, the time zone — EST, CST, MST, or PST. This `Zon_Time_piece` class will also add public and private member functions to those that it inherits from its base class. A sample `main` function (from `zontimpc.cpp`) that creates and manipulates `Zon_Time_piece` objects is

```
void main()
{
    Zon_Time_piece t1, t2;
    t1.set(12,0,'A','E');
    t1.display(); cout << endl;
    cout << "Enter a time (hh:mm xM xST): ";
    t2.enter();
    t2.display(); cout << endl;
    t2.update(12, 59);
    t2.display(); cout << endl;
}
```

Some sample runs, two of which contain run-time errors, are

```
12:00 AM EST
Enter a time (hh:mm xM xST): 8:19 pm PST
8:19 PM PST
9:18 AM PST

12:00 AM EST
Enter a time (hh:mm xM xST): 2:04pm AST
Time_piece error: 2:04 PM AST

12:00 AM EST
Enter a time (hh:mm xM xST): 13:00pm MST
Time_piece error: 13:00 PM
```

The Zon_Time_piece **Class Interface** The complete class interface, also from zontimpc.cpp, is

```
class Zon_Time_piece : public Time_piece
{
public:
    // modifiers
    void set (int h, int m, char mrd, char zn);

    // accessors
    char get_zone() const { return zone; }
```

```
    // IO functions
    void display( ostream& outs = cout) const;
    void enter ( );

protected:
    char zone; // 'E', 'C', 'M', or 'P'
    void validate_zone();
};
```

The set ***Member Function Definition***   The set member function of the Zon_Time_piece class must assign the values of its four parameters to the four corresponding data members: hr, min, merid, and zone. However, setting the first three of these can be done by calling the base class's set member function.

```
void Zon_Time_piece::set (int h, int m, char mrd, char zn)
{
    Time_piece::set(h, m, mrd); // call base class's set fn.
    zone = zn;
    validate_zone();
}
```

The use of scope resolution (highlighted in the preceding code) to call the base class's set member function is necessary. Otherwise, the compiler assumes that the call is to the Zon_Time_piece class's set member function, and issues a compiler-dependant error message, which for Turbo C++ 4.5 is "Too few parameters in call to 'Zon_Time_piece::set (int,int,char,char)' ".

■ QUESTION   How should you complete the following definition of the Zon_Time_piece class's display member function.

```
void Zon_Time_piece::display( ostream& outs) const
{
    _____;
    outs << ' ' << zone << "ST";
}
```

Answer   The completed line is

```
        Time_piece::display(outs);
```

Other Member Functions   The definitions of enter and validate_zone are at the PWS Web site. Note that none of the Zon_Time_piece class's member function implementations directly accesses the base class's data members.

Additional Data Members and Constructors The version of the `Time_piece` class discussed in Chapters 18 and 19 did not have explicitly provided constructors. Therefore, the descendant `Zon_Time_piece` class does not need to provide constructors, although it may do so. Suppose, however, that the `Zon_Time_piece` class is a descendant of a `Time_piece` class that does have explicitly provided constructors. Such a version is provided at the PWS Web site in the `time_pc3.h` file. Its constructors are

```
Time_piece () { /* do nothing */ }

Time_piece (int h, int m, char mrd)
    : hr(h), min(m), merid(mrd) // initializer list
{ validate(); }
```

The `Zon_Time_piece` *Class Constructors* The `Zon_Time_piece` class can now provide its own no-argument and four-argument constructors, making use of the base class's constructors in the process. Notice in the following implementations that the base class constructors are "called" in initializer lists.

```
Zon_Time_piece ()
    : Time_piece() { /* do nothing */ }

Zon_Time_piece (int h, int m, char mrd, char zn)
    : Time_piece(h, m, mrd), zone(zn)
{ validate_zone(); }
```

27.4 An `Ord_Int_list` **Class**

The examples of inheritance provided in the previous two sections extended the base `Time_piece` class by adding member functions and/or data members. In some cases, inheritance is useful for modifying, rather than extending, the behavior of the base class.

In this section, we use inheritance to modify the `Int_list` class, first introduced in Chapter 18, to create an `Ord_Int_list` class. The version of the `Int_list` class that we will use is in the file `int_lst2.h`. It is identical to the version of Chapters 18 and 19 except that the access modifier for data members is `protected` rather than `private`.

The *Ord_Int_list* ***Class Interface***   The interface for the `Ord_Int_list` class is given here. It overrides the behavior of its base class's `add` member function. Also, it disables the inherited `sort` member function (which is now of no use to a client program) by "hiding" it in its `private` section.

```
class Ord_Int_list : public Int_list
{
public:
    void add (int elt);
    // override Int_list's add member function
    // so that list is kept in sorted order

private:
    // hide Int_list's sort member function
    void sort();
};
```

■ **EXAMPLE**   The following `main` function, from `ordlist1.cpp`, produces the output shown. Notice that elements are added to the list in sorted order, and that `Ord_Int_list` objects still have access to functions `display`, `length`, and `retrieve` from their base class.

```
void main()
{
    Ord_Int_list L;
    L.add(31); L.add(10); L.add(20); L.add(6);
    L.display(); cout << endl;

    for (int i=L.length(); i>= 1; i--)
        cout << L.retrieve(i) << ' ';
    cout << endl;
}
```

```
6 10 20 31
31 20 10 6
```

Output

Overriding the Inherited *add* ***Function***   The `Ord_Int_list` class will override the `add` function that it inherits from the `Int_list` class by redefining it. Notice that this definition directly manipulates the `protected` members of the `Int_list` base class, and that it uses the technique of Section 14.5 for inserting the new element into the sorted vector `Elts`.

```
void Ord_Int_list::add (int elt)
{
    len++;
```

```
if (len >= Elts.length())
    Elts.resize(8 + Elts.length());
for (int i=len-1; i>=1; i--)
    if (Elts[i] > elt)
        Elts[i+1] = Elts[i];
    else
        break;
Elts[i+1] = elt;
}
```

Other Ways to Define *add*   Our implementation of the function just given has not taken full advantage of inheritance. The three highlighted lines of the preceding definition can be replaced by the single statement

```
Int_list::add(elt);
```

because the base class's add member function has to increment the length of the Elts vector and, if necessary, resize it. Be aware that failing to use scope resolution to indicate that this is a call to the Int_list class's add function would result in infinite recursion!

An even shorter version of add could replace the statements to move elt into its correct, sorted position by the call

```
Int_list::sort();
```

to the base class's sort function. Although this significantly reduces the amount of code to write, and places no burden on the programmer to understand the implementation of the base class, it may be very inefficient, depending on the sorting algorithm used in the base class's implementation.

The Derived Class's *sort* ***Member Function***   Because no client program of the Ord_Int_list class can call sort, it is not necessary to provide a definition for it in the derived class.

27.5 An Improved String Class

In Chapters 6 and 16, you learned to use some of the member functions of a String class that is a subset of the ANSI-ISO C++ draft standard. The file bastring.h at the PWS Web site contains the complete C++ source code for the interface and implementation of this class. If you are using a different string class, such as that provided by Borland in cstring.h, you may have only the compiled object code, not the C++ source code, for the implementation. The important point here is that, regardless of which version you are working with, the String class is implemented in such a way that a programmer can extend it through inheritance *without understanding the details of its implementation* — another example of the power of information hiding.

Creating an xtString ***Class*** To illustrate how we can extend the String class, consider the following extended string class interface, xtString. It adds member functions for returning the reverse of a string and for converting a string to uppercase.

An Extended String Class, xtString ***(from*** xt_str.h***)***

```
class xtString: public String
{
public:
    xtString reverse() const;
    // return reverse of calling xtString object

    void to_upper();
    // Change calling xtString object to uppercase
};
```

Member Function Implementations The implementations of these new member functions are

```
xtString xtString::reverse() const
{
    // Construct a copy of the calling object
    xtString rev(*this);

    char tmp;
    int len = rev.length();
    for (int i=0, j=len-1; i<len/2; i++, j--)
        {
        tmp = rev[i]; rev[i] = rev[j]; rev[j] = tmp;
        }
    return rev;
}
```

```
void xtString::to_upper()
{
    for (int i=0; i<length(); i++)
        (*this)[i] = toupper((*this)[i]);
}
```

Notice in the highlighted expression how the *i*th character of the calling String object is accessed.

A Test Program for the *xtString* **Class** The following main function, from str_tst.cpp, both tests and demonstrates the new xtString class member functions. Notice that this derived class has inherited the base class's no-argument constructor, getline function, and overloaded operator<<.

```
void main()
{
    xtString s, rev_s, up_s;
    cout << "\Enter a string: \n";
    getline(cin,s);
    rev_s = s.reverse();
    cout << rev_s << endl;
    up_s = s; up_s.to_upper();
    cout << up_s << endl;
}
```

```
Enter a string:
Reverse me, now!
!won ,em esreveR
REVERSE ME, NOW!
```

Sample run

■ Exercises

Programming Problems

1. Implement the following additional Btr_Time_piece class member functions given that the base class's data members are private.

```
bool operator != (Btr_Time_piece T);
    // return true if calling object is
    // not equal to T; false if it is.
void enter_24hr( )
    // enter time in 24 hour format
void display_military( )
    // display time in military format
    // (See Section 11.10)
```

2. Create an Int_set class by inheritance from the Ord_Int_list class of this chapter by
   (a) overriding the add member function so that an element that is already in the list will not be added again,

(b) overriding the display function so that sets are output enclosed in curly braces, with spaces separating elements, and

(c) adding overloaded operators +, *, and - for set union, intersection, and difference and operators ==, !=, <, <=, >, and >= to take the place of the usual set comparison operators =, ≠, ⊂, ⊆, ⊃, and ⊇.

3. The file frac_cl3.h contains a version of the Fraction class in which the private access specifier has been changed to protected. Create by inheritance from Fraction a class called NR_Fraction whose objects are always displayed and stored in normalized, reduced form.

(a) Which member functions must be overridden?

(b) Which inherited member functions should be hidden in the derived class?

(c) Which member functions can you override without accessing the protected data members directly?

4. The following Sphere class interface and implementation are from sphere.h.

```
class Sphere
{
public:
    // constructors and destructor
    Sphere() { }
    Sphere(double r) : radius(r) { }

    //  accessors
    double get_radius() const { return radius; }
    double get_volume() const
        { return 4.0/3.0 * PI * radius * radius * radius; }

    // modifiers
    void set_radius (double r) { radius = r; }

    // Display
    void DisplayStatistics() const;

private:
    double radius; // radius of sphere
}; //  end Sphere class interface

void Sphere::DisplayStatistics() const
{
    cout << "Radius = . . . " << get_radius() << endl;
    cout << "Volume = . . . " << get_volume() << endl;
}
```

A named sphere is a sphere with a name. Create a NamedSphere class by inheritance from the Sphere class so that a client program can do the following:

(a) Construct a NamedSphere with a given radius and name.

(b) Get or set the radius of a NamedSphere.

(c) Get or set the name of a NamedSphere.

(d) Display all statistics of a NamedSphere, in the form

```
Name = . . . . Volleyball
Radius = . . . 5
Volume = . . . 523.6
```

Longer Assignments

5. Implement and test the following xtString class member functions.

```
void remove_all (xtString t);
// remove all occurrences of t from
// calling xtString object

void replace_all (xtString old_s, xtString new_s);
// replace all occurrences of old_s by
// new_s in the calling xtString object

bool is_palindrome() const;
// return true if calling xtString object
// is a palindrome; false otherwise

bool is_integer() const;
// return true if calling xtString object
// represents an integer; false otherwise

long to_integer() const;
// return the integer value represented by
// the calling xtString object
```

6. Rewrite the program rpn.cpp of Section 24.3 using the is_integer and to_integer functions of the previous problem in place of the RPN program's free functions is_operator and to_int.

C++ Reserved Words

asm	delete	if	return	try
auto	do	inline	short	typedef
break	double	int	signed	union
case	else	long	sizeof	unsigned
catch	enum	new	static	virtual
char	extern	operator	struct	void
class	float	private	switch	volatile
const	for	protected	template	while
continue	friend	public	this	
default	goto	register	throw	

ASCII Characters

Left/right digits	ASCII American Standard Code for Information Interchange									
	0	**1**	**2**	**3**	**4**	**5**	**6**	**7**	**8**	**9**
0	nul*	soh	stx	etx	eot	enq	ack	bel*	bs*	ht*
1	nl*	vt*	np	cr*	so	si	dle	dc1	dc2	dc3
2	dc4	nak	syn	etb	can	em	sub	esc*	fs	gs
3	rs	us	sp	!	"	#	$	%	&	'
4	(	)	0	3	,	—	.	/	0	1
5	2	3	4	5	6	7	8	9	:	;
6	<	0	>	?	@	A	B	C	D	E
7	F	G	H	I	J	K	L	M	N	O
8	P	Q	R	S	T	U	V	W	X	Y
9	Z	[	\	]	^	—	`	a	b	c
10	d	e	f	g	h	i	j	k	l	m
11	n	o	p	q	r	s	t	u	v	w
12	x	y	z	{	|	}	~	del		

*These nonprinting characters are discussed further in Appendix C.

NOTES:

All shaded characters are nonprinting control characters.

Character code 32 (sp) prints a space.

Character codes for digits are contiguous.

Character codes for uppercase letters are contiguous, and character codes for lowercase letters are contiguous; further, the difference between the code for an uppercase letter and its lowercase equivalent is 32.

Escape Sequences

Meanings and Escape Sequences for Some Frequently Used Control Characters			
ASCII code	Abbreviation or character	Meaning	Escape sequence
0	nul	null	'\0'
7	bell	bell	'\a'
8	bs	backspace	'\b'
9	ht	horizontal tab	'\t'
10	nl	newline	'\n'
11	vt	vertical tab	'\v'
13	cr	carriage return	'\r'
27	esc	escape	'\x1B'

Other Commonly Used Escape Sequences			
ASCII code	Abbreviation or character	Meaning	Escape sequence
34	"	double quote	'\"'
92	\	backslash	'\\'

C++ Operators — Precedence and Associativity

In the following table, operators are grouped by precedence, from highest to lowest, and any two operators in the same box have equal precedence. Thus, * and / have equal precedence, as do < and >. *Associativity* refers to the order in which operators of equal precedence are evaluated— left associative operators of equal precedence are evaluated from left to right, whereas right associative operators of equal precedence are evaluated from right to left.

Operators	Meaning(s)	Associativity
( ) ::	grouping scope resolution	left
( ) [] -> . ++ --	function call or type cast subscripting indirect member access direct member access postfix increment postfix decrement	left
++ -- ! - + & * new delete	prefix increment prefix decrement logical not unary minus unary plus address of dereference memory allocation memory deallocation	right

Operators	Meaning(s)	Associativity
* / %	multiply divide modulus	left
+ −	add subtract	left
<< >>	stream insertion (output) stream extraction (input)	left
< <= > >=	less than less than or equal greater than greater than or equal	left
== !=	equal not equal	left
&&	logical and	left
||	logical or	left
= *= /= %= += −=	assign multiply and assign divide and assign modulus and assign add and assign subtract and assign	right
,	comma (evaluate)	left

The following operators are not covered in this book:

	`sizeof`
bitwise operators	`~, &, |, ^, <<, >>`
member access	`.* ->*`
conditional	`?:`
assignment	`&=, |=, ^=, <<=, >>=`

Author-Provided Function Libraries and Classes

```cpp
// ourtools.h
// For "Using C++", by Hennefeld & Burchard
#ifndef _OURTOOLS_H
#define _OURTOOLS_H

#include <iomanip.h> // ios, setiosflags, setprecision, resetiosflags
#include <fstream.h> // ostream and ofstream
#include <stdlib.h> //  exit fn.

// Virtual printer:
// This file provides an alternate output source for programs.
// UNIX users will need / to modify the drive and path specification.
ofstream vprn ("C:\\VPRINTER.OUT");

// Simplified floating point output formatting:
void fixed_out (ostream& out, int d)
// display floating point numbers on stream outs in fixed-point format
// with exactly d digits to the right of the decimal point
{
    if (d<0) d=0;
    out << setiosflags (ios::fixed | ios::showpoint)
        << setprecision(d);
}
```

```cpp
void scientific_out (ostream& out, int d)
// display floating point numbers on stream outs in scientific
//(exponential) format, with exactly d digits of precision
{
   if (d<1) d=1;
   out << setiosflags (ios::scientific | ios::showpoint)
       << setprecision(d-1);
}


void default_out (ostream& out)
// display floating point numbers on stream outs in the default format
{
   out << setprecision(6)
       << resetiosflags (ios::fixed | ios::scientific | ios::showpoint);
}


void Assert (int cond, char err_msg[])
// If cond is false(0), display err_msg, then terminate program.
// (NOTE: This function is similar to the apassert function
// recommended by the AP Computer Science Advisory Board)
{
   if (!cond)
      {
      cerr << "\nASSERTION FAILED:\n\t"
           << err_msg << endl;
      exit(1);
      }
}
#endif


// myfuns.h
// Library of user-defined functions for "Using C++",
// by Hennefeld & Burchard. NOTE: Students may wish
// to add their own utility functions to this library.
#ifndef _MYFUNS_H
#define _MYFUNS_H
#include <math.h> // for floor, ceil, pow, labs fns.
```

```
long max (long a, long b)
// return max of a and b
{
    if (a > b)
        return a;
    else
        return b;
}

double round (double x)
// Return the value of x rounded to the nearest integer
{ return floor(x+0.5); }

double round (double x, int d)
// Return the value of x rounded to d decimal places.
{
    double pow10; // 10 to the d power
    double x_rnd; // rounded value of x
    pow10 = pow(10,d);
    x_rnd = x * pow10;
    x_rnd = floor(x_rnd + 0.5);
    x_rnd /= pow10;
    return x_rnd;
}

long gcd (long a, long b)
// Return the greatest common divisor of a and b.
// Uses the Euclidean algorithm. (See Exercise 8.5.)
{
    long r;
    a = labs(a); b=labs(b);
    while (b>0)
        { r = a%b; a = b; b = r; }
    return a;
}

long lcm (long a, long b)
// Return the least common multiple of a and b.
{ return (a/gcd(a,b)*b); }

#endif
```

```
// bool.h
// Implements bool data type in case the compiler you are
// using does not provide this Draft C++ Standard type.
#ifndef _BOOL_H
#define _BOOL_H
    #undef true
    #undef false
    typedef int bool;
    const int false = 0;
    const int true = 1;
#endif
```

```
// bastring.doc (See also bastring.h)
///////////////// String class //////////////////////////////////
//
// For "Using C++" by Hennefeld & Burchard
// Implements a subset of the ANSI/ISO Draft C++ Standard
// string class. See Chapters 6 and 16 for discussion,
// details, and examples of using this class.
//
// const unsigned int NPOS = (unsigned int)(-1);
// Description: Constant whose value is the largest unsigned
//              integer for a given implementation. This varies
//              depending on size of int data type in bits.
// Sample uses: See documentation for function find, below.
//
// Constructors / destructor
// String();     // Zero argument constructor
// Condition(s): Calling object has not been declared.
// Description: Constructs an empty string.
// Sample calls: String s1, s2; // s1 and s2 are empty strings
//
// String(const String& src); // copy constructor
// Description:  Constructs a string whose initial value is src
// Condition(s): Calling object has not been declared.
// Sample calls: If s is a String object, then
//         String t(s); // t constructed with initial value s
//         String v=s; // v constructed with initial value s
// Notes: Copy constructor is used when
//              1) passing strings to functions by value, or
//              2) returning a function result by value.
//
```

```
// String(const char* pChs);
// Description:  Construct a String object whose initial value
//               is a String literal.
// Condition(s): Calling object has not been declared.
//               (This is true for all constructors!)
// Sample calls:
//     String t("one"); // t constructed with initial value "one"
//     String v="two"; // v constructed with initial value "two"
// Notes: This constructor is used for implicit or explicit
//        conversion of a String literal to a String object.
//     s1 = t + String("one"); // s1 is now "one + one"
//                             // where conversion is explicit
//     s2 = v + "one";         // s2 is now "two + one"
//                             // where conversion is implicit
//
// String (char ch);
// Description: Construct a String object whose initial value
//              is a char literal or variable.
// Sample calls:
//     String t('a'); // t constructed with initial value 'a'
//     char ch = 'Z';
//     String v=ch;   // v constructed with initial value 'Z'
// Notes: This constructor is used for implicit or explicit
//        conversion of a char to a String object.
//     s1 = t + String('B');     // s1 is now "aB"
//                              // where conversion is explicit
//     s2 = 'y' + v ; // s2 is "yZ", where conversion is implicit
//
// ~String(); // Destructor
// Description:  Deallocates memory used for the characters
//               of the calling String object
// Sample calls: Cannot be explicitly called; it is called
//               implicitly when a String goes out of scope.
//
// String& operator = (const String& src);
// Description: Assign String object, src, to calling object
// Condition(s): The calling object has been constructed. (This
//        holds for all member functions other than constructors.)
// Sample calls:   String s("abcd"), t, v;
//                 t = s; // t is now "abcd"
//                 v = s + "EFG"; // v is now "abcdEFG"
//
// String& operator = (const char* src);
// Description: Assign String literal, src, to calling object
```

```
// Sample calls:    String s;
//                  s = "A string"; // s is now "A string"
//
// String& operator = (char ch);
// Description: Assign char literal or variable, ch,
//              to calling object
// Sample calls:  String s, t; char ch='X';
//                s = ch; // s is now 'X'
//                t = '4';; t is now '4'
//
// const char& operator [] (int index) const;
// Description: Constant subscripting operator. Returns char
//              in position index of the calling object, or causes
//              a fatal error, with diagnostic message, if index
//              is out of bounds.
// Condition(s): 0 <= index and index < length()
// Sample calls:  String s("abcde");
//                char ch = s[2]; // ch is now 'c'
//                cout << s[0]; // outputs 'a'
//                ch = s[5]; // causes fatal bounds error
//
// char& operator [] (int index);
// Description: Non-constant subscripting operator. Returns a
//              reference to the character in position index of
//              the calling object, or causes a fatal error as
//              described for the const version of this function.
// Condition(s): 0 <= index and index < length()
// Sample calls: String s("abcde");
//                s[2] = 'X'; // s is now "abXde";
//                s[0] = toupper (s[4]); // s is now "EbXde";
//
// char* c_str() const;
// Description: Returns the null ('\0') terminated char array
//         data member of the calling string object. This accessor
//         function is used for calls that require a "C-style"
//         char array rather than a String object.
// Sample calls: String file_ID = "NAMES.DAT";
//                ifstream names_in; // input file stream
//                names_in.open (file_ID.c_str());
//
// unsigned int find (const String& T, int start=0) const;
// Description:
//     Find the first occurrence of T within the calling object
```

```
//     and return the index of the first character.  If T is not
//     found, then return NPOS.
// Sample calls:    String s("123abc123XYZ"), t("abc");
//                  unsigned int n = s.find(t); // n is now 3
//                  n = s.find("123"); // n is now 0
//                  n = t.find(s);      // n is now NPOS
//                  n = s.find('2', 5); // n is now 7
// Notes: Use NPOS to check for success/failure of find:
//         if (s.find("it") == NPOS) cout << "Not found";
//         else                      cout << "Found";
//
// unsigned int length() const;
// Description:  Return the length of the calling object.
// Sample calls:
//      String s, t("123ABC");
//      cout << s.length(); // outputs 0
//      int n = t.length(); // n is now 6
//      cout << t[t.length()-1]; // outputs 'C'
//
// String substr (int start, unsigned int len = NPOS) const ;
// Description: Return the substring of length len starting at
//         position start. If len is the default value, NPOS, or
//         if len >= length() - start, then all chars from start
//         through length()-1 are returned. Note that start < 0
//         is the same as start == 0; if start >= length() the
//         null string is returned.
// Sample calls:
//         String s ("0123456789"), t;
//         cout << s.substr(2,4); // displays "2345"
//         t = s.substr(6); // t is now "6789"
//         t = s.substr(12); // t is now ""
//         cout << s.substr(-5, 2); // displays "01"
//
// String& operator += (const String& str);
// Description: Concatenates a copy of str onto the calling obj.
// Sample calls:   String s("QW");
//                 s += 'E'; // s is now "QWE"
//                 s += s; // s is now "QWEQWE"
//                 s += "RTY" // t is now "QWEQWERTY"
// Notes: The memory reserved for the calling object will
//         be automatically increased.
//
```

```
// String& insert (int where, const String& S);
// Description:  Inserts S into the calling obj. at pos. where.
// Condition(s): 0 <= where and where <= length()
// Sample calls:  String s("abcde"), t("123");
//                s.insert(5, 'f'); // s is now "abcdef"
//                s.insert(2,t); // s is now "ab123cdef"
//                s.insert(0, "XY"; // s is now "XYab123cdef"
// Notes:  The memory reserved for the calling object will
//         be automatically increased.
//
// String& remove (int start, unsigned int len = NPOS);
// Description:  Removes len chars from the calling object,
//         starting at position start. If len is the default value,
//         NPOS, or if len >= length() - start, then all chars from
//         start to the end of the calling object are removed.
// Condition(s): 0 <= where and where < length()
// Sample calls:  String s("01234567890abc");
//                s.remove(10); // s is now "0123456789"
//                s.remove(2,4); // s is now "016789"
//                s.remove(2,7); // s is now "01"
// Notes: The memory reserved for the calling object will
//         be automatically decreased.
//
//////////////////////////////////    non-member functions
// ostream& operator << (ostream& os, const String& str);
// Description: Outputs a string to a file or the monitor
//
// istream& operator >> (istream& istrm, String& str);
// Description: Scans over whitespace, then reads contiguous
//              non-whitespace characters from istrm into str,
//              stopping on the next whitespace character in istrm
// Sample calls:  See Sections 6.5 and 11.5 of the text.
//
// istream& getline
//         (istream& istrm, String& str, char delim='\n');
// Description: Reads all characters from istrm, up to but not
//              including the first occurrence of delim, into str;
//              the first occurrence of delim is removed from istrm
// Sample calls:  See Sections 6.5 and 11.5 of the text.
//
// String operator + (const String& lstr, const String& str);
// Description:  Returns concatenation of lstr with str
// Sample calls:
//      String s("abc"), t;
```

```
//        t = s + "de"; // t is now "abcde"
//        s = "123" + s; // s is now "123abc"
//        t = "QWE" + "RTY" // illegal. Must explicitly convert
//                          // one of the operands to a String
//        t = "QWE" + String("RTY"); // t is now "QWERTY"
//
// Comparison operators
// bool operator <    (const String& lstr, const String& rstr);
// bool operator <=   (const String& lstr, const String& rstr);
// bool operator >    (const String& lstr, const String& rstr);
// bool operator >=   (const String& lstr, const String& rstr);
// bool operator ==   (const String& lstr, const String& rstr);
// bool operator !=   (const String& lstr, const String& rstr);
// Description:  Compare strings lexicographically using the
//               ASCII ordering of characters; return true (1)
//               or false (0)
//////////////////////////////////////////////////////////////////////


// bavector.doc - (See also - bavector.h)
/////////////////// Vector Class Template ////////////////////////////////
//   See Chapter 13 for an introduction to this class.
//
//      template <class EltType>
//      class Vector
//
//      Note: The Vector element type, EltType, must have a
//            no-argument constructor and assignment operator
//
// Vector(); // Zero-argument constructor
// Description:  Creates a Vector of size zero.
// Sample calls:
//    Vector<int> n;   // creates an empty Vector, n, of int elements
//    Vector<String> s // creates an empty Vector, s, of String elements
// Note: An empty Vector created with this constructor can
//       be enlarged by using the resize member function.
//
// Vector(int sz); // One-argument "size" constructor
// Description: Create an uninitialized Vector of sz elements,
//              indexed from 0 through sz-1
// Sample calls:
//    Vector<int> n(12);
//       creates a Vector, n, of 12 int elements, n[0]..n[11]
//    Vector<String> s(5)
//       creates a Vector, s, of 5 String elements, s[0]..s[4]
```

```
//
// Vector(const Vector& v); // Copy constructor
// Description: Create a Vector that is a copy of v.
// Condition(s):  The vector under construction must have
//                the same element type as Vector v
// Sample calls:
//   Vector<int> m (n);
//       Creates m, a copy of n.
//   Vector<String> t = s;
//       Creates t, a copy of s.
// Note: This constructor is also used for passing a Vector
//       parameter by copy (value) and for returning a Vector
//       from a function by copy.
//
// ~Vector(); // Destructor
// Description:  Deallocates memory in use by a Vector
// Note: Cannot be explicitly called; it is called
//       implicitly when a Vector goes out of scope.
//
// Vector& operator= (const Vector& Rhs); // Assignment operator.
// Description: Assign the Rhs vector to the calling Vector object.
// Condition(s):  The calling Vector must have been declared
//                and have the same element type as Rhs
// Sample calls:
//   m = n; // m will be destroyed, then assigned the contents of n
//   m.operator=(n); // alternate syntax for the above call.
// Note: The return type, Vector& permits cascading, as in
//           (m = n).resize(2*n.length());
//       which copies n to m, then doubles the size of m.
//
// EltType& operator[] (int index); // Non-constant subscripting
//                                  // operator
// Description: Return a reference to element number index
//              of the calling Vector object
// Condition(s): If index is negative, or greater than or equal to
//               the length of the calling Vector object, the program
//               will terminate with an error message.
// Sample calls:
//     n[3] = 27;   // assigns 27 to n[3]
//     s[0] += "XXX"  // appends "XXX" to String s[0]
//
// const EltType& operator[] (int index) const; //Const subscripting
//                                              //operator
```

```
// Description: Return a copy of element number index
//              of the calling Vector object
// Condition(s):  If index is negative, or greater than or equal to
//                the length of the calling Vector object, the program
//                will terminate with an error message.
// Sample calls:
//    int p = n[2]; // retrieves a copy of n[2]
//    cout << s[k] << endl; // displays String s[k], or a fatal
//                          // error message if k is out of bounds
//
// int length() const; // length accessor function
// Description:  Return the current length of the calling Vector object
// Sample calls:
//    int len = n.length();
//    cout << s.length();
//
// void resize (int newsz); // resize modifier function
// Description: Dynamically change the size of the calling vector//
//              object, while preserving the contents of the calling
//              object.
// Condition(s): Data may be lost if newsz if less than the length
//               of the calling object.
// Sample calls:
//    n.resize(20); // change size of n to 20
//    s.resize( 2*s.length()); // double the size of s
//////////////////////////////////////////////////////////////////////


// bamatrix.doc  (See also, bamatrix.h)
/////////////////// Matrix Class Template ////////////////////////////
//       See Chapter 15 for an introduction to this class.
//
//   Declare and implement an 2-dim array-like data type that provides
//   automatic index range checking and that can be resized dynamically.
//
//   Note: The Matrix element type, EltType, must have a
//         no-argument constructor and assignment operator
//
// Matrix(); // Zero-argument constructor
// Description: Creates an empty Matrix
// Sample calls:
//    Matrix<int> n;   // create an empty Matrix, n, of int elements
//    Matrix<String> s // create an empty Matrix, s, of String elements
```

```
// Note: An empty Matrix created with this constructor can
//       be enlarged by using the resize member function.
//
// Matrix(int rows, int cols); // Two-argument "size" constructor
// Description: Create an uninitialized rows x cols Matrix, with
//              rows indexed from 0 to rows-1 and cols indexed
//              from 0 through cols-1
// Sample calls:
//    Matrix<int> n(4,6);
//       // create a 4 x 6 Matrix, n, of int elements
//    Matrix<String> s(5,5)
//       // creates a 5 x 5 Matrix, s, of String elements
//
// Matrix ( const Matrix & mat); // Copy constructor
// Description: Create a Matrix that is a copy of mat.
// Condition(s):  The matrix under construction must have
//                the same element type as Matrix mat
// Sample calls:
//    Matrix<int> m (n);
//       // Create m, a copy of n.
//    Matrix<String> t = s;
//       // Create t, a copy of s.
// Note: This constructor is also used for passing Matrix
//       parameters by copy (value) and for returning a Matrix
//       from a function by copy.
//
// ~Matrix(); // Destructor
// Description:  Deallocates memory in use by a Matrix
// Note: Cannot be explicitly called; it is called
//       implicitly when a Matrix goes out of scope.
//
// const Matrix& operator = (const Matrix & Rmat); // Assignment
// Description: Assign the Rmat Matrix to the calling Matrix object.
// Condition(s):  The calling matrix must have been declared
//                and have the same element type as Rmat.
// Sample calls:
//    m = n; // m will be destroyed, then assigned the contents of n
//    m.operator=(n); // alternate syntax for the above call.
// Note: The const modifier on the return type prevents cascading.
//
// int numrows( ) const; // accessor function
// Description: Return the number of rows of the calling Matrix obj.
// Sample calls:
//    int len = n.numrows();
```

```
//     cout << s.numrows();
//
// int numcols( ) const; // accessor function
// Description: Return the number of cols of the calling Matrix obj.
// Sample calls:
//     int len = n.numcols();
//     cout << s.numcols();
//
// const Vector<ItemType>& operator[] (int index) const;
// Vector<ItemType>& operator[] (int index);
// Description: Constant and non-constant subscripting operators.
//            Return row number index of the calling Matrix obj.
// Conditions: 0 <= index and index < numrows()
//            Causes a fatal error, with diagnostic message, if
//            index is out of bounds.
// Note: The return type is a Vector, since single subscripting
//       returns an entire row of a Matrix. Double subscripting
//       is used to access or modify a single Matrix component.
// Sample calls:
//     cout << n[2][4]; // output the element in row 2, col 4
//     s[0][0] = "Row 0, Col 0"; // Assign a string to s[0][0]
//
// void resize( int newRows, int newCols ); // resize modifier
// Description: Dynamically change the number of rows and cols of
//         the calling Matrix object, while preserving the contents
//         of the calling object.
// Condition(s):  Data may be lost if newRows < numrows() or if
//                newCols < numcols().
// Sample calls:
//     n.resize(20,n.numrows()); // change number of rows of n to 20
//     s.resize(2*s.numrows(), 2*s.numcols());
//                // double the number of rows and cols of s
//////////////////////////////////////////////////////////////////////
```

F

Binary Representation of Integers

Internal Representation of Data   C++ program instructions are translated into binary by the compiler; the data that the program manipulates is also represented internally in binary. Data can be in the form of whole numbers, or integers, such as 0 and -17; real numbers with a fractional part, such as 3.14159; individual characters such as Y or N; or messages such as "Please enter your age:". Each of these kinds of data has a different internal representation. In this section, we look briefly at the binary representation of non-negative integers.

Converting Non-negative Binary Integers to Decimal   In decimal or base-10 arithmetic, there are 10 digits, 0 through 9, and a place value system based on powers of 10. The decimal integer 2073 is a compact representation for

$$
\begin{aligned}
&(2 \times 10^3) &+\quad &(0 \times 10^2) &+\quad &(7 \times 10^1) &+\quad &(3 \times 10^0) \\
=\ &2 \times 1000 &+\quad &0 \times 100 &+\quad &7 \times 10 &+\quad &3 \times 1 \\
=\ &2000 &+\quad &0 &+\quad &70 &+\quad &3
\end{aligned}
$$

In binary or base-2 arithmetic, there are only two digits or bits, 0 and 1, and the place value system is based on powers of 2.

■ **EXAMPLE**   The decimal equivalent of 10110_2 is 22_{10}. To see this, expand 10110 in powers of 2 as follows.

$$
\begin{aligned}
&(1 \times 2^4) &+\quad &(0 \times 2^3) &+\quad &(1 \times 2^2) &+\quad &(1 \times 2^1) &+\quad &(0 \times 2^0) \\
=\ &1 \times 16 &+\quad &0 \times 8 &+\quad &1 \times 4 &+\quad &1 \times 2 &+\quad &0 \times 1 \\
=\ &16 &+\quad &0 &+\quad &4 &+\quad &2 &+\quad &0 \\
=\ &22_{10}
\end{aligned}
$$

CAUTION The rightmost, or least significant, bit represents $2^0 = 1$, *not* $2^1 = 2$. ■ ■■■

Because the only digits in base 2 are 0 and 1, it is not necessary to write out the first line in as much detail as in the previous example. Beginning from the rightmost binary digit, write down the decimal value of the power of 2 represented by each 1 in the binary number, then add these values.

■ **QUESTION** What is the decimal equivalent of the binary integer 1001011?

Answer

$$
\begin{array}{ccccccc}
1 & 0 & 0 & 1 & 0 & 1 & 1 \\
\downarrow & & & \downarrow & & \downarrow & \downarrow \\
64 & + & & 8 & + & 2 & + & 1 & = & 75_{10}
\end{array}
$$

■ ■■■

Converting Non-negative Decimal Integers to Binary A somewhat more difficult problem is to start with a non-negative decimal integer and produce its binary equivalent. Two different methods are used to accomplish this conversion.

Method 1: Repeated Subtraction For rather small decimal values, consulting a table of powers of 2 and using *repeated subtraction* can quickly lead to the binary equivalent.

■ **EXAMPLE** To find the binary equivalent of 83_{10}, we first subtract the largest power of 2 that is less than or equal to 83. We then repeat this process with the difference, 19, continuing until the difference is 0.

Powers of 2

i	2^i
0	1
1	2
2	4
3	8
4	16
5	32
6	64
..	..

$$
\begin{array}{cccc}
83 & 19 & 3 & 1 \\
-64 & -16 & -2 & -1 \\
\hline
19 & 3 & 1 & 0 \quad \text{STOP!}
\end{array}
$$

This gives 83 as the sum $64 + 16 + 2 + 1$, so we can write

$$83_{10} = 1\ 0\ 1\ 0\ 0\ 1\ 1_2$$

■ ■■■

Method 2: Repeated Division by 2 For larger decimal values, the process of repeated subtraction can be tedious and error prone. (Further, it is more difficult to program the computer to do decimal to binary conversion this way.) An alternative method for producing the binary equivalent is to use *repeated division by 2*.

■ **EXAMPLE**   **(Repeated Division by Two)**   To find the binary equivalent of 90_{10}, we first divide 90 by 2, getting a quotient of 45 and a remainder of 0. We repeat this process with 45, stopping when the quotient is 0.

						stop!
45r0	27r1	11r0	5r1	2r1	1r0	0r1
2/90	2/45	2/22	2/11	2/5	2/2	2/1

Notice that the remainders, in the order that they were produced, are 0, 1, 0, 1, 1, 0, and 1. These are the bits of the binary equivalent of 90, but in reverse order. Thus, $90_{10} = 1011010_2$.   ■ ▬

Why Reverse Order?   To get a further sense of why the remainders are used in *reverse* order, consider what happens when you apply the process of repeated division to the number 6852, using 10 rather than 2 as the divisor. For example,

685r2	68r5	6r8	0r6
10/6852	10/685	10/68	10/6

Notice again that the remainders are produced in reverse order: 2, 5, 8, 6.

     In general, when you repeatedly divide by a base, b, the *first* remainder will be the *last* base-b digit, the *second* remainder will be the *second from last* base-b digit, and so on.

Streamlining the Process   The process of repeated division by 2 can be streamlined by starting at the bottom, and working up, as illustrated here. The bits of the decimal equivalent of 90 are "stacked up" by this process — they can then be "unstacked" and written one at a time to produce 1011010, the binary equivalent of decimal 90.

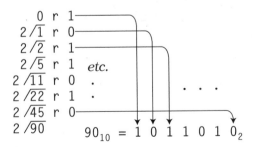

Notice that repeated division by 2 requires no table of powers of 2. (This method can also be used to produce the base-n equivalent of a decimal number for values of n other than 2.)

■ **PROBLEM**   Use the methods of *repeated subtraction* and *repeated division by 2* to produce the binary equivalents of 94_{10} and 99_{10}.

Solution   **Repeated subtraction of**   **Repeated Division by 2**
powers of 2

$$
\begin{array}{ccccc}
94 & 30 & 14 & 6 & 2 \\
-64 & -16 & -8 & -4 & -2 \\
\hline
30 & 14 & 6 & 2 & 0
\end{array}
$$

$94 = 64 + 16 + 8 + 4 + 2$

$\quad\ = 1\ 0\ 1\ 1\ 1\ 1\ 0_2$

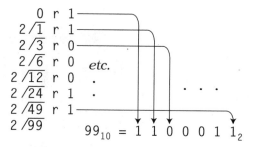

$$
\begin{array}{l}
0 \ \text{r} \ 1 \\
2\,\overline{/1} \ \text{r} \ 1 \\
2\,\overline{/3} \ \text{r} \ 0 \\
2\,\overline{/6} \ \text{r} \ 0 \quad etc. \\
2\,\overline{/12} \ \text{r} \ 0 \\
2\,\overline{/24} \ \text{r} \ 1 \\
2\,\overline{/49} \ \text{r} \ 1 \\
2\,\overline{/99}
\end{array}
$$

$99_{10} = 1\ 1\ 0\ 0\ 0\ 1\ 1_2$

■ **Exercises**

1. Convert each of the following binary integers to decimal.
    (a) 1011   (b) 10000100   (c) 11111

2. Continue counting in binary up to 16 decimal.
    Decimal: 0, 1, 2, 3,   4, . . . ,   16
    Binary: 0, 1, 10, 11, 100, . . . , 10000

3. Make a table of powers of 2 from 2^0 through 2^{12}.

4. Use the method of *repeated subtraction of powers of 2* to convert each of the following decimal integers to binary.
    (a) 41   (b) 1027   (c) 112

5. Use the method of *repeated division by 2* to convert each of the decimal integers of Exercise F.4 to binary.

6. (a) What is the largest decimal integer that can be stored in 4 bits? (*Hint*: $1111_2 = \underline{\hspace{1cm}}_{10}$.)
    (b) How many different values can be stored in 4 bits?
    (c) Answer parts (a) and (b) for 8 bits, then 15 bits.
    (d) Give a formula for the number of values that can be stored in k bits and the largest decimal integer that can be stored in k bits.

Formatting Output Using Manipulators from `iomanip.h`

In addition to the `setw` manipulator introduced in Section 6.2, the library file `iomanip.h` provides the manipulators `setprecision`, `setiosflags`, and `resetiosflags` for specifying the exact format of output to a stream.

setprecision (digs)   Used to set the number of digits of precision for floating point output to `digs`, which has a default value of six. This manipulator is **persistent** — that is, the last value specified stays in effect until a different value is specified. For example,

```
double x = 12.374859654321,
       y = 9.8765432109876E12;
cout << x << " " << y << endl;
cout << setprecision(10);
cout << x << " " << y << endl;
cout << setprecision(3);
cout << x << " " << y << endl;
```

Fragment

```
12.3749  9.87654e+12
12.37485965  9.876543211e+12
12.4  9.88e+12
```

Output

Notice that, depending on its value, a floating point number may be displayed in either fixed-point or scientific (exponential) format. Neither format is a default.

Formatting Flags   The class `ios` (for input/output specification) contains several named constants, called **specifiers**, or **flags**, for specifying the format for output. Scope resolution (`ios::`) must be used with these flags. Some of the most useful of these, along with their functions, follow.

`ios::fixed`	display floating point values in fixed decimal format.
`ios::scientific`	display floating point values in scientific (exponential) format.
`ios::showpoint`	display floating point values with a decimal point and trailing zeros.

setiosflags (ListOfFlags) This manipulator sets the formatting flags in `ListOfFlags`, where `ListOfFlags` is a sequence of one or more flags separated by the **bitwise-or** operator, |. For example,

```
cout << setiosflags(ios::fixed | ios::showpoint);
```

specifies that floating point output to `cout` is to be in fixed-point format with the decimal point shown.

The following program illustrates various combinations of output flags. Each formatting statement is followed by an explanatory comment, and each output statement is followed by a comment containing the output (highlighted) that it produces.

```
double x = 9876.0, y = -12E8, z = 123.456789;

cout << " " << x << " " << y << " " << z << endl;
// default output format and precision
// 9876 -1.2e+09 123.457

cout << setiosflags (ios::showpoint);
// ensures that decimal point shows
cout << " " << x << " " << y << " " << z << endl;
// 9876.00 -1.20000e+09 123.457

cout << setiosflags (ios::fixed) << setprecision(2) ;
// sets flt. pt. format to fixed, with 2 digits
// after the decimal point (as in outputting currency)
cout << " $" << x << " $" << y << " $" << z << endl;
// $9876.00 $-1200000000.00 $123.46

cout << resetiosflags (ios::fixed | ios::showpoint)
     << setprecision(6);
// resets flt. pt. format to default state,
// and shows up to 6 digits of precision
```

```
cout << " " << x << " " << y << " " << z << endl;
// 9876 −1.2e+09 123.457

cout << setiosflags (ios::scientific) << setprecision(3);
// sets flt. pt. format to scientific, accurate to
// 5 digits, 3 of which follow the decimal point
cout << " " << x << " " << y << " " << z << endl;
// 9.876e+03 −1.200e+09 1.235e+02

cout << resetiosflags (ios::showpoint | ios::scientific)
    << setprecision(8);
// resets flt. pt. format to default state,
// and shows up to 8 digits of precision
cout << " " << x << " " << y << " " << z\ << endl;
// 9876 −1.2e+09 123.45679
```

The functions `fixed_out`, `scientific_out`, and `default_out` in `outrtools.h` (see Appendix E) use combinations similar to those illustrated here.

Selected Exercise Solutions

Chapter 1

1. Because each electronic switch can be in one of two states, it can be considered to be a binary digit, or bit. Information can thus be represented in binary form using the binary number system for numbers and ASCII codes for characters.

4. A byte is eight binary digits (bits). One K, or kilobyte, is $2^{10} \approx 1000$ bytes. One M, or megabyte is $2^{20} \approx 1,000,000$ bytes. One G, or gigabyte, is $2^{30} \approx 1,000,000,000$ bytes.

6. Go through the n bottom cards of the deck to find the one with the smallest number. An algorithm for this is:

Mark *the first of these* n *cards by placing a paper clip on it.*
For each of the remaining n − 1 *cards:*
    If the number on the card is smaller than the number on the card that is currently marked, then move the paper clip from the currently marked card to this card.

---

11. A programming paradigm is a general framework or model for designing and organizing programs. Two different programming paradigms currently in use are the procedural paradigm and the object-oriented (OO) paradigm.

Chapter 2

2.
```
// 02-02.CPP
#include <iostream.h>

void main()
```

```
{
    int feet, inches;
    feet = 5;
    inches = 12 * feet;
    cout << inches;
}
```

4. (a)   (c)

```
10510    x = 5
         y = 10
```

5.
```
tot_cents = 10*dimes + pennies;
cout << dimes << " dimes and " << pennies << " pennies"
     << endl;
cout << "equals " << tot_cents << " cents." << endl;
```

Chapter 3

2. (a) 1437.2   (b) 0.546   (c) 0.00546

4. (a) 3   (d) 3.25   (f) illegal

5. (b) 5   (d) 1   (f) 32

6. (b) m is 5 and x is 5.3

7. (b) `seconds += 60 * minutes;`

8. (a) `salary = salary + bonus;`

  (c) `annual_int_rate = annual_int_rate / 100.0;`

9. (a) `(x + y)/(2*w)`

12. The value assigned to salary will not be 34000 as intended, because 34000 exceeds the maximum value that can be stored as an int. (This assumes 16-bit integers.)

16. (a)   (b)

```
4 Hi there.      1 Hi 2 Hi 3 Hi there.
Bye now.         Bye now.
```

Chapter 4

2. The condition `age < 65` is redundant.

```
if (age >= 65)
    cout << "You may retire.";
else
    cout << "Keep working.";
```

4. `false`
   `true`

6. **(a)** `OK`   **(b)** `NO`

8. **(b)**
```
cin >> age >> height;
if (age >= 16 || height <= 76)
   cout << "More information needed";
else
   cout << "Play basketball!";
```

10. **(a)** The segment on the right will not compile, because there are two separate statements on the `true` branch. Use curly braces to make these two statements into a single compound statement.

11. **(b)** `OK to cross bridge`   **(d)** `Do not cross bridge!`
                                          `Too wide or too high`

12. **(a)** `Quadrant IV`   **(c)** `Quadrant III`

Chapter 5

1. **(b)** 5.12   **(e)** 64.0   **(h)** 12.0   **(i)** 2.0

2. **(b)** 2.0   **(d)** 1.8

3. **(a)** 2.0   **(c)** 1.0

5. **(b)** true   **(d)** true   **(f)** `'p'`   **(h)** `'<'`

6. **(b)** 1253.6 1254 1.254

10. **(e)**
```
void display_pt (float x, float y)
{ cout << '(' << x << ", " << y << ')'; }
```
   (f)
```
bool is _leap (int yr)
{
   if (yr%4==0 && (yr%400==0 || yr%100!=0))
      return true;
   else
      return false;
}
```
   (h)
```
int mins_past_midnight (int hour, int minute, char meridian)
{
   int mins;
   if (hour==12)
      hour = 0;
   mins = hour*60 + minute;
   if (meridian=='P')
      mins += 12 * 60;
   return mins;
}
```

Chapter 6

2. ABCDEFG
   ```
      -3.8
      47.2
   -3.841
   47.16
   ```

4. Eyenstein, Alfredo
   Eyenstein, Alfredo Q.

6. ```
   String LFI_name (String first, char init, String last)
   {
       String ret_val; // value to return
       ret_val = last + ", " + first + ' ' + init + ".";
       return ret_val;
   }
   ```

8. The statement `cin >> model;` will input only the first word (ACME) of the computer model. It should be replaced by the statement

   ```
   getline (cin, model); // input complete line
   ```

   Of course, this requires that the statement

   ```
   cin.ignore (80, '\n'); // skip to next input line
   ```

   be inserted immediately after `cin >> ans;`

Chapter 7

1. (a)   (c)   (e)
   Hi Hi Hi there.   "silent" infinite loop   (nothing)
   Bye

2. (c) ZXVTR/

3. (b) ```
   int prod=1;
   for (int i=1; i<=6; i++)
   {
       prod = prod*2;
       cout << "2^" << i << "=" << prod << endl;
   }
   ```

4. (b) 8
       12
       18
       26 18

6. (b) The output of the program is unpredictable because the initial value of sum is "garbage."

8. No
   Yes

Chapter 8

1. For m=20:
   10 0
   5 0
   2 1
   1 0
   0 1

3. **(b)** Sum first exceeds 100 when you add 7 squared
   Sum is 140

5. **(b)** 12 10
   10 2
   2 0
   gcd is 2

7. **(b)** `cout << "**";`
   `    for (i=1; i<=n; i++)`
   `        cout << i << "**";`

8. Output for k=3:   3 9 27 81 OUT

9. **(a) (ii)** 60

   (b) The least common multiple, or *lcm*, of *m* and *n*.

11. **(a)** Max: 20
    11 25

    Max: 30
    7 34

    Max: 40
    7 43

    Max: -1

12. **(a)** 0 ADGJM
    1 BEHKN
    2 CFILO

13. **(c)** `for(int i=1; i<=rows; i++)`
    `    {`
    `    int j;`
    `    for (j=1; j<i; j++)`
    `        cout << ' ';`
    `    for(j=rows+1-i; j>=1; j--)`
    `        cout << "*";`
    `    cout << endl;`
    `    }`

Chapter 9

1. 0 10

3. ABRA CADABRA
   ABRACADABRA CADABRAKAZAMM

5. **(b)** 12 3
      29 3

7. ```
void ins_to_yd_ft_in (int tot_ins, int& yd, int& ft, int& in)
{
    yd = tot_ins / 36;
    tot_ins = tot_ins % 36;
    ft = tot_ins / 12;
    in = tot_ins % 12;
}
```

# Chapter 10

3.

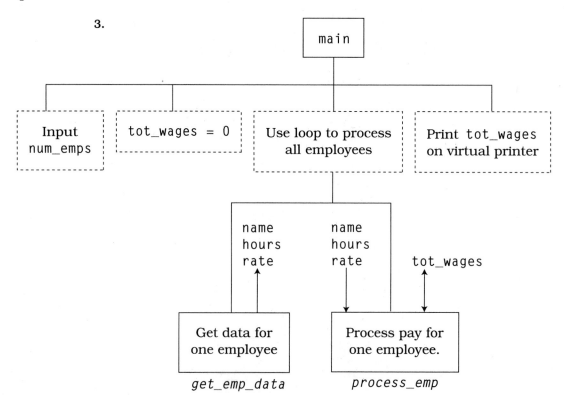
```

4. ```
int rand_int (int n)
{ return rand() % n; }

int rand_int (int a, int b)
{ return rand() % (b-a+1) + a; }
```

6. Notice that the call rand_int(10) is equivalent to the call rand_int (0,9). The parameters n (of the one-parameter version) and b (of the two-parameter version) don't have exactly the same meaning — they are off by one. Further, the implied lower bound, 0, of the one-parameter version, corresponds to the parameter a of the two-parameter version. (Because a ≤ b, it makes sense for a to be the first parameter.) But, because all default parameters must follow any nondefault parameters in the function header, this combination does not fit the pattern for using default parameters.

8. ```
What should I
enter to stop this?
What 4
 should I 9
enter to  9
top 3
```

Chapter 11

1.
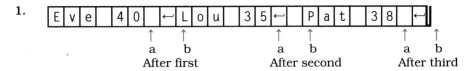

3. (a) There will be a fourth execution of the getline statement, although there are only three lines of data. The fourth execution will read no characters into line.

(b) ```
while (emps_in >> ws && !emps_in.eof())
```

```
Eve 40  7
Lou 35 6
Pat 38  7
```

6. (b) ```
#include <iostream.h>
#include <fstream.h>
#include "bastring.h"
#include "ourtools.h"

void main()
```

```
            {
            String source_file, dest_file;
            String line;
            ifstream old_file;
            ofstream new_file;

            cout << "Copy from what file? "; cin >> source_file;
            cout << "Copy to what file? ";   cin >> dest_file;

            old_file.open(source_file.c_str());
            Assert (!old_file.fail(), "Error opening source file.\n");
            new_file.open(dest_file.c_str());
            Assert (!new_file.fail(), "Error opening destination file.\n");

            getline(old_file, line);
            while (!old_file.eof())
                {
                new_file << line << endl;
                getline(old_file, line);
                }

        old_file.close();
        new_file.close();
        }
```

Chapter 12

2. **(a)** 1510?   **(b)** 10?   **(c)** ?

6. **(b)** Curves and straight lines

7.
```
if (month == 4 || month == 6 || month == 9 || month == 11)
    cout << "30 days";
else if (month == 1 || month == 3 || month == 5 || month == 7 ||
         month == 8 || month == 10 || month == 12)
    cout << "31 days";
else if (month == 2)
    cout << "28 or 29 days";
else
    cout << "Invalid value for month.";
```

Chapter 13

2. **(a)** The vector nums has size zero.

   (b) An element type was not given for the vector, the size was given in []
   rather than (), and the index for nums in the for loop should be in [].

4. **(a)** 12   8   4 23 19   5

6.

	i	x[i]==x[i-1]	count	output
Pre-loop			1	
Loop iterations	1	14==14 (true)	2	
	2	22==14 (false)	1	14 2 occurrence(s)
	3	25==22 (false)	1	22 1 occurrence(s)
	4	25==25 (true)	2	
	5	25==25 (true)	3	
	6	25==25 (true)	4	
	7	38==25 (false)	1	25 4 occurrence(s)
	8	38==38 (true)	2	
	9	40==38 (false)	1	38 2 occurrence(s)
Post-loop	10		1	40 1 occurrence(s)

8.
```
Vector<int> concat (const Vector<int>& v1, const Vector<int>& v2)
{
    tot_len = v1.length() + v2.length();
    Vector<int> v3(tot_len);
    for (int i = 0; i < v1.length(); i++)
        v3[i] = v1[i];
    for (int i = v1.length(); i < tot_len; i++)
        v3[i] = v2[i - v1.length()];
    return v3;
}
```

10.
```
Vector<int> merge(const Vector<int>& v1,
                  const Vector<int>& v2)
{
    Vector<int> v3(v1.length()+v2.length()); // merged vector

    int i1=0, i2=0, i3=0; // indexes in v1, v2, and v3, resp.
    // merge until all elts of one vector have been copied to v3
    while(i1<v1.length() && i2<v2.length())
        if (v1[i1]<v2[i2])
            { v3[i3]=v1[i1]; i3++; i1++; }
        else
            { v3[i3]=v2[i2]; i3++; i2++; }

    // append remaining elements of v1 or v2 to v3
    while(i1<v1.length())
        { v3[i3]=v1[i1]; i3++; i1++; }
```

```
    while(i2<v2.length())
       { v3[i3]=v2[i2]; i3++; i2++; }
    return v3;
}
```

Chapter 14

1. (a) 2   (b) 1   (c) -1

2. (c)

Loop body iteration	Vector segment under consideration	mid	Compare to_find and V[mid]	Narrow search or return
1	V[0]..V[8]	4	"Gil" < "Ida"	last = mid−1
2	V[0]..V[3]	1	"Gil" > "Eva"	first = mid+1
3	V[2]..V[3]	2	"Gil" > "Fay"	first = mid+1
4	V[3]..V[3]	3	"Gil" == "Gil"	return 3

3. Trace of select_sort for V = {44, 55, 20, 12, 60, 32}

Loop iteration	ctf	index_min	At end of iteration: V[0] . . . . . V[5]
1	0	3	12 55 20 44 60 32
2	1	2	12 20 55 44 60 32
3	2	5	12 20 32 44 60 55
4	3	3	12 20 32 44 60 55
5	4	5	12 20 32 44 55 60

5. V = {60, 20, 30, 40, 50, 10}

7.
```
template<class Etype>
bool is_sorted (Vector<Etype> V, int size)
// determine whether V[0]..V[size-1] is sorted
{
    for (int i=0; i < size-1; i++)
       if (V[i] > V[i+1])
            return false;
    return true;
}
```

Chapter 15

1. (b)

M	0	1	2
0	9	5	1
1	10	6	2
2	11	7	3
3	12	8	4

2. (b)
```
Matrix<String> strMat(10,2);
    for (r=0; r<10; r++)
        for (c=0; c<2; c++)
            strMat [r][c] = "EMPTY";
```
4.
```
void display (const Matrix<int>& M)
{
    int r, c;
    for (r=0; r<M.numrows(); r++)
        {
        for (c=0; c<M.numcols(); c++)
            cout << setw(4) << M[r][c];
        cout << endl;
        }
}
```
6. (a)
```
template <class EType>
    void fill (Matrix<EType>& M, const EType& fill_val)
    {
        int r, c;
        for (r=0; r<M.numrows(); r++)
            for (c=0; c<M.numcols(); c++)
                M[r][c] = fill_val;
    }
```
(b)
```
Matrix<char> chMat(4, 6);
fill (chMat, '?');
Matrix<String> strMat(10,2);
fill (strMat, String("EMPTY"));
```

Chapter 16

1. (b) 0 7 65535
4 65535

(*Note*: Depending on the compiler, NPOS may have the value 4,294,967,295 rather than 65535.)

4.
```
bool is_integer (String s)
{
    if (s.length()==0)
        return false;
```

```
        int start=0; // position of first digit
        if (s[0]=='+' || s[0]=='-')
           if (s.length()==1)
              return false; // "+" and "-" aren't integers
           else
              start=1;

        for (int i=start; i<s.length(); i++)
           if (!isdigit(s[i]))
              return false;

        return true;
     }
```

6. ```
   void Ltrim (String& str) // IN-OUT
   {
        int len = str.length();
        if (len == 0) // nothing to do
           return;
        // Find leftmost non-whitespace character
        for (int i=0; i<len; i++)
           if (!isspace(str[i]))
              break;
        if (i<=len)
           str.remove(0, i);
   }
   ```

Chapter 17

1. **(c)** ```
        // Output name as FIRST M. LAST
        cout << user_name.first << ' '
             << user_name.mid_init << ". "
             << user_name.last << endl;

        // Output name as LAST, FIRST M.
        cout << user_name.last << ", "
             << user_name.first << ' '
             << user_name.mid_init << ".\n";
   ```

3. **(b)** ```
   for (int i=0; i<employees.length(); i++)
        if (employees[i].salary > 35000.00)
           cout << employees [i].name << endl;
   ```

5. ```
   void get_date (date_str& d)
   {
        char sep; // separator between MM, DD, and YYYY.
        cin >> d.month >> sep >> d.day >> sep >> d.year;
   }
   ```

7.
```
void display(Time_piece_str T)
{
    cout << T.hr << ':';
    if (T.min<10)
       cout << '0';
    cout << T.min << ' ';
    cout << T.merid << 'M';
}
```

Chapter 18

1. The first and third errors are as follows.

   - `clock.validate()` is a private member function.
   - `cout << "Hr: " << clock.hr << endl;`
     should be:
     `cout << "Hr: " << clock.get_hour() << endl;`
     because `clock.hr` is a private data member.

3. The follow code fragment makes clever use of the `get_mins_past` member function to achieve the desired result:
```
Time_piece time;
int start; // initial time as minutes past midnight

cout << "Enter a time: "; time.enter();
start = time.get_mins_past();

time.update(1,0);
while(time.get_mins_past() > start)
   {
   time.display(); cout << endl;
   time.update(1,0);
   }
time.display(); cout << endl;
```

5.
```
bool subset(const Int_list& L, const Int_list& M)
{
    int elt;
    for (int i=1; i<=L.length(); i++)
       {
       elt = L.retrieve(i);
       if (!M.contains(elt))
             return false;
       }
    return true;
}
```

6. (b) `if(f.get_num()!=0)`

```
      {
      Fraction r(f.get_den(), f.get_num());
      r.normalize();
      cout << "Reciprocal = "; r.display(); cout << endl;
      Fraction prod(f.get_num()*r.get_num(),
                   f.get_den()*r.get_den());
      prod.normalize();
      prod.reduce();
      cout << "Product = "; prod.display(); cout << endl;
      }
   else
      cout << "No reciprocal\n";
```

(d) `f_nrm = f;`

```
    f_nrm.normalize();
    f_nrm.display(); cout << endl;
    f.display();
    if (f.get_den() > 0)
       cout << " is normalized\n";
    else
       cout << " is not normalized\n";
```

Chapter 19

1. (b) 30   **(d)** 1335

3. $120 = 60*2$—in `set_mins_past` when called by `set`
$-1680 = 120 + 60*(-30) + 0$; then $= -1680\%(24*60) = -240$; then
$1200 = -240 + (24*60)$—in `update`
Final values: `hr` $= 8$, `min` $= 0$, `merid` $=$ 'P'

5. The additional lines would be

```
L.add(20);   5  { ?,  7, 25, 30, 14, 20, . . . . }    false
L.sort();    5  { ?,  7, 14, 20, 25, 30, . . . . }    true
L.add(40);   6  { ?,  7, 14, 20, 25, 30, 40, . . }    true
L.add(5);    7  { ?,  7, 14, 20, 25, 30, 40,  5, . . } false
```

7. (a) Using direct access:

```
      bool Int_list::is_empty() const
      { return len==0; }
```

(b) Using member functions only:

```
      int Int_list::max_elt() const
      { // exercise 7b (using member functions)
        if (length()==0)
           return INT_MIN; // from limits.h
```

```
            if (sorted)
               return retrieve(length());
            int max = retrieve(1);
            for (int i=2; i<=length(); i++)
               if (retrieve(i) > max)
                  max = retrieve(i);
            return max;
   }
```

9. The values of num and den after each call are given in comments.

```
Fraction f(15, -10); // num = 15 and den = -10
f.normalize();        // num = -15 and den = 10
f.reduce();           // num = -3 and den = 2
f.set(f.get_den(), f.get_num()); // num = 2 and den = -3
```

10. **(b)** `double Fraction::as_double() const`
    `{ return double(get_num()) / get_den(); }`

11. The integer multiplications of the alternative version are probably faster than the floating point divisions of the version given in Section 19.7. However, when f is 90,001/100,000 and g is 180,002/200,000, the multiplications 90,001*200,000 and 100,000*180,002 performed by the alternative version both involve wraparound because the product exceeds the largest 32-bit integer, and the values produced by wraparound may cause the alternative version to return an incorrect result.

Chapter 21

2. Insert the line `template <class Etype>` before the first line.
   Replace every occurrence of `Int_pair` with `Pair`.
   Replace every occurrence of `long` with `EType`.

4. `template <class EType>`
   `void Pair<EType>::display (ostream& outs)`
   `{ outs << '(' << val1 << ", " << val2 << ')'; }`

6. The stream insertion operator, `<<`.

8. `(2h, Ac)`

9. **(a)** This is pass by value.
   (b) The parameter passing will require extra memory for the copy and time for making the copy.
   (c) Pass by constant reference.
   (d) `contains`

11. **(a)** If a list is unsorted, it is unlikely that replacing one element will restore it to sorted order.
    (b) `remove`

```
(c) template <class EltType>
    void List<EltType>::check_sorted ()
        // Go through list to see if it is sorted.
        // Set sorted to true if so, false if not.
    {
        for (int i=1; i<length(); i++)
            if (Elts[i] > Elts[i+1])
                {
                sorted = false;
                return;
                }
        sorted = true;
    }
```

Chapter 22

1. Memory:

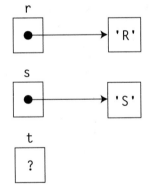

Before first cout *statement*

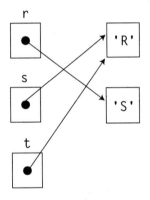

Before second cout *statement*

Output

2. Memory:

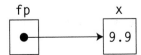

A run-time error ocurs because the statement attempts to deallocate memory that was allocated statically, not dynamically.

4. **(a)** 77   **(b)** 0 0
In both fragments, p becomes a dangling reference.

6. s is of type int rather than int*. The compiler errors produced by Turbo C++ 4.5 are

```
s = new int;  // Cannot convert 'int *' to 'int'
*s = 0;       // Invalid indirection
```

8. **(a)** Time_piece( ) { } // 0-arg. constructor

```
Time_piece (const Time_piece& T) // copy constructor
: hr(T.hr), min(T.min), merid(T.merid) {   }
```

10.
```
double x[4];

cout << "Enter four floats:\n";
for (i=0; i<4; i++)
   {
   cout << (i+1) << ": ";
   cin >> *(x+i);
   }

cout << "You entered: " << endl;
for (i=0; i<4; i++)
   cout << *(x+i) << endl;
```

Chapter 23

1. **(b)**
```
NodeType *last;
if (head==NULL)
   last = NULL;
else
   for (last=head; last->next!=NULL; last=last->next)
      { /* All code is in loop header! */ }
```

   (d)
```
NodeType* front = new NodeType;
front->name = "Vark"
front->next = head;
head = front;
```

2. **(b)** `NodeType* last_node (NodeType* head);`
      `// return pointer to last node of the list pointed to by head,`
      `// or NULL if the list is empty`

   (d) `void insert_front (NodeType*& head, String new_data);`
      `// insert a new node containing new_data at the front`
      `// of the list pointed to by head.`

3. **(a)**
```
NodeType* head = NULL;
for (int i=5; i>0; i--)
   {
   NodeType* curr = new NodeType;
   curr->data = i*i;
   curr->next = head;
   head = curr;
   }
```

6. First, the `search` function's `prev` and `curr` parameters are of type `NodeType*`, so `NodeType` would have to be made public rather than private. Second, these changes would give client programs direct access to the nodes of an `Ord_link_list` object, violating the security provided by having `search` and `Node Type` as private members.

8. **(a)** The body of the `for` loop would be written
```
entry = phone_list.retrieve(i);
phone_list.remove(entry);
entry.change_extension(1000 + 10*i);
phone_list.insert(entry);
```

   (b) The calls to `remove` and `insert` in the previous code fragment both require searching the list, either to find the item to remove or to find the correct insertion point. This is much less efficient than the call to `replace` in the original code fragment because `replace` uses indexing to locate the *i*th element, and changes it "in place"—that is, without removing and inserting.

9. **(a)**
```
template <class EType>
Ord_link_list<EType>&
Ord_link_list<EType>::operator= (const Ord_link_list& Rhs)
{
   if (this != &Rhs)
      copy (Rhs);
   return *this;
}
```

   (c)
```
template <class EType>
void Ord_link_list<EType>::destroy ()
```

```
      {
        NodeType* temp;
        while (head!=NULL)
          {
          temp = head;
          head = head->next;
          delete temp;
          }
        len=0;
        head=NULL;
      }
```

Chapter 24

1.
Iteration	S (bottom -> top)	Q (front -> rear)
1	A B C D E F G	F
2	A B C D E F	F E
3	A B C D F	E E D
4	A B C E	E D D C

2.

	Value	Operand stack (bottom -> top)
(b)	8	10 9 11
(d)	4	30 7 0

3. **(b)** A B C + − D /   **(d)** A B − C D E − / +

4. **(a)** 2 + (5 * 9 − 11)   **(c)** (30 % 7 + 8) / 2

6. **(a)**
```
template <class EltType>
void Stack<EltType>::pop(EltType& item)
{  item = get_top(); pop();  }
```

7. **(b)**
```
template <class EltType>
void Queue<EltType>::dequeue (EltType& elt)
{
    Assert (!is_empty(),
        "\"Queue empty\" error in dequeue.");
    elt = front->data;
    NodePtr tmp = front;
    front = front->next;
    delete tmp;
    if (is_empty()) rear = NULL; // Optional.
    len--;
}
```

Chapter 25

1. **(c)** `Done 1 2 5 10 21`

2.

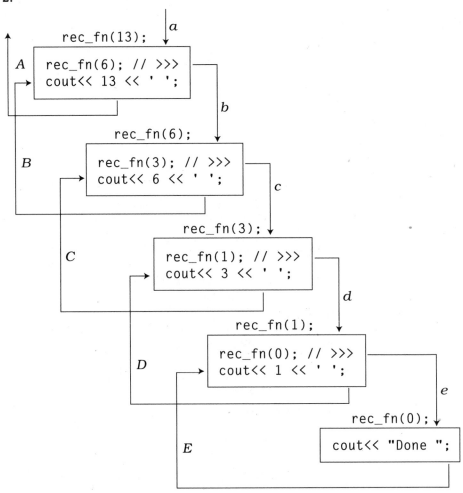

3. **(b)** −20

5. **(a)** It returns the sum $2 + 4 + \ldots + n$.
   (b) It goes into infinite recursion because the condition of the terminal case is never satisfied.
   (c) `if (n<=1)`
   `    return n;`

6. For various values of n, the table at right gives the value of fib(n) and the number of calls, c(n), required to calculate fib(n). Note that the values of c(5) and c(6) agree with the trace tables when the initial call to fib is counted.

Because fib(7) = fib(6) + fib(5), it follows that c(7) is c(6) + c(5) + 1, where c(6) and c(5) are, respectively, the number of calls to calculate fib(6) and fib(5), and the additional call is the initial call to fib(7). In general, c(n) = c(n−1) + c(n−2) + 1, which is 2*fib(n) − 1.

n	fib(n)	c(n)
1	1	1
2	1	1
3	2	3
4	3	5
5	5	9
6	8	15
7	13	25

7. **(b)**
```
bin_search (v, "Ida", 0, 11)
bin_search (v, "Ida", 0, 5)
bin_search (v, "Ida", 3, 5)   ← returns 4
```

8. **(b)** For the call move_pile (2, 'A', 'C', 'B') the code executed is

```
move_pile (1, 'A', 'B', 'C') ;
cout << "Move A to C << endl;
move_pile (1, 'B', 'C', 'A') ;
```

and from part (a), we know the pattern for moving one disk, so the output is

```
Move A to B
Move A to C
Move B to C
```

(c) For the call move_pile (3, 'A', 'C', 'B') the code executed is given at left, and the output that it produces is given at right. Note that the output in boxes is known from the pattern established in part (b) for moving two disks.

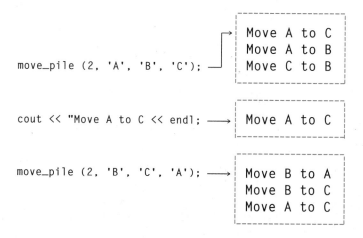

```
move_pile (2, 'A', 'B', 'C');        Move A to C
                                     Move A to B
                                     Move C to B

cout << "Move A to C << endl;   →    Move A to C

move_pile (2, 'B', 'C', 'A');   →    Move B to A
                                     Move B to C
                                     Move A to C
```

10. One parameter change fn

```
lo = 0 hi = 6
lo = 1 hi = 5
lo = 2 hi = 4
lo = 3 hi = 3
eybdooG
```

Chapter 26

2. For the first version of bubble sort, the number of comparisons is the same whether the vector is or is not sorted. The following table gives the number of comparisons on each of the 19 passes.

Pass	1	2	3	. . .	19
Comparisons	19	18	17	. . .	1

The total number of comparisons is $19 + 18 + 17 + \ldots + 1 = 19 \times 20/2 = 190$.

4. For the first version of bubble sort, the number of comparisons for sorting vectors of size 10, 40, and 800 are, respectively, $9 \times 10/2 = 45$, $39 \times 40/2 = 780$, and $799 \times 800/2 = 319,600$. The step-counting experiment of Section 26.3 produced, respectively, 42.5, 760.4, and 318,344 as the average number of comparisons made by the early exit version for sorting random vectors of size 10, 40, and 800. Except in the case of vectors that are nearly sorted and for which the small values are not far out of place, the early exit version does not save many comparisons.

6.

Value(s) of n	ct	floor $(\log_2 n)$
1	1	0
2, 3	2	1
4 . . 7	3	2
8 . . 15	4	3
16 . . 31	5	4
2^n . . $2^{n+1} - 1$	$n + 1$	n

7. V = {12, 40, 29, 32, 20, 55, 58, 80, 70} part_index = 5
W = {40, 40, 40, 32, 40, 12, 40, 80, 58} part_index = 6

8. (a)

```
quicksort(V,0,8)  {32, 20, 28, 42, 70, 81, 59, 62, 55} part_index = 3
quicksort(V,0,2)  {28, 20, 32, 42, 70, 81, 59, 62, 55} part_index = 2
quicksort(V,0,1)  {20, 28, 32, 42, 70, 81, 59, 62, 55} part_index = 1
quicksort(V,0,0)  terminal case
```

```
quicksort(V,2,1)  terminal case
quicksort(V,3,2)  terminal case
quicksort(V,4,8)  {20, 28, 32, 42, 62, 55, 59, 70, 81} part_index = 7
quicksort(V,4,6)  {20, 28, 32, 42, 59, 55, 62, 70, 81} part_index = 6
quicksort(V,4,5)  {20, 28, 32, 42, 55, 59, 62, 70, 81} part_index = 5
quicksort(V,4,4)  terminal case
quicksort(V,6,5)  terminal case
quicksort(V,7,6)  terminal case
quicksort(V,8,8)  terminal case
```

Chapter 27

1. ```
void Btr_Time_piece::display_military()
{
    int mili_time;
    int mins = get_mins_past();
    mili_time = 100*(mins/60) + mins%60;
    cout << setfill('0') << setw(4) << mili_time
        << setfill(' ');
```

2. **(a)** ```
void Int_set::add (int elt)
{
    if (!contains(elt))
        Ord_Int_list::add(elt);
}
```

   (c) ```
Int_set Int_set::operator+ (const Int_set& S) const
{
    Int_set Union = *this;
    for (int i=1; i<=S.size(); i++)
        Union.add(S.retrieve(i));
    return Union;
}
```

3. **(a)** The constructors, set, operator+, and enter.

   **(b)** normalize and reduce

   **(c)** All of them. As an example:
   ```
NR_Fraction NR_Fraction::operator+ (NR_Fraction f2) const
{
    Fraction sum;
    sum = Fraction(get_num(), get_den()) +
        Fraction(f2.get_num(), f2.get_den());
    sum.normalize();
    sum.reduce();
    return NR_Fraction(sum.get_num(), sum.get_den());
}
```
```

5.
```
int xtString::is_palindrome() const
{
    xtString ltr_dgs; // Letters and digits of this string

    // copy letters and digits of calling object to ltr_dgs
    for (int i=0; i<length(); i++)
        if (isalnum((*this)[i])) // ith char is a letter or digit?
            ltr_dgs += (*this)[i]; // append to ltr_dgs

    ltr_dgs.to_upper();
    return (ltr_dgs.reverse() == ltr_dgs);
}
```

Appendix F

1. (b) $132 = 4 + 128$

2. Decimal: 5,   6,   7,   8,   9,   10,   11,   12,   13,   14,   15
Binary: 101, 110, 111, 1000, 1001, 1010, 1011, 1100, 1101, 1110, 1111

3.

P	2 to the p
0	1
1	2
2	4
3	8
4	16
5	32
6	64
7	128
8	256
9	512
10	1024
11	2048
12	4096

4. (c) $112 = 64 + 32 + 16 = 1110000_2$

5. (c)
```
  1 ÷ 2 =    0 r 1     So 112₁₀ = 1110000₂
  3 ÷ 2 =    1 r 1
  7 ÷ 2 =    3 r 1
 14 ÷ 2 =    7 r 0
 28 ÷ 2 =   14 r 0
 56 ÷ 2 =   28 r 0
112 ÷ 2 =   56 r 0
```

6. (d) The number of values that can be stored in k bits is 2^k. These values range from 0 to $2^k - 1$.

Index

Index of Source Code References

Index of references to .cpp, .h, .dat, and .doc files available from the PWS Web site.